TRADIVOX
VOLUME X

TRADIVOX

CATHOLIC CATECHISM INDEX

VOLUME X

Jean-Joseph Gaume

Edited by
Aaron Seng

SOPHIA INSTITUTE PRESS
MANCHESTER, NEW HAMPSHIRE

This book is an original derivative work comprised of newly typeset and
reformatted editions of the following Catholic catechisms, once issued with ecclesiastical
approval and now found in the public domain:

Gaume, Jean-Joseph. *The Catechism of Perseverance*. 2nd English ed.,
translated from the 10th French ed. Vol. 1. Dublin: M. H. Gill & Son, 1883.

English translations of papal encyclicals are from the Vatican website
(http://w2.vatican.va/content/vatican/en.html) © Libreria Editrice Vaticana.
All rights reserved. Used by permission.

Scripture references follow the Douay-Rheims Bible,
per the imprint of John Murphy Company (Baltimore, 1899).

Printed in the United States of America. All rights reserved.

Cover and interior design by Perceptions Design Studio.
Unless otherwise noted, all illustrations are in the public domain.

Sophia Institute Press
Box 5284, Manchester, NH 03108
1-800-888-9344

www.SophiaInstitute.com

Sophia Institute Press® is a registered trademark of Sophia Institute.

ISBN 978-1-64413-368-2

LCCN: 2022940870

The Manner of Execution at Tyburn.

Dedicated with love and deepest respect
to all the English Martyrs and Confessors.
Orate pro nobis.

CONTENTS

Acknowledgments   xi

Foreword   xiii

Series Editor's Preface   xv

THE CATECHISM OF PERSEVERANCE, VOL. 1 (GAUME, 1883)

Brief of Gregory XVI   5

Approbations   7

Author's Preface   11

Introduction   14

1. Vocal Teaching of Religion   56

2. Written Instruction   61

3. God: In Himself, His Attributes, and Proofs Of   67

4. Creation: The First Day   80

5. Creation: The Second Day   85

6. Creation: The Third Day   90

7. Creation: The Third and Fourth Days   96

8. Creation: The Fourth Day (Continued)   103

9. Creation: The Fifth Day   110

10. Creation: The Fifth Day (Continued)   117

11. Creation: The Sixth Day   127

12. Creation: The Sixth Day (Continued)   134

13. Creation: The Sixth Day (Continued)   141

14. Creation: The Sixth Day (Continued)   146

15. Creation: The Sixth Day (Continued)   153

16. Fall of Man   164

17. Divine Justice and Mercy   168

18. History of Job   176

19. Knowledge of Religion   181

20. Antiquity of the Christian Religion   189

21. Religion; Messias Foreshadowed: Adam and Abel   199

22. Messias Foreshadowed: Noe   209

23. Messias Foreshadowed: Melchisedech   213

24. Messias Foreshadowed: Isaac   217

25. Messias Foreshadowed: Jacob   220

26. Messias Foreshadowed: Joseph   225

27. Messias Foreshadowed: Paschal Lamb   230

28. Messias Foreshadowed: Manna   235

29. Messias Foreshadowed: Sacrifices and the Brazen Serpent   238

30. Messias Foreshadowed: Moses   243

31. Messias Foreshadowed: Josue   246

32. Messias Foreshadowed: Gedeon   250

33. Messias Foreshadowed: Samson   254

34. Messias Foreshadowed: David   259

35. Messias Foreshadowed: David (Continued)   263

36. Messias Foreshadowed: Solomon   267

37. Messias Foreshadowed: Jonas   271

38. Messias Prophesied by David   275

39. Messias Prophesied by Isaias   280

40. Messias Prophesied by Micheas, Jeremias, and Joel   284

41. Messias Prophesied by Ezechiel and Daniel   287

42. Messias Prophesied by Daniel (Continued)   291

43. Messias Prophesied by Aggeus, Zacharias, and Malachias   296

CONTENTS

44. General Recapitulation: Application of the Foregoing
to Christ   300

45. Messias Prepared For: Up to the Assyrians   303

46. Messias Prepared For: Judith   308

47. Messias Prepared For: Tobias   311

48. Messias Prepared For: Esther   317

49. Messias Prepared For: Greeks and Romans   323

50. Messias Prepared For: Heliodorus, Eleazar, and the
Machabees   329

51. Unity of Religion and of the Church   333

52. Influence of Religion   339

Endnotes   347

About This Series   387

ACKNOWLEDGMENTS

THE publication of this series is due primarily to the generosity of countless volunteers and donors from several countries. Special thanks are owed to Mr. and Mrs. Phil Seng, Mr. and Mrs. Michael Over, Mr. and Mrs. Jim McElwee, Mr. and Mrs. John Brouillette, Mr. and Mrs. Thomas Scheibelhut, Mr. and Mrs. Kyle Barriger, as well the visionary priests and faithful of St. Stanislaus Bishop and Martyr parish in South Bend, Indiana, and St. Patrick's Oratory in Green Bay, Wisconsin. May God richly reward their commitment to handing on the Catholic faith.

FOREWORD

The Catholic faith remains always the same throughout the centuries and millennia until the coming of our Lord at the end of the time, likewise "Jesus Christ is the same yesterday, today and forever" (Heb 13:8). The Catholic faith is "the faith, which was once delivered unto the saints" (Jude 1:3). The Magisterium of the Church teaches us solemnly the same truth in the following words of the First Vatican Council: "The doctrine of the faith which God has revealed, is put forward not as some philosophical discovery capable of being perfected by human intelligence, but as a divine deposit committed to the spouse of Christ to be faithfully protected and infallibly promulgated. Hence, too, that meaning of the sacred dogmas is ever to be maintained, which has once been declared by holy mother Church, and there must never be any abandonment of this sense under the pretext or in the name of a more profound understanding. May understanding, knowledge and wisdom increase as ages and centuries roll along, and greatly and vigorously flourish, in each and all, in the individual and the whole Church: but this only in its own proper kind, that is to say, in the same doctrine, the same sense, and the same understanding (cf. Vincentius Lerinensis, *Commonitorium*, 28)."[1]

An authentically Catholic catechism has the function of learning and teaching the unchanging Catholic faith throughout all generations. The Roman Pontiffs indeed, taught: "There is nothing more effective than catechetical instruction to spread the glory of God and to secure the salvation of souls."[2] Saint Pius X said, that "the great loss of souls is due to ignorance of divine things."[3] Therefore, the traditional catechisms have enduring value in our own day and age, which is marked by an enormous doctrinal confusion, which reigns in the life of the Church in the past six decades, and which reaches its peak in our days.

I welcome and bless the great project of the "Tradivox" in cataloguing and preserving the hundreds of long-lost Catholic catechisms issued with episcopal approval over the last millennium. This project will convincingly show the essentially unchanging nature of the apostolic doctrine across time and space, and so I invite the faithful of the entire world to support this historic effort, as we seek to restore the perennial catechism of the Church. The project of a catechism restoration on behalf of "Tradivox" will surely be of great benefit not only to many confused and disoriented Catholic faithful, but also to all people who are sincerely seeking the ultimate and authentic truth about God and man, which one can find only in the Catholic and apostolic faith, and which is the only religion and faith willed by God and to which God calls all men.

+Athanasius Schneider, O.R.C.,
Titular Bishop of Celerina
Auxiliary Bishop of the Archdiocese of Saint Mary in Astana

PREFACE

S OME are surprised to find that when a given Catholic is asked to "look something up in the catechism," he may well respond: "Which one?" The history of the Catholic Church across the last millennium is in fact filled with the publication of numerous catechisms, issued in every major language on earth; and for centuries, these concise "guidebooks" to Catholic doctrine have served countless men and women seeking a clear and concise presentation of that faith forever entrusted by Jesus Christ to his one, holy, Catholic, and apostolic Church.

Taken together, the many catechisms issued with episcopal approval can offer a kind of "window" on to the universal ordinary magisterium — a glimpse of those truths which have been held and taught in the Church *everywhere, always, and by all*. For, as St. Paul reminds us, the tenets of this Faith do not change from age to age: "Jesus Christ yesterday and today and the same for ever. Be not led away with various and strange doctrines" (Heb 13:8-9).

The catechisms included in our *Tradivox Catholic Catechism Index* are selected for their orthodoxy and historical significance, in the interest of demonstrating to contemporary readers the remarkable continuity of Catholic doctrine across time and space. Long regarded as reliable summaries of Church teaching on matters of faith and morals, we are proud to reproduce these works of centuries past, composed and endorsed by countless priests, bishops, and popes devoted to "giving voice to tradition."

In This Volume

Within the impressive scope of catechisms found in the Catholic manuscript tradition, the vast majority were composed in question-answer format, reflecting their typical use in settings of oral instruction. Even so, a significant minority were composed in longer explanatory form, at times even adopting the style of homiletics or popular narrative. This was especially true in the nineteenth century: as the means of printing and distribution continued to advance, sectarian government restrictions began to lessen on Catholic publishers, and the field of pedagogical studies came into its own. Many catechisms composed in this period appeared as multi-volume works, tending to be considerably more comprehensive in their treatment and offering readers more material for study, instruction, and prayer. They also held the advantage of being able to offer more penetrating engagement with issues of their own time, particularly as they applied unchanging Christian moral principles to new questions that arose in their immediate surround.

If these multi-volume works could be said to constitute a subgenre of Catholic catechisms, then the literary historian must point to Msgr. Jean-Joseph Gaume's *Catechism of Perseverance* as its most remarkable example. Originally published as an eight-volume collection with the formidable title: *Catéchisme de Persévérance, ou Exposé de la Religion depuis l'origine du monde jusqu'à nos jours* (Paris: 1838), this larger catechism represented a certain summation of the reputable French prelate's most consuming concern and lifelong project, which was to foster an integrally Catholic approach to education.

Born in Franche-Comté in the wake of the French Revolution, Abbé Gaume knew firsthand what disastrous effects could be expected from systematic education that abandoned its roots within scripture and tradition, or neglected to study "pagan sources" within the necessary Christian framework, or worse: gave such sources priority in the classical curriculum. As a professor of theology, seminary rector, vicar-general, and later prothonotary apostolic under Pope Bl. Pius IX, Gaume published several theological and historical works that frequently returned to this theme of reforming education for youth, which he saw as especially vulnerable to the pagan revival that had commenced with the Renaissance and borne its natural fruit in the murderous frenzy of the Revolution; ideas that continued to insinuate themselves long after the guillotines had been removed from the public square. The zeal with which he pursued his campaign for a new approach to Catholic education—a true *révolution*, as he himself called it—led to the publication of numerous articles and smaller books on the topic (some of them quite controversial in the academia of his time), as well as his celebrated *Catechism of Perseverance*.

This was a catechism composed on a grand scale, combining doctrinal instruction with compelling stories, thematic prayers, literary excerpts, historical anecdotes, and more, all with a view to offering a complete and systematic course in religious instruction for those "that have made their first Communion to persevere in the study and practice of religion." Many parishes and schools adopted it as an entire teaching script for a four-year curriculum in religious education, and it was generally received with high praise. It became popular not only in France, but in many different European language editions as well: fascinating iterations were still appearing as late as 1924, as witnessed by the appearance of an illustrated abridgment in phonetical Cree, intended for priests in northern Canada. Sadly, the size and scope of the French original precluded the publication of new English editions by the turn of the century, although reprinted summaries continued in some places. The present Tradivox volume and the three that follow it together comprise the first republication of Abbé Gaume's catechism in nearly 150 years, newly typeset from the second Dublin edition of M. H. Gill & Son. The length of these four volumes has necessitated a smaller typeface and endnotes throughout, but our only notable changes to this text have been to simplify the Table of Contents and section headers, remove the appended summary questions, and omit two deficient anthropological footnotes from Lesson 23.

This volume includes Abbé Gaume's sweeping overview of creation and human history leading up to the incarnation, offered from the supernatural perspective that "Jesus Christ is the immortal King of ages, the Alpha and the Omega, the center to which all rays converge." In the dizzying religious indifferentism of our own age, it is bracing to find here the classical doctrine that there is only one true religion, which has existed from the first: "The religion that we profess has always existed, since, from the beginning of the world, the expectation of Jesus Christ has been its soul. ... Faith in Jesus Christ has been the faith of all ages." One is likewise struck by the many anecdotal glimpses of the "religion and science" debates of the early nineteenth century, and perhaps even more by Abbé Gaume's claims of how natural science, once "the arsenal in which impiety sought for weapons against the faith," now "renders homage to religion." The *Catechism of Perseverace* is one of the earliest catechisms to address what has now become a veritable cult of "scientism"—and its treatment of the Catholic doctrine of creation is especially intriguing in this regard.

As with all of Abbé Gaume's works, the whole is characterized by beautiful phrasing and heartfelt conviction, as he seeks to "lift a little the veil which conceals so many wonders." Amid these many wonders is a palpable ascetical dimension that affords a glimpse into the true spiritual warfare accompanying all study and exercise of the faith:

> Man is a soldier; he must preserve his union with the new Adam, and advance towards perfection sword in hand. Hell and the old enemy have made a thousand efforts to render this warfare most perilous to us. ... Sometimes they raised up heresies to change the truth,...sometimes they raised up scandals,...sometimes the double crime of heresy and scandal,...reviving the savage sway of the strongest arm, and replunging the world into that state of misery and abjection in which it groaned under paganism. ... [Even so,] on every point of attack the new Adam places a sentinel.

With this spiritual combat in mind, it is consoling to find just such a "sentinel" in Abbé Gaume's *Catechism of Perseverance*: a catechism that, in the words of the contemporary archbishop Nicolas-Augustin, "contains at once the soundest instructions on the faith, morality, and liturgy of the Catholic Church, and of itself alone, forms a little religious library that we would wish to see in the hands of all the laity and clergy of our diocese."

EDITORIAL NOTE

Our *Catholic Catechism Index* series generally retains only the doctrinal content of those catechisms it seeks to reproduce, as well as that front matter most essential to establishing the credibility of each work as an authentic expression of the Church's common doctrine, e.g., any episcopal endorsement, *nihil obstat*, or *imprimatur*. However, it should be noted that especially prior to the eighteenth century, a number of catechisms were so immediately and universally received as reliably orthodox texts (often simply by the reputation of the author or publisher), that they received no such "official" approval; or if they did, it was often years later and in subsequent editions. We therefore include both the original printing date in our Table of Contents, and further edition information in the Preface above.

Our primary goal has been to bring these historical texts back into publication in readable English copy. Due to the wide range of time periods, cultures, and unique author styles represented in this series, we have made a number of editorial adjustments to allow for a less fatiguing read, more rapid cross-reference throughout the series, and greater research potential for the future. While not affecting the original content, these adjustments have included adopting a cleaner typesetting and simpler standard for capitalization and annotation, as well as remedying certain anachronisms in spelling or grammar.

Woodcut depicting an early method used in the production of Catholic catechisms, circa 1568.

At the same time, in deepest respect for the venerable age and subject matter of these works, we have been at pains to adhere as closely as possible to the original text: retaining archaisms such as "doth" and "hallowed," and avoiding any alterations that might affect the doctrinal content or authorial voice. We have painstakingly restored original artwork wherever possible, and where the rare explanatory note has been deemed necessary, it is not made in the text itself, but only in a marginal note. In some cases, our editorial refusal to "modernize" the content of these classical works may require a higher degree of attention from today's reader, who we trust will be richly rewarded by the effort.

We pray that our work continues to yield highly readable, faithful reproductions of these time-honored monuments to Catholic religious instruction: catechisms once penned, promulgated, and praised by bishops across the globe. May these texts that once served to guide and shape the faith and lives of millions now do so again; and may the scholars and saints once involved in their first publication now intercede for all who take them up anew. *Tolle lege!*

Sincerely in Christ,
Aaron Seng

TRADIVOX

VOLUME X

THE

CATECHISM OF PERSEVERANCE;

OR,

AN HISTORICAL, DOGMATICAL, MORAL, LITURGICAL, APOLOGETICAL, PHILOSOPHICAL, AND SOCIAL EXPOSITION OF RELIGION.

FROM THE

BEGINNING OF THE WORLD DOWN TO OUR OWN DAYS.

BY MONSIGNOR GAUME,

APOSTOLIC PROTHONOTARY, DOCTOR IN THEOLOGY, VICAR-GENERAL OF MONTAUBAN AND AQUILA, KNIGHT OF THE ORDER OF ST. SYLVESTER, MEMBER OF THE ACADEMY OF THE CATHOLIC RELIGION (ROME), &c.

Jesus Christ, yesterday, and to-day; and the same for ever.—*Heb.* xiii. 8.
God is charity.—1 *John*, iv. 8.

Translated from the Tenth French Edition.

IN FOUR VOLUMES.

VOL. I.

Second Edition.

DUBLIN

M. H. GILL & SON, 50 UPPER SACKVILLE STREET

1883

THE

CATECHISM OF PERSEVERANCE;

OR,

AN HISTORICAL, DOGMATICAL, MORAL, LITURGICAL,
APOLOGETICAL, PHILOSOPHICAL, AND SOCIAL
EXPOSITION OF RELIGION.

FROM THE

BEGINNING OF THE WORLD DOWN TO OUR OWN DAYS.

BY MONSIGNOR GAUME,

APOSTOLIC PROTHONOTARY, DOCTOR IN THEOLOGY, VICAR-GENERAL OF MONTAUBAN
AND AQUILA, KNIGHT OF THE ORDER OF ST. SYLVESTER, MEMBER OF THE
ACADEMY OF THE CATHOLIC RELIGION (ROME), &c.

———————

Jesus Christ, yesterday, and to-day; and the same for ever.—Heb. xiii, 8.
God is charity.—1 John, iv. 8.

———————

Translated from the Tenth French Edition.

IN FOUR VOLUMES.

VOL. I.

Second Edition.

DUBLIN
M. H. GILL & SON, 50 UPPER SACKVILLE STREET
1883

Nihil Obstat:
THOMAS O'SULLIVAN,
Censor Deputatus

Imprimatur:
+ PAULUS CARD. CULLEN,
Archiepiscopus Dubliniensis

Brief

OF HIS HOLINESS GREGORY XVI

To the Author.

The author of the *Catechism of Perseverance* had the honor of presenting to the holy father a copy of this and his other works. While staying at Rome, he was frequently admitted to a special audience with the supreme pontiff. On these occasions, he heard from the lips of the vicar of Jesus Christ the kindest words and the most flattering encouragements. A few days after the last of these interviews, His Holiness was pleased to send him the following Brief, accompanied with the cross of the Order of St. Sylvester:

GREGORY XVI, POPE,
TO OUR BELOVED SON,
J. Gaume,

Priest, Canon of the Cathedral of Nevers.
Beloved son, health and apostolic benediction.

The rewards of praise and honor, together with other marks of Our Pontifical benevolence, We are accustomed most willingly to bestow on those persons, especially ecclesiastics, who, distinguished for talent and virtue, and professing a devoted attachment to this Chair of Peter, place all their glory in deserving well of the Catholic religion. Wherefore, it being perfectly evident to us that, adorned with the most admirable qualities of mind and heart, and recommended by a piety, an integrity of life, and a gravity of manners known to everyone, you apply yourself with all earnestness, care, and labor to procure the good of the Catholic religion, to which you have rendered no small service indeed by the works that you have published; aware, also, that you profess toward Us and this Apostolic See a singular regard and veneration, We have thought it fit to give you some mark of Our good will toward you. Wishing, therefore, to honor you in a particular manner; having, in the first place, for this purpose alone, absolved you, and declaring you absolved, from any excommunication, suspension, interdict, or other ecclesiastical censure, sentence, or penalty whatsoever, which you may perchance have incurred: We create and nominate you by these presents, and in virtue of Our Apostolic Authority, a Knight of the Order of the Golden Militia, lately restored by Us, and invested with new splendor, and We associate you to the rank of the other knights that compose it. Accordingly, We permit and authorize you to wear the cross of the said order, and to enjoy each and every privilege, prerogative, and favor that the other knights of the said order enjoy or may or shall enjoy, save and except the faculties withdrawn by the Council of Trent, having the approval of this Apostolic See: all Apostolic Constitutions and Decrees, and other things whatsoever, to the contrary, notwithstanding. Now, We wish that you should wear the emblem of the order, namely, an octangular golden cross, bearing, in the center, on an enameled silver ground, an image of the Supreme Pontiff St. Sylvester, and suspended from the breast by a red and black ribbon, embroidered with red, on the left side of the garment, according to the usual manner of the knights, and to the form prescribed in Our Apostolic Letter of the 31st October, 1841, regarding the said order: otherwise, you will forfeit the advantages of this grant. Finally, that you may be still better acquainted with Our good will in your regard, We have ordered that the cross itself should be forwarded to you.

Given at St. Peter's, Rome, under the Fisherman's Ring, on the 29th day of March, 1842, the twelfth year of Our Pontificate.

A. CARD. LAMBRUSCHINI.

Approbations

From Monsignor the Archbishop of Bordeaux.

Ferdinand Francis Augustus Donnet, by the divine mercy and the favor of the Holy
Apostolic See, Archbishop of Bordeaux and Primate of Aquitaine:

Having become personally acquainted with the book entitled *The Catechism of
Perseverance; or, an historical, dogmatical, moral, and liturgical exposition of religion from the beginning of the world to the present day*, by the Abbé Gaume, Canon of Nevers, we approved
and now again approve of this work for our diocese. Useful to the faithful of every age
and class, the reading of this book will be especially so to the young, and to those who are
charged with their education. The *Catechism of Perseverance* is a summary of many works
on religion, and alone supplies their place; its doctrine is taken from the best sources; the
style is clear, attractive, vivid, and forcible; the plan immense, embracing at once a history
of Christianity, with our religious orders, an exposition of dogmas, and an explanation
of morals, as well as of the sacraments and the ceremonies of the Church: the method
employed by the author is that which was followed with so much success by the Greek
and the Latin fathers, and which, in fine, it was the earnest desire of Fenelon and many
other great bishops to see revived amongst us.

Given at our archiepiscopal palace, Bordeaux, under our seal and signature, and the
signature of our secretary, the 26th December, 1839.

> + FERDINAND.
> Archbishop of Bordeaux.
> By order of Monsignor the Archbishop,
> H. DE LANGALERIE,
> Hon. Sec. Genl.

From Monsignor the Bishop of Gap, nominated to the Archbishopric of Auch.

Nicholas Augustine De La Croix D'Azolette, Bishop of Gap nominated Archbishop
of Auch:

We have read and examined the work entitled *Catechism of Perseverance*, by the Abbé
Gaume, Canon of Nevers, and we have found that the esteemed author treats in a
learned and attractive manner of the creation, the fall, and redemption of man, and the
establishment, propagation, and preservation of Christianity: in a word, that this work,
under so modest a title, contains at once the soundest instructions on the faith, morality,
and liturgy of the Catholic Church, and, of itself alone, forms a little religious library that
we would wish to see in the hands of all the laity and clergy of our diocese.

> Paris, 25th January, 1840.
> + N. A., Bishop of Gap.
> Nominated to the Archbishopric of Auch.

From Monsignor the Bishop of Belley.

Alexander Raymond Devie, Bishop of Belley:

In accordance with the reports that have reached us regarding the work entitled *The Catechism of Perseverance, or an historical, dogmatical, moral, and liturgical exposition of religion, etc.*, by the Abbé Gaume, Canon of Nevers, and from the knowledge that we ourselves possess of it, we are anxious to recommend its use to the clergy and laity of our flock; they will find in it an explanation of doctrine, and a history of religion, replete with interest. Ecclesiastics, especially, will be able to draw from it a multitude of arguments, illustrations, and historical sketches for the explanation of the ordinary catechism, and, more particularly still, for their discourses from the pulpit, or for those assemblies or reunions which now take place in a great many parishes, to fortify the rising generation in the doctrines and practices of religion.

> Belley, 7th February, 1840.
> + A. R. Bishop of Belley.

From Monsignor the Bishop of Saint Flour.

We, Frederick Mary Gabriel Francis De Marguerye, by the grace of God and the authority of the Holy Apostolic See, Bishop of Saint Flour:

Having had the work entitled *Catechism of Perseverance*, by the Abbé Gaume, Canon of Nevers, examined, we are desirous to recommend its perusal to the clergy and laity of our diocese. We have read the first five[4] volumes ourselves with the liveliest interest; and we congratulate the Abbé Gaume on having conceived the idea of a work that, under the modest title of *catechism*, contains an admirable history of religion, with an exposition of its proofs, its mysteries, its morality, and the immense benefits for which man and society are indebted to it here below, while awaiting the rewards of eternal justice hereafter. It is impossible to read this series of lessons, equally instructive and affecting, on the origin of the world and of man, on our renovation in Jesus Christ, on the happy influence of the evangelical law in promoting the welfare of nations and individuals, on the combats and triumphs of the Church, on the beauty of Catholic feasts, at the same time so poetic and so social that they relieve the weary Christian's heart, sinking under the burden of labor and sorrow, and give a foretaste of paradise; it is impossible to read these pages without admiring, without esteeming, and without soon practicing a religion so full of consolations for the present and so rich in hopes for the future. Hence, we have witnessed with pleasure the circulation of the *Catechism of Perseverance* through our diocese, and we have requested our clergy to recommend its perusal in Christian families, well assured that it will produce abundant fruits of salvation and peace.

> Given at Riom-ès-Montagnes, during the course of our pastoral visitation, 30th May, 1841.
> + FREDERIO,
>   Bishop of Saint Flour.

From Monsignor the Archbishop of Reims.

Thomas Mary Joseph Gousset, Archbishop of Reims, etc.

We have examined the work entitled *Catechism of Perseverance; or, an historical, dogmatical, moral, and liturgical exposition of religion*, by the Abbé Gaume, Canon of Nevers; we have found nothing contrary to the doctrine of the Church in it, and it appears to us equally useful to the laity and to ecclesiastics charged with the duty of explaining to the people the dogmas of religion, the morality of the gospel, and the ceremonies of Catholic worship. Hence, we desire to see the work spread through all the parishes of our diocese.

Reims, 4th November, 1841.
+ Thomas,
Archbishop of Reims.

From Monsignor the Bishop of Soissons and Laon.

Jules Francis De Simony, by the divine mercy and the favor of the Holy Apostolic See, Bishop of Soissons and Laon, senior suffragan of the province of Reims:

The *Catechism of Perseverance*, by the Abbé Gaume, is a work known and appreciated. The testimonials that it has received from many of our venerable colleagues; the praises that have been given it by such of our clergy as we have deputed to examine it; and, in fine, the knowledge that we ourselves have personally acquired regarding it, lead us to approve and recommend its use throughout our diocese, as a work most useful for its depth and abundance of doctrine, and most admirable for the elegance of its style and the clearness of its arrangement.

Given at Soissons, 15th April, 1842.
+ Jules Francis,
Bishop of Soissons and Laon.

From Monsignor the Bishop of Agen.

John De Levezon De Vesius, by the divine mercy and the favor of the Holy Apostolic See, Bishop of Agen:

Having acquired a knowledge of the work entitled *The Catechism of Perseverance; or, an historical, etc.*, by Monsignor J. Gaume, Canon of Nevers, we are happy to say that the doctrine contained in the work is conformable to Catholic doctrine, and that the method adopted by the author is clear, and well calculated to engrave on the minds of the faithful the history and the truths of our holy religion.

We therefore approve the work for our diocese, and recommend its perusal.

Given at Agen, under our signature and seal, and the signature of our secretary.
+ John,
Bishop of Agen.
By order, Deyche, Can. Sec. Gen.
Agen, 8th November, 1842.

From Monsignor the Bishop of New Orleans.

We are happy to join our recommendations to those of so many illustrious European prelates who have honored with their approbation the *Catechism of Perseverance*, by the Abbé Gaume, Canon of Nevers. The knowledge that our brief moments of leisure have allowed us to acquire personally of the work, and particularly the testimony that is rendered to its merits by numerous ecclesiastics of our diocese, who continually avail themselves of it with the greatest fruit, make us desire most earnestly to see it in the hands, not only of all the clergy, but of all Christian families in our diocese. The *Catechism of Perseverance* is alone amply sufficient to enlighten the minds of the laity in our provinces, and to supply priests in the pastoral office with subjects of solid instruction on faith and morals, as well as on the liturgy of the Church.

+ Ant., Bishop of New Orleans.
New Orleans, 20th February, 1843.

From Monsignor the Bishop of Nevers.

We, Dominic Augustine Dufêtre, by the grace of God and the authority of the Holy Apostolic See, Bishop of Nevers:

We consider ourselves dispensed from the necessity of praising the *Catechism of Perseverance*, by the Abbé Gaume, our Vicar-General. This work, of which new editions have followed one another so rapidly, has taken its place among the best treatises on religion, and we are not aware of any other in existence so complete.

We believe it called to produce the happiest fruits among the faithful, but we recommend it above all to the youth of both sexes. The good that it has wrought in the bosom of the *Catechism of Perseverance* in our episcopal city is a sure guarantee with us of what it may accomplish elsewhere.

We have the most ardent wish that this book, to which we give our fullest approbation, may be circulated more and more throughout our diocese, and become the book of every family. We exhort our fellow laborers to encourage its perusal as much as possible, and to take it themselves as their guide in those instructions which will be so necessary for children after their first Communion, in order to secure their perseverance.

Given at Nevers, under our signature and seal, and the signature of our secretary, 15th February, 1845.
+ Augustine Dominic,
Bishop of Nevers.
By order,
Delacroix,
Canon Secretary.

Author's Preface

Where are we? Is there any hope of salvation still left for society? Or, rather, is the end come, and should we hide our heads?

Such are the questions addressed every day to one another by men accustomed to reflect on the great interests of the human family. We ask the latest news regarding society, as we should inquire about an army whose destruction was every day threatened, or of an agonizing patient whose death seemed every moment at hand. These questions ought not to astonish us, so critical is our situation; and certainly they are sufficiently important to merit our consideration.

This is not the place to examine and characterize the symptoms of life or death that the social body exhibits at the present day.

It only concerns us to state a principle, which is admitted by all great and upright minds, namely, that the world will not recover from its present crisis but inasmuch as religion is allowed to resume her sway. And if you inquire by what means can religion again form the rule of faith and morals, the answer will be returned in one voice: religion cannot enter into minds or hearts but through the rising generations.

If the justness of the answer were not self-evident, its proof would be furnished in the incredible zeal with which the emissaries of iniquity and the apostles of deceit labor continually for the destruction of youth.

Such is, then, the grand problem of our period: to make the rising generation truly and sincerely Christian. It is a great matter; a matter of life or death.

On the one hand, it is to the young that the future belongs; on the other, there are no true creeds, no pure morals, no peace in the family, no happiness in society, outside of Christianity. This is the simple fact; let him who has eyes to see, see it: no one is required to prove the existence of the sun.

But, in order to fix the coming generations immovably in Christianity, despite the fickleness of their hearts, despite the storms that rage around them, even from the cradle, despite the scandals of word and deed that are everywhere to be met with, and, above all, despite the vanities of the world, so directly opposed to everything that Christians should believe, and love, and practice; what, I ask, are the transitory lessons of childhood? Superficial instructions, which the weakness and levity of young people hinder from being understood or remembered, and which, never sinking into the depths of the soul, cannot make that impression which is capable of determining their conduct in afterlife.

Inquire of those venerable priests who, every year, receive at the holy table so large a number of youthful Christians, how many persevere? They will reply in the anguish of their souls by showing you perhaps here and there a few children, sad remains left as it were by a miracle out of the general shipwreck in which the rest perished. They will tell you that, especially of late years, their ministry has seemed reduced to the agonizing farce of enlisting victims for corruption and impiety.

Formerly it was not so: the child found in the family circle the means of perseverance. But, since religion has generally deserted the domestic hearth, it has been forced, under pain of beholding the rising generations perish like those before them, to supply for the absence of parental care by extraordinary solicitude, and by instructions more coherent, specific, and consecutive than previously, continued even beyond that critical age in which the rising passions begin to show their violent nature, and so often drive the inexperienced minds and hearts of youth far from the paths of virtue.

11

Examine now the question; turn it, and consider it on every side; and say do you know any better means for attaining the end we have in view than the establishment in every parish of a "Catechism of Perseverance after First Communion."

What we know for certain is that supreme pontiffs have most warmly encouraged this means of salvation, so imperatively called for by the circumstances of our time.[5] What we also know for certain is that the pious bishops who govern our churches perfectly coincide on this matter with the pastor of pastors; hence, they eagerly establish branches of this invaluable association throughout their dioceses.

Other parochial associations have undoubtedly done, and still do, much good. Yet it seems to us that they are not so directly adapted to meet our actual wants.

Established chiefly with a view to nourish piety, they suppose in their members an extensive knowledge of the truths of faith; for their only desire is to give meat to the strong, not milk to children. The information that they fail to communicate would indeed be supplied in better times by the teaching of the family.

At the present day the world is greatly changed: our youth are no longer possessed of a sufficient knowledge of religion. To think of forming them to piety without first laying a solid foundation of instruction is merely to build upon sand; it is to calculate on those affectionate sentiments which adorn a heart of fifteen years for its maintenance in virtue through all the disorders and perplexities of afterlife. Surely there is no straighter road to numerous and bitter disappointments.

The Catechism of Perseverance, having for its object, as its name denotes, to secure perseverance in the study of religion and the practice of our religious duties, we regard it, with our superiors in the faith, as the best means for making the generations of the present day sincerely Christian.

Providence, which never fails to place the remedy near the evil, brought forth this eminently useful work amongst us at the precise moment when the family, forgetting its noble vocation, ceased to be a domestic church: this was about the middle of the seventeenth century.

Paganism, which had drawn away so many of the higher classes, soon opened the door to that corruption of morals and deplorable indifference which are the scourge of our own day.

About that time, the venerable M. Olier was appointed pastor of Saint Sulpice, Paris. He took possession of his parish in 1642.

Such were the ignorance and immorality that reigned throughout his district that it was termed the "sink of Paris." Its name was a byword. Yet the zealous pastor was not discouraged. He saw that there was one means left him of renewing the face of that land and purging it of its iniquities—the education of the young—and to this he applied himself with heroic zeal. O holy priest! may the world bless thee, while heaven crowns thy merits!

"Catechisms Preparatory for First Communion," but, above all, "Catechisms of Perseverance," were established: nothing was neglected to ensure their success. While the new apostle planted and watered, God gave the increase; and before very long, thanks to the "Catechisms," the parish of St. Sulpice was changed: its shame was taken away, and from being one of the most abandoned, it became one of the most edifying in Paris.[6]

Directed with like zeal by the successors of M. Olier, the "Catechisms of Perseverance" continued to produce similar fruit. Such was the state of affairs till the period of the French Revolution. At this disastrous epoch, the "Catechisms" shared the fate of every other public exercise of religion. But on the return of calmer days, they were quickly reestablished: a beginning was made in the year 1804.

Never had this great means of salvation been more necessary. Hence, the reopening of the "Catechisms " of St. Sulpice was a signal for the establishment of a great number of others throughout the capital and the provinces. The most consoling experience has continually justified the patronage that so many distinguished prelates and venerable priests have at all times bestowed on this precious institution.

Called ourselves to direct, during the space of twenty years, one of these "Catechisms," we also must render glory to God for the blessings bestowed on the work. That we may contribute, as far as lies in our power, to facilitate its propagation, we now publish, for the ninth time, the complete course of our instructions.

We present it, first of all, to our brethren in the ministry. A complete exposition of Christianity, in its history, its dogmas, its morality, its worship, its letter, and its spirit, with all that can enlighten the mind, touch the heart, or warm the imagination; in a word, religion, such as in our eyes it ought to be presented, especially at the present day, in order to be accepted, embraced, and practiced: this is the work that we present to them, according to the measure of our ability, under the title of the *Catechism of Perseverance*.

To you also, Christian parents, masters and mistresses, who place education before instruction, virtue before knowledge, the interests of eternity before those of time, we present this work. You will find in it the means of rearing up children truly useful to society, by making them pious Christians, capable of rendering an account of their faith and their hope.

And to you also, our young friends, the only hope of the future, we present this work. Like ourselves, the unhappy children of an age of skepticism and turmoil, you wearily seek the precious treasure of truth for which your hearts were made. Alas! some sophists, coming forward with their deceitful systems, have presented to you an unintelligible abstraction or a dangerous utopia. What they never can or could present to you, this work presents to you.

Do not let its name inspire you with contempt or disgust. Do not suppose that it is a dry and barren abridgment, cut up into questions and answers. Under the simple title of *catechism*, which literally means "vocal instruction," you will find the most interesting history that ever charmed your leisure hours, the most admirable philosophy that you ever studied, nay, we venture to say it, an epic poem of such thrilling interest that never before did your heart beat with the perusal of anything so enchanting.

This name, though commonplace, is not unpoetic. It reminds you of two great epochs in the history of mankind—that of the patriarchs and that of the early Christians—the tents of Sennaar and the catacombs of Rome: poetic reminiscences, if ever there were any; memorable periods, when truth had for its sole interpreter the venerable voice of the aged patriarch, whitened with years, or the still more venerable voice of the pontiff, rich with the trophies of his sufferings.

There are other persons still to whom we venture to present this work.

Among the multitudes advanced on the road of life, many persons are to be met with who have only heard of Christianity in the vaguest manner. They entertain only some passing thoughts and crude ideas on this most important of all subjects. Others, still more unfortunate, scarcely know the incarnate Son of God—the most beautiful of the children of men—in any way but through prejudices and calumnies bequeathed to them by the last century and communicated to them in their early education. At the same time, the necessity of believing and loving makes itself felt in their inmost souls.

Like the Romans of the second century,[7] alluded to by Tertullian, they are inclined in prosperity to turn their eyes toward the capitol; but when adversity seats itself at their doors, they hasten to raise their sorrowful looks toward heaven: this is the moment in which they become Christians. Unfortunately, their Christianity, not being established on the basis of a profound conviction, which is the result of sound instruction, their beautiful sentiments vanish with their fears and griefs.

What is the greatest want of all such persons at the present day but a full and complete exposition of the faith? We endeavor to supply it to them. Here they will find no bitterness, no polemics, but a simple history of Christianity.

This work, then, we present to you, O men, whosoever you are, that wander without star or compass on the stormy sea of life, ignorant whence you came, what you are, or whither you go; and whose hearts, the constant scene of indescribable struggles, become too often the victims of some cruel deception, and, alas! at times of inconsolable sadness.

This work, like an inspired philosopher, will teach you to know yourselves; like a tender comforter, it will pour a salutary balm over the wounds of your soul; like an experienced mariner, it will direct your barque toward the shores where there are neither sighs nor tears.

Pause a moment. Can you refuse to hear us? We would speak to you of God and of yourselves.

Let us tell you the plan that we have adopted.

Introduction

St. Augustine, being asked by a deacon of Carthage the best method of teaching religion, replied to the question by writing an admirable treatise, entitled: *De Catichezandis Rudibus:*[8]

"The true manner of teaching religion," says the great bishop of Hippo, "is to ascend to the words: 'In the beginning God created heaven and earth,' and to develop the whole history of Christianity down to the present day. Not that one should relate the old and the new testament from beginning to end: the thing is neither practicable nor necessary. Make an abridgment thereof; insist especially on that which appears most important, and pass lightly over the rest. By this means, you will not weary the mind of him whose ardor you would excite, nor overburden the memory of him whom you should instruct. Now, to show the whole connection of religion, remember that the old testament is a figure of the new; that the Mosaic religion—the patriarchs, their lives, their alliances, their sacrifices—are so many figures of what we now behold; that the whole Jewish people and its government, are only a great prophecy concerning Jesus Christ and his Church."[9]

Such, according to St. Augustine, should be the manner of teaching the letter of religion. Its spirit, according to the same holy doctor, the faithful interpreter of our divine master, consists in the love of God and our neighbor. The following are his remarkable words:

"You begin your narration, then, with an account of the creation of all things in a state of perfection, and you continue it down to the present state of the Church. Your only object will be to show that everything which precedes the incarnation of the Word tends to manifest the love of God in the fulfillment of this mystery. What do we learn from Christ himself, immolated for us, but the immense love which God has testified for us in giving us his only Son?

"But if, on the one hand, the principal object of the Word in coming on earth was to teach men how much they are beloved by God, and if this knowledge has no other object than to enkindle in the hearts of men a love for God by whom they have been first loved, and a love for their neighbor, in accordance with our Savior's precept and example; if, on the other hand, the scriptures before Jesus Christ are intended only to announce his coming, and if everything subsequent to him speaks only of Christ and charity, is it not evident that not only the law and the prophets, but even the whole new testament may be reduced to these two great precepts: the love of God and the love of the neighbor?

"You will render a satisfactory account of everything you relate; you will show the cause and the end of all events to be love, in such a manner that this great idea shall be ever present to the eyes of the mind and heart. The twofold love of God and the neighbor being the term or limit of everything you have to say, you will describe what you relate in such a manner as to lead the listener to faith, from faith to hope, and from hope to charity."[10]

Such is the plan which we have endeavored to follow. Could we anywhere select a better? Will the youth of the nineteenth century be lost, if we introduce St. Augustine as a catechist? Hence, an exposition of religion from the beginning of the world until our own day; religion before, during, and after the preaching of our Lord Jesus Christ; religion in its letter and spirit: this is the object of our work.

The course of our lessons continues for four years.

FIRST YEAR

God.—During the first year, we give some indispensable ideas on the twofold manner in which religion has been taught, as well as on scripture and tradition, the two great sources of all religious truths; then, ascending to that beginning which precedes all beginnings, we adore in his ineffable essence the God of eternity, who has made both time and every creature existing in time. The perfections of this adorable being engage all our attention. We speak of his power, his wisdom, his goodness, his liberty, his immutability, and his providence.

After having contemplated him in himself, we contemplate him in his works. With the "morning stars"[11] we assist at the magnificent spectacle of the creation of the universe. Every day of the great week which it occupies adds a new portion to that word, which we may read in the clearest characters on the brow of every creature: namely, God.

All things speak to us of the unity, power, wisdom, goodness, and providence of the great being, who watches with equal care over those immense worlds, careering along their majestic courses from age to age, and the blade of grass, which, springing forth with the sunrise, withers, perhaps, with the day. Hymns of gratitude and admiration ascend unconsciously from our lips, and nature becomes the first great book in which the Christian child learns to know and to love its God.

In this manner, we follow not only the advice and example of St. Augustine and the most illustrious fathers of the Church, but even the formal invitation of the Holy Ghost. "Ask now the beasts," the divine Spirit says, "and they shall teach thee: the birds of the air, and they shall tell thee. Speak to the earth, and it shall answer thee; and the fishes of the sea shall relate to thee the wonders of their Creator."[12]

We know that our great masters in the art of teaching religion, such as St. Basil, St. Gregory, St. Ambrose, St. Augustine, and St. Chrysostom, regarded it as a sacred duty to explain to their people the work of the six days.[13] If we are not sufficiently acquainted with the grounds of their conduct, we shall be informed on the matter by the eloquent patriarch of Constantinople.

"You inquire of us," says St. Chrysostom, "how God taught men to know him before there were any books. How? In the same manner that we ourselves have adopted, to lead you to the knowledge of this supreme being. We have conducted you in spirit through the whole universe; we have shown you heaven, earth, the sea, the plains, the fields, the riches and varieties of nature; we have searched into the elements of the different productions; and, uniting our voices in one glad transport of admiration, at the sight of so many wonders, we have cried out: 'How great are thy works, O Lord! how profound are thy thoughts!'"[14]

Thus, the fathers of the Church began the teaching of religion, as God himself began it. They explained, before all things, that great book in which the Creator has been pleased that the children of men should first read of his existence and his adorable perfections.

"We are also asked," continues St. Chrysostom, "why, the book of the scriptures being so useful, it was not given to the world from the beginning. The reason is because God wished to instruct men by the objects of nature, and not by books. If God had begun our instruction by means of characters intelligible only to the learned, the ignorant would have been but little benefited. The rich might have purchased books; but the poor could not. To derive any advantage from them, it would have been necessary to understand the language in which they were written; therefore, they would have been useless to the Scythian, the Indian, the Egyptian, in a word, to every man unacquainted with their language.

"Such is not the case with the grand spectacle of the universe: whose language is understood by every nation of the earth. This book is laid open without distinction to learned and ignorant, to rich and poor. Hence, the prophet does not say that the heavens *testify*, but that they *relate*, the glory of God: eloquent preachers, indeed, whose auditory is the whole human race."[15]

According to the admirable models that we have selected, we begin our teaching of religion by an explanation of the work of the six days. In an age when men understand nothing but what falls under their senses, an explanation of this kind appears more necessary than ever. It renders the great truths of religion palpable, so to speak. It brings God back into every part of the physical world, from which the materialistic science of the last century had banished him, and the indifferentism of the present still endeavors to keep him separated. The universe is no longer for man an empty temple. God is everywhere present, animating all things, preserving all things, vivifying all things.

Does his august presence say nothing to the heart? Can it be that a man, surrounded by so many wonders, whose harmony, and end, and meaning, we shall be careful to explain to him, will fail at length to become more grateful and more Christian? Whatever one may say, when we make nature serve religion, does it not correspond with the intentions of the Creator, and do we not imitate an example, which has often been given us in the gospel by the divine teacher of the human race?

In this admirable record, we show inferior creatures, pointing always to superior ones, those which precede calling on those which follow, and all, together, acknowledging man: man, the center of so many rays; man, the keystone of nature's magnificent dome; man, the mediator, representative, and pontiff, by whom all creatures, descended from God, should continually ascend again to God. For these reasons, man appears last on the scene.

"Acknowledge," says again the eloquent patriarch of Constantinople, "the inexhaustible goodness of the sovereign Lord of nature in regard to man. He begins by preparing a splendid banquet, served with as much elegance as variety; by constructing a palace for the ruler of the new empire containing in itself everything that is beautiful and select. When everything was thus completed, he creates man, to take possession of so many treasures, and to become the master of nature. It is thus, when an emperor is about to enter a city, all the members of his suite take care that everything may be found in proper order on the arrival of their sovereign."[16]

It is no longer difficult to understand the meaning of that salutary expression: "Man, acknowledge thy dignity, and beware of degrading thyself by any conduct unworthy of thy greatness!"[17]

We speak of the creation of man, his glory, his power, his primitive royalty. We follow him to the terrestrial paradise; we enjoy his delighful abode. We hear the Creator giving our first parents his easy command: "Thou shall not eat the fruit of the tree of the knowledge of good and evil."[18] Such is the homage required by the Lord of creation from his noble vassal. Is it too much? Happiness, in the fullest extent of the word, is attached to the fidelity of our first parents.

Here we speak of that happiness which should be our rightful inheritance; in other words, of the state of man before his fall.

Primitive state.—Formed in a state of grace and supernatural justice, man was endowed with a clear knowledge of God, himself, and nature; so much for the understanding. Framed to know, as the eye is to see, the intellect of the first man was satisfied. In this respect, therefore, there was happiness.

He loved God with a strong, tender, pure, and tranquil love, and in God and for God he loved himself, as well as all other creatures; so much for the heart. Framed to love, as the fire is to burn, the heart of the first man was satisfied. In this second respect, therefore, there was happiness.

Exempt from infirmities and diseases, he was never to be acquainted with death. In his body, therefore, he was happy. In a word, united to that being who is the very source of happiness and immortality, man enjoyed an ample share of happiness and immortality.[19]

Hence, in the primitive state, God could exercise his dominion over man without resistance, and through man over all creatures: *omnia in omnibus* (all in all). For man, truth, charity, and immortality; between God and man, an intimate union; glory for God, peace for man, order and harmony for the whole creation!

Then reechoed from all parts of the universe that magnificent canticle, which the angels, four thousand years later, should again proclaim to the earth, when the Desired of Nations had come to repair his work: "Glory be to God on high, and peace on earth to men of good will!"[20]

Fall and redemption.—Such was man, such was the world in the days of innocence. Scarcely have we studied this beautiful page in our history—for, alas! the happiness of man on earth is written in a single page—than we arrive at that tremendous catastrophe whose remembrance is at once so deep and so universal that it is found engraven at the head of the theology of every nation.

Man is fallen! Almost choked with sorrow at this terrible blow, a deep sigh escapes us, and we involuntarily exclaim, alas! alas! and for ever alas! But, behold, a voice is heard in the twilight of ages, which cries out: O *felix culpa!* (O happy fault!) Presently the conduct of the Almighty toward his fallen creatures justifies the adoption of these marvelous words.

Far from destroying the human race upon the spot, as it deserved, far from treating it as he had treated the rebel angels, God allowed it a time of trial in which to recover itself. This was not enough; man should be furnished with a superabundance of means, to reacquire the goods which he had forfeited through his own fault, and to obtain even greater. To whom are we indebted for so unmerited a favor? Here begins the great mystery of mercy.

As the adorable Trinity had taken counsel regarding the creation of man so it now takes counsel in order to save him. The eternal Word offers himself to his Father, as a victim of expiation for guilty man: the mediation is accepted. From this moment, it takes effect; grace is restored, with new privileges.[21] The supernatural bond which, before the commission of sin, had united man to God is renewed. This reunion, or rather this second union, the mediator of which is Jesus Christ, is called *religion.*[22]

Hereby, we clearly see that all religion is but one great grace, a grace diversified in a thousand ways; that its dogmas, its precepts, its sacraments, the ceremonies of its worship, so various, and so beautiful, are like so many channels, which convey the waters of this fountain to our minds, our hearts, and our senses. It is not without reason that, at the very outset, we thus present religion from a point of view at once so just and so calculated to touch the heart. The ignorance of man, and, above all, his vicious inclinations, too often persuade him that religion is a burdensome yoke, and a present from the hand of God anything but desirable. Victims of this deplorable error, a great many persons never submit to the salutary prescriptions of faith, except from fear; others, whose case is still more deplorable, either abandon these prescriptions entirely, or live in a criminal indifference to them.

Hereby, we also see that the religion of Jesus Christ, or Christianity, is as ancient as the fall of man.[23] Thus is made palpable that great truth, which it is so important to remember at the present day, namely, that Christianity is the religion of ages; that there never has been, and it is impossible there ever could be in the future, any other religion; for, in the state of fallen nature, there is no religion without a mediator, and there is no other mediator than Jesus Christ, because there is no other man-God than he.[24]

We next show, in a few pages, the certainty of revelation, the truth and necessity of religion, and the obligation of all men, both rich and poor, kings and people, to observe one great law; also, the folly, the guilt, and the misery of that indifference, which so rapidly conducts our modern world either to an abyss itself in the bloody saturnalia of anarchy, or to sink under the yoke of the most frightful despotism that ever oppressed the human race.

To reestablish and perfect the primitive union of man with God is the mission of the mediator. To accomplish it, he should remove sin from the world, sin which alone had thwarted the divine plan. In order to satisfy the divine justice, he should be a victim; to repair in man the sad ravages of sin, he should be a teacher and a physician. In the Person of the mediator, the human race should triumph fully and perfectly over sin and its consequences, as, in the person of the first Adam, sin had unfortunately triumphed over man in his mind, his will, and his body.

Now, as it is evident, that by our union with the first Adam, we have become miserable and guilty,[25] so it is evident that it is only by our union with the second Adam that we can be saved. The aim of temporal life, the labor of every man, should therefore be to unite himself with Jesus Christ in a complete and permanent union; commenced on earth, this union will be perfected only in heaven, where, as in the early days of the world, God will be all in all.

Such, in a few words, is the divine plan of redemption.

This admirable design was not unveiled by God at once: he wished to disclose it little by little, and to prepare the way for its reception. It was also necessary that man should understand, by a long experience, the need he had of a Redeemer. Yet the divine wisdom and goodness told him enough of it, according to times and circumstances, to console him in his misfortunes, to support his confidence, and to elevate his works to a supernatural rank; though not so much as to take away the merit of faith, or to dazzle his eyes with too brilliant a light.

God proportions himself to the wants and strength of man. He makes the sun of revelation rise like the sun of the physical world, gradually. The gentle breaking of dawn prepares the eye for the brighter rays of the aurora; and these in turn dispose it to endure the effulgence of midday. The spiritual is in many respects analogous to the material world, and we are careful in our explanations not to deviate from this providential system.

This is the reason why, beginning at the origin of time, we pursue through the course of ages the progressive manifestation of the great mystery of redemption. As it rests either on Jesus Christ already come, or Jesus Christ to come, it is still Jesus Christ we seek, follow, show everywhere, from the first to the last of our lessons. Historical facts are merely links between the promises, the figures, and the prophecies. That which predominates in every one of our instructions is the grand image of the Messias.

In this manner we realize the views of St. Augustine, who desires that throughout the old testament we should behold only one object, Jesus Christ.[26] The Lamb sacrificed from the beginning of the world, the heir of bygone ages, and the world to come of the future age; the cornerstone uniting the ancient and the modern people; the center of all things in the intellectual, moral, and political orders: Jesus Christ was yesterday, is today, and will be forever. It is of him that all the scriptures speak; is it not of him that this whole work should speak? Hence, as we have said above, Jesus Christ regenerating the world is the center; the Alpha and the Omega; the beginning, the middle, and the end of our catechism.

Having shown in what the nature, system, and object of Christianity consist; having learned that, according to the eternal counsels of the divine Wisdom, the Redeemer should not come immediately; we seek that which the divine goodness should do for man, in order to console him during a delay of four thousand years.

Now, there is not much trouble in conceiving what God should do:[27] 1) to promise the Redeemer to man; 2) to give some sign by which he might be recognized on his arrival; 3) to prepare the world for his reception and kingdom.

This is what God does, in a manner worthy of his infinite goodness and his profound wisdom. We show, in point of fact, that from the fall of man till the coming of the Messias, it is to the latter all-important event that the counsels of God are directed. Therefore, the successive explanation of the promises, figures, prophecies, and preparations, for the approach of the Messias follows.

The Messias promised. — To strengthen the heart of man against despair, and to make him learn patience during four thousand years, God should first, as we have seen, promise man a Redeemer.

And hence the king of creation has scarcely fallen from his throne, when a first promise, like a ray of hope, shines before his eyes, all wet with tears: "From the woman shall be born a son, who shall crush the serpent's head."[28] Adam understands this mysterious word, and faithfully transmits it to his children. During two thousand years, this first promise was the only hope of the human race. Although given in very general terms, it sufficed to uphold the courage of the just in those days, and to render their works meritorious.

The second promise was more specific. It was made to Abraham, and settled on the posterity of the holy patriarch. As ages rolled on, and man became capable of more enlightened views, new promises succeeded one another in terms more and more precise. It is admirable to follow the links of this long chain of divine promises, which, mutually explaining, conduct us step by step from various nations to a particular people, from this people to a particular tribe, and from this tribe to a particular family. Arrived there, God pauses; the promises are ended, but not so our uncertainties.

It is true that man is assured of receiving a Redeemer, and that this Redeemer shall spring from the family of David. But in the family of David, which shall exist, without being confounded with any other, until the ruin of Jerusalem and the Jewish nation, that is to say, during a space of more than a thousand years, there will be many whom we must reject. If then some new lights do not break in upon us, it will be impossible to recognize among so many persons that Son of David who is to save the world. Here is, therefore, the human race exposed to the danger either of disowning its Redeemer, when he shall come with outstretched hands to raise it from its fallen state, or of attaching itself to the first impostor of the race of David who shall call himself the Messias: the risk is grave. But let us be reassured; God provides for it: he will supply us with certain marks, by which we may distinguish, among the posterity of David, that child to whom the world shall owe its salvation.

The Messias pointed out. — Here, as in the promises, we show that God accommodates himself to the weakness of man, and makes the truth known only by insensible degrees. The mind is developed like the body.

He begins by sketching in certain great personages the characteristic marks of the liberator. During more than three thousand years, that is, from Adam to Jonas, there appear many distinguished personages, who all point out the Messias, in some circumstances of his birth, life, death, resurrection, or triumph. God overrules a thousand events, and establishes a great variety of ceremonies and sacrifices, which are like so many scattered strokes, whose combination forms a distinct outline of the Desired of Nations. Among all the figures of the Messias, the most significant were the sacrifices. Every day saw the blood of victims shed; the perpetual sacrifice of the lamb, in the Temple of Jerusalem, reminded the Jewish people of the future victim, whose sacrifice should replace all others, to which it had previously given their merit: a standing mystery, with which the whole people were well acquainted.[29]

If, in the catechism, we have explained only a limited number of these wonderful figures, it is because we should keep within reasonable bounds. We have selected those which the sacred authors and the fathers of the Church mention as the most striking, and which assist in the explanation of a great number of historical facts. The figures which we develop form a portrait so exact, and so exclusively correspond to the Messias, our Lord Jesus Christ, that it is impossible not to recognize him as their type and model.

Then, unless one maintains that all these admirable resemblances are only the result of chance; unless one denies the testimony of the fathers of the Church, and even of the sacred writers of the new testament, it is necessary to admit that, in these figures, God has really desired to furnish an outline and a description, by which the Messias should be represented and known.[30]

At the same time, we must confess that these different traits do not suffice; the sketch is not the portrait, and yet it is the portrait we want. These scattered rays of light, mixed with shadows more or less dark, at best produce but a misty light, and convey but a yet vague knowledge of the future Messias. Now, God wills that this description shall be so clear, so characteristic, so circumstantial, that it shall be impossible for man, unless he is voluntarily blind, to be deceived, or to fail in recognizing his Redeemer.

It is necessary then to dispel the clouds, to give the finishing touches, to put an end to all uncertainties. How, then, does God act?

In his infinite wisdom he raises up the prophets. Associating their understanding to his infinite intelligence, he reveals to them the secrets of the future. Before their eyes he places the Desired of Nations, and directs them to depict him in such accurate and minute terms, that it will be the easiest thing possible to distinguish among the children of David that one who should save the world. What, then, are the prophecies? They are the complete description of the Redeemer, promised from the origin of time, and prefigured under a thousand different forms.

"In fact," says one of our most celebrated Oriental scholars, "we clearly find, by an attentive examination of the sacred text, that all the prophecies, during the four thousand years which preceded the Messias, form only one great circle, whose radii meet in a common center, which is no other, and can be no other, than our Lord Jesus Christ, the Redeemer of the human race, involved in guilt since the fall of Adam. Such is the object, and the only object, of all the prophecies; they concur in pointing out the Redeemer in so clear a light that he cannot be mistaken. They form altogether a most perfect picture. The more ancient prophets draw the faint outline; others, in succession, complete the details left unfinished by their predecessors; the nearer they approach to the event, the brighter the colors glow; and when the painting is finished the artists disappear. The last, as he retires, is careful to mention the personage who should draw aside the veil: 'Behold I will send you,' says he, in the name of the eternal, 'Elias the prophet (John the Baptist) before the coming of the great and dreadful day of the Lord.'"[31]

In the catechism we give the description such as it has been left by the prophets. With this at hand, we seek among the children of David, who lived before the destruction of the second Temple, which, according to the prophets themselves, the Messias should enter, him to whom it answers in every respect and particular. Our search is neither long nor troublesome. Like the navigator who, on the appearance of the desired shore, cries out, in a transport of enthusiasm: "Land! land!" we soon fall on our knees, and, in the liveliest sentiments of admiration, love, and gratitude, proclaim the adorable name of the babe of Bethlehem.

In explaining the prophecies, we are careful to illustrate an essential fact, but one which is, perhaps, too little observed,[32] namely, that the prophets never fail to authenticate their predictions concerning the Messias by the announcement of events near at hand, or, if remote, whose accomplishment should be as visible as the sun at noon. We shall here cite a single example.

Who can doubt the truth of the oracles of Isaias regarding the Redeemer, when he compares the words of this great prophet regarding the city of Tyre with subsequent events? At the time Isaias spoke, Tyre was one of the greatest and most powerful cities in Asia, perhaps even the most opulent city in the world. Yet the prophet announces in distinct terms that this queen of the sea shall one day be no more than a miserable village, occupied by a few poor fishermen, who will wash their nets on the very beach, where anchored of old the proud ships of every nation. Such a village is Tyre today. It is not left only to the impious Volney, standing on its ruins, and reading Isaias, to cry out, "The oracle is fulfilled!" But, blind man! if this oracle is fulfilled, then the others, of which it is the proof, are also fulfilled: *Noluit intelligere ut bene ageret* (He was unwilling to understand, lest he should be obliged to change his life).

We also show how incontrovertible is the proof of the divinity of religion drawn from the prophecies. As a matter of fact, God alone knows the future, that future which, depending on the free election of human wills and passions, escapes all our calculations. The gift of this knowledge, which makes the created intelligence a participant in the lights of the uncreated intelligence, is one of the greatest miracles that God can work. But God cannot work miracles in favor of deceit. Therefore, Jesus Christ, whom he has announced so many ages beforehand, by the agency of a great number of prophets, unknown to one another, as the Redeemer of the world, the ambassador of heaven, the Messias promised from the origin of time, is not an impostor; nor his religion a fable. To deny this conclusion is to extinguish in oneself the last ray of reason, and to take one's place among the lower order of creation.

A last point, on which we equally insist in our explanation of the prophecies, is the admirable means chosen by God to place above all suspicion the antiquity and genuineness of the sacred books. A copy of every prophecy was deposited in the Temple of Jerusalem, and confided to the guardianship of the priests. Numerous other copies were in the hands of the people, who made them the subject of constant reading in their homes and synagogues. How impossible to alter a work possessed at the same time by millions of persons unknown to the author!

This is not all. By an admirable arrangement of providence, the Jewish nation ceases to be the only depository of the scriptures about two centuries before the coming of the Messias. At the request of an idolatrous king, their ancients or doctors, to the number of seventy-two, make a translation of the holy books. Deposited in the most famous library of the world, this translation is placed beyond the reach of any falsifying attempt. When the auspicious moment arrives it will be impossible for the synagogue to deny or to alter the testimonies of Moses and the prophets in favor of the Messias; this translation we still possess.

Since the coming of the Messias, these same books have been found in the hands of two societies, diametrically opposed to each other. How unlikely, nay impossible, that there could be collusion between them. It is precisely of the Jewish people themselves that God avails himself to prove to demonstration the antiquity and genuineness of the prophecies; it is to the people most interested in destroying or altering these documents that their guardianship is confided.

Though convicted in the sight of the world of the greatest crime and the most inconceivable folly, their zeal is no less impassioned at the present day for these sacred books.

The Jews preserve them religiously, love them as the miser loves his treasure, and even at the peril of life, bear testimony to them. What do I say? Not only has God made the Jewish nation the incorruptible guardian of the prophecies, but he has made the Jews their indefatigable propagator. Behold the reason why this people cannot take root in any part of the earth! Behold the reason why it is scattered everywhere without a home, bearing to all places, in its wandering career, and reading to all nations with whom it comes in contact, the books which it does not understand.

This is not yet all. During eighteen centuries, by a singular prodigy in the annals of the world, this people, or rather this corpse of a people, is preserved, without ruler, without pontiff, without country, without altar, without sacrifice, everywhere rejected, everywhere despised, isolated among the nations, accommodating itself to all climates, the last remnant of antiquity, surviving the ruins and revolutions of ages without mixture or confusion, a people evidently designed to serve as an everlasting witness to the Messias.[33]

Now, we say that the Jews were sufficiently acquainted with these promises, figures, and prophecies, to expect with confidence and to recognize with ease the future Redeemer.

First, they all believed in the coming of a Messias; this was the chief article of their creed, the foundation of their religion. They knew well that the Messias should be born of Abraham, in the line of Isaac, Jacob, Juda, and David. This divine Messias, himself conversing among them, one day asked: "What think you of Christ, whose son is he?"[34] They immediately answered, without any hesitation: "David's."[35] If they knew that the Messias should be man, they also knew that he should be God. Addressing our Lord, the high priest spoke in these terms: "I adjure thee by the living God, that thou tell us if thou art the Christ the Son of God."[36] It is manifest that the Jews did not separate the idea of the Son of God from that of Christ. Elsewhere, astonished to hear Jesus speak of his death, they exclaimed: "Is not the Christ to live for ever?"[37]

As for the figures, especially the sacrifices, "the more enlightened," says St. Thomas, "had an explicit knowledge of them; the others had all the intelligence necessary to discover in them, at least obscurely, the different characteristics of the Redeemer."[38]

Is there question of the prophecies? They tell you confidently that, according to the prophets, Christ should be born in Bethlehem of Juda, should deliver the house of Israel, should be King. And how, in fact, can it be supposed that they had not an understanding of the book, placed expressly in their hands to announce to them the restorer of the world, and which, from its first to its last page, speaks only of him?[39]

First, then, the promises, figures, and prophecies were given for the Jews; but they were also, and even in a higher degree, given for us. To us, Christians, they reveal the admirable plan of our redemption, begun at the origin of time, and developed without interruption during a long course of ages.

Thereby they establish our faith on an immovable basis, showing us that the Christian religion extends its roots even to the earliest days of the world, that it is the inheritor of all things great, and that it is impossible for a religion, whose founder, mysteries, struggles, and victories are announced, prefigured, and foretold ages before, not to be the work of God. Moreover, the prophecies which have already been verified are a guarantee to us for the accomplishment of all those which relate to future ages; and, thus, the certainty of our faith reposes both on the past and the future, according to the remark of St. Augustine.[40]

The way for the Messias prepared. — God employs five hundred years to give, by the instrumentality of prophets, a complete description of the Messias. The place of his birth, the time of his coming, every detail of his conduct is foretold. What remains? A few moments will show. When a great king, tenderly beloved by his people, and impatiently expected home after a period of absence, is about to enter into the capital of his kingdom, every one is anxious to adorn the way, to open the gates, to increase the general enthusiasm; in like manner, when the eternal Word, the immortal King of ages, the Desired of Nations, was about to make his entrance into the world, it pleased the eternal Father to prepare his way, to open the gates, to dispose the minds of men for his reception, and to make all events whatsoever concur in the establishment of his eternal kingdom. A grand and majestic preparation, which begins to be felt at the vocation of Abraham, and becomes evident five hundred years before the arrival of the Messias.[41]

Here we develop the divine plan, and show, on the testimony of the prophets, that all political events anterior to the Messias, and particularly the four great empires, which, according to Daniel, would precede his coming, concur, each in its peculiar manner, to the establishment of the kingdom of the Desired of Nations, by whom, and for whom, all things have been made.

Now, if we consider that these four great empires are raised up only during a long course of ages; that they are prepared for one object by a multitude of events, such as wars, victories, and alliances, of which both East and West have been the scene from the remotest antiquity; in fine, that they are developed, only by absorbing all surrounding kingdoms: then we see clearly that these four empires bear the whole world to the feet of Jesus Christ; like those mighty rivers, which bear to the ocean, not only the waters of their source, but also the waters of their innumerable tributaries.

It is thus that sacred and profane history unite to give us a palpable proof of the sublime saying, that "Jesus Christ is the heir of all things";[42] that all ages refer to him; and that not only the Jewish, but every other nation on the face of the earth, has borne him in its womb.

On the authority of the prophets, we show that the first of the four great empires predicted by Daniel, that of the Assyrians or Babylonians, was providentially intended to oblige the Jews to preserve intact among them the sacred deposit of the promise of a liberator, together with his perfect worship.

We show that the second great empire, that of the Persians, was intended to bring about the birth of the Messias in Judea, and to secure the accomplishment of the prophecies, according to which he should be known as the Son of David, and should enter into the second Temple.

We show that the third great empire, that of the Greeks, was intended to prepare men's minds for the kingdom of the Messias, and to facilitate its establishment, by diffusing everywhere the language in which the gospel should be announced, or by drawing the Jews forth into all known countries, or by spreading over the world, through the Alexandrian translation, a knowledge of the holy books, securely lodged beyond the reach of Jewish falsification.

We show, in fine, that the fourth empire, that of the Romans, was intended to smooth the way for the preaching of the gospel, by overthrowing the barriers that still separated different races, and by levelling the face of the earth and laying down everywhere vast, noble, and extensive roads; also, to fulfill the celebrated prophecy of Jacob on his deathbed, and to put the finishing stroke to the preparation for the gospel, by having the Messias born at Bethlehem.[43]

Admirable philosophy of religion! which, in three lines, contains the universal history of the whole world, during four thousand years:

> All for Christ.
> Christ for man.
> Man for God!

Yes, truly admirable philosophy of religion! whose sublimity astonishes the learned, and whose simplicity adapts itself to the capacity of the meanest intelligence. Experience has demonstrated to us that it is not one of those exalted studies which are too elevated for simple minds.

Thus, God, man, the world; Jesus Christ promised and described, with the preparations for his arrival; such are the subjects of our lessons during the first year.

SECOND YEAR

Life of the Messias. — The times are fulfilled. We issue from the region of shadows and figures to enter on that of lights and realities. What is our first duty henceforward, unless, in accordance with the advice of the holy bishop of Hippo, to present the gospel as the divine commentary on, and accomplishment of, the old testament?[44]

Hence, we hasten to show, with the fathers of the Church, that religion, born with the world, known by the patriarchs, developed under Moses and the prophets, has been perfected under the gospel. We add, with St. Ambrose and St. Thomas, that the Church is an intermediate state between the synagogue and heaven; the Jew had only shadows, without the reality; the Christian possesses the truth, hidden under veils; the saint beholds God, face to face.[45] The old testament is revealed in the new; and the new will be revealed in heaven.

In this manner, we show young Christians that their religion, like God, who is its author, enjoys an everlasting duration; that it was yesterday, that it is today, that it shall continue throughout eternity. Still, though always the same, it has not been always equally developed. It has had a continual progress; from Adam to the Messias, the promises, figures, and prophecies, went on developing themselves successively.[46] Like the sun, it rises only gradually from the eastern horizon, till at noon it pours forth in the richest profusion its sparkling rays; like the tender acorn, it is only with years that it becomes the majestic oak; like man, in fine, it must pass through the various stages of existence, without ever losing its individuality.

When, then, we have sketched the general state of minds, and the particular condition of Judea, at the time of the coming of the Messias, we show the Son of the holy Virgin of Juda, engaged from the time of his birth, not in founding a new religion, but in perfecting the old, in regard to dogma, morality, and worship, replacing weak elements by sacraments full of grace and efficacy; abolishing all those rites that were peculiar to the Jewish people; proclaiming the object of his mission in these luminous words: "I am not come to destroy the law and the prophets, but to fulfill and verify them":[47] attaching thus his work to the ancient work, or rather teaching us that the old and the new testaments are but one great edifice, of which he is the foundation-stone.[48]

Obliged to abridge the account of his marvelous works, we endeavor to relate, in detail, those in which he more conspicuously appears as victim, model, teacher, physician, in other words, as the Redeemer and Savior of the human race. We pass lightly over the rest. Having shown him in his birth, in his life, in his instructions as the man-God, we consider him in his death, dying as a God-man, and proving his divinity more incontestably by his death than by his life.

To the scene of his sorrows we conduct our Christian children. Who does not love to visit the place of his birth? Calvary was our cradle; we bring forward even the infidel to prove it. From Calvary, we pass with our Savior to the tomb; thence we follow into limbo him who was "free among the dead,"[49] preaching the gospel to the just souls, and spreading through their shadowy abodes the light of liberty.

The three days marked by the prophets are rolled away; the Son of the eternal arises from the tomb, conqueror of sin and of death, which is the satellite of sin. We point out his enemies confounded, reduced to the extremity of purchasing for silver the lying depositions of sleeping witnesses. Then come the principal proofs of the resurrection of the Messias, which is the pledge of our resurrection, and the basis of Christianity. We relate his various apparitions, and the tests to which his condescension induced him to submit, in order to convince the apostles.

Here we draw a syllogism, whose magnificent premises are formed of four thousand years of promises, figures, prophecies, and preparations, literally realized in our Lord Jesus Christ, and whose necessary consequence is the divinity of our Savior.

Moreover, by an examination of general facts, we show that our Lord is truly the Messias, promised to the human race, and expected by all people.

The first fact is that, at the period of his birth, the expectation of a Messias, who should renovate mankind, had disappeared after a long existence and wide diffusion, according to the acknowledgment of unbelievers themselves, from every nation, except the Jewish. But this exception itself is entirely in our favor. It was formally predicted that the Jews would not receive the Messias when he should come,[50] so that if they had received him as our Lord Jesus Christ, he would not have been the Messias, or the prophets would have spoken falsely. Thus everything contributes to render unquestionable the certainty of his divinity.

The second fact is that our Lord has really accomplished the mission of the promised Messias, the Desired of Nations, in all its extent. What should the Messias do? One single thing, containing everything in itself: "Take away the sins of the world,"[51] or, according to the word of God himself to the first woman: "Crush the serpent's head."[52]

Now, we show that our Lord has really removed sin. In regard to God, he has rendered an infinite homage to the divine majesty and an infinite satisfaction to the divine justice. The crib and the cross are glorious proofs of it. In regard to man, he has been obedient to death, and even the death of the cross, in order to take away a disobedience, whose guilt was infinite. In regard to God and man, he is both God and man, in order to reunite in the most perfect manner those whom sin had separated.[53]

He has remedied all the consequences of sin, viz.—ignorance, concupiscence, death; in his divine Person, man has known God perfectly, has been fully freed from concupiscence and death, and reigns today triumphant in heaven. And then we show the head of the serpent crushed, that is, the empire of the devil overthrown from its foundations by the teaching and miracles of our Lord. Meanwhile, his apostles, heirs of his power, and preachers of his doctrine, go forth in his name to scatter to the winds the temples and idols that are honored from one end of the world to the other. All these truths, recorded in the life of our Lord, are historical facts. "Now, the facts regarding Jesus Christ," observes the philosopher of Geneva, "are better proved than those regarding Socrates, of which no one doubts."

The Messias is the new Adam.—Thus, in the Person of the man-God, the human race has been perfectly restored to its true life; but it is necessary that each one of us should individually participate in this restoration: otherwise, "Christ will profit us nothing." Here comes forward naturally the explanation of a fundamental truth, without a knowledge of which one cannot understand anything of Christianity.[54] Let us hear it from the lips of the most sublime interpretor of divine thoughts, the most profound searcher into the mystery of redemption.

St. Paul beholds only two men in the world: the first Adam, and the second Adam, or our Lord.[55] The first represents the human race fallen; the second represents the human race restored. It was the union of the whole human race with its first head that rendered it guilty and miserable; it is its union with the second head that renders it just and happy. The union of the human race with the first Adam was a complete,[56] though moral union. This is the reason why man has been degraded in every part of his being.

What, then, must we do to be regenerated? We must, replies the great apostle, bear in ourselves the image of the heavenly man, as we have borne in ourselves the image of the earthly man; we must become the children of the new Adam, by a communication of his Spirit and his divine being, as we were born children of the first Adam by a participation in his sinful flesh.[57] Hence, for each of us, there is an indispensable necessity to be united with the new Adam.[58]

Union of man with the new Adam. — The indispensable union, which has just been pointed out, is acquired in the present life by means of faith, hope, and charity. "These three virtues," says the incomparable St. Thomas, "added to the nature of man by the mercy of his Redeemer, raise him to a godlike union, by rendering him, according to the saying of St. Peter, a participator in the divine nature. Faith elevates the mind, enriching it with supernatural truths, made known by a divine light. Hope elevates the will, by directing it toward the possession of a supernatural good promised to us. Charity elevates the heart, by forming a tender union between it and the supernatural good, its object."[59]

To believe, to hope, to love: such are the three fundamental acts of cooperation required from us by the new Adam, in order that we may be united to him. Thence, in fact, flows the whole economy of our sanctification on earth, and our glorification in heaven. Faith commences our union with God; hope continues it; charity completes it.[60] This view, at once so luminous and comprehensive, being established, we pursue, in our work, the following order and connection in the different parts of the Christian doctrine or catechism, properly so-called:

Faith, with its object, God, the essential truth; also, revealed truth, the Creed.

Hope, with its object, God, the sovereign bounty; what it promises us, grace and glory; the means of obtaining grace, prayer and the sacraments.

Charity, with its object, God, the supreme good; also, what it requires from us, either by itself or its sinless spouse, the commandments of God and of the Church.

Next, we treat of the causes which dissolve this divine union: the passions, with their attendant, sin; then, the preservatives against that only evil — namely, the virtues opposed to the corrupt inclinations of the human heart.

It is here, especially, that a perfectly regular system is necessary. Between all the parts of the Christian doctrine there exists an intimate relation with which it is most important to be acquainted. Should anyone have the misfortune to despise it, or the imprudence to neglect it, the chapters of the catechism would succeed one another, without any rational order. Each part would form, in some manner, an isolated whole; the subject going before would not evoke that which follows; the fundamental truths would not appear in a sufficiently clear light — perhaps they might even be found in a secondary rank: the teaching would be deprived of its energy and perspicuity, in the absence of its logical connection. Henceforward, the child would not understand whither he went, and his wearied memory would soon allow those doctrines to escape, whose explanation had been presented to him with as little regularity or harmony as might be found among a handful of needles thrown on a table.

The first advantage of the plan which we have followed is that it avoids this inconvenience.

The second is that it places in the rank of honor suitable to them the three great virtues of faith, hope, and charity, showing them forth as the three sources of salvation, the three foundation courses of the edifice of religion.

The third is that it is as simple as fruitful; for it embraces, without an effort, every part of the Christian doctrine: every part entering naturally into the place assigned it by logic, like the various pieces of a beautiful mosaic work, in the copy of some grand old masterpiece.

The fourth is that it is most secure. Amongst others, it has been followed by Bellarmine, in his Roman Catechism, solemnly approved by many sovereign pontiffs.[61]

In this the learned cardinal was but a disciple of St. Augustine, who continually desires that all instruction on religion should lead to faith, hope, and charity.[62]

Thus, we delight in saying it, for our general plan, St. Augustine; for our secondary plan, St. Augustine together with Bellarmine: such are the masters, in whose footsteps we follow. Let us pass on to a development of the matter.

Union of man with the new Adam by faith.—The admirable economy of Christianity, to which we have just referred, and the indispensable conditions of our salvation, were the particular subjects of our Savior's conversation with his apostles during the forty days which elapsed between his resurrection and ascension. It was then that he gave them an understanding of the scriptures, and instructed them in the depths of the mysteries of the kingdom of God![63] On this account, we place at this epoch a detailed explanation of his whole doctrine.

The Savior was not content with saying in general, "He who believeth not shall be condemned";[64] but, entering into details, he taught his apostles the various truths which they should preach to the world, and which man should believe in order to be united with his Redeemer, and participate in the benefits of redemption. The apostles composed an abridgment of these truths.

This is the place in which, after having shown the necessity of faith, we explain the Catholic Symbol or Creed. In it are summarized the fundamental truths of religion and philosophy.

God, one in nature, three in Persons: the Father—the work of creation and the government of the world; the Son—the work of redemption; the Holy Ghost—the work of sanctification; and, as a consequence, the Church, with its magnificent hierarchy and immortal constitutions.

Man, mysterious compound; created innocent, degraded by his fall, subjected to trials; surrounded with the means of regaining his primitive perfection, together with other advantages, and obliged to render an account when his days are ended, of the use he has made of the opportunities afforded him; happiness or misery without change or end, the inevitable lot which awaits him after the last judgment.

The world, created by God, regulated by the laws of a universal providence, and destined to be consumed by fire, on the day marked out for it by him, who first drew it forth from nothing.

These are the truths, in a few words, which the Creed reveals to us on the great subjects: God, man, and the world.

To understand this Creed in all its sublime simplicity, compare it with the creeds of the thousand sects which have in turn appeared upon the earth. Remark particularly how every one of its articles destroys some of the absurd theories divulged by pagan philosophers on God, man, and the world: dreams renewed again with such daring effrontery by some of our impious moderns. Every word is a ray of light, dissipating a portion of the darkness in which man's reason has been enveloped since the fall; and the whole assemblage of rays is but the bright sun of truth, before whose presence all darkness disappears, like the shadows of night before the king of day.

Let anyone examine the Creed with impartiality, and say whether anything can be found in the world more perfect, more useful, more consoling, or more venerable.

Modern philosophers! so jealous of your knowledge, know that it is to the Catholic Creed you are indebted for your intellectual superiority over other nations, in both past and present times; to it you owe your deliverance from the gross errors and infamous superstitions of the Senate and the Areopagus. It alone has substituted for the despondent doctrine of a blind destiny and an inexorable fatality, the consoling belief of a universal providence, which rules the world, and watches over man, as man himself watches over

27

the apple of his eye. Let him who chooses say now whether the Christian dogmas are useless in themselves, or contrary to reason.

The Creed being the truth, it follows that the mind which receives it receives something of God.[65] The divine thoughts of the new Adam replace our human, false, imperfect thoughts, inherited from the first Adam. Thus is effected our intellectual union with, or rather transformation into, the Redeemer. On this account, every believer may say: "It is not I, a son of the old Adam, who live, but Jesus Christ liveth in me."[66]

Union of man with the new Adam by hope. — We have seen how magnificent are the operations of faith in the intellect. Reaching into the future, this messenger of eternity brings to the pilgrim of time, "the substance of things hoped for";[67] opens to his eyes a new heaven and a new earth; shows him God, not only as the author of nature, but as his Father, Redeemer, and last end; unveils to him his origin and destiny; traces the way for him, and, by its omnipotent power, supports him to the end of his journey. Elevated into a new region of existence, the understanding has no longer anything to desire but the clear vision of the truths which it possesses.[68]

Nevertheless, by faith our union with the new Adam is not complete; it is perfected by hope. In point of fact, man is not all mind, he is also will; consequently, unless these future realities are to be considered as torments instead of benefits, the goods of the supernatural world can no more remain an object of mere idle contemplation than a treasure presented to the grasping hands of a miser, or food to the perishing looks of a starving man; they must be accessible to the will. Now, it is hope that assures us of their possession.

Raising the will above the transitory goods of this life, it places God and the new heaven and earth of eternity, with the means of obtaining them, in a word, the substance of those future goods, at the head of all its undertakings and actions.[69] It is the queen of immortality, ennobling the desires of man, supporting him in his continual combats, assuaging his sorrows, and caressing his soul. It is the fiery chariot of Elias, transporting us to the heavens, raising us above ourselves, and holding us suspended between heaven and earth, between time and eternity. Such are the properties and effects of hope. It elevates our will, by setting before us a divine object, and filling us with divine tendencies. Under this new head, the Christian can say: "It is not I, a son of the old Adam, who live, but Jesus Christ liveth in me."

Now, among the means of acquiring the supernatural goods which hope presents to the laudable ambition of man, who is enlightened by faith, there is one in particular which may be said to embrace all others: it is grace—grace, so perfectly defined as "the beginning of glory."[70]

We have seen at the outset of our lessons that man was created in a supernatural state, that is, destined for a happiness which the conditions of his simple nature did not require. We have also seen how sin degraded him, but how Jesus Christ restored him to his primitive state, that is, returned to him again the right of seeing God face to face in heaven. With much reason, therefore, is religion, which conducts man to supernatural felicity, termed a *grace*, a gratuitous favor, a magnificent alms. It evidently follows, hence, that man, of his own natural strength, cannot arrive at the triple union, of which we have spoken, with the new Adam; for such an effort grace is necessary. This was the case with man before his fall, as the supernatural state in which he was created shows. With much more reason, then, is grace necessary to him after the injury done to all his powers by original sin.[71] Grace is, therefore, the great object of hope.

Now, grace, the powerful and universal succor granted in consideration of the merits of the new Adam; grace, by which God lowers himself and becomes present to man; grace, by which man, strengthened and illuminated, reascends to his supernatural state, is obtained by two principal means: prayer and the sacraments.

Prayer, the mysterious power which brings the creature close to the Creator, is an indispensable condition of the supernatural union of man with God. Hence, among all people may be found an uninterrupted practice of prayer, from the beginning of the world. Hence, also, the precept, by which the new Adam lays down and formulizes the necessity of this fundamental act of religion: "Pray always, without ceasing"[72]—a precept at once positive and negative. To pray is not less necessary for the life of the soul than to breathe is for the life of the body.

It is easily seen that we here mean *prayer* in the general acceptation of the term.[73] We call it, therefore, the soul or life of Christianity. Among the early Christians, prayer and Christianity were synonymous. With them a Christian was a man who prayed.[74] Even among the savage tribes of the New World, the same beautiful and just idea is found. In their language, Christianity is styled, not "religion," but "prayer"; to become a man of prayer is to become a Christian.

To this view succeeds that of prayer, strictly so called. St. Augustine, with his loving heart, his mighty genius, and his piercing intellect, is joined by Tertullian and St. Cyprian, in the explanation which our catechism affords of the most beautiful of all prayers, the Lord's Prayer.

The second means of obtaining grace is the sacraments. In order to meet the requirements of the twofold nature of man, uniting both his soul and senses to his Redeemer; in order to preserve him in humility, a permanent condition of his restoration, by placing before his eyes the omnipotence of him, who, in the order of grace as well as in the order of nature, has need only of the weakest instruments for the accomplishment of the mightiest works; in order to supply all the wants of our supernatural life, God, in his profound wisdom, has instituted the sacraments.

Sensible signs, they captivate the outward man, by rendering palpable to us, through the elements which serve as their matter, the marvelous effects wrought by them on the inward man; sacred signs, they reveal, in the supernatural order, the sovereign dominion of him who reigns as absolute master in the natural order; permanent and varied signs, regulated by spiritual laws, they do for the maintenance of the life of the soul that which creatures and physical laws do incessantly for the maintenance of the life of the body. Admirable harmony! which displays, with so much splendor, the finger of God, and the intimate relations established between nature and grace, by him who is the author of both!

Indeed, there are seven things necessary for man in order to lead, preserve, and utilize his natural life: he must be born; he must grow; he must be nourished; he must be healed, if wounded; he must recover his strength, if sick; he must be surrounded by authorities, invested with the power of maintaining order and promoting the public welfare; in fine, he must be perpetuated. All these things are equally necessary for the spiritual life, and, in consequence, explain the reasons of the seven sacraments.

By baptism we are born again in the new Adam; by confirmation we grow; by the Eucharist we are nourished; by penance we are healed; by extreme unction the strength of our soul is renewed for the last combat; by holy orders we are surrounded with the ministers of religion; by matrimony the faithful are perpetuated.

To the foregoing harmony there is joined another not less admirable. As, in the firmament, all the planets gravitate toward the sun, so, in the Church, all the other sacraments gravitate toward the Blessed Eucharist. "The Eucharist," says St. Thomas, "is the end of all the other sacraments; for all refer to it, and find in it their perfection."[75] Baptism makes us capable of receiving it; confirmation renders us more worthy of receiving it, or assists us to preserve the divine union wrought by it; penance puts us in a fit state again, if made unfit by sin; extreme unction maintains us in this state against the most violent attacks of the devil at the last moment; in fine, holy orders and matrimony perpetuate the Blessed Eucharist by perpetuating the Church.

Since, on the one hand, the Eucharist is the end of all the other sacraments, the supreme mystery of faith, and love, and unity, or, as St. Thomas says, the consummation of the spiritual life; and, on the other, the Eucharist is our Lord Jesus Christ himself, perpetually incarnate in the midst of the world; there follow, hence, two great consequences, eminently calculated to place this august sacrament in the high rank of honor which belongs to it.

First, under the gospel, as under the law, Jesus Christ is ever the Alpha and the Omega of religion; everything refers to him, and to our union with him. From the moment of original sin there has been no salvation for man, except in a union with Jesus Christ, through the three possible modes of faith, hope, and charity—consequently, by communion, the Jew could and should believe in Jesus Christ to come, could and should hope in him, could and should love him, could and should communicate with him, by participation in the victims which represented him.[76] Like the ancient worship in general, this figurative communion was only a shadow of the real Communion, reserved for the law of grace. Hence, that admirable expression of St. Ambrose: "The Jew had shadows, without the reality; the Christian possesses the truth, hidden under veils; the saint enjoys the truth, without veils."[77]

Secondly, the Eucharist is the same in the spiritual as the sun in the physical world. Everywhere its light and heat diffuse innumerable blessings to mankind. By it the whole creation, flowing continually from the bosom of the Creator, continually returns thither again. The eyes have only to be opened to behold the accomplishment of this mysterious law.

All creatures tend to a state of perfection, that is, to pass from a life less perfect to one more perfect; but, to do so, they must lose their peculiar life. Thus, inorganic bodies, air and water, for example, lose their peculiar life, in order to take that of some other creature to which they are assimilated; the vegetable, in its turn, is absorbed by the animal, and acquires a new life; the vegetable and the animal, being absorbed by man, acquire a still nobler life. God, in fine, draws man to himself, and communicates to him his divine and immortal life. Then man can truly say: "It is not I who live, but God, who lives in me." Who will not here adore, in silent love and admiration, the touching mystery by which is accomplished the grand transformation that leads the world to unity?

Treating of the sacraments, we are careful not to omit an explanation of those admirable ceremonies and sublime prayers which accompany their administration. Is it possible to find anything more venerable, more instructive, more eminently philosophical, and yet, we are obliged to say it, more generally unknown than the liturgy? How many rites and usages whose signification carries the mind back to the earliest days of the Church, or raises it to the contemplation of the most sublime mysteries, remain as a dead letter to us, a species of unintelligible hieroglyphic, of which the ignorant Catholic is unable to render an account, and at which the still more ignorant skeptic does not hesitate to scoff!

Besides the advantage of enlightening the Christian's piety, our explanation of these beautiful ceremonies has that also of proving the constant tradition of the Church on each of the sacraments: a tradition of fact—more striking, it appears to us, and more easily grasped, than the tradition of oral testimony.

Union of man with the new Adam by charity.—United to the new Adam by faith, which, according to the expression of the fathers, deifies the mind, by hope, which deifies the will, and by Communion, which deifies the whole being, has man anything more to desire or to do? Certainly. That God whom he receives under passing veils, the new heaven and earth of eternity, all those supernatural goods which faith shows him in the distance, and hope promises him, he must endeavor with his utmost power to unite himself to, in a complete and permanent manner, becoming rich with their riches, happy with their happiness, and perfect with their perfection.

To believe is not sufficient for the fervent Christian, to hope is not sufficient for him, to possess imperfectly and temporarily is not sufficient for him: he wishes to enjoy, to enjoy completely, to enjoy eternally; for joy is union, and union is love, and love is the most noble and imperative want of man, the first and the last commandment of the new Adam, the fulfillment of the law and the prophets, the end of faith and hope, the supreme bond of perfection on earth, and the essence of felicity in heaven. Hence, the expression of St Bernard: "With reason does the apostle define faith, 'the substance of things hoped for.'[78] It is, indeed, as impossible to hope for that in which one does not believe as to paint in the air. Faith says: God has prepared ineffable joys for his faithful servants. Hope says: they are reserved for me. Charity says: I run to possess them."[79]

We now see that faith and hope are only means to arrive at charity; it is therefore evident that man cannot, ought not, limit himself to these two virtues: the new Adam calls him to a more perfect union. Communion itself is but a means, not an end; it is a nourishment intended for the renovation of our strength, that we may continue our work. Man is here below a laborer, whose day is not ended.

When then he is weak with the warfare of well-doing, the labor of virtue, he acquires fresh vigor by communicating; on his departure from the sacred table, burning with a holy ardor, he returns to his work, and his work becomes love in action; for love does not solely consist in the contemplation of the perfections of God, but also in the accomplishment of the divine will. "We love God," says St. John, "if we keep his commandments, and his commandments are not heavy."[80] The reason is now plain why, in the order of our lessons, we place charity after faith and hope, the commandments after the Creed and the sacraments.

Now, if the Creed is the tutor of our weak reason and the chief regenerator of our thoughts, the decalogue is the guardian of our heart and the chief regenerator of our affections. We do ourselves an incalculable amount of good by carefully considering the meaning of each commandment. Human love, degraded by the primitive fall, is inclined to abandon itself to everything beneath it. A proof of this humiliating truth is easily found in the irreligion of both ancient and modern times. Our poor heart, like the idolatrous priest, who searches in the reeking entrails of victims for the secrets of heaven, having wandered among all creatures, and roamed through all pleasures in search of happiness, is at length obliged to exclaim: Vanity! falsehood! affliction! Truly it is a merciless deception and a fearful torment, from which the Redeemer has been pleased to deliver us, by recalling us to the only objects worthy of our affection!

All the commandments are reduced to two: the love of God, and, for the love of God, the love of the neighbor; hence, in our neighbor, it is God himself whom we love.

O love of God! thou greatest want of man, the first law of his existence, the precious treasure carried away by the robber-serpent, recovered but by the new Adam, and restored to the human race for its happiness and glory in time and eternity, thou descendest to the world by the decalogue! This sacred code is the organic law of charity: its end is to regulate, to nourish, and to protect its manifestation, to nourish and protect it in the midst of a thousand dangers.

Hence, in the decalogue, there are two kinds of precepts: positive and negative. By the first, the new Adam teaches us that we should love God, and man for the love of God. The first Adam brought misery on himself and his posterity by violating this primordial law; the second Adam places all our happiness in a return to the sweet law of love.

Thus, by regulating our affections, Jesus Christ shows himself truly the Savior of our hearts, as by teaching us what to believe, he shows himself the Savior of our minds. In a word, the decalogue delivers the heart of man from the degrading yoke of concupiscence, as the Creed delivers his mind from the wretched yoke of ignorance.

By the negative precepts the new Adam protects our heart against every foreign, inimical, usurping love. All that can be the object of a legitimate love—the life of our body and the life of our soul, the peace of families, the sanctity of the marriage tie, our property, even our reputation—he surrounds with a barrier more sacred than could be afforded by the whole collection of human laws.[81]

Hence follows the truth, unfortunately so little known, that each of the commandments of God is a benefit, a pledge of happiness, even on earth.[82] Such is the supremely just point of view, from which we exhibit this divine code. Is anything more important? Alas! is it not because so many unfortunates consider it a painful yoke that they trample it under their feet? No, no, mistaken men! the decalogue would not fetter your liberty, but perfect it; nor retard your pace, but regulate it; it would not embarrass your steps, but direct and enlighten them.[83]

A traveler advances toward a magnificent city, in which not only his beloved family, but an immense fortune, awaits him. Between him and the desired city there lies an unfathomable abyss. Thick darkness overspreads the way. He has neither guide nor lantern. Across the abyss there is only one narrow, unsteady plank. The unfortunate man is accustomed to make false steps: his numerous and deplorable falls heretofore have been but too convincing a proof of his weakness.

Tell me, now, if a charitable guide came forward to take this traveler by the hand, if he erected on each side of the dangerous plank a strong barrier, if he suspended around the place a number of bright lamps, so that it would be impossible for any one to go astray, or to fall into the abyss, unless by deliberately leaping from the brink or parapet into it, would you regard these fences as impediments, these lamps as insults, so many cares as wrongs done the traveler? Would this friendly guide deserve the name of a tyrant for having lent his hand and secured a prosperous journey to a stranger beset with so many perils?

The application is easy; the traveler, subject to so many false steps, is man on earth. The blessed city, where fortune, glory, a beloved family await him, is heaven. The dark abyss is hell. The narrow, frail, trembling plank is life. The kindly guide is God. The barriers and the lamps are the commandments of the Lord.

Let the blinded man now say that the decalogue is an obstacle to his liberty; as for us, O my God! we shall always acknowledge that it is our sweetest support, and consequently, one of thy greatest benefits; and, not to fall into the bottomless pit, we shall always be careful not to offend against it.

As, by believing in the Creed, our mind is united, so, by accepting the decalogue, our heart is united to the new Adam. In fact, the decalogue is charity. See how soon the heart, that is humble and pliable under the law of love, overflows with divine instincts. The new Adam becomes the principle and life of its affections. The regenerated man can say, from this point of view also: "It is not I, a son of the old Adam, who live, but Jesus Christ liveth in me." Henceforward, there are found in him, as in the man-God, but two loves: the love of God, and the love of his neighbor; though, indeed, the two are but one; and thus he finds himself conducted back to the primitive unity of the state of innocence, when all was pure, holy, noble, and great in man.

Volumes upon volumes would not suffice to explain the riches, honors, and advantages which are contained, for the benefit of nations and individuals, in this decalogue, alas! so little known, and so unmeritedly violated in our hapless days. How sadly is human love degraded! Moderns, beware! already you have made more than one step toward paganism. Imprudent men, in trampling under your feet the decalogue, the bases of your ancient glory, you sport with the thunderbolt!

End of our union with the new Adam. —Having shown, as well as we could, the nature, necessity, and conditions of our union with the Redeemer, we seek what object the Word proposed to himself, in uniting himself so closely to us. We learn it immediately from himself: "I am come, that they may have life, and may have it more abundantly";[84] that you and I may be one;[85] it is, that we may live by his life on earth and in heaven.

Here the life of the new Adam is proposed for universal imitation. The great physician, who has descended from heaven for the benefit of mankind, who lay groveling on the earth, is not content with pouring a salutary balm over the wounds of the human race; nor even with placing it on the road again, and saying, "Walk"; but, like the royal eagle, which encourages its young ones to fly, by flying before them, he takes his divine flight toward heaven, in the presence of man, teaching man to follow him thither. In his tender goodness, he passed through all the stages of man's existence, and sanctified them, teaching us to do likewise.

The new Adam is then our model; as we have borne the image of the terrestrial man, it is necessary that we should also bear the image of the heavenly man. Yes, heaven is closed against every one who does not bear an exact resemblance to our Redeemer!

He is the model of every age, state, and condition. Christ is man; such is the point of view from which we present him.

He is the model of our interior life—it is according to his judgments, affections, thoughts, and desires, that those of all men should be formed. What has the new Adam thought, what has he loved?[86] Such should be the touchstone of all human thoughts and affections. O admirable philosophy, contained in these few words!

He is the model of our exterior life—his conduct may be summed up in one expression: "He did all things well."[87]

He is the model of inferiors—his life may be expressed in the words: "He was subject."[88]

He is the model of superiors—"He went about doing good."[89]

He is the model of all sufferers, whether superiors or inferiors—"May it be so, O Father, for so it hath seemed good in thy sight."[90]

This essential part of religion is not explained in any catechism, at least, according to our view, as it should be explained. In general, the Savior is only shown as our model during his mortal life; while, in fact, it is otherwise.

Lest future generations should forget his example, or falsely imagine that it was intended only for certain times or places, the new Adam has established his permanent abode amongst us in the Holy Eucharist. Dwelling in town and country, in every climate and every age, he repeats from his tabernacle, and will continue to repeat to all future generations, the lessons which he once gave in Judea; he presents the same example today as he did eighteen centuries ago; and he exhorts us to attend to him in the same words which were heard of old along the banks of the Jordan: "See, and do all things according to the pattern which was shown thee."[91]

O men! whoever you are, weigh well this truth. It will give you wondrous light to understand the lessons which continually emanate from the tabernacle. From this pulpit of truth, the great master of heaven utters, in the simplest and sweetest tones, the grand maxims of Christian perfection. Think well on it; if it is true, that, in consequence of his incarnation, the new Adam bore the title of master and the character of teacher of justice; if he fulfilled his duties so worthily during the course of his mortal life, it is no less true that he still conducts the school of all virtues in the adorable sacrament of the Eucharist.

If we cannot contemplate him living amongst men in the exercise of an ardent charity, a profound humility, an extreme poverty, a boundless generosity, and an unwearying patience, without feeling within us a desire of following and imitating him, with how much more reason should we be affected with similar sentiments, when we consider him, glorious as he is, still residing in our holy tabernacles, and giving us a continual example of the selfsame virtues!

The end of our union with the new Adam is then to sanctify us in time, and render us happy in eternity. Sublime and delightful union! which, transforming man into God, restores the human race to its primitive perfection; but a union, which, alas! at any time during the period of our earthly trial, may easily be broken![92]

In order to inspire a sovereign horror of sin, we speak here of that frightful evil, which alone can destroy, in regard to each of us, the benefit of our redemption, separate us for-ever from the new Adam, and by making us depart this life more guilty than we entered into it, fix our abode irrevocably in the company of the devil and his angels. To preserve young Christians from this dreadful evil, this only real evil, we endeavor to show it to them in its causes, its progress, its occasions, its effects, its punishments, and its remedies.

Perpetuity of our union with the new Adam. — The forty days which our Lord should remain on earth after his resurrection drew to an end. The divine master had instructed his apostles in the mysteries of the kingdom of God. He had given them the understand-ing of the scriptures. The admirable economy of man's redemption, the object for which the incarnate Word was born into the world, lived, died, and rose again; the necessity for all men to unite themselves to him by faith, hope, and charity; the end of this union in time being the imitation of his life, and in eternity the participation of his glory; the only cause which can sever this holy union, and render Christ unprofitable to us, is sin; all these matters were henceforward known to the apostles, who were charged with instructing the whole world regarding them.

Was there anything else still to be done by the new Adam? Yes; to secure the preser-vation and provide for the propagation of his divine work, in order that all men coming into the world might gather its fruits. He would not himself impart instruction, person-ally, much longer; his earthly mission was fulfilled; he was about to ascend to the right hand of his Father. How would he perpetuate the benefit of redemption, and render it accessible to all persons, even to the consummation of time?

He substitutes another for himself; he selects a vicar on whom he will confer the plenitude of power which he has received from his Father, and to whom he will confide the care of perpetuating and extending the great work which he himself has come to begin. Never will man be elevated to a higher dignity; never will a more formidable responsibility be laid upon the shoulders of a mortal.

Who will be this viceroy of the Son of God? O abyss of mercy and wisdom! Even he, who, but a few days ago, thrice denied his master at the voice of a servant. All that is most weak is chosen for the work that is all important! A reed to support the world! A great sinner to be the teacher of faith, and the father of Christians! In a word, the vicar of the new Adam will be the apostle St. Peter. How sublime and affecting are the circumstances of his consecration!

When a king wishes to confide some important charge to one of his subjects, he looks for a guarantee or security; so does Jesus Christ. This divine shepherd, who came to shed his blood for the salvation of his sheep, is on the point of quitting them. Before confiding to St. Peter so precious a flock, he required some guarantee or security. But what can he expect from a poor, illiterate fisherman, without any other fortune than a boat and its nets? The greatest and safest pledge that man can give, namely, love; but a love carried even to heroism, a love ready to sacrifice itself for the service of its master and the interests of its charge.

Such is the meaning of these admirable words, so earnestly repeated: "Simon, son of John, lovest thou me more than these?" It is only after having obtained the assurance of this love, proof against every trial, that the divine shepherd says to him: "Feed my lambs, feed my sheep."[93] Everything that breathes of paternal devotedness in authority, everything that breathes of filial gentleness in submission, consequently everything that is indestructible in the social bonds, is contained in this model consecration of the chief of all superiors; a consecration unique in the annals of the world, and displaying in itself alone more social philosophy than all the books that were ever written. Absolute power to govern the Church, the right of confirming his brethren, the primacy of honor and of jurisdiction, infallibility as supreme teacher in faith and morals; such are the prerogatives of Peter, ever living in his successors.

Having appointed a supreme head to the Church, the new Adam associates co-operators with him. He approaches his apostles and says to them, with all the majesty becoming the greatness of the occasion: "All power is given to me in heaven and on earth; go, therefore, teach all nations, baptizing them in the name of the Father, and of the Son, and of the Holy Ghost."[94]

Judges of the faith with St. Peter, the apostles and their chief form the teaching Church. Jesus Christ calls it his body, that is, the visible organ of his Spirit, by which he addresses the world. He promises to be with it, even to the consummation of the world, as the soul is with the body. Now, Christ does not die; his Church, therefore, will be an immortal body, which, by the constant renewal of its members, shall never fade away.

Henceforward, it will be through the instrumentality of his Church that the new Adam will teach, develop, and propagate his doctrine to the end of time. By the Church must all men be born again to him. "No one can have God for his Father, who has not the Church for his mother."[95]

We have scarcely departed from the sublime ordination of St. Peter, when a new spectacle presents itself to our eyes: the Savior ascends to heaven. The model of man in time, he continues to be the same in eternity. The firstborn among the dead, chief of the human race, he solemnly, in the name of all mankind, his brethren, takes possession of heaven; of heaven, his noble conquest, and the eternal home of man; of heaven, the happy abode of all those who shall have profited by his redemption.

There we contemplate him before the throne of his Father, in the divine character of advocate and high priest, always interceding for us, always watching over us, always opposing the infinite merits of his labors and sufferings to the avenging justice; with one hand holding the helm of the Church, which he guides among the quicksands to the heavenly shore; with the other, placing crowns of immortality on the heads of his happy children, according as they arrive safely at the end of their course.

We now return to earth. With the apostles, we enter the upper chamber to await the descent of the Holy Ghost, who is to animate the Church. Here begins our third year.

THIRD YEAR

Christianity established. — As before the coming of the Messias, all the designs of God tended to realize the work of the redemption, so in the same manner after the coming of the Messias, all the designs of God tend only to maintain and extend this work. Thus, the restoration of all things in Jesus Christ is the pivot around which all the events of the world revolve, and is the final end of all the designs of God; a sublime end, to which concur, whether knowingly or unknowingly, willingly or unwillingly, both kings and peoples.

We have shown the accomplishment of this great law during the four thousand years which preceded the coming of the Redeemer. If we were to stop there, our task would be incomplete. Religion would not be known in its magnificent entirety, and our teaching, being deficient, would not meet the views of the great master whom we follow.[96] The exposition of religion, from the time of Pentecost down to our own days, is then as necessary as its anterior history; it is even much more interesting, whether because it is less known or because it touches us more closely.

If it is admirable to assist at the first appearance and gradual developments of this divine tree, whose roots are hidden in the night of ages, how much more admirable is it to see it extending its protecting branches over the whole world, sheltering beneath its generous foliage, and nourishing with its vivifying fruit, the generations who pass it by on their way to eternity; to see it beaten by the storms, and yet as immovable as the rocks; ever attacked by the consuming worms of heresy, scandal, and impiety, and yet always preserving its vigor, youth, and inexhaustible fertility! a continual miracle! before which man, enlightened by faith, falls on his knees, and, in a transport of admiration, exclaims: "O work of God, inexplicable to reason!"[97]

Such is the picture which we unfold before the eyes of youthful Christians during the third year of the catechism.

Before ascending to heaven, the divine Word had created the body of the Church, observing in the formation of regenerate man the same order which he had followed in the formation of fallen man. The consecrated apostles, the disciples attached to the apostles, the various orders of the established hierarchy, the laws and regulations promulgated, formed, so to speak, the body of the Church. Yet a little while, and the Spirit from on high shall come to give life to this immortal body. The ever memorable day of Pentecost breaks upon the world; the Holy Ghost descends to the cenacle, and rests upon every one of the assembled company. The soul is joined to the body; the Church is animated.

With the apostles, we depart from the upper chamber; we follow them in their evangelical journeys. We speak of the persecutions, and other gigantic efforts of hell, to stifle the work of redemption. We sketch the history of the most illustrious martyrs. To make young Christians acquainted with the manners of their forefathers in the faith, we relate in detail the customs of the early Christians; we trace their footprints at Jerusalem, at Antioch, at Corinth, at Rome; we descend into the catacombs.

With the torch of science and of history in our hand, we seek our way along the galleries and through the oratories of this subterranean city. Every monument that we meet with bears witness to the angelic virtues, the patient sufferings, and the lively faith of our glorious ancestors. We see them, in this dark abode, raising their innocent hands to heaven; reciting, with extended arms, their fervent prayers; celebrating their fraternal *agapae*, and offering the holy mysteries, either to prepare themselves for martyrdom, or to obtain the salvation of their haughty persecutors, whose golden chariots roll with fury above their heads. These ever-interesting places are hallowed with such sweet reminiscences, that we cannot too frequently conduct thither or too long retain there the Christians of the present day.

Herein we imitate the Church herself, who, in an age of coldness and indifference, returns again to the forgotten paths of the catacombs, and opening on all sides these ancient tombs, reanimates the piety and faith of her children by presenting to them the traditions and monuments of her infancy.[98]

Faithful imitators of the Savior, our forefathers were obliged to bury themselves in the bowels of the earth for three long centuries, as he himself had lain buried in the tomb for three days. The catacombs were the tomb from which, full of life, the chaste spouse of the man-God should arise victorious to ascend the throne of the Caesars, as he had arisen from his tomb, the conqueror of death and hell, to reign eternally over the world.

The divinity of Christianity being rendered as evident as the existence of the sun by the mere fact of its establishment,[99] despite the efforts of all human antagonism, we show its admirable effects upon the world. For this purpose we compare man under paganism with man under Christianity.

Examining in detail the various positions in which man may be found, and the various relations under which he may be regarded, we behold the universal influence of Christianity: over the intellectual, moral, and physical man, by enlightening, sanctifying, and consoling him; over society, by restoring the true ideas of right and duty; over the domestic circle, by leading it back to its primitive perfection, which excludes divorce and polygamy; over the father, by making him no longer a despot, but a venerable and amiable representative of our Father who is in heaven; over the mother, by declaring her the companion, and not the slave, of man; over the child, by presenting it as a sacred deposit to its parents, and abolishing the barbarous privilege of forsaking, killing, or selling it; over the slave, by proclaiming him his master's brother and equal before God; over the poor, by calling them the dear friends of Christ; over the stranger, by considering him as a welcome neighbor; in fine, we show what ought to be written in letters of gold, Christianity everywhere relieving the weak, by substituting for the brutal dominion of might, the sweet law of love.[100]

Comparing thus the pagan with the Christian world, we show the new aspect which all things have taken under the influence of the gospel. Everyone perceives in particular what he owes to Christianity, and is obliged to bless that beneficent religion, and God who is its author.

Thanks to the priesthood, to the Church, the world is become Christian! After so many salutary improvements have been made in manners, laws, and institutions; in a word, after so many human beings, children of the old Adam, have shared in the life of the new Adam; should we not think that the world, now rendered happy and become grateful for so many benefits, should repose in the bosom of a profound peace, and that Christianity should enjoy, uninterruptedly, the fruit of its laborious triumph? Yes, so it would appear; but, in reality, it cannot be so.

The effects of sin in regard to man are weakened, but not destroyed, by redemption; this work will only be consummated in heaven. Until we arrive there, we shall have warfare: intellectual warfare, "there must be heresies";[101] moral warfare, "it must needs be that scandals come";[102] physical warfare, "through many tribulations we must enter into the kingdom of God."[103] All these things are necessary, that our temporal life may be what God desires it to be: a trial, a meritorious trial, but a painful trial. Man is a soldier; he must preserve his union with the new Adam, and advance toward perfection, sword in hand.[104]

Hell and the old enemy have made a thousand efforts to render this warfare most perilous to us, and the work of redemption unavailing in regard to nations and individuals. Sometimes they raised up heresies to change the truth, and destroy the intellectual man; sometimes they raised up scandals to substitute concupiscence for charity, to exchange a sensual for a supernatural life, consequently to destroy the moral man; sometimes the double crime of heresy and scandal, or some other particular crimes, drew on kingdoms a series of pestilences, wars, famines, injustices, and disorders, which tended to destroy the physical man, by reviving the savage sway of the strongest arm, and replunging the world into that state of misery and abjection in which it groaned under paganism.

Thus, to ruin the work of redemption in the intellectual, moral, and physical man, will be the continual aim of the devil, and of the evil principle which exists within us.

On every point of attack the new Adam places a sentinel. Here we develop his admirable system of defense and conservation. Happy the man who comprehends it! for him history has no secrets, he sees the plan, the object, the importance of every event; the more deeply he thinks, the more clearly he perceives that Jesus Christ is the immortal King of ages, the Alpha and the Omega, the center to which all rays converge. Thanks to this luminous knowledge, his reason is enlightened, his judgment formed, his heart inflamed; an admiration of religion becomes the habitual sentiment of his soul, and he renders an account of all things in the world with a superiority and a justness of conception, which in vain may be sought for among philosophers without faith. All our efforts in this part of the catechism are directed to lift a little the veil which conceals so many wonders.

Christianity preserved; the priest, the saint, the religious orders. — The universal and constant preserver of the work of redemption, namely, the priest, will bear the same characteristics, and fulfill the same offices, as Jesus Christ himself, whose substitute he is. Like the Word incarnate, he must be:

I. An offerer of sacrifice, in order to apply to all generations the merits of the sacrifice of the cross, by perpetuating it on the altar; a living victim, too, he will immolate himself for the sins of the people. By this uninterrupted expiation, he will preserve for the world the chief fruit of redemption, which is the union of heaven and earth, and draw down continual graces on mankind, preventing their crimes from ever erecting again the wall of separation, raised by the revolt of the first Adam, and overthrown by the sacrifice of the second. Such will be the permanent characteristic of the priest, such the office prevailing over all others, such the principal duty imposed by the Savior: "Do this for a commemoration of me."[105]

In the order of history, as well as of dignity, the mission of offering sacrifice precedes that of preaching the truth and judging consciences; what man particularly requires is expiation. Hence, the apostle St. Paul, commenting on the words of the divine master, says, in express terms: "Every high priest, taken from among men, is ordained for men in the things that appertain to God, that he may offer up gifts and sacrifices for sins."[106] Hence follows the list of his other duties.

II. A teacher, in order to prevent, by the continual dissemination of Christian truth, the ruin of the work of redemption in the human mind: "You are the light of the world; go, teach all nations."[107]

III. A model, in order to prevent, by the shining example of his virtues, or, in other words, by the practical love of supernatural goods, concupiscence, or the irregular love of sensible things, from ruining the work of redemption in man's will: "You are the salt of the earth; let your works so shine before men, that they may glorify your Father who is in heaven."[108]

IV. A physician for all human miseries, in order to prevent, by an unwearying and universal charity, the ruin of the work of redemption in the physical man, through a return to pagan degradation, and to the sufferings which were its natural consequences: "Cleanse the lepers, heal the sick, do good to all."[109]

Anointed ministers of God! such is your mission. Was there ever a nobler? The several offices of expiator, intercessor, teacher, model, and physician, are always to be characterized in him, but with more or less splendor, according to the requirements of times and places; or, in other words, according to the needs of the divine work. The priest, then, is the preserver of Christianity; is it possible to conceive a juster or a more exalted idea of him, to remind him more efficaciously of the obligation he is under of practicing all virtues, or to inspire the people more fully with that respect and love which they owe to him?

Now, as the evil principle which fights against Christianity is found wherever there are men, always armed, always seeking to undermine and destroy the divine work, so the priest is likewise found everywhere, watching, night and day, as the shepherd over his flock, or as the watchman on the ramparts of a besieged city. So much for ordinary times.

But sometimes the danger increases. The wolves roaming about the fold become more numerous and more fierce. The enemy attacks the fortifications more desperately; already his foot is on the battlements. The isolated pastor becomes too weak to defend his sacred trust. It is then that is heard on all sides the cry of alarm, and that individual pastors have recourse to the pastor of pastors; or that, assembling from the neighboring quarters, they themselves employ one united effort as the surest means of banishing the wolves from the sheepfold and the enemy from the fortress; in other words, of arresting heresies and scandals. The means here referred to are councils.

We relate, according as we meet them in the course of time, the history of these august assemblies. The historical exposition of their occasions, decisions, and results shows not only the literal accomplishment of the divine promise, "I am with you all days, even to the consummation of the world,"[110] but also the absurdity of the reproach which is sometimes made against the Church of creating new dogmas.

Witnesses of the ancient faith, the pastors are content with rendering testimony to the constant belief of their particular Churches; their only fear is, lest a single word should be added or taken away, lest the slightest innovation should be made in doctrine. See what passes at Nice; the same is followed ever afterward.

Arius attacks the divinity of our Savior. The bishop of Alexandria raises the cry of alarm; the bishops from the four quarters of the world are convoked: they assemble at Nice. Do they say: "We have discovered, and now declare, for the first time, that the Son of God is consubstantial with his Father"? No; but they say: "We render testimony to the faith of our Churches, and we depose that they have always believed, and still believe, in the divinity of the Word; the doctrine of Arius is opposed to the ancient doctrine, it is an innovation; we, the guardians of the ancient faith, condemn both the innovation and the innovator." Thus, it is not a new faith they establish, it is only the ancient faith they profess.

In the same manner, when the bishops assembled at Trent from all parts of Christendom, and condemned the errors of Luther and Calvin, it was not on the holy scriptures alone, but also on the decisions of preceding councils, the constant sentiment of the fathers, and the immemorial practices of the Church, that they founded their decrees.

Is this an act of absolute despotism on the part of the bishops? Far from it; it is, on the contrary, an act of docility to an authority more ancient than theirs. They received the law before imposing it on others, and if one among them should refuse to bow to its yoke, he would immediately incur an anathema and be deposed. The simple Catholic, then, who submits to their decision, does not merely yield to the personal authority of his pastors, but submits to the entire body of the Church, and the Church herself submits to the authority of Jesus Christ, by obeying the command which he gave her to bear testimony to him in Jerusalem, and in Samaria, and even to the extremities of the earth, till the consummation of time.[111]

And now the days have come when the evil principle, gathering fresh courage, wages a fiercer war, and spreads the conflict wider. It is then that, from the ever-fruitful womb of the Church, the Almighty brings forth a new array of defenders. We speak of those extraordinary saints, those men powerful in word and work, who appear from time to time in the day of trial. They are always endowed, in the most eminent degree, with the qualities required by the circumstances of the time, so that their mission is evident.

But, as we have seen, hell can only attack man in three ways: in the intellectual man, by error; in the moral man, by scandal; and, in the physical man, by a return to pagan abjection and slavery. So on this account—how admirable!—we behold three kinds of saints, and only three.

I. Apologist saints (the word *apology* is occasionally employed throughout this work in its original sense of "defense" or "justification")—men raised up for the defense and propagation of truth, that is, to prevent the ruin of the work of redemption in the intellectual man. It has been remarked before our time that they not only appeared at the very places which most needed them, but at the precise moment when truth was in the greatest danger. This fundamental observation, which renders the continual action of providence over the Church so evident, we are careful constantly to place before the minds of youth.

Another remark, not less interesting, is that religion's most illustrious apologists appeared in the first ages. These apologists are not the Tertullians, nor the Athenagorases, nor the Clements of Alexandria, but the men of the people, the poor, the ignorant, and the old; weak women, young virgins, timid children; in a word, the martyrs; these are the most illustrious witnesses of the truth, the most eloquent apologists, by whose blood its triumph was secured. "How, indeed," says Pascal, "can we refuse to believe in witnesses who allowed themselves to be strangled for the testimony which they give?" We show that the testimony of blood, the apology of torments, is found by religion as often as it is required.

II. Contemplative saints—raised up for the defense of the work of redemption in the moral man, they trample underfoot honors, riches, pleasures, all the passions, and by a supreme contempt of transitory things, recall the human heart to the love of supernatural things.

Certainly if all the evils of the world proceed from an inordinate love of creatures, how useful to the repose of society and to the happiness of nations are those persons who, by their example, contribute more efficaciously than all philosophers with their writings, and legislators with their laws, to destroy this guilty love. History still shows them to us, always appearing at the very moment when human love, being degraded by scandals and tepidity, and become sensual, steps forward to seize its fallen scepter.

Thus, by the side of vice, you always observe the contrary virtue! It is a counterpoise, an innocent victim laden with the expiation of guilt. This is one of the most admirable harmonies of the moral world, and a proof of the oracle, the Lord "hath disposed all things in number, weight, and measure";[112] a profound saying, of which the spiritual world offers us much more resplendent proofs than the material. We know that the physical creation would be instantaneously overthrown, if the law of gravity by which it is regulated, were for a moment disturbed; a similar fate would await society, if the band which holds so many opposing forces in spiritual equilibrium, were at any time withdrawn.

III. Infirmarian saints—raised up for the comfort of the poor, sick man, that is to say, for the preservation of his life and corporal well-being, consequently to prevent the physical man from falling back into that state of misery, abjection, and wretchedness, from which the Redeemer rescued him; the lives of these saints are a long series of devoted acts for the relief of every misfortune. The fruits of redemption are thus preserved in the physical man. Here, also, history shows them to us, appearing on the earth like so many consoling angels, at the precise moment when the feeble and the helpless are most closely threatened with calamities and scourges.

All these saints have their special mission. This does not, however, prevent them from bearing the other characteristics of those whom Jesus Christ selects to preserve his kingdom. We merely distinguish them by their prevailing characteristic, which we recognize in their works. Every age presents us with some of these providential personages. According as we meet with any of them, we exhibit his life for the admiration and imitation of young Christians: Can we offer them a surer guide-book from earth to heaven?

The religious orders.—If the preceding part of the divine plan for the preservation of Christianity is admirable, there is another part not less so. There are found, in the life of the Church, some fearful epochs, when one would be tempted to say the powers of hell must prevail. The winds of heaven break loose from their chains with unprecedented violence; a furious tempest, bursting over the barque of Peter, threatens to engulf it and the work of redemption in the abyss, and thus replunge mankind into the degradation of paganism. The warfare is likely to be long and bloody, the engagement is general along the whole line; never has the world run such risks. It is in the midst of this crisis that God brings forth from the treasure house of his love, a new auxiliary force for the cause of redemption; we have named them the religious orders.

Assembled under the same banner, acting as one man, appearing on the very day when their presence became necessary, these great bodies will last until they triumph in the warfare their mission has confided to them. Now, as we have already remarked, there are only three modes in which hell can attack Christianity: intellectually, morally, and physically. Behold a striking coincidence! we have three kinds of religious orders, and only three.

I. Apologist or learned orders—for the preservation, defense, and diffusion of truth; that is, to prevent the ruin of the work of redemption in the intellectual man.

II. Contemplative orders—for the protection of the work of redemption in the moral man. You see them, with a noble contempt of all earthly things, elevate human love toward supernatural goods, act as a counterpoise to scandal, and prevent concupiscence from resuming its ancient dominion. Pure victims, ever immolated though ever living; angels of prayer, prostrate day and night between the vestibule and the altar; they do more for the repose of the world and for purity of manners than kings with their governments, magistrates with their laws, and philosophers with their maxims. A poor convent of Carmelites prevents a greater number of disorders than the jails punish.

III. Infirmarian orders—consecrated to the relief of all human miseries, we find them watching over the cradle of the newborn infant, and by the bedside of the dying old man; in the garret of the beggar, and in the dungeon of the prisoner; waiting for the traveler on the summit of the Alps, and descending after the miner into the depths of Potosi; in a word, posted at every point where hell can attack the work of redemption in the physical man.

How beautiful art thou, O holy religion! considered in thy means of preservation. Tower of David! a thousand bucklers hang upon thy walls. Blessed art thou, O priesthood! house of God, army of Israel, now watching on the walls of Jerusalem, now praying on the mountain, now fighting in the plains. Blessed are ye, O saints of God! beneficent stars that the Almighty sends forth above the horizon of a guilty world, to dissipate the murky clouds of error and vice. And blessed, also, are ye, O religious orders! most powerful auxiliaries in the work of redemption. Wonders of the world! it suffices to know you, to deplore without measure the blindness of the men who would suppress you. To pray to God and to devote yourselves to his service, to give the world an example of detachment and of all virtues, to cultivate the desert, to reclaim lands deemed uninhabitable, to create resources for myriads of families, to teach the young gratuitously, to diffuse all kinds of useful information among the peasantry, to undertake and accomplish immense scientific labors which would exceed the powers of a single individual, to offer an asylum to the penitent, a refuge to the unfortunate, a home to the innocent, to exercise a sweet and generous hospitality, to guide the traveler, to help the poor and the sick, to comfort the afflicted, to provide for the spiritual and temporal wants of a neglected population; these are your works! Ah, ye senseless or wicked defamers of religious orders! are these the works you call useless, are these the lives you call infamous?

We say of the religious orders, that which we have said of the saints: they all bear the characteristics of the Redeemer, but each is distinguished by some special one. This portion of the catechism, in which we relate their history, is one of the most interesting in our work, and is well calculated to render plain as noon-day the continual preserving action of providence. It has, moreover, for our age at least, the powerful attraction of novelty.

The priesthood, the saints, the religious orders; such are the three means established by the new Adam for the maintenance of Christianity. They are all contained in one, which is the Church; for it is in the Church, and by the Church, that saints are born; it is in the Church, and by the Church, that religious orders are formed.

To preserve the work of redemption, even to the consummation of the world, notwithstanding the incessant attacks of hell and the devil, is the first duty which the Savior owes to himself; the second is to propagate it.

Christianity propagated. — All men are children of God. For all, without distinction of country or condition, the divine blood has been poured out on Calvary.[113] God wishes that all men should come to the knowledge of the truth, and participate in the blessings of which the mediator is the source.[114] If, then, the greatest mark of love that God can show a Christian people is to preserve their religion for them, the greatest proof of mercy that he can give to nations, seated in the shadow of death, is to allow the light of the gospel to shine upon them.

Hence, the necessity of missions; and their existence in the world since the descent of the Holy Ghost. We give a history of the principal ones which have taken place in the various centuries, from the establishment of the Church down to our own day: the field is immense. Nothing, it appears to us, is better calculated to elevate the mind, or move the heart, than this glorious picture of evangelical conquests. Everything in it is particularly interesting to the young, it speaks to their imagination, which delights in the wonderful, and engages their most generous affections.

On the one hand, the unknown people to whom the missionaries carry the good news, the profound degradation in which they are found, the progress of the gospel, the change of these barbarous men into fervent Christians; on the other, the labors, heroic devotedness, and unwearying patience of the missionaries, the innumerable dangers to which they are exposed, the incredible privations to which they condemn themselves; all contribute to reanimate our fervor, and to make us bless our good God, who, having drawn us also, in the persons of our forefathers, from the night of paganism, has caused us to be born in the midst of the admirable light of the gospel.

Let us add that the periods and the successes of the different missions give us a new proof of the unfailing providence which watches over the Church. When the sacred torch is extinguished by a guilty people in one place, we immediately see it lighted among a new people in another. We are not aware of any occurrence in history more regular or more instructive.

And, then, all these wonders of former days are renewed again in our own day! Considering these savages, who become Christians under the action of the gospel; these barbarians, who are transformed into civilized men; these martyrs, who joyfully shed their blood for the faith; all these miracles, which adorn the history of the early Church, and which modern impiety has dared to call in question; are not all these calculated to confound that impiety and to reanimate our faith, when we see similar occurrences taking place in our own day, and at the hands of Catholic missionaries alone?

It is thus, that, faithful to the advice of St. Augustine, we form a series of brilliant rings, the long chain of Christian ages, and trace the history of religion from the beginning of the world down to our own time, until our narrative ceases at the mission to Corea.

FOURTH YEAR

Christianity rendered visible; exterior worship. — It is not enough to present religion to the mind and the heart of man. To gain his whole being, it must also be presented to his senses; hence God has written it in sensible signs. That which the visible is to the invisible world, exterior worship is to the dogmas and the precepts of Christianity; it is a mirror, in which we see with our eyes and touch with our finger the truths of the supernatural order, just as we behold the truths or the laws of the natural order in the physical world.

By exterior worship is conveyed a knowledge of the teachings of faith and the rules of morality; the fall of man, his redemption, hopes, duties, dignity. What more shall we say? Exterior worship is to religion that which the word is to the thought; a true expression, now pleasant, now joyful, now terrible, now sad, according to the nature of the truths which it communicates. In a word, the exterior worship of Catholicity is Christianity presented to the senses.

Sunday. — After having gone back to the days of old, and shown the venerable origin of Catholic worship, its necessity, and its harmony with all our wants; after having described in detail the sacred places where our holy ceremonies were anciently carried out, and proved that there is not a single part of our churches which is not rich with the most pleasing memories, we explain the office of the solemn day, which is so well named the Lord's day. The Holy Sacrifice of the Altar, the divine office, the benediction, all pass in review. Hereby we show how worthy the Catholic worship is of the true religion; that is, how reasonable, noble, and holy it is, and how proper to captivate and purify the senses, elevating them to the contemplation of eternal things: above all, we endeavor to show how instructive and how deserving it is of our veneration.

Suppose that a navigator, deserving of credit, should announce to the learned of Europe, on his return from a foreign voyage, in which he had visited some previously unknown islands, that he had met with a people who, during the last eighteen hundred years, preserved unchanged their language, faith, manners, laws, customs, rites, even the form of their dwellings and garments; that all these things are remarkable for splendor, or wisdom, or genius, and are rooted in the most venerable traditions, the greater number of which go back to the very origin of time, and are connected with the most extraordinary events in the annals of the human race, so that, to know this people, to enter into their temples, to witness their religious ceremonies, to understand the motives of their actions, is to be transported, as it were, by enchantment, eighteen centuries back and more, and to become acquainted with the most wonderful mysteries of man, and to behold some of the most eventful scenes of remote antiquity.

Now the unaccountable ardor which is manifested at the present day to explore the ruins of the past is an assurance of what would happen; archaeologists, philologists, tourists, amateurs, would hasten to our ports and set sail for the land of this monumental people. Most probably governments themselves would send out scientific expeditions, commissioned to gather the most reliable traditions, to study the most interesting inscriptions, and to explore ruins more venerable than those of Thebes or of Ninive.

Well, such a people exists; it is the Christian people, it is the Catholic Church. Youthful lovers of antiquity! too long have you remained in admiration at the threshold of our cathedrals; enter the sanctuary. There you will discover the mysterious thought, whose marvelous expression delights you, and your admiration will increase, for you will find the spirit of that monument whose dead letter only you at present understand. Be Christians in the practical sense of the word, and from simple spectators, as you were, you will be changed into poets of art; for, do not forget, in the arts, that thing is dead to this life which flourishes not for the other.

When, on a Sunday, you behold the priest at the altar, making his accustomed gestures with a mathematical precision, repeating the selfsame prayers which have been so long in use, far from your minds be an ignorant criticism, far from your lips be the language of impiety; recollect your thoughts, penetrate the mystery, and say to yourselves:

"Behold the antiquity of the faith! Behold the perpetuity of Christianity! While everything else changes, while everything around it falls, religion alone remains ever the same. That which the priest now does at the altar is done this day in every quarter of the globe by thousands of other priests; that which they all do has been done in like manner for the past hundred years, for the past ten hundred years, for the past eighteen hundred years. The basilicas of Constantinople and the catacombs of Rome were witnesses of the same sight. In the priest I behold Chrysostom at Constantinople, Augustine at Hippo, Ambrose at Milan, and Clement at Rome. He extends his arms to pray, I behold the Christian of the early days; he places his hands over the sacred offering, I behold Aaron taking possession of the victim; he unfolds a linen cloth on which rests the adorable host, I behold the winding-sheet of Calvary in which the great victim of the human race was laid. All antiquity is unrolled before my eyes. Eighteen centuries disappear, and I hear the voice of the Son of the Eternal: "One jot or one tittle shall not pass of the law,"[115] and I behold with my eyes the accomplishment of his declaration: "Heaven and earth shall pass away, but my word shall not pass away."[116]

Not only do the august ceremonies of the holy sacrifice exhibit before our eyes the venerable antiquity of the Church, but the most ordinary customs of our holy assemblies proclaim it also in the simplest and sweetest language. For instance:

"The practices of the primitive Sunday are still observed among us. At our High Masses, we have the bread broken among the faithful, the reading of holy books, the gifts made to the poor and to captives; what St. Justin acknowledged to Marcus Aurelius, we still do after sixteen hundred years.

"In memory of the bread distributed among the faithful, behold the blessed bread which two choristers carry on a little carriage, adorned with white hangings and surrounded with lighted tapers.

"In memory of the voluntary gifts of the early Christians, made for the relief of the poor and the redemption of captives, the priest and his assistants now make the collection! These ask for the sick and for poor orphans; those for prisoners. This little girl, with the red velvet purse, petitions you for means to purchase bouquets of white flowers for the altar of Mary. This old man, with his black belt sprinkled over with silver tear-drops, is a member of the Confraternity of a Good Death, he asks you for alms to procure coffins for the poor.

"In memory of the Acts of the Apostles and the books of the prophets, which the lectors read formerly in the assemblies of the faithful, the subdeacon and the deacon now read similar lessons. Listen again: the pastor in the pulpit reads the gospel of the day; and, in accordance with the recommendation of the apostle, prays for pontiffs and kings, rich and poor, the sick and the helpless, travelers and exiles.[117]

"Religion has arranged these things so; it leaves no sorrow without consolation, no misery without relief, no want without assistance, and every Sunday it presents us with a specimen of each of its good works as a choice bouquet.

"If haughty minds despise a High Mass, it is because they know not that it recalls the memory of ancient manners and holy customs. What a wonderful thing that, in all Christendom, there is not a village or hamlet which does not, every eight days, present, even to the most erudite, innumerable reminiscences of antiquity, memories of the Caesars and of the amphitheatre, the catacombs and the martyrs."[118]

This explains and justifies the astonishing expression of the most loving, and perhaps the most inspired soul of the sixteenth century: "I would give my head," says St. Teresa, "for the least ceremony of the Church."

Division of time.—Having explained in detail the Sunday, as well as the affecting, instructive, and yet ill-understood ceremonies of the divine office and the adorable sacrifice, having noticed also the profound wisdom of the Church in the constant use of the Latin tongue, since an immortal doctrine requires an unchanging language, we pass on to the days of the week, to the months, and to the ecclesiastical year. First comes the Christian definition of time.

Time is a period of trial, imposed on all free creatures before arriving at their end. Since the fall, time is the delay granted by the divine justice to guilty man, that he might recover himself. In this simple definition, what an abundant source of salutary thoughts and sentiments! To the definition of time succeeds the division of the year adopted by the Church, a division eminently philosophical, its three parts correspond to three parts of the catechism, as these in turn correspond to the state of religion before, during, and after the preaching of Jesus Christ.

The first part of the year, which comprises Advent until the Nativity of the Messias, traces for us again the four thousand years of preparation, with the hopes and sighs of the ancient world, such as we have explained them in the first part of our lessons.

The second, which extends from Christmas to the Ascension, comprises the whole mortal life of the Redeemer, and corresponds with our second year.

The third, in fine, which commences at Pentecost and terminates at All Saints, recalls the life of the Church, as developed in our third year.[119] Thus, the life of the Church, the succession of feasts, the divisions of the year, which picture to us the whole history of the human race and of Christianity, end in the feast of heaven. Thus, everything conducts us thither; heaven is the end of all.

Feasts. — After the example of the great writers on sacred science, we show our Christian feasts to be an apprenticeship for heaven; a feeble yet comprehensive and constantly recurring image of the eternal feast: blessed art thou, O holy religion! whose tender goodness has moved thee to scatter some flowers and plant some shady trees along the sorrowful road which man must tread before arriving at his happy country.

The very name of *feast* is to him a lesson of sublime philosophy. This name, which contrasts so strangely with the tears, toils, and turmoils of life, recalls to man his whole destiny, past, present, and future; leads him to the fear of God, to encouragement, to resignation; reminding him of his redemption, and the pure eternal joys which await him. Feasts do still more: they detach man little by little from a sensual life, while they afford him solace in his pains, and prepare him for a future state of bliss.

Oh, how much love and wisdom on the part of the Church, or rather of our heavenly Father, in the institution of feasts! How much cruelty and madness on the part of those who would abolish them, or degrade them by their misconduct! What evils on humanity! Poor laborers and artisans, ye who earn your bread in the sweat of your brow, sorrowful children of Eve, for you the festival days were chiefly established! It was not only the interests of your souls, but those of your bodies, that the Church, your mother, had in view in the institution of these solemnities.

Society itself is not less interested in their faithful observance. It is a truth that a cessation of labor on certain days affects even the foundation of kingdoms, and that a violation of days of repose compromises the material well-being of society — a truth unhappily disregarded at the present day more than at any former period. We cannot too often repeat that religion, which at first sight seems to have no other object than the happiness of the next life, secures also the happiness of the present.

Although our principal aim is to make known the Catholic feasts from a historical, dogmatical, moral, and liturgical point of view, still we are careful not to pass over in silence their admirable harmony with the seasons of the year, as well as with the wants of the human heart.

Each of our great solemnities is celebrated in the season most proper to develop the sentiments which it is calculated to inspire. In this manner, nature joins with religion to promote the good of man, and by so doing, contributes through him to the glory of God, who is the beginning and the end of all things. One example, amongst others, will suffice to illustrate a truth which is not sufficiently appreciated.

Suppose that Christmas, instead of being celebrated in winter, were celebrated in the beautiful days of summer, would you not feel your tender compassion for the newborn babe of Bethlehem diminished?[120] How difficult to excite in our hearts, when sinking under the burden of an oppressive sultriness, those lively sentiments of pity which we should entertain for an infant benumbed with cold! But place Christmas on the 25th of December, and immediately you will feel, almost in spite of yourself, a tender sympathy for the divine infant, who is born at midnight, during the dreary winter season, in a damp cavern, exposed on all sides to the piercing blasts of the cold north wind. We need not be surprised; the one supposition produces discord between the event and the season; the other, harmony.

Descending still more into these mysterious harmonies, we show that, during the course of the year, there is not a truth which the Church does not preach, not a virtue which she leaves unproposed for our imitation, not a fibre of our souls which is not stirred by this admirable variety of her feasts; so that we are moved to say of every solemnity that which has been said of every Christian maxim: If it did not exist, it ought to be invented.

The foregoing is the manner in which we teach the letter of religion.

Spirit of religion. — As to the spirit, we also follow the great master who has served us as our guide. The whole of our lessons, the magnificent exposition of Christianity, has no other end than to place in clear relief this greatest of truths: God loves man,[121] having had but one design from the beginning of the world, that of making man happy, and bending to this kind and merciful thought both heaven and earth, peoples and kingdoms, the ancient world and the modern.

How, henceforward, can anyone have a heart capable of loving, or a mind capable of linking two ideas; in a word, how can anyone be a man, and deny this consequence: It is a duty, but a duty as sweet as it is sacred, to love so good a God, and, for the love of him, to love our neighbor, who is his image and our brother?

Thus, the love of God above all things, and, for the love of God, the love of our neighbor as ourselves; such is the summary, the conclusion, the moral end of each of our lessons, the grand sentiment which predominates throughout the catechism. Even though we had wished it, could we arrive at any other conclusion? Is not the redemption of the world the center to which all rays converge? Does not each of our instructions explain some one of the means adopted by God to prepare the way for it, to realize it, to maintain it, or to extend it? Now is not the redemption the great mystery of the charity of God toward man?[122] How, then, can we terminate each of our lessons but by an act of gratitude and love?

Should anyone reproach us for this constant repetition, we would find our justification in the conduct of the beloved disciple, and indeed in the very natures of God and man. Worn out with age, the apostle of love used to be carried to the church, and all his instructions consisted of these few words, which he continually repeated: "My little children, love one another." His disciples, astonished to hear him always repeat the same thing, asked him the reason; he returned them an answer, worthy of him who had the ineffable privilege of resting on the bosom of our divine master: "Because, if you do this, it is enough."

In the very natures of God and man, we find a justification for that saying of St. Augustine, which serves us as a compass on our course: "Explain everything by love." One law, that of attraction or gravity, which may be called "the mutual love of bodies," regulates the physical world. One law, that of charity, regulates the moral world. In their essence, these two laws are but one. Whence proceeds this inexhaustible fecundity, this marvelous power? God is charity, and God has made man to his image. If God is charity, man is love. To love is life, not to love is death.[123] Henceforward it will be understood why God has given to man but one law, the law of charity.[124] It will also be understood why we continually lead back the minds and hearts of young Christians to this fundamental point. Happy shall we be if, by frequent repetition, we succeed in inspiring some of them to be ever faithful to this law of charity, which is the only end of the catechism; the summary of the law, the prophets, and the gospel; the proper object of man's life in time and eternity, and the end of all the works of God!

Religion in eternity. — The great law of charity leads us to speak of religion beyond the tomb, and assists us to comprehend what it shall be. Thus, having journeyed down the six thousand years which separate us from the origin of man, having followed the majestic river of religion, which, descending from its source in heaven, spreads fertility and life throughout the world, and beheld in imagination its progress to the end of time, we arrive at the threshold of eternity. Time is no more; everything connected with it has ended.

Will it be so with religion? No; religion shall still subsist when time shall be no more. On the one hand, the relations of which it is the expression are as immutable as the nature of God and that of man, on which they are founded; a sacred bond shall exist between God and man, as long as it will be true that God is the Creator and Father of man, and man the creature and child of God. Now this will be true forever and ever. On the other hand, the work of religion cannot be completed within the limits of time. What does this religion of charity desire; what does the Catholic Church, the only depository of this religion, desire in civilizing nations, instructing kings and subjects, forming them to virtue, and consoling them in all their affections? It desires to repair little by little, in regard to all the generations that appear on earth, the sad consequences of original and actual sin. It desires to restore, as far as human corruption permits it, the great law of charity, whose sovereign dominion formed the happiness of the early days of innocence, and whose transgression has inundated the world with a deluge of crimes and tears. It desires to prepare the human race for a complete deliverance.

This deliverance, of which we draw a picture in the four volumes of the catechism, is only begun on earth; its perfection is reserved for eternity, to which, as we have said, religion conducts us. When time ends, then the religious, social, and domestic hierarchies; the distinctions of nations and families; laws, threats, and promises; the regulations of penance, festivals, and sacraments; in a word, the whole system of the universe, which has been organized only to establish and develop charity during our period of trial, must vanish before the aurora of eternity. The noblest virtues, even faith and hope, will remain at the threshold of the immortal abode; charity alone shall enter.

The reason for this glorious privilege is that charity is everything; it is the very soul and essence of virtues. The principal virtues have in it their merit, the secondary their cause. On God's side, love is everything, since to create, to preserve, to redeem, and to glorify, is to love; in like manner, on man's side, to correspond by love to the love of God is the whole man. Indeed, all true virtues are but the varied manifestations of charity.

Let us hear the admirable St. Augustine defining all virtues by means of love. "If virtue," he says, "conducts us to a blessed life, I affirm that virtue is nothing else than the love of God. I hesitate not to define faith, a love which believes; hope, a love which expects; prudence, a love which discerns; justice, a love which renders to everyone his due; humility, a love which annihilates itself; obedience, a love which submits itself; courage, a love which wages war; and so of the rest."[125]

Hence it happens that the blessed city above contains only three descriptions of inhabitants—God, angels, and men; the first is charity by essence, the others are charity by grace. Thus are verified both the scriptural expressions: "God is charity,"[126] and he has "made man to his own image,"[127] and the mysterious call which God and humanity have been continually addressing to each other since the beginning of the world: "The Spirit and the bride say, 'Come.'"[128] This call is the termination of all things, as it is the termination of the last of the inspired books. When, for the last time, the bride says, "I come," all shall end.

At this solemn moment will be revealed, in all the splendor of their glory, to assembled angels and men, both the sublime unity of the divine plan, and the no less sublime excellence of charity, like an edifice disencumbered from its scaffolding. Charity, disengaged from all that which was done for it, but which was not itself, will appear as the only law of the world, the soul of virtues, the center of events; as an august queen to whom ages and empires have been tributary, and who, the only survivor of the ruins of time, will enter triumphant into the glorious city of God, there to develop, without rival or hindrance, her beneficent reign, commenced at the origin of the world, and continued with so much labor throughout the course of ages.

Relying on the authority of the faith and the teaching of the fathers, we venture to utter a few words on this blessed eternity, the last benefit of religion, the ineffable reward of our short sufferings and light labors, the brilliant crown of the work of redemption, the beautiful solution of all the problems of life, the eternal repose of order, restored by grace and consummated by glory. Of a truth, in heaven all things shall be perfect.

For God, heaven is the accomplishment of all his designs; it is the full and perfect enjoyment of his works, the complete manifestation of his glory, the sweet reign of a beloved Father in the midst of his devoted children; it is the immense, eternal overflowing of his love upon them, and the similarly eternal overflowing of their love toward him; in a word, it is all in all, the fulfillment of the desire expressed by the Son of the Eternal, when instructing the human race: "Father, thy kingdom come, thy will be done on earth as it is in heaven."[129]

For creatures in general, it is the fulfillment of the desire expressed in their name by the great apostle: All creatures groan and travail in pain, expecting their deliverance from corruption and their participation in the glory of the elect.[130]

For man in particular, it is the fulfillment of all his legitimate desires in regard to body and soul; it is the accomplishment of the wish expressed in the name of the whole human race by the royal prophet: "I shall be satisfied when thy glory shall appear."[131]

Yes, what light is to the man almost blind, who would fain behold it in all its splendor, heaven is to man; what health is to the sick man, who endures a thousand pains, heaven is to man; what peace is to the miserable, who pass their days and nights in grief, heaven is to man; what the recovery of a lost scepter is to a dethroned king, heaven is to man; what a limpid stream is to the traveler dying of thirst, heaven is to man; what a return to his native country and the bosom of a beloved family is to the exile, heaven is to man; finally, that which a full and secure enjoyment of all good things—repose, immortality, happiness, and glory, is to a man eaten up with desires, broken with labors and sorrows, and condemned to tears, infirmities, death, and torments, heaven is to the human race.

Such is the picture, however imperfect, that we trace of the complete restoration of our nature and of all things, in order to excite in the souls of young Christians an efficacious desire of one day participating therein, and to remind all, in the language of the great apostle, that the pains of this life, the sacrifices which religion imposes on us, are not worthy to be compared with the glory and felicity which await us in heaven.[132]

ADVANTAGES OF THE METHOD HERE ADOPTED

1. The exposition of religion in its letter, in its spirit, in its history, in its dogmas, in its morality, in its worship, in its relations with man and society, in its means and end in time and eternity; such, as we have seen, is the object of this catechism.

We may speak of the superiority of the catechism without any danger of vanity. The fundamental idea does not come from us. We have already said that it comes from St. Augustine. Even the form frequently belongs to other fathers of the Church. Far from attributing to ourselves that which belongs to another, we make it our glory, in so sacred a subject, to have said nothing of ourselves.

If, now, we consider the plan of this catechism in itself, we shall find that it is the most complete of all those that have appeared till the present day.

The greater number of catechisms, even those most developed, say little of the old testament, and nothing of the history of the Church. With a few exceptions, all are silent on the work of the six days. A great many omit the feasts of the Church. There is not one which subordinates to Christianity all the events of the world, whether before or after Jesus Christ, and which renders an account of everything by means of Christian data. There is not one, it seems to us, which endeavors to show religion in its relation to the wants of man and society: an essential task, which we have endeavored to fulfill, less by reasonings than by facts, so as to defy the most active imagination to discover in the intellectual, moral, or physical man, a single real misery which religion does not solace, a single rational desire which she does not indulge, a single legitimate sentiment which she does not satisfy. Hence, the concluding truth follows: that Catholicity contains, and it alone contains, the means necessary for fallen man to recover himself. Out of it, everything is indefinite, incoherent, incomplete, inefficacious, illusory. This teaching of religion, in accordance with the counsel of St. Augustine, is then the best, we even venture to say the only means of making Christianity known in its magnificent entirety.

2. This complete exposition of religion dispenses with the laborious and often useless assistance of argumentation.[133]

As the best means of proving the power of motion is to walk, so the best syllogism in favor of Christianity is to show it as it is. To what man in his senses did it ever occur to prove that the Pyrenees and pyramids are not mere shadows? These imposing masses have remained immovable for thousands of years; behold the proof of their solidity! In like manner, we do not say: We are not about to prove that Christianity is divine, social, beneficent, its dogmas sublime, its morality pure and amiable, its worship magnificent and tender. We content ourselves with saying: "Behold Christianity!"

When, from the summit of a solitary mountain, in the perfect calm of a beautiful summer night, one beholds the queen of the firmament advancing majestically along her path to take possession of her throne in the midst of innumerable twinkling stars, does one inquire for syllogisms to make him believe in the magnificence of the heavens, or does he not rather exclaim in a transport of admiration: "The heavens show forth the glory of God, and the firmament declareth the work of his hands"?[134]

In like manner, when one scans with the mind's eye the vast horizon of ages, and beholds the magnificent edifice of Christianity, starting with the origin of the world, developing gradually its immense proportions, withstanding the tempests of six thousand years, surviving the ruin of all human institutions, and resisting the passions of the vulgar, the persecutions of the great, and the rage of hell, how shall he fail to exclaim: "The finger of God is here"?[135]

When one sees all the parts of this grand masterpiece so perfectly united to one another, that each and all are indispensable to the general harmony; when one considers this religion, ever young notwithstanding its great age, ever in advance of reason and progress notwithstanding its miraculous immovability; when one reflects on this wondrous fact, ever ancient and ever new, which explains everything, and without which nothing can be explained; in a word, when one contemplates Christianity in its magnificent entirety, must he not exclaim: O noblest work of the Almighty! O mystery which reason cannot fathom! Will he any longer seek to have its divinity proved by the contemptible aid of syllogisms? He indeed would be deserving of pity, who, at the sight of the heavens, would not acknowledge the existence of God; much more deserving of pity should he be, who, at the sight of Christianity, in the magnificence of its history and the splendor of its benefits to the human race, would not fall on his knees, and, in a transport of love and admiration, adore its divine author.

Let us add, with one of the fathers of the Church, that religion is an illustrious princess, a daughter of heaven, all radiant with immortal gems, and that it does not become her to enter the lists with error, the ignoble offspring of hell or human frailty; it is enough for her to appear in all the splendor of her majesty; her presence is victory. Let us add from another father: Bear in mind, that to discuss the truth of a religion, which we see confirmed by the blood of many witnesses, is a dangerous experiment. Yes, it is very dangerous; after the oracles of the prophets, the testimony of the apostles, and the torments of the martyrs, to call in question the faith of ages, as if it were born but yesterday.[136]

Moreover, the complete exposition of religion contains in itself all the most conclusive reasonings in favor of Christianity, since it establishes, in an incontestable manner, the truth of these three propositions, which are the abridgment of all religious demonstrations: 1) either there is a true religion, or men have been fools for six thousand years; 2) either the true religion is found in Christianity, or nowhere; 3) either Christianity is found in the Catholic Church, or nowhere.

If this broad method dispenses with all particular proofs, it also renders all objections vain and ridiculous; and this is an inestimable advantage!

Spread out on a table, before the eyes of an ignorant man, all the little wheels that form the interior of a clock; on every one of them he will be able to raise a multitude of difficult questions. He will imagine that he sees a thousand defects in regard to size and harmony; perhaps he will even deny the possibility of setting such mechanism in motion. Now as long as the pieces remain scattered about, it will be folly to expect him to understand their relations. Would you think of convincing him by argument? Alas! you would only run the risk of defeating yourself on every point, or at least of wearying yourself in vain efforts, while you would probably entangle more and more the ideas of your opponent, and confirm him in his erroneous views.

But let the clockmaker, without saying a word, take up the different pieces, arrange each one in its place, and strike the pendulum; what becomes of doubts and objections? In like manner, when Christianity has been exhibited in all its magnificent harmonies, what becomes of the *how* and the *why* of unbelief?

3. This teaching is the best remedy for the great evils of our period: carelessness, ignorance, rationalism.

Carelessness or indifference is the daughter of doubt, and doubt is the daughter of false reasoning. The father of this fatal reasoning was the new paganism of the Renaissance; its powerful interpreter, the monk of Wirtemberg; its most ardent missionaries, the school of Voltaire; its victim, our age; its effects, the evils which we endure, to say nothing of those which await us.

Attacked on all sides, and still remaining on all sides the master of the field, Christianity has been receiving for several years past the intellectual homage of a large number of the vanquished. The heart only remains indifferent; it refuses to submit, because it fears the noble conqueror, and it fears him because it does not know him. And hence we describe him such as he is, the friend of hearts, the King of love. On his part, we say to rebellious hearts: "Many sins will be forgiven you, if you love much." And to weary and broken hearts, the victims of a cruel deception — alas! their number is too great — we announce his invitation: "Come to me all ye who groan under the burden of anguish, and I will refresh you; living under my law, you will find joy and repose."

As for ignorance, it does not at first sight appear credible that our age, we speak of the enlightened portion, the portion who manifest a desire to believe, hope, and love, should be a much greater stranger than the preceding one, to the knowledge of Christian doctrine. Yet a little consideration will show that such a result is but natural. The eighteenth century, though it became a libertine when an adult, had nevertheless received at the parental hearth a religious education. Not so with the nineteenth century; the days of its childhood rolled away without an allusion to religion. The Republic, which cradled it amongst us, only whispered in its ears the names of Greece and Rome. In the lyceums and the bivouacs of the First Empire, it learned to adore nothing but glory.

At a later date, no doubt, religion was called into our colleges, but in reality far from her sanctuary, on an abandoned altar, what could she do but pray, and, like Rachel, shed unceasing tears over the lot of her children, whom vice and impiety too often tore from her maternal tenderness and devoured before her eyes? The people of our age then ignore religion, though they understand the need there is for it, and though they feel favorably inclined toward it. This latter tendency arises from that conservative instinct which grows more earnest in the hearts of nations as well as of individuals in proportion as their dangers become greater. But still this noble sentiment can go astray, especially if there is no one found to present before its eyes the glorious lamp of true doctrine, shining in all its purity. Now, to remedy these two great evils of carelessness and ignorance, is there a better means than a clear and complete exposition of the faith?

Another misfortune, which we also owe to the audacious reasonings of the last century, and to some additional causes which it would take too long to enumerate, is the anti-Christian tendency which predominates in a certain class of society. Hence has proceeded, along with the bold and repeated denial of the divinity of the Son of God, the opinion, unfortunately so widely spread, that religion is only a tolerated thing in the world, and Jesus Christ a kind of dethroned monarch, who does not deserve either to be consulted or obeyed. Our age, which has not time to doubt, accepts these gross falsehoods as oracles, and makes them the rule of its conduct. Hence, the innumerable chastisements and bloody revolutions with which the earth is desolated. Now, from our teaching, it follows:

I. That the divinity of our Savior is the starting point of every reasonable mind, and the foundation-stone of all true philosophy.

II. That, far from being merely an accessory thing in the world, Christianity, on the contrary, is the soul of everything, the pivot around which the whole government of the universe revolves. It is like the sun in the center of the planetary system. It carries in its arms both rulers and races, and that endless variety of causes, immediate and remote, which contribute to the formation or the dissolution of kingdoms, and to the promotion or the decline of art, science, literature, peace, war; in a word, men, with their virtues and passions; so that, in fact, Christianity is the limit of everything.

III. That, far from being a dethroned monarch, who deserves no regard, or esteem, or obedience, Jesus Christ is the immortal King of ages; that today, as heretofore, as ever, it is he who raises up empires and abases them, who glorifies and preserves them, if they are docile to his laws, or breaks them as vessels of clay if they presume to say with the Jews: "We will not have thee reign over us."[137]

Indeed, the attentive reader of this catechism will find the whole history of the world divided into two great epochs. First, the period before the Messias; those long four thousand years, including the great week of the creation, may be summed up in a few lines: "All for Jesus Christ" (that is, for the establishment of his kingdom). "Jesus Christ for man. Man for God." Before his eyes pass all events both particular and foreign to the Jewish nation, rolling on to Jesus Christ, as rivers roll on to the ocean. Secondly, the period after the Messias; the eighteen centuries flown by since the birth of the babe of Bethlehem may be summed up in similar terms: "All for Jesus Christ" (that is, for the preservation and extension of his kingdom). "Jesus Christ for man. Man for God."[138] So that the whole creation, descended from God, ascends continually again to him through Jesus Christ, unless it is degraded.

Were you to suppose that the portion of creation which is degraded, that is to say, which revolts against Jesus Christ, is withdrawn from his dominion and ceases to contribute to his glory, you would deceive yourself. God, the Creator of all things, says to every king, to every nation, to every newborn infant: "Thou art placed in the world to know, love, and serve Jesus Christ, my Son, the King of kings, the Lord of lords, to whom I have given all nations for an inheritance; behold thy law! Honor and glory for thee, if thou observe it; shame and misfortune for thee, if thou violate it. But whatever thou be, whether an observer or a violator of this immutable law, thou wilt contribute no less to the glory of my Son, thou wilt continue as much under the authority of his hand."

The book of history lying before us, we show this law accomplished with the utmost accuracy. From the Jewish people down to the French empire we see, at any given point, the nations happy as long as they recognize Jesus Christ for their king, and miserable from the moment in which they revolt against him.

The closing period of our panorama is the time of that powerful man, who lately made the world tremble at the very sound of his name. Called by God to restore a little life to the agonizing French people, this wonderful man collected in his iron hand the scattered elements of the ancient monarchy, rebuilt the sanctuary, triumphed over his enemies, and grew greater and greater, so long as he showed himself the servant of the great master, who had brought him to the front rank. But, scarcely had he struck against the rock, when his star declined, his power diminished, and his laurels were torn into fragments by the most dreadful disasters. Divested of everything, and reduced to the condition of a prisoner, he went to expiate in the midst of the ocean, the crime of his rebellion against the Lamb; and, from the summit of the lonely rock where he expired, there might be heard a warning voice to kings and nations: "Let my example serve you as a lesson; there is no one strong against God; be the pliable instruments of the Lord and his Christ, or, like me, you will be leveled with the dust."

Thus is shown, in all ages, the royal power of Jesus Christ; thus empires and emperors, whether they wish it or not, must be the tributaries of his crown. If they are docile to his laws, he preserves and glorifies them, and their happiness consolidates his dominion by teaching others to love him; if they dare to revolt against him, he crushes them to atoms, and the echoes of their destruction consolidate his dominion by teaching others to fear him.

Such is the philosophy which springs forth with splendor from the complete teaching of religion. Admirable philosophy! because it is true; and true, because it is Christian. Philosophy, most proper to heal the maladies of our period! for now, more than ever before, it can confirm its lessons by examples. Philosophy truly divine! which fully satisfies the religious soul by showing it the supreme Lord of the world, seated on his immovable throne, holding in his hand the reins of empires, and making kings and peoples, nay, the very passions of men, subservient to the accomplishment of one only design—the redemption of the human race through Jesus Christ.

There is enough—do you not think so—in this simple knowledge to overthrow from their bases all the theories, so unworthy of being called philosophical, with which our era is inundated, and of which we are the unfortunate victims. There is enough, too, it appears to us, to extend immeasurably the horizon of our intelligence, and to elevate genius to the loftiest regions of truth.

Another evil under which our century labors, and which arises from its deplorable ignorance, is the mania of reforming religion, of arranging religion according to the variable opinions of the moment, according to the laws of "give and take," in a word, of adapting Christianity to the views of everyone. What remedy is there for this evil? The best, without a doubt, is a complete exposition of the Catholic faith.

From this universal teaching it is shown, as St. Augustine desires, that Christianity is not the work of man but of God; that it has not come forth imperfect from the hands of its author, but perfect; that if it requires developments, the duty of bringing them forth belongs not to man but to God, and to God alone; in fine, that Christianity, as immutable as God himself, is, in its manifestation, as ancient as time and as durable as eternity, since Jesus Christ, who is its life, was yesterday, is today, and will be forever, always the same.

Hence follow two equally necessary consequences: 1) that only one true religion is, at any period of the world's history, possible; and 2) that it does not belong to any man for any era to modify religion, or to degrade it, by subjecting it to the state, from the supreme rank which it holds as its birthright; so justly, indeed, that it alone has the absolute, eternal right to repeat that celebrated expression: *Aut Caesar aut nullus.* "I am everything or nothing."

Thus is cut away with a single stroke the root of the various sects, which are all founded on the possibility of a new worship, that is, on the pretended insufficiency of the true worship; definitively, on the possible existence of a religion other than actual Christianity; a supposition as dangerous as it is absurd, renewed in our days by a class of men worthy of a better cause.

It is thus that religion, presented as it should be, suffices to dissipate all the errors which the passions or the frailties of man can oppose to it; in the same manner as it suffices for the sun to appear above the horizon, shining in all his splendor to dissipate the shadows of night, and the clouds with which the unchained winds have blocked up his path.

IV. Presenting every fact, every idea, in its relation with the general plan of religion, our teaching has the advantage of clarifying all particular kinds of knowledge, and of giving to each, along with the place which suite it, the degree of importance which it deserves.

At the present day a great many persons, oppressed with doubts, occupy themselves with the study of religion, but they often do so without guide or compass, without any fixed or well-conceived plan. Hence, many efforts, though conscientious, are fruitless; many long steps, if you please, but little true progress; stones and mortar scattered about, but no buildings raised; the only result is a vague religiosity, without any real action or change of conduct.

Let us digress for a moment to observe that the remark which we have just made on the study of religion applies with equal force to the acquirements of human knowledge. At the present day, specialities are everywhere, general science nowhere; this is the complaint of men most distinguished for their learning. How could it be otherwise? Religion, the necessary bond of minds and thoughts, because the source and center of all truth, no longer rules over our scientific investigations, to enlighten them, to direct them, to coordinate them, and to dignify them by attaching them to a superior unity. The religious data being the generating principles of science, and the only means of attaining to a solution of its most difficult problems, it follows that science without religion is a book from which both the beginning and the end have been torn.

Let us return to the study of religion, and give a few examples. If you take the isolated history of Judith or Esther, you have a dramatic episode certainly, but nothing more. If, on the contrary, you study it in the general economy of religion, the facts immediately acquire a high degree of importance. You see that they correspond admirably with the sublime plan of providence for the preservation among the Jewish people of the great promise of the liberator. The same must be said of the history of Cyrus, of Alexander, of Augustus, etc.

If you pass from the domain of facts to that of ideas, you will see why in such a century such an idea was brought to light, and propagated by some distinguished personage, or, perhaps, by a religious body. It is the same with regard to great virtues. The known relation of all things with the general plan of providence gives them at once, in your eyes, the importance which they deserve. You see them in their cause, in their effect, in their connection with the actual state of the Church and the world, with the occurrences, ideas, and manners of the period. All your particular studies are elevated and ennobled; nothing is lost. The light shines on your intellect, and an immovable faith, a just appreciation of men and ideas, a high philosophy of history, perhaps some sudden illumination of genius, will be the happy fruit of your study.

V. This teaching has the precious advantage of placing all that is most wonderful, convincing, and beautiful in religion within the reach of the meanest capacity.

Religion is founded on facts. I mistake: it is altogether but one long series of facts, alternately simple and sublime, tender and terrible, always luminous as the sun; its teaching ought then to be historical; such is ours.

If sometimes the necessary explanation of a dogma or a precept occupies the greater part of a lesson, we are careful to add to it, as a practical illustration or confirmation, some sketch or sketches taken from history analogous to the subject. From this historical mode of teaching we draw the double advantage of being understood by youthful Christians, and at the same time of forming their hearts to virtue, by making them acquainted with their models, their progenitors in the faith—the patriarchs, the prophets, the martyrs, and the principal saints of all ages.

Is there a better means of exhibiting to their tender imaginations pure and noble images, of tracing for them the way of life, or of facilitating their comprehension of pious books and pastoral instructions in which the great characters that figure in the old and the new testament, or in the history of the Church, are displayed, to persons who are less acquainted with them, than perhaps with the heroes of profane antiquity, and even with the divinities of mythology?

Hence, also, another advantage: it is a specific for the indifference of our age; it is a clear manifestation of the important place which the plan of redemption must ever occupy consequently in the maintenance of even the temporal happiness of the world by the priesthood, at present so much despised; by the saints, whose lives were accounted folly; and particularly by the religious orders, whose usefulness is so often and so pompously denied by men of wealth, who understand no laws but those of business, who care for no other life than that of profit and loss; among demagogues, the enemies of everything that retains an image of order; and among the ambitious, who basely covet their dwellings and other properties.

VI. Finally, this teaching supplies the most efficacious of all remedies for that egotism which at present gnaws our souls, and which draws so many other evils in its train.

It makes Christianity not only known but loved. The unhappy age in which we live no longer understands how to love properly, for either it does not love at all, or else it loves that which is evil. The violation of this primordial law is the cause of the unheard-of revolutions with which society is torn asunder, the disorder being ever in direct proportion to the infraction of the law. Soon would this unfortunate age be healed, if it only opened its heart to love, for love is God: "God is charity."[139]

To aid in the accomplishment of this salutary duty, our teaching renders so palpable the benefits of God or of religion in regard to each of us, and to each part of our being in every condition and age, as to be easily appreciated, so that nothing can be clearer than that to attack Christianity, to despise it, to abandon it, or to remain indifferent to its salutary precepts, is not only ingratitude but spiritual suicide.

Thus it is that the method of St. Augustine, making known the true spirit of religion, which is love, develops in the soul of youth this divine sentiment much more than fear. We are not the slaves of Sinai, but the children of Calvary. For the well-beloved of the Word made flesh, who has become our brother, we desire that God should appear less as an angry judge or a severe master than as a tender Father and an affectionate friend. Hence, the continual care that we take, conformably to truth, to present religion as an immense benefit. Nothing is more important than to exhibit from this particular point of view the commandments of God and of the Church. Is it not, perhaps, on account of having been accustomed from infancy to regard these holy laws as a painful yoke that so many persons trample them under their feet? Hence, also, a similar care to deduct from every fact, from every explanation, this grand truth: God loves man.

From Adam to ourselves, the testimony of all times is invoked. To every age we put the question: Has God loved you? And every age replies by offering to our consideration the numerous and special proofs of God's love toward it. If, then, you glance over the whole exposition of religion during the four years of this course, you will find the most pleasing and varied of all possible histories, the complete history of God's charity toward man. On whatever point you fix your looks in the succession of ages, you will find the affecting proof of this great truth, which ought to soften a heart of bronze:

God is a Father, who created man high priest and king of the world, who loaded him with honor and happiness, and who, though grossly insulted by this favored creature, has never ceased for a single instant, from the beginning of the world, to labor for the amelioration of the human race (degraded by a willful separation from its Father), to console it, to encourage it, and to move heaven and earth in order to supply it with the means of recovering with advantage its lost bliss.

Magnificent history! which, in a single word, *love!*, comprises, with regard to the heart, God, man, the world, time, and eternity; as, with regard to the mind, it comprises all things also in another single word, *Christ!*

Christ and love! these two words contain all our teaching, both as to the spirit and the letter. Therefore they are placed as an epigraph to this work. May they be the eternal motto of our minds and hearts!

Structure of this catechism.—A word regarding the form that we have given to this treatise on religion. Every part contains fifty-two lessons; one for each week in the year. It has appeared to us more convenient to make the narrations consecutive, than to break up the lessons into questions and answers. In this manner the catechism may serve as a reading-book for persons who are advanced in their knowledge, while the summary of questions and answers appended to each volume will facilitate its comprehension and assist the memory.[140] We have had the abridgment printed apart for children. It is a text which they may learn by heart, and of which the catechist will find the full development in the large work, or in the authors whom we have cited with all possible precision on every subject.

Since the last edition of the large catechism, we have composed two other catechisms, entirely modeled on the first. One is addressed to children of seven years, the other to children who are preparing for their first Communion. In these two works, as in the *Abridgment* already published, will be found the same plan, the same definitions, the same answers; the only difference is as regards quantity. Thus, the child who knows his *Little Catechism*, knows the one-fourth of the *Catechism for First Communion;* the child who knows the *Catechism for First Communion*, knows the half, or nearly so, of the *Abridgment* intended for those who have made their first Communion; then comes the large work, which completes all the others.[141]

This unique collection of catechisms, developed according to the various ages, and always remaining closely alike, presents the inestimable advantage of a perfectly uniform progress in religious instruction. Either we are mistaken, or youth should find therein a great facility of being instructed; and masters, a powerful means of elevating youth safely, and almost without an effort, to the fullness of the science of Christianity. To attain this double end has been for us, during the course of long years, the constant object of a labor that was unremitting, and less easily sustained than perhaps one would imagine. In so noble an aim, we trust that our efforts have not fallen too far below the mark.

Catechism of Perseverance

Lesson 1: Vocal Teaching of Religion

The old shepherd. — A traveler from a distant country found himself at nightfall near the entrance to a vast forest; he could neither go back nor yet remain where he was: necessity compelled him to advance through the darkness. As he was about to bury himself in the dreadful obscurity, he perceived an old shepherd, of whom he inquired the way.

"Alas!" said the shepherd, "it is not easy to point it out to you; the forest is cut up by a thousand pathways, which turn and cross in every direction, and all, except one, end in the abyss."

"What abyss?" asked the traveler.

"The abyss that surrounds nearly the whole forest. But this is not all," continued the shepherd, "the forest is not safe; it is infested with robbers and wild beasts. There is one enormous serpent, which makes frightful ravages; few days pass without our discovering the remains of some unfortunate travelers who have become its prey. The climax of the evil is that it is absolutely necessary to cross the forest in order to arrive at the place to which you are going. Moved with compassion, I have taken up my station at the entrance of this dangerous passage, to instruct and protect travelers; at intervals along the way are my sons, who, animated with the same benevolent sentiments as myself, discharge the same office. Allow me to offer you my services and theirs; if you choose, I will accompany you."

The candid air of the old man, the tone of truth in which his words were uttered, gave the traveler confidence; he accepted the offer. With one hand the shepherd seized a lamp, and enclosed it in a strong lantern; with the other he took the traveler's arm. They set out.

Having journeyed on for some time, the traveler began to feel his strength decline.

"Lean upon me," said his faithful conductor to him.

The traveler, thus supported, continued his journey. Soon the lamp began to shed only a feeble light.

"The oil is failing," said he to the shepherd, "our light will soon go out; what will become of us?"

"Have courage," replied the old man, "in a little while we shall find one of my sons, who will put fresh oil in our lamp."

He was not deceived. A light soon appeared at a short distance. It shone in a little cabin by the roadside. At the well-known voice of the shepherd, the door was opened. A seat is offered to the weary traveler; some simple but substantial food repairs his strength. After a delay of three-quarters of an hour, he continues his journey, accompanied by the old man's son.

From time to time the traveler meets with new cabins, renewed attentions, new guides; he walks thus the whole night. The first rays of dawn begin to illumine the eastern sky, when he arrives safe at the end of the dangerous forest. Now he understands, in its full extent, the service which has been rendered to him by his kind guides. Before his eyes, he beholds a frightful abyss, from whose hideous depths the dull roar, as of a distant torrent, breaks upon his ear.

"See," said the guide, "this is the abyss of which my father told you; no one knows its depth; it is always covered with a multitude of brambles, which the eye cannot penetrate." Saying these words, he heaved a deep sigh, and turning aside, wiped away the tears which began to roll down his cheeks.

"What is the matter?" said the traveler. "Why do you appear so afflicted?"

"Alas!" replied the guide, "how should I be otherwise? Can I look on this abyss without remembering the many unhappy victims who are every day lost in it? My father, my brothers, and I offer our services, but few accept them. The greater number of those who walk a few hours under our guidance accuse us of wishing to frighten them with vain alarms; they despise our advice; they leave us, but very soon they lose their way, and perish miserably. Some are destroyed by the great serpent, others are murdered by robbers, and others again are buried in this abyss. The only way across the abyss is this little bridge before us, and we are the only persons acquainted with the road which conducts to it. Pass over with confidence," said he, turning, and tenderly embracing the traveler, "in a little while you will have the broad daylight; yonder is your city!"

The traveler, filled with gratitude, thanked his kind guide, whom he promised never to forget, and advancing at a rapid pace, quickly crossed the little bridge; a few hours more, and he reposed tranquilly in the bosom of his beloved family.

Necessity for the Catechism of Perseverance. — Young Christians! this history renders palpable to you the necessity for the *Catechism of Perseverance*, of which I am about to speak to you. Are not you, also, travelers from a distant country? This forest is the world, or the present life; these robbers are the enemies of your salvation; this dreadful serpent, the devil; this dark and fathomless abyss, hell; all these paths, which traverse the forest in so many different directions, are the roads, alas! too numerous, which conduct to eternal misery; the only way, which terminates at the little bridge, is the narrow way to heaven.

As for the charitable shepherd who waits at the entrance of the forest, and who offers the assistance of his arm and his lantern to the traveler, you easily understand that he represents the divine pastor, who descended from heaven to succor and "enlighten every man coming into the world";[142] the sons who aid the generous old man in his charitable work are the ministers of the Lord, devoted to the care and guidance of the traveler; the lamp which is borne by the shepherd and his sons is the light of faith, which, according to the expression of St. Peter, "shineth in darkness."[143] It is unnecessary to explain to you what is meant by the persons who accept the advice of the old man and his sons, and by those who reject it. During the course of the journey the lamp threatens to go out: it is important that you should understand the meaning of this portion of the allegory.

The lamp of religion has been lighted and placed in your hands by the instructions which you received before first Communion; but do not be offended if I tell you that the oil in your lamp must soon fail. What, indeed, are the lessons of your childhood? Very elementary instructions, capable of imparting only a faint, superficial idea of a science with which you should be much better acquainted. I will not say that levity or dissipation prevented you more than once from understanding or remembering them; no, your conscience will speak to you on the matter for me.

It will tell you that in religion there are many things which you do not know well, and many others which you do not know at all; it will assure you that it is the greatest temerity to think of traversing the wilderness of life with a scanty supply of religious knowledge; it will show you, on all sides, a multitude of young persons who have fallen victims to their imprudence; it will convince you that the knowledge of religion is more necessary now than at any previous time.

I. Because there exists at the present day a great number of persons who do not study, do not know, do not love, do not practice religion; who live as if there were no God, no heaven, no hell, no eternity; as if they had neither a soul to save nor duties to fulfill; who even attack the truths of religion, and, like madmen, mock at those who reverence them.

II. Because among the number of these wretched beings there may be some very dear to you. And who knows? Perhaps providence has destined you to enlighten them and to lead them back to God. What a reproach would you make to yourself if you should fail to correspond with so noble a vocation! And could you fulfill it if you were unable to render an account of the faith that is in you? You are well aware that with the knowledge you possess at present, the task would be above your strength.

III. Because, during the evil days in which heaven has placed your existence, many miseries and sorrows, perhaps many great misfortunes, await you on the highway of life. Do not rely upon men for consolation; religion alone can pour a salutary balm over your wounds, she alone will remain faithful when all others abandon you, she alone will sweeten the bitterness of your sorrow and wipe away your tears, she alone will smooth with a mother's tender care your weary pillow, she alone will support your courage at the last moment. But if religion be a stranger to you, if you do not know her language, or the feelings of her maternal heart, what can you expect? Now, I repeat, you are not sufficiently acquainted with religion, and if you cease to study it, why in a few years you will not know it at all; my word is the word of experience.

IV. Because the false maxims which you every day hear so pompously repeated in your ears; the dissoluteness, the corruption, the indifference, and the scandals of every kind which you meet with at every step, and under every form, more especially the seducing clamor of your own passions, amid the terrible storms that will soon burst over your weak heart; in fine, because the world, the devil, the flesh, have all united for your destruction, and have formed a league, more terrible at the present than at any former period.

In the midst of so many tempests, how will you, weak reeds, support yourselves? In the midst of so many enemies, how will you, unarmed soldiers, defend yourselves? In the darkest part of the night the divine lamp will be extinguished, unless you quickly replenish it with a fresh supply. This supply awaits you on the road; and you should profit by it: it is the *Catechism of Perseverance*.

O how appropriately is this salutary help termed the "Catechism of Perseverance!" Yes, it is a catechism where you will find all the means to persevere. You will find there strong and consecutive instructions, in harmony with the condition of your minds; salutary instructions, which will not only preserve but develop the lessons you have already received. New oil being thus frequently supplied to your lamp, you will not fear being left without light in the midst of darkness, nor run the risk of losing the only path which conducts to the bridge over the abyss.

In the ministers of the divine shepherd you will meet with safe and charitable guides. Their wise counsels will be to your souls that which the old man's arm, the friendly cabin, the hospitable table, were to the wayworn traveler. Thus, constantly guided and protected, you may hope to traverse in security the dangerous and tortuous path of the forest.

But the *Catechism of Perseverance* is not only useful inasmuch as it increases your light: its most precious advantage is that it supports your feeble virtue. In all things, union is strength. Well, at the Association of the "Catechism of Perseverance" you will find its strength, whether in the example or in the prayers of a great number of other young persons, with whom you will form but one heart and one soul. Without this union, as isolated travelers you would with difficulty traverse the desert of life. I shall explain my meaning:

When travelers resolve to penetrate the immense deserts of Africa, they first assemble in large numbers and form caravans. If they undertook their perilous enterprise alone, they would likely either perish of want, or become the prey of wandering tribes of Arabs; but united in one company, they have little to fear. I cannot too often repeat to you, my dear friends, that you have to traverse a desert, a thousand times more dangerous than any in Africa: that to travel this desert alone, you would probably perish; but joined with others the project is quite feasible. Now, it is at the Association of the "Catechism of Perseverance" you will meet with this company of young travelers who are making the same journey, and who, if you choose, will admit you into their society.

Memories which the word "catechism" recalls. — But, perhaps, the name of *catechism* inspires disgust, awaking in your minds some strange ideas, not very agreeable or flattering. You say to yourselves: "We are still to have dry, barren, elementary, metaphysical instructions; then, a weariness of listening to them, a difficulty of remembering them — in a word, a repetition of things which we imagine we know sufficiently well already, to be able to teach others. A catechism after first Communion! Is it to make us begin our school days again?"

How many rash judgments! — I should rather say prejudices! You have had, but a moment ago, the answer to all these objections, whose weakness will appear to you more and more evident on an attentive examination. Nevertheless, once again have the goodness to hear me.

Signification of the word "catechism." — The word *catechism* may call forth the unpleasant recollection which you attach to it; but, here, its meaning is quite different. Under so common a name are concealed the most beautiful history you have ever read, and the most varied and complete instruction that you can desire: both presented to your mind, to your heart, and to your imagination, in a manner capable of interesting and pleasing you. Even in this name of *catechism* there is nothing, as you shall see, but what should recall the sweetest reminiscences.

Catechism means "vocal teaching"![144] It applies especially to the elementary teaching of religion. Now, religion was taught by word of mouth from the beginning of the world until the time of Moses, and from the commencement of the Christian era until after the persecutions. Thus, the word reminds us at once of the tents of Senaar and the catacombs of Rome, the unaffected manners of the patriarchs and the still more beautiful manners of our fathers in the faith. This manner of teaching, much more interesting than bare study, was perfectly adapted to the first ages of the world. The patriarch traveled always in the company of his family. His long life supplied him with the means of instructing his children well. Abraham had lived for more than a century with Sem; Isaac was seventy-five years old when his father, Abraham, died, from whom we are not told by history he was ever parted. The record of the other patriarchs is similar.

The patriarchs and the early Christians. — Thus, the memory of past things was easily preserved in the traditions of old men, who naturally delighted in relating stories, and who usually had the leisure to do so. Moreover, the patriarchs were careful to perpetuate the remembrance of extraordinary events by altars and similar monuments. These were the books which future generations were to explain to their little ones. Abraham raised altars in various places where God had appeared to him.[145] Jacob consecrated the stone which had served him as a pillow during his mysterious dream of the ladder[146] which reached to heaven; he also named Galaad (Witness Heap) the heap of stones which was the sign of his alliance with Laban.[147] To these examples we may add many others.

The names which the patriarchs gave to these places or monuments likewise expressed the whole history of the events which occurred there. And when the patriarchal family arrived with their numerous flocks near the well of Rachel or the stone of Bethel, the children inquired with eagerness what meant these names and these stones. At the signal of the patriarch all seated themselves attentively under the shadow of a palm tree, and the old man, with white hair, narrated a history that was doubly interesting, for it was a family history and a religious history at the same time.

Thus was transmitted, from generation to generation, a knowledge of God, of the creation of our first parents, and of the great religious truths which God had revealed to man. The magnificence of the heavens and the voice of the patriarch declared at the same time the wonderful works of God. For more than two thousand years the teaching of religion was accomplished by word of mouth. This was the primitive catechism.

The same mode of teaching was adopted at the commencement of the Christian era. The Redeemer of the world, the teacher of all nations, conveyed his lessons by word of mouth: he wrote nothing. It was not till many years after his glorious ascension that his apostles committed his doctrine to writing. Even then their teaching did not become less vocal. Neither the gospels nor the epistles were ever placed in the hands of those about to be initiated into the Christian dispensation, and this for very important reasons. First, because vocal teaching was easier, safer, and more in harmony with the weak minds of the neophytes; next, because it was necessary to preserve the holy books from falling into the hands of the profane. This kind of reserve was in perfect accordance with the command of our Savior: "Beware of casting your pearls before swine."[148] In fine, it was feared that catechumens, becoming disgusted, might take occasion from the knowledge which they had acquired to hand over the doctrines of Christianity to derision, or, having altered them, to provoke by their calumnies the persecutions of the pagans.

Grounds of vocal teaching.—On this account instruction was imparted by word of mouth, and always with the utmost caution. It is necessary to be acquainted with this holy custom of our fathers in the faith in order to understand: 1) the meaning of these words which recur so frequently in their discourses: "The initiated know what I mean";[149] 2) the reason why the catechumens were sent out of the church before the celebration of the holy sacrifice; 3) the reason why there are certain truths to which the fathers have rarely alluded in their writings; and 4) the reason why the teaching of religion was then called by the name of *catechism.*

In imitation of the patriarchs, who gave to memorable places such names as would easily recall the events which had happened there, the first Christians had also their monumental writings. To supply the place of books, they had engraved on the walls of the catacombs, on their lamps, on their rings, on a thousand articles of which they made daily use, the principal emblems of the old testament and several of the new. All this we shall see in the third part[150] of the catechism.

When therefore a pagan or a Jew desired to embrace Christianity, there was no sacred book placed in his hands; nor was he instructed in the fullness of the truths of faith. The principal object in the first instance was to make the former feel the insufficiency of the law of Moses—the latter the vanity of idols, as well as the absurdity of profane philosophy. They were taught, moreover, the moral precepts of the gospel, and the general dogmas of religion, such as the unity of God, the general judgment, the resurrection of the body, and the history of the old and the new testament: other things were passed over in silence.

After the catechumens had been subjected to long trials, and when the time of receiving baptism drew near, the Creed and the Lord's Prayer were explained to them. This instruction was given in particular assemblies called "scrutinies," because the faith and dispositions of those who should be baptized were examined in them. The Creed and the Lord's Prayer were then put in writing, that all might learn them by heart. Eight days afterward, at the next scrutiny, these prayers should be recited, and the manuscript which contained them returned, lest it should fall into the hands of the profane. This was called the "Return of the Symbol."[151]

In fine, when the catechumens had been sufficiently tried, and they were deemed worthy of receiving baptism, whose grace they persisted in soliciting, they were assembled at the baptismal font, on the Vigil of Easter or of Pentecost—solemn and glorious nights, universally consecrated to the regeneration of adults. There, before being plunged into the blessed water, the bishop explained to them openly the necessity and effects of the first of the sacraments. On their departure from the baptismal waters they were conducted, clothed in white robes, to the assembled faithful, with whom they should henceforward be associated. The bishop then ascended the pulpit, and, drawing aside the veil which had previously concealed the holy mysteries, displayed them in full to the neophytes. Instructions on the institution, nature, and effects of the Eucharist, and on the pious sentiments of faith and love which its reception demanded, continued during every day of the first week. Such was the general practice of the Church, till the fifth century.[152]

We have now shown the signification and origin of the word *catechism*, and the pleasing memories with which it is hallowed. When it sounds in our ears, may it bring to our hearts the remembrance of the first ages of the world, with the pure and simple manners of the patriarchs—the remembrance of the early Christians, with their respect for the sacred mysteries, with their persecutions, with their innumerable virtues! For this one word comprises the double history. May it, above all things, lead us to an imitation of the admirable examples which they have left us.

PRAYER

O my God! who art all love, I thank thee for having established these "Catechisms of Perseverance." Thou hast been pleased, enlightening my mind by a profound knowledge of religion, to support my heart in the practice of virtue; grant me the grace to correspond with this benefit, to which many owe their salvation.

I am resolved to love God above all things, and my neighbor as myself for the love of God; and, in testimony of this love, I shall assist, with a great desire to profit thereby, at the *Catechism of Perseverance*.

Lesson 2: Written Instruction

Intention of God in regard to his own people and all nations, in having the old testament written.—We have seen that from the beginning man could learn the existence of God and the other great truths of religion, either by reflection on the wonders of nature or by attention to the discourses of the aged. Such were for him, during a space of two thousand years, the two great sources of instruction. At a later period, the simplicity of faith seemed to have almost disappeared with the pure manners and the long lives of the patriarchs; the passions gradually assumed sway, and, by depraving the heart, blinded human reason.

The posterity of Abraham would perhaps have followed the example of other nations, and idolatry had reigned everywhere; but God, who watches over the human race, was not pleased that it should be so. To render the teaching of religion more sacred and secure, he engraved his holy law on stone. His ordinances were written out by Moses; Aaron and the priesthood were charged with the duty of teaching religion, and maintaining it free from error. The guardian of the sacred books, the synagogue, watched both day and night over their safekeeping, and decided such religious questions as arose among the people.

Then came the prophets and other inspired writers, who, for reasons worthy of the infinite wisdom of God, wrote their predictions and the history of the chosen people. All these books together are called the old testament. The word *testament* means "alliance." The old testament is then the alliance which God made with the people of old, in particular with the Hebrew people. It is a magnificent contract, which includes, on one hand, the desires and promises of God; on the other, the engagements of Israel. Its end, like that of all the other works of God, is to secure the happiness of man on earth and in heaven, through the instrumentality of Jesus Christ.

The old testament: Its objects; its parts.—The old testament is composed of many parts:

I. The works of Moses, divided into five books, and therefore called the Pentateuch: namely, Genesis, in which is found an account of the creation and the great events which took place until the departure from Egypt; Exodus, which relates the miraculous journey of the Israelites through the desert, and the promulgation of the law in the outset of their travels; Leviticus, in which are recorded the various ceremonies of religion, and the ordinances regarding priests and Levites; Numbers, so called, because it begins by numbering the children of Israel — a book which contains the wisest regulations for the maintenance of order amongst an immigrant and naturally rebellious people; in fine, Deuteronomy, that is, the second law, because it consists of an abridgment of all the laws previously published, accompanied with explanations and additions, in favor of those who were not born, or had not arrived at the use of reason, when they were first given.

II. Historical books, which contain a history of the people of God in general: namely, the book of Josue, that of the Judges, the four books of Kings, the two books styled Paralipomenon (which are a kind of supplement to the books of Kings), that of Esdras, that of Nehemias, and the two books of the Machabees (a special history of some holy and illustrious personages); also the books of Ruth, Tobias, Judith, Esther, and Job.

It will be asked, why did God cause the history of his people to be written? Besides the necessity of preserving the truths of religion intact, it was his intention to show the Israelites the fidelity with which he observes an alliance. On his side, he never fails in the fulfillment of his promises: abundant benedictions, a profound peace, are the portion of his people, as long as they are faithful to the conditions of the contract; chastisements of every kind fall upon them, as soon as they prevaricate. Another reason was to show all people that he is the ruler of the world; and that, holding in his hands the destinies of empires, he makes everything subservient to one immutable design, the redemption of mankind through Jesus Christ. This is, in general, what we learn from the historical books of the old testament; and it was to perpetuate these important truths to the end of time that God was pleased they should be written.

III. The old testament contains several books of instruction and prayer: namely, the Psalms of David (to the number of 150), Proverbs, Ecclesiastes, Solomon's Canticle of Canticles, Wisdom, and Ecclesiasticus. It was not enough to have established the conditions of his alliance with the people of Israel; God desired to reap the fruits of this alliance in the formation of their hearts to virtue. On this account the books of which we have spoken were written; they abound with the wisest maxims, the safest counsels, and the clearest directions, for the regulation of one's conduct. If all other ancient legislators are only children in comparison with Moses, all other ancient philosophers are as nothing in comparison with the inspired sages, who drew up this admirable code of morality.

IV. Prophetical books, namely, those of the four great prophets, Isaias, Jeremias, Ezechiel, and Daniel, to which should be joined that of David, the first of all[153] (enumerated before); also those of the twelve who are called minor prophets, either because they wrote less, or that we possess less of their writings: their names are, Osee, Joel, Amos, Abdias, Jonas, Micheas, Nahum, Habacuc, Sophonias, Aggeus, Zacharias, and Malachias.

Almighty God did not wish his people to be ignorant that the alliance which he had contracted with them was only of a temporary nature. On the contrary, he desired that they should have continually before their minds the thought of a more perfect alliance, cemented by a purer blood — a new alliance, which should one day replace the old — an alliance, of which the Messiah, prefigured by Moses, should personally be the mediator and high priest.

He desired these things 1) that his people should not place their confidence in the vain shadows and worthless victims of the law; and 2) that they might enter willingly into the new alliance, when the Redeemer should come to proclaim it. For these reasons, and that the people of Israel might easily recognize the Redeemer, God was pleased to announce his coming many ages beforehand; and, by the instrumentality of a long succession of prophets, to depict his character with the utmost precision.

Thus all the holy books written after Moses tended to maintain the alliance, facilitate its accomplishment, to impart its true spirit, and to prepare Israel for a more perfect alliance.

It is necessary also to know that, by the side of these written instructions, God allowed vocal instructions to subsist, at least in part. All religious truths were not consigned to books. There were some that tradition alone was commissioned to transmit from generation to generation. This is a fact, of which we find the proof in the very words of Moses.

This holy legislator, drawing near his end, said to the children of Israel, "Remember the days of old, think upon every generation; ask your fathers and they will declare to you, your elders and they will tell you."[154] He did not say: "Read my books; consult the history of the world, which I have written and left to you." They would do so, undoubtedly; but, without the assistance of the tradition of their fathers, they should never be able perfectly to comprehend these books.

Moses was not content with recording in writing the prodigies which God had wrought in favor of the Jewish people; after the example of the patriarchs, he preserved the remembrance of them by the establishment of certain religious observances at their annual recurrence, a species of monument, the meaning of which he directed the old to explain to the young: What necessity for these precautions if everything was written? Thus, before the coming of the Messiah, the two great sources of religious truth were tradition and scripture.[155] It has been the same ever since, as we shall immediately see.

New testament: Its parts. — The new testament is the new alliance which God has made, no longer with one people, but with the whole human race, through the ministry of Jesus Christ. The books in which are written the conditions of this divine contract form what is called the new testament; they number twenty-seven.

I. Historical: which record, along with the lives of our Lord and the apostles, the history of the new alliance, the manner in which it was accomplished, and the admirable effects which followed it. These books are the gospels of Sts. Matthew, Mark, Luke, and John, and the Acts of the Apostles (written by St. Luke). As at the beginning of the world, God did not write the law which he gave to Adam, so, at the beginning of the new alliance, our Lord did not write the doctrine which he gave to his apostles. This heavenly doctrine was delivered by word of mouth for several years, until the moment arrived when, for imperative reasons, the apostles found themselves obliged to commit it to writing.

II. Instructive: such are the epistles or letters, which the apostles wrote to their disciples, or to the Churches which they had founded. We count fourteen from St. Paul, of which one is to the Romans, two to the Corinthians, one to the Galatians, one to the Ephesians, one to the Philippians, one to the Colossians, two to the Thessalonians, two to Timothy, one to Titus, one to Philemon, and one to the Hebrews. There is one from St. James to the Jews dispersed throughout the world. There are two from St. Peter to the Jews in Asia. There are three from St. John, the first to the faithful of his time, the second to the Lady Electa, and the third to Caius. Finally, one from St. Jude to all new Christians in general, completes the list. The end of all these writings is to explain the new alliance, and to impart its spirit. This spirit, like that of the old testament, is simply the love of God and the neighbor.

III. Prophetical: only one of this class, the Apocalypse of St. John. As the old alliance prepared the way for a more perfect alliance, announced by the prophets of the Jewish nation, so the new alliance, founded by Jesus Christ, prepares the way for a still closer union with God in heaven. The prophet of the new law, the apostle St. John, was charged with the duty of describing to us some of the ineffable joys which are reserved for us.

In short, we say that the Pentateuch contains the alliance of God with the Jewish people, as the gospel contains the alliance of God with the Christian people. The other historical books of the old testament relate to us the manner in which God and the Jewish people observed their engagements. On the one hand, we see God as faithful to his promises as to his threats; on the other, the people, alternately rebellious and submissive, receiving without fail their merited chastisement or reward. This mixture of goods and evils was the sanction of the alliance, and wonderfully contributed to its observance, since hope and fear are the two great motive powers in all human actions. The prophetical books are intended not only to announce a future alliance, but to maintain the people in fidelity to their engagements. They point out what is to be hoped or feared, according as men obey or prevaricate. The moral books are intended to secure the observance of the alliance in its spirit. By the side of the old testament rests a tradition, which preserves the unwritten truths. The whole of the ancient law conducts to the new.

Similarly, in the new testament, the history of the Church is intended to show the manner in which God and the Christian people observe their august alliance, sealed by the blood of the Redeemer. On the one hand, we see God during eighteen centuries dispensing either recompenses or chastisements, according to the faithfulness or the unfaithfulness of Christian nations; on the other, Christian nations either happy or miserable, according as they are docile or rebellious. So that, at the head of every page of the history of a Christian people, we may read these words: "Nations are elevated by faithfulness, and degraded by unfaithfulness to the alliance of Calvary." Thus we see that the whole history of the world, under the old as well as under the new testament, is intended to maintain this double alliance, and to teach mankind by a consideration of punishments and recompenses, as the return for their obstinacy or tractability, to be faithful to their God.

Tradition, inspiration, authenticity, and genuineness of the old and the new testaments. — By the side of the gospel rests a tradition, which preserves a great number of truths not written in the new testament.

Moreover, as the old alliance conducted to the new, so the new conducts to heaven.

The evangelists and apostles did not write all the instructions of the Savior. They say so themselves in express terms. "To know them," they add, "it is necessary to consult tradition."[156] Let us here remark that protestants who, after the example of the Samaritans, reject tradition to confine themselves to scripture alone are in continual contradiction with themselves. How, for example, do they know that the Bible comes from God? How do they know that baptism by infusion is valid? So of other truths which they are compelled to admit on the sole authority of tradition, which, nevertheless, they despise.

The different works composing the old and the new testament are called the Bible, that is to say, the book of books. Everything that is grand may pass away, but these divine pages, the immortal archives of humanity, will not pass away. Borne in triumph from century to century, like the ark of the ancient alliance across the sandy desert, the Bible will continue to relate to future generations the existence of God, his alliance with man, his judgments, and his glory, until the arrival of the solemn moment, when the Church, having reached the threshold of eternity, books will cease, for truth shall be seen then without shadow and without veil.

From these simple, but essential considerations, let us pass to the inspiration, authenticity, and genuineness of the Bible. All the books of holy scripture, together as well as apart, are inspired, that is to say: 1) God revealed immediately to the sacred writers, not only the prophecies which they should announce, but all the truths which they could not know by natural light or human means alone; 2) he led them, by a particular motion of his grace, to write, and directed them in the choice of those things which they should commit to writing; and 3) he watched over them, by a special assistance of the Holy Ghost, and preserved them from all error whether in regard to essential facts, or dogmas, or morals.[157]

As to the authenticity and genuineness of the Bible, we say that a work is authentic when it truly belongs to the author whose name it bears, and genuine when it is such as it came from the hands of the author. There is nothing more certain than the inspiration, authenticity, and genuineness of the books which compose the old and the new testament.

To prove this positive fact, the following is the mode adopted once by a very enlightened ecclesiastic. He found himself in the midst of a numerous company, among whom one well instructed in profane sciences, but quite ignorant in regard to religion (the class is legion at present), permitted himself to be carried away with an attack on the inspiration, authenticity, and genuineness of the Bible.

"Since your attack is directed against so many points," said the ecclesiastic, "permit me to divide the defense: it is important that nothing should be confounded. I will first prove to you the inspiration and authenticity of our holy books: I trust we shall speedily be of one mind."

Everyone drew near the disputants; silence ensued; and the ecclesiastic, addressing his opponent, said: "I am happy, sir, to have an encounter with an educated man; great minds and upright hearts were made to know the truth; religion is afraid only of the half-learned. Do you doubt the authenticity of the works of Plato, Virgil, Horace, Cicero, or Caesar?"

"Never has such a doubt entered into my mind," replied the gentleman.

"And how do you know that these works were composed by the great geniuses whose names they bear?"

"How do I know? Why, as we know all the facts of antiquity. Because the whole world grants it, and has always granted it. I should be the first to call him a fool who would refuse to admit such a testimony."

"Well, sir, a testimony a thousand times more forcible, a thousand times more certain, assures us that the books of the old and the new testament were inspired by God, and written by the men whose names they bear. Have you now ever known a person who died, or declared himself willing to die in defense of the authenticity of the works of Virgil or Plato?"

"No, certainly not; such a man has yet to be found."

"Well, sir, thousands of Jews and Christians have died in defense of the inspiration and authenticity of our holy books, and thousands of others are ready to die for the same cause. What do you think of that? Are witnesses, who lay down their lives for their depositions, to be considered suspicious?"

"I have not reflected on these things."

"But there is further proof. The testimony, which assures me of the inspiration and authenticity of the Bible, is much more ancient than yours; it is considerably weightier: it is that of two great peoples, the Jewish and the Christian, whose united existence extends over a period of more than 3,500 years. How does the matter seem to you now? Is such a testimony insufficient to render the faith of a Christian reasonable and legitimate? Are we only weak-minded creatures when, relying on such a proof, we believe in the authenticity and inspiration of our sacred books?"

"I think, my dear Abbé, you will soon convert me."

"I hope so; for you cannot defend yourself without inconsistency. I now pass on to the genuineness of the Bible. On this point, as on the others, I am sure you will not be slow to share my conviction. I appeal to yourself. How do you know that the works of Plato, Caesar, or Virgil have come to us, such as they left the hands of their authors?"

"Ah! I see what you are coming to; you are about to prove the genuineness of the Bible, as you have proved its inspiration and authenticity — showing that it is supported by an evidence more certain than that whose authority leads me to the belief of the genuineness of the works of Plato or Virgil."

"You anticipate me."

"Well, I await your proofs."

"Here they are: history is a very faithful witness, and you know better than many that thousands of Jews and Christians have died in defense of the statement, that our holy books have come to us such as they left the hands of their authors, without increase, diminution, or change; whilst you also know that no one has ever given his life in testimony of the fact, that the works of Virgil or Plato are such today as when they were written by their authors. But, sir, I will go still further with you, and show you that not only have our holy books never been altered, but that it has always been impossible to alter them."

"Let us see; if you succeed in your task, I will certainly lower my colors."

"I take you at your word; mark now!" An increased degree of attention was immediately observable amongst the auditors. "We shall first take the books of the old testament.

I. "It was impossible for the Jews to alter them before the schism of the ten tribes. How, I ask, could one, at the present day, alter the Civil Code of France? If any forger attempted it, would he not be immediately discovered? In the same manner, how could the Jews alter a book which was respected much more amongst them than the Civil Code is amongst us; a book which was found in every family, and meditated on daily; whose original was devoutly preserved in the tabernacle, and read on certain festivals by the priests to all the assembled people? Suppose an attempt were made at alteration—thousands of voices would immediately exclaim against it. Yet there does not exist a single vestige of any such complaint. Moreover, the alterations would undoubtedly have borne on whatever was humiliating to the national pride, or mortifying to the passions. Well, nothing of the kind has been retrenched.

II. "It was impossible for the Jews after the schism of the ten tribes. If the two tribes which remained faithful to the descendants of David had desired to alter the books of the law, how would the other tribes, their mortal enemies, have consented to receive these alterations? Nevertheless, the Pentateuch of the Samaritans, or of the ten separated tribes, is absolutely the same as that of the Jews.

III. "It has been impossible since the coming of the Messiah. At the beginning of this epoch the books of the old testament were in the hands of the Jews and the Christians, two bodies diametrically opposed to each other. If, then, the Jews had altered the old testament, the Christians would have accused them of their baseness, and have refused to accept their alterations. The tables being turned, the same consequences would have followed in regard to the Christians. Yet the old testament which is found in the hands of the Jews, that old testament which was deposited in the royal library of Alexandria 250 years before Jesus Christ was born, is absolutely the same as that of the Christians. So much for the old testament.

"As for the new, any alteration in its regard has been equally impossible.

I. "It was impossible before the schism of the Greeks. Indeed, sir, you will easily admit that it is impossible, without its being speedily discovered, to alter a book which is found in the hands of thousands of persons scattered over the surface of the earth. There would have been complaints, for Christians have always shown themselves extremely sensitive on this matter. In connection with this, I wish to mention for you an incident related by St. Augustine. An African bishop, preaching to his people, desired to substitute for a word in the gospel another word which appeared to him more appropriate. The people revolted. Affairs came to such a pass that the bishop was obliged to retract what he had said, and to restore the ancient word; otherwise the people would have abandoned him.[158] And the material proof that the new testament has never undergone the least alteration is that the copies in the hands of the Christians in the East are absolutely conformable to those which are used by their brethren in the West.

II. "It has been impossible since the schism of the Greeks. If the Latin Church had endeavored to change the new testament, the Greek Church, its mortal enemy, malignantly punctilious and vigilant, would have been far from accepting what seemed but sacrilegious alterations: it would have cried out against them with all the energy of its hatred. Now, no complaints have ever been heard of this; and the new testament which that Church uses at this day is in all points conformable to that of the Latin Church."

"Reverend sir, I return you thanks, I surrender my arms; it is glorious to me to have been defeated; I acknowledge that I have never reflected on the arguments which you have adduced."

"It is not to have been defeated but enlightened. As I said, noble minds are ever the admirers of the truth: I congratulate you on being amongst their number. These proofs, to which many others might be added, suffice to show that the faith of a simple Catholic, who, on the authority of the Church, believes in the divine origin of the Bible, is perfectly well founded, and that the most erudite man in the world can oppose nothing reasonable to it.[159] Let us all, whoever we be, learned or ignorant, conclude hence that we owe to the sacred books an entire faith and a most profound respect: in every part they are the true word of God."[160]

Here the discussion ended. The praises of the company were divided between the ecclesiastic, who had proved the inspiration, authenticity, and genuineness of the Bible, with as much perspicuity as modesty, and his adversary, who had displayed the rare courage of sincerely yielding to the evidence of truth.

Let us add that we owe the same faith to tradition as to scripture; for both are equally the word of God. "All scripture," says St. Paul, "inspired of God, is profitable to teach, to reprove, to correct, to instruct injustice, that the man of God may be perfect, furnished to every good work."[161] "Stand fast," he says elsewhere, "and hold the traditions which you have learned whether by word or by our epistle."[162]

PRAYER

O my God! who art all love, I thank thee for having given us thy holy law, and for having written it, that the passions of men may never be able to alter it. Grant me a great respect for thy holy word.

I am resolved to love God above all things, and my neighbor as myself for the love of God; and, in testimony of this love, I shall listen to the words of the gospel with the most profound respect.

Lesson 3: God: In Himself, His Attributes, and Proofs Of

God considered in himself. — We have already said that the first truth which the catechism teaches is that there is only one God.

Be silent, O heaven and earth! Children of men, I pray you, be attentive. Before all ages, above all the heavens, beyond all worlds, there was, there is, an eternal, infinite, unchangeable being, who is his own principle, end, and felicity. The whole creation, with its stars and systems, every one of which comprises in itself unnumbered smaller worlds, is but a reflection of the glory of this great being. He is everywhere, he sees all things, he hears all things. O being of beings! who am I, a weak mortal, to speak of thy greatness? Silence is the only hymn that is worthy of thee: "Silence will give praise to thee, O God, in Sion." (*Silentium tibi laus, Deus, in Sion.*)

And, first, what name shall we give thee? "Being above all beings," replies one of those who this day contemplates thy ineffable essence. "Being above all beings" is the only name that is not unworthy of thee! Alas! what language can name thee, of whom all languages together are unable to frame an idea?

"Thou art incomprehensible, because from thee have emanated all intelligences. Everything celebrates thy praise: that which speaks, by its voice; that which does not speak, by its silence. Everything reveres thy majesty: both the animate and the inanimate creation. To thee are addressed all desires and all tears; to thee ascend all prayers. Thou art the life of life, the center of motion, the end of everything; thou art alone, thou art all! O vanity of human expressions! All these names belong to thee; yet none of them can designate thee. Alone in the immensity of the universe, thou art nameless. How shall we penetrate beyond the heavens, into thy inaccessible sanctuary? Being above all beings! this is the only name that is not unworthy of thee."[163]

Such is God!

And God is not a being without personality. He has revealed himself: Father, Son, and Holy Ghost, three distinct Persons in one and the same divinity.

Proofs of the existence of God.—What man has ever doubted the existence of God? The impious may, indeed, say in his depraved heart: "There is no God;"[164] but to affirm it with a sincere conviction—no, he never can do so. The first real atheist is yet to be seen. And, in fact, unless a man has lost his reason, how is it possible for him to deny the existence of a being, whose presence is more gloriously manifest than that of the sun at midday in a cloudless sky? Hence, we will content ourselves with adducing only three proofs of the existence of God.

1. *The necessity of a Creator.* There is no effect without a cause. A mansion presupposes an architect; a painting, an artist; a statue, a sculptor. The earth with its gigantic mountains, and its fertile plains, and its lakes, and rivers; the sea, with its immensity, and its foaming waves, its regular currents, and its monster inhabitants; the heavens, with their resplendent, enormous, innumerable worlds: all presuppose an omnipotent cause, the source of so many wonders.

What is this cause? Are these wonderful works their own cause? All reply to us in their eloquent language: *Ipse fecit nos, et non ipsi nos*—"It was God who made us, and not we ourselves."[165] No, they did not make themselves, for they are not God; the earth is not God, the sea is not God, the heavens are not God: in these creatures there are none of the incommunicable properties or characteristics—such as eternity, independence, immensity, liberty, spirituality—which belong only to the being of beings.

What is then the cause, which has produced so many wonders? Chance? But chance is nothing; it is a meaningless word which man employs to conceal his ignorance. We say that a thing happens by chance, to signify that we do not know its cause; but it has a cause, nevertheless. Chance then is nothing; and it has made nothing in the world.

What then is the creative cause of the universe? Man? Truly history is inexcusable for not having preserved the name of the astronomer who constructed the sun, and fixed all the stars in the firmament; the name of the geologist who erected the Alps and the Pyrenees; and the name of the chemist who produced the ocean. Alas! all the men in the world could not make a little fly, or a grain of sand; and yet they made the universe!

Thus, on the one hand, it was neither chance nor man that made the wonders which everywhere meet our eyes; on the other, these admirable works have neither existed always nor made themselves, since they have none of the properties of a necessary being; what remains then but that they are the work of the eternal, infinite, and omnipotent being, whom the language of every nation terms God?

2. *The testimony of mankind.* Yes, all people have named him, for all have believed in the existence of this being, who is the source of all other beings.[166] Go to the human race in its cradle; follow it through all the different regions which it has successively inhabited; let no climate, no nation, no class escape your observation; pass from the civilized to the barbarous; search among the degenerate tribes who have planted their tents on the burning sands of Africa, or the savage hordes who wander over the vast savannahs of America—everywhere you will hear the name of God; everywhere you will discover mankind by the traces of the altars which they raise to the glory of the great being above, by the odor of the

sacrifices which they offer in his honor, and by the sound of the hymns and canticles which they send up before his eternal throne. Traverse the world: it will be easier for you to find a city built in the air than to meet with a people having no knowledge of God.

It must be that this great idea of God is very deeply rooted in the human heart, when man, reduced even to the condition of the irrational beast, and wallowing in the mire of the grossest vices, allows, nevertheless, to escape him the name of God, and raises his suppliant looks to the abode of this eternal being. Such is the remark made by Tertullian to the pagans of his time. "Do you desire," he says, "that I should prove the existence of God by the simple testimony of the soul alone? Well, although buried in the dungeons of sin, held fast by the chains of prejudice, weakened by passion and concupiscence, the slave of false divinities, yet, when the soul awakes from its languor, like a man recovering from drunkenness or fever, in the very first instant of its health, it proclaims the name of God, and invokes the only being who can assist it: 'Great God! Good God!' are the words that come naturally to the lips of every man. *Omnium vox est*—it is the voice of all! O testimony of the soul, naturally Christian—*O testimonium animae naturaliter Christianae!* And, when it utters this language, it is not to the capitol it looks, but to heaven, the abode of the living God, from whom it comes."[167]

It is, therefore, true that both man and the world vie with each other in proclaiming the existence of God in such a manner, that the folly of those so-called atheists, who attempt in the face of this double testimony to prove the contrary, is in itself a proof of the existence of God.

3. *The absurdity of atheism.* We call those atheists who deny the existence of God. If you desire to know how much their system deserves to be abhorred and deplored, listen to their creed:

"I believe all that is incredible.

"I believe that there are effects without causes! paintings without artists, clocks without clockmakers, houses without masons.

"I believe that the first man made himself, or that he grew up under an oak, like a mushroom.

"I believe there is no good or evil, virtue or vice; that to murder or to support my father is the same thing.

"I believe that all men are fools; that there is more sense in my little finger than in all human brains.

"I believe that I am a beast; that between me and my dog there is no difference, unless that it has a tail."

This last article is the only one on which the atheist has not gone far astray. If you imagine that we have placed all these absurdities gratuitously to the account of the atheists, you deceive yourself. Not only are they the strict consequences of their principles, but we even find them written in every character throughout their works. What venomous reptiles, then, does one press to his bosom, when he denies the existence of God! The foregoing are not the only ones; listen to the sum of the atheist's decalogue:

"Thou shalt satisfy all thy inclinations and passions."

This is the first and greatest commandment of atheism. Indeed, since there is no God, no soul, no duty, no good, no evil, no heaven, no hell, everything ends with death. Therefore, to eat well, drink well, sleep well, gratify all one's inclinations, is the true religion, the grandest philosophy: whoever follows any other rule of conduct is a dupe. The second commandment is no less important than the first:

"Thou shalt regard all men either as obstacles or instruments."

If instruments, thou shalt make them serve to thy good as much as possible; if obstacles, thou shalt destroy them without remorse. If it be necessary to crush them to pieces in a mortar, thou shalt crush them; if it be necessary to rob them, thou shalt rob them and retain their property unblushingly; if it be necessary to lie, thou shalt bear false witness audaciously.

You see that such morality is the morality of wolves; it establishes war among all; it converts the world into a vast den of thieves, and allows no other protection than that of the highwayman. These are the frightful maxims of atheism; written, avowed, practiced—at least in part; for happily man is usually better or worse than his principles. Such is the creed, such is the decalogue of atheism. Hence, we repeat, there never has existed a man so complete a fool as to maintain such a system on the grounds of a sincere conviction, and to deny, with his hand upon his heart, the existence of God.

Another proof. Be that as it may, it is well to remind our "freethinkers" of the language of one of the most powerful geniuses of modern times. Napoleon, when at St. Helena, was once discussing with a general the existence of God; he expressed himself thus: "You ask me, What is God? and if I know what I know. Very well! I will tell you. But answer in your turn: How do you know that a man has genius? Is genius something that you have seen? And is genius really visible? Ah! we see the effect and from the effect ascend to the cause. We seek, we find, we affirm, we believe—is it not so? Thus, on the field of battle, when the action begins, if suddenly we perceive the plan of attack to excel in promptness and adroitness, we are in admiration at it and exclaim: 'A man of genius!' In the midst of the conflict, when victory appears uncertain, why are you always the first to seek for me? Yes, you cry out for me, and on all sides the cry is repeated: 'Where is the Emperor! What are his orders!' What is the meaning of this cry? It is the cry of instinct, denoting a general belief in my genius. Well! I also have an instinct, a belief, a certainty—the cry escapes me in spite of myself, when I reflect on nature and its phenomena—I admire and exclaim: 'There is a God.'

"My victories make you believe in me; well! the universe makes me believe in God. I believe, because of that which I see around me, because of that which I feel within me. These wondrous effects of the divine omnipotence, are they not more striking and eloquent realities than any of my victories? What are the grandest movements on a battlefield compared with the movements of the heavenly bodies? Since you believe in genius, tell me, I pray you, whence does the man of genius derive that flow of ideas, that sublimity of conception, that quickness of thought, peculiar to him? Answer me.—Whence comes all this?

"You cannot, I see. Well! I should be in the same predicament; and no one has any further information on the matter than you and I: nevertheless, that peculiarity, which distinguishes several individuals, is a fact, as positive and evident as any other fact. But if there is a difference in minds, there must be a cause, and the cause is someone makes this difference: it is not you nor I, and 'genius' is only a word, that teaches nothing of its cause. Someone will say perhaps: 'They are organs,' a piece of nonsense allowable in a trifler! but which does not suit me—do you understand?

"Effects prove the cause; and divine effects make me believe in a divine cause. Yes, there exists a divine cause, a supreme reason, an infinite being; this cause is the cause of causes—this reason is the fountain of all intelligence.—There exists an infinite being before whom, General, you are only a little atom, and I, Napoleon, with all my genius, only a real nothing, a genuine nothing. Do you hear me? I feel this God, I see him, I have need of him, I believe in him; if you do not so too, well! so much the worse for you."[168]

To the eloquent demonstration of this great man, let us add the simple but decisive reasoning of a child. Some years ago, a young man, a native of one of the provinces, was sent to Paris, to complete his studies. Like many others, he had the misfortune to meet with bad companions. His own passions, together with the impious language of his comrades, soon led him to a forgetfulness of the pious lessons of his mother, and to a contempt of religion. He came to the point of wishing, and at length of saying, like the senseless creatures of whom the prophet speaks: "There is no God; God is only a word." Incredulity always begins by saying these things as it were in a passing way; it is a plant that takes root only in corruption. After many years' residence in the capital, the young man returned to the bosom of his family.

He was invited one day to a very respectable house. There was a large company assembled. Whilst every one talked about news, pleasure, or business, two little girls, each twelve or thirteen years of age, were reading together, seated in the recess of a window.

The young man, approaching, said: "What romance, ladies, are you reading with so much attention?"

"We are not, sir, reading any romance," they replied.

"Not a romance! What book, then, pray?"

"We are reading the *History of the People of God.*"

"*The History of the People of God!* Do you, then, also believe that there is a God?"

Astonished at such a question, the young girls looked at each other, their faces covered with blushes. "And you, sir," said the elder, "do you not believe it?"

"I believed it once," replied the young man, "but since going to reside in Paris, where I have studied philosophy, mathematics, medicine, and politics, I have been convinced that God is only a word."

"As for me, sir," answered the little girl, "I have never been in Paris; I have never studied philosophy, or mathematics, or those other fine things which you know: I know little more than my catechism. But since you are so learned, and say there is no God, will you tell me, what does an egg come from?"

The child pronounced these words in so clear a tone of voice as to be heard by a portion of the company. A few persons drew nigh to know what was the matter; others followed; and, finally, the whole company assembled round the window to hear the dialogue. "Yes, sir," continued the child, "since you say there is no God, be so good as to tell me, what does an egg come from?"

"An amusing question! an egg comes from a hen."

"And what does the hen come from?"

"The young lady knows as well as I: a hen comes from an egg."

"Very well; but which of the two existed first, the egg or the hen?"

"I certainly do not know what you want to make of your eggs and your hens; but, in a word, that which existed first was the hen."

"There was, then, a hen which did not come from an egg?"

"Ah! pardon me, miss, I was not paying attention; it was the egg that existed first."

"There was, then, an egg which did not come from a hen? Answer me, sir."

"Ah!—if—pardon me—I mean—because—you see——"

"What I see, sir, is that you do not know whether the egg existed before the hen, or the hen before the egg."

"Well! I say it was the hen."

"Be it so. There was, then, a hen which did not come from an egg. Tell me, now, who created this first hen, from which all other hens and eggs have come?"

"With your hens and your eggs, you seem to take me for a girl from the poultry yard."

"Pardon me, sir, I merely ask you to tell me, whence came the mother of all hens."

"But, to end the matter——"

"Since you do not know, permit me to tell you. He who created the first hen, or the first egg, whichever you please, is the same being that created the world, and we call him God. You cannot, sir, without God, explain the existence of an egg or a hen, and yet you pretend, without God, to explain the existence of the world!"

The young infidel asked no more questions; he stealthily seized his hat, and disappeared: "As much ashamed," remarked one of the company, "as a fox that had been caught by a hen."

To this little sketch we shall add another. A short time ago one of our pretended atheists was traveling in a public conveyance. All along the way, which was considerable, he never ceased to outrage the feelings of his fellow travelers with his impious jargon. Arrived at a place for changing horses, he began to look out of one of the carriage windows, and, seeing some little girls on their way home from the schools of the Sisters of Charity, he addressed himself to the nearest.

"My little one," said he, with a mocking air, "I will give you a penny if you tell me what is God."

The little girl, understanding the mockery, left her place, and drawing near to the carriage, said to him: "God is a pure Spirit, sir, and you—you are only a beast." Thereupon, she made a low courtesy, and tripped away again, smiling, to rejoin her companions. The rest may be imagined.

From the existence of God, let us pass on to his adorable perfections.

Perfections of God.—God is an infinite, eternal, incomprehensible Spirit, who is in all places, who sees all things, who can do all things, who has created all things by his power, and who rules all things by his wisdom. To name God is to name a being above all, a being properly such, a being infinitely perfect. From this incontrovertible idea of God we deduce, by a chain of evident consequences, all the essential attributes of the divinity.

I. *Eternity.* Since God is infinitely perfect, it follows that he has no other principle outside of his own existence, that he is by himself, and necessarily of himself. Having never received an existence, he is always the same being. He is eternal, that is, he has neither beginning nor end. *He who is*, is his name—*I am who am:* sublime, incommunicable definition, which he applies to himself![169]

Here, let us reflect that we are made to the image of God, and are obliged to copy in our lives the perfections of this adorable model. For it is written: "Be ye perfect, as your heavenly Father is perfect."[170] To imitate this chief perfection, let us reply to all finite, perishable creatures, when they come to solicit the affections of our hearts: I am greater than you, and born for greater things; I am immortal, and in all my actions I look to eternity.

II. *Independence.* Since God is preeminently great, an infinite being, he cannot have a superior or an equal: otherwise, he would be limited in his perfections, and would not be God. Let us, the images of God, be piously independent of men, of creatures, of our own passions, of everything that is not according to the will of our only master.

III. *Immensity.* Since God is an infinite being, it follows that he cannot be bounded, or fettered, or confined by any cause, by any place, nor in any one of his perfections: infinite in the fullest sense, he is as immense as he is eternal. Let us, the images of God, imitate our model by the immensity of our charity and the abundance of our good desires.

IV. *Unity.* Since God is an infinite being, it follows that he is one, and that there is no other: beyond the infinite, what can exist but nothingness or images of the infinite? Let us, the images of God, be like him; let God be everything to us, as he is everything to himself. Let the motto of the seraphic St. Francis be ever ours: "My God and my all!"

V. *Immutability.* Since God is an infinite being, he cannot lose anything, or acquire anything, modify or change himself, have new thoughts or desires—he is ever the same, because he is immutable. Let us, the images of God, be ever immutable in truth, in charity, in the practice of all virtues; woe to the inconstant!

VI. *Liberty.* Since God is infinite, no external cause can interfere with his operations. He has then freely created the world in time, without having arrived at any new act or design: he was pleased from all eternity to do so, and the effect followed in time. What he created freely he governs freely. Let us, the images of God, never allow our hands and feet to be bound by the shameful chains of sin: How could we endure the thought that we, children of God, should become slaves of the devil?

VII. *Spirituality.* Since God is infinite, it follows that he has no body by nature, save in the incarnation of the Word; for a body is limited, imperfect, subject to change and decay. God is, then, a pure Spirit. A simple and invisible being present everywhere, without mixture or form, he cannot be seen by our eyes, touched by our hands, or fall under the cognizance of our senses. Hence, when you hear mention of the hands, arms, feet, ears, or eyes of God; when you hear of his being moved with sentiments of anger or hatred, beware of taking these words literally in a material or human sense. Such language is only figurative, the Divine Majesty thus condescending to adapt itself to the capacity of our weak understanding.

A like occurrence happens in the daily intercourse of men. When we meet with persons of little education, we borrow their own language to make them understand us. So, when we hear of the hands, arms, ears, and eyes of God, the meaning is that he has made all things, that he can do all things, that he hears all things, and that he sees all things; by his hatred and anger, we understand that he cannot endure sin, and that he punishes it as it deserves. Let us, the images of God, be like angels in mortal bodies, that the life of the senses may be ever subject in us to the life of the spirit, until the happy day when both shall be absorbed in the life of God himself, to whose likeness we shall be assimilated.

VIII. *Intelligence.* Since God is infinite, it follows that he knows all things, past, present, and future; or, rather, there is neither past nor future with God, but all things are present to him. The world is one of his thoughts; he comprehends it; he penetrates a thousand times better into it than we can, or than we can penetrate into any of our own thoughts.

As God sees all things present, it follows that the knowledge which he has of human actions does not interfere in the least with our liberty. In point of fact, the actions of men do not occur because they are foreseen by God; on the contrary, they are foreseen by God because they will occur. To maintain otherwise, would be to maintain an absurdity and a blasphemy; an absurdity, since it would pretend that God sees them not; blasphemy, since it would annihilate the liberty of man.

The reason is plain. If the actions of men occur because God foresees them, it is evident they must occur, whether we will or not; if not, God should be deceived. The following reasoning would then be strictly logical: either God has foreseen that I shall die a month hence, for example, or, he has not foreseen it; if he has foreseen it, whatever I shall do, whatever precautions I may take, I shall die; if, on the contrary, God has not foreseen it, whatever I shall do, whatever imprudence I may be guilty of, even though I should refuse all kinds of nourishment, or cast myself headlong from the top of a tower, I shall not die. The absurdity of such reasoning at once illustrates the absurdity of the proposition, that the actions of men are necessitated by the divine prescience. Let us, images of God, behold the past with a single glance, to humble ourselves and return thanks; the present, to profit by it; and the future, to prepare for it. And since God sees all things, let us always remember that he sees us.

God sees me. These three words have heretofore prevented, and still prevent, more sins than all the preachers in the world. The thought that God is everywhere fills the reflecting soul with awe, confidence, and love; the remembrance of the presence of God is the school of virtue. The saints and patriarchs of the old testament were particularly careful to walk always in this holy presence. "As the Lord liveth, in whose presence I stand."[171] This was their motto, their battle cry, their familiar expression. David was not content with praising the Lord seven times a day. "I set," says he, "the Lord always in my sight, for he is at my right hand, that I be not moved."[172]

Why should we not imitate these great men, our models and masters? What more proper than the thought, *God sees me*, to encourage us in well-doing, to console us in affliction, and to maintain us in our duty? Would we ever dare to do before God that which we should blush to do before men?

To all the perfections which we have mentioned, add power, sanctity, goodness, truth, mercy, justice, in the highest degree, and you will have some idea of the great being, whom the tongues of all nations term God.[173] How great he is! but, at the same time, how good! for all these adorable perfections he turns to the welfare of his creatures. He has not abandoned the world to the winds of fortune after drawing it from nothingness; but, as a king governs his states, or a father his family, so God governs the universe. This thought leads us to speak of providence.

Providence.—Let us begin by clearly explaining this beautiful word which so many persons pronounce without understanding its meaning. Providence is God's government of the world, or God's action over creatures to preserve them and to conduct them to their end. It supposes the employment of all the divine perfections, but especially power, wisdom, and goodness. It extends to all creatures, the least as well as the greatest; that is, God watches equally over the slave and the monarch, the infant and the old man, over the insect that is crushed beneath our feet and those glorious orbs that roll over our heads. He preserves all alike, and conducts each to its appointed end. The very hairs of our head are numbered, says our Lord himself, and not a little bird falls to the ground without the permission of our heavenly Father.[174]

Now there are two kinds of creatures; material and spiritual. Accordingly we have providence in the physical and in the moral order.

Providence, in the physical order, is that continual action by which God preserves all creatures, the heavenly bodies, land, sea, plants, animals, etc., and directs them to their final end.

Providence, in the moral order, is that continual action by which God preserves spiritual creatures, angels and men, and directs them to their end.

It is easily understood that the laws of providence which direct inanimate creatures are not the same as those which direct free and rational creatures. On the first, God imposes his will without ever allowing them the liberty to wander from it. Thus the sun is not free to rise or not to rise daily, the sea is not free to ebb and to flow at its pleasure, the animals are not free to change their mode of feeding, hunting, and dwelling. It is otherwise with rational creatures. God has given them laws, which, by the rewards he promises and the chastisements he threatens, he invites them to observe: they can do so or not, as they choose. Being free, it is their duty to honor God by the voluntary submission of their minds and hearts to his supreme commands.

It follows, hence, that irrational creatures, of necessity, attain the end for which God has created them. For them there is neither merit nor demerit, good or evil; consequently, neither recompense nor chastisement. On the contrary, as rational creatures either arrive at or wander from their last end by the free exercise of their wills, so they may lay up for themselves a store of merit or demerit, good or evil; consequently, recompense or chastisement.

Now the last end to which providence conducts all material or spiritual creatures is the glory of God, that is to say, the manifestation of his adorable perfections. Hence David tells us: "The heavens show forth the glory of God, and the firmament declareth the work of his hands."[175] It is the same with regard to the earth, the sea, the animals, the least blade of grass, which it is impossible to contemplate without being struck with admiration at the infinite power, wisdom, and goodness of the Creator which is displayed therein. The last end of man is also the glory of God. He has been created as a beautiful mirror, wherein the power, goodness, wisdom, spirituality, and the liberty of the celestial workman are reflected. It suffices to see him, in order to adore, in the silence of admiration, the great being by whom he has been formed.

Besides this last end, which is the glory of their author, all creatures have a particular end. For inanimate and irrational creatures, this particular or definite end is the good of man. This is the reason why they all serve for his use. As to man himself, his particular end is salvation, that is, happiness for all eternity; if he glorifies God on earth, God promises in return to glorify him for all eternity in heaven. But whether man secures his salvation or not, God will no less attain the last end which he proposed to himself in man's creation.

If we refuse to be monuments of his goodness, we shall be monuments of his justice, and God will be no less glorious, that is to say, no less good, no less wise, no less powerful;[176] in the same manner as the sun is no less luminous, no less beneficent, though we close our eyes against its rays or flee from its heat. Nevertheless, God, who is goodness itself, wishes with all the might of his love that men should arrive at eternal beatitude, and for this purpose supplies them with all the means of doing so. Such is the idea that we should have of providence; let us now show that it exists.

Proofs for the existence of providence. — There exists a providence in the physical order; that is, God preserves and directs all material creatures to the end for which he has created them, his glory and man's good. This providence is exercised not only over the universe as a whole, but over every separate, even the smallest, part thereof; the wren, the worm, the ant, the blade of grass. Let us come to proofs.

1. Who better than the Creator himself can reveal to us the existence of providence? Here are his oracles — let us be attentive and listen to them: My wisdom "reacheth therefore from end to end mightily, and ordereth all things sweetly."[177] And elsewhere the prophet exclaims: "There is no other God but thou, who hast care of all."[178] But let us hear even the word of the Son of God exhorting us to consider the smallest creatures, that we may be convinced of the existence of a general and a particular providence in the physical smallest: "Behold," he says, "the birds of the air; they sow not, neither do they reap nor gather into barns, and your heavenly Father feedeth them."[179] It would be necessary to relate the whole of the sacred history, from one end to the other, if we were to quote all the facts which show that God disposes, as master, of the elements, that he directs all things in nature to his own glory and to man's good, that he directs the course of the sun, that he raises or appeases the storm, that he kindles or extinguishes the lightning, in fine, that he directs all nature to his own glory and man's welfare.

2. All nations have recognized a providence in the physical order. There is no doubt about the belief of Jews or Christians. As for pagans, although incredulous depositaries of revelation, they admit this sacred dogma. Notwithstanding the errors peculiar to various philosophical sects, they believed so little in chance, in fate, in blind destiny, that they carried even to superstition their belief in the government of the physical world by intelligent beings superior to man. Hence, in their opinion, every element, every portion of the universe, was placed under the protection of some deity or divine agent; hence they imagined there were gods of every description and in every place, gods of heaven, gods of the earth, gods of the sea, gods of fire, gods of fountains, gods of forests, gods of seasons, gods of harvest, gods of vintage, and of many other things

3. But setting aside all these reasons, to ask if there is a providence in the physical order — in other words, to ask if there are laws regulating the preservation of the universe and the direction of every material creature in it, is a question whose solution presents no difficulty to anyone with eyes to see. Indeed, the constant succession of the same phenomena necessarily supposes a constant cause producing them. Now this constant cause is called law, for we recognize a law by the permanence of its effects. If, then, we see effects in the universe which are constantly reproduced in the same manner; if, for

example, we see the sun constantly running his course in the heavens, enlightening and fertilizing the earth, we have no hesitation in concluding that there is a constant cause for this fact, and we say: "There is a law, in virtue of which the sun is so regular."

In the same manner if we examine any other portion of the universe, the earth with the animals that inhabit it and the vegetables that cover it, the sea with its ebb and flow and the fishes that disport in it, and everywhere find certain effects a thousand times repeated, we conclude that there are unvarying causes, the principles of these facts, and we say: "There are laws presiding over all these phenomena." Millions of creatures throughout the universe present the same spectacle. We should, therefore, naturally conclude that there are laws presiding over the preservation and direction of the world in general, and over every creature in particular.

It remains to be seen who has established these laws, for there are no laws without a legislator. This wise, this powerful legislator of the universe must be God, or man, or chance; there can be no other. It is not chance that legislates, for chance is nothing; it is not man, as we are well aware; it must be God. There is, therefore, a divine providence governing the physical creation.

To the foregoing observations, let us add two remarks: 1) As God established the laws of the physical world freely, so he can freely modify them or dispense with them, and he frequently does so when we pray to him for this purpose; hence, when plagues, epidemics, famines, inundations, droughts, threaten us, we pray to God to remove them from us, and, under similar circumstances, all people have done so before us. 2) The constant repetition of the same effects is so little due to chance, that the impious apostles of this blind deity do not claim the honor of it for their master, even in the smallest things, as the following anecdote will show.

The leading philosophers of the last century were one evening assembled together. After a supper, seasoned with atheism, Diderot proposed that he should name a counsel for God, and the lot fell accordingly on the famous Abbé Galiani. The Abbé took his seat and thus began: "One day, at Naples, a man took six dice in a box before my eyes, and laid a wager he would throw a pair royal of six. At the first throw he turned out six. I said: 'It is possible to do so once, by chance.' He returned the dice into the box, and a second, a third, a fourth, and a fifth time, always threw six. 'By Bacchus,' I cried out, 'the dice are loaded.' And so they were. Philosophers! when I consider the regularly recurring order of nature, those regularly revolving cycles of an endless variety of details, that sigular direction for the preservation of a world such as we see, ever turning up in spite of a hundred million other chances of perturbation and destruction, I am forced to cry out: 'Certainly nature is loaded.'" This original and sublime sally of wit rendered the adversaries of providence mute.

We shall not here more fully develop the proofs of a providence in the physical world; the near explanation of the work of the six days which we are about to enter upon will supply us with a more convenient opportunity. Let us pass on to consider providence in the moral order.

There is a providence in the moral order, that is, God preserves his rational creatures, men and angels, and directs them to the end for which they were created, his glory and their felicity. Man alone will engage our attention at present.

First let us remark that, in the moral as in the physical order, we find a general as well as a particular providence. The first is the action by which God directs the human race, kingdoms, revolutions, and great events of this world to his glory and our salvation. The *Catechism of Perseverance*, reaching from the creation of the first man down to our own days, will be the glorious history of this providence, which, before Jesus Christ, conducted all events to the accomplishment of the great mystery of redemption, and, after Jesus Christ, has been conducting all events to the preservation and propagation of his great work of reparation. We are then relieved from proving just now the existence of a general providence in the moral order.

As to a particular providence, if a full historical proof of it were required, we should recount the history of each people, of each family, of each individual person. We should behold God enlightening every race, every family, and every man that cometh into the world, revealing and preserving the truths to be believed, imposing duties, and supplying the means to practice them. We should see him speaking in every language, adopting every tone, and suiting the manifestation of his laws to the capacity of each people, family, and individual. We should see him recommending the observance of his commands by the promise of future recompense or the threat of future chastisement. What do I say? rewarding or punishing, even in this life, nations, families, and individuals, according as they are docile or rebellious to his law.

Beautiful study! which leads triumphantly to one conclusion, that clearly demonstrates the existence of providence. The history of every nation is summed up in two lines—virtue and reward, crime and punishment. That is to say, fidelity to the divine laws which should govern nations is followed by happiness; disobedience to them is certainly followed by misery. On one hand behold the law, on the other the approval. This is providence; for the same facts are reproduced in all quarters of the globe, and have ever been so, as far back as we can travel into the twilight of time. Oh, truly! "it is virtue that elevates nations, and sin that renders them miserable."[180] Immortal inscription over providence! which should be written at the head of the constitutions of every people, as it is written at the head of every page of their history!

If, from the social order, we pass to the domestic order, we shall see that the same laws of providence are exemplified in regard to every family, and our own conscience will tell us that they are equally fulfilled in regard to everyone of us.[181] Exceptions only confirm the rule, and prove the existence of an eternity, in which God will reward all men according to their works.

Other proofs.—To the foregoing let us add some other proofs of the existence of providence:

1. *The testimony of God himself.* A thousand times, in the old and the new testament, he exhorts mankind, his well-beloved creatures, to place all their confidence in him, to cast all their cares into his bosom, to be assured that he watches over them as the apple of his eye. Adopting the most gracious forms, he represents himself to the consideration of man as a vigilant shepherd guarding his flock, as a father who arises before day to labor for the benefit of his children, as a friend desirous that we should speak to him in terms of intimate familiarity. He imposes it on us as a sacred duty to have recourse to him in all our wants, both of body and soul.

The most touching proof of his tenderness is the prayer which his divine Son vouchsafed to teach us: "Our Father, who art in heaven." Tears come into our eyes when we hear this God, our brother, begging us with earnestness to place all our confidence in our heavenly Father. "Ask and you shall receive, seek and you shall find," etc. And why? "If you who are imperfect know how to give your children the good things which they ask of you, how much more will your heavenly Father give you the good things which you ask of him. Verily, verily, I say to you, all that you ask with faith shall be given you."[182]

2. *The testimony of all nations.* To the voice of heaven is joined that of earth, in proclaiming the consoling dogma of a providence in the moral order. Jews, Christians, even pagans, are unanimous on this fundamental point; they have all believed that man lives under the government of a God who is offended by the commission of crime, who is pleased by the practice of virtue, and whose justice may be appeased or bounty merited. Hence, with all people, there have been prayers, sacrifices, a religion.

It is on considering this universal fact that one of our most celebrated theologians exclaims: "The dogma of a providence is the faith of the human race, the worship rendered to the divinity in all times and places attests the confidence of mankind in the power and care of the Creator. A natural instinct leads us to raise our eyes to heaven in our wants and sufferings; even the impious, by their blasphemies against providence, demonstrate that they believe in it. This is what Tertullian calls the testimony of the soul naturally Christian."[183]

3. *A providence in the physical order demonstrates a providence in the moral order.* If, indeed, as the sight of the universe proves, God takes so much care of inanimate and irrational creatures, of the blade of grass which springs forth at morning and dies at evening, and of the sparrow which is sold for a farthing; if he watches with so much solicitude over our body that not even a hair of our head can fall to the ground without his permission; if he provides with so much attention for our food and clothing; if all these cares are not unworthy of him, will it be unworthy of him to be occupied with the care of a creature nobler than all others, the masterpiece of his hands, his living image, and for whom all material creatures received their existence?

If he gives nourishment to the little ravens that invoke him, will he refuse the most precious nourishment, truth, to the soul that asks him for it? Whilst he has established so many wise laws for the preservation of material creatures, will he abandon to chance, like vessels without a rudder, intelligent creatures, alone capable of rendering him the homage that is worthy of him? And whilst he shows a paternal tenderness for the very insects, will he be without eyes, or ears, or hands, or heart for man? Oh, no! a thousand times no, cry out with one voice, from one end of the globe to the other, both the generations that live today and those that lie buried in the dust of the tomb. It were a crime to think it, a blasphemy to utter it.

You will perhaps meet with perverse men, who, to shake your faith in providence, will tell you that it would be imposing too painful a burden on God, to require of him to watch over the whole universe. The only answer you need make them is to ask them whether the sun grows weary by enlightening nature. They will then tell you that it is unworthy of God to concern himself about weak and imperfect creatures. Answer them boldly: You do not know what you say; the preservation of the world is only a continuation of the act of creation; if it was not unworthy of God to begin the miracle, why should it be unworthy of him to continue it? Rather, as the miracle of the creation occupied only six days, while that of the preservation of the world has already occupied nearly six thousand years, the latter must be much more glorious to God than the former.[184] They will then ask you how it happens that virtue is unfortunate and vice triumphant. You will first answer them with the assent of every people and tribe, that all does not end on earth; that there is a world to come, where matters will be restored to order, for every one will there be dealt with according to his works; that God sometimes punishes crime in this life, lest we should doubt of his vigilence, but does not always punish it lest we should doubt of the future judgment. You may even, without having recourse to the other life, say to them boldly: It is false that, even on earth, virtue is not happier than vice.

This is the manner in which you may draw up the inventory of the evils that press upon humanity:

I. There are some evils common to all men, such as weakness in infancy, infirmity in old age, death. So far the lot of virtue is at least equal to that of vice.

II. There are many diseases and miseries that are the consequences of sin. The largest share of these evils is undoubtedly the portion of the wicked; for the wicked are intemperate, imprudent, irritable, dissolute. Their vices are so many causes of disease and misery to them, while the contrary virtues are so many sources of happiness to the just.

III. There is another kind of suffering to which we must pay particular attention, in order to compare and properly estimate the respective lots of the wicked and the just: it is the punishments which human laws have sanctioned, and the courts of justice decreed. For whom have these laws been made? for the innocent or the guilty? It happens, sometimes, without doubt, that the innocent man is condemned: this is the misfortune of the period, a deplorable exception to order. But, in the ordinary course of things the sword of justice falls only on the guilty heads of the wicked.

IV. Suffering becomes so much the more painful in proportion as a man is less resigned to bear it. Now, who has the greater amount of resignation? the virtuous man or the vicious? From which party proceed the most heartrending complaints? By whom are committed the many thousand suicides that France is counting annually for the last forty years?

Thus, in reality, and as a simple matter of fact, the good man suffers less than the bad, and this suffices to show that no one has a right to accuse providence of the kind of injustice laid to its charge when people say that the condition of virtue here below is more painful than that of vice.

Finally, you do not, perhaps, know what interest these men can have in denying providence; we shall unfold to you their shameful secret, or rather they betray it themselves: if the dogma of providence is the consolation of the just, it is the terror of the wicked. Accordingly, they will tell you that God is too great to concern himself about man; that our actions matter little to him, since they cannot affect his felicity. We cannot be deceived here. This is the language of a corrupted heart that wishes to abandon itself to evil without fear or remorse. This alone should make us suspect it.

Would you desire to refute them? Content yourself with answering: It is truly strange that you wish to free yourselves from every duty toward the Creator, on those very grounds which rather prove both the importance of your duties and the guilt of him who offends against them. You refuse to adore God, and why? Because he is too great, too perfect; that is, too worthy to be adored. You refuse to obey God, and why? Because he is too powerful, too wise; that is, he has too many claims on your obedience. You refuse to love God, and why? Because he is too just, too holy, too good; that is, too amiable. It is no longer to be wondered at, that, having prepared such excellent reasons, you await in repose the terrible judgment that will decide your eternal lot. You say again that God is indifferent to our crimes, because they cannot disturb his felicity; and is then the slave, who wings a murderous arrow at his master, or the unnatural son, who raises his sacrilegious hand against his father, less guilty because the object of his fury escapes unhurt? It is not success that constitutes a crime, but the will to commit it.

V. But to put to silence completely all the objections of deists or indifferentists, it suffices to expose their system: this is the best proof of a providence.

The absurdity of deism proves a providence. We call those deists who, admitting the existence of God, deny his providence, either in the physical or moral order, and, consequently, remain indifferent as to what regards religion. The following is their creed:

"I believe in God, who has created all things, but concerns himself about nothing; who abandons his works to chance, like to an unnatural mother, who, having giving birth to the fruit of her womb, casts it into the street.

"I believe in a God, who says to me at the moment of my creation: 'I create thee to adore or outrage me, as it pleases thee; to love or hate me, according to thy fancy; truth, error, good, evil, everything about thee is a matter of indifference to me; thy isolated existence has nothing to do with my counsels; thou vile production of my hands! thou dost not deserve that I should look upon thee; begone from my sight; depart from my thoughts; frame thy own law; direct thyself; in fine, be thy own God.'"

If the creed of the deist is absurd, his decalogue is no less so. Here it is, reduced to its simplest form:

"Thou shalt admit or reject all religions alike. Whether thou art a Catholic at Rome, a protestant at Geneva, a Mahometan at Constantinople, or an idolater at Pekin, is all one. In religious affairs, day and night, white and black, yes and no, are all the same thing. To eat well, drink well, sleep well, and follow all one's inclinations, is the only true religion. It is also that of us, deists."

Now, this pretended religion, a hundred times more injurious to the divinity than atheism, reduces man to the level of the brute, opens the door to every crime, affords society no other protection than that of the robber; allows no hope to the weak, no consolation to the miserable, no encouragement to the just, no restraint to the wicked; and thus establishes a morality worthy only of swine and wolves. It is, therefore, false. "For," says one of themselves, "truth never injures." And this is the best proof that the doctrine of deists is not the truth.

In conclusion, we shall see in the catechism that there is a true religion; that there is one only, as there is one only God; that this religion comes from God; that it is indispensable; that an eternity of happiness will be the just recompense of those who venerate, and an eternity of torments the just chastisement of those who shall have despised this holy religion, the sovereign law of him who created man, and endowed him with reason and liberty.

PRAYER

O my God! who art all love, I return thee thanks for having made thyself known to us; enlighten those who know thee not. I adore thee; I love thee; I consecrate to thee all that I have, and all that I am.

I am resolved to love God above all things, and my neighbor as myself for the love of God; and, in testimony of this love, I shall frequently say to myself: "God sees me."

Lesson 4: Creation: The First Day

God considered in his works. — After having contemplated God in himself, let us contemplate him in his works; they will relate his glory, and, better than all arguments, explain his infinite perfections to us. We have seen that God has existed from all eternity; not so with us. In the beginning, nothing of all that we see around us existed; nor did we ourselves exist. There was no heaven, no earth, no sun, no mountains, no rivers, no sea, no animals, no men, no angels.

God resolved to create all these things. But how would he do so? Where would he find materials with which to form this magnificent universe? You are aware that when a man desires to build a house, he requires a supply of stones, brick, wood, iron. The first cabin should still be unconstructed, if man had to create its materials. But God's power is very different from ours: "He spoke, and all things were made";[185] for he who can do all things accomplishes whatever he desires by a simple word.

From all eternity God had conceived the idea of the world. At the time marked out for it, he uttered his thought; that is, he expressed his thought outwardly by his Word; in short, he spoke, and all things were made. The mode in which man, the image of God, performs his works may give us an idea of the creation. When a man desires to build a house, for example, he begins by conceiving an idea of it; then, at the fixed time he says: "Let the house be built." If the effect does not immediately follow the expression, it is because man, not being omnipotent, cannot accomplish what he desires by a command. He must supplement his weakness by a multitude of laborers and materials, all which requires time. But it is no less true that man's works are the expression of his thoughts, as the world is the expression of God's thought.

To know how powerful and fruitful was the Word that created the universe, let us hear the account of the creation with the same sentiments of admiration penetrating our souls as if we had been present at this great work, and had seen, at each word of the Creator, that wondrous multitude of creatures, so various and so perfect, spring forth from nothingness. Before our eyes will be unfolded a magnificent book, the first in which God desires that the children of men should read the lesson of his existence, glory, power, goodness, and all his other perfections.

Work of the six days: First day. — This admirable book was written by God in six days. Whether each of these days was a revolution of twenty-four hours, or a longer space of time, a question left to the disputations of philosophers.[186] What is important to remark is that God was not pleased to create the world instantaneously or suddenly, but gradually, hereby to teach us that he is free to act as he pleases. The following is the order in which he called forth creatures from nothingness:

In the beginning God created heaven and earth. — "In the beginning"; that is, at the beginning of all things, when God began to create the world.

Heaven and earth. — Moses desired, first of all, to point out the creation of the universe in general, whose principal parts, in our regard, are heaven and earth. In these few words he places the whole before our eyes. He then descends to particulars, mentioning what was done on each day of the great week.[187] How many doubts are cleared away in the few words: "God created heaven and earth!" How many errors dissipated? How many salutary truths revealed? What would our reason do without this light, save perchance ever seek, but never find.

First expression as the basis of science. — This first expression of the Bible is the basis of modern science. By these luminous words it ought to be delivered from those absurd cosmologies, from which pagan antiquity could never free itself, and which, condemning the human mind to grope eternally in the dark, have chained it down in the pitiable condition that every one sees. The impious science of the last century has plunged into chaos, because it has rejected the true basis of the edifice. Actual science emerges from darkness in proportion as it becomes biblical.

Consider, again, what majesty, and, at the same time, what simplicity there is in these few words: "In the beginning God created heaven and earth!" We feel that it is God himself who instructs us regarding a wonder at which he himself is not surprised, because he is superior to it. An ordinary person would endeavor to make the magnificence of his expressions correspond to the grandeur of his subject, but he would thereby only exhibit his weakness. The divine architect, who amused himself in the formation of the world, as he says himself, relates the account of it without any emotion.[188]

The earth was without form and void;[189] that is, without ornaments, without men, without animals; in a word, deprived of all that which embellishes it at present.[190] God was pleased to create the earth without its magnificent adornments (though he might easily have acted otherwise), that man might not regard the earth as rich and fruitful of itself. He must learn that originally it was without fertility, without inhabitants, without beauty; that, of itself, it should have ever remained as worthless and unproductive as on the day of its creation; and that the riches with which it at present overflows are not its own, but are the gifts of an invisible hand.

Darkness covered the face of the deep. — By this *deep* we are to understand the deep waters that enveloped the earth on all sides, forming with it a single globe.[191] Thick darkness covered the face of all; by this we should understand not only the privation of light under which the whole universe labored, but also a very thick mist, rising to a considerable height, which concealed the surface of the waters, even when light was made. This circumstance has appeared even to God to merit particular attention. He says to Job,

"Who shut up the sea with doors, when it broke forth as issuing out of the womb, when I made a cloud the garment thereof and wrapped it in a mist as in swaddling bands?"[192]

There are few persons who have not observed that rivers, lakes, and much more the sea, become enveloped during the night, at certain seasons of the year, with a thick fog, which at daybreak appears like a closely-napped counterpane under which the waters lie tranquilly asleep. It was almost thus that during the general darkness or night in which the world was at first plunged, God held the immense abyss tranquilly asleep, as in the cradle of its infancy, under a misty coverlet, waiting for a future time to set free this terrible ocean, he himself being ever its master, alike to calm it to rest or to agitate it by the storm.

And the Spirit of God moved over the waters.—These words denote that operation of God which prepared the waters and the earth for fecundity. See the beautiful and affecting comparison. The waters were covered with a mist which served them as garments and swaddling bands; and the "Spirit of God moved over them." Like a bird that extends its wings over its little ones to protect them, or even rests on its eggs to hatch them, so the vivifying Spirit brought to light, if we may so speak, the infant world, animated it with its breath, and inspired it with life and heat.

Image of baptism.—In this occurrence, we find a beautiful figure of another birth, much more miraculous to eyes enlightened by faith. Our Lord, speaking to Nicodemus, says to him: "Amen, amen, I say to thee, unless a man be born again of water and the Holy Ghost, he cannot enter into the kingdom of heaven. That which is born of the flesh is flesh, that which is born of the Spirit is spirit. Wonder not that I say to thee, thou must be born again."[193] Our Lord compares the Spirit of God imparting a secret virtue to the waters for a first birth, with the same Spirit rendering efficacious the waters of baptism for a second birth. He shows in our creation the model of our reformation. He warns us that we have received from our first origin a carnal birth only, having lost the Holy Spirit whose vivifying heat had animated it. And that we shall be forever excluded from heaven unless we receive a new birth, of which the Spirit of God and the waters must be as heretofore the principal.[194] This is not the only time in which we shall have occasion to remark, that God observes the same laws in the regeneration as in the creation of man.

And the Lord said: Let there be light; and light was made. And God saw that the light was good, that is, conformable in all respects to the rules and designs of the divine Wisdom. "He separated the light from the darkness, and called the light day, and the darkness night."[195]

Creation of light; its rapidity of propagation.—Light is the first work and the first benefit of the Creator; it should, then, be the first subject of our gratitude. Without light, all nature would be as if it were not, and the beauties and wonders which the divine Wisdom has scattered everywhere would be valueless to man, who ought to be their admirer. But what is light? Here begins a long chain of mysteries that confound our reason. The mysteries of nature, inexplicable though evident, teach us to believe in the still more elevated mysteries of religion, though we cannot comprehend them. All that the most learned philosophers have said regarding light is little more than conjectural.

Some assert that light is a fluid substance, in which we live as fishes in the sea, and which becomes visible when it is excited and set in motion by the sun or some other inflamed body. Others say that light is nothing but fire, which, by an infinitely subtle emanation or flowing forth of its particles, strikes gently on our eyes at a proper distance.

If light is incomprehensible in its nature, it is still more so in its effects and properties. The rapidity with which it moves is prodigious; its molecules travel at the rate of about 200,000 miles a second. If it traveled only with the velocity of sound, it would require 14 years to come from the sun to us, while at present it accomplishes the distance in about 8 minutes.[196] In this short space of time, a ray from the sun passes over many millions of miles. Still more: the observations of astronomers teach us that the rays of a fixed star, in order to reach us, perform a journey which a cannonball, discharged at the greatest possible velocity, and careering onwards at a uniform rate, would require 100,400,000 hours to travel.

The expansibility of light is no less incomprehensible. The extent to which it spreads has no other limits than those of the universe itself; and the immensity of the universe is so great, that it far exceeds the grasp of the human intellect. The proof of the inconceivable expansibility of light is that the most distant known objects, the heavenly bodies, may be seen by the naked eye, or with a telescope; and if we had optical instruments that would carry our vision as far as the boundaries of light, we should thereby discover, perhaps, new orbs, placed at the extremity of the universe.

But why does light diverge on all sides with such astonishing swiftness? It is that an innumerable multitude of objects may be perceived at the same time by an innumerable multitude of persons, and that every moment man may be able to enjoy the universe as far as his eye can reach. Why are the particles of light almost infinitely rarified? It is that they may paint the objects on even the smallest eye, without blinding by their brilliancy, or hurting by their heat. Why, in fine, are the rays refracted in so many ways? It is that we may more clearly distinguish the objects that are presented to our eyes.

It is, then, true, that in the creation of light, as in that of all other things, God proposed to himself the happiness and the advantage of man. What gratitude do we owe to thee, O Father of light, for thy wise and beneficent arrangements!

Colors; their advantage.—One admirable property of light is that of coloring objects, and thus enabling us more easily to recognize them. Instead of a charming landscape, adorned with everything that spring and the hand of man could render delightful, let us imagine the country all covered with snow. The light of the sun, as it appears above the horizon, is powerfully reflected by the universal whiteness. The brightness of the day is considerably augmented. Everything is clearly visible; yet everything is confounded; the objects can only be guessed at. The effect of the uniform whiteness, notwithstanding its brilliancy, is that we cannot discern the habitations of men from rocks, trees from the hills where they grow, or cultivated from uncultivated lands. We would see everything, and yet we would hardly know anything. Such would have been, very likely, the aspect of nature if God had given us light without the property of color.

But, thanks to this property of light, which paints and adorns everything around us, all creatures are recognized at a glance; each kind wears its particular dress. Whatever serves us has its characteristic mark; we require no effort to search out what we seek; its color announces it to us. To what delays and perplexities should we have been exposed if it had been necessary at every moment to distinguish one thing from another by some tedious process of reasoning. Our whole life would have been employed in study rather than in action. But it was not the design of our heavenly Father to engage his children in idle speculation. We easily see that he has concealed from us the nature of beings, that we may fix our attention more steadily on the wants of life and the exercise of virtue. The earth was not made to be a dwelling-place for disputants and dreamy philosophers, but for a society of brethren united by the bonds of reciprocal wants and duties.

It was with this view that, instead of the long and tedious mode of discussion, God was pleased to grant to the human race, and even to animals which are so serviceable to man, the convenient and expeditious mode of distinguishing objects by color. Man opens his eyelids in the morning; and behold, all his inquiries are at an end. His work, his utensils, his food, whatever he desires, is at hand. No embarrassment about it; color is the friend that guides him securely by the hand whither he should go.

The intention of enabling us easily to distinguish objects was not the only one that contributed to the formation of colors. God concerns himself in regard to our pleasures as well as our necessities. Was it not his design to place us in an agreeable abode, when he adorned all parts of the universe with such beautiful and various paintings. Remark the inimitable skill of the divine artist. The heavens, and everything to be seen from afar, are painted in bold outline; grandeur and magnificence of color are their characteristics. Delicacy and fineness of touch, with all the graces of miniature, are found in objects that are destined to be viewed closely: as leaves, birds, flowers.

This is not all. Lest uniformity of color should become wearisome, the earth changes its dress and ornaments according to the seasons. It is true that, during winter, the heavenly painter conceals his picture beneath a great white curtain. But winter, which deprives the earth of a portion of its beauty, procures it a rest that is useful to it, and still more useful to the husbandman. While man, the master of the earth, is confined within doors during the winter to what purpose would the earth be arranged in its ornaments? At the return of spring the curtain rises, and the spectator of the universe beholds the gorgeous picture with a new and ever increasing admiration.

Colors, which produce so beautiful an effect on nature, are no less beautiful in embellishing civil society. What elegance do they not add to our dress and furniture? But of all the services they render to us, there is none that pleases us more than that of gratifying our inclinations, and serving us in various ways. The most ordinary colors serve for general purposes; the gayest and brightest are reserved for grand occasions. They add a charm to our festive days, and by their brilliancy infuse a secret joy which is peculiarly their own. When we are in affliction we lay aside the gay and put on sombre colors. In this way they share in our mourning, and administer consolation to us by alleviating our sorrow.

Light possesses another property quite as wonderful as those of which we have been speaking. It is that of being one of the principal fertilizers of nature. The most advanced school of science believes itself in a condition to prove this fact, foreshadowed by an ancient father of the Church: that all material creatures are only transformations of light on some terrestrial base. If this is really so, see the analogy which exists between the created light, that renders fruitful and beautifies the visible world, and the uncreated light, that embellishes the invisible world.

The Word of God, the eternal light, essentially fruitful, has made all things; and the created light gives to all parts of the material world their proper being, and the modifications that distinguish them, so that we may say of light what is said of the divine Word itself: "It shines everywhere and always."

The analogy between the created and the uncreated light is perceived not only in their effects, but also in the laws that regulate them.

It is by the Word of God that we know all truth in the supernatural order: he enlightens every man coming into this world. It is by the created light that we know all things in the order of nature; it also enlightens the eyes of every man coming into this world. Man, who comprehends everything in nature by means of light, does not comprehend what light is. It is the same in the supernatural order. Man dares to deny what his senses cannot perceive, what he cannot touch with his finger, and, nevertheless, he only sees and knows what matter itself is by means of light, which yet has nothing of matter in it;[197] what a contradiction!

The uncreated light, which possesses in a superior degree all the properties of created light, is spread by means of the Word with a rapidity that is truly astonishing; it enlightens all minds, whenever and whenever it meets them; it never fails in its efficacy; it teaches how to distinguish all things, the true from the false, the good from the bad, the perfect from the imperfect; it colors, embellishes, and gives a character to the various objects which come under our knowledge, and seek our love. It is precisely the same with created light. These few words on the analogy between the twofold lights which enlighten our twofold nature, may suffice to teach us in what manner we should study the works of God, and thus verify the profound saying of the apostle St. Paul: The visible world is only an expression of the invisible.[198]

After having created the light, God separated the darkness from it. This means that he appointed an order and succession between light and darkness. Since that moment, day and night have followed each other without intermission. One would say they were like two children who had peacefully divided the paternal inheritance between them, and who were never known, in the lapse of ages, to encroach upon the limits originally assigned to each of them.

PRAYER

O my God! who art all love, I thank thee for having created light for me, and thereby procured me so many means of enjoyment. Do not permit that I should ever abuse thy gift to commit evil. Enlighten my soul with the light of thy truth — a light which is only feebly represented by that which strikes my eyes.

I am resolved to love God above all things, and my neighbor as myself for the love of God; and, in testimony of this love, I will often raise my eyes to heaven.

Lesson 5: Creation: The Second Day

Creation of the firmament; its extent. — God said: "Let there be a firmament made amidst the water, and let it divide the waters from the waters. And God made a firmament, and divided the waters that were under the firmament from those that were above the firmament, and it was so done. And God called the firmament heaven."[199]

The firmament is the starry heaven; it appears to our eyes like an azure dome, from which the sun, moon, stars, and other heavenly bodies are suspended.[200]

It is in the heavens that the greatness and power of God shine forth most resplendently. To have some idea of the extent of the heavens, we must know: a) that the sun, which appears to us so small, has a diameter 112 times that of the earth; in other words, about a million miles — that its size is about 1,330,000 times that of the earth — in fine, that its distance from the earth is about 114,000,000 miles;[201] b) that a cannon ball, traveling at the rate of 9 miles a minute, would occupy 125 years in passing from the earth to the sun, or 600,000 years to the nearest fixed star;[202] and c) that the fixed stars are so many suns, which transmit, even to us, not a borrowed, but their own light — suns which the Creator has scattered by thousands over the illimitable fields of space. Let us hereby endeavor to conceive how powerful is he, who, by a single word, made all these things. He is the same God, who, for the love of us, became a little child, and who, hidden under the appearance of bread, gives himself to us in the Holy Communion!

If the fixed stars can be seen by us at such an immense distance, it is because they quite equal the sun in size, and because their apparent littleness is simply the effect of their fearful remoteness from us. They are then so many suns, which have been withdrawn from us, to preserve us from their heat, without depriving us of the joy of their light. Moreover, if that whiteness, which is called the Milky Way, is, as the telescope declares it to be, only a vast mass of stars or suns, still more distant, then the hand of God has cast worlds along this way, with as much profusion as the sands are scattered along the seashore.

Those enormous spheres that roll in such variety over our heads are like so many terrible engines, the least collision with one of which would be sufficient to shatter our globe into a thousand fragments; but the same hand that has suspended them in space has marked their route. An unerring calculation has regulated the consequences of their weight, motion, and velocity; there is no danger of any unforeseen obstacle or secondary cause, disarranging their course.

And, in the midst of this immensity, what is the handful of earth that we inhabit; what are provinces and kingdoms in comparison with these mighty worlds? A few atoms that sport in the air, and that are hardly perceptible in the rays of the sun. And what am I in the midst of all? Ah! how I am lost in my own nothingness! Nevertheless, O abyss of goodness! it is for us that God has made all these magnificent works.[203]

The excellence of the beings which God has made is not measured by their weight. Man has received a mind, a will, a soul. It is to this little creature that God communicates a knowledge of his works, while he refuses it even to the sun. It is for man's use and benefit he designes the rich apparel of the heavens. God invites no other visible creature to praise him. What dignity for man to have a Father who covers the earth with good things for him, and even intends the heavens for his service! What gratitude do we owe to a God who treats us with so much honor!

To judge merely by the testimony of our senses, we should imagine that above our heads is an immense dome painted blue, and that the stars are only little brass-headed nails fastened into it. We have seen that the apparent smallness of the stars is due to their amazing distance.

Its color. — As to the blue color of the firmament, it happens a) because the atmosphere, or the mass of air surrounding us, is not of itself perfectly transparent, and b) because this atmosphere is usually charged with strata of light waters—both of which causes combine in refracting the rays of the sun. A bluish color is natural to water, either dense or ratified, particularly when the volume or water is great. The atmosphere ought then to be of an azure color, and this color is more or less clear in proportion to the quantity of rays with which it is penetrated.

It is from this mixture of air and water that God has formed the color of the glorious vault above, which everywhere rejoices the sight of man, and serves as the beautiful ceiling of our palace. Such a wonder demands from us more than admiration, for it is standing proof that we are the object of our Creator's most tender regards.

Indeed, God could have made the heavenly vault either brown or black; but these dark sombre colors would have cast a gloom over all nature. Red and white would have answered no better. Yellow is reserved for the aurora; moreover, an entire vault of a golden color would not have thrown out the stars in sufficient relief, so as to render them easily discernible. Green would indeed have been an appropriate background; but it is with this beautiful color God has decorated the earth: it is the carpet which he has spread out beneath our feet. Blue, without sadness or harshness, has at the same time the advantage of determining the color of the stars, and thus showing them in proper relief. Hence, the divine decorator selected it in preference to the others.

How terrible is the aspect of the heavens, when covered with stormy clouds! But how beautiful, how majestic, what simplicity of color, when the heavens are serene! The halls of kings, decorated by the skill of the most experienced artists, are nothing in comparison with the chaste grandeur of the heavenly dome. And who has painted the heavens so beautifully, who has decorated them so richly?

By a truly kind consideration, the heavens do not always preserve a uniform tint. So far from it, their color changes many times even in a day. In the morning we have gentle gleams brightening by degrees the horizon, until the starry azure of night pales away, to prepare our eyes for the splendor of midday. And when evening is come, the sun does not withdraw its light in a moment: soft gleams, like those of morning, prepare us for the darkness of the night. To pass suddenly from a clear effulgence to a profound obscurity would be very inconvenient. Such a sudden passage would injure, if not destroy, the organs of sight. Many travelers, surprised by the nightfall, would be in danger of wandering; and the greater number of the birds would be in danger of perishing. Thanks be to thee, O heavenly Father! thou hast anticipated all these inconveniences.

Let there be a firmament in the midst of the waters. — After having stretched out the heavens, or the firmament, as a magnificent pavilion, God was pleased that its situation should be in the midst of the waters; so that there are waters above the firmament and others beneath it. God caused the greater portion of the immense bodies of water which surrounded the earth to evaporate, reducing them to such imperceptible atoms, that, no longer forming a regular mass, and acquiring a rapid motion upwards, they arose so high, that there remained a vast abyss between them and those with which the earth was still covered. As this space formed a part of the heavens or the firmament,[204] it deserved to bear the same name: the *firmament* was then the separation of the waters, or the space between the waters that had been elevated and those that were left on the earth.

Thus, above our heads, and beyond the firmament, is an immense quantity of water — a formidable ocean — kept there by the hand of the Almighty alone.[205] Hurtful or useless here below, this water is valuable elsewhere. If we are but imperfectly acquainted with its material utility, there are decided advantages of a superior order for which we are indebted to it. It says to us continually: "I have yielded my place to mankind, who ought to be just and innocent." And to the early inhabitants of the world it said: "I am ready to return again to the earth, to punish ingratitude and irreligion."

It was undoubtedly with views such as these that God informed the fathers of the human race regarding the separation of the waters, some of which are suspended over our heads, and the rest are only confined by the limits which his hand has placed. When the impenitence of the human race had led God to repent of giving existence to man, he restored matters to their original state. He burst asunder the boundaries that held fast the sea; and, not content with pouring down torrents of rain, he even opened the floodgates that served as a barrier to the waters above. Then the earth was anew plunged and enveloped in water, as on the day of its birth: this was the deluge. "All the fountains of the great deep," says the scripture, "were broken up, and the floodgates of heaven were opened."

A portion of the immense quantity of water connected with the earth remains below the firmament, and composes our seas, our lakes, and our rivers. These are called the inferior or lower waters, of which we shall have something to say when treating of the third day.

Air. — Let us again make a remark on the space which reaches from earth to heaven. It is filled to a considerable height with a heavy elastic fluid, called air. The whole of this mass of air surrounding the earth, and serving it as a kind of garment, is called the atmosphere.

It is necessary to know that the force with which a column of air presses on a square inch is about fifteen pounds weight. Thus, a man of ordinary stature really supports a burden of over 21,000 pounds. How is it, then, that we are not crushed? The thought seems capable of disturbing us; but our uneasiness is changed into admiration, when we learn that the small quantity of air contained within our body, and which is continually renewed, suffices to maintain an equilibrium with the dreadful burden that presses on us on all sides.

These internal and external forces destroy each other, or rather they are not felt at all, because they are equally balanced. They, nevertheless, positively exist. We can give an evident proof of it: when the air is pumped out of the body of an animal, the animal is crushed beneath the weight of the external air, and dies instantly. When, on the other hand, the air that is around an animal is pumped away from it, as may easily be accomplished by an air pump, the air within it presses out with such violence that the animal becomes extremely swollen, and dies, as in the former case.

Thus, the small quantity of air that is within our body is capable of annihilating a force of more than 20,000 pounds. This is one wonder; the second is not less strange. The air within us, in its effort to be free, would tear our body to pieces. This dreadful design is frustrated by the air around us. The mere equilibrium of these destructive forces is, therefore, our only security; were it destroyed we should instantly perish. But no; the hand that formed these astonishing forces to put all nature in action has moderated them with such precision, that the impetus of the one is just equivalent to the resistance of the other.

You will perhaps ask why the air, which is so close to us, and which acts on us with so much energy, is not visible. The answer to this question will be a new proof of the existence of a providence, attentive to all our wants. If the air were visible, the view of all other objects would be less distinct. Every particle of the air having then sufficient extent to reflect the light clearly, we should only be able to see as through a cloud of dust, or as we see in a dark chamber which is penetrated by a few gleams from the sun. By rendering the air totally invisible, God has been pleased to reveal the exterior of his works more manifestly to us; while, at the same time, he conceals from our eyes that which it is not necessary for us to see.

Indeed, if the air were visible, vapors would be still more so. Accumulations of smoke would then disfigure the beautiful picture of the universe. Life itself would become uncomfortable and troublesome. We should continually perceive on all sides the perspiration of animals, the exhalations from kitchens, from the streets, and from inhabited places everywhere: society would be unendurable. Nevertheless, as exhalations, which cease to be hurtful after undergoing the process of dispersion in the upper regions of the air, might, not being seen, injure or even suffocate us, God has been pleased to warn us of their proximity by the sense of smell, and to deliver us from their dangers by the gentle action of the wind.

But, whatever delicacy our heavenly Father has given to the particles of the air to render them invisible, he has at the same time given them sufficient solidity to render them capable by refraction of moderating the intensity of the rays of light. To this arrangement we are indebted for the twilight, which is so advantageous to the human family.

When the sun sinks in the West, we should be totally deprived of light, and should enter straightway into utter darkness. This, nevertheless, does not happen. We still see the day continuing an hour, often even longer, after sunset: this is the evening twilight. A similar twilight, or more properly, an aurora, precedes the rising of the sun next morning. Owing to the wonderful manner in which God has formed the air, we are indebted for this useful increase in the length of our daylight. He has so proportioned the air to the light, that when a ray of the latter enters the mass of the former perpendicularly, it continues its course in a straight line, but when it enters it obliquely, it becomes, as it were, broken, and comes to us in a slanting direction.

Thus, when the sun is rising, many of his rays, which are not sent toward us, and ought to pass above us, meeting with the body of air that surrounds us, are bent into it, wing their flight to the earth, and reach our eyes. This is the reason why we see day a long time before the appearance of the sun in the morning, and still enjoy it when that luminary has disappeared in the evening.

Finally, when the sun has sunk to a certain degree below the horizon, the air ceases to break and transmit its rays to us. It is then that thick darkness warns man to cease his labors. If the moon and the stars still watch for our service, their light is soft and gentle, and incapable of disturbing our repose.

The vehicle of odors and sound. — The air produces other effects still more marvelous. It is a messenger that brings us from all sides, even from afar, tidings as useful as they are prompt, of what it is important for us to know, whether good or ill. It is the vehicle of odors. Transmitting them to us, it informs us, for instance, of the quality of our food. As it announces to us by delicate sensations that which is pleasing to our nature, or suitable for our use, so likewise it warns us, with equal fidelity, when to flee an unwholesome region, or to shun a poisonous atmosphere, and remove far from an infected dwelling.

If the air, by wafting to us different odors, proves itself a faithful watchman, it is no less so by the various sounds with which it strikes our ears. Indeed we may consider these sounds as so many couriers, whom it every moment sends to us, that they may inform us of what is going on, frequently even at a considerable distance, and that we may profit by their advice.

This is not all; it even informs us of what passes in the minds of others. Different thoughts occupy my mind; they are known only to myself; they cannot be seen. How shall I communicate them to my hearers? I form, by the motion of my tongue and lips, some words, whose different articulations are the signs of certain thoughts. By this means, the persons who hear the sound of my lips and tongue become acquainted with the thoughts of my mind. They reflect on these same thoughts, and their hearts become affected with similar sentiments. The air then, so to speak, is the interpreter of the human family, and unites minds together in one common bond of fellowship. How wonderful is the first birth of the word in the understanding; how wonderful in its external incarnation, and again in its new birth, in the minds of its auditors!

It not only unites those who are near, and may communicate their thoughts orally, it moreover establishes a correspondence between those whom distance separates by wide intervals. The inhabitants of a city cannot see what passes outside the walls; those who know that the enemy is attacking one of the gates cannot, by their mere voice, make known their wants to the citizens who are at the extremity of the city. The air immediately comes to their assistance. The sentinel sounds the tocsin. In a second, that is in the sixtieth part of a minute, the air bears the sound of that knell a distance of 1,080 feet. Another second or two, and the sound is heard all over the city. Thus, the news of the danger is made known in far less than half-a-quarter of a minute. On the spot, every one runs to arms, and the enemy is repulsed—the victory is due to the air!

The air then is, after electricity, the swiftest and most diligent messenger we can employ. But if it astonishes us by the speed of its journeys, what shall we say of the fidelity with which it delivers its message? Without confusion it conveys to the audience the full harmony of the concert; it brings us, without the least mistake, all the regularity of the measure, the graceful cadences, the semitones, say, even the least inflections of the voice. Now it flashes, sparkles, thunders; anon, it languishes, trembles, dies; again it is reanimated, becoming in turn wild and enthusiastic, or soft and tender; thus it enters so deeply into all the passions, whose transports are so admirably represented by music, that the audience are carried away in a flood of excitement. What an abuse would it be if we should ever employ this valuable servant to convey from us words offensive to truth or modesty! Nay, rather may it ever bear from us the accents of prayer and charity.

Rain and wind.—Under the hand of our heavenly Father, the air diversifies its employments, in order to promote our comforts, and to supply our wants. Water is one of those things that are essential to the fertility of the earth, and, consequently, a necessary condition of our existence. It must be drawn from the sea, and dispersed over the land; the air is charged with this office. Like a pump, it raises a sufficiency of water, which it distributes on the surface of the earth according to the directions of the Creator.

Sometimes the air is agitated; it then takes the name of the wind. When highly excited it roars and whistles, but it purifies the world. Without it, great cities would soon become like so many cemeteries. Again: the air warms us and cools us in turn. Its services are always accompanied with the utmost grace: hence it removes, without our notice, those gases which might tarnish or infect us. But we are like those whimsical and inconsiderate masters who never acknowledge the merits of their domestics, in whose conduct they can see nothing but defects. Perhaps we have not even once remarked the assiduous services which the winds have rendered to us a thousand times over; on the contrary, the least breath of air is sometimes enough to offend our delicacy!

Finally, the greatest benefit of the air is that it enables us to live; it enters into our lungs, and abides there during the time that is necessary to supply strength and motion to the organs of our body. When it has lost its energy it departs; fresh air from without replaces it, and thus prolongs our life. A perfect image of prayer, by which we should continually breathe in God and for God!

PRAYER

O my God! who art all love, I thank thee for having placed all creatures at my service. The heavens in which thou appearest so mighty, the air in which thou appearest so admirable, are the benefits of thy paternal hand; grant that I may ever refer them to thy glory and my salvation.

I am resolved to love God above all things, and my neighbor as myself for the love of God; and, in testimony of this love, I will promptly obey my superiors.

Lesson 6: Creation: The Third Day

The Sea.—God said: "Let the waters that are under the heaven be gathered together into one place, and let the dry land appear; and it was so done. And God called the dry land earth, and the gathering together of the waters he called seas; and God saw that it was good." God said again: "Let the earth bring forth the green herb, and such as may seed, and the fruit-tree yielding fruit after its kind, which may have seed in itself upon the earth; and it was so done."[206]

You will lend me all your attention to hear the explanation of these commands. Prepare also your minds for admiration, and your hearts for gratitude; we have to speak of new wonders and new benefits. God, having separated the waters into two portions, and left on the earth only such a quantity as was suited to his designs, commanded the lower waters to assemble in one place, that the earth might become visible.[207] He called these waters the sea. This command, that "the waters under heaven should be gathered into one place," which here seems only a mild expression, was, according to the psalmist,[208] a terrific menace and a voice of thunder. Instead of flowing tranquilly, the waters rushed, as it were, terror-stricken, and appeared ready to abandon, not only the earth, but, if possible, even the universe, so quickly did they pile themselves on one another like huge mountains, in order to vacate the place which they had seemed to usurp, since God thus chased them from it.

In this precipitate obedience, the affrighted waters were on the point of carrying destruction in all directions; but an invisible hand controlled them with the same ease as a mother controls her infant, which she wraps in its swaddling clothes, and lays in its cradle. This is the simple comparison under which God himself represents to us the work he then accomplished. "Who shut up the sea with doors," he says to Job, "when it broke forth as issuing out of the womb, when I made a cloud the garment thereof, and wrapped it in a mist as in swaddling bands? I set my bounds around it, and made it bars and doors, and said: Hitherto thou shalt come and shalt go no farther; and here thou shalt break thy swelling waves."[209]

The sea abandoned only that portion of the earth which God was pleased to un-cover; it quitted the regions which he had resolved to people, and occupied those which he had destined for its abode. Thus, the terrible infant was laid in its bed; since that moment it has remained tranquilly at rest, the limits of its cradle a grain of sand assigned to it by God.

The tide. — Nevertheless, the waters of the sea, assembled in their immense reservoir, might corrupt, and afterward diffuse their malarious vapors, so as to render the earth uninhabitable. The creative Wisdom provided against this inconvenience. The same God who forbade the sea any departure from its bed, ordered it at the same time to observe a continual motion; and the obedient sea, twice every day, pushes its waters for six hours in one direction, and then again for six hours in the opposite direction. During six thousand years it has never failed a single time. This motion is called the ebb and flow. It is peculiar to all seas; if it is more observable in the ocean than elsewhere, it is because this motion is more necessary, the quantity of water there being greater.

Thus, the object of the continual and miraculous movement of the waters of the sea is to prevent them from corruption, which would necessarily follow from repose. The sea renders us other services also; for it is on our account the sea exists, and on our account it is ever agitated. First, the tides drive back the waters of rivers, make them ascend in a body far inland, and thereby so deepen the beds of the rivers as to admit the passage of enormous vessels, laden with foreign merchandise, to the quays of our great cities; which otherwise would be altogether impracticable to vessels of heavy burden. These vessels have usually to wait a short time for the rise of the tide, when they cross the shallows, and arrive at their destination in safety. On the ebb of the tide, the rivers continue to afford their ordinary advantages to those who dwell along their banks.

The Christian is, moreover, indebted to the continual motion of the sea for another blessing, namely, that of being presented with an instructive lesson on the instability of human life. What is life but a constant ebb and flow? ever increasing, ever diminishing; everything in it is inconstant; there is no lasting happiness here. We navigate an ever-changing sea. Let us beware of being lost in its depths; rather let us endeavor to reach the port in safety.

The flux and the reflux of the tide are the first means by which God preserves the waters of the sea from corruption; the second means is the saltness of its waters.

Saltness of the sea. — To maintain the sea effectually in its purity, it is the duty of the ebb and the flow to scatter about every day the salt with which it is impregnated. Without this constant agitation, the salt would quickly settle down to the bottom, and in such case the sea would not only cease to nourish the fish, whose variety and delicacy we so much admire, but its stench would infect the whole world with its deadly poison. Happily the creative Wisdom foresaw all these consequences, and arranged everything in number, weight, and measure.

This saltness of the sea, which already interests us so much by its preservation of the water and its support of the fish, procures us another advantage. The heavier saline particles resist the heat and the air, whereby evaporation is effected, and its measure fixed. The more the heat and the air meet with saline particles to resist them, the less they meet with particles of water to yield to them. The salt, which increases the weight of the water, moderates therefore its evaporation, and we are indebted to the saltness of the sea for the exact quantity of sweet, or as it is more generally termed, soft water, which the sun raises to supply our wants. Without the resistance of the salt, the sun would raise a much greater mass of vapor, which would afterward inundate, not fertilize, the earth. The half, perhaps the three-fourths of our time, it would be raining; so that the earth should become a complete marsh. Thus, we may in all truth say, that if the sea were not salt, we should die of starvation.

Extent of the sea. — The same just proportion is also found in the extent of the sea. It covers about two-thirds of the globe. At first sight it would seem much more advantageous if the Creator had converted into habitable land the immense space occupied by water—that is, the seas, the lakes, and the rivers. To reason thus is to show our ignorance.

If the ocean were reduced to half its present extent, it could only furnish half its ordinary amount of evaporation. We should then have only half the usual quantity of rain; our rivers would be reduced to half their size; the earth would no longer be sufficiently irrigated. The sea then has been established the grand reservoir of water, that the warmth of the sun may draw from it a proper quantity of vapor, which shall afterward fall in rain upon the earth, and become the source of streams and rivers. If the extent of the sea were less than it is, the most highly cultivated districts would soon be converted into deserts.

Let us give another proof of the admirable Wisdom which presided over the division of land and water. If God had left on the surface of the globe a greater portion of water than it at present contains, the land portion must have become one vast uninhabitable morass; if, on the other hand, he had reduced the quantity of water, the land would not have been sufficiently fertilized to nourish the seeds sown in it; we should have neither plants nor trees. The soil of the earth should be so hard as to permit us to walk on it, and so soft as to permit us to cultivate it. Without sufficient solidity we should sink in it; and unless it were sufficiently pliable or porous, it would be impossible for water to percolate, or plants to strike root in it

Navigation. — Moreover, what would become of the advantages that we now derive from commerce, if this great body of water did not exist? It was not the design of God that any one portion of the earth should be totally independent of, or separated from, all the others; on the contrary, he desired that intimate relations should exist amongst all mankind: this is rendered possible by the sea. How could we amass our treasures of wealth, or render all parts of the world tributary to our needs and our pleasures, if it were not for navigation? Thus, the sea, far from being a means established by Almighty God to keep nations apart, and confined within narrow limits, is, on the contrary, a means intended to unite all men together in the bonds of friendship, and to facilitate the transport of merchandise, which would otherwise have been very inconvenient.

Perhaps we have never reflected seriously on the advantages of navigation; perhaps we have never thanked the Creator for them. Nevertheless, we are indebted, either directly or indirectly, to navigation for many things which are now almost indispensable to our existence. The aromatic herbs and medicinal plants; the rare stuffs, the beautiful dyes, the woods, the corn, the precious fruits, etc., that come to us from distant countries—all these would be wanting, or at least could only be procured with great difficulty and expense, if there were no ships to convey them to our shores. To what a pitiable condition should we be reduced if the only mode of transit for these goods were by land! The following calculation will enable us to understand this better. A good-sized vessel carries five hundred tons; now, at the rate of two-and-a-half tons to a two-horse wagon, putting difficult hills and bad roads out of the question, it would require two hundred such wagons to convey a fair cargo overland.

In fine, a crowning benefit of navigation, consequently a most important service, rendered to us by the sea, without which there can be no navigation, is the propagation of the gospel, even to the most distant regions of the globe. Ye peoples and tribes, children of men, seated of old in the shadow of death, return thanks to God, who has created the ocean! Without the mighty highways of the sea, which the apostles of truth, the bearers of good tidings, traverse with such rapidity, you would perhaps still be buried in the darkness of error. But it is now time to quit the sea; the land calls for our attention.

Let the dry land appear. — When the waters retired into the immense basins which the hand of the Almighty had prepared for them, the dry land, that is, the earth, appeared. The design of God in uncovering the earth was to render it fertile, to adorn it with soft verdure, to diversify it with plants and trees, to enliven it with animals, and give it to man as his abode. But he left it for some time dry, bare, and sterile, to show us what it is of itself. He desired even that it should take its name from its natural aridity, in order that those who would one day be tempted to regard it as the source of all the beauties that decorate it, might remember its early poverty: "Let the dry land appear! And God called the dry land earth."

Herbs and their color. — A new creature, then, appears before our eyes. That earth, our nursing mother, was much abashed at this moment, for she was undressed and barren. God hastened to adorn her with a garment, worthy alike of his munificence and his goodness. He said: "Let the earth produce the green herb," and in an instant the earth was arrayed in the most superb dress.[210] Immortal garment! as bright, as new, as beautiful, after the lapse of six thousand years, as on the day it first adorned the earth!

What strikes us here particularly is the choice which God made of green in the earth's raiment. This color, so agreeable to our eyes, shows us it was the same hand that colored nature, and that formed the eye of man to be its spectator. If all the fields were tinted white, who could endure their brilliancy? If red, who could support their harshness? If darkened with sombre colors, what pleasure could anyone feel in gazing on the dreary landscape? A gentle green is the golden mean between these extremes.

Moreover, green has such a relation with the structure of the eye, that it refreshes instead of wearying, fortifies instead of exhausting. What is still more remarkable is that there exists so great a diversity of shades in this color, that there is not a single plant whose green is precisely as light or as dark as that of another. These delicacies of touch prevent monotony, and bear testimony to the exquisiteness of the brush of the divine artist who decorated the universe. Do not so much wisdom and goodness say anything to our hearts? Do they impose no duty on us?

Exuberance of plants. — When creating the rich sward God said: "Let the earth bring forth the green herb bearing seed in itself!" This is more wonderful than anything we have yet related; for hereby God engages himself to preserve the life of plants, and to impart to them a species of immortality. Indeed, how many plants require no labor or culture! They perpetuate themselves independently of any care of ours. How wretched would our meadows appear, if we were obliged each year to sow and water them anew!

Our heavenly Father has dispensed us from this care; he himself attends to it. What an immense multitude of plants he cultivates for the pleasures or the wants of his children! In a field, a thousand feet square, there are hundreds of thousands of blades of grass, and in a square foot, more than a thousand species thereof. The fields are odoriferous, and the combination of a thousand different essences forms an exquisite perfume, which the air, our Creator's faithful messenger, kindly conveys to us. And — wonderful still! — amongst plants and herbs, those which are the most useful to us as food or medicine, are the most numerous.

But why has the Creator multiplied so wonderfully the productions of the vegetable kingdom? First, for our health and strength; secondly, for the beasts that serve us. The prairies are the storehouses of animals.

Propagation of plants. — It is not only in the immensity of the number of plants that the greatness of our heavenly Father shines forth, but also in their wonderful productiveness. One alone may produce thousands — nay, millions. A stalk of the tobacco-plant sometimes yields as many as 40,320 seeds. If, now, we calculate its productiveness in the space of four years, we shall find that one of these seeds will multiply to 2,642,908,293,365,760,000 other such seeds. An elm, twelve years old, has often 5,000 grains of seed; what an astonishing number of trees would it propagate in a few years!

When we consider that the same rule holds good, in due proportion, with regard to all other plants, we are amazed that the earth has not been altogether eaten up by them.

What, then, is the continual miracle that preserves vegetation within its limits? It is principally this: a countless multitude of animals derive their subsistence from herbs and plants, of which they annually consume so great a quantity, that if God had not endowed the vegetable kingdom with an extraordinary degree of productiveness, we might well fear their total extinction. Here appears one of those beautiful harmonies, so usual in the works of God. If the multiplication of plants were less rapid than it is, many animals would perish of hunger; and, on the other hand, if that of animals were more rapid than it is, many species of plants would be quickly consumed, and many species of animals would quickly disappear. But thanks to the happy equilibrium established between the animal and vegetable kingdoms, the occupants of each increase in a just proportion.

When commanding plants to bear their seed, God gave them, as we have seen, a kind of immortality. Let us pause a moment to consider how this immortality is effected: in other words, how plants are reproduced. In doing so, we shall only follow the counsel of our Savior, who, to animate our confidence in God, exhorts us to examine in what manner the lilies of the field are produced and preserved.

In all kinds of plants we distinguish four parts: the root, the stem, the leaf, and the grain or fruit. A little seed falls on the ground; you need not fear, it will not perish; God watches over it as well as over the whole world. Let us pursue the operations of the divine agriculturist. He begins by covering the grain of seed with a little clay, which is not so heavy as to break it, but is sufficient to protect it against the cold that would freeze it, the heat that would scorch it, the winds that would carry it away, and the birds that would eat it. See now what happens. He calls both heat and moisture to swell the grain. Its cover bursts, and from it you see two little germs spring forth; one ascends, the other descends. That which ascends is the stalk, that which descends is the root. Who was it that told these little germs thus to separate, and take each such different directions? But let us follow the plant in its development.

I. *The root.* The root is intended to fix the plant, which would otherwise fall to the ground and perish of damp, or be carried away by the winds; and also to procure nourishment for the stalk: hence, the root is hollow in the middle. Through this little canal are drawn up, by means of the heat, the juices, which the root finds in the earth. But here is the danger! All the juices, or varieties of moisture, with which the earth is filled, do not suit every plant; and there are myriads of species of plants.[211] But do not fear, the root will not be deceived; it will only select those which are suited to it. By whom has it been taught to make these fine distinctions? In what school, or under what master, did it graduate in chemistry?

But there is another difficulty. Sometimes the juices proper to a plant are only to be found at a distance from it. What will the root do? Take notice again! Under the hand of providence, the root will stretch out right and left its little filaments to examine the nature of the aliments contained in the soil, and to report on their various qualities. But a fresh difficulty arises. The root is perhaps separated from its desired nourishment by a stone or a trench; how will it act? The faithful provider creeps softly round the stone, or dashes boldly under the trench.

When the juices have reached the top of the root, they meet with the neck, a kind of joint or knot pierced with holes like a sieve. Here they are purified, as in the alembic of a distiller, or after the manner in which a mother softens and sweetens the panado which she is about to present to the lips of her little infant. Here also, between the root and the neck, is placed a kind of leaven, which, mixing itself with the juices, communicates to them those qualities that are proper for the plant: and hence proceeds that variety of taste which we find in fruits.

II. *The stem.* In proportion as the root buries itself beneath the earth, the stem or stalk raises itself aloft. It is pierced with a multitude of little canals, through which the juices ascend and descend in connection with the root. The manner is somewhat similar to that in which the blood circulates through the veins of our bodies, supporting our life. As the stem rises above the earth, it forms knots or joints. These serve to strengthen it, as well as to purify more and more the nutritious fluids transmitted by the root. Placed one above another, they allow nothing to pass but what is most delicately refined. When the stalk becomes strong, it requires a more abundant supply of nourishment, just like an infant that is growing rapidly. The root, which is the stalk's nurse, would then run the risk of exhaustion, and the stalk might die of hunger, if God had not provided for this danger: the Father, who nourishes all things that live, comes to the assistance of his work: he does so by means of leaves.

III. *The leaf.* On the side of the little stalk, or the branches, which may be regarded as a portion of the stalk, appears a bud, which gradually increases in size: it is the leaf. The side of the leaf that turns toward the sun is smooth and glossy. Why so? In order that it may more easily be warmed by the rays of the sun, and may afterward communicate its heat to the stalk. The stalk will hereby be strengthened and enlarged, and the circulation of its fluids stimulated. The side of the leaf that turns toward the earth is rough and covered with little hairs, hollow within. Why is there such a difference? It is another admirable invention of the divine gardener. All these little hairs are open to receive the surrounding air, to gather in the warm vapors that rise from the earth, and thus contribute to the nourishment of the stalk. Quite as skillful chemists as the root, these little hairs admit none but suitable particles of air or vapor. Now, the nourishment gathered by the root and the leaves might become superabundant, and the plant be choked. How does providence arrange for this new danger? In this manner: all these little hairs that cover the underside of the leaf become like so many pores, which, perspiring, reject the useless and noxious fluids that should not be retained.

IV. *The seed or fruit.* We have now passed over the root, the stem, and the leaf; all concur to one end: the formation of the seed or fruit. When the stalk has reached its full height and maturity, we see a little thing, like a case or ball, appearing somewhere on its upper part. This little case contains all that is most precious in the plant. We also see with what tender care it is watched over by providence. It is covered with three or four envelopes, tightly fastened, to protect it against cold, heat, insects, wind, and rain.

The first of these envelopes is pretty hard; the second is finer, and in texture is more beautiful than silk or muslin; the third or the fourth, which encloses the seed, is inimitable for softness and delicacy. It is so made in order not to injure the little grains. In proportion as the seeds grow, the envelopes expand; at length the latter open, but very gradually, lest the little occupant should be exposed to the danger of perishing. When the seeds have attained sufficient strength, the downy coverings disappear, just as an infant is set free from its swaddling clothes.

The precious seeds are destined to give birth to new plants; therefore their birth must be celebrated with the utmost joy and magnificence. When the child of a king is born into the world, it is wrapped in costly stuffs. Its cradle is ornamented with gold, and its apartments are richly decorated. The air which it first inhales is purified—nay, often perfumed with sweet odors. Its birth is hailed with transports of gladness. All these things are repeated by our heavenly Father in favor of the fruit of the meanest plant.

Leaves of exquisite fineness and texture, adorned with beautiful and varied colors, wrap it in swaddling clothes, and form its cradle. Around it float the richest perfumes. The feathery songsters, the musicians of our good God, returned from their distant journeys, or recently liberated from their nests—nay, all nature, awakened by the breath of summer, and decked in the richest attire, hastens to welcome the arrival of the little stranger. Here it is born, here it grows, in the midst of the harmonies of sweet sounds, and in an abode more gorgeous than the palace of a king.

Examine all these things minutely, and, if you can, prevent your lips from saying with the divine Savior: "I declare that not even Solomon, in all his glory, was so richly decked, and so royally lodged. Men of little faith! if your heavenly Father takes so much care of the herbs of the field, which live but today, and on the morrow are thrown into the fire, what will he not do for you?"[212] How, then, can you distrust providence?

When the new grains of seed are sufficiently formed to become, in their turn, the mothers of new plants, the stalk droops its head; it says to God: "My task is done." The seed falls to the ground. Then begins again, for the formation of other plants, the wonderful process which we have just described. Should the plant be propagated afar off, God gives to the little grain feathers, and, when it is ready to depart, commands the winds to carry it away. The winds obey, and, wafted by these faithful messengers, it goes to rest in the place designed for it by providence. There it gives birth to new generations of seeds, becomes the parent of numerous colonies, and, like a zealous missionary, relates to other men the omnipotence and the wisdom of the Creator. Oh, may we profit of its eloquent discourse!

Seeing the care, and, so to speak, the gentleness with which God watches over the least plant, the humblest flower, the blade of grass that we trample beneath our feet, would we not imagine that it should live for ever? Yet from morning till evening is its life; the morrow sees it parched by the sun; on the day after it falls under the sickle. What then should we think of the immense ocean of beauties to be found in God, since he scatters them with such profusion over a little plant, that lives but a few hours? What, in fine, should we think of the care which he lavishes on our immortal souls, made to his glorious image?

PRAYER

O my God! who art all love, I thank thee for having given us the sea to supply us with rain and dew, for having decorated the earth so beautifully as our abode, and for having provided so tenderly for even the smallest plants. It is for me that thou hast done all these things: grant me the grace to profit by so many benefits!

I am resolved to love God above all things, and my neighbor as myself for the love of God; and, in testimony of this love, I shall offer my heart to God every morning.

Lesson 7: Creation: The Third and Fourth Days

Continuation of the third day. — It would not sufficiently display the magnificence of the Creator, or his goodness toward man, that the earth should be adorned with green turf, and enameled with odoriferous flowers. A new word must complete the embellishment of the abode intended for the future king of creation. God said: "Let the earth bring forth…the fruit tree, yielding fruit after its kind, which may have seed in itself upon the earth. And it was so done."[213]

Before this word, the earth was little more than a meadow or a vast kitchen-garden. But suddenly, when the word was uttered, it became an immense orchard, abounding in all sorts of trees, bearing a thousand species of fruits, which should succeed one another, according to the seasons. O men! open your eyes, the eyes of your souls, and behold here again the wisdom and the goodness of your heavenly Father!

I. *In the creation and variety of fruit trees.* What a source of pleasure in the endless variety of fruits that naturally follow one another, or that, by skill, may be preserved during the entire year! Among the fruit trees there are some which bear only at one season, others at two seasons of the year. There are also some which seem indifferent to all the seasons;

orange trees, for example, bear at the same time blossoms, green fruits, and ripe fruits. God has made them thus for reasons that invariably tend to our advantage.

First, he gives us an instructive lesson, by showing us the freedom with which he can diversify the laws of nature, and at all times do with everything whatever it pleases him. Next, he speaks to our hearts. Does not the tree, whose branches are laden to the ground under the weight of its exquisite fruits, which announce their flavor by their delicious odors and brilliant colors, at the same time that they amaze us by their abundance, seem to say to us: "Learn of me the greatness and the goodness of God, who formed me for thee. It is neither for him, nor for myself, that I am so rich. He stands in need of nothing; and I cannot use what he has given me. Bless him, then, and repay him for me! Return him thanks; and, since he has appointed me the minister of thy pleasure, do thou become the minister of my gratitude!"

On all sides are similar invitations repeated. At every step we meet some new species of them. See then, O men! how the divine Wisdom has delighted in the formation of creatures. In some cases the fruit is hidden within, as in the walnut; while in others a stone is found, as the peach, whose velvet skin is radiant with the most beautiful colors. The voices of all creatures demand our gratitude, as well as reproach us for being unthankful. The saints understood this mute language, and we, like them, should listen to its pleading. It is related of a venerable solitary that, seeing the herbs, the flowers, the shrubs along his path, he would strike them gently with his staff, saying: "Be silent, be silent, I understand you; you upbraid me with my ingratitude; be silent, be silent, I will now love and bless him who made you for me."

II. *In the relations of fruit trees with climates and seasons.* All these trees which, at the word of the Creator, appear on a single day, and in one country, in order to instruct and charm Adam, who was soon to follow them, are intended for different places. The acid fruits will be more common in warm countries, where they are more necessary—citrons, for example. The fruits of sweeter and more varied tastes—apples and pears, for example—will be more abundant in more temperate regions. The same rule holds good in regard to other fruits, which we receive from shrubs and plants; they are all in perfect harmony with the climate and the season. Why have we these fruits in the midst of summer and autumn? Ah! it is because our blood, warmed by the sultry air or by oppressive labor, requires refreshment. May we not truly be called—allow me the expression—the spoiled children of our heavenly Father?

The month of June furnishes us with melons, strawberries, raspberries, currants, and cherries.

The month of July supplies our tables with peaches, apricots, and several species of pears.

The month of August seems almost lavish in its store of rich fruits: figs, late cherries, and delicious pears.

The month of September provides us already with a few grapes, some winter pears, and apples.

The presents of the month of October are various sorts of pears and apples, and the exquisite fruit of the vine.

Such is the wise economy with which our good Father distributes his gifts. On the one side, he prevents too great an abundance from being burdensome to us; on the other, he procures us a long succession of enjoyments. It was not alone to minister to the luxury of the rich, but likewise to satisfy the wants of the poor, that God so multiplied the fruits; for a much smaller quantity would be required, if there were only question of perpetuating the trees themselves. It is then evident that the Creator was pleased to provide by them for the nourishment of men, especially the poor. In fruits, he gives the poor an inexpensive, nutritious, and wholesome food; and so agreeable, that they have no reason to envy the costly, but often unwholesome, dishes of the rich.

III. *In trees that do not bear fruit.* Let us first observe, still with regard to fruit trees, another attention of our heavenly Father. These trees never rise to any great height. The object of providence is evident: What would we do if we had to gather pears or peaches on trees as lofty as the pine or the poplar? The creative word mentions only fruit trees: this means indeed every tree bearing fruit. But we properly call fruit trees those which serve to our nourishment; the others, however, confer many advantages. First, their fruits are the nourishment of a multitude of birds and insects, useful to man. The apothecary draws medicine from them; the artist, colors. Then again, to how many uses do not the wood of these trees serve?

The oak, whose growth is exceedingly slow, and which only puts on its leaves when all other trees are clothed with theirs, furnishes the hardest wood; and the art of man has employed this wood in works of carpentry, joinery, and carving, which seem to defy the action of time. Soft or light wood serves for other purposes; and, as it grows more rapidly and abundantly, it is also of more general utility. To the wood of trees we are indebted, in a great measure, for our ships, our houses, our fuel, our furniture, and a thousand other things of indispensable necessity, or very great convenience. It is the most natural material of fire, without which we could not cook our food, nor carry on our manufactures, nor preserve our health.

Without doubt, the sun is the very soul of nature; it communicates life and motion to all things; but we cannot turn into fire any of its rays for the purpose of cooking our food, or the melting or fashioning of our metals. Its place is supplied, in many of our operations, by wood, whose greater or less quantity affords us the various degrees of heat and flame necessary.

These trees are also eloquent preachers of the wisdom and the goodness of the Creator. Those which abound in resin and pitch, such as pines and firs, are reserved for mountainous regions, which are often for a long time covered with snow. The warm and glutinous substance that holds the place of sap in these trees protects them from the inclemency of the seasons. Ever preserving their verdure, they are likewise an emblem of immortality, as those which cast their leaves in autumn, to resume them again in spring, are emblems of the resurrection.

This is not all. While God has ordained that the greater number of trees and plants should repose during winter, after the labors of the three preceding seasons; yet, by preserving the foliage of many other trees, such as the holly, juniper, and holm, he is pleased to show us that he is absolute master of all things, and is subject to no law of necessity. Still he does not use his liberty according to caprice; his arrangements tend to the benefit of man, who is the beloved child he has always in view. Without the perpetual verdure of certain smaller trees, what would be the resource of the rabbit, hare, deer, roebuck, and so many other animals which serve to man's use, though he has not the trouble of taking care of them.

IV. *In forests.* The first thing that strikes us is their magnificence. What a difference between those noble trunks, that stretch their branches toward heaven, as if to carry even to the clouds the glory of God, and those little plants, that we cultivate in our fields! The forests are the Creator's gardens; what a difference between his and ours! Ours are spacious when they contain a few acres; his cover whole countries; their number is almost countless, and the height of some of the trees amazing.

Still, all these trunks, so well nourished, are only a few feet distant from one another. Who has been able to undertake this work, and conduct it to perfection? Who is the gardener that was so careful in planting this multitude of trees? Who has been able to prune and water them? God. To him belong the forests. Though he gives increase to all other productions of the vegetable kingdom, yet the forests are peculiarly his work. Alone he has planted them; alone he has maintained them; alone he has defended them, during centuries, against the rage of storms. Alone he has drawn from his treasure-houses the rain and the dew that were necessary to renovate their verdure, and to endow them with a kind of immortality.

The divine Wisdom has distributed the forests over the surface of the earth with more or less abundance, but always in a just proportion. They help to purify the air; they afford us a cool and agreeable shade; they adorn nature by sweetly diversifying the landscape; they afford shelter to a multitude of animals, that are of invaluable service to us. It is in the forests that God provides a safe retreat for an immense number of the brute creation. There he provides sufficiently for all; there, in the lonely solitude, he clothes, nourishes, and lodges them. To some he gives strength; to others cunning; to this one agility; to that one blind fury—all which propensities tend to draw man from indolence, by drawing him from a false security. Everywhere we recognize the wisdom and the goodness of him who made all things for our wants, and even for our pleasures.

Treasures contained in the interior of the earth. If the riches that cover the surface of the earth call forth, as they well may, our gratitude and our admiration, what should our sentiments be when we know that the bowels of the earth contain other treasures, so numerous and so varied, that it would require whole volumes to explain them in detail? In turn, we see the diamonds, the precious stones, the marbles, the building stones, the metals. Let us merely say a word of these last: their utility being more general, they more particularly claim our attention, and awake our gratitude.

I. *Gold.* Gold is the king of metals. It is neither from caprice nor prejudice that man prefers it to all the rest. The advantageous idea we have formed of it is founded on its real excellence. If it is not the heaviest or the densest of metals, it has, at all events, the most beautiful color—that which most nearly approaches to the warm glow of fire. It is the most ductile and the most malleable of the metals—the one that lends itself most easily to whatever we desire to do with it. From an ingot of this metal, two feet long, three inches broad, and three inches deep, one might draw out a thread that would reach from Paris to Lyons. Unlike other metals, it does not soil the hands that work it. The slightest portion, the merest trace of it on any other substance, suffices to impart a degree of splendor and brilliancy; it embellishes everything it touches.

To these excellent qualities there is added another which raises it to the highest rank among metals—namely, that it cannot be corroded by rust, nor diminished by fire. It is not, therefore, to be wondered at that men should, in all ages, have adopted so perfect a substance as a mode of payment for merchandise. Even the scarcity of this beautiful metal makes us content to receive a small portion of it in exchange for a large quantity of goods. How useful! How advantageous to commerce! Have we ever reflected on our duty to thank him who has made us a present of it?

We have spoken of the chief use of gold; let us examine some of its other uses. This metal is converted into most beautiful and valuable ornaments, in the hands of skillful workmen, whose ingenuity is no less admirable than the material on which they labor. Goldsmiths convert it into a thousand articles: some of them, being small and inexpensive, are suited to the fortunes of private individuals; others, being much larger and more elaborate, suit the grandeur of temples and the opulence of kings. With this metal, jewelers very much increase the lustre of precious stones, which would otherwise be deprived of much of their brilliancy. Embroiderers sometimes ornament the surface of silk and woolen fabrics with delicate threads of this precious metal; at other times they weave these threads with bright colors, and trace on the fabric a variety of beautiful designs; or again they skillfully imitate the brilliancy and gaiety of flowers—the flexibility of leaves sporting with the wind, or even the animated expression of a painting. Gilders understand how to overlay other metals, as well as woods, with gold, and to employ it in gorgeously decorating the wainscoting of halls, the ceilings of palaces, and the domes of majestic temples.

II. *Iron.* If gold is unquestionably the most perfect of metals, still there are others which have many properties that render them highly valuable to us. The vilest of all, the coarsest, the most full of alloy, the most sombre in its color, the most liable to corrosion by rust, in a word, iron, is really the most useful. It possesses one quality which suffices to raise it, in a certain sense, above all other metals: it is that of being the most tenacious.

Plunged hot into cold water, it thereby acquires a degree of hardness which renders it still more valuable to us. In this state it serves, with its strong bars, as a guard for our houses, and protects our most precious treasures. Binding together wood and stone, it places us beyond the reach of the insults of the winds, and the attacks of robbers. Gold even, and diamonds, are not secure, unless protected by iron. It is iron that furnishes navigators, clockmakers, and all the various workers in art with the utensils they require to break, strengthen, scoop out, cut, polish, and adorn other materials—in a word, to produce the various commodities of life.

In vain should we be possessed of gold, silver, and other metals, if we had not iron with which to fashion them: they would all be softened away, one against the other. Iron alone subdues the rest, and crushes them without itself bending or breaking in the effort. Hence, it was under the figure of a beast with iron teeth that the Creator was pleased to prefigure, in the lapse of ages, the future Roman Empire, which was to overthrow and destroy all other existing empires. Of the innumerable articles of furniture, machinery, and even food, which every day and every instant offer us their services, perhaps there is not one but owes its form to iron. We can at present justly compare the value of iron with that of all other metals. These are very useful; but iron is indispensably necessary.

Reading the history of the discovery of America, we have perhaps been surprised to find that the savages were wont to give their conquerors a great deal of gold in exchange for a billhook, a spade, or some other iron instrument. We can now understand that they had good ground for doing so, since they knew that iron would render them services which they could not obtain from gold.

It is then true, O my God! that man cannot raise his eyes on high, or make a step on earth, or dig a few inches beneath his feet, but everywhere he finds the treasures that have been prepared for him. He can everywhere see that he is the object of a tender love, which has provided for all his wants, everywhere placing something to occupy his mind, something to call forth the exercise of his industry, and thereby to win his heart. Can he, in the midst of so many benefits, be ungrateful?

But the kindness that is so manifest in the excellent qualities of the metals, which God has placed in the bosom of the earth for us, is still more apparent in the exact proportion which he has established between the amount of these metals, and the measure of our necessities. If some man had been employed to create the metals, in a just proportion for the wants of the human race, he certainly would not have failed to place more gold in the earth than iron. He would have imagined that he had displayed his generosity in giving but sparingly the metal that is most contemptible, and bestowing with profusion that which we most admire. God had acted quite otherwise.

As the value and convenience of gold proceed in a great measure from its scarcity, God has given it with economy. This scarcity, of which ingratitude complains, is a new benefit. On the other hand, iron enters generally into all the wants of life. It is to place us in a position of providing for these wants easily, that providence has scattered iron everywhere. Thus, there is no mere ostentation in the gifts of a paternal providence. The chief characteristic of this liberality is that it studies not that which procures an empty honor for the donor, but that which procures a substantial advantage for the recipient. A precious lesson to us, and a new subject of gratitude!

Let us now pass on to the fourth day of the great week, and we shall behold new wonders.

Fourth day.—The fourth day God said: "Let there be lights made in the firmament of heaven, to divide the day and the night, and let them be for signs, and for seasons, and for days and years; to shine in the firmament of heaven, and to give light upon the earth. And it was so done.

"And God made two great lights: a greater light to rule the day, and a lesser light to rule the night, and the stars.[214] And he set them in the firmament of heaven, to shine upon the earth; to rule the day and the night, and to divide the light and the darkness. And God saw that it was good. And the evening and morning were the fourth day."[215]

At this fourth command a new spectacle appears. Let us contemplate, in the silence of admiration and love, the wonders that present themselves to our consideration, and the profound wisdom of the Creator, of whom they are monuments ever ancient and ever new.

I. *The creation of the sun.* Light existed already: the succession of days and nights was regulated; the earth was fertile—everything it should produce was formed; it was decked out with flowers, and laden with fruits. Every plant and tree was not only in its present state perfect, but it had, moreover, all that was necessary to perpetuate or multiply it. Of what use, then, will the sun be, after all that we attribute to its virtue is already done? What does it come to do to the earth, which is more ancient than itself, and which has heretofore done without it? Of what will it be the father? And by what strange blindness will men regard it as the principle of all that preceded it?

It is an observation, of which we frequently meet the proof, that the world was created with a particular design to prevent the errors of nations; consequently, with a supposition of the fall of man, one of the saddest consequences of which has been the rise of idolatry. The most ancient and general kind of idolatry is that which had the sun and moon for its objects. God, who foresaw this guilty error, was pleased that, even by the history of creation, the family of Adam, and afterward that of Noe, should regard the sun only as a new arrival in the world, less ancient than the day, younger than the flowers, and less necessary than any of the effects that are attributed to it.

As, at the present day, the danger of idolatry is almost past, and that of ingratitude almost universal—for the first temptation of man was to adore everything, and the last with which we are threatened is to adore nothing at all—we need not fear to consider the sun with overmuch attention, especially as the perfections of the Creator are rendered visible by it.[216]

II. *Its distance from the earth.* Though God has placed the sun in the firmament, it is for the advantage of the earth. He has regulated the distance of the one by the necessities of the other. He has placed between the heat of the sun and those things which it should assist such a due proportion as to be always salutary to them. With a greater separation, the earth should be frozen; with a less, it would be burnt up. Behold the unerring calculations of the heavenly mathematician! He requires to enlighten and warm a globe of 25,000 miles in circumference. He desires only one furnace for the purpose. What, then, must be the size of that furnace, and at what distance from the earth must it be placed? He speaks; and, at his word, a fiery globe, 1,330,000 times larger than the earth, glides into boundless space. But the rays of fire, which issue from a flaming globe, a million times larger than the earth, must have an astounding activity, while they remain concentrated, and act together. They must then divide, so that when they arrive at the earth, they may shed no more than the requisite degree of light and heat. At what distance must the earth be placed, that these rays, on their arrival, may be sufficiently divided to enlighten man, without blinding him, and to warm him without burning him? What do you think? If this problem had been presented to some of our astronomers, do you not think it would be still unsolved? But God, infallible in all his operations, only speaks the word, and the sun is placed at the distance of 114,000,000 miles from the earth. And the experience of six thousand years has proved the accuracy of these calculations.

III. *Its motion.* By reason of the rotundity of the earth, if the sun were immovable in the midst of the heavens, it would only enlighten and warm the half of our globe, supposing the latter to be also immovable. It was then necessary that this great luminary should keep continually marching round the earth, or that the earth itself, turning on its axis, should successively present the various parts of its surface to the rays of the sun. The divine organizer was not unmindful of this necessity. He has commanded the sun to rise every day, and to enlighten, during the space of twenty-four hours, the different portions of the earth. During six thousand years the sun, obedient, has risen every day without fail, and journeyed along his course, without ever wandering from the line marked out for him. It will easily be understood here that we speak only according to sensible appearances, and do not enter into any controversy with our great astronomers on their systems.

Behold with what a profusion of colors he adorns nature, and with what magnificence he is himself clothed! Like a young bridegroom, who goes forth from the nuptial chamber on the most solemn day of his life, the sun appears above the horizon, as the friend whom heaven and earth expect, and who behold him with delight. His splendor is full of sweetness. The universe greets his arrival; the eyes of all creatures are fixed upon him; and, to receive the salutations of all, he renders himself accessible to all.

But everywhere he is commissioned to dispense light, heat, and life. Consider, therefore, how he unites, with the graceful dignity of a bridegroom, the rapid progress of a giant! Behold how he urges forward, how he speeds his onward course, much less concerned with his attire than his duty, anxious only to announce the news of the Prince who has despatched him! Running along the hills of heaven, he dispenses more heat in proportion around, as he ascends, until he reaches his meridian, vivifying all that he enlightens. Nothing escapes his light, or withdraws itself from the influence of his heat; he reaches, by his flaming arrows, even to those places which his radiant beams cannot penetrate.

A natural and very beautiful image of him who came to enlighten the world, and who so worthily combined the characteristics of spouse and ambassador! From the bosom of his Father, he came forth, full of ardor, to run his course like a giant; and, like the sun, he returned again to the point from which he had departed, after having, like that beautiful daystar, passed along, doing good.

IV. *Its rising.* If every day the sun pursued the same route, a great portion of the earth would be uninhabitable, either because the darkness should be continual, or the heat or the cold excessive. Moreover, this uniform method would but ill display the wisdom of God, and his care in the government of the universe. Therefore, it is not so.

No day, to speak precisely, is equal to that which precedes or that which follows it. It is then necessary that every day the sun should both rise and set at different points. This is the reason why, according to the expression of the prophet, each day carries a new order to the following day which succeeds; and every night finds marked out for it by the preceding night at what precise moments it must begin and end. Thus, nature, in suspense, learns at each instant from him who conducts it, what it must do, and how far it must go.

How many wonders have we here presented for our consideration! Who has said to the sun: "Do not begin to shine tomorrow where you began this morning, and do not end this evening where you ended yesterday?" And who has measured the interval between two sunrises, that its limits might not be passed? Who has commanded the sun, on its arrival at a certain point, to retrace its steps, and forbidden it, on any consideration, to travel farther? This is the manner in which, every day, every hour, every moment, the heavens declare the glory of their author. Their language is neither rude nor strange. The voice of the heavens is clear, strong, sweet, intelligible, and familiar. It resounds from one end of the universe to the other. Greeks and barbarians, Scythians and Indians,

Christians and idolaters, understand alike the words of these eloquent preachers—the heavens—and all mankind is instructed by the wisdom of their discourses.

V. *Its light.* It would seem as if God had been careful to assemble in this beautiful star all the qualities that are most proper to exemplify the perfections of the divinity. Like God, the sun is one; whatever is rich or splendid appears annihilated, and vanishes in its presence; it sees everything, it acts everywhere, it animates all things, it is always the same. Is it not surprising that, during so many ages, the sun should not diminish in size, and that its light should be as bright and plentiful today as on the first day it illumined the earth?

If we had been consulted, before the creation of the sun, on the best mode of enlightening the world, how many lamps should we have imagined necessary? Who could convince us that one might suffice; that, placed at a certain distance, it would enlighten the universe by a single glance; that it would pass from East to West, without any visible guide, without any apparent support, without chariot, without engine; and that, after a multitude of centuries, it would be as brilliant and as perfect as on the day it came forth from the hands of its Creator?

We now understand what we owe, not to the sun, but to him who created it, and who every day makes it rise alike on the good and the bad; and, worthy children of our heavenly Father, let us love all men as our brethren.

PRAYER

O my God, who art all love, I thank thee for having bestowed on us all the riches of heaven and earth; how can I testify to thee my admiration and gratitude? For so many benefits, thou askest my heart in return; I give it to thee without reserve.

I am resolved to love God above all things, and my neighbor as myself for the love of God; and, in testimony of this love, I will never fail at my prayers before and after meals.

Lesson 8: Creation: The Fourth Day (Continued)

I. *Beauty of the moon.* The same word that created the sun, and suspended it in the firmament to preside over the day, created also the moon and the stars as its suite. The moon, like a kind and gentle queen, was appointed to preside over the night, that is to say, to moderate the darkness of the clouds by her gentle lustre: night is the time of her triumph. She draws the objects around us from obscurity, and her mild light agreeably enlivens the face of nature. The moon herself is one of the most beautiful objects in existence. She rejoices our eyes by the sweetness of her radiance, and varies the scene by a continual change of form and position.

Like the sun, she learns every day from the sovereign master of the universe, the place where she must rise or set. Every day, from West to East, she moves back her place of rising. At one time she appears in an ash-colored robe, fringed round with a simple band of gold. At another time she puts on a dress of purple, and mounts the horizon larger than usual; then she gradually diminishes, and grows more pale as she rises. In proportion as day flees away, her light becomes more brilliant, and of more use to man. But whether she appears by glimpses or in full, she everywhere bestows new ornaments on nature.

How sweet, yet how capricious!—sometimes starting out suddenly from the midst of clouds, and surprising us with her smiling countenance; again, hiding herself under a silken veil, and allowing us to search for her! Now, she darts her soft rays across the thick foliage of the woods; anon, she weaves for herself, of the clouds around her, a crown of various hues. Then, again, as the sun approaches, the moon lays down her scepter; she disappears—but to appear again.

What agent in nature has been appointed to light this beautiful lamp, and to bring it to us with so much regularity?

II. *Its utility.* O men, how long will you have eyes, and see not? How long will you have hearts, and yet not love? Employ your reason, and you will discover, in the visits of the moon, nothing but the utmost attention to your wants. This body, ponderous and opaque as it is of itself, has been placed so near the earth, that it gives us more light than all the stars together, though, they are so many immense suns.

Let us here remark the wisdom and the goodness of the Creator. He has removed the stars to such a distance from us that night, of which we stand in need, suffers nothing from their light; and he has placed the moon so close to us that she becomes a magnificent mirror, in which a large portion of the sun's light is reflected for our convenience. It is true that the carriage of this mirror round the earth occasions some irregularities; but they are limited: and hence, we rarely have eclipses. If it were not for the provision that has really been made against inconveniences, we should have a dozen eclipses of the moon, and as many of the sun, every year. Any apparent irregularity, therefore, that exists is only a new benefit, and a new evidence of the profound wisdom that ordained it.

Let us pass on to other greater benefits. Does man desire to begin his journey before day, or prolong his journey after sunset? The moon, in its first quarter, presents itself immediately after the sun withdraws, and offers itself to be his guide. Does he, anticipating the aurora, desire to begin his journey before the break of day? The moon, in its last quarter, awaits him, as a guide, many hours before the dawn. If he is at liberty to delay his journey till the time of full moon, the orb of night will give him, so to speak, days of uninterrupted light for twenty-four hours. With this assistance he may avoid the heats of summer, or expedite in safety, and at his wish, that which he could not safely entrust to the light of day.

But would not a clear night at all times have been more desirable? God unites almost everywhere a number of advantages together, so that the excellence of his presents may be enhanced by the variety of their services. The moon is not only destined to soften the sadness of night by a light which prolongs or replaces that of the sun; she is also intended to act as a sentinel near the palace of man, and to announce the tidings of the hour, at different stations, as she beats her rounds.

The sun should serve, by his revolution in a year, to regulate the order of rural labors. But the moon, by her revolution round us in twenty-nine days, changing her form, as we say, at each quarter of her journey, should serve to regulate the civil order, and the ordinary affairs of society. Under a new phase every seven days, the moon is a beacon to all nations, offering them such short and regular divisions of time, as are most convenient in fixing the duration of operations in detail.

Thus, the Hebrews, the Greeks, the Romans, and nearly all the ancients used to assemble at the time of the new moon, to acquit themselves of certain duties of piety and gratitude. On this day was announced everything that could interest them during the month. The full moon assembled them again in the middle of the month. The other two quarters were terms as easily remembered. Even at the present day, the Turks, the Arabians, the Moors, and many other races throughout the world regulate the order of their calendar entirely according to the phases of the moon.

If we are less attentive to the moon than they, it is not because she has ceased to render us the same services as to the rest. We are dispensed from all care on the matter by the convenient computations that are placed in our hands by experienced astronomers; nevertheless, these calendars of theirs are regulated by observations on the course of the moon. They are adjusted in advance by the counsels which this vigilant satellite never fails to supply, until he who appointed her our sentinel judges it proper to change her office, by changing the condition of man, in whose service she is engaged. What a happy condition shall that be! in which we shall no longer require the sun or the moon to enlighten us, but the Lamb will be our light, and the light, too, of the whole heavenly Jerusalem! Yes, happy condition, indeed! Mayst thou be the object of all our desires and labors!

God also made the stars.—It belongs only to God to speak with this indifference regarding the most astounding spectacle that adorns the universe. He says in one word that which cost him only a word! But who can measure the power of that word?

I. *Number of the stars.* Let us go out a moment during the calm of a beautiful summer night, as God made Abraham go out from his tent, to consider the heavens: "Having brought Abraham forth abroad, God said to him, Raise thine eyes to heaven, and count the stars if thou canst."[217] And Abraham looked up to the stars, and was content with admiring them; for he could not count them. Nor can any man count them: they are innumerable. Since the invention of the telescope, thousands of new stars have been discovered; and, in proportion as astronomical instruments are perfected, the number of discoveries is increased. With much reason, then, may we suppose that the number of stars lying buried in the illimitable abysses of space exceeds all human calculation.

We are aware that the magnitude of the sun, as well as that of several planets which revolve round it, far surpasses that of the earth on which we dwell. And who knows but among the other heavenly bodies there are many which do not yield to these in any respect, and whose volume may be still greater? Their astounding distance from us causes them to appear as mere specks, shining in the firmament. But in reality they are, for the most part, so many suns, whose wondrous dimensions can only be guessed at by man. It is then true that thousands of worlds roll in space; and that we only see the smallest portion of the mighty army that is ranged above our heads in the most beautiful order.

Do you yet desire anything more admirable? He who has scattered a million luminous globes along the boundless prairies of the firmament, as the husbandman scatters grain in his field, holds these enormous masses suspended in space. He requires no columns to uphold the majestic dome of heaven; nor is there any danger of its falling under its frightful weight. He has kept it as it is today for thousands of years, and will continue to do so till the end of time, that it may relate to all generations the glory of its author.

II. *Their motion.* The stars present to an attentive mind another subject of astonishment. These immense bodies are in continual motion. They revolve on their axes, as wheels on their axles. Many of their attendant stars revolve in immense orbits. For each of these a particular path or orbit is marked out. They never wander from it, though they travel at a speed which almost baffles imagination. By a resolution of two forces—the centrifugal and the centripetal; the former drawing them away from their center, the latter toward it—they are continually retained in their orbits. Many of the fixed stars are supposed to be centers of distinct solar systems.

Although there are thousands of celestial bodies moving in space, yet not a single interruption or collision ever takes place amongst them. They appear to us to be thrown about the firmament in strange confusion; and yet the most perfect order and harmony reigns amongst them. For thousands of years they have risen and set regularly in the same manner. Millions of soldiers belonging to this celestial army, ever on the march, return in succession to the scenes of their early bivouacs; and able astronomers announce, even a thousand years beforehand, their exact course and position. O God, how great thou art! and what is man that he should dare to rebel against thee?

III. *Their utility.* What is the use of so many wonders? What means the host of heaven, with their watchful sentinels? Simply to contend with our ingratitude, our pride, and our indifference; and to secure the triumph of such great dogmas as the existence of God, his power, his majesty, and his goodness. It suffices to render mankind inexcusable, that they should listen to the eloquent army of the heavens, or gaze on the magnificent book of the firmament, written in characters of flame.

This is not all. These enormous globes are placed at so fitting a distance from the abode of man that they produce a beauty which enchants his eyes, and a regularity which adds not a little to the happiness of his pilgrimage. By this admirable arrangement, these radiant fires are converted into resplendent lustres, depending from the magnificent canopy which overhangs his dwelling. On all sides they shine and sparkle, and the dark azure of their background throws out their brilliancy in bolder relief. Yet their beams are mild; for so immense is the space in which their rays are scattered, that they are softened and cooled a long time before their arrival at the dwelling-place of man. Thanks to the precautions of our Creator, we enjoy the sight of a multitude of fiery worlds, without being disturbed by apprehensions about the chill of night or the tranquility of our sleep!

But it is not merely to adorn the palace of man with rich gildings and paintings, that God unveils every day the magnificent dome of the heavens: he desires to bestow some more positive advantages upon us. Among the stars that we can easily distinguish, there are some whose position is always in the same region of the heavens: the chief of these is the polar star. There are others which we see rising slowly above the horizon, describing immense arcs, and setting again in another quarter of the horizon.

The first class of stars regulate the journeys of man by land and sea, showing him, amid the darkness, a portion of the heavens whose aspect remains unchanged, and thus preserving him against the danger of wandering. But as, from time to time, the clouds may intercept the view of these stars, which have been given to man as his guides, God has attached such a secret virtue to steel touched by a magnet, that if a bar of it be suspended in equilibrium, it will immediately turn one end—and always the same end—in the direction of the pole-star. Hence has arisen that useful instrument, the mariner's compass, which renders such amazing services to navigation. To it the mariner is indebted for information regarding the position of his invisible guides; and his course is at all times free, notwithstanding the unsettled state of the weather.

The second class vary their situation considerably as regards us, rising and setting at a different time each day, though among themselves they always observe the same order. These variations are so regular, that they fix the succession of our labors, and determine the limits of the seasons with the nicest precision. The mere experience of heat or cold would be too uncertain a rule, too liable to accident, to determine us in the selection of a time for the cultivation of our land, or a voyage across the ocean.

Man also finds an abundance of instruction on these matters, by seeing the sun's motion through the different constellations of stars, and which he travels uniformly in the same course year after year. We know well the track of this beautiful luminary.[218] We give a name to each of those clusters at which he rests as he passes on his route. Man knows the exact duration of his sojourn in each of his twelve abodes. He can name the point in the zodiac which is favorable to whatever operations we may have to undertake, whether by land or sea.

The sun and moon have been appointed to separate the day and night—to mark times, seasons, and years. Directing man and his labors, these admirable clocks have never yet gone a minute astray. Do you know the name, do you know the dwelling-place of him who constructed them? But why have we this perpetual succession of day and night, of light and darkness? O ye who inquire thus, prepare your minds for admiration, and your hearts for gratitude! Let us bring forward new proofs of the wisdom and the goodness of your heavenly Father. Already you are familiar with the advantages of the day; learn also those of the night.

I. *Its benefits: Instruction.* Night is nothing. It is merely the interruption of the passage of light toward us. But even nothingness itself is fruitful in the hands of God. It is his glory to have drawn all creatures from it; and, every day, he still continues to draw from it, in favor of man, not alone new creatures, but salutary instructions and benefits. Accordingly, night, by concealing nature from us, reminds us of that nothingness from which we have been taken, and plunges us again into that state of obscurity and imperfection which preceded the creation of light. Hereby, we better understand the inestimable value of day.

But its shades are not destined merely to relieve the beauties of the grand picture of the universe; and to make us more humble by an experience of the darkness that is natural to us, or more grateful for the return of a light that is not due to us. However useful may be the lessons which we thus derive, it would be sad indeed if, to instruct us, it were necessary to impoverish us. That which seems lost to our life, by the deprivation of light for many hours of the day, is restored to us abundantly by the repose which is secured to us in return.

II. *Repose.* Man is born to labor: it is his vocation and condition. To be able for it, it is necessary that his blood should be continually supplying him with a fresh and exquisitely delicate and subtle matter, which sets in play the tissues of his brain and the various muscles of his body. But the waste that is every moment taking place of this matter would soon reduce him to a state of extreme languor and exhaustion, if he did not repair his strength by a fresh supply of nourishment. Now, food cannot be digested, or its effects distributed properly through the body if the body is constantly in action. It is necessary that the labors of the head, of the arms, of the feet, and of the various other members of the body should be interrupted, that the heat and energy expended upon them may assist the functions of the stomach during the inaction of the other members of the body. Without repose we should quickly perish; and it is night that procures it for us. How many workmen who, during the day, spend their strength in some fatiguing yet necessary employment, bless the night, when it comes to suspend their labors, and brings them rest and sleep!

III. *Sleep.* We ourselves should bless God for not having left the use and arrangement of this necessary repose to times selected by our wavering and capricious reason. As a good Father, he takes care himself to lull his child to sleep. He has made sleep an agreeable necessity for us, without allowing us to understand it or to control it. Sleep is a state perfectly incomprehensible to us. Man is so little acquainted with the nature of sleep that he can neither yield himself to it when it flies from him, nor decline it when it comes to him. God has reserved to himself the disposal of this repose, whose time and measure he is well aware would be but ill-regulated by human fancy.

But if we do not understand the nature of sleep, ah! how much do we feel the benefit of it! It suspends the sighs of the afflicted, as well as the painful feeling of their misery. To be happy, then, they require only a bed; when sleep closes their eyelids, all their wants are satisfied. Sleep makes no distinction between the king and the beggar; both find in it a treasure which money cannot purchase. Now, the messenger whom God has selected to carry this universal benefit to us is the night.

Consider with what precaution and respect it acquits itself of its interesting commission! It does not come abruptly to extinguish the lamp of day, and deprive us of the sight of the objects with which we are engaged. Far from surprising us in the midst of our labors or journeys, the night advances with slow steps, and extends its shadows by little and little. It is only after having informed us, with courtesy, that it is necessary to take some repose, that it completes the task of veiling nature. It deprives man of the light of the universe, that it may deprive him of the use of his senses; it then draws a veil over our eyes, by closing our eyelids.

During the time that man reposes, it kindly keeps watch against the disturbance of his tranquility. Not only does it extinguish light, but it suppresses sound, by imposing silence on all things around him: the horse, the cow, the animals in general, are asleep as well as man. One sound only is uninterrupted: it is the clock, as it marks the progress of the hours: for it is good that man, on his awaking, should remember his *last* hour.

Night disperses the birds, too, into their different retreats. How often does it seem to soothe the very winds, that throughout the abode of man there may reign for many hours a universal calm! Thus we see that night is charged with securing the repose of the king of nature, and causing his sleep to be respected by all creatures. In these considerate attentions of providence, can we fail to recognize the solicitude of a tender mother, who, to put her little one asleep, removes light and noise from the precincts of its cradle?

IV. *The preservation of our life.* Without night we should perish, not only of fatigue, but of hunger. If the sun were to remain ever above our horizon, he would burn all that he causes to spring up. But night, succeeding day, imparts to the air a degree of coolness and freshness, which reinvigorates everything—the faded leaves, the parched earth, the weary animals.

It is to the night, also, we are indebted for the dew which not only rejoices our eyes at morning with its pure and crystal drops, all sparkling like rubies in the sunshine, but even supplies the place of rain for a considerable time, and thus preserves the flowers and the plants and the corn. Without night we should be deprived of the treasures that are peculiar to countries separated from us by immense seas; for the astronomer would not be able to supply us with his learned calculations, on which the success of navigation so much depends.

This is not yet all. Without night, men, obliged to travel or to toil, would be continually exposed to the rage of savage beasts. During the daytime, providence restrains these beasts in forests and caverns; but if the daytime were continual, hunger would compel them to quit their retreats, and they would speedily attack men, more feeble and less swift than themselves.

By appointing limits to the day, and causing night to succeed it, God has placed men in security and the beasts at liberty. The natural horror that men have for darkness obliges them to return to their houses during the night; and the natural fear that beasts have of light prevents them from wandering out of their dens during the day. When man has arrived at home, they may issue from their abodes: they are not allowed to seek their prey until the hand of the Lord has provided for the safety of man.

Then, when night has fallen, and there is no one in the fields, we hear the roaring of lions and the howling of wolves, which teach us who the master is that watches over man during the day. But when sunlight appears, all the beasts, the enemies of man, hasten to leave his place free; an invisible shepherd chases them into the woods with his crook. It seems, then, as if all these animals had changed their nature, they become so peaceable.

Either they sleep, or they are as quiet as if asleep; a superior power holds them captive; and, unless one imprudently approaches their dens, there is nothing to fear. On the other hand, when the sun begins to dissipate the darkness of the night, man, full of spirit and strength, feels the love of labor renewed within him: his house seems cheerless and wearisome to him, and the outer world full of attractions. Happy, if he knows how to recognize in this admirable order the paternal hand of one who arranges all things for his good!

Last duty of the sun and moon. — The last commission given to the sun and moon is to mark the seasons. Consider with what respectful attention and fidelity they acquit themselves of this duty. There is no hurry in their movements. The sun, after having withdrawn his heat in winter, returns it to us in spring; but he so regulates its quantity, that plants may have time to shoot forth and grow strong, without any danger of being either destroyed by late frost, or prematurely developed by untimely warmth. In the same manner, summer departs by degrees, so that the fruits of autumn may have time to ripen little by little, without being exposed to injury from the cold or winter.

Every season varies our pleasures, and indemnifies us by one class of benefits for another which it takes away; but at the same time that this very variety imposes new duties upon us.

I. *Spring.* Nature, which was dormant during the winter, resumes a new life. The little birds return from their distant wanderings, and begin again their joyous songs.

These numberless musicians, borne on the wings of the wind, visit in turn the cottages of their native land, and renew their gratuitous concerts at every door. In spring their melodious songs are all for us at home; in winter they are for others on a foreign shore. The meadows put on a brighter green. Through the soft verdure we see the early flowers. Sweet perfumes and agreeable colors salute us on our way. The trees gradually unfold their magnificent foliage, and prepare a shelter for man against the rays of the sun. A striking image of youth, as it is also of the general resurrection, spring dilutes our hearts with early hope; and at the same time leads us also to a detachment from everything that passes away with time. How long will these beautiful days, and these fresh, delicate flowers last? O man! how long will thy years, and the flowers of thy youth and vigor last? But console thyself: spring will pass, only to return again; and thou shalt die, only to be born again—yes, to be born again, and never more to die.

II. *Summer*. The sun continues his course; nature assumes a different appearance; it is the beginning of summer. Fruits of every kind present themselves to our eyes, and invite us to taste them; cornfields put on their golden hue; vast numbers of newly-fledged birds issue from their nests, and the whole feathered tribe, entoning both day and night the praises of their Creator, rejoice the soul of man, who, at this season, is almost ever in the open air. Who can count the benefits bestowed on us by our heavenly Father during summer? It is the happy season when he pours out most abundantly the treasure of his benedictions. Nature, after having revived us by the genial warmth of spring, is continually occupied during summer in providing us with everything that is not only necessary for our existence but delightful to our senses, and capable of awakening in our hearts the liveliest sentiments of gratitude and love.

Like the other seasons, summer is a preacher that announces many salutary truths to us. "See!" it says, "the reaper prepares to gather in his harvest. His scythe lays low the corn right and left, and behind him the fields are empty and forsaken. Mortals! such is your destiny. All flesh is as grass; and all its glory, as the flower of the field. Behold these busy bees! Let their anxiety to gather and store their honey teach you to lay up in time such treasures of wisdom and virtue, as may form your consolation in the winter of old age."

III. *Autumn*. The earth has received the heat of which it had need. The Lord directed the sun to pause, and to retrace his steps, not precipitately, but gradually, in order that by a temperate heat the maturity of the fruits might be consummated, and especially that full perfection might be given to that precious liquor which rejoices the heart of man. What activity reigns in every department of labor! The barns and storerooms are filled; goods of every description are to be had in abundance. In every quarter man lays up provisions for the winter; but he does not limit his thoughts to the necessities of the approaching winter. If he were to put all his stock in granaries, fire might burn it, robbers might plunder it; he confides a large portion of it to the safekeeping of the earth, assured that, at the return of spring, this faithful guardian will restore it to him with interest. But the men that hoard up, the birds that migrate, the leaves that fall, the skies that darken, the days that shorten, all the emblems of decay that surround us, do they say nothing to the heart?

IV. *Winter*. Every day man requires rest; and in the same manner every year the earth requires rest, that it may recruit its strength, exhausted in the service of man. Without winter, nature, impoverished and fatigued, would be able to produce nothing; and we should die of hunger. Hence the necessity, in the designs of providence, for the four seasons: spring prepares for us, summer ripens for us, autumn lavishes on us, the rich productions of the earth; winter repairs the strength of our nursing mother. When, then, she has deprived herself of everything for our sake, God directs the sunshine to keep away from her, as a tender mother removes the light that would hinder her child from sleeping. He does still more: he spreads over the earth a thick covering of snow, in order to keep it warm.

Although the snow appears to you cold, yet it is in reality an excellent coverlet that secures the earth against the piercing north wind, and keeps alive beneath its downy folds such heat as is necessary for the preservation of seeds, plants, and trees. The snow is, moreover, a powerful manure: melted by the sun, it sinks gradually and deeply into the earth, and thus vivifies and nourishes the roots and tubers of the plants. Hence we see that in the wildest of the seasons, our heavenly Father is concerned about the well-being of his children; and that, without requiring any labor from us, he prepares in the silence of his laboratory the rich treasures of nature! Children of so good a Father, let us lay up for ourselves the rich treasures of grace by redoubling our charity during this severe season, feeding the hungry and clothing the naked.

PRAYER
O my God! who art all love, I thank thee for having established the day, the night, the seasons, for our advantage; may thy praise be ever on my lips, thy love ever in my heart!

I am resolved to love God above all things, and my neighbor as myself for the love of God; and, in testimony of this love, I will conform myself in all things to the will of God.

Lesson 9: Creation: The Fifth Day

Fifth day. — God said also: "Let the waters bring forth the creeping creature having life, and the fowl that may fly over the earth, under the firmament of heaven.[219] And God created the great whales and every living and moving creature which the waters brought forth, according to their kinds; and every winged fowl, according to its kind. And God saw that it was good. And he blessed them, saying: Increase and multiply, and fill the waters of the sea; and let the birds be multiplied upon the earth. And the evening and morning were the fifth day."[220]

Hitherto we have seen a crowd of wonders appear at each word of the Creator. What will be the effect of that which we are now about to hear? Is there anything still to be produced? The sky shines forth in all its splendor, the earth is arrayed in its beauty; plants and fruits have each a variety and a perfection that we are never weary of admiring. Shall anything be born of the sea, which God has hitherto seemed to look upon as an obstacle to his designs, and which has separated from the earth as if in anger? Thy threatening voice, O Lord, hath put it to flight. Yes, it is to the sea that God speaks; and immediately it is filled with an innumerable multitude of new creatures, different from all others. They are not like the plants, which must be rooted in one place; they have motion and life. But let us, in imagination, transport ourselves to the shores of the sea, and descend into its fathomless depths. There we shall find such wonders as magnificently display the infinite power and wisdom of the Creator.

I. *Creation of the fishes.* — The waters of the sea are full of salt and bitterness: Should we not hence conclude that they are naturally sterile? How is it, then, that they give birth in an instant to a countless multitude of living and animated creatures? How is it that, in the midst of water, so impregnated with salt that we can hardly bear a drop of it on our tongue, the fishes live and sport in perfect health and wonderful vigor? How is it that in this water, whose very appearance makes us sad and pensive, they can grow strong, and supply us with a description of meat which the luxurious prefer to that of the most exquisite birds? These are things which appear impossible to us, yet which, we must admit, have been accomplished. At every step we clearly perceive that in nature as in religion, God requires of us to believe in things which he does not judge it proper we should comprehend, and that, content with showing us the reality of his wonders, he demands of us the sacrifice of our intellect, or rather of our ignorance, regarding the nature of that which he has done, and the manner in which he has performed it.

How does it come to pass that, though the fishes cannot leave the sea, where scarcely anything grows, to seek on land the good things with which it superabounds, yet God has made them so voracious that they mutually devour one another? O creative Wisdom, if thou art not here in fault, thou mayest well sport with difficulties! How shall this new race be able to subsist? The Creator provides for it: he multiplies them so prodigiously, that the number destroyed is always far below that which remains for their reproduction.

At least, the smaller races will soon be annihilated by the greater, which regard them as their prey, and continually pursue them, especially as in the ocean plains there are neither barriers nor ramparts—the way is open, all things are in common. There, as elsewhere, the Lord comes to the assistance of the tiny and the feeble. He has given to the smaller fish a motion swifter than to the larger ones. When pursued they run to hiding-places where the shallow water will not allow their enemies to pursue them. God has given them a foresight proportioned to their weakness and their danger.

But, by saving the little ones, will you condemn the large ones to perish? Is it not to be feared that fishes of enormous size, such as the whale, would be unable to find wherewith to nourish themselves; for there are few fishes on the high seas, and these immense monsters cannot approach the shore without danger of being stranded? Nevertheless, their hunger is very great, and they have a stomach or rather a gulf, capable of containing anything. How, then, shall these monsters be nourished? Yes, they too shall be supported. For them the seas are peopled with myriads of little animals[221] whose preservation is a new wonder. Thus, the providence of God reaches to all creatures. And that monster, which is the king of the sea, and sports among its billows, expects from the Creator, just as the smallest fishes, and even more so than the smallest among them, the nourishment of which it has need.

II. *Their preservation.*—All the animals that people the air, that roam over the earth, or that dwell within its bowels, have this in common, namely, that they breathe air; without air, they should die upon the spot. If you plunge them into water for a little while, they perish. Yet the water has its inhabitants which live in its bosom, and perish when you withdraw them from the element that has been assigned to them. O man! in so many admirable arrangements, do you not recognize the power of the Creator, who sports with difficulties? But how can the blood of fishes—for they have blood—circulate? Why does it not freeze or coagulate under the great cold of the sea? How can fishes live under mountains of ice? The land animals have feathers, or down, or fur, to protect them against the cold. We find nothing of this kind among fishes. What have they then to resist the effects of an element colder than air?

Ask your memory: it will tell you that the first thing you meet with on touching a fish is a kind of sticky substance, with which the whole body is covered. Then you find a coat of strong scales, well-fastened and united, and overlapping one another, in much the same manner as the slates of our houses, but with infinitely greater art. This is only one garment. Before reaching the flesh, you meet with a new layer of oily matter, which envelops the fish from head to tail. The scales, by their hardness, prevent the fish from injuring itself against pebbles or gravel; the scales and the oil together, by their opposition to water, secure to the fish its heat and life. It would be impossible to present the fish with robes lighter or more impenetrable to cold.

Thus, whithersoever we go, our eyes meet with a wisdom ever fruitful in new designs, and never inconvenienced by any resistance in the materials that it employs. Unlike the plant, the fish is not confined to the district where it came into life; it moves, it travels abroad. To pass from one place to another, it must brave the fury of the most terrible element: Who will ensure its life? How shall it direct its course? Providence provides for all. One example out of a thousand will suffice to make us appreciate here, as elsewhere, the divine interposition. There is a little mollusk called the argonaut or paper, nautilus or navigator. This marine curiosity has eight arms, and, of its own substance, builds a shell in the form of a ship. After having taken in a sufficient supply of water to serve it as ballast, it raises two of its arms, and thus hoists as a sail to the wind the membrane that unites them; it plunges two others into the sea as oars; and employs a fifth as a helm. Thus fitted out, it traverses the ocean, with sail and oar, being its own ship, pilot, and cargo.

This is not all: What if a storm threatens, or an enemy comes in view? The industrious mariner lowers his sail, pulls in his oars and helm, fills his hold with water, and sinks into the deep. Then when the danger is over, he turns his barque upside down, creates a vacuum within, and immediately ascends to the surface; then he puts his vessel once more in order, unfurls his sail, and abandons himself to the pleasure of the winds. When will man be able thus to escape the fury of the tempest?[222]

III. *Immense size of some.* — Imagine you see an animal 90 feet in length, with breadth and depth in proportion; an animal whose bones, like tall trees, serve for the construction of boats; an animal whose blubber produces 120 casks of oil; an animal, in whose enormous skeleton a party of 24 musicians could give a concert;[223] an animal whose movements make the water of the sea boil as in a storm; an animal whose head alone is sometimes 20 feet long,[224] and whose tail is about 20 feet broad, is sufficiently strong to fling the long-boat of a ship full of men into the air; an animal which, notwithstanding its extraordinary dimensions, ploughs the waves with extreme rapidity; finally, an animal, by whose side an elephant is no more than a little dog: this monstrous animal, the sovereign of the seas, is the whale.[225] And the great God, who created it, who guides it as a shepherd guides a lamb, condescends to obey the children of men! Does so wondrous a thought suggest nothing to my heart?

The whale has no teeth, but it carries in their stead, on the sides of its mouth, an immense number of blades or plates, twelve or fifteen feet long, and usually called baleens. They are fixed in the upper jaw, on each side of the palate, and form with the tongue an enormous sieve. The water, gulped in at each opening of the mouth, escapes through the interstices of the baleen plates, without, however, carrying away the little animals that are contained in it. The elastic blades, to the number of many hundreds in each whale, serve, under the name of whale-bone, for a multitude of purposes, with which every one is acquainted.

IV. *Their utility.* — Whales and all other large fishes, whose appearance spreads terror among those which they make their prey, seek the high seas, for fear of running ashore along the coast, where they could not find sufficient water to float them. The invisible hand that drew them forth from nothing impels them to inhabit places which the others desert. It nourishes them under the ice of the polar regions, or sends them, as a means of support, to the inhabitants of those dismal countries. The flesh is edible, the oil most valuable, the bones and skin most useful for the construction of boats, in which the natives can carry on their maritime operations.

Do you know how the whale is caught? The whalers approach as closely as they can with safety to themselves, and dart their harpoons into it. To a ring in each harpoon a very long rope is attached from the boat. The animal, on being wounded, plunges into the deep sea, with the harpoon sticking in it. In vain it endeavors to free itself from the deadly weapon; loss of blood completes its exhaustion, and soon its monstrous carcass, rising to the surface of the water, becomes an easy prey of the daring fishermen.[226]

Men are not the only enemies of the whale. Many large fish, or, if you choose, many sea monsters wage a most bloody war against it, and thus retain within due limits the propagation of the giant of the ocean. Among the enemies of the whale, one of the principal is the octopus or devil fish.[227]

Imagine you see an animal from eighteen to twenty feet long, its other dimensions in proportion, and weighing between four and six thousand pounds. Like the hippopotamus, its color is a reddish brown. Its head has the shape of a parrot's bill. Round its body are eight arms, from five to six feet long. These arms, as flexible as strips of leather, are provided along their sides with an immense number of suckers. Woe to the inhabitant of the deep that comes in contact with this monster! It embraces its prey in its viscous arms, charged, we are told, with some paralysing influence, and, by means of its powerful cupping-glasses, drinks in a few minutes the last drop of its victim's blood.

If the whale, by the material advantages that we derive from it, teaches us to love the Creator, the octopus, by its repulsive figure, and especially by its frightful arms, teaches us to fear the devil, a much more terrible and dangerous enemy than any marine monster. This is a salutary lesson, of which man stands at all times in need.

The greater number of the other kinds of fish range themselves near our shores. Some are always with us; others, such as the herring, come to us every year in shoals. We know the time of their periodical visits, and we make good use of this knowledge. It is from the northern seas, the home of the whale, that herrings and other such migratory fish come. At certain seasons, they fly before the wrath of the whale, and thus cast themselves on our shores. The progress of these aquatic hosts is animated, not only by the fear of a pursuing enemy, but also by the relish of numberless insects which dwell along our coasts, and which are regarded as dainty food by these inhabitants of the deep. When nearly all are captured, during summer and autumn, the remainder return, it is believed, in winter to the polar regions, where they give birth to new generations, which visit us the following year.

Several species of fish, such as the salmon and the shad, enter the mouths of our rivers with the utmost eagerness, and endeavor to ascend to their source. Why so? In order to communicate the advantages of the sea to persons whose situation is inland. What hand directs them with so much kindness and consideration for man, if not thine, O Lord! though, alas! a goodness so visible but rarely excites our gratitude?

He also created the birds, according to their kinds. — That omnipotent word which peopled the profound abysses of the ocean was followed by another, which filled the vast regions of the air with joyous inhabitants. Like the fishes, the birds were born of the sea. What new miracle is it, that this element should produce two such different kinds of beings? We have descended into the depths of the sea: it is time that we should now arise, and travel through the air. We shall find here a race of itinerant musicians, who publish to the world the admirable wisdom and goodness of the Creator.

I. *By the structure of their bodies.* Covered with oil and scales, particularly flexible toward the tail, supplied with an abundance of fins, the body of the fish combines all the qualities necessary to defend it, with ease and grace, against the element in which it must live. No less admirable is the structure of birds. The very sight of their body shows us that a most just proportion has been observed between them and the subtle and delicate element which has been assigned them as their abode. The body of the bird is neither very solid nor equally thick throughout.

Perfectly adapted for flight, it is pointed in front, and thus cleaves the air. The wings, convex without, concave within, form on each side two levers, which keep the body in equilibrium, two oars in effect, suited to the element in which they must move. The tail counterbalances the head and neck, and answers all the purpose of a helm, while the wings row. This helm not only keeps the bird steady in its flight, but enables it to rise, fall, or turn as it chooses. The tail no sooner turns to one side, than the head turns to the opposite direction.

The bones of birds, though sufficiently solid to hold the members together, are yet so hollow and slender, that they scarcely add anything to the weight of the body. All the feathers are skillfully constructed and arranged, as well to uphold the bird as to defend it against injury from the air. The feet are formed in such a manner that, when they are pressed in the middle, the claws naturally grasp the body that presses them. It follows that the talons of a bird clasp the object on which they rest more or less tightly, in proportion as the movement of that object is more or less rapid.

"Thus," remarks Chateaubriand, in his *Genius of Christianity*, "when we see at night-fall, in winter, the ravens perched on the bleak summit of an aged oak, we imagine that, ever awake and attentive, they only hold fast to the branches with incredible difficulty, amid whirlwinds and clouds. Nevertheless, heedless of danger, and challenging the tempest, they are rocked to sleep by the angry elements. The cold north wind itself attaches them to the branches, from which we might suppose that it would cast them to the ground; and thus, like old sailors, whose hammocks are suspended from the shaking beams of the ship, the more they are rocked by the storm, the more soundly they sleep."

II. *By their preservation.* He who created those millions of birds of every species watches over each one of them, with as much care as over the universe. Nothing that could contribute to their preservation or welfare has been forgotten. Let this thought both instruct and console us. If our heavenly Father takes so much care of a little sparrow, which may be purchased for a farthing, what will he not do for us, who cost him the last drop of his blood? To enable the birds to make journeys, even of a considerable distance, along whose stages it might not be easy to find inns or provisions, and to pass the long winter nights without eating, God has placed under their throat a little pouch, which is called the crop or craw, and in which they reserve a stock of nourishment. The liquor, with which the food is here saturated, assists digestion. The gizzard, which admits only a very small quantity of food at a time, does the rest by the help of little sandy or pebbly grains, which the bird employs the better to break its food.

The little aerial traveler having been supplied with the necessary provisions, the only question now is, how to secure him against wet and cold. To solve it, he should have a coat which neither the rain nor the air could penetrate. Accordingly, we find that his body is covered with feathers, which are furnished with a soft and warm down at one extremity, and with a kind of long double beard at the other. This beard, or rather these two rows of thin barbs, are not only curved, but closed as neatly in line, as if the operation had been performed by scissors. Every one of these barbs is itself a new quill, supporting two rows of barbules, so exceedingly small that they are scarcely perceptible; yet they effectually obstruct every passage by which the air could reach the body.

All this delicate attention, which we should certainly have overlooked, did not yet satisfy providence. Lest this necessary arrangement might be disturbed by rain, the Creator has supplied the birds with a means of rendering their feathers as impervious to water as to air.

Besides the little reservoir, full of oil, placed at the end of each feather, all birds have another, much larger, at the extremity of the body.[228] This reservoir has many little openings; and when the bird finds its feathers dry or tossed, it taps the reservoir with its bill. It thus extracts an oil or fatty liquid, which is reserved in its glands; and afterward, passing the greater number of its feathers through its bill, communicates to them the oil, by means of which they at once glisten brightly and the crevices in them are filled up. After this operation the rain can only roll off the bird; it finds all the avenues by which it could reach the skin perfectly closed.

The inmates of our poultry-yards, enjoying good shelter, are not so well provided with this liquor as birds that live in the open air; which explains the reason why a wet hen looks so very miserable. On the other hand, swans, geese, ducks, and all aquatic fowl in general, oil their feathers from their very birth. The supply is in exact proportion to their needs. Even their flesh contracts the taste of oil; and every one may remark that one of their most ordinary exercises is to refresh or to arrange their feathers.

Still there is a general waste in nature; and, notwithstanding all the care the birds may take of their plumage, their garments will yet grow threadbare. This brilliant army desires to throw off its old uniform; it wishes to render honor to the powerful monarch who is its commander-in-chief. To himself, therefore, when the season of moulting approaches, the numberless regiments have recourse. He opens his magazines, and condescends himself to become their clothier and outfitter, as he is their guide and support. Autumn is the period of the general distribution. Every bird divests itself of its old attire, and receives *gratis* a new suit. Winter now approaching, they set its severity at defiance. On the return of the following year, the dress being again worn out, each individual receives a new supply from the storehouse of him who created and preserves the universe.

But from one distribution to another, it is necessary that the aerial beings of this little world should labor. Like man, they must earn their bread: their life must be divided between labor and the joy of music. For this purpose these little creatures are supplied with all the instruments and organs suitable to their occupation and their mode of living. Two or three examples will suffice to explain what we mean, and to fill us with admiration for providence.

The greater number of small birds, such as the sparrow, live on slender grains, which they find in the neighborhood of our houses and in the fields. It does not cost them much to procure their food or to break it. Accordingly, their bill is small, and their neck and claws short: this suffices. Not so, however, with snipe and many others, that have to seek for snails and worms in the midst of clay and mud. The Creator has provided them with a very long neck and bill. Thus furnished, they dig and rake, and lack for nothing.

The woodpecker, whose manner of living is quite different, is quite differently formed. Its beak is pretty long, and exceedingly hard; its tongue is of an immoderate length, sharp, with a number of little points, and moistened with a sort of glue at the end. It has short legs; two claws before, two behind: both hooked. All these appliances have reference to its manner of seeking its food and of living. This bird derives its subsistence from little worms or insects that live in the heart of the branches, or more commonly under the bark of old trees. It is an ordinary thing to find under the bark of fallen trees the retreats of these little creatures, even to a considerable depth.

The woodpecker has need of hooked claws, to grasp the branch or bark on which it rests. Long legs would be useless for bringing out that which is beneath the bark. But a strong and sharp beak is necessary, because the bird is obliged to examine, by strokes of its beak along the branches or the bark, in what part the wood is rotten. It stops where the stroke sounds hollow, and pierces the bark with its beak. It next pushes its beak into the hole which it has made, and either screams or whistles into the hollow of the tree, in order to detach and set in motion the insects that are asleep. It then puts its tongue into the hole, and by the help of the small bristling darts and very cohesive gum to which we have alluded, gathers up as many of the little insects as it can discover, and thus makes its repast.

We have often seen it strike the side of the tree, opposite the retreat of the little insects, and then run swiftly to the hole. One who did not understand this stratagem might take the woodpecker for a fool; but he is no such thing. These strokes are intended to awake the insects, without awaking their suspicions. If a few taps are insufficient, the wood-pecker renews the operation, until its prey comes within reach of its tongue.

Examine, in like manner, various other birds, and you will find that there is not one unprovided with organs adapted to its mode of life. This harmony is so much the more admirable, as the objects which exhibit it seem less important; and clearly proves that all things are the work of infinite Wisdom.

III. *By their nests.* This infinite Wisdom is still more apparent in the skill with which birds build their nests. How can we contemplate, without emotion, that goodness which gives skill to the weak and foresight to the unthinking? First of all, who has taught them that they have need of nests; who has told them to build these nests, that their eggs may be preserved warm and safe; who has informed them that the heat will not gather round the eggs if the nest be too large, or that there will not be room for the little ones if it be too small? How do they know the exact proportion to place between the size of the nest and the family that must inhabit it?

What astronomer has prepared an almanac for them, that they may not be deceived as to the time of building, or be overtaken by any distress? What mathematician has drawn out the shape of the nest? What architect has shown them how to select a suitable site, and to build on a solid foundation? What mother has advised them to strew the under part of the nest with the softest materials, such as wool and down? And, when these materials fail, who has inspired them with that generous charity, which leads them to pluck away from their breasts as many feathers as are necessary to form a comfortable cradle for their little ones?

And when spring arrives, and the trees unfold their leaves, behold, we see a thousand workers beginning their labors. Masons, carpenters, weavers, all astonish us by their ingenuity. Are you acquainted with their school of art? You will see some carry long straws into some hole in an old wall; others plaster their little edifices near the windows of a church; others again pull away a hair from a horse, or the little piece of wool which the sheep has left hanging on the brier. Each one chooses such materials as suit its purpose.

But if you desire to view more closely that admirable wisdom which directs all these artisans, enter an aviary, where a great variety of birds are collected. Place in a corner whatever is necessary for the construction of their nests, such as little bits of dry wood, bark, leaves, hay, chaff, moss, hair, cotton, wool, silk. Examine with what judgment the several inhabitants come a shopping to this market. This one desires a little moss; another seeks for a feather; another disputes about a leaf; two others want a little tuft of wool, and sometimes a very sharp contest is the consequence. The general result of which is that dispute about each one carries away as much as he can pull to his own side. In fine, every species has its own taste, its own peculiar style of living and of furnishing. Then the houses being built, they never fail to carpet and curtain the interior with little feathers, or wool, or silk, to promote a beneficial warmth round them and their little ones.

And for all this work, what organs have they? Look at the swallow: its nest is a structure altogether different from other nests, which seems to surpass the capabilities of the builder. It does not build with little branches and hay; it employs only mortar and cement, and goes along so solidly, that we find it difficult to break its work. Still it has no bucket to carry water, no barrow to wheel sand, no shovel to temper the mortar, no trowel to lay it on. How, then, can it produce such excellent workmanship?

A hundred times a day it may be seen passing and repassing over the neighboring lake. With its wings raised, it moistens its breast on the surface of the water; afterward, mixing this moisture with dust, it tempers and prepares a suitable mortar, which it carries away and works with its bill. Suppose now it were possible to reduce the most experienced architect in the world to the size of a little swallow. Leave him no arms, no instruments, no materials. Leave him only his knowledge of science, and a bill; the swallow has only a bill, and no acquaintance with science. Set both to work; and see which of them will succeed better!

IV. *By their instinct.* Here we cannot but admire the wondrous influence of a supernatural wisdom. When the nest is made, and the eggs are laid, the habits of our artificers completely change. The birds assuredly know nothing of the contents of their eggs, or of the principles on which the theory of hatching is founded. Yet these little creatures, so active, so restless, so volatile, forget in a moment their natural propensities, to fix themselves on their frail brood during the necessary time. At last the little ones come forth from their shells. How many new cares for the parents till the young troop can pass away from them! Now they feel what it is to be burdened with a family: they must provide for seven or eight, instead of two. The warbler and the nightingale must labor then like the rest. Goodbye to music now: there is no time for it; at least very little. Every one must be afoot before sunrise. During the day the food must be distributed with great equality; each little inmate must receive its due portion in turn, without ever being supplied twice in succession.

What do I say? The tenderness of these parents goes so far as to change their natural dispositions: new duties are accompanied with new characteristics. There is question now, not only of nourishing their young, but of guarding and defending them, of making head against the enemy, and even of paying penalties in their own person. To be better understood, let us select an illustration from the birds that we have every day before our eyes.

Follow a hen, lately become the mother of a family: she is no longer the same. If she finds a grain of wheat, or a crumb of bread, or something larger that may be divided, she does not touch it. She informs her little ones of it by a cry which they well understand; they run to her quickly, and all the good luck is theirs. The mother limits herself to her frugal repasts. Heretofore, naturally timid, she has known only how to flee. At the head of her little troop of chickens, she is now a heroine that knows no danger, that dashes into the face of even the strongest dog. Yes, she would face a lion, so great is the courage inspired by her new dignity.

Occasionally I have seen one in another attitude, not less pleasing. Some person had placed duck eggs under her, and they came forth most successfully. The little ones, on breaking their shells, had not the shape of her other children. But the hen believed herself their mother, and, on this account, she found them quite to her liking. She guided them about as her own, with the most perfect good faith in the world; she assembled and warmed them under her wings; and wherever she led them, it was with that authority and in the exercise of those rights which belong to a mother. She had always been perfectly respected, followed, and obeyed by the whole of her troop.

Unfortunately for her honor, a stream came in her way: behold, in the twinkling of an eye, all the little ducklings run to the water! The poor mother was in the utmost consternation. She followed them with her eye along the bank; she gave them advice, and reproached them for their temerity. She went to and fro, imploring assistance, and recounting her sorrows to the whole world; she returned to the water, and commanded the imprudent to return; but the little ducks, delighted to find themselves in their natural element, continued to take their diversion. The hen, on her side, remained inconsolable until she had gathered once more under her wings her little waddling family, which, at the earliest opportunity, should again afflict her in the same manner. In what school, may I ask, did these little ducks learn that water was their element? It certainly was not in the hen's school.

PRAYER

O my God! who art all love, I thank thee for having created the fishes and the birds for our use. I bless thy providence, which watches with so much care over all creatures, and which lavishes so many benefits on me. Increase my confidence and love toward thee!

I am resolved to love God above all things, and my neighbor as myself for the love of God; and, in testimony of this love, I shall say my morning prayers with true devotion.

Lesson 10: Creation: The Fifth Day (Continued)

I. *Instinct of birds (continued)*. We have seen with what admirable instinct birds are endowed to build their nests, to hatch their eggs, to nourish their young. This instinct goes even so far as to foresee danger, and to distinguish the enemy that would injure them. Out of a thousand examples, we shall take one, which will be so much the more intelligible as it is the more familiar.

Observe a turkey at the head of her little ones. Sometimes we hear her utter a doleful cry, for which we cannot divine the cause. Immediately all her little ones crouch under the bushes, or the grass, or whatever else is at hand: they disappear. If there is nothing to cover them, they stretch themselves on the ground, and seem to be dead. They may be seen in this posture for half an hour at a time, and often much longer. The mother, meanwhile, looks upwards, quite alarmed, redoubles her distress, and repeats the strange cry which had cast down all her little ones.

Persons who notice this mother's embarrassment and uneasiness look up into the air in search of the cause. By a careful examination they at length discover, under the clouds that traverse the heavens, a black spot, barely visible. This is a bird of prey, which, though almost concealed from the spectator's view, does not escape the vigilant eye of our little mother; this is the cause of her alarm, and of the panic throughout the camp. We one day saw a family of this class remaining for four consecutive hours fastened to the ground, the mother all the while in the greatest agitation, while the bird of prey swept, ascending and descending, above their heads.

At length the pursuer disappears. The mother changes her note; she utters a cry which restores life to her little ones. They run to her from all sides; they flap their wings; they proclaim a victory; they have a thousand things to tell her. They seem to relate all the dangers they ran, and to hurl maledictions after the base wretch that threatened their lives. How astonishing is all this! Who can have informed this mother of an enemy that never did her any harm? How did she perceive this enemy at so considerable a distance? What telescope did she employ? On the other hand, what lessons has she given to her family on the manner of distinguishing, as occasion may require, the meaning of her different cries, and of regulating their actions in accordance with her language?

The admirable harmony between the organs of this fowl and the use to which she turns them—nay, this collection of wonders in structure and instinct—is every day presented to our view. Who remarks them and thanks providence for them? Oh, how well does the maternal solicitude we have described justify the comparison of which our Lord makes use in the gospel! Nothing can show us his tender goodness in more beautiful or touching language: "Jerusalem, Jerusalem, how often would I have gathered thy children together, as the hen gathereth her chickens under her wings, and thou wouldst not."[229] Every page shows us the power, the wisdom, and the goodness of the Creator, and invites our hearts to confidence and love. Let us proceed to a new chapter in their history, no less interesting than the preceding. May it produce in us those salutary impressions which the inspired penman who has written it wishes.

II. *Their migrations.* The lives of birds are full of instruction.[230] Birds do not dwell continually in the same place; they change their abodes according to the seasons. In spring, we are visited by crowds of nightingales; in summer, by quails. All these birds disappear on the arrival of the cold weather toward the end of autumn. The joyous army takes up its winter quarters in some warmer climate. The granaries there are more abundantly filled; the great caterer has anticipated all their wants. It is true that our pilgrims have no provisions for the journey; they do not even know the way. It matters not; neither the number of miles, nor the perils of the sea, nor the darkness of the night, can terrify or stay them. Confiding in him who calls them, they expect to find the way, and along the way lodgings and provisions: and they are never disappointed.

When the moment of departure approaches, you see them making their preparations. Every class has its special mode of traveling, as in an army every corps has its special characteristic and duty. See! some set out alone; others, with their tender family; others, again, in a little company. Soon the body of the army moves; the numerous troops who compose it have chosen as the locality of their rendezvous some lonely field or the belfry of some village church. Here are the wild ducks; there the swallows.

The signal to depart being given, the first of these two latter classes arrange themselves either in a long line, or in two lines meeting as in the letter V. The duck at the angle is the leader; and by cutting the air, facilitates the passage of all the others. This bird is charged with its commission only for a time; when it grows tired, it passes round to the end to rest itself; then another takes its place, and so on. The second class, much smaller and lighter, form themselves into a compact mass, with which the air is sometimes darkened. Many remain in Europe, concealing themselves among reeds and in marshes, to await in a dormant state the return of spring. Men, whose veracity cannot be called in question, have proved this by actually taking some of them out of water in a condition apparently lifeless, at a time when the whole race had vanished from the face of the country, and restoring them to animation by means of a gentle warmth.

The precaution that they take beforehand to oil their feathers well, and to bury themselves in banks with their backs outward, secures them against moisture: this regards the sand marten. As for our chimney and window swallows, they emigrate in autumn to warmer countries. Numberless bands of them may be seen gathering along the shores of the Mediterranean. When all have waited for a few days on some elevated spot in expectation of a favorable moment, the innumerable legions start together, and cross the ocean; they are sometimes met in full sail; and again they are seen resting on the rigging of ships, when contrary winds oppose their passage. We are assured that, in the month of October, our swallows make their appearance at Senegal, where they spend the winter and change their feathers.

On the return of spring, each one hastens to revisit the town, the village, the cottage, or the old window, where it had left all its affections, because it there found hospitality during the preceding year.

How many wonders! If the rigor of the season or the want of nourishment told the birds to change their residence, one could more easily understand it; but how does it happen that, when the weather permits them to remain, and they still find abundance of food, they do not defer their departure beyond the time specified? What traveler has come to inform them that they shall find suitable meats and climates elsewhere? What chairman has summoned the council, in which the day of leaving should be fixed on? In what language have the mothers told their little ones, born only a few months ago, that they must quit their native land, and journey to a foreign clime? Why do those that are held captive in cages seem so restless at the time of departure, as if afflicted because they cannot join their companions?

What is the name of him who announces to the assemblage, by sound of trumpet, the resolution taken, that all may be found ready? Have they a calendar to show them the precise day on which it is necessary to set out? Have they officers to maintain discipline among so immense a number; for, before the edict, no one stirs, and the day after the departure we see neither stragglers nor deserters? Have they a compass to direct them safely toward the shore at which they desire to arrive, without the slightest danger of being put out of their course by wind, or rain, or darkness? Are they, in fine, under the influence of an infallible reason, superior to the reason of man, who dares not to venture across the ocean without a thousand precautions? Ye, who pretend not to believe in God—answer!

All, we may say, are now departed. Adieu to their sweet society! Adieu to their delightful music! A few only remain: the lonely sparrow, the innocent wren. Poor little things! What will become of you during the long winter? Who will warm you? Who will feed you? Father of all things that breathe! hast thou forgotten them? No, no. For them, there will be some mild rays of the sun, a bushy fir tree, a thatched roof; for them, the juniper tree will be covered with fruit; for them, the berries of the sweetbriar will be softened into jelly; and the little solitaries will have a table and a roof. It is thus, O truly maternal providence, that nothing escapes thy loving solicitude!

It is true, then, that God is everything to the birds. Those that migrate have certainly neither charts nor compass, nor wagons, nor guides, nor reason; nevertheless, they all arrive without fail. Those that stay behind are also lodged, and warmed, and nourished by his goodness. But if he takes so much care of the birds, of which a couple may be bought for a penny, what care will he not take of us, for whom not only the birds but the whole world has been created?

III. *Their utility.* Yes, the birds have been created for us; their flesh nourishes us, their feathers serve us in a thousand ways, their songs delight us. They free the country from a multitude of insects and smaller reptiles, of which an excessive number would be a plague. This is probably the most important, though least appreciated, of all the services that birds render to us. Since the opportunity presents itself for entering into some details on this matter, it is only proper that we should embrace it. Such knowledge, besides, will afford a triumphant reply to the objections of infidelity against the wisdom of providence.

Ever since the revolt of the first man, which brought death into the world, we find war and death in every department of nature; but providence holds a just balance between the belligerents, so that life and order subsist, notwithstanding the causes that lead continually to ruin and disorder. Let us cite a few illustrations:

The insect is the natural enemy of vegetables, on which it lives; but its insatiable appetite and wondrous fecundity would constitute an unparalleled overplus in the means of destruction, which should end in the annihilation of the whole vegetable kingdom, if the supreme Wisdom did not place by its side a most efficacious moderator. This moderator is the bird, which wages war to the utmost limits against the countless hosts of its prey.

Unfortunately, man has become, in his turn, the most ruthless enemy of the bird, on account of finding its flesh extremely delicate; and, as in all things, the lord of creation tends to extravagance, so instead of economizing this precious aliment and exquisite luxury, he wastes it. He has pursued to death his most useful servant, the only one that could arrest the progress of myriads of little gnawers, often invisible to our eyes, generally inaccessible to our hands.

Indeed, nearly all birds feed on insects that destroy our food: even those birds whose presence has been for a long time erroneously regarded as noxious. Thus, a Norman farmer, who had guarded his field against the supposed plunder of crows, perceived at length, on opening a few of those he had killed, that their stomachs contained nothing but worms, the larvae of beetles, and some other descriptions of ravaging insects.

And those poor larks, whose beautiful song cannot preserve them from the shot or the snare of the fowler, are also most valuable assistants to the agriculturist. They wage incessant war against crickets, grasshoppers, spring beetles, the wheat-fly, and the mole cricket in general. Now, an idea may be formed of the services which might be rendered to us by these poor songsters when we state that the injury done in 1856 to wheat, by some little spoilers (a yellow worm larva of the beetle species), in the department of the Moselle alone, was estimated at four million francs.

About sixty years ago the vines of Beaujolais and the neighboring districts were invaded by a host of warblers, tomtits or titmice, and other such birds, who kept pecking away from morning till night at the leaves and stalks, so that their noise resembled that of grasshoppers. At the present day, in consequence of the war that has been waged against them, we scarcely see one of them amongst the vines, but in their stead, myriads of caterpillars, moths, etc., swarming everywhere; so that the committee of taxation have valued at more than three million francs annually, the damage caused by the cabbage-garden pebble moth alone in the twenty-three communes of Mâconnais and Beaujolais.

The sparrow itself, the sparrow so much decried by Valmont de Bomard, who desired that a reward should be given for its head: the sparrow has lately been acknowledged one of the greatest protectors of our harvests. So much so that England, Prussia, and Hungary, which had previously carried on a war of extermination against it, have been obliged to restore it at considerable expense, because they found that without the sparrow there was no crop secure from a host of invisible enemies.

The signal for war against the sparrow was given in the last century by Frederic, king of Prussia. This royal philosopher learned that, every year, at least two million bushels of grain were consumed by sparrows in his states. The disorder was intolerable: its progress should be instantly arrested. In consequence he issued a proclamation, offering a reward for every sparrow's head that should be brought to him. Every Prussian became a sportsman: the unfortunate sparrows disappeared. The war was waged with such vigor that in less than a year there was nothing rarer than a sparrow in the kingdom of Prussia.

The people looked forward to a magnificent crop, and the philosophical king did not regret having given a little lesson on wisdom to providence. But what happened? The following year immense multitudes of caterpillars and locusts, freed from their enemies, devoured the harvest. The desolation was such that Frederic, humbled and confounded, found himself obliged to repeal his law as soon as possible, and to forbid, under severe penalties, that any one should kill a single sparrow throughout the whole extent of his dominions.

The goldfinch administers justice among the insects that destroy wood; the starling disencumbers it from a multitude of vermin that injure it. The blackbird and the thrush dispose of the slugs, worms, and insects that feast on the vine. The cuckoo has a special relish for shaggy caterpillars, which other birds cannot swallow. Yet all these eminent services cannot stay the rapacity of man: fowlers and poachers seem to have given the command for the destruction of the aerial tribe. To take only a few examples we find that in the department of the Eastern Pyrenees, all the heights are covered with snares at the time of the passage of the birds; and on some more fortunate days, there are sometimes as many as ten thousand of these little tourists taken prisoners. Again, the lapwing or peewit, which is so exceedingly serviceable to man, since it defends him against the frightful ravages that are caused by shell-worms, even through such extensive works as the dikes of Holland, is the object of a most cruel hatred and persecution.

It is, therefore, high time to put an end to this insane war, not only in France, but in the other countries of Europe. In conformity with the desire of an eminent Berlin naturalist, the protection of useful birds, and all are such, should be made an article of international law.[231]

To draw to a close, let us add that the birds are musicians, placed by our heavenly Father near our abodes — near the abodes of the poor especially — to soothe our afflictions, and to relate his benefits. This is so true that singing birds are usually found nowhere but in inhabited places; that when man reposes, they are silent, and only begin their song again to greet his waking; and, in fine, that it is their delight to meet him on his way, and to cheer his soul with their sweet refrains.

See the innocent lark: it eats a few of our grains, it dwells in some of our fields; but it pays for its board and lodging with its glorious concerts. When man walks the country on a beautiful summer day, the vigilant musician springs from its resting-place at the sound of his footsteps; it mounts upward singing — still upward — still upward — and continues its song till man can no longer hear it; when its lord has passed, it descends again, and rests itself, but only to begin anew.

Let us also pause a moment, to hear the little sermon of St. Francis of Assisi. This earthly seraph, this matchless figure of the simplicity and sanctity of the children of God, had regained a portion of that dominion over animals which was lost to us by sin. He had a special love for larks: obedient to his voice, these little musicians used to gather around him to hold their concerts. At his death, an innumerable multitude of them were seen fluttering over the roof of the house in which his body lay, and celebrating, in songs of more than ordinary joy, the everlasting happiness of their friend.

The good saint loved larks so much that he was accustomed to compare his religious to them.

"The larks," he would say, "have a little crown on their heads; and you have a cowl. This article of dress, peculiar to country children, informs you that you should imitate their humility and innocence.

"The larks are of an ashy color; your habit is much the same. It says to you: 'Remember man that thou art dust, and into dust thou shalt return.'

"The larks live in poverty, gathering, without solicitude for the morrow, the grains that they find on the earth; you make profession of poverty. Without uneasiness you live on the bread of alms; your granaries are the providence of God and the charity of the faithful.

"The larks have scarcely partaken of the food prepared for their nourishment, when they rise straight toward heaven even till they are lost to view, singing songs of gratitude to God, the Father and nourisher of every creature; thus do you act, my brethren, for you eat the bread of angels with thanksgiving—I mean the bread that the good angels inspire the faithful to give you.

"The larks are also called *a laude*,[232] because they continually praise the Lord by their joyous canticles; thus should you act. Despise earthly, and aspire after heavenly things; regard yourselves as pilgrims on earth and citizens of heaven; never forget that you are called to praise the Lord continually by the triple canticle of prayer, sanctity, and preaching."[233]

We also, whatever our state may be, should endeavor to be as pleasing as the larks in the sight of the good God.

It is time to take up again the thread of our discourse. A new day opens to us, a day whose light will display wonders superior to all those which have heretofore passed before our eyes.

Sixth day.—The sixth day God said: "Let the earth bring forth the living creature in its kind, cattle, and creeping things, and beasts of the earth, according to their kinds. And it was so done. And God made the beasts of the earth according to their kinds, and cattle, and everything that creepeth on the earth after its kind. And God saw that it was good."[234]

Truly, my God! thou seemest, in continually creating new difficulties, not only to amuse thyself before me, but to take a pleasure in bewildering my mind. Yesterday thou didst command the sea to produce fishes and birds, and it obeyed thee. I have not yet recovered from my astonishment; and today thou dost again address the earth, commanding it to bring forth new creatures into the world. But is it not already covered with millions of trees and plants? Are not all its energies exhausted? Where will there be room for any new arrivals? Every place seems full.

Be silent, my reason! Recollect thy thoughts; and prepare thyself to adore. And thou, my heart! make ready to love.

Land animals.—At the sixth word of the Creator, three new kinds of animals spring into existence from nothingness. Of those with which we are already acquainted, some swim in the water, others fly in the air. Now we have a description that walk on the earth, and come somewhat nearer to ourselves. They, too, are divided into three classes. The first class are domestic animals; the second, reptiles and insects; and the third, wild beasts. Here, again, the prescient goodness of the Creator appears with the utmost splendor.

I. *In the docility of domestic animals.* By domestic animals we understand all beasts of burden, appointed to obey man; to assist him in his labors, to supply for his deficiency of strength, to furnish him with garments and food. God, to whom all the consequences of creation were known from the beginning, prepared thus for man, fallen into the state of sin and condemned to penance, a number of obedient domestics that should share his toil, and relieve him from it altogether when it might be found too painful. He commanded the animals of great strength to use their powers only for the service of man: to carry burdens without reluctance, to love our dwellings more than their liberty, and to respect the voice even of a child that might be appointed to guide them.

To what must we attribute the gentle dispositions, the perfect docility of domestic animals? Only to the order which God has given them to obey man as their master. If you have any doubt upon the matter, endeavor to tame lions, tigers, bears, and wolves; endeavor to assemble them in flocks, and to entrust them to a shepherd; endeavor to make them till your fields, draw your carts, or work your machines: succeed in it you will never.

II. *In their temperance.* Not content with giving man a multitude of strong and obedient animals, God was pleased to take upon himself their support. Moreover, he created them with inclinations so temperate as to be entirely for our advantage. While savage animals eat much, and would quickly ruin a master by expense, the greater number of domestic animals eat little and labor much: a little grass, even the driest, or the smallest description of our grains, suffices them. They expect no other recompense for their services. God has earned his foresight even further still: he has been pleased that their food should be found everywhere. The plains, the valleys, the mountains, are all like so many tables, ready laid, and supplying them with an abundance of nourishment.

III. *In their services.* For the little that we give them, see how much they return us! If we have occasion to pass rapidly from one place to another, behold the horse is at hand, and appears sensible of the honor done him in requiring his services. He studies the manner of pleasing his master. At the least sign he starts off; he is always ready to walk, or to trot, or to gallop when he knows the will of his rider. Neither the length of the journey nor the unevenness of the road, nor ditches, nor even rivers can discourage him. He clears everything; he is like a bird that cannot be stayed. Is there question of his master's defense, or of an attack upon the enemy? He dashes into the presence of armed men; he fears no danger. The sound of the trumpet, and the signal for the affray, only arouse his courage; and even the flashing of the sword cannot make him recoil or turn aside.[235]

Turning now to the ox; consider how it moves along with measured steps. Less active, less pleasing in shape than the horse, this new domestic is not, however, less useful to us. Our fields require to be sown: place a yoke upon its neck, attach the plough to the harness, and it will patiently trace the furrows for you. When the time of reaping arrives it will assist you to carry your abundant crop into your barns. At a later period it will convey the surplus of your produce to market; it will bring you wood for firing during the winter: you have only to speak to it, it is always ready to obey.

These two animals have their merit; but there is another, whose services are much more generally employed, and whose existence is a new manifestation of that maternal providence which so many proofs have already rendered sensible to us. The horse and the ox are expensive; and their maintenance is somewhat costly. The rich alone, or at least the man of easy circumstances, can purchase and keep them; the poor cannot. Yet it is the poor that have most need of help. Will the poor man, who bears for us the burden and heat of the day, be alone in his painful labors? Will no one come to share them with him? Ah! in the order of nature, as in that of grace, God is not unmindful of the poor and the little. For these children of special regard he has expressly created a new servant: it is the ass.

Instead the noble air of the horse, we find substituted in the ass most humble deportment; and for the strength of the ox, a patience which no labor can exhaust.

The ass does not move very quickly, but it moves regularly, and for a long time together. It renders its services with perseverance; and what is a great matter in a domestic, it makes no account of them. Easily pleased with regard to food; the first thistle it meets with answers its purpose. It never imagines anything due to it; it never displays any unhappiness or discontent: whatever is given to it is well received. It is the faithful companion of peasants and laborers, who are themselves the bone and sinew of states, and the sustainers of our lives.

To what a condition would vinedressers, gardeners, masons, and the great majority of country people, that is, two-thirds of mankind, be reduced, if it were necessary for them to employ other men, or horses, or oxen, for the transport of those articles which they sell and purchase. The ass, ready for all these things, is continually under orders. It carries fruit, vegetables, hides, coal, wood, tiles, brick, plaster, lime, straw, manure. Whatever is most abject is its ordinary lot. How great an advantage for so many persons to have a tractable, vigorous, indefatigable animal, that, with little expense and no conceit, supplies our towns and villages with all sorts of provisions!

Now, what shall we say of the dog, that faithful friend, which God has placed so near man, for the sake of company, aid, and defense? The services rendered to us by dogs are as different as their species or kind. The mastiff guards our houses during the night; the shepherd dog knows both how to make war on wolves and to discipline the flock; the hound unites swiftness with strength, to diversify our pleasures.

The spaniel charges itself alternately with the discovery of what has been lost, and the amusement of its master's children. Should its master become poor or infirm, this faithful companion will share his misery, and almost seem to weep with him. Should he become blind, then it leads him from door to door; and we hardly know which to compassionate more—the affliction of the unfortunate master, or the mournful and suppliant air of the faithful servant—when the poor blind man dies, the world misses him not; for he is poor, and the poor have no friends. No one, therefore, will lament over his grave—no one but his dog: between the dog and the master, friendship lasts even to death.

Man finds in the horse, the ox, and the ass convenient modes of transit; in the dog he finds a trusty guard and a faithful guide. But there are other things still more necessary to him, namely, food and raiment; these he finds chiefly in his flocks. It is plain that the cow, the goat, and the sheep, have only been placed near man to enrich him. We give them a little grass, or the liberty of gathering through the commons whatever is most useless; and these creatures return in the evening to pay for the kindness that has been shown them, in streams of milk and cream. The night is no sooner passed than they purchase, by a new installment, their nourishment for the coming day.

The cow alone furnishes sufficiency along with bread for a whole family, covering our tables with riches of the most varied kind. The goat is the poor man's cow, as the ass is his horse. O tender providence, we find thee everywhere! and what a wonder is here! How does it happen that a withered and juiceless herb, from which we find it impossible to extract anything nutritious, becomes the source of milk? Ah! it is caused by a blessing, whose nature we do not understand, but whose effects we every day perceive. We are so accustomed to these occurrences that, perhaps, we have never thought of thanking him, who is their author, for them. Henceforward, my God! it shall not be so: gratitude and thanksgiving shall take the place of indifference and forgetfulness.

The sheep, content with being clad in winter, gives us its fleece in summer. Thus, according to the beautiful words of St. Martin, it fulfills the gospel precept by keeping one coat for itself and giving us the other. Ye rich of the world, do ye understand the lesson that condemns your luxurious superfluities?

It is therefore true that the domestic animals are only placed near us solely for our benefit. If anything diminishes our esteem for the services which they render us or the presents which they continually make us, it is their frequency, their daily repetition. We cease to think of them as benefits. The facility of obtaining them seems to lessen their value. But this is really what should increase it. A never-ceasing liberality deserves a continual gratitude; and the least we can do, when we receive a favor, is to condescend to notice it.

Insects in general. — The second class of beings, which the sixth creative word summoned into existence, are insects and reptiles. If it is true that the power and wisdom of God shine forth resplendently in the great works of nature, it is no less true that they also shine forth resplendently in the little.[236] Both equally astonish our minds and call forth the gratitude of our hearts. Let us read attentively this new page in the great book of the universe. God himself invites us to it in a special manner: the very ant will be a school of wisdom for us.[237] Before commencing, let us cast a rapid glance over insects in general.

I. *Their dress.* If God has not judged it unworthy of him to create insects, is it unworthy of man to consider them? Their smallness appears at first sight sufficient to justify the contempt in which they are too often held; but that is really a new reason why we should admire the skill and mechanism of their structure, which combines so many vessels, fibres, veins, muscles, a head, a heart, a stomach, and such wondrous motive power in a little particle, which is often almost invisible. Vulgar prejudice regards them either as the effect of chance or the refuse of nature. But attentive eyes discover in them the manifestation of a wisdom which, far from neglecting them, has taken particular care to clothe them, to arm them, and supply them with everything necessary for their condition.

Yes, the Father of the family has clothed the insects not with clumsy attire, like the children of the poor, but with garments of the richest description, shaped with matchless art. In their robes, on their wings, through their headdress, are lavished blue, green, red, gold, and silver, diamonds even, fringes, and plumes. It is only necessary to see a firefly, a butterfly, a simple caterpillar, to be struck with this magnificence.

To luxury of garments is added luxury of perfumes. The rich of the world purchase exquisite essences and odoriferous cosmetics at a high price, in order that their dress may be redolent, and their features beautiful. Without any expense there are some insects provided with a perfume so sweetly fragrant, that there is nothing else in nature analogous to it. Science has made the most strenuous efforts to lay hold on it, and to subject it to the service of man. We refer to the little insects, with bodies of emerald, speckled with black, which you and I have often crushed beneath our feet, and which are called cicindelae, or tiger-beetles.

II. *Their armor.* The same Wisdom that amused itself in the brilliant decoration of insects has vouchsafed to arm them from head to foot, and to fit them for waging war, whether offensive or defensive. If they are not always so fortunate as to catch that which they wait for, or to escape from what would be injurious to them, they are, nevertheless, provided with all that is best adapted to ensure success in either case. They have, for the most part, strong teeth, or a double saw, or a sting, or darts, or very effective pincers. A coat of mail, formed of scales, protects their entire body. The more delicate are furnished on the outside with a bushy nap, which saves them from shocks that they could not well sustain, and from friction that would be very injurious to them.

Nearly all find safety in the swiftness of their flight. They steal away from danger: some by the help of their wings; others with the assistance of a thread, fastened to which they plunge headlong down from the leaves where they live, far from the enemy that seeks them; others by means of their hind feet, whose sudden spring casts them instantaneously beyond the reach of harm. Finally, when strength fails, stratagem is resorted to. The continual war, which we observe among animals, is one of the most wonderful harmonies of nature. While it furnishes many with their ordinary nourishment, and delivers man from an excessive number of them, it still preserves enough of them to ensure their perpetuation.

Who would not be enchanted to see the Creator of worlds occupied with the adornment and outfitting of those insects that we despise? What should be our surprise, were we to examine in detail the skillful organization by which they live, and the instruments by which they all labor, each one according to its profession, for each has its own!

III. *Their dexterity.* Some are spinners, and they spin marvelously well, having two distaffs, as well as fingers, to fashion their thread; others are weavers, and make cloth and nets, for which they are provided with rolls and shuttles. Others are woodcutters; they build in wood, and have received two bill-hooks with which to cut their way. Others, again, are chandlers, and the shop in which they work their wax is furnished with scrapers, ladles, and trowels. Many are carpenters and joiners: besides the saw and nippers with which these are provided, they also carry an auger which they lengthen, twist, and untwist at will. By means of this instrument they secure very convenient board and lodging for themselves and their families, in the heart of fruit, under the bark of trees, often even in the hardest wood. The greater number are excellent distillers; they have a trunk which, more wonderful than that of the elephant's, serves some as an alembic for producing a syrup, which man has never been able to imitate; with others, it serves as a tongue for tasting, while nearly all employ it as a tube for sucking. In fine, they are all architects, building palaces which, for convenience, elegance, and finish, leave nothing to be desired.

Let us adduce, as an example, the home of the mason-fly. This fly, which is black, and about the size of a wasp, is found in warm countries, particularly in the Isle of Bourbon. When spring returns it may be seen flying around the houses, and entering the apartments on its reconnoitering expeditions. Its choice soon settles on the cornice of a ceiling, or the corner of a gilt frame. Immediately it sets to work. As the bee carries wax, it carries agglutinated clay which it fastens to the selected spot. During the long days it multiplies its journeys, until it has succeeded in building a house about the size of a pigeon's egg.

The little cells inside are constructed with a skill of which man would hardly be capable. The cradles being prepared, the eggs are laid. The children will be lodged, but who will nourish them? The mother will take care of that. After laying the egg, she begins her journey again. She tears away such spiders' nests as she finds, gathers up the young spiders, administers a sort of chloroform to them, and lulls them to sleep, then places them in the little cells whose entrance she carefully plasters. When the young flies are so far advanced in life as to move about, they find waiting for them some fresh and tender meat, a nourishment suitable to their age. In a very short time they break through the doors of their apartments, and find their way into the open air, where they proclaim the wonders of that providence which takes care of all things that breathe.

If insects are well made up in the arts, they are no less experienced in the sciences. They are all chemists, botanists, astronomers, mathematicians. It never happens that they are deceived regarding the qualities of a flower or a plant proper to nourish them, or the season in which they should undertake special labors, or the proportions which they should observe in their buildings. And now where are all these great scholars educated? Can you mention the names of the professors who lecture the silkworm? Can you tell me where are printed the classical works which the ants study? Can you inform me in what city is the university where the bees graduate?

IV. *Their organs.* What shall we say of their organs? There are a few insects that, with excellent eyes, are still further blessed with the possession of two antennae, or horns, which shelter their eyes, and, preceding the body in its progress, particularly in darkness, examine the way, and feel and discover, by a delicate touch, anything that could soil, hurt, or moisten them. If the horns become wet by contact with any noxious fluid, or strike against any hard body, the little creature is warned of its danger, and turns aside. Some of the horns are formed with knots, like those of lobsters, to give them more solidity; others are covered with little feathers, or velveted like a brush, to be secure against moisture.

Besides these helps, and many others, as various as the species of the creatures for which they are designed, the greater number of insects have also received the power of flight. Some have four wings; others, whose wings are so exquisitely fine that the least rub would tear them, have two strong scales which rise and fall precisely like two wings, but which are really intended to serve only as shields for them. You see, for example, these shields in cantharides and cockchafers. If that which we find in insects causes us so much admiration, how much more admiration would that which lies concealed from our vision and our reason occasion in us, if it were made manifest to us! That which we know, however, is sufficient for a noble heart, to make it adore and love the Creator of so many wonders.

PRAYER

O my God! who art all love, I thank thee for having placed at our command so many creatures that aid us, that guard us, that nourish us; grant, O Lord, that we may always avail ourselves of them, so as to love thee more!

I am resolved to love God above all things, and my neighbor as myself for the love of God; and, in testimony of this love, I shall be faithful to the good resolutions which I make in the morning.

Lesson 11: Creation: The Sixth Day

I. *The ants.* — Now that we have cast a rapid glance over insects in general, let us pause a moment to consider some of those marvelous miniatures more closely: our study will be repaid by useful instruction. Let us enter, for example, the school of the ant. The learned governess is at home: let us, then, take our places and attend.

The ants are a little nation, forming a regular republic, and having their own laws and police. They dwell in cities of their own, intersected by many streets, which lead to the different public establishments. One portion of the citizens harden the clay; they prevent it from crumbling by means of a coat of plaster which they spread over it: these are the state masons. Others, those which we ordinarily meet abroad, are the carpenters. With unwearying activity they gather up pieces of wood to arch the streets in the manner of an arcade; over these beams they run lengthwise a number of twigs; then suddenly transformed into slaters, they heap on all a pile of rushes, grass, and straw. At the first glance, these works seem very irregular; but this apparent disorder conceals an amount of art and design which we quickly discover on examination.

Under this hillock, which conceals their abode, and whose shape facilitates the running off of the rain, are found galleries which, communicating with one another, resemble very much the streets of a city. They terminate at the chief storerooms, of which some serve for provisions, and others for the eggs of the ants, and the little worms which the eggs bring forth.

As for provisions, our republicans are well off. They accommodate themselves to every kind of food. They may be seen running about with wondrous eagerness, one carrying a fruit kernel, another a dead fly. It is not allowed to these little travelers to go wherever they choose: there are some appointed to make expeditions of discovery. On their report, all turn out to make a general assault on some very ripe pear, or bit of sugar-cake, or pot of jam. They will go from the foot of a garden, even to the third story of a dwelling-house, to reach this pot. They look upon anything of this description as a perfect sugar quarry, as a new gold mine, which they have succeeded in discovering; but still, to go and return, the march must be regular, the whole population must assemble on the one road.

The way is often long and tortuous. But providence has supplied these travelers with a means of never wandering. Like the caterpillars, the ants leave traces wherever they pass. These traces are not perceptible to our eyes; they are known rather by their smell. It is acknowledged that the ants quickly recognize scent. If we run our finger several times across a wall, which ants pass up and down, we shall stop their progress quite short. The guiding line is broken; and we see them hesitating, retreating, turning right and left, until at length one, more daring than the rest, ventures to open a passage, and leads the way.

After having passed the summer in continual labor and flurry, the ants confine themselves within doors during the winter, enjoying peacefully the fruits of their toil. Yet there are good grounds for thinking that they do not eat much during the wintertime, and that they are rather buried in a torpid or dormant state, like so many other insects. Thus, their ardor to lay up provisions, tends less to secure them against the winter, than to supply them during the harvest with what is necessary for their little ones. These, from the moment of their issuing forth out of the egg, are nourished with a care which engages the whole nation. The care and protection of youth is justly regarded as a matter of state importance.

This is not the only lesson afforded us by the ants. The delicate structure of their organs, their untiring industry, their unwearied diligence, the political wisdom and wise economy of their republic, the tender care which they take of their little ones, and many other peculiarities, show forth resplendently before our eyes the wisdom of that great being, who is both their and our Creator.

Of all the works of God there is not one but is useful and worthy of admiration, however useless or harmful it may appear at first sight. Our trees have not a leaf, our meadows not a blade of grass, our flowers not a stamen that is useless; and even the flesh-worm has not been made in vain. God has been pleased to make known to us the usefulness of some of these creatures, that we may not doubt of the usefulness of the others, though that may lie hidden from us. Little ants! so despised, you can teach us this truth; and, if we profit by your lessons, we shall never quit one of your habitations without having made progress in wisdom.

II. *The bees.* — We have visited a republic; let us now enter and survey a monarchy; for, you perceive, we are launched into politics. With the bees one alone directs the whole nation. That bee is not only the people's queen, but she is, moreover, the people's mother. From this prerogative proceeds that extreme affection which all the bees have for her. You see her nearly always surrounded with a circle of bees, whose sole occupation is to render her little services. Some present her with honey; others pass their trunk lightly from time to time over her body, to remove anything that might soil her dress. When she walks, all those that are in her way range themselves in lines at a respectful distance from her.

The vast majority of the nation consists of workers. To them we are indebted for the construction of those beautiful combs, in which the very perfection of geometrical symmetry appears. They gather their materials from flowers: the wax is made from the pollen of stamens. It is with their trunk or antennae that they suck up the honey. What a subject for admiration! Present one of these trunks to any one you please, and he will say: "It is the leg of a fly; what good is it?" Nevertheless, this instrument is such that, with its aid, a bee can lay up more honey in a day than all the chemists in the world could gather in a year.

While one portion of the bees are thus engaged in gathering wax and honey to fill their storehouses, others are occupied with different labors. Some build cells with wax; others polish and perfect the work. These cover with a waxen lid the cells that contain the honey; as it must be preserved for the winter, this precaution is most necessary. Those give food to the little ones. All have their special employments.[238]

Those that go to the country are allowed nothing to eat; it is supposed that they will not forget themselves. Those employed about the cells have a very fatiguing labor. They pass and repass their mouth and feet, and the hinder extremity of their little body over all the work: they never cease their toil till everything is polished and perfect. As they require to eat from time to time, and yet must not cease their work, a few of their companions are always ready to give them something when they seek for it. They make known their wants by signs: the worker that is hungry lowers her trunk before the dispenser, and this means that she wishes for some food. The dispenser opens her bottle of honey, and pours out a few drops on the trunk of her sister. The little repast finished, the work is resumed, and the process continues as before.

But why all this activity? For whom is all this delicious nectar intended? Ah! it is for me, it is for the mouth that has so often allowed words of sin to escape it. My God, pardon my ingratitude!

III. *Silkworms.*—If bees furnish us with what is most exquisite in our nourishment, silkworms supply us with that which is most select in our raiment. Thus, in the order of nature, as in that of grace, God avails himself of the weakest instruments to accomplish the greatest things. Yes, silk, which for a long time was confined to the use of kings, and was sold with weights of gold, is prepared for us by a little insect that seems good for nothing but to be trampled under our feet.

The silkworm makes from a portion of its nourishment a thick and gummy liquor, which it reserves in a little long bag, hidden in the interior of its body. The creature has under its mouth a kind of plate, which consists of a skin pierced with many holes. By two orifices in this plate it exudes the liquor with which its bag is replenished. These little channels are like two distaffs, which continually supply the matter from which it makes its thread. A single worm will give as much as two thousand feet of silk.

Thus, an insect which we scarcely deign to recognize with a look, becomes a blessing for whole provinces, an important article of commerce, and a source of incalculable riches. Millions of men live by it alone. When it has fulfilled its task, and its life draws to a close, it wraps itself in the precious threads which it has spun for the public. They serve it as a funeral shroud, as a tomb: it is hidden, it is lost. Is it dead? No; it transforms itself there, and becomes a butterfly.

These two creatures are totally different. The first is wholly terrestrial, and crawls with difficulty; the second is agility itself, it no longer tarries on the earth, it disdains to touch any gross substance. The first has a repulsive appearance; the second is decked with a variety of colors. The one confines itself stupidly to a coarse description of food; the other flits from flower to flower, lives on honey and dew, continually varies its pleasures, enjoys the liberty of nature, and embellishes it besides, and decorates itself alone. What a graceful image of our resurrection! It is thus, O my God, that thou hast scattered on all sides, through the fields of nature, such rays of light as give us a relish for heavenly things, and enable us to understand the most sublime truths!

IV. *Reptiles and wild beasts.*—In the first part of the sixth day, God also made reptiles and wild beasts. We shall confine ourselves to a few general reflections concerning them. Applied to whatever appears a disorder in nature, they may not, in our eyes, always justify a providence: such justification is unnecessary. But they will show forth, with new splendor, the power and the wisdom of the Creator.

The world is a work of infinite power, wisdom, and love. It bears in flaming characters the stamp of its origin. After every creation God said: "It is good." That is, "it corresponds perfectly with my idea, and with the end which I have proposed to myself. The world is good, since it relates my glory; the world is good, since it teaches sinless man my existence, my power, my wisdom, my love for him; the world is good, since it corrects sinful man, prevents him from forgetting me, and, by recalling him to me, recalls him also to himself."

Thus, the end of the visible, like that of the invisible world, is the glory of God and the salvation of man. All the creatures, whose destiny we have hitherto made known, prove this truth eloquently. Others, whose use is less known to us, or which even seems injurious, or at least useless to us, speak the same language.

Since we have come to the reptiles, let us begin with the serpents. These animals, whose look terrifies and sting kills us, manifest, nevertheless, the power and the wisdom of God. 1) Serpents have a surprising amount of dexterity and agility; some of them are of an immense size and wonderful strength; 2) they deliver us from a multitude of animals and insects, whose excess would destroy the country; thereby, they maintain an equilibrium between various kinds of creatures; 3) a far more important advantage is this: they teach sinful man to dread the mighty and terrible God who created those thousands of animals, of which one alone would be sufficient to desolate a kingdom.

Let us add that the instinctive aversion, with which the thought of a serpent inspires us, reminds us of the fall of our race, which was wrought by the devil under the form of a serpent. Worms, lizards, snails, and other such creatures of a size more or less developed, of a figure more or less repulsive, of a manner of living more or less mysterious, have each a reason for their existence. This reason or end, though often concealed from our view, is, we are certain, the glory of God and the good of man. Let us speak particularly of the mole and the hedgehog.

In a commune of the canton of Zurich, there was question lately of choosing a mole-trap. An intelligent observer was anxious to convince his fellow citizens that, though it might be useful to prevent too great a multiplication of moles, still it would be imprudent to wage war against them to the last extremity, considering that the mole does not eat the roots of any plant, but nourishes itself principally with destructive insects. "A distinguished naturalist," he said, "examined carefully the stomachs of fifteen moles, collected in different localities; he did not find a single vestige of a plant or the root of a plant, but only the remains of white worms and earthworms. If, as is pretended, the mole eats vegetables, some of them should also be found, especially as they are digested with greater difficulty. Not content with this experiment, he enclosed some moles which he had procured with considerable difficulty in a case, full of clay, partly covered with fresh grass; he then placed in the case some white and earth worms also. He proved afterward that in nine days, two moles had consumed 341 white worms, 193 earthworms, 25 caterpillars, and 1 mouse, skin and bone, which had been put living into the case. He next gave them some raw meat, cut into little morsels, and mixed with vegetables. The moles ate the meat, and did not touch the vegetables. Then he gave them nothing but vegetables, and in twenty-four hours they all died of hunger. Another naturalist has calculated that two moles destroy 20,000 white worms in a year."

Let us now see another little animal, against which the dogs bark and growl, which they strangle when they can, which the laborer pursues and kills, and whose very name is used to denote a surly character, without doubt, on account of the thorns that bristle on its back, for it is naturally of a mild and inoffensive disposition: we mean the hedgehog. Like the mole, it deserves to be treated by cultivators with respect and consideration. While the mole destroys the worms, which it meets in subterranean passages, the hedgehog, a no less skillful hunter, waits for the hours of evening. From seven till nine o'clock, as day declines and the worms make their appearance on the surface of the soil, it turns out from under the bushes, and eats a great quantity of them. It nourishes itself almost exclusively with worms: these are its favorite dish.

The hedgehog is a hibernating animal. As soon as the cold weather sets in, it hollows out the earth in some furry ditch, makes a little cavern there, brings in a supply of dry leaves on its spikes, and arranges them round its covert, until it has a sufficiency to preserve it against the frosts. Does it gather a stock of provisions, as some fruit occasionally discovered near its den might lead one to suppose? The matter is very doubtful. What would be the use of provisions when it is certain that, according to the habits of marmots, it goes to sleep at the approach of winter, and never awakes until the beautiful days of spring?

From April till October the fields with us are divested of fruit. On what does the hedge-hog live during this period? It would require a large quantity of apples, as well as spacious storerooms, if it were to live on fruit alone. It is not five or six that would nourish it during seven months. The worms are evidently its chief article of consumption during this period. There remain October and November, we shall say, the time of gathering fruit, two months during which it might commit some ravages. Are we not aware that frosts frequently occur at this season; and that the chilly little animal anticipates them, and hibernates?

Its taste for fruit has consequently very little time to be indulged, while its predilection for worms has at least seven long months for exercise. This, then, is the marauder, which is so severely punished for a few apples seen near his abode; which, during four months, is asleep, during seven, eats worms, the plague of grain, and, during one, has only a very doubtful dessert indeed. This is the night-rover, who is tracked and pursued, when, on the contrary, we should watch over his safety, and regard him as a patron of agriculture. In the providential scale of creation, not a being is useless, not a species can be enfeebled or destroyed without some present or future evil resulting to humanity. Peace, then, to these innocent creatures!

There are wild beasts as well as reptiles. The design of God in filling the mountains and the forests with animals of every kind, of which we take no care, was to show us the extent of his providence, and his particular watchfulness over living beings, though hidden in solitudes and rocky fastnesses. Without houses, without meadows, without stores of provender, without any assistance on the part of man, these animals are better supplied with everything they require, swifter in the chase, stronger, better fed, more polished as regards their fur, more regular as regards their figure, than the greater number of those for which men are the purveyors.

Like serpents, wild and ravenous beasts serve a variety of purposes:

1. They show us the extent of providence.

2. They hold us in awe, teaching us to tremble before him who has created so many terrible animals, and whose hand alone retains them in lonely places.

3. They punish sinful man, who, by his first disobedience, merited that whatever had been submissive to him previously, should in future refuse to obey him. When man was perverted he was banished from the place where everything had been regulated in accordance with his innocence; and he found his place of exile suited to the fulfillment of the penance which had been imposed on him. This is one of those beautiful harmonies which we meet with at every step, in the physical as well as in the moral world.

4. These voracious animals are also useful to man, since they carry far from his dwelling and eat those carcasses which, lying exposed on the earth, would infect the air and engender diseases.[239]

5. By waging war they diminish the number of other animals, which, becoming too numerous, would destroy the fruit of our harvests or injure our domestic animals. The hand that restrains them stays them at the precise moment, when they have made a proper amount of carnage among the animals that are prejudicial to man. This amount is sufficient to prevent their doing mischief, but insufficient to prevent their propagation or interrupt the accomplishment of their providential mission.

6. By forming a cincture of terror around inhabited countries, they teach man that he is made to live in society, and that death awaits him if he should dare to break the sacred bonds which unite him to his brethren, and which form his strength and security.

7. They are the life, if not the wealth, of numerous savage tribes who eat their flesh and sell their fur. As, every year, providence sends into our European seas, myriads of fish, whose capture constitutes a very important branch of trade; so, every year, the

same providence crowds the immense forests of America with innumerable multitudes of cariboos, elks, martens, buffaloes, black and silvery foxes, etc., the hunting of which is to the inhabitants what agriculture and manufacture are to us.

If, from serpents and savage animals, we pass to insects, we find the same wisdom and the same harmonies. "What," says someone, "is the use of caterpillars and so many other unseemly insects? Could not the world go on without them?" The ignorant and the impious alone put such questions. The man, whose mind is illumined with the twofold light of science and faith, shrugs his shoulders when he hears them. No; all these things are anything but useless.

Destroy the worms and the caterpillars, and you take away the life of birds. Those birds which we sometimes eat, and which rejoice us with their songs, have no other milk during their infancy. From the depth of their cradles, they address their cry to the Lord, and he multiplies a nourishment suited to their delicate condition; it is for them that he scatters everywhere the caterpillars and the worms.

By an admirable coincidence, the birds do not come forth from their eggs until the caterpillars are in the fields, and the caterpillars disappear when the birds, grown strong, are able or willing to content themselves with another kind of nourishment. Before April, there are no caterpillars or broods; in August or September, both caterpillars and broods are all, or nearly all, gone. The earth is then covered with grain, and with refreshments of every other kind for the birds.

As long as the birds had a safe supply in the caterpillars, it was just that these should also have some safe supply for themselves. Therefore, they had free play on plants and herbs. They have their right, as well as we, to the verdure of the earth: their charter is drawn up in due form like ours, since it is precisely the same. When, then, we take it ill to see the caterpillars and other insects exercising their right, they can refer us to Genesis 1:29-30. With this title at hand, their counsel might summon us before any tribunal, and it would not be in our favor that an impartial judge should decide the contest.

The association of insects with man, in the permission to use the herbs and fruits of the earth, becomes occasionally inconvenient to us. We complain, and, in doing so, we are unjust, since they only exercise their right. We are blind, since we do not see, or we pretend not to see, their utility. We are selfish, since if these worms, these caterpillars, these flies, these ants, etc., were to gather us honey or spin us silk, though at the expense of a million other creatures, we should make much account of them; but because they slightly hurt a few plants that we use, we imagine ourselves authorized to exterminate them!

Moreover, we must remember well, that the evil of which we speak has been foreseen and ordained. Man does not require merely to live; he also requires to be instructed. His ingratitude is confounded when insects take away that which God has liberally displayed before his eyes. His pride is no less so when the Lord sets in motion the armies of the divine vengeance, and calls up against man the caterpillar, the locust, and the fly, instead of bears, tigers, and lions. To humble those men who believe themselves strong, rich, great, independent, what instruments does he employ? Worms or midges.

It is also very necessary that man should be continually reminded that the earth is a place of exile, and his life a period of trial. Whatever disturbs his amusements, whatever interrupts his enjoyments, whatever scatters clouds over his life, is a heavenly messenger that says to him: "Remember, there is no true happiness in this world." Oh, if he would understand this lesson which the very insects give him in their own manner, concupiscence should be extinguished or restrained within just bounds; and society should be in peace, for the heart of man would be in order!

It is, then, true that everything has its object and use in nature, inasmuch as "all things that God has made are good in their time."[240] Because our feeble reason cannot penetrate the motives of his works, does it belong to us to criticize his infinite wisdom, and to think of diminishing, extending, and modifying whatever we choose in the order of nature? Reason teaches us that we should judge of the uncertain by the certain. Now, everything that we discover in the study of creation reveals the existence of an intelligence which is infinite, and which disposes of all things in number, weight, and measure. It only remains, therefore, for us to adore, not to criticize; and this distinction we plainly do not understand.

V. *Harmonies of the world.* — All things are related to one another in the visible as well as in the invisible world. Take away an insect, a blade of grass, an atom, and you break the chain of being, you overthrow the general equilibrium, you disturb the universal harmony. For this insect, this blade of grass, this atom, like the ideas of which they are the expression, are connected with other ideas or other atoms, and through these, with whatever is most considerable or important in the whole creation. If one were to say that they were related with nothing, what, then, would be the meaning of their existence?

Thus, these little productions of nature, that shortsighted men judge useless, are not particles of dust on the wheels of the mighty machine of the world; they are the smaller wheelwork, fitted into the greater. There is nothing isolated. Every being has its peculiar action, whose sphere is determined by the rank which it holds in the universe. A mite has not very much power, but it joins with other creatures, whose action reaches to the greatest distance. Thus, the limits are extended more and more; and this marvelous progression rises, by degrees, from the sphere of the mite to that of the angel.

All parts of the universe act in concert with one another. Animals depend on vegetables, vegetables on minerals, minerals on the earth, the earth on the sun, and so on; the balance of the universe is held in the hand of the Ancient of Days.[241]

Species and individuals have a relation to the greatness and solidity of the earth. The greatness and solidity of the earth have a relation to the place which it occupies in the universe. The physical corresponds with the moral order. Both have for their end the happiness of intelligent beings. From these relations, which exist between all parts of creation, and in virtue of which all parts tend to one common end, results the harmony of the universe.

All creatures rely and call on one another. Between the highest and the lowest, the angel and the mite, the number of intermediate creatures is almost infinite. The sum of all these degrees forms the universal chain, the magnificent chain, which binds all beings, embraces all worlds, unites all spheres. There is only one being outside this chain: he who made it.

A thick cloud hides the most beautiful portions of this chain from our eyes; we can only see some scattered links of it, very indifferently put together in the natural order. However, as much of it as is visible we behold winding its serpentine course over the earth, down into the mines, through the sea, up into the air, and away into the ethereal realms, where we can no longer distinguish it, except by some odd fiery spark, cast here and there. That which sparkles before our eyes inflames our heart, and that which escapes our looks, humbles our reason: visible or invisible, it instructs and improves us. This is the very purpose for which God made it.

VI. *The world is a book.* — As the receptacle of an author's thoughts, every book is made to be read. The world, which is God's book, is the expression of his thoughts. God has only expressed his thoughts in order to make himself known, consequently loved and served; for the manifestation of his thoughts reveals an infinite power, an infinite wisdom, an infinite love. The visible world, then, is only the transparent envelope of the invisible. Every creature is like a letter, or a word, in God's great book. Now a book, through the characters which compose it, does not show the thoughts of an author; it only gives signs for those thoughts. If they are not known, you cannot understand what the author means. In the same manner, if we are content with looking on the great book of the universe, as animals look on it with eyes of flesh; if we rest on the signs and characters without endeavoring to comprehend their meaning, we shall not correspond with the designs of God, we shall be guilty before him.

Pagans do not read the Bible. Nevertheless, says the apostle St. Paul, they are inexcusable, and they shall be condemned for having held the truth captive, closing their eyes against the light.[242] "But how," asks St. Chrysostom, "is the truth manifested to their eyes? What prophet, what evangelist, what doctor supplies the place of a Bible? None of these," he answers, "but God's book, the universe."[243]

The heavens relate his existence and his infinite power; the earth, his goodness; the sea, his terrible wrath; the smallest creature, his loving tenderness. The bees preach obedience and charity to us; the sheep, meekness and detachment; the birds, purity; the seasons, death; the insects that die in order to be born again new creatures, full of elegance and beauty, our resurrection. There is not a virtue, not a truth, not a duty, but has its chapter in the great book of the universe; and this book is intelligible to all.

Happy is he who chooses to read it! New harmonies continually meet his eye, and delight his heart. The work becomes a temple to him; everywhere he beholds God present. At every moment he feels himself pressed by this presence, now majestic, now paternal, now holy, now dreadful, now consoling. God is near, God is afar off, God is here, God is there. He is above, he is below, he is around. See the flower—he is there; see the star—he is there. He is in the fire and in the water, in the zephyr and in the tempest, in the light and in the darkness, in the atom and in the sun. He is around me in the warmth which vivifies me, and within me in that air which supports my life.

He hears all things: the sublime canticles of the seraph, and the joyous songs of the lark, and the buzzing of the bee, and the roaring of the lion, and the murmuring of the stream, and the bellowing of the ocean, and the creeping of the ant, and the rustling of the leaf.

He sees all things: from the mighty sun which enlightens the universe, down to the little insect, which is hidden beneath the leaves of grass or under the bark of the tree, and the fishes that are lost in the depths of the ocean. He sees all animals, with the movements of their muscles, and the circulation of their blood. He sees the thoughts of my mind, the beatings of my heart. He knows the wants of the little bird that opens its bill to ask for food. He also knows my desires. He feeds, warms, clothes, protects all creatures that breathe. He is my Father: Can he, then, forget me?

The man who reflects on these things is just and good; mindful of the omnipresence of God, his heart is pure, his hand generous, his life holy, his peace uniform, his countenance serene, his death tranquil, his eternity glorious. Happy is he who knows how to read thus the great book of the universe!

PRAYER

O my God! who art all love, I thank thee for having created this magnificent universe for me: I adore thee equally in that which I do, and in that which I do not comprehend; for, in all things, thou art equally wise, powerful, and good; grant me the grace to read, with eyes of faith, the great book of the universe!

I am resolved to love God above all things, and my neighbor as myself for the love of God; and, in testimony of this love, I will often say: "God is here!"

Lesson 12: Creation: The Sixth Day (Continued)

God then said: "Let us make man to our image and likeness, and let him have dominion over the fishes of the sea, and the fowls of the air, and the beasts, and the whole earth, and every creeping creature that moveth upon the earth. And God created man to his own image, the image of God."[244]

"And the Lord God formed man of the slime of the earth, and breathed into his face the breath of life, and man became a living soul."[245]

The great book of the universe is written; but, what is the use of a book if there is no one to read it? What is the use of a magnificent picture if there is no one to admire it? Now, there is neither reader nor admirer in existence. The angels have no need of this book or this picture. They know the author in himself; they read his thoughts in his divine essence; they behold him face to face. In regard to animals and plants, this grand spectacle is as if it were not: they have no intelligence. Again, then, what is the use of this book? What is the use of this picture?

And then, for what purpose are all these creatures and all these magnificent harmonies? The globes, scattered through space, roll on with majesty; but what is the object of their motion? The sun enlightens the earth; but the earth is blind, and does not require light. The heat, the rain, the dew, cause the seeds to germinate, and cover the plains with harvests and fruits; but these are lost riches: there is no person to gather or consume them. The earth nourishes an innumerable host of animals; but these animals are good for nothing, in the absence of a master, who should turn to account their useful qualities, and concentrate, so to speak, their services.

The horse and the ox are endowed with strength, capable of drawing or carrying the heaviest burdens: but this strength is useless. The sheep sinks under the weight of its wool: but there is no person to accept its present. The cow and the goat are inconvenienced with the abundance of their milk; but this abundance is superfluous. The earth contains stones suitable for building houses, and metals suitable for fabricating all kinds of things; but there is no guest to be lodged; there are no workmen to employ these materials. The surface of the earth is a magnificent garden; but it is not seen. All nature is a gorgeous spectacle: but no one is aware of it. A creature, then, is wanting, without whose presence all others would be valueless.

What more shall we say? The world is like a magnificent palace, adorned with everything calculated to render it an agreeable residence. Like so many lustres, millions of stars, suspended from the dome of heaven, shine both day and night. The whole earth is covered with a rich green carpet, enameled with flowers of every description; the air is balmy with the most agreeable perfumes; the trees are laden with fruit; the streams are murmuring; the fishes are sporting in the water; the birds, like so many musicians, make the hills and the valleys ring with their sweet concerts; the beasts of the field await in respectful silence the master who will command them: all is ready.

"This is the manner," says St. John Chrysostom, "in which, when an emperor is about to enter a city, all persons attached to his service anticipate him, in order that on his arrival everything may be prepared for his reception."[246] But for what king has God destined this glorious kingdom? Who shall be the reader of this magnificent book? Who shall be the admirer of this gorgeous masterpiece?

Let us recollect ourselves and lend an ear.

After casting a last look over his work, and seeing that it is all good, God enters into himself, deliberates with himself, consults with himself. Then, suddenly rising from this mysterious council, he says: "Let us make!!!"

Explanation of the words: "Let us make man." — What new expression is this? Who is, then, the extraordinary being about to appear, for whom it is necessary that the Creator should consult and deliberate within himself beforehand?

It was not in this manner that the heavens and the earth were created: one word drew them forth from nothingness. "Let them be"; and they were. A command is proper for slaves; but, when a master is concerned, God changes his language. To recommend the king of the world to all his subjects, God begins to honor him by treating him almost as an equal.

"Let us make!!!" But to whom does God speak? To someone who acts like himself; to another self; to the Son, by whom all things have been made; to the Holy Ghost, omnipotent, co-equal and co-eternal with the Father and the Son, and who, moving over the waters, vivified chaos, as the bird vivifies its nest: the Trinity begins to be declared.

"Let us make!!!" And what will be made? An ordinary angel? No. A seraph? No. A spectator will be made for the grand scene that has been painted; a reader for the magnificent book that has been written; a king and a high priest for the universe! Would you desire to know his name? He is called man!!!

Yes, this masterpiece from the hands of the Almighty, this being whom all nature invites with eagerness, and awaits with respect, is man, is you, is I. "Let us make man to our own image and likeness!!!"[247]

Let us fall on our knees, and while the whole creation honors us, adore in silence the God who has made us so great. Let a noble pride abase our heart; let us recognize our dignity, and let us fear to degrade, by unworthy acts, the august image, which the divine hand has engraven on our forehead and in our heart.

Man is then the king of the world, the most noble of visible creatures. Let us pause a moment to consider him.

Man in his body. — Everything in man, even that which is exterior, marks his superiority over all other living beings. While animals, bent toward the earth, are obliged to look toward it alone, man, on the contrary, holds himself erect; his attitude is one of authority. His head, clothed with beautiful hair, presents a majestic front, an open brow on which are traced the characters of his dignity; a divine fire animates his features; his eyes look up to heaven, whence he has come, and to which he is destined, and he casts them around on nature, which has been made for him. His ears, whose extreme delicacy permits him to seize the slightest whispered sound; his mouth, upon which rests an amiable smile, and is, moreover, the organ of speech; his hands, priceless instruments, masterpieces of art; his chest, broad and gracefully rounded; the figure of his body, in general tall and well defined; his legs, like beautiful pillars, so admirably adapted to the edifice which they have to support; his feet, a narrow base, but only more wonderful in regard to their solidity and motion; finally, his majestic carriage, his bold and steady step, all combine to announce his dignity and nobility.

Admire now how wonderfully the position and structure of each of his senses correspond with the object for which it was intended.

The eyes, as sentinels, occupy the most elevated place. Thence, discovering objects at a distance, and in due time they warn the soul of what it should do. A lofty place befits the ears, in order to receive sounds, which naturally ascend. The nostrils ought to be in the same situation, because odors also ascend, and because they require to be near the mouth, that they may assist us to judge of the nature of our food and drink. The taste, which makes known to us the qualities of what we partake of, resides in that portion of the mouth through which food must pass. As for the touch, it is spread over the whole body, in order that we may not be attacked by heat or cold, or receive any other impression, without being immediately made aware of what has happened to us.

Remark also that the senses are arranged according to the order of their dignity and importance. The eyes occupy the highest rank, because sight is the most noble and useful of all the senses. Then come the ears; and so of the rest.

As to their structure, who but a God infinitely wise could form our senses so artistically? To speak only of the sight: he has surrounded the eyes with thin coverings, transparent in front, that we may see through them, and sufficiently strong in their texture to keep the eyes in the right position. The eyeballs move freely in their sockets, to avoid easily what might be hurtful to them, and, at the same time, to cast their glances whithersoever they list. The eyelids which cover the eyes are soft and polished under the surface, so as not to incommode the action of the eyes. Whether the fear of accident obliges us to close the eyelids, or that we simply desire to open them, the eyelids are made so as to be always ready, and one or other of these movements is instantaneous. The lashes are a kind of pallisade, defending the eyes from whatever could hurt them when they are open; and, by closely covering them, enable them to repose tranquilly when sweet sleep lulls them to rest, and hinders their use to us. Our eyes have, moreover, the advantage of being concealed under and defended by prominences; for, on one side, to arrest the sweat which flows from the head and forehead, they have the eyebrows, and on the other, to guard them from below, the cheeks.

Who can tell the wonders of which the eye is the instrument? Millions of objects, mountains, rivers, forests, houses, whole cities, kingdoms of many miles in extent, are painted at the same time, and without any confusion, on a little mirror, not a line in diameter. A thing more astonishing still is that all these objects are painted in an inverted manner on our eye, and yet we see them in their natural position!

We can examine thus the structure of all our senses, and we shall discover in each the profound wisdom of its inventor. If we enter next into the interior of the human body, the very great number of its parts, their surprising variety, their delicate formation, their marvelous harmony, the infinite skillfulness of their arrangement, will cast us into such raptures of astonishment that we shall only recover ourselves to lament that we cannot sufficiently admire so many wonders.[248]

The bones, by their solidity and connection, form the skeleton of the edifice; the ligaments unite the parts together, and the muscles, like so many springs, set them in play; the nerves, by winding themselves through the various parts, establish a close communication between; and all the arteries and veins, like gentle streams, carry life and refreshment everywhere. Placed in the center, the heart is the principal agent, destined to effect the motion of the blood, as well as to dispense it; the lungs are important instruments for inhaling air, an important element of life, and for expelling noxious elements; the stomach and the various intestines are warehouses and laboratories, in which are prepared the materials that are necessary for the work of daily repair; the brain, which is like an apartment for the soul, is spacious, and furnished in a manner suitable to the dignity of the master who occupies it; the senses, faithful and obedient servants, warn their master of whatever it is fitting he should know, and contribute both to his pleasures and his wants.

At the sight of so many wonders we must exclaim, with a celebrated physician of antiquity, Galen: "O thou, who has formed us! I believe that in describing the human body I sing a hymn to thy glory. I honor thee more by disclosing the beauty of thy works than by filling temples with the perfumes of the sweetest incense. True piety consists in knowing myself; then, in teaching others, how great are thy goodness, thy wisdom, and thy power. Thy goodness appears in the equal distribution of thy presents, giving to every man the organs that are necessary for him; thy wisdom is seen in the excellence of thy gifts; thy power is made manifest in the execution of thy designs."[249]

To the eyes of reason, then, how noble is our body, and, to the eyes of faith, how venerable! Purified in the waters of baptism, consecrated many times by the holy unction and a participation in the divine flesh and blood, the living temple of the Holy Ghost, a member of the man-God, destined for immortal glory, a vessel of honor—Oh! may we never make it a vessel of opprobrium!

Man in his soul. — After having formed man's body from the slime of the earth, God breathed into his face the breath of life, and man became living and animated: this means that God united to a material body a spiritual soul. Our soul is then a breath which has come forth from the mouth and heart of God; it is that free, spiritual, immortal principle, which thinks within us, which loves, which desires, which reasons, and which essentially distinguishes us from all other living creatures.

To endeavor to prove that we have a soul would be to insult the universal belief of the human race. Indignation and contempt are the only answers worthy the absurdities of materialism. "I can pardon many things," said Napoleon, "but I hold the atheist and materialist in abhorrence. How can you expect that I should have anything in common with a man who does not believe in the existence of the soul; who believes that he is a heap of mire, and who desires that I should be like himself, a heap of mire, too?"[250]

But how shall we describe the excellence of the human soul? I have seen the beauties of the earth; I have admired the magnificence of the heavens; I have contemplated the masterpieces of art: Have I seen the beauty of a soul? No. The soul is something so noble, so perfect, so exalted above all corporeal substances, that it is as difficult for me to form an idea of the beauty and perfection of a spirit, as for a blind man, who has never seen the light, to picture to himself the brilliancy or the exquisite variety of colors. Whilst my body, the masterpiece of creation, grows old and changes, my soul, ever entire in its substance, remains the same; it has no acquaintance with the ravages of disease or the wrinkles of old age. Whilst my body, drawn down by its weight to the earth, lives only in the present, my soul embraces every period of existence.

It lives in the past, ascends to the origin of time, and, conversing with generations that are buried in the dust, resuscitates them from the tomb. It lives in the present, and, without quitting itself, travels through the universe. In the twinkling of an eye it passes from pole to pole, from the East to the West; visits nations, and observes their manners, customs, and laws; penetrates the secrets of nature, and discovers the properties of plants and minerals; descends into the bowels of the earth to explore their structure, and to extract therefrom the riches that lie concealed therein; then, as if for mere amusement, mounts to the heavens to calculate the extent of the firmament and the dimensions of the stars. It lives in the future, whose secrets it penetrates by sound reasonings and conjectures; and this is not the least part of its glory.

From the limits of this mighty universe, it sweeps away beyond suns and worlds, and mounts even to the throne of that being, who is the source of all other beings; and, though he dwells in light inaccessible, it discovers him by its intellect, and unites itself to him by love. Sublime union! which, deifying it, leaves far beneath it the alliances of princes and monarchs! After these things, will you still ask me what is the value of my soul!? I address the same question to the learned and the wise, to heaven and earth, and for an answer they weary themselves in eloquent words, or they confine themselves to a silence still more eloquent. I speak to God himself; and this great God, this Almighty being, taking me by the hand, leads me to the summit of a mountain, and there, drawing aside a curtain stained with blood, shows me his only and co-eternal Son dead on a cross, and says to me: "Behold the price of thy soul!" *Anima tanti vales!* O my soul, so much art thou worth! Full of this noble thought, let us enter calmly into a few details on the perfection of our soul.

1. *Our soul is spiritual.* — That is, it has neither the least length, nor depth, nor breadth; it has no figure; it cannot be seen by our eyes, or touched by our hands, nor apprehended by any of our senses. That our soul is spiritual is easily proved. As a matter of fact, the operations of our soul are recollection, thought, and will. Nothing can be more spiritual than these three operations. Now, if our soul were not spiritual, neither would its operations be spiritual; hence recollection, thought, and will would be material things. We might then see them, touch them, divide them, weigh them. We could then say, for example, a pint of ideas, a yard of desires, a hundred-weight of recollections — a red thought, a white thought, a blue thought; a round wish, an oval wish, a triangular reminiscence.

Now, all the world would ridicule him who should utter such language. Why so? Because every one feels that we cannot attribute material qualities to recollection, thought, or will.

And, therefore, recollection, thought, and will are not material things. The soul, which is their principle, is not material either; for the modifications of any being are always of the same nature as that being itself; or, rather, they are only that being itself modified in such or such a manner. Thus, recollection denotes our soul remembering or calling anything to mind; thought, our soul thinking; will, our soul willing or desiring anything.

The soul of man is, therefore, spiritual, like God, who created it to his image.

2. *Our soul is free.*—This means that it can, according to its liking, do what it pleases, act or not act, decide in such or such a manner. In this respect it differs from all other creatures that surround it.

The sun, for example, is not free to rise or not rise every morning, to travel one way instead of another, to advance or recede as it chooses. It is compelled to do everything that it does. On this account it does regularly and invariably the same thing. Nor are animals free. Hence, they always show the same habits, the same tastes, the same operations. Now, if the animals were free; if they had within themselves the principle and rule of their conduct, as we have within us the principle and rule of our conduct: they would vary matters, as we do; they would every day invent, reform, and perfect; and they would, like us, do a hundred important and rational things.

The swallows today, for example, would no longer build such nests as their progenitors used to build a hundred years ago. The Chinese swallows would not build in the same style as the French. Even in France, the swallows of the capital would be careful not to lodge or live like their provincial friends. The Parisian swallows should regulate the fashions for all the rest; in a short time this very fashion should be ridiculed, as fit only for Goths, when it would come into their heads to establish another. This is the manner in which affairs are conducted among ourselves. Why not, also, among the swallows? The reason is because they obey a superior immutable will, which constrains them always and everywhere to execute its commands.

It is quite otherwise with our soul. The soul acts or does not act, it wishes or it does not wish; while doing one thing it perceives perfectly well that it might do another instead. If the action is good, the soul experiences joy; if bad, remorse: for it feels that it is free not to act improperly. There is no person among us unacquainted with this sentiment of pleasure or pain, which follows the commission of a good or a bad action. But this sentiment should not be experienced by us if we had not been free to act as we choose: we could not then merit either recompense or chastisement.

What would you say, for example, of a man who should break his clock because it went rather fast or slow? You would say: "His conduct is absurd, he is a fool." Yet no one says of a father that his conduct is absurd, that he is a fool, when he corrects his child for doing wrong. We might say it, indeed, if we were not free; for then all things would be equal, since all things would be compulsory. In this supposition it would be absurd and unjust to punish vice and reward virtue; or, rather, there would be neither good nor evil, neither vice nor virtue: we should move as mere machines. Accordingly, God would be unjust to reward some and to punish others; but, if God were unjust, he would no longer be God, he would no longer be anything: the world would be an effect without a cause. Such is the abyss into which we fall, after a few steps, if we deny the free will of the soul.

3. *Our soul is immortal.*—This means that our soul will never die; that it is even impossible it should die. The body dies when the parts that compose it are separated: when the head, the feet, the arms, the heart, are scattered in different directions. But our soul has no parts: it has no head, no feet, no arms, no heart; these parts cannot then be separated from it; it cannot, therefore, perish.

One thing alone could annihilate it, namely, the omnipotent will of him who created it. Well, so far is God from wishing to destroy our soul, that he declares, on the contrary, in express terms, he wishes to make it live forever, as long as himself, during all eternity. The wicked, he says, shall go into everlasting punishment, but the just, on the contrary, into life everlasting.[251]

To this voice from heaven is joined that of all the nations on the earth, proclaiming the dogma, at once terrible and consoling, of the immortality of the soul. "This is what nature cries out," says St. Augustine; "this is what is impressed on our heart by the Creator; this is what all men know, from the infant school to the throne of Solomon; this is what shepherds sing in the plains, what pastors teach in the holy place, what the human race declares throughout the universe."

You see that to deny the immortality of the soul is to give the lie to God, to reason, to mankind. It is, moreover, to accept the following absurdities: 1) that God has been merely sporting with us in giving us an invincible desire of immortality; 2) that heretofore all the nations of the world have been in error, except a few libertines, who alone have had common sense; and 3) that the lot of the assassin will be the same as that of the innocent victim—that St. Paul and Nero, the saints who have lived in the practice of every virtue, and been the benefactors of humanity, and the wicked, who have sullied themselves with every description of crime and been the scourges of humanity, must be treated in the same manner. Is not the maintenance of such doctrines the encouragement of every kind of iniquity? Can there be a surer means to make the world a haunt of brigands and a den of ferocious beasts? These consequences are frightful; therefore, the principles that occasion them are false and abominable.

Man's resemblance with God.—Before creating man, God meditated within himself, and said: "Let us make man to our own image and likeness."[252] As an artist considers and studies the person whose portrait he desires to produce on canvas, so God, after considering and studying himself, expresses his own divine features on man. How admirable is the resemblance between the copy and the original! The image of God is engraven on our soul; in it we resemble him.[253]

God is one in nature; our soul is one in nature. In God there are three distinct Persons; in our soul there are three distinct faculties: the memory, the understanding, and the will. God is a pure Spirit; our soul is a pure spirit. God is eternal; our soul is immortal; nothing bears a closer resemblance to eternity than immortality. God is free; our soul is free. God knows the past, the present, and the future; our soul remembers the past, is acquainted with the present, and conjectures the future. God is present everywhere; our soul is present in all parts of our body—this wondrous microcosm—and, in the twinkling of an eye, makes a tour round the world. God is just, true, holy, good, merciful; such was the soul of Adam before his fall, and such is also ours after his fall, for it has the idea and sentiment of justice, truth, sanctity, goodness, and mercy.

God is infinite; our soul is infinite in its desires. Nothing finite can satisfy it. All that is limited wearies, straitens, disgusts it. The uneasiness and misery which the soul experiences, render testimony to its dignity; for there is a greatness in being miserable and inconsolable, when one is deprived of an infinite good. God is the most perfect of all beings; man is the most perfect of all visible beings. God depends on no one; man depends on no one but God. God is the sovereign master of heaven and earth; man is king over everything around him. All things belong to God; all earthly things are for man, and man for God.

How great, then, are we, since we are formed on the model of God himself!

PRAYER

O my God! who art all love, I thank thee for creating me to thine own image and likeness; never permit that I should disfigure thine image by sin.

I am resolved to love God above all things, and my neighbor as myself for the love of God; and, in testimony of this love, I will make the sign of the cross with much respect.

Lesson 13: Creation: The Sixth Day (Continued)

Man created as king of the universe. — Man was created to be king. His titles to royalty are expressed in the very words of his creation. God says, "Let us make man to our image and likeness, that he may rule over the fishes of the sea, the birds of the air, the beasts, the whole earth, and all the reptiles that move under heaven." Never was power more extensive; never was scepter more lawfully borne.

Before his rebellion, Adam exercised his authority peacefully over all nature. The animals were not in any way a source of terror to him; nor was he in any manner a terror to them. We see them all assembled familiarly together, like servants in the house of their master, whose orders they are ever ready to execute. Witness the serpent's conversation with Eve.[254] It is sin that, disturbing this admirable order, has changed the dominion of man. Nevertheless, man is not so completely divested of his primitive sway as not to retain some honorable vestiges of it.

First, while punishing his infidelity, and condemning him to earn his bread in the sweat of his brow, God was pleased to lighten and sweeten his painful labors. Man is still allowed the full exercise of his power over the domestic animals. He speaks, and his numerous servants hasten to obey him. The sheep surrenders its fleece to him, and the silkworm prepares a rich robe for him. The bee supplies him with honey; the dog keeps sentry at his door; the ox cultivates his land; the horse carries his burdens, as well as himself whithersoever he pleases.

As for the wild animals, it is his business to recover, at least in part, by strength or by skill, that dominion which, in the state of innocence, he exercised over them by mildness. He draws them, into his snares; captures, kills them with his domestic animals. When he requires some game for his repast he sends his dog, and, with very little trouble on his own part, receives what he desires. The most enormous and even ferocious animals, such as the elephant, the whale, the tiger, and the lion, become his tributaries.

He commands not only the animals, but all inanimate creatures; and no creature commands him. He avails himself of the services of all; but none presume to tax his service. He makes use of the stars to regulate his labors, and to direct his course in the midst of the ocean or the desert. At his voice, the oaks descend from the summits of the hills; stones, iron, slate, gold, and silver spring forth from the bosom of the earth, to raise or to embellish his habitation. The hemp and the flax strip themselves that their fibres may furnish him with garments. The ductile metal is molded in his hands; the hardest marble yields to the force of his fingers. The rocks fly in splinters, and open to him a passage; the rivers turn aside from their beds, to irrigate his fields, and work his mills.

If he should be attacked, the whole creation comes to his assistance: wood and stone erect barriers against his enemies. Niter, charcoal, and sulphur unite with iron to place him beyond the reach of insult. If it happens that a superior power overcomes his skill and precautions; if an army of flies, for example, is sometimes stronger than he, it is because he himself has a master, of whom he must be mindful.

Does he wish to change his climate; to pass beyond the seas, and carry thither the supplies of his produce, or bring back the commodities of other countries which he has selected? The winds and the waves lend him their wings for this purpose to convey him round the globe. His vessels place at his feet the rarities of the four quarters of the earth. His desires are fulfilled from one end of the world to the other. He holds communication with the most distant regions, whenever he chooses, without quitting his home. At one time, with the quickness of thought, electricity transmits his desires beyond the sea — nay, flashes round the globe many times in a minute — at another a bird gives him its feather, a plant its bark, and a mineral its color: with these, he depicts his thoughts on paper. The writing departs, and, without any trouble to him, passes by millions of men, leaps over mountains, sweeps across oceans, and manifests his wishes to persons who are eight or ten thousand miles distant from him. While living, he imparts information to the whole world; and, when dead, transmits it to the most remote posterity.

He acts in the world like the omnipotent Wisdom that created it. With a stroke of his brush he changes a coarse canvass into a scene of enchanting perspective. The chisel and the graver at hand, he animates the marble, and makes the bronze breathe. With the help of a microscope, which he has invented, he discovers new worlds in invisible atoms; then, exchanging his microscope for a telescope, he scans the heavens, and contemplates the moon and the brilliant army of stars. Returning into his house, he discovers the laws of the celestial bodies, traces their orbits, measures the earth, and weighs the sun.

It is then true that all nature is in the hands of man like a toy in the hands of a child. Notwithstanding his fall, he still preserves a considerable portion of the power that was given him in those sublime words: "Let him rule over the fishes, and the animals, and the whole earth."

Man is not a constitutional king. His royalty in regard to the world is not an empty honor; it is real. He commands, and he enjoys. We have seen that he commands; we shall see now that he enjoys. Placed in the body, as in a palace, his soul has five faithful ministers, who bring it in turn, sometimes together, the homage of the universe. These ministers bear the names of sight, hearing, smell, taste, and touch. By their means man is enabled to enjoy all creatures without exception.

Usufructuary of the universe. — From the firmament, where the most distant stars have a dwelling, down to the surface of the earth, all that is visible lies within the domain of the eye; the soul is indebted to this beautiful organ for the enjoyment of so many beauties continually presented to it. All sounds, which may be varied in so many wondrous ways, are within the domain of the ear: thanks to it, no melody or harmony may escape the enjoyment of the soul. All scents belong to the domain of smell: hence, no perfume may escape the enjoyment of the soul. All savors belong to the domain of taste: consequently, no deliciousness must escape the enjoyment of the soul. Finally, the domain of touch shall equally contribute to give pleasure to the soul.

Thus, the whole world is reduced to the service of man; and, by this service to unity. The whole material creation is comprised in the extent of those sensations, whose organs are found in the human body, and their term in the soul. Do you imagine that, in order to enjoy his immense domain, man is obliged to make painful efforts? Not at all; this enjoyment costs him nothing, and may be had at any moment. Still this is not the most wonderful arrangement of the divine Wisdom. It has been pleased that all those creatures, such as animals and plants, which man holds continually under his hand, should have a general and necessary bond with all other creatures in the universe. Thus it has appointed that the least blade of grass should have need of the earth, the air, the dew, the wind, the rain, the light, the warmth of the day, the coolness of the night, the influence of the seasons: in a word, of all things else.

The vegetable creation has a close relation with the animal. In their turn, animals of every kind, namely, those that live in the water, on the earth, and in the air, collect around them an infinity of things, which seem to escape man and to render him no immediate service. Afterward, these creatures, the inhabitants of water, earth, and air, coming themselves to man as their master, place at his disposal every portion of the universe. It is thus that he enjoys whatever he desires without an effort.

A familiar example will place the matter more clearly before you, and show you how every man, even the poorest, is a king, who enjoys the whole universe. See this poor child, as he eats the piece of bread which you have given him; despise him not; he is a young king who unconsciously places a tax on all creatures, on all the conditions of society, nay, even on God himself.

1. This morsel of bread supposes flour. The flour supposes a baker, who kneaded it; water, which moistened it; an oven, which baked it; fuel, which warmed the oven; a mill, which ground the wheat; stone, iron, and wood for the construction of the mill; steam, winds, currents, or animals, to turn the wheels of the mill; men with a knowledge of mathematics and mechanics, to build the mill; and workers, to manage the mill. The flour supposes also bags to carry it; the bags, webs; the webs, weavers; the weavers, yarn; the yarn, spinners; the spinners, tow; the tow, hemp.

2. This morsel of bread supposes wheat. The wheat supposes a laborer, who sowed it; a plough, with oxen or horses, that prepared the ground; soil, that received the seed; sunshine, that warmed it; rain, that fertilized it. The rain supposes clouds; the clouds, seas and rivers, from which they were evaporated; the rivers, mountains in which they rose, and plains through which they flowed. The wheat also supposes the four seasons: autumn, in which it is sown; winter, in which the earth gathers strength to nourish it; spring, in which it grows; and summer, in which it ripens.

3. This morsel of bread supposes a harvest-man, who reaps, thrashes, and winnows the wheat. These processes suppose sickles, flails, and fans. The sickles suppose miners, who draw metal from the bowels of the earth; forgers, who cast it; ironmongers, who dress it. The flails suppose wood; the wood, foresters who hew it, and turners who shape it. The fans suppose bushes—osier, for example—and basket-makers, who manufacture them.

The baker, the miller, the laborer, the harvest-man, all the workmen who prepare the utensils necessary for agriculture, have need of clothes, hats, and shoes. These different things suppose in their turn tailors, hatters, and shoemakers, as well as flocks and shepherds. Each state of life here mentioned supposes others, up to the highest and down to the lowest in society. Society supposes a power, which makes laws for the protection of property. The execution of these laws supposes magistrates, police, and jails. The laws suppose knowledge; knowledge, study; study, colleges, professors, and books. We have not yet told all. This morsel of bread supposes the protection of the laborer, not only against domestic, but also against foreign enemies. This supposes fortifications, armies, guns, and that multitude of arts and professions which war brings in its train.

4. This crumb of bread supposes not only the grain of wheat which formed it, but also the grain that gave birth to the grain which formed it; and so on, back to the first of these grains of wheat. This first grain supposes a God infinitely powerful, who created it—infinitely wise, who made it grow—and infinitely good, who gave it to us.

So you see, heaven, earth, water, fire, men, and God himself work in concert for the production of a piece of bread. The man who eats it enjoys therefore, by the very fact, the whole universe. Unlike the animals, he enjoys the universe with intelligence, and every moment of the day and night, from the first moment of his existence till his last breath. For, day and night, heaven, earth, water, fire, men, and even God, labor to prepare not only a piece of bread, but all that is necessary for our nourishment and clothing. Have we ever thought of these things? Judge hence how full of egotism, and how great a monster is the man who lives in this world only for himself.

High priest of the universe. — "How great," exclaims a saint of the first ages, "is the ingratitude of man! While I languish in sloth, all creatures labor for me. The sun and the moon are always on the march, to scatter everywhere their precious light and heat. While I render myself guilty of some sin, abusing my mind to think on evil, my heart to desire it, and my body to commit it, the earth is exhausted in preparing bread for my nourishment. The bees fly by brooks, and valleys, and meadows, to gather sweet honey for my tongue, which pronounces so many unjust and unbecoming words. The sheep divest themselves of their fleece to supply me with garments, in which I so often indulge my vanity.

"The grapes await impatiently the heats of summer, in order to ripen and please my taste, and rejoice my heart, which so often dishonors him from whom it holds its existence. The fountains and the rivers flow night and day, to water the fields and make a thousand beautiful flowers spring up under my feet, which so often walk in the ways of iniquity. The birds endeavor by their melodious songs to charm my ears, which so often take a guilty pleasure in lying and impure discourses. All the creatures of the universe exhaust themselves in satisfying my wants and my pleasures; and I nearly always abuse creatures, and scarcely ever think of thanking him, who, by their ministry, lavishes so many benefits on me!"[255]

All creatures then obey man as their king; all refer themselves to him as to their end; he enjoys all, and none enjoy him. On whatever side you turn your eyes or direct your thoughts you behold millions of different creatures concentrating in man, as the radii of a circle meet in its center.

But is it in man that all creatures should rest? Is he their last end? No; else he should be God. What, then, do creatures ask of him when coming to give themselves to him, and lose themselves in him? What should he do with them and with himself? He should refer all to the great God, who is above him: for all things come from God, and should return to God. "It is for myself," says the Lord, "that I have made all things."[256] All creatures, therefore, should flow on to God, as rivers to the ocean.

Now, of themselves, creatures cannot tend to God, that is, cannot honor him in a manner pleasing to him or worthy of him. They have no mind to know him, no heart to love him, no mouth to bless him, no freedom to adore him; they are not acquainted even with themselves or their perfections. The diamond is not aware of its value or its brilliancy: How can it thank God for either? The sheep does not know him who clothes and nourishes it: How can it return him thanks? The trees and the birds, the sun and the earth, are ignorant of the source from which flowers, and fruits, and gorgeous plumage, and melodious voices, and heat, and motion, and fertility proceed: How, therefore, can they be expected to feel gratitude toward God?

Nevertheless, it is necessary that all these creatures should thank and love their author, and celebrate his praises in a manner worthy of him. Man alone is capable of doing so; for he alone is free. He alone has a mind to know, a heart to love, a mouth to bless the Creator. He alone, then, is strictly obliged to do so; because he alone is able to do so, and because he alone enjoys all creatures at each instant, while no creatures ever enjoy him.

We see that without man all nature is dumb; with him, on the contrary, it sings an everlasting canticle of praise to the Creator. By man's mind, it knows him; by man's heart, it loves him; by man's mouth, it blesses him; by man's freedom, it adores him! What, then, is man in the midst of the universe? He is as a high priest in a temple; his victim is the world and himself; the sword that immolates it is his will; the fire that consumes it is his love.

A worshipper, composed of a body, which unites him with material creatures, and a soul which associates him with the angels; a living abridgment of the universe, all whose perfections culminate in him; a high priest, placed between visible and invisible things; a king, inferior only to the angels and God: man alone fulfills, in its full extent, the object which God had in view in the creation of the world. Man is commissioned by all other creatures to pay, in their name, the debt which they owe to him from whom they have received their being. He is their life, their understanding, their heart, their voice, their mediator, their deputy. The less religious they are of themselves, the more imperative is the duty which they impose on man to be religious for them.[257]

Coronation of man. — After having made known to Adam his twofold dignity of king and high priest, God took him by the hand, and led him into the magnificent abode prepared for him. It was a beautiful garden, planted with all kinds of trees, and watered by a copious fountain, from which flowed four great rivers. Two of these rivers are at present unknown, the Gehon and Phison; the other two still remain, the Tigris and Euphrates.

Notwithstanding these particulars, no one at present can tell the precise place where the terrestrial paradise was situated. But it is the teaching of faith that it was a material place, situated on the eastern part of our globe as regards us, and not far from Mesopotamia and Armenia, where the Tigris and Euphrates still flow. To represent the terrestrial paradise, like one of our gardens or parks, however beautiful and extensive they may be, would be an erroneous idea. The terrestrial paradise was immense: it seemed an abridgment of the world.

In that wonderful place were assembled all kinds of creatures which the Lord God had drawn forth from nothingness—not only plants, but fishes, birds, animals, living peaceably among themselves, and perfectly submissive to man. The beasts, by their gentleness and grace; the fishes, by their sports; the birds, by their songs, and the exquisite variety of their brilliant plumage; the flowers, by their gorgeous colors and perfume; the plants, by their strange qualities and vigorous growth; the trees, by their sweet fruit, their magnificent figure, and their lovely foliage; even the serpent itself, which as yet possessed nothing repulsive: all contributed to embellish the abode of the king of nature. The paternal goodness of God made an eternal spring reign there.[258]

It would be superfluous to extend the description of the terrestrial paradise. All that we can say is that it was worthy of man, the king and high priest of the universe, the visible representative of the Creator of worlds. How solemn was the moment in which our first father, guided by God himself, entered his dwelling! How bright was the day which illumined this triumphant entry! Without doubt, the seraphim, witnesses of this tender and sublime spectacle, sang a new canticle, with accompaniments, on their golden harp, and all nature responded in a shout of gladness!

How beautiful was man himself! To form an idea of it, ah! let us not look on man at the present day, degraded by sin, furrowed with wrinkles, discolored by sadness, bending under the weight of his sorrows, uncrowned, and fallen. Man today is only a wreck, a ruin. But, at that time, like a statue of the richest and purest metal, coming forth from the workshop with all the dazzling splendor of gold, man was really perfect, a paragon of excellence. He was beautiful, admirably beautiful, because he was the living image of God, and nothing had yet[259] altered this image. As the sun shines in a cloudless heaven at noon, so the grace and majesty of God himself shone in innocent man.

Soon a new spectacle succeeded the first: Adam was crowned with honor and glory. What remained, except the ceremony of investiture in connection with that magnificent empire of which the Creator had made him ruler? Accordingly, the Lord God brought all the animals before Adam, that they might receive their names from him, whose subjects they were to be. Adam imposed a name on each, and this name expressed perfectly its character and qualities. They still bore these names when Moses wrote. Whatever name Adam gave to an animal was not only expressive of his dominion over it, but illustrative of his profound acquaintance with its nature, for to name is to define.

Henceforward, all the animals recognized the sway of man, and submitted to it without constraint. It was so, as long as Adam remained faithful. Could it be otherwise? The innocent Adam ruled the world with justice and equity; that is, he turned all creatures toward the end for which God had drawn them from nothingness, and placed them under his dominion. Each of them served man as a step by which to ascend to the Creator. Each of them was a mirror in which were reflected to the eyes of man the power, the wisdom, and the goodness of the Creator. Every service that they rendered him evoked from him an act of gratitude and love toward God. Thus, the whole creation, descended from God, ascended again continually to him, through the intermediation of man.

Since the fall, all things have been changed. Instead of raising man to God, as pictures remind us of the persons whom they represent, creatures too often serve only to make man lose the thought of God. The fault is not theirs; it is man's. We are heirs to the first man's fault. On this account the sight and the enjoyment of the universe, instead of awaking our gratitude, dissipate our minds. We make use of the benefits that are showered on our heads and scattered under our feet, like the stupid animal that greedily eats some wholesome kernel without ever raising an eye toward the beneficent hand that cast it down.

Still more, we employ creatures to degrade ourselves. They become in our hands instruments of pride, avarice, and corruption both for ourselves and others. We hold, in a state of oppression,[260] those creatures which we refer to ourselves alone, and whose natural destination leads them necessarily to God. We stop them on the way instead of employing them as guides. We constrain them to lament in secret the order of providence which prevents them from withdrawing themselves from our depraved use. We oblige them to entreat God to be delivered from the share that we force them to take in our corruption.

Hence, first, all creatures, having become so many instruments of sin in the hands of man, will become at the end of the world so many instruments of the divine vengeance, as slaves, who have long been held captive, may be seen, on the day of their liberation, bounding with fury, and breaking on the head of their haughty and tyrannical master the chains with which he had loaded them.

Hence, secondly, all creatures await in sighs the general resurrection, when the saints, no longer subject to sin, will employ them for the glory of God. Then will they be fully and eternally redeemed from slavery, and will participate in the glory of the children of God.[261]

Hence, thirdly, they will be purified at the end of the world by fire. Sinners, cast into hell, will no longer be in a condition to contaminate creatures which they will no longer be allowed to use. The just, fully and perfectly reestablished in order, will take possession of the universe; and heaven and earth, created only for them, will be inhabited only by them. The whole creation will fulfill its destiny by returning to God, who, as in the days of innocence, but in a yet more perfect manner, will be all in all.[262]

PRAYER

O my God! who art all love, I thank thee for having laden me with glory and power. What shall I render thee for the world, which thou hast given me? But, above all, what shall I render thee for thy blood, which thou hast shed for me?

I am resolved to love God above all things, and my neighbor as myself for the love of God; and, in testimony of this love, I shall every day mortify some one of my senses.

Lesson 14: Creation: The Sixth Day (Continued)

Happiness of man in the state of innocence. — The image of God, a king, the great usufructuary, the high priest of the universe — man, coming forth from the hands of his Creator, was enriched with all the natural gifts which the divine liberality could bestow on a creature. These precious gifts were so many means in the hands of man to arrive at a natural beatitude, that is to say, at a happiness proportioned to his twofold or corporal and spiritual nature. For this purpose God granted them to him: it was necessary only that man should make a good use of them — a use conformable to the will of their author.

We can easily understand that God, who is wisdom and goodness, could not, in creating a free and reasonable creature like man, composed of a body and a soul, refuse him natural helps for the functions of life, nor the means necessary for the fulfillment of the divine orders, nor even a reward for his fidelity. The created nature of man and the creative protection of God demanded these things. But God did not owe to man an exemption from the miseries and accidents of life, from infirmities and sicknesses, from old age and death, from the combat of concupiscence, and the blandishments of passion. Adam might have been created in this state of simple nature, without having any reason to complain of his Creator, or any ground to say that man was not good, because in all these imperfections, natural to a finite being, there is no evil—of sin.

In this manner man might have arrived at a natural happiness, that is, at the satisfaction of all his faculties. His mind would have known, his heart would have loved God indirectly, or by means of creatures, in which, as in a beautiful mirror, the divine power, wisdom, and goodness were gloriously reflected. He would have enjoyed his God during the time marked out for him by a providence as liberal in its rewards as it is wise in its counsels.

Such, we repeat, was the state of simple nature, in which man might have been created: God, however did not will it so. Not only should man come forth from his hands with all the privileges and all the gifts of a perfect nature, exempt from misery and weakness, but, moreover, destined for a supernatural end. This was, so to speak, a new creation, which perfected the first.[263] Thanks to this new benefit, his whole nature was exalted. It is no longer a dark and secondary, but a clear, immediate, and intuitive vision of his God that must form his happiness.

This destiny, infinitely nobler than the first, required proportionate means for its attainment. God gave them, and Adam received supernatural habits of all virtues, faith, hope, and charity, new strength, greater knowledge, and a thousand other special privileges, which placed him in a condition to arrive at his sublime destiny.[264]

If Adam had not fallen from this sublime state, he would, without passing by the way of death, after loving, adoring, and contemplating God for some time in creatures, as in a mirror and through a veil, have gone to behold that great being face to face and as he is in heaven, in the company of the angels.[265]

Thus, not only did man come forth from the hands of the Creator adorned with all natural gifts and destined for a natural happiness, but even enriched with all supernatural gifts and destined to see God face to face. In a word, man at his creation was constituted in a state of grace and supernatural justice.[266]

In this purely gratuitous state, innocent man was perfectly happy. According to the admirable saying of the scripture, he was "upright" (*Fecit hominem rectum*);[267] that is, he was in perfect order. His reason was subject to God; the inferior powers of his soul and body were subject to reason.[268] His mind knew clearly everything which it should know; his heart loved, with a strong, pure, and tranquil love, everything that it should love, and nothing which it should not love; his body enjoyed a perpetual health and youth. All this was only the beginning of a much greater happiness in heaven, that is to say, of a clearer knowledge and a more perfect love.

Such was man, as he came forth from thy hands, O God! and as he knew himself. We may imagine what were the transports of his gratitude and love, on seeing that which his Creator had done for him, within him and without him—on considering that which was prepared for him in the present and in the future life.

Creation of the woman.—So many benefits were still insufficient for the inexhaustible goodness of the divinity. God wished to double the happiness of man by giving him a companion, who should share it with him. Free from jealousy and passion, forming only one heart and soul, these two innocent creatures, in the communication of their thoughts, their sentiments, the delightful impressions of their gratitude, should increase their mutual felicity, and assist each other to advance every day in perfection.

When, then, all the animals had passed before Adam, and he had imposed a name on each of them, the Creator wrapped him in a mysterious sleep. He selected this time to create a spouse for man. The omnipotent artificer took away, without pain, one of

147

the sleeping Adam's ribs, and filled up its place with flesh. As from a little slime he had formed the body of man, so from his rib he formed another body, to which he united a rational soul: he thus created the woman, endowed with the same advantages, and elevated to the same supernatural state as the first man.

She was the first object presented by God to the father of the human race, when he awoke, informing him of the manner in which she had been made, and that she was a part of himself. At this sight, at this account, Adam, who had not found a being like himself among all those which had passed under his eyes, cried out: "This is bone of my bone, and flesh of my flesh;...wherefore, a man shall leave father and mother and shall cleave to his wife; and they shall be two in one flesh."[269]

God, in his turn, addressing these two new creatures, destined to be his first images on the earth and the first parents of all men, said to them: "Increase and multiply; fill the whole extent of the earth."[270]

It was thus that God, associating woman with man, gave a queen to the visible world, and instituted the holy society of marriage, which, from the beginning, consisted in the indissoluble union of one man with one woman, for the continuation of the human race. It follows, hence, that divorce is contrary to the primitive institution of marriage. If God tolerated it in the time of the old law, it was only with regret, and on account of the hard-heartedness of the carnal Jews.[271] Accordingly, the eternal Word, the restorer of all things, hastened, after his appearance on the earth, to abolish divorce, and to reestablish conjugal union in its primitive state. Blessed change! which restored to the family its happiness and dignity, and to society peace and order.

God then said to our first parents, and through them to the whole human race: "Rule over the fishes of the sea, the fowls of the air, and all living creatures that move upon the earth. Behold I have given you every herb bearing seed upon the earth, and all trees that have in themselves seed of their own kind to be your meat; and to all beasts of the earth...that they may have to feed upon."[272]

These words give man a right to the plants and the fruits of the earth; but he renders himself unworthy of the gifts of God if he abuses them, or is ungrateful for them. These words also secure nourishment to the animals. And hence, from the moment in which they were pronounced, the earth has never ceased to produce the nourishment necessary for the subsistence of the millions of living creatures that inhabit it. The omnipotent virtue of the Word of God has placed an admirable harmony between the food of each animal and its appetite. Wheat has the property of nourishing man; and grass of nourishing the horse and the elephant. So that a bundle of hay, from which one could never draw as much nourishment as would preserve the life of an infant, suffices to maintain the existence of the largest and the strongest animals.

"All things that breathe turn their eyes toward thee, O Lord!" says the royal prophet.[273] "All creatures expect of thee that thou give them food at a convenient time;...thou wilt open thy hand, and fill them with the effects of thy goodness."[274] The cares of thy providence extend even to the smallest birds. Shall we, who are created to thine image and likeness, have so little faith as to fear that thou wilt ever forget us?

In the midst of the terrestrial paradise, in which God had established our first parents, were two trees, remarkable among all the rest. The first was "the tree of life"; the second, which has become so sadly celebrated, was "the tree of the knowledge of good and evil."

The first was so called because its fruits contained a vivifying property, capable of preserving and restoring the failing strength of man. For man, though destined by a gratuitous privilege not to die, would still have grown weak, enfeebled, exhausted even, if he had not such a preservative against the infirmity and decay inseparable from his nature. St. Augustine says admirably well that the tree of life was a figure of the Word incarnate, whose vivifying flesh maintains the life of the soul, and communicates immortality to it.

The second tree was destined to put the fidelity of our first parents to the test. They had already a knowledge of good; nothing was wanting to them but the experimental knowledge of evil: sad knowledge! which was wholly unnecessary either for their happiness or their perfection.

We now see Adam and Eve established in the terrestrial paradise, endowed with all the advantages, and invested with all the authority that became the king and the queen of the world. Up to this time the Creator had only spoken to them of their prerogatives. It was just that man should be reminded of his condition. Created free, he should, by the dependent acts of his will, merit the eternal recompense which was promised to him. Moreover, if he was the king of the earth, he was also a vassal of heaven: in this character, he should render homage to his Lord. By thanksgiving and love he should refer back to God the whole creation which had come forth from God. Such was his mission; such was the fundamental condition of his royalty, of his very existence.

By a new mark of goodness, God, who might have required from his noble subject numerous and difficult kinds of homage, was content with asking one solitary external act of good will. "This vast universe," said he to our first parents, "belongs to you; the sea with its fishes, the earth with its plants and animals, the air with its birds, are yours; this garden of delights, in which I have placed you, is for your use; eat of the fruit of all the trees, which my hand hath planted—I except only one: the tree of the knowledge of good and evil. You shall not touch it. The day in which you violate my prohibition you shall die."

What could be more just in itself than such a command? What easier to fulfill? Could anything be better calculated to secure its observance than the terrible threat with which God accompanied it? "You shall die": that is, your body shall die, and your soul shall die another kind of death still more frightful; and you shall remain dead, or separated from me, for all eternity; not only shall you yourselves die, if you prevaricate, but you shall condemn all your posterity to death also, while, on the other hand, if you be faithful, you shall secure to yourselves forever the privileges and happiness which you enjoy.[275]

This precept was a kind of summary of all the duties of man.[276] His fidelity in complying with it should be the sacred bond that would unite him forever with God. Constituted at his creation in a state of supernatural justice, he had all the graces necessary for its observance. Let him show himself ever faithful and obedient, and the long chain of beings, of which he is the first link, being attached to God, then, peace to man, glory to God, harmony and order to the universe will result.

O father of the human race! love this easy precept, love it for God, love it for thyself, love it for us, love it for itself—yes, love it for itself, for it is the fundamental title of thy glory.

Society of man with God.—The last trait of the greatness of man and of his superiority over the animals is the intercourse which he holds with his Creator by religion. The observance of a precept was, in regard to our first parents, an essential condition of this august society. Wrapped in the thickest clouds, the animals are ignorant of the hand that formed them. They enjoy existence, and never think on the author of their life. Man alone rises to the divine source of all things; and, prostrate at the foot of the throne of God, worthily adores that ineffable goodness which created him.

In consequence of the eminent perfections bestowed on our nature, God vouchsafes to reveal himself to man: he guides us by the hand in the ways of happiness. The various laws which we have received from the supreme Wisdom resemble so many bright lamps placed at regular distances along the road which conducts from time to eternity. Enlightened by these heavenly lights, man advances in the career of glory—already he seizes the crown of life— and encircles with it his immortal brow.

Adam, who felt himself full of courage and penetrated with gratitude, probably regarded the law of abstinence from a single fruit as a light trial on his virtue, and, perhaps, imagined the advantages attached to so easy a precept henceforward secure for his posterity. Alas! he did not know to what a temptation his fidelity should soon be exposed.

God, whose power is infinite, and whose wisdom sported itself at the creation of the world, had drawn many kinds of creatures from nothingness. Some, visible and purely material, as earth, water, minerals, plants; others, at once visible and invisible, material and spiritual, men; and others, again, invisible and purely spiritual, angels.

Thus, there were no leaps in nature, no breaks in the magnificent chain of beings. All the links were connected by relations more and more perfect, until, on our arrival at man, this chain dazzles our weak reason by the greatness of its glory. But the chain of creation does not terminate with man; he is not, he cannot be, the brightest link.

Creation of the angels. — God is the source of life. He scatters it abroad in every form: vegetative, animal, intellectual. According as life is more or less perfect, it marks the hierarchy of beings. Now, it becomes more perfect, in proportion as a being approaches nearer to God, in other words, is less material and more spiritual. If, then, man sees below him myriads of creatures less perfect than himself, millions of other creatures appear above him, more perfect than he: and among these, again, are various degrees of perfection, according as they approach nearer to the ocean of all perfection.

In that world, which is vastly superior to ours, and whose extent bears as little relation perhaps to the visible world as the sun to a grain of sand, the celestial hierarchies shine like so many resplendent galaxies. There beam on all sides the angelic choirs. In the center of these august hosts shines the sun of justice, the orient from on high, from whom all the stars borrow their light and their splendor. Celestial hierarchies! annihilate yourselves in the presence of the eternal! for your existence is from him. The eternal is from himself, "He is who is." He alone possesses the plenitude of being; you possess only its shadow. Your perfections are streams; the infinitely perfect being is an ocean, an abyss into which the cherubim dare not look!

Such is the angelic world. Its creation is, beyond question, the most beautiful work of the six days. To pass it over in silence would be to mutilate our explanations. Moreover, this world has so great an influence on our own, touches us so closely, that nothing can be more interesting for us than to study its inhabitants and wonders: a knowledge of its history is necessary for the comprehension of our own.

Besides, before taking up one's residence in a city, or joining a community, a person seeks to know something of those with whom he must spend his life. Now, we are to dwell eternally with the angels in heaven; we are to become like them: let us begin, then, to use the words of a great pope to make some acquaintance with them.[277]

I. *Their nature.* — The angels are intelligent and invisible creatures, purely spiritual, and superior to man. Faith teaches that there are good and bad angels. Their existence is even a necessity of the creation. "The decree of the creation being supposed," says St. Thomas, "the existence of certain incorporeal creatures is a necessity. In fact, the principal end of the creation is good. Good or perfection consists in the resemblance of the created being with the Creator, of the effect with the cause. The resemblance of the effect with the cause is perfect, when the effect imitates the cause according to its manner of production. Now, God produced the creature by the intellect and the will. The perfection of the universe, therefore, requires that it should have intellectual and incorporeal creatures."[278]

Thus, that there are angels, and that the angels are personal beings, and not myths or figures, is a truth taught by revelation, confirmed by reason, and attested by the belief of the human race. Nearly every page of the scripture speaks of their existence.[279] Beings perfectly intellectual in their nature, the angels have nothing to learn from material creatures, and a body would be useless to them. It follows, hence, that they cannot, like human souls, be essentially united to bodies, and become one person with them. From thè air or some other preexisting matter, they can, nevertheless, assume bodies, and give themselves an accidental form.

The appearance of angels under sensible forms is a fact continually repeated from the beginning of the world, both in the old and the new testament, in the history of the Church, and the lives of the saints. These apparitions are not mere imaginary visions. An imaginary vision passes only in the mind of him who sees it: it escapes others. Now, the angels who appeared to Abraham were distinctly seen by the patriarch, by his family, by Lot, and by the inhabitants of Sodom. In the same manner, the archangel Raphael, who appeared to Tobias, was seen by him, by his wife, by his son, by Sara, and by all Sara's family.

Since the angels have no bodies, it follows that they are incorruptible and endowed with a beauty, an intelligence, an agility, and a strength, altogether incomprehensible to man. Free from languors and maladies, they have no need of nourishment or repose; they know neither the weaknesses of infancy nor the infirmities of old age.

They are beautiful. God is perfect beauty, and the fountain of all beauty. The more a being resembles him, the more beautiful it is. The soul is more beautiful than the body, because it is a more perfect image of the eternal beauty. The angel, in its turn, because an incomparably more perfect image of this beauty, is incomparably more beautiful than the human soul. We have an instinct of the angelic beauty; for, to denote the highest degree of sensible beauty, we say, "beautiful as an angel."

They are intelligent. The beauty of the angels is the radiance of their essential perfection, and their essential perfection is intelligence. Who will tell us its extent? St. Thomas replies: "The angelic intelligence is godlike, that is, the angel acquires a knowledge of the truth, not by the sight of sensible things nor by reasoning, but by intuition or a simple glance."[280] In possession of a principle, the angels immediately know what it contains, even to its most remote consequences. Thus, there can be no falsehood, or error, or deception in the mind of an angel.[281] The knowledge of the angels extends to all the truths of the natural order. The whole universe, heaven and earth, have nothing hidden in their regard; and, since they are confirmed in grace, they know the greater number of truths in the supernatural order.[282]

We say the "greater number," for, until the day of judgment, the angels will receive no new communications on the government of the world, and especially on the salvation of the predestined.[283]

Thus, our Lord, speaking of his second coming, says that even the angels do not know its day or its hour. There are also other things of which God has reserved the secret to himself alone. Such, for example, is the perfect knowledge of hearts, and of future events, which depend on the free concurrence of wills. This knowledge is an incommunicable prerogative of the divinity.[284] But if the angels have not a positive knowledge of the secrets of hearts, we must admit that they are much better able than we are to form a conjecture from external signs.[285] This conjectural knowledge extends also to future events.

They are agile. A finite angel, in its nature, cannot be everywhere at the same time; but such is the rapidity of its movements, that it may almost be regarded as ubiquitous. The angel, says St. Thomas, is not composed of different natures, so that the movement of the one might be hindered or retarded by the movements of the other; as happens with man, in whom the movement of the soul is restrained by the organs of the body. Now, as no obstacle retards or hinders the angel, it moves with all the plenitude of its strength. In its regard space disappears. Hence, it can pass from place to place in the twinkling of an eye, without any intervening lapse of time.[286]

They are strong. Like their other qualities, the strength of the angels takes its rise from the essence of their being, which participates more abundantly than any other in the divine essence—infinite strength. Accordingly, the strength of the angel surpasses everything that we know of strength in nature, and it is exercised over the world and over man.

Over the world: there are angels who impart motion to it. Material creatures, inert of their own nature, are created to be set in motion by spiritual creatures, as our body by our soul.[287] Such is the strength of the angels that one of them would suffice to put the whole planetary system in motion, and to carry the most enormous bodies wherever it desired with a rapidity that baffles all calculation. If, then, God permitted it, an angel could easily throw the world into confusion, or transport a whole city from one place to another, as happened with the holy House of Loretto, which angels carried from Nazareth to Dalmatia, and from Dalmatia to the place where it now receives the homage of the Catholic world.[288]

Over man: in virtue of the great law of subordination, spiritual beings of an inferior order are subjected to the action of spiritual beings of a superior order. Hence, man is sub- jected, body and soul, to the angelic powers, and they are not subjected to him. It would be necessary to run through the whole scripture if one desired to adduce the various operations of angels on the body of man. Let us merely mention the prophet Habacuc, carried by an angel from Palestine to Babylon, in order to bring some food to Daniel, shut up in the lions' den; the army of Sennacherib, king of Assyria, of which 185,000 men were cut to pieces by an angel in one night; the exterminating angel, to whom a few moments sufficed for the destruction of the firstborn of all men and beasts (except those of the Israelites) throughout the whole extent of the kingdom of Egypt; all the inhabitants of Sodom, struck blind by the angel who delivered Lot.

As for the soul, the angels can, and really do, act on it, in a manner—now ordinary, now extraordinary—to an extent which it is difficult to realize. The understanding owes its most precious light to them. "Revelations of divine things," says the great St. Denis, "come to men through the ministry of angels."[289] Every page of the old and new testament, from first to last, justifies the words of the illustrious disciple of St. Paul, Abraham, Lot, Jacob, Moses, Gedeon, Tobias, the Machabees, the Blessed Virgin, St. Joseph, the holy women, the apostles, are instructed and directed by these appointed spirits as administrators over man and over the world. We shall soon see that the guardian angel fulfills, in a less remarkable way, no doubt, but not less really, the same duties in regard to the soul confided to its care.

As to angelic operation on the human will, the universal experience of mankind testifies how many inspirations of good angels are efficacious in leading us to virtue, and, on the other hand, how often the suggestions of the wicked angels are efficacious in leading us to vice. The devils fascinate the imagination with deceitful representations, which hide the deformity of evil and give it the semblance of good; they agitate all the inferior part of the soul, and excite concupiscence. But the good angels disperse the mists of error and the dark clouds of the passions, lead back the senses to their original purity, and produce a kind of internal light in the soul, by means of which the soul is enabled to see things in their true character.[290] Such are, in their nature, the admirable creatures whom we call the good angels; and one day we shall be like them, intelligent, beautiful, agile, and strong.[291] O man! what thought more capable of moving thy heart?

The angels were created[292] at the same time as heaven and earth: such is the formal doctrine of the Church.[293] But what day of the great week illumined their birth? The answer to this question matters little. St. Augustine and St. Gregory think that the angels were created at the same time as the heavens.

As for the rest, if Moses has not been more explicit regarding the creation of the angels, the reason is, according to St. Thomas and the two holy doctors whom we have just cited, because he had grounds to fear that the Jewish people, whose propensity toward idolatry was known to him, might take occasion from their acquaintance with the matter to introduce some superstitious worship.[294] It may also be said that God did not wish we should know more regarding the angels than he has been pleased to reveal to us, lest our actual condition should make us find something dangerous in it. Finally, it may be added, with the generality of interpreters, that the principal object which Moses had in view was to relate the order of the creation of the visible world.[295]

II. *The bad angels.* — All the angels were created in a state of innocence and justice,[296] but they were no more impeccable than man. Being free, they should, like man, undergo a trial. The beatific vision and immutability in good were the recompense which they should gain by a proper use, with the assistance of grace, of their free will. God, therefore, subjected them to a trial. Every trial, before being meritorious, must be essentially costly or painful. What was the trial of the angels?

Decreed from all eternity, the dogma of the incarnation of the Word was, in due time, proposed to them for their adoration. Human nature preferred to the angelic nature! An obligation to adore a man-God — their inferior become their superior. At this revelation the pride of Lucifer rebelled. He cried out: "I protest against it. Are we to be cast down? I will ascend. Is my throne to be lowered? I will raise it above the stars. I will sit on the mountain of the covenant. It is I and no other that shall be like the Most High."[297] One third of the angels of various hierarchies answered: "We also protest against it."

At these words an archangel, no less brilliant than Lucifer, cried out: "Who is like to God? Who can refuse to believe and to adore that which he proposes for the faith and adoration of his creatures? I believe and I adore." The majority of the celestial hierarchies answered: "We also believe, and we also adore." Such is the great battle that took place in heaven, and of which St. John speaks in these terms: "There was a great battle in heaven; Michael and his angels fought with the dragon; and the dragon fought and his angels."[298]

These few words contain treasures of light. In them, and in them alone, is found the real origin of evil. Punished as soon as guilty, Lucifer and his adherents, changed into horrible devils, were precipitated into the depths of hell, which their pride had dug for them.[299]

Here, let us admire, with humble gratitude, the wide difference which the divine mercy placed between them and us. The door of penance is open to men during the whole time of their life, while the bad angels found themselves, immediately after their fall, in that state in which sinful men will find themselves immediately after their death.[300] The eternal damnation of the reprobate angels, like that of men, consists in the loss of the beatific intuitive vision and in the pain of fire. It is needless to seek for any other proofs on the matter, besides these words of our Lord to the wicked: "Depart from me, ye cursed, into everlasting fire, which was prepared for the devil and his angels."[301] They have suffered this punishment since the moment of their fall, as sinners suffer it from the moment of their death.[302]

PRAYER

O my God! who art all love, I thank thee for having crowned our first parents with so much glory and happiness. I thank thee for having made us so great, as to establish us, by means of religion, in communication with thee: grant us the grace to carry faithfully thy amiable yoke.

I am resolved to love God above all things, and my neighbor as myself for the love of God; and, in testimony of this love, I shall every day make an act of humility.

Lesson 15: Creation: The Sixth Day (Continued)

1. *Malice of the angels.* — If the dogma of the incarnation, considered in itself, suffices to explain the fall of the angels, it explains this fall still better, when viewed in its effects. On the one hand, this mystery is the foundation or the keystone of the whole divine plan; on the other, it is the special object of the eternal hatred of Satan. What evil had our first

parents done the demon to become the object of his hatred? None. What, then, was the cause of that murderous hatred which condemned them to innumerable miseries in this life and to death eternal? Satan pursued, persecuted, and hated in them the eternal Word, whose privileged friends and brethren they should become, by means of the incarnation.

That which Satan did against our first parents, he does against us. On earth, as in heaven; over the whole extent of the globe, as in the terrestrial paradise; today, as at the beginning of time, and on to the end of ages: it is always the Word made flesh that Satan pursues in human nature. "The sin of Lucifer and his angels," says a celebrated commentator, "was a sin of ambition. Having a knowledge of the mystery of the incarnaion, it was only with jealousy they beheld human nature exalted above angelic nature. Hence, their hatred against the Son of the woman, that is, our Lord Jesus Christ; their war in heaven; and the war which they still wage to the utmost on earth."[303]

This bloody, incessant war alone explains the grand enigma which we call the life of man in this valley of tears. Unable to prevent or oppose the decree of the hypostatic union between the divine and human nature, Lucifer and his satellites are continually, and in a singular manner, endeavoring to frustrate its effects. From their poisonous mouths they breathe into the world three great errors, to which all the errors of both ancient and modern times may be referred. These three monstrous errors, which have unceasingly tended to predominate over the human race, are: pantheism, materialism, and rationalism. These three errors may be comprised in one, which is their beginning and their end, namely, Satanism.

As is easily seen, these errors tend to render radically impossible the belief in the dogma of the incarnation. Pantheism: if all things are God, the incarnation is useless. Materialism: if all things are matter, the incarnation is absurd. Rationalism: if the highest wisdom is to believe in reason alone, then the incarnation is chimerical. Thus, the incarnate God is the eternal object of the hatred of Satan. Here is the origin of heresies, schisms, persecutions, of temptations of individual persons, and of social revolutions. In other words, this is the explanation of the great battle, which, once commenced in heaven, is continued on earth, to end in an eternity of happiness or of misery.

Thus, the constant occupation of the bad angels is to tempt man, in order to frustrate the ends of the incarnation. "The devil," says the apostle St. John, "is that great dragon, that old serpent, who is called Satan, and who seduces the whole world."[304] And St. Peter: "The devil is like a roaring lion, that goes about night and day seeking whom to devour."[305] The hatred of these reprobate spirits against man is so great that the injury which they do to themselves, through the shame of their defeat, is not capable of diminishing their fury. "They even attack," says St. Chrysostom, "those whom they have no hope of vanquishing, through the sole motive of wearying them, disquieting them, and troubling them, if they can do nothing else."[306]

The whole man is the object of the devil's hatred. Not content with destroying our soul by sin, he brings upon us all the temporal evils in his power. Hence, the scripture calls him the great murderer. Death, which he introduced into the world by the introduction of sin; the excesses to which he was carried against Job—houses overthrown, flocks scattered, children deprived of life in one day, whether by fire from heaven or earthquakes, or violence of winds, and, in addition to all, Job's body covered with ulcers from head to foot; the corporal vexations, by which he torments the possessed; the human sacrifices, which he has required from all ancient, and still requires from all idolatrous, nations; his apparitions, under frightful forms to so many solitaries; his threats, always followed by their effects, when God does not arrest his fury: all are so many proofs of that enemy whose hatred was announced at the beginning of the world, and which never grows old.[307]

The devils not only hate man in his person, but they also detest him and attack him in his goods, and in the elements necessary for his existence and his security. A great portion of the evils that afflict us come from these malevolent spirits. In union with all other bodies of men, even pagans, the Church has always believed in the dreadful power which God has left to the devils over creatures, and in the use which they make of this power to injure mankind. Hence, among pagans formerly, as among idolaters at the present day, we find sacrifices and expiations to appease malicious divinities. Hence, in the Church, we find prayers, exorcisms, blessings on creatures, particularly on those which are to serve for the administration of the sacraments and the general requirements of religion.

The jealous hatred with which the devil is animated against the Word incarnate, and against us, leads him not only to do to man all the spiritual and temporal injury that lies in his power, but even to usurp the place of the divine mediator, by having himself adored as God. Such was, and such still is, the nature of idolatry. Under a thousand forms, and by a thousand artifices, the bad angels have succeeded in securing for themselves divine honors.

We have seen all ancient peoples, the Jewish excepted, prostrate before their altars. Even at this day, in Hindustan, in Japan, in China, in Tibet, in Africa, Lucifer takes from the Word incarnate that place which he could not snatch from him in heaven. "All the gods of the nations," says the prophet, "are demons": *Omnes dii gentium daemonia*.[308] "Nothing," says Eusebius, "proves better the hatred of the demons against God than their rage to pass for gods, carrying away in his sight the homages that are due to him. It is on this account that they employ divinations and oracles, striving to draw men from the worship of the true God, and to plunge them into the bottomless abyss of impiety and atheism."[309]

2. *Power of the bad angels.* — The hatred of the angels is set in motion by a power, the extent of which it is impossible to calculate. Beauty excepted, the bad angels still retain all their natural gifts. "Although the devil," says St. Gregory the Great, "has lost happiness, still he has not lost the excellence of his nature, whose energy surpasses that of men."[310]

St. Thomas teaches the same doctrine. "The angels," says this great doctor, "are not like a man that one can punish by taking away his hand or his foot: simple beings, one can take away nothing from their nature. Hence, this axiom of St. Denis: 'The natural gifts remain entire with the fallen angels.' Consequently, their natural faculty to know has not been in the least altered by their revolt."[311]

It is the same with their other natural qualities: agility and strength. The natural intelligence of the fallen angels, like that of the good angels, is deiform. We must understand hereby that they know the truth in the twinkling of an eye, without reasoning, without effort, in itself and in all its consequences. In their regard no error can be possible, except in things of the supernatural order, or that God himself limits their knowledge.[312]

As for the future, their knowledge far surpasses ours. If there is question of things which must necessarily happen in the future, the demons know them in their cause with certainty. It is much the same with future contingencies, which most frequently happen, the demons know them by conjecture, as the physician may know beforehand the death or the recovery of his patient. Among the demons this conjectural knowledge approaches so much the nearer to certainty, as they understand causes more universally and more perfectly: as the same manner as the foresight of a physician is so much the surer, as he has had more experience. With regard to future events of a purely casual or fortuitous nature, these are known by God alone.[313]

What we have said of the agility and strength of the good angels applies also to the demons. It is unnecessary to repeat the explanations already given. Let us only add that the power of the demons is limited by the divine Wisdom, so that they cannot do to us, nor to creatures in general, all the evils that they would. Accordingly, God never permits them to tempt us beyond our strength. With the assistance of grace, we can always resist them, and by the victories that we gain over them, advance the work of our sanctification, and increase our merits. Such is, at least in part, the object of providence in the power which has been left to the devil.

Let us also add that the power of the demons has been greatly diminished since the incarnation. This diminution of power appears especially in what relates to sensible apparitions, in possessions and corporal vexations. All these things have been much less common among Christians than they formerly were among pagans, and are among idolaters at the present day. "The obstinate malice of the devil," says St. Cyprian, "holds out till one comes to the salutary waters of baptism, but it loses its strength in this sacrament."[314]

On which account we must carefully remember that Christianity alone having withdrawn the world from the sway of Satan, the world returns again to that sway, in direct proportion as it throws off the yoke of the Redeemer. Nothing, then, is less surprising than the allusions, the oracles, the table-turnings, and all the other practices of somnambulism, magnetism, and spiritism, that have become so common within the last few years in Europe and America. Modern nations turn their back on Christianity, and Satan returns with all his array of deceitful trumperies that heretofore secured his dominion over man.

Hence, to believe, and, with much more reason, to teach that agreements, divinations, conjurations, apparitions, communications of every kind with the devil, whose possibility and reality the scripture and the history of all nations attest, are almost unknown in our days, would be a great and a most fatal error.

It is the same with regard to the practices and actual manifestations of artificial somnambulism, magnetism, and spiritism; they are not always jugglings, nor the effects of purely natural causes. Taken altogether, they are nothing else than the reproduction of the superstitious practices of ancient paganism and the restoration of the kingdom of Satan. On this account the Church condemns them, as well as the writings that are disseminated to propagate them. In consequence, it is forbidden to read such writings, or to take part in, or even assist at, such practices, on any pretext whatsoever.[315]

3. *Habitation of the bad angels.*—Speaking of the fall of Lucifer and his accomplices, St. Peter says that God precipitated them into hell, where they are tormented, and held in reserve until the day of judgment.[316] Moreover, the same apostle exhorts us to vigilance, by warning us that the devil, like a roaring lion, goes continually about, seeking to devour us.[317] St. Paul, on his side, calls Satan the prince of the powers of the air, and warns the human race to clothe itself with its divine armor, that it may be able to resist the attacks of the devil. "As for us," he says, "the warfare is not against enemies of flesh and blood, but against princes and powers, against the rulers of this world of darkness, the malicious spirits who inhabit the air."[318]

Accordingly, the habitation of the fallen angels is hell, and the air that surrounds us; but let them be in hell or in the air, their pain is always the same, for they everywhere carry hell about with them. Such is the teaching of all the fathers and all the doctors of the Church.[319]

Providence has never permitted that this dogma, of such importance to the life of the human family, should be forgotten, even by pagans. Out of many, let us select the testimony of Porphyry. "It is not without reason," says the prince of pagan theology, "that we believe the bad demons are subject to Serapis, who is the same as Pluto. These malicious spirits are invisible and imperceptible to the senses of man, for they are not clothed with a solid body. All, moreover, have not the same form, but they are fashioned on a variety of models. The forms distinguishing each of these spirits is sometimes visible, sometimes invisible. Occasionally, some even change their appearance, and these are the most wicked,...their corporeal forms are perfectly monstrous. With a view to glut their passions, demons of this kind dwell more willingly and more frequently near the earth, so that there is no crime which they do not attempt to commit. A mixture of violence and duplicity, they have subtle and impetuous motions, as if they were dashing from an ambuscade, now practicing deceit, and again having recourse to violence. They do these and such like things in order to turn us aside from the true and proper worship of the gods, and to attract us to themselves. They take a pleasure in everything strange and disorderly; they rejoice when we fall into error.

The bait, which they make use of to attract the multitude, is everything that inflames the passions, the love of pleasures, of riches, of power, of voluptuousness, or of vainglory. Thus they foment seditions, wars, and all the consequences that follow from such things. They are the fathers of magic;…every house is full of them. On this account we banish them, and purify our habitations, as often as we pray to the gods."[320]

With his usual penetration, St. Thomas discovers the reason for the double abode of the fallen angels. "Providence," says the Angelic Doctor, "conducts man to his end in two ways: directly, by leading him to good—this is the ministry of good angels; and indirectly, by exercising him in the conflict against evil—it is becoming that this second mode of procuring the good of man should be entrusted to the bad angels, that they may not be altogether useless in the general order. Hence, for the latter, two places of torment: one, by reason of their fault, is hell; the other, by reason of the exercise which they must give man, is the cloudy atmosphere that surrounds us. Now, the business of the salvation of man will continue till the day of judgment: till then, therefore, will continue the ministry of the good, and the temptation of the bad angels. Hence, until the last day of the world, the good angels will continue to be sent to us, and the bad to inhabit the lower strata of the air. Yet, it belongs to those who are in hell to torment the persons whom these draw there; in the same manner, as a number of the good angels remain in heaven with the souls of the saints. But, after the day of judgment, all wicked men and angels will be in hell, and all the good in heaven."[321]

4. *Good angels: their number, their hierarchies.*—If the power and the number of the bad angels terrify us, that which we are about to say of the good angels is well calculated to console us. However numerous the former are, the number of the latter is considerably greater: St. Augustine expressly teaches it.[322] Besides, that which the apostle St. John says of the predestined of all nations, namely, that their number is innumerable, can be said with much more reason of the celestial spirits. It is admitted that the number of the angels will be much greater than that of the saints.

Theologians remark, following the fathers, that the terms, *thousands* and *millions*, of which the scripture makes use when speaking of the angels, do not mean a definite number; they say that the sacred authors only employed such expressions, in the absence of any others suitable, to denote an extraordinary number, which might be regarded as in some manner infinite.[323]

However great this number may be, yet there is no confusion or disorder among the angels. The Almighty God, who maintains so wonderful a harmony between thousands of suns, suspended above our heads, and rolling in space, maintains also, among the celestial host, an admirable order and a marvelous subordination. The angels are divided into various hierarchies, of which each contains different choirs, not equal in dignity but all duly subordinated.

According to the etymology of the word, *hierarchy* means "a sacred government."[324] A government comprises at once the prince himself and the multitude ranked under his orders. God being the Creator of angels and men, there can only be, in his regard, one hierarchy, of which he is the supreme hierarch. It is the same with regard to the incarnate Word. The King of kings, the Lord of lords, to whom all power has been given in heaven and on earth, he is the supreme hierarch over angels and men—consequently over the Church, both triumphant and militant.

If we consider the sacred government in its relations with the multitude, we call a hierarchy, "an assembly of beings submissive to one and the same law." Now, beings are not subject to the same laws unless because they have the same nature and the same functions. It follows hence, that all the angels not having the same functions, the angelic world is divided into several hierarchies. If the angels form distinct hierarchies, the reason for it lies in their relative perfection. This perfection is so much the greater, as the angels participate more abundantly in the perfections of God: that is, as they have a more or less clear, more or less general knowledge of the truth.

"This knowledge" says St. Thomas, "marks three degrees among the angels, for it can be regarded in a triple relation:

"I. The angels can see the reason of things in God, who is the first and universal principle. This manner of knowing is the privilege of those angels who approach nearest to God, and who, according to the beautiful saying of St. Denis, abide in his vestibule. These angels form the first hierarchy.

"II. They can see it in universal created causes, which we call 'general laws.' These causes being numerous, the knowledge is less clear and precise. This manner of knowing is the portion of the second hierarchy.

"III. They can see it in its application to individual beings, inasmuch as these depend on 'particular laws.' Thus do the angels of the third hierarchy know."[325]

There are then three hierarchies among the angels, and there are only three: there is no room for a fourth. In fact, these three hierarchies owe their existence, in a certain sense, to the three manners in which it is possible to know the truth, namely: in God, in general causes, and in particular causes; or, as the sublime Areopagite says, to the "more or less abundant life," which the angels composing them enjoy.[326]

Revelation also discovers to us three choirs or different orders in each hierarchy. We call an angelic choir or order, "a multitude of angels resembling one another in the gifts of nature and grace, and in the similarity of their offices."[327] Every hierarchy contains three, and only three: more would be too many; less too few. Indeed, every hierarchy forms a sort of small state. Now, every state necessarily comprises three classes of citizens, neither more nor less.

"However numerous they may be," says St. Thomas, "all the citizens of a state are reduced to three classes, according to the three things which constitute a well-ordered society, namely, the beginning, the middle, and the end. Hence, we everywhere see three orders among men: some in the first rank, the aristocracy; others in the last, the populace; and others, again, in the middle, the citizen or burgesses.

"It is the same among the angels. In each hierarchy there are three different orders. Like the hierarchies themselves, these are distinguished by the natural excellence of the angels composing them, and by a difference of office. All offices refer necessarily to three things, the beginning, the middle, and the end."[328]

Hence, composed of three great hierarchies, and each hierarchy divided into three distinct orders, the angelic world is presented to our view as a magnificent army, ranged in the most admirable order.

The first hierarchy comprises the seraphim, the cherubim, and the thrones.

The second hierarchy comprises the dominations, the principalities, and the powers.

The third hierarchy comprises the virtues, the archangels, and the angels.

To the first hierarchy belongs the consideration of the end; to the second, the universal disposal of the means; and to the third, the actual application of the means. The knowledge, which the angels of the first hierarchy draw from the very bosom of God, are communicated by them, as far as is required, to the angels of the second hierarchy; and by these again to the angels of the third hierarchy, who afterward share the same with men.

The seraphim are the most sublime creatures that God has drawn forth from nothingness. They owe their name to their inflamed love. Placed at the head of the hierarchies, they approach, as far as the finite can approach the infinite, the divine Trinity, the eternal furnace of all love.

The cherubim come immediately after the seraphim. Their name signifies fullness of knowledge. With their gaze steadily fixed on the face of the eternal, they contemplate the inmost reasons of things, in their source, in order to communicate them to the inferior angels.

The thrones are so called, because these angels, resplendent with beauty, are raised above all the choirs of the inferior hierarchies, to whom they convey the orders of the great King, while sharing with the seraphim and the cherubim the privilege of seeing the truth clearly in God himself, the cause of causes.[329]

The dominations: to dictate and to command is the business of the dominations. These angels are so called, because they rule over all the angelic orders charged with the execution of the commands of the great monarch, as the commander-in-chief of an army rules over all the generals placed under his orders.

The principalities: that we may continue the comparison, the principalities, whose name denotes leaders according to the sacred order, represents the superior officers, who appoint the various movements and exercises for their subordinates, in accordance with the general orders of the commander-in-chief. Princes of nations, these powerful spirits conduct each one, in that which concerns it, to the accomplishment of the divine plan.

The powers: invested, as their name denotes, with a special authority, these angels are commissioned to remove obstacles that interfere with the execution of the divine commands; they banish the evil spirits, who continually besiege kingdoms, in order to turn them from their appointed end.

The virtues: their name denotes strength, which they exercise on the material world, presiding immediately over the laws that regulate it, and maintaining the order which we so much admire.

The archangels: between the angels and us there exists a constant intercourse shadowed forth by the ladder of Jacob. To descend the steps of this mysterious ladder and fulfill important missions amongst men on certain solemn occasions—to preside over the government of provinces, dioceses, religious bodies: such are the twofold office of the archangels, whose name denotes superior angel, or princes among the angels properly so called.

The angels: The last order is that of the angels. *Angel* means "messenger." As all the heavenly spirits are employed to notify the divine thoughts, the name of angel is common to them. To this office the higher angels add certain prerogatives, from which they derive their peculiar names as already explained. The angels of the last choir of the last hierarchy, adding nothing to the ordinary occupation of envoys, retain the simple name of angels. In a more direct and more constant relation with man, they watch over his twofold life, and bring him, every hour, the light and the strength of which he has need, from his cradle to his grave.

5. *Offices of the good angels.*—To enjoy the sight of an immense army in all its grandeur, we should see it in motion. In like manner, to form a high idea of the brilliant hosts of heaven, of the place which is occupied by the good angels in the designs of providence, it is fitting that we should study them in their exercises.

I. *The good angels praise the Lord.* It is of faith that the good angels enjoy the intuitive vision. Our Lord assures us of it in express terms;[330] the splendor of the Divine Majesty penetrates them with a respectful fear and an incomprehensible love. Isaias saw them prostrate before the throne of God; he heard them answering one another, and saying, eternally: "Holy, holy, holy is the Lord, the God of armies; the earth is full of his glory."[331] St. John, another witness of the same spectacle, saw them around the throne and heard them crying out, night and day, without ceasing: "Holy, holy, holy is the Lord Almighty, who was, and who is, and who is to come."[332]

II. *They preside over the government of the visible world.* It has always been a general conviction that divine providence governs the world by the ministry of angels, and that their ministry extends even to corporeal elements and inanimate creatures. "The angels," says Origen, "preside over all visible things, earth, air, fire, and water, that is, over the principal elements, the animals, the celestial bodies. Their ministries are divided. Some take care of the productions of the earth; others preside over wells and rivers; some, again, preside over the winds; others, over the sea."[333]

Several fathers of the Church speak in no less formal terms; even pagans have acknowledged this truth. "If it is unbecoming for a king," says Apulius,[334] "to govern all things by himself, much more would it be so for God. We must, then, believe that, in order to preserve his majesty, he is seated on a sublime throne, and rules over all parts of the universe by celestial powers. It is, in fact, by their ministry that he governs this lower world. To do so costs him neither trouble nor calculation, things which are inseparable from the ignorance and the weakness of man."[335]

III. *They preside over the government of the invisible world.* Ministering spirits sent to procure the sanctification of the elect, the angels execute the will of God in regard to men. It is certain that he has almost always made use of their services in the wonders which he has wrought, in the graces which he has bestowed, and in the just judgments which he has executed in favor of his Church, as well under the old as under the new testament.

The celebrated apparitions made to Abraham, Lot, Jacob, and Moses, are a proof of it.[336] An angel delivers the Hebrews from the slavery of Egypt,[337] precedes them in the desert, and conducts them into the promised land![338] It is an angel who commissions Gedeon to deliver Israel from the bondage of the Madianites;[339] who predicts the birth of Samson;[340] who causes the law to be respected during the captivity of Babylon;[341] who delivers the children from the furnace, and Daniel from the lions' den;[342] who fights in company with the Machabees;[343] in a word, in all the dangers and tribulations that encompass the Jewish people, it is the angel of the Lord who delivers them.[344]

Under the new testament, the angels take a part in all the circumstances of the birth, infancy, life, death, resurrection, and ascension of our Lord. They preside over the birth of his precursor;[345] announce to Mary the great mystery, which should be wrought in her;[346] and inform the shepherds that a Savior is born to them.[347] They warn Joseph to flee into Egypt;[348] and direct him to return into the land of Israel.[349] They approach Jesus Christ to serve him in the desert.[350] They strengthen him in his agony.[351] They publish his resurrection. Finally, they accompany him in his ascension, and thus accomplish his prediction that the angels of heaven should be seen ascending and descending on the Son of Man.[352]

They watch, in like manner, over the apostles of the infant Church. The apostles are put in prison: an angel opens the doors, and allows them to depart.[353] The deacon Philip is sent by an angel to the road leading from Jerusalem to Gaza, that he may instruct and baptize the envoy of the queen Candace—a conversion which will soon effect many others in Ethiopia.[354] An angel appears to the centurion Cornelius, and orders him to send for the apostle St. Peter, from whom he shall receive instruction and baptism.[355] It would be useless to multiply the authorities; we find them everywhere in the new testament; everyone knows them.

IV. *They keep guard over the human race.* The different services of angels in regard to creatures are referred, like creatures themselves, to the salvation of man. Hence, it is chiefly to the guardianship and care of the human race that the celestial intelligences are appointed. "God," according to Lactantius, "sends his angels to guard, and, as it were, to cultivate the human race;[356] they are our guides and tutors."[357]

V. *They guard empires.* There is mention in the tenth chapter of the prophet Daniel, of the archangel Michael, who is styled there one of the first princes; also, of a prince of the kingdom of the Persians, and of a prince of the Greeks. The context does not permit us to doubt that all these princes are angels. Such is also the general interpretation both of the commentators and fathers. From this passage and some others they conclude, as a certainty, that every nation or kingdom has its tutelary angel. St. Basil positively distinguishes national from individual guardian angels, and proves, by scripture, the existence of both these angelic ministries. The other fathers of the Church teach the same;[358] and one among them declares that this truth is founded on the testimony of the scripture.[359]

VI. *They guard each Church.* That which St. Basil, St. Epiphanius, St. Jerome, and many other ancient writers say of kingdoms and nations, they also say of each particular Church, which they do not doubt is placed under the protection of a special tutelar angel. Origen states in several places that it would be too long to prove it.[360] Eusebius of Caesarea is no less formal. "God wishes," he says, " that every angel should watch as a guardian over the Church committed to it."[361]

St. Gregory Nazianzen believed the same thing. Hence, in the beautiful discourse which he delivered when quitting Constantinople, and bidding a tender farewell to all that had been connected with that great metropolitan Church, he placed in the first rank the holy angels, who were the protectors of it.[362] All the fathers were persuaded, with St. Ambrose, that God is not content with establishing a bishop over each flock, but that he has likewise appointed an angel to guard it.[363]

VII. *They guard the universal Church.* If each particular Church has a tutelar angel, with much greater reason must we suppose that a very large number of angels watch continually over the welfare of the universal Church. "The celestial powers," says Eusebius, "guard the Church of God."[364] St. Hilary represents them as surrounding the sheepfold of Jesus Christ, and fulfilling in its regard the duties of soldiers, who are appointed to the defense of a city.[365] St. Gregory of Nyssa compares them to that tower which is mentioned in the Canticle of Canticles, and from which hung an immense number of bucklers, to teach us that these blessed spirits protect and defend the Church in its continual warfare against the powers of darkness.[366]

VIII. *They guard each one of us.* Every man has a guardian angel destined to enlighten, defend, and guide him during the whole course of his mortal life. This consoling truth is, next after dogmas expressly defined, one of the best founded in scripture and tradition. Although it is neither expressed in formal terms in the holy books nor absolutely defined by the Church, it is, nevertheless, received by the unanimous consent of this same universal Church. It has, moreover, so solid a foundation in texts of scripture, understood according to the interpretation of the holy fathers, that one cannot deny it without very great temerity, and almost without error.[367]

The Lord, says the royal prophet, has appointed his angels to keep you in all your ways. All the holy fathers understand this passage, not only of our Lord, but also of all men, and more especially the just. Besides, Jesus Christ himself says that the angels of children continually behold the face of their heavenly Father.

"The angels," writes Origen, "have a care of our souls, which are confided to them, as tutors have a care of their pupils."[368] "We have learned from scripture," says Eusebius of Caesarea, "that each one of us has an angel, whom God has given us for our guidance."[369] "The dignity of our souls is so great," adds St. Jerome, "that each one, from his very birth, has an angel appointed to guard him."[370] "Every soul," continues St. Anslem, "is confided to an angel, at the same time that it is united to its body."[371] Tradition cannot, on this matter, be more general, more uninterrupted, or more uniform.

6. *Advantages we derive from the guardian angels.* — Although the salvation of our souls is the principal object of solicitude with our tutelar angels, yet they extend their care so far as to procure us the goods of this life also: they preserve us from accidents, to which we are all exposed, and deliver us from evils when we have fallen into them. They will carry you in their hands, says the scripture, lest you should hurt yourselves against a stone; the Lord will send his angels round those who fear him, and he will deliver them from all their tribulations.[372]

During the period of infancy, and in journeys, we are exposed to more immediate dangers. It is, then, also, that our guardian angels redouble their solicitude, according to the expression of St. Augustine.[373] The holy angels procure us temporal goods, by preventing the demons from injuring us. "The Lord," says Origen, "has given us the angels as charitable tutors, in order that the bad angels and their prince, who is called the prince of this world, may not be able to do us any harm."[374]

"Our weakness," adds St. Hilary, "could not resist the malice of the evil spirits without the assistance of our guardian angels."[375] "God aiding," says St. Cyril, "we have nothing to fear from the powers of darkness, for it is written: 'The angel of the Lord will encamp round those who fear him, and will deliver them.'"[376] The guardian angels are not content with enabling us to avoid the snares of the devil, and turning us away from vice; they also assist us in the practice of all the virtues.[377]

They offer our prayers to God, joining their own with them. "I presented thy prayer to the Lord," said the angel Raphael[378] to Tobias. We also read in the Apocalypse of an angel, who stood before the altar, with a golden censer and a large quantity of incense, that he might use them in offering the prayers of the saints on the golden altar that is before the throne; and the smoke of the incense, joined with the prayers of all the saints, rising from the hand of the angel, ascended before the throne of God.[379]

"Our guardian angels," resumes Origen, "offer our prayers to God through Jesus Christ, and they also pray for him who is confided to them."[380] "It is certain," says St. Hilary, "that the angels preside at the prayers of the faithful."[381] "The angels," adds St. Augustine, "not only bring us the favors of God, but they also offer him our prayers." "Not that God is ignorant of them," he says elsewhere, "but the more easily to obtain for us the gifts of his mercy and the blessings of his grace."[382]

Many holy fathers, whose testimony we have quoted, extend the assistance of the angels to all men in general, so that each person in particular, and without exception, has a guardian angel who never leaves him. Others seem to confine the assistance of guardian angels to the just alone, and only for the time during which they persevere in justice. This apparent contrariety is easily reconciled.

The angels have a more special care of the just, in proportion to their fervor in the practice of virtue; so that sin seems to remove them to a distance, inasmuch as it interrupts or diminishes more or less the effects of their vigilance. It is thus that the holy fathers themselves explain the objection. "The angels," says St. Basil, "are always near each faithful soul, unless they are banished by evil actions."[383] Does he mean to say that they entirely abandon sinners? No; but that they do not take the same care of the wicked as of the just. "The guardian angels," continues this holy doctor, "assist those more specially who give themselves to fasting."[384] St. Thomas teaches expressly that the angel guardian never abandons sinners entirely.[385] In another portion of these lessons, we shall speak of our duties toward the holy angels.[386]

Such is the invisible world that surrounds us; such its inhabitants; such their relation with us.

Greatness of man. — And now, O man, thou sublime being, measure, if thou canst, the greatness of thy dignity! Occupying, by thy body, the highest place in the scale of material beings, thou seest beneath thee, yet tending toward thee, thousands of other creatures, linked to one another. From the blade of grass to the cedar of Lebanon; from the drop of dew to the immense ocean; from the atom to the sun; from the mite to the elephant: all the material creation is referred to thee. King of the earth, thou art the vassal of heaven!

Occupying, by thy soul, the first step in the spiritual world, thou art the bond of two worlds. Below thee, thou seest only material creatures; above thee, only spiritual substances: and even these substances, though of a nature superior to thine, are referred to thee. O man, thou sublime being, measure, if thou canst, the greatness of thy dignity!

Let the thick veil, which hides the invisible world from thee, rise before thine eyes! What a spectacle! On thy left, millions of rebel angels, day and night moving round thee, scattering their snares under thy feet, and exhausting their strength and their genius to bring thee under their banner; on thy right, innumerable legions of tutelar angels, ever with arms in hand to protect thee; above thee, the Eternal, contemplating thee from his throne, and offering thee with one hand a crown, with the other his support!

Why this great battle between heaven and hell? Why this incessant strife? It is because thou art destined to be the prize of the conqueror. Why so many addresses on the part of God himself? Why so many opposite solicitations from Lucifer with his angels, and Michael with his angels? It is because thy will alone can turn the scale, and decide the victory. Dost thou now comprehend the mysterious deliberation of thy God before creating thee? Dost thou now comprehend why, after having created thee, he treated thee with so profound a respect?[387] Dost thou now, in fine, comprehend why thou wast the last act of the creative power? O man, thou sublime being, measure, if thou canst, the greatness of thy dignity?[388]

It is by man, then, that God terminates the work of the sixth day, and crowns the act of creation.

The Lord God saw at that time all the things which he had made, and he found that they were very good. At the close of each day, he was content with saying of every separate work that it was good. But today, when he considers all at one glance, when he compares them one with another, and with the eternal prototype of which they are the expression, he finds their beauty and perfection transcendent.

The universe appears to him like a magnificent painting, to which he has just given the last touch. Every part has its meaning; every stroke, its grace and beauty; every figure is well placed, and produces a charming effect; every color is well chosen: altogether it is marvelous—the very shadows improve it.

Perhaps you will ask me why the scripture says that God so frequently approved and admired his own works. It was to teach us the admiration which they should excite in us, the study which we should make of them, and the reflections which they deserve. Moreover, it was to confound beforehand our weak reason, which, in its ignorant pride, imagines that it finds defects and unprofitableness in the works of God. Truly, it well becomes man to discover that to be evil which God has found good! It was, in fine, to confound our stupidity, which does not reflect, and our ingratitude, which does not return thanks for the gifts of God; we remain ignorant and cold, though we live in the midst of astounding prodigies, we ourselves being among the most incomprehensible of them.

Let us henceforward shun this reproach: let us often consider with gratitude the sublime spectacle of the universe. A spectacle worthy of God may well be worthy of us. Is that which he admires, beneath our admiration? Can that which produces complacency and joy in him, produce no effect in us?

After having completed his work, God rested on the seventh day. The expression, *God rested*,[389] does not mean that God ceased to act, for he every day creates new spirits, human souls; and, since the beginning of the world, he has never ceased to preserve the universe by his power, and to rule it by his wisdom. "My Father," says the Son of God, "worketh until now, and I work."[390] The universe is not, in regard to God, what a palace is in regard to its architect. The palace, once built, subsists without the help of the architect, and survives him for centuries. But the works of God cannot continue in existence unless the same will that created them preserves them—creating them anew, so to speak, every moment.

The rest, then, which God takes is not a cessation from action; much less is it the consequence of a weariness like that which the laborer feels after his day's toil. An infinite power cannot be exhausted, and is never weary. Hence, the scriptural expression merely denotes that after the works of the sixth day God ceased to produce any new kinds of creatures. He had, in some manner, come forth from himself and his eternal repose to create the universe; he returned to his original state in the sense that, after the six days, his power ceased to be made visible by any new works.

On this account he blessed the seventh day, and sanctified it. In memory of this mysterious rest to which God returned, he specially appointed the seventh day of the week for his worship. He wished that this day should be for man a day of repose and thanksgiving. Free from the bodily labors that distract us during the week, and leave us only a few moments to think of God, we can, by the help of this holy leisure, recall to him our minds and hearts, meditate on his wonders, thank him for his benefits, lay before him our wants, study his law, and, above all, engage ourselves in the consideration of that eternal repose to which we are invited, and toward which all our thoughts and desires should tend.[391]

PRAYER

O my God! who art all love, I thank thee for having created on my account this world, and the angels themselves, whom thou hast appointed to defend me; grant that I may never do anything unworthy of myself.

I am resolved to love God above all things, and my neighbor as myself for the love of God; and, in testimony of this love, I shall every day recommend myself to my good angel.

Lesson 16: Fall of Man

Stratagem of the devil. — Crowned with honor and glory, our first parents enjoyed, in the terrestrial paradise, all that could satisfy reasonable creatures. Around them, a world submissive to their commands; before them, a life of exquisite delights here, and an eternity of ineffable joys hereafter; above them, an omnipotent Father, watching over them with love.

Alas! these paternal looks were not the only ones fixed on them: Lucifer also beheld them. This guilty angel, who had forfeited his own happiness, resolved to make our first parents the companions of his ruin, by making them the accomplices of his guilt. O cruelty! he attacked these two innocent creatures, in order to destroy the whole human race in its origin.

Of the various creatures before him, the serpent appeared most suitable for his design. He took possession of the body of this animal, the most cunning, the most clever, the most wily of all those which the Lord had created on the earth. Under this figure he addressed himself to the woman, whom he knew to be naturally weak, inquisitive, and credulous. He first flattered her with the love of liberty; and, feigning compassion, asked her: "Why has God not allowed you to eat freely of all the fruit in this garden?"

Imprudence of Eve. — Eve, instead of closing her ears against the envenomed voice, as a testimony to God of her fidelity, answered the seducer: "We have permission to eat of the fruit of all the trees in paradise, except this one in its midst; as for it, the Lord has forbidden us to eat of it, or even to touch it, lest perhaps we should die."

This beginning of the conversation was a grand presage of the success of the temptation: so true it is, that we must never reason with the enemy of our salvation. It succeeded too well with the tempter not to pursue his advantage. The lying spirit then dared to say, contrary to the formal assurance of God, that it should not be so. He even had the boldness to attribute this prohibition of God to a feeling of base jealousy. "You are very simple," he said, "to allow yourselves to be frightened in this manner. God knows that the day in which you eat of this fruit your eyes shall be opened; you shall be as gods knowing good and evil."

Thus, the first fault of our mother was to enter into conversation with the tempter; the second was to cast her looks on the fruit of the forbidden tree. Instead of turning away her eyes, as from a thing that was prohibited her, she took a pleasure in beholding this dangerous object. The fruit was beautiful; it seemed that it ought to have an exquisite taste. The promises of the tempter were fluttering. Curiosity, vanity, and presumption induced a forgetfulness of God, and banished fear. The woman, seduced, laid her hand on the forbidden fruit. She ate of it.

Frailty of Adam.—The tempter was in admiration with himself. But he wisely judged that Adam was too well instructed to be taken in so gross a snare.[392] He did not attempt to deceive, but to weaken Adam. If Eve could only be employed to tempt her spouse to a compliance, the archfiend might rely on the victory. She defended herself as poorly from this attack as from the first. She then presented the fruit to Adam, who was not seduced by the demon, but allowed himself to be overcome by an easy condescension toward his wife.[393]

He ate the fatal fruit, which deprived him of his innocence, and made him lose in a moment the privileges that he had been honored with; these privileges he might have transmitted to his posterity, at the sole cost of doing himself a short and slight violence.

Until this moment, Adam and Eve had remained naked, as they were created. They did not blush at their nakedness, because they were clothed with the robe of innocence. Stripped of this innocence, their eyes were opened, and the knowledge of their state became the first effect of their prevarication. Such were the sad lights that they derived from their fault: the knowledge of good and evil, so vauntingly recommended by the tempter, extended no farther. They availed themselves of it, to cover themselves as well as they could with fig-tree leaves, of which they made themselves large cinctures. Hence, let us never forget that though our garments be of linen, or purple, or silk, they should remind us of the sin and shame of our first parents. What vanity, then, can we take in them?

Goodness of God.—Suddenly, they heard the voice of the Lord, as he walked in the garden in the afternoon. These words mean that the Lord hastened to make the culprits feel their guilt, in order to penetrate them with a lively remorse for it. Infinite goodness! After our first parents had transgressed the law given them, the Lord did not cease to show himself merciful in their regard, but, ever like himself, he remembered that he is a Father and a physician. As a Father, he beholds a son degrading his nobility, and renouncing his high destinies, to crawl in the mire; and, yielding to paternal tenderness, he cannot leave the guilty one without succor—no, he takes a compassionate interest in the fallen, to elevate him by degrees from his baseness, and to reestablish him in his lost rights. As a physician, he runs with eagerness to the sick man, lying on the bed of suffering, whether the benefit of his skill has been sought or not. This is the manner in which God acts with man.[394]

Meanwhile, the guilty, having heard the voice of the Lord in the garden, ran to hide themselves among the trees in the garden. How strange a folly, to imagine oneself hidden from the all-seeing eye of him who fills all places! You call those servants insolent, who, to avoid the presence of their irritated master, run away and hide their troubles and terrors in the nooks and corners of the house. Thus, Adam and Eve, for want of an asylum, seek it in the very house of the master whom they have outraged, among the trees of his garden.

Notwithstanding their precautions, the sovereign judge soon discovers them. Behold the culprits in his presence! Let us recollect ourselves a moment, and, in the silence caused by our sorrow and dread, let us assist at the examination: it is our first parents who are about to be judged. Let us hear attentively the answers of the accused, and the sentence that shall be passed, as well on them as on the perfidious instigator of their crime.

Let us recollect first the threat which God had made to our first parents: "The day on which you eat the fruit of the tree of the knowledge of good and evil you shall die."[395] Death of body and soul was to be the punishment of their guilt. The conduct of God toward the rebel angels established a terrible precedent: the human race deserved to be on the spot precipitated into hell, and the justice of God seemed moved to the rigorous execution of the sentence. What will this God, who is at once a judge and a Father, do? How will he reconcile the pleadings of his tenderness with the rights of his justice? Let us follow this momentous trial.

Interrogation of the guilty. — The Lord God calls Adam, saying: "Adam, where art thou?" He calls him by his name, to encourage him. Adam replies: "I heard thy voice in the garden, and I was afraid, because I was naked, and I hid myself." The Lord asks: "How didst thou know thou wast naked, but because thou didst eat the forbidden fruit?"

These first questions show us in its full light the inexhaustible clemency of the judge. He need not have addressed a single word to the guilty, but have pronounced at the moment the sentence of death, which he had threatened. He does not do so: he represses his just indignation, and listens to the culprit's defense.

What will the accused answer?

"The woman whom thou gavest me for a companion, presented me with the fruit of this tree, and I did eat of it." He cannot deny his crime; but, instead of humbling himself, and having recourse to the clemency of his judge, he casts the blame of his act on the woman whom God has given him. He seems to accuse God himself of being the first cause of his ruin. Such an excuse could not be admitted. The Lord does not deign even to consider it. Adam being convicted of disobedience, he interrogates the other culprit.

"Why," he says to the woman, "hast thou done this?" That is, thou hast heard the complaint lodged against thee by thy husband; why hast thou become the instrument of his and thy misfortune?

Eve answers: "The serpent deceived me, and I did eat of the fruit." She defends herself no better than her spouse. As Adam had cast his fault on Eve, so Eve endeavors to cast it on another culprit. The Lord presses his questions no further. If he were to act otherwise, it would not be to procure information, for nothing is concealed from him. He desires to show his clemency toward the guilty, and to afford them an opportunity of presenting their justification, if in their power.

Sentence against the devil. — After having received the declaration of our first parents, the Lord addressed himself to the instigator of the crime, not to hear any defense, not to enter into any investigation of the matter; but to pronounce sentence. Without asking him why he had done so to Adam and Eve, the Lord says: "Because thou hast done this, thou art cursed among all animals and beasts of the field; thou shalt crawl on thy belly, and thou shalt eat the dust all the days of thy life. I will place enmity between thee and the woman, between thy race and hers. Her race shall crush thy head, and thou shalt lay snares for her feet."[396]

We are impatient to know why it is the serpent and not the devil, the instrument and not the author of the crime, that is punished. Here, again, we shall see shining forth the tender love which God bears us.

The father, who has been robbed of a beloved son by an assassin's sword, first vents his fury on the murderous weapon, which he breaks into fragments. God acts here in like manner. He chastises the serpent, which the demon had employed for a criminal purpose, by inflicting on it a perpetual punishment, to make us understand by this sensible image how odious the demon is to him; and, since he displays so much rigor against that which was only the instrument, I leave you to imagine the treatment which the author of the outrage receives. As the curse pronounced against the demon, who is banished far from us into hell, produces no effect apparent to our eyes, God is pleased to give us a sensible representation of it in the punishment of the serpent, which is condemned to crawl on the earth and to eat the dust.

Mercy and justice toward our first parents. — The sentence being pronounced on the devil, the judge turns toward our first parents. But, O infinite mercy! even before acquainting them with their sentence, he allows to shine on their eyes, in the very condemnation of the tempter, the bright rays of hope.

And first, in saying that he would put enmity between the race of the woman, and the race of the serpent, he gave them to understand that they should not undergo death the very day of their sin, as they might have expected. If they were condemned to it they should have time to prepare for it, and render it meritorious. Then, adding that the race of the woman should crush the serpent's head, he taught them that the evils of which they were the victims would be repaired.

With this twofold assurance, our first parents awaited, without disquietude, the sentence of a judge who showed himself so clement. Mercy had indeed conquered; but still there was something due to justice.

The Lord then turns toward the woman, less guilty than the devil, but more guilty in a certain sense than the man,[397] and says to her: "I will multiply thy sufferings; thou shalt bring forth children in the midst of the most bitter sorrows; thou shalt be subject to man, and he shall have dominion over thee."[398] Observe the divine clemency even in the severity of the chastisement. The sorrows of childbirth will be balanced by consolations, which will soon make them forgotten. And woman, by her gentleness and resignation, will regain a portion of her dignity, and sweeten the dominion of man.

There still remains the father of the human race, the king of the visible world, the well-beloved of his God. The Lord addresses him, saying: "Because thou hast preferred the voice of thy wife to my command, and hast eaten of the forbidden fruit, the earth, which of itself, and without compulsion, would have provided for thy wants, will henceforward present thee only a cursed and ungrateful soil. All the days of thy life it will require the most wearisome labor to obtain from it, against its will, the bread which thou shalt purchase in the sweat of thy brow. It will be covered with briars and thorns, through which thou wilt gather the herbs that will serve thee as a portion of thy nourishment. Such will be thy condition till, worn out with labors, and subjected to death, thou shalt return into the earth, from which thou wast taken; for dust thou art, and into dust thou shalt return."

This terrible sentence strikes the culprit throughout his whole being. His understanding darkened, his will inclined to evil, his body overwhelmed with sorrows: all will henceforward attest the greatness of his fault and the severity of God's chastisements. Nevertheless, Adam should find himself happy in being let off so easily. In the midst of all these evils, the choicest good still remains to him, namely, hope; in other words, time and means to repair his misfortune. He is much better treated than the rebel angels. Although threatened with the same punishment, he can recover heaven: they shall never be able to do it. Now, when one has not lost heaven irreparably, what are all other losses?

The Lord God, whose paternal heart suffers from the strokes which his justice inflicts on the guilty, hastens to give our first parents an affecting mark of his goodness; for it is in little attentions that kindness shows itself most. To spare them the shame of their nakedness, he himself provides them with garments made from the skins of beasts.

This mournful scene of the first judgment of God takes place in the very garden where the crime was committed. To moderate the bitterness of their grief, the Lord again consoles his two creatures. At this moment the first woman received from her husband the name of *Eve*, or "Mother of all the living": an inspired name, which, raising the dignity of the woman, foretold the Blessed Virgin, and strengthened the hopes of the guilty. It only remained to execute the sentence. The Lord spoke, and our parents departed overwhelmed with sorrow from the terrestrial paradise, never to enter it again.[399] A cherub, with a fiery sword, came and stood at the entrance, to refuse admission to the first man and all his posterity.

The penance of Adam and his burial on Calvary. — Exiled a short distance from this place of delights, and obliged to cultivate the earth for his support, Adam spent a long life of 930 years bewailing his unhappy transgression. His penance was so humble and so persevering that, in consideration of the future liberator, he recovered the special friendship of God, in whose love he died.[400] The father of the human race, or at least his head, was buried on Calvary, at the very place where, 4,000 years after the creation, stood the cross of the Redeemer.

It was fitting, say the fathers of the Church, that our Lord, coming to redeem the first Adam, should choose to suffer at the place where he had been buried, and thus, while atoning for his sins, should also atone for all his race. It had been said to Adam: "Thou art dust, and into dust thou shalt return";[401] and, on this account, Jesus Christ came to find him at the place where the sentence had been executed, in order to deliver him from the curse, and, instead of the words, "Thou art dust, and into dust thou shalt return," to say to him: "Arise thou that sleepest, and come forth from thy tomb."[402]

Thus, the name *Calvary*, which signifies "skull," unites in one prophecy the burial of Adam with the tomb of our Lord, all the sacrifices and mysteries of the old with those of the new law. This is one of those beautiful harmonies, which we meet with at every step in the order of grace as well as in that of nature, and which disclose a Wisdom that nothing can escape.[403]

PRAYER

O my God! who art all love, I thank thee for not having abandoned man after his sin—what do I say, O my God?—for having promised us a Redeemer, who should restore with interest the goods that we had lost.

I am resolved to love God above all things, and my neighbor as myself for the love of God; and, in testimony of this love, I shall resist temptation as soon as I perceive it.

Lesson 17: Agreement between the Divine Justice and Mercy in the Punishment and Transmission of Original Sin

The Indian king. — In reward for the attention with which you have followed the preceding lessons, we shall begin this one with a little story. A king of the Indies was setting out for the chase with his principal officers. Arrived at the place of general meeting, his highness withdrew from the company, and concealed himself in the depth of a forest. After some time he heard at a short distance a very animated conversation, the meaning of which he desired to understand. He drew near softly, and concealed himself behind an immense palm tree. It was a wood seller and his wife, who complained bitterly of the miseries of life. The woman, particularly, spoke loud against God and our first parents. "Ah!" said she, "if I had been there instead of Eve, never should gluttony or curiosity have made me disobey."[404]

The king allowed them to continue without any interruption. When they had done, he went forward, and seeming not to have heard anything, said to them: "You are very miserable; if you desire it, I shall change your lot; you have only to follow me."

The look, the tone, the appearance of the unknown, easily convinced the two wood gatherers. It is so easy to convince us, when happiness is promised us. "Come with me," said the king; and, on the spot, quitting their labor and their tools, they walk after him.

The distance is pretty long. At length the end of the forest is reached. The officers and royal suite are here assembled. The monarch ascends his palanquin, and, to the great astonishment of all the court, brings his two new friends with him. Arrived at the palace, he provides them with garments and apartments suitable to their new position. Numerous officers are placed under their orders. All persons are anxious to serve them, because they behold in the new guests their master's favorites.

Some days pass thus in joy and abundance; and the wood seller and his wife congratulate themselves and bless the king. However, he one day called them to him, and said: "You know the state from which I lately withdrew you: you are now happy. It depends upon yourselves to possess always the happiness that you now enjoy; if you be faithful to my orders, your children shall also participate in the same advantages. I annex only one condition to my favors: you may eat of all the meats every day brought to you, with the exception of one, which shall be placed at the center of the table, in a rich golden dish, adorned with jewels, and covered. The day on which you touch it you shall die. Do not forget: the fate of yourselves and your children depends on your fidelity."

The king then retired, and our fuel gatherers praised to the skies the goodness of one who was pleased to attach their happiness, and that of their children, to such an easy condition.

The hour of repast arrives; the golden dish is placed on the table. Its elegant shape, the fretwork that adorns it, the precious stones that enrich it, quickly arrest the looks of the two guests, who, for the rest, used always to eat alone. The woman especially is unable to draw her eyes from the brilliant object; but, through respect for the orders of the king, she goes no further. At the next repast the dish is again placed on the table. The more it is seen, the more beautiful it seems. A desire springs up in the heart of this new Eve; still, she dare not yet manifest it.

The following days, the same sight and the same desire. At length, after two months, curiosity carries the day. The woman said to her husband: "As long as this dish is on the table every kind of food is insipid to me; I should be happy if I could only see what it contains: it is not my intention to eat anything out of it." "Beware!" replies the husband, "beware of such a thought; the king has declared his will on the matter: the day on which we touch this dish we shall die." "But," answered the wife, "we can touch it without anyone seeing us; I shall just raise the cover ever so little, take a peep, and be satisfied." The husband has not the courage to displease his wife. "Allow me," he says, "to assist you; the danger will be less."

The wife, all eagerness, stretches forward her head, while the husband gently lifts the fatal cover. But, O misery! a tiny mouse rushes about the dish! The wife, alarmed, screams; the husband lets the cover fall; the little prisoner escapes and vanishes.

The king, who chanced to be in an adjoining apartment, at once proceeds to ascertain the cause of the noise, and detects the guilty pair in the deed. "Is it thus," he says to them in an angry tone, "that you respect my commands? You shall undergo the punishment with which I threatened you." At these words, he orders them to be put to death. On the moment, the only son of the king comes forward, and, casting himself on his knees before his father, exclaims: "Pardon, pardon them; if a victim is required for thy justice, behold me, my father; I offer thee my life." The king accepts the mediation of his son, whom he condemns to death instead of the two culprits. The young man is conducted to the scaffold. He dies. Through the merits of his death the two criminals preserve their lives, and obtain all the means necessary to recover the advantages of which they have deprived themselves by their fault.

"Only," says the king to them, "you shall not recover the goods which you have lost, unless by availing yourselves of the means for which you are indebted to the death of my well-beloved son. This is the trial which I appoint you. You shall undergo it far from my palace; take your rags, and the road that leads to the forest. If you be faithful, and love my son, I will restore you all the goods that you have lost, and others even greater. All your children, even to the last generation, shall enjoy them after you; moreover, you shall want for nothing as regards body or soul. If you should have need of anything, you shall ask it, and on the spot you shall be satisfied."

Is there, we ask, a shadow of injustice or cruelty in the conduct of this good king? On the contrary, is he not full of justice and mercy?

Original sin. — And now, that which we suppose to have passed in the Indies took place in the terrestrial paradise. The conduct of this king exactly represents to us the conduct of God.

I. Before being drawn from nothingness, our first parents were less than wood gatherers: they were nothing; they had no right to anything. When giving them their existence, God could have created them in a state inferior to that in which they came forth from his hands.

II. The fulfillment of the command which God gave them, after having laden them with honor and glory, was very easy; it was also a matter of the utmost importance, since on it depended the happiness of our first parents and their descendants.

III. This command was most clear. "The day on which you eat of the fruit of the tree of the knowledge of good and evil you shall die." No equivocation or ambiguity here. Adam and Eve had, moreover, all the graces necessary for its observance; they could not pretend forgetfulness or ignorance. They remembered this precept so well, in its precise sense, and in the terrible consequences of its violation, that the woman herself said to the serpent: "The day in which we eat of this fruit we shall die."

IV. It was most just. God had certainly a good right to impose this prohibition on creatures whom he had drawn from nothingness, and to annex to their fidelity a continuance of the privileges, both for themselves and for us, with which he had endowed them. God is the master of his gifts; he can grant them on whatever conditions he pleases: And who amongst us can consider that to be difficult which he imposed on our first parents? If they became prevaricators, in spite of so many considerations and so many means of preservation, to whom could they complain of the punishment inflicted on them?

V. In executing the threats which he had uttered against them, God remained perfectly just. What, now, were the consequences of original sin in regard to our first parents? They extended to the present and the future life. In the present life, some affected the body, and others the soul. As for the body, the effects of original sin for our parents were death and all the miseries of life. As for the soul, the loss of sanctifying grace, that is, the forfeiture of the supernatural state, or of the right to see God in his essence, and of the power to merit; also, concupiscence, that is, a violent inclination to evil, and ignorance, which darkened to their eyes the truths, of which, before their fall, they had a clear knowledge. The result of original sin for our first parents in the future life was hell, that is, the pain of loss, which consists in the eternal privation of God, and the pain of sense, which is eternal fire. Let us not forget that in Adam and Eve, guilty of their own free choice, the sin that we term *original* was actual: accordingly, it merited for them the torments of hell.

Such is the teaching of the Catholic Church, the infallible organ of truth. "If any one," says the holy Council of Trent, "does not admit that the first man, Adam, by transgressing the command of God in the terrestrial paradise, lost thereby the sanctity and justice in which he had been established, and incurred by his prevarication the anger and indignation of God, and consequently death itself, with which he had been previously threatened by God, and along with death, captivity under the power of him who had thenceforth the empire of death, namely, the devil; and, in fine, that the whole person of Adam was changed and degraded, in body and in soul, by the effect of that disobedience: let him be anathema."[405] Thou art just, then, perfectly just, O my God! in the punishment of our first parents; thou art no less so in regard to their posterity.

Effects of original sin. — In effect, as to us, the consequences of original sin are in this world: with regard to the body, subjection to sufferings and death; with regard to the soul, the loss of sanctifying grace, and with it the right to eternal happiness; also, ignorance in the mind and concupiscence in the will. Let us again hear the oracle of truth itself. "If any one asserts," says the holy Council of Trent, "that the sin of Adam was hurtful only to himself, and not to his posterity, and that the justice and sanctity which he had received from God, were lost only for himself, and not for us at the same time; or that, sullied with the sin of disobedience, he only transmitted corporal pains to the human race, and not sin itself, which is the death of the soul: let him be anathema. For he contradicts the apostle, who tells us that 'sin entered into the world by one man, and by sin death, and thus death passed to all men by him in whom all have sinned.'"[406]

Such are the evils that original sin causes us in this life. Now, the contrary goods, that is, sanctifying grace or a supernatural union with God, the right of the intuitive vision in heaven, an absolute dominion over our passions, exemption from sorrow and death, were not due to us. They were so many gifts of the pure liberality of the Creator. Such is also the doctrine of Catholic theology. St. Augustine, in particular, the experienced interpreter, so safe in matters of reason and faith, teaches this doctrine formally; and the whole Church applauded the condemnation of Baius, who had maintained the contrary.[407] As for the effect of original sin in the other life, with respect to us, it is a matter of faith that it deprives us of heaven, that is, of the intuitive vision of God, unless it be effaced by baptism. The words of our Lord are formal: "Unless you be born again of water and the Holy Ghost, you cannot enter into the kingdom of heaven."[408]

Transmission of original sin. — With regard to us, then, God has been just in the punishment of original sin. And, in reality, it is no more contrary to divine than to human justice, to include children in the condemnation of their father, by depriving them of the gratuitous privileges which they should have enjoyed if their father had continued faithful.

But does the loss of heaven necessarily involve the pain of hell, so that a child of Adam who dies with original sin alone is condemned to the punishment of a miserable eternity? Without entering into any details on the various opinions enunciated on this matter,[409] we shall quote the words of one of the most celebrated defenders of religion. "Original sin," says Bergier, "was, in Adam and Eve, a sin of self-will, committed with reflection; therefore, it rendered them deserving of eternal punishment. It is not the same in our regard. We may say that God does not condemn to hell the souls that are guilty of this fault alone. It is permitted us to believe, with St. Thomas,[410] that God deprives them only of supernatural beatitude, to which they have no right. The Faculty of Theology in Paris, in the censure of *Emile*, declared that this opinion was not blamable."[411]

Though no one can solve the question with certainty, still it is beyond all doubt that God will never do an injustice to any person, and that his conduct can never be the subject of a reasonable accusation.

It is a mystery, indeed — the condemnation of all in the person and for the fault of one — but it is a mystery as certain as it is unassailable.

Alas! yes, it is certain that man is born degraded. Now, he is not degraded unless because he is fallen; and, under a good God, he did not fall, unless because he was guilty. All kinds of proofs assemble in a body to confound the impious of our days, who dare to deny the transmission of original sin.

The Bible, the book by excellence, to whose truth such illustrious homage is rendered by modern science, continually proclaims this dreadful mystery. "Who is free from stain?" cries out the patriarch of sorrow from the bosom of the Gentile people. "No person, not even the child of a day old."[412] And the royal prophet: "I have been conceived in iniquity, and formed in sin in my mother's womb."[413]

And the most sublime interpreter of the counsels of God, the great apostle: "As by one man sin entered into the world, and by sin death, so death has passed to all men by him in whom all sinned...And as the condemnation is for all by the sin of one, so justification and life are for all by the justification of one," who is Jesus Christ.[414]

To the words of St. Paul are joined those of all the great men who are the glory of Christian ages, the Athanasiuses, the Augustines, the Chrysostoms, the Thomases of Aquin. To our modern scoffers we might address the interpellation of Clement of Alexandria to the heretics of his time: "No person, according to the scripture, is exempt from sin, though he should have lived but one day. Let them tell us then, where has the newborn babe sinned, or how has one, who never performed an action, fallen under the curse of Adam?"[415]

"Children are baptized," adds Origen, "to be forgiven their sins. What sins? When did they commit sins? What reason can there be for baptizing children, unless it is found in this passage: 'No person is free from stain, though he should have lived but one day'? It is because baptism effaces the sin in which they are born that little children are baptized."[416]

Repeating this wondrous tradition, the Catholic Church strikes with anathema any person who dares to deny the transmission of Adam's sin to all his posterity.[417] Is it necessary to summon pagan generations of past ages from their tombs, or to call as witnesses nations that are still seated in the shadow of death? They will answer us with one voice, either from the depths of their tombs, or from the recesses of their forests: "Yes, we were born guilty." "The first man and woman," say the Parsees (Guebres, or Persian fire-worshippers), "were in the beginning pure, and submissive to Ormuzd, their maker. Ahriman saw them, and was jealous of their happiness. He approached them under the guise of a snake, presented fruits to them, and persuaded them that he was the author of mankind, of animals, of plants, and of the beautiful universe in which they dwelt. They believed him, and henceforward Ahriman was their master. Their nature was corrupted, and this corruption infected their posterity."[418]

One of the most remarkable of Mexican traditions is that of the mother of our flesh, the woman of the serpent, fallen from her first state of innocence and happiness.[419]

What mean the expiatory rites that we find among all peoples for the purification of the infant on its entrance into life? This ceremony usually takes place on the same day as a name is given to the child. This day, among the Romans, was the ninth for boys, the eighth for girls.[420] It was called *lustricus*, on account of the lustral water which was employed to purify the newly born.[421] Similar rites are found among all nations. This fact is so evident that Voltaire himself is obliged to admit it. "We notice," he says, "that the Parsees have always had a baptism. Baptism is common among all the ancient nations of the East."[422] And elsewhere: "The fall of degenerate man is the foundation of the theology of all ancient nations."[423]

And, without having recourse to these foreign authorities, do we not find within ourselves the proof of our degradation? What, in effect, I ask you, are these strange compounds of good desires and bad inclinations, of greatness and meanness, of truth and error, of virtue and vice, that are manifested within us from childhood? Who are these two enemies that we carry within us, and that make our whole life a continual warfare? You cannot deny what we all are; and, certainly, he would be deserving of pity who should fail to see that man, at present, inclined to evil from his youth, is only a sad wreck.

Granted that these things are so; after all, how has the crime of one man infected his whole race? How can children justly bear punishment for the fault of their father? This is what the arrogant reason of our century asks with greater assurance than ever. As an answer, we would first remind it of the preceding explanations on the effects of original sin; then, descending into the depths of the mysteries of human nature, say, with a pagan philosopher:[424]

"There are some collective beings, who can be guilty of certain crimes, as well as individual beings. A state, for example, must be taken as a whole, like an animal which always continues the same, and whose identity is not altered by age. The state, then, being one, as long as the association maintains unity, rewards and punishments for all that is done in common are justly distributed to it, as they are distributed to a single individual.

"But if a state can be considered from this point of view, it ought to be the same with regard to a family proceeding from a common stock, which imparts to it that mysterious energy, or essence, or qualities, which extend to every individual of the line. Beings, that come from generation, do not resemble productions of art. Among the latter, when a work is finished, it is immediately taken out of the hands of the workman, and no longer forms a part of him; it is, indeed, by him but not of him. On the contrary, that which is begotten proceeds from the very substance of the generating being; so that it receives of him something which is most justly punished or rewarded for him, because this something is himself."

Such is evidently the case with the human race. "What are we?" says St. Augustine, "what are all men but a continuation of Adam, one and the same man perpetuating himself through centuries with his various qualities and vices?" *Omnes nos unus Adam.* (We are all but one Adam.) Hence, St. Paul sees among all men only two men: the first Adam, of whom we are all, by our corporal birth, the defiled continuation and reproduction; and the second Adam, our Lord Jesus Christ, of whom we become, by a spiritual birth, the sanctified continuation and reproduction.[425]

These considerations, which cast some light on this profound dogma, are of a nature to satisfy an upright and reflecting mind, as well as to close the mouths of vulgar wranglers, by showing them that the object of their attacks is not at all contrary to reason.

Thus, we repeat, on one side, the terrible mystery of the transmission of original sin is certain; on the other, it is unassailable. The reason is evident: since God is infinitely good, just, and holy, we must necessarily conclude that the transmission of original sin is not contrary to infinite goodness, justice, or holiness. In one word, God is just, and we are punished: this is the sum of all that it is indispensable for us to know—the remainder is only a matter of pure curiosity.

Let us fear nothing: God has never done, and never will do, a wrong to any person. Such is the grand answer to all difficulties, that our own mind or the minds of others can raise on this mystery, or on any other mystery that we meet with in religion. We are happy to say it is also the answer counseled by the great master who is our guide. "Although I may not be able," says St. Augustine, "to refute all the arguments of heretics, I see, nevertheless, that we must hold to that which the scripture clearly teaches us, namely, that no man can come to life and salvation without being united to Jesus Christ, and that God cannot condemn any one unjustly, or unjustly deprive any one of life and salvation."[426]

Justice and mercy in regard to our first parents.—God, then, was just, perfectly just, in punishing Adam and Eve, and in including all of us in their punishment. What is particularly affecting is that we see shining through this conduct, so severe in appearance, an infinite mercy.

I. Instead of putting our first parents to death on the very day of their fault, as he had a right to do, he allows them time and means to do penance.

II. To avenge them on the devil, he promises the woman that she shall one day crush the serpent's head. As shown in the development of the work of the redemption, God makes two announcements to our first parents: one, that he shall restore them all the goods they have lost; the other, that they shall really become like him, in order to confound the pride of Satan, by accomplishing, in its full extent, the promise which he deceitfully has made them: "You shall be as gods."

III. This redemption will be so abundant, the goods it will procure to the human race so vastly transcending the evils caused by original sin, that the Church does not hesitate to exclaim, when speaking of Adam's misfortune: "O happy fault! O truly necessary sin! since it merited for us such a Redeemer."[427]

IV. From the moment of this fall, God has no other thought than that of repairing it: to save man must be his only affair; it must be the center from which all his designs will radiate; in fine, it must be the end of all his works.

. We are struck with astonishment at the wondrous ease and boundless mercy with which God forgives the father of the human race. Let us endeavor to cast some light on this abyss of wisdom and goodness: the noblest use of reason is to guide man to faith.

Harmony between justice and mercy in the mysteries of the incarnation and passion. — "By his sin man becomes the enemy of God, and it is necessary that the reciprocal hatred (that is, separation or opposition) between God and man should be changed into a reciprocal love, so that God and man may be again able to form a true society. But man cannot be reconciled with God, unless he is pardoned. Nor can God be reconciled with man, unless he is satisfied. These relations are necessary in connection with a being infinitely just and good.

"But God, infinitely just, cannot surrender the rights of his justice: he will then punish man with infinite rigor. On the other hand, God, infinitely good, and desiring to save man, will pardon him with infinite goodness. How can these things be reconciled? To punish man with infinite rigor is to put him to death in the midst of the most frightful torments; and to pardon him with infinite goodness is to preserve him safe and sound with all his privileges. Can God himself, omnipotent as he is, destroy and preserve man at the same time?

"Yes, he can: he can destroy one man in place of all men; he can preserve all other men in consideration of one man put to death. 'As the fault of one alone has rendered all men guilty, so the justice of one alone renders all men holy.'[428] Human justice can afford us an idea and example of such compensation."[429]

Witness, out of a thousand, that celebrated fact in the history of France: in 1347, Edward III, king of England, laid siege to Calais. Irritated at the prolonged resistance of the inhabitants, he pressed them so hard that they were ultimately obliged to sue for peace. Edward refused to grant it, unless they delivered into his hands six of the principal citizens to be treated as he should decide.

Eustace de St. Pierre offered himself as one of the six victims. Five others were found to follow his example. With ropes round their necks, and dressed in their shirts, they went to present the keys of the city to the English king. This fierce conqueror had absolutely determined on their death. The executioner was already sent for. It was only the abundant tears and the repeated entreaties of his queen that ultimately stayed his fury.

To this example we might add many others. And certainly it is a great mercy, when a whole family, when a whole population, when the whole human race is deserving of death, to remain satisfied that only one man should suffer in the place of all the rest.

"This is what God does. He destroys one man instead of all men. The man to be destroyed in place of all men must, then, be infinitely hated by God, since he will be laden with the infinite crimes of all men. At the same time this man, to whom all other men will owe their pardon, must be infinitely loved by God, since he will merit for all the forgiveness of their offenses.

"Now, God cannot hate any one infinitely, except a being laden with sins; nor love any one infinitely, except a being infinitely amiable, as himself, as God. This man then will be God: he will be a God-man.

"The God-man will then be destroyed instead of all men, to satisfy the justice of God; and mankind will be pardoned and preserved, through the merits of the God-man. The God-man will, then, be the mediator, the Savior, the Redeemer of the human race, and the founder of a new covenant between man and God."[430]

Thus, the Redeemer will unite in himself two great characteristics opposed to each other. He will be at once a prodigy of glory and of humiliation, the object of the complacency and of the severity of God. On the one hand, burdened with all the iniquities of the world, he will experience in his life and death whatever is most rigorous: he will be a man of sorrows. On the other, like God, and God himself, he will feel all the tenderness of God, and glorify God in the worthiest manner.

Such, then, is the harmony between the justice and the mercy of God in the punishment and the pardon of original sin. Man, a finite being, was incapable of atoning for an infinite wrong: he could not renew the supernatural bond, which had united him to God, and which sin had broken. God himself selects a victim, whose merits are infinite: the victim is sacrificed, sin is expiated, the supernatural bond is repaired, and all men are saved.

It is now easy to understand the astonishing facility with which God forgives our first parents. From all eternity, the incarnation of the Word was foreseen. God had continually before his eyes the immolation of this great victim. The sin of man was, in a certain sense, expiated before it was committed.

The fatal disobedience takes place. The eternal Word presents himself to his Father; he shows himself dying on Calvary. His mediation is accepted; and, the divine justice being fully satisfied, mercy is displayed with the utmost splendor in regard to the guilty.

It is also easy to understand how men, who lived before the coming of the Redeemer, were saved: they were saved in consideration of the merits of the future Redeemer. Though accomplished only in the plenitude of time, the voluntary sacrifice of the Lamb slain from the beginning of the world, *agnus occisus ab origine mundi*, appeased the anger of God, and procured time and means for men to recover his friendship.

Doctrine of St. Leo and St. Thomas: Necessity of faith in the Redeemer. — "Let no one, then," says St. Leo, "complain of the conduct which God has observed in the work of the redemption. Let no one say that Our Lord has been too late in being born according to the flesh, as if the times that preceded his birth were deprived of the fruit of the mysteries which he has wrought in the last ages of the world. The incarnation of the Word, decreed in the counsels of God from all eternity, produced before its accomplishment the same effects as it has since produced. Never, in the most remote antiquity, was the mystery of the salvation of men without its effect. That which the apostles preached, the prophets had long before foretold; and the work of the Savior cannot be regarded as too long deferred, since it has always been the object of faith.

"It is from no new line of conduct, then, or tardy compassion that God has provided for the redemption of the human race, by effecting the incarnation of his only Son. But from the earliest days of the world, he appointed one and the same cause of salvation for all men and all ages.

"True, the grace of God has been poured out more abundantly since the temporal birth of Jesus Christ; but it did not then begin to be communicated, for by it alone the saints of all bygone ages were sanctified. The profound mystery of God's love, the belief of which is now established throughout the earth, is of so efficacious a nature, that even when it was only predicted and prefigured, all those who by faith attached themselves to the promise which God had made, drew the same fruit from it as those who, since its accomplishment, have shared in its salutary effects. It was by faith that all the saints who preceded our Savior were justified and made members of the mystical body of Jesus Christ."[431]

Thus, salvation has never been possible but by Jesus Christ, and through faith in Jesus Christ. All men, without distinction of climate, age, or nation, have been obliged to believe in the great mystery of the redemption. As all men were condemned in the first Adam, on account of being united to him, so all men must be united to the second Adam, in order to be saved. The essential bond of this union is faith in him.

Let us hear the prince of theologians, St. Thomas, speaking of the necessity of faith in Jesus Christ. "There is not," he says, "according to the apostle, any other name under heaven by which men can be saved. Therefore, it is necessary that the mystery of the incarnation of the Word should be believed, in some manner, at all times, and by all men."[432] This belief has been different, according to times and persons.

"Man, before his fall, had an explicit faith in the incarnation of the Word, inasmuch as this incarnation had for its end the consummation of glory, but not inasmuch as it had for its end the deliverance of man from sin, through the death and resurrection of Jesus Christ.

"After sin, the mystery of the incarnation was believed, not only as to the incarnation, but also as to the passion and the resurrection, by which the human family have been delivered from sin and death. Otherwise men would not have prefigured the passion of Jesus Christ by the sacrifices in use before the law and under the law. The more enlightened knew explicitly the meaning of these sacrifices. The less enlightened, believing that these figurative sacrifices were established by God, found in them a veiled knowledge of Jesus Christ. Add to this, that they knew the mystery of the incarnation more distinctly in proportion as the time for its accomplishment drew nearer."[433]

PRAYER

O my God! who art all love, I adore the justice, and I bless the mercy, which thou dost display in the punishment of original sin. I thank thee for promising us a Savior: grant that we may profit by his merits.

I am resolved to love God above all things, and my neighbor as myself for the love of God; and, in testimony of this love, I shall every month renew my baptismal promises.

Lesson 18: History of Job

Men have always had the grace necessary to believe in the Redeemer. — Faith in the Redeemer having been always necessary for salvation, we must conclude that all men, without distinction of age or nation, have had the grace necessary to believe in the mystery of the redemption. The reason of this is because God wishes the salvation of all men without exception. He has, then, given to and preserved for men the lights and graces necessary to save them, so that salvation has never been impossible to any person.

We know well that the Jews had always a sufficient knowledge of the future Redeemer, in order to be saved. Was it the same with the Gentiles? How did they obtain or preserve the necessary knowledge and faith concerning the mystery of the redemption?

Proofs from reason; historical evidence. — We cannot fathom the abyss of the counsels of God, nor count up all the means that he has of communicating himself to his beloved creatures; yet there are many things known to us on the matter.

1. The Gentiles were, like the Jews, the descendants of Adam and Noe. They had, then, a knowledge of the condition of the first man, of his fall, of his early promises of a restorer. Wandering from the same paternal home, they carried these traditions with them: their history attests it.[434] Vestiges of the belief in a Redeemer are to be found even in the oracles of the Sibyls and in popular songs.[435]

There were some among the Gentiles who foretold the coming of the Messias: witness the holy man Job. St. Augustine says that providence allowed this man, though in the midst of heathenism, to belong to the true religion, in order to teach us that among pagans there were others also who formed a part of one holy and universal society.[436] Witness, too, the famous tomb, mentioned by St. Thomas, which was opened some centuries after the coming of the Messias, and in which was found a golden plate, on the breast of the deceased, with this inscription: "Christ will be born of the Virgin; and I believe in him. O sun, thou wilt behold me again in the times of Constantine and Irene!"

2. The great doctor adds that the revelation of the Messias was made to a large number of pagans. "If some," he adds, "were saved without this revelation, yet they were not saved without faith in the mediator; for, although they had not an explicit faith, they had an implicit faith in divine providence, believing that God would save men by means pleasing to himself, and according to what his Spirit had revealed to those who knew the truth."[437]

Thus, neither pagans nor Jews could ever be saved without, at least, an implicit faith, according to the explanation of St. Thomas, in the mystery of the redemption. "Moreover," says a great theologian, "our Lord having died for all men, who were, who are, and who will ever be, we must conclude that God has always given and still gives to all men, even to infidels, the graces of salvation, which, as a consequence, tend either directly or indirectly to bring them to the knowledge of Jesus Christ. If they corresponded with these graces, God would certainly grant them others more abundant. Consequently, there is no infidel condemned for want of faith in Jesus Christ, but for having resisted grace."[438]

Job: A witness and a prophet of the Redeemer. — The most celebrated of all the prophets of the Messias, among heathens, is undoubtedly the holy man Job. His life, full of grand instruction and useful examples, naturally finds place here. A perfect model of patience, a real hero in adversity, he seems to have been specially chosen by God to offer in his person, to all posterity, the admirable spectacle of a virtuous man struggling with adversity, but who, encouraged by the thought of heaven, shows himself superior to the miseries of the present life. Let us give his interesting history.

Job's history. — A man dwelt in the land of Hus, a country of Arabia: his name was Job. Simple and upright he feared the Lord, and avoided evil. He had seven sons and three daughters. Besides this fine and numerous family, he possessed that kind of property which then constituted the wealth and patrimony of the most distinguished families. Seven thousand sheep, three thousand camels, five hundred yoke of oxen, five hundred she-asses, and a proportionate number of attendants and domestics, made him one of the richest princes in the East.

He brought up his daughters near him. As for his seven sons, he had given them houses and lands. Abundantly provided with everything necessary for their maintenance, they lived apart at their different homes. One of the greatest cares of the virtuous father was to promote peace and union among his children. Hence, he willingly consented that his sons should invite the rest of the family to their houses at least once a year, on their birthdays. He then sent his three daughters along with their brothers, and allowed them to attend the feast.

When the festival day, whether it occurred seven or ten times a year, was over, he assembled all his children, instructed them on their duties, and disposed them, by his holy lessons, for the sacrifice which he wished to offer to the Lord on behalf of each of them. "Because," he said, "these are young people, who might easily allow some indiscreet word to escape them — how do I know but they have offended God in their hearts?"

With this fear, he rose early in the morning; and as among the ancient nations it was princes and heads of families who acted as priests on behalf of their subjects and their children, he immolated victims to the Lord, a holocaust of expiation.

What an admirable example, in a Gentile prince, of a simple faith and a truly paternal vigilance! Such an example, common heretofore in all the states of Christendom, is almost forgotten nowadays. Yet these are the domestic virtues and practices encouraged by religion, which draw down the blessings of God, delight the angels, and drive the devils to despair. By the faithful fulfillment of all the duties of a good father, Job, without knowing it, prepared his heart for a victory over all the powers of hell.

One day the blessed angels, interested in the salvation of men, appeared in the presence of the Lord to receive his orders, and to execute them. Satan, enraged with jealousy against all good persons, also made his appearance, soliciting permission to tempt men and to persecute them. "Satan," said the Lord to him, "whence comest thou?" "I have gone round the earth," Satan answered, "and visited it everywhere." The object of God in asking this question was to derive honor before his enemy from the fidelity of a virtuous man. The Lord is pleased in being glorified; and generous souls should find it the sweetest portion of their reward to give him pleasure.

"While traveling through the world," continued the Lord, "didst thou observe my servant Job? He has not his like on the earth. He is a simple and upright man, fearing

God, and avoiding evil." "It is no wonder," replied Satan, "that Job lives in the fear of God. Is it for nothing he serves thee? Thou hast made him rich and powerful; thou dost protect his family, his goods, his person; thou dost bless all his undertakings: every day increases his fortune. But change thy conduct toward him; lay thy hand ever so little on him; at least allow me some liberty: thou shalt very soon see whether his virtue will continue, or that he will not rather curse thee to thy face."

"Go," said the Lord to Satan, "I abandon to thee whatever Job possesses; only do not touch his person." Satan departed, and to its fullest extent used the liberty that God had granted him. Job was not expecting any conflict, but the saints are always sufficiently armed by their spirit of faith, and no attacks can find them unprepared.

One day, when Job's eldest son, according to the custom which we have mentioned, entertained his brothers and sisters, a messenger came running to Job, and said: "Thy oxen were ploughing, and thy asses were feeding near them, and the Sabeans[439] came and took them all away. They put all thy servants to the sword; I alone have escaped, and am come to tell thee."

He was yet speaking when another came to Job, and said: "Fire from heaven has fallen on thy flocks and thy shepherds; they are all burnt to ashes; I alone have escaped to bring thee the sad news."

This messenger had not finished speaking before a third came who said: "The Chaldeans[440] came in three great troops; they fell upon thy camels, and led them off; they slew all thy servants; I am the only one that did not perish in the massacre."

Before the end of this account another messenger arrived, who said: "Thy sons and thy daughters were at table in the house of their eldest brother, when suddenly there came from the desert an impetuous wind, which shook the four corners of the house. The house fell on thy children, and they were all crushed under its ruins; they are dead; I alone have escaped, and am come to tell thee of the dreadful accident."

After this last blow, Job arose, and rent his garments. Then, having shaved his head, he fell with his face on the ground and adored the Lord, saying: "I came forth naked from my mother's womb, and I shall return naked into the womb of the earth. The Lord gave me all; the Lord has taken all away. As it has pleased the Lord, so has it happened to me. Blessed be his name!"

Previously to this heroic effort of faith and courage, Job was to be pitied. He ceases to be so, when religion reigns supreme in his heart. If all afflicted persons were to follow this example, we might, indeed, still see great calamities on the earth, but we should never see misery inconsolable.

Still Job had not reached his final trial. One day, continues the sacred writer, the angels presented themselves before the throne of God, and Satan also stood there. "Whence comest thou, Satan?" said the Lord to him, as before. "I have gone round the earth," he answered, "and visited every place." "Hast thou considered my servant Job?" asked the Lord, "thou hast excited me against him; I have abandoned to thee his goods and his children; has he loved me less, or has he rebelled against me?"

"I am not surprised at it," replied Satan, "a person is consoled for every loss so long as he has health and life. But stretch out thy hand over his person; strike his flesh, and let pains creep through his bones; and thou shalt see whether he will not curse thee to thy face."

"Be it so," answered the Lord, "I abandon him to thee; only I forbid thee to take away his life." This gave the tempter great latitude. He turned his powers to account without delay. Having gone forth from the presence of the Lord, Satan struck Job with a frightful ulcer, which reached from the crown of his head to the soles of his feet. Poor and sick, and presenting a most disgusting appearance, Job was obliged to seat himself on a dunghill, and with the fragments of a broken dish to clean away the matter that flowed from his sores. In the soul of the just man so many sufferings raised no trouble; on his tongue, no murmur or indiscreet word. It was then that the devil employed the last means, and, to his mind, the most certain, for disturbing the patience of his unfortunate victim.

Job had a wife. She ought to have been his consolation. For indeed the assiduous cares of a wife, whose soul is penetrated with sentiments of religion, can considerably alleviate the sorrows of an afflicted and virtuous man.[441]

Friends had known her rich, influential, honored, the mother of many children: she had now lost everything on earth. The misfortune was that she was not contented with the hopes of heaven that still remained to her. Job, unlike his wife, still continued to bless God. More piqued, perhaps, at the constancy of her husband than at her own degradation, she said to him, in a tone of bitter irony: "Remain still in thy simplicity; continue to praise God; he treats thee in a manner well calculated to deserve thy gratitude. He is a very beneficent master indeed. Come, bless him for the last time, and die."

With a calmness, which ought either to have converted or maddened his wife, Job answered her: "Thou hast spoken like one of those foolish women from whom sorrow takes away the use of reason. If we have received good things from the hand of the Lord, why should we not also receive evil?"

In the midst of pains of every kind, the holy man did not utter a single complaint, did not yield to the least of those senseless transports which attack the providence of God and take away from the transitory afflictions of time all the merit that they have for eternity. It was then, truly, that faith in the true God afforded the world a spectacle worthy of the admiration of men and angels, namely, a just man battling with adversity and rising superior to misfortune.

The visit of his friends. — The rumor of Job's woes and disgrace soon spread through the countries bordering on his states. Three lords or petty kings, his particular friends, agreed to pay a visit of condolence to their old companion. These princes were named Eliphaz of Theman, Baldad of Sucha, and Sophar of Naamath.

At some distance from their friend, they cast their eyes upon him, but they could not recognize him. Having drawn nigh, they raised a loud cry; tears fell from their eyes; they rent their garments, and covered their heads with dust; they seated themselves on the ground, and for seven days and seven nights observed a great silence. Thus, the sum of Job's consolation was to see these men dismayed, their countenances dejected, their eyes bathed in tears.

At length, Job breaks the silence. Submissive as he is to the decrees of God, he delivers an eloquent discourse, showing how God regards the sorrows of his friends, at a time when their complaints, though lively and bitter, are humble and respectful.

"Let that day perish," he says, "in which I was born! Let that day be turned into darkness! Let God himself no longer look upon it! Let no light ever shine upon it!"

His friends answered him, that the evils of which he complained had fallen on him justly; that if he were not guilty of some secret crime, God would not afflict him so much. Job repeated and maintained that he was innocent, and that God sometimes tries the just by adversity.

It was in one of his answers to his friends, that the holy man allowed to escape him his immortal profession of faith in the divine Redeemer, who would yet unveil the secrets of hearts, and render to all men according to their works, after having raised them from the dead, and summoned them before his tribunal.

"Have pity on me, have pity on me," he says, "at least you, my friends, for the hand of the Lord has touched me. Why, thirsting for my ruin, do you also persecute me, reproaching me with crimes of which I am innocent? But, since you insult me with your reproofs, and seem to feast on my miseries, I shall find in my faith that comfort which you refuse me. Would that the language and the sentiments of my heart were written and preserved for posterity! Would that they were engraven on lead with a pen of steel or cut on stone with a chisel! Yes, I know that my Redeemer is living, and that I shall arise from the earth on the last day. I shall be clothed again with my skin, and in my own flesh, I shall see my God, the witness of my innocence; I shall see him myself, with my own eyes, myself and not another, and my eyes will contemplate him: this hope is laid up in my bosom."

What a magnificent prophecy! It must have been that the belief in a future Redeemer was very general in those remote times, when a prophet of the Gentiles, situated in a distant region of the East, could proclaim it with such precision.

Notwithstanding all his protestations of innocence, the friends of Job persisted in maintaining that he was guilty, and that his faults were the occasion of the evils that overwhelmed him. God, who beheld these combats, and who was preparing a victory for Job, did not delay very long to declare in his favor, and to confound his calumniators. But a few rather strong words had escaped Job. Patient under his sorrows, the liveliness of his zeal had carried him a little too far against the blindness of his friends and the unfairness of their judgments. The Lord gave him a charitable admonition on the matter. Though addressed to the holy man, it was also a lesson for the princes, his friends.

The Lord begins by enumerating the wonders of nature. All the questions that he puts to Job, and that at first sight appear foreign to the subject at issue are admirably connected with it. The Lord reasons thus: you cannot understand the order of nature, and you wish to search into that of grace; you do not know the laws by which my providence directs the inferior creatures that you see, and you wish to explain those by which I govern the superior world! Truly divine reasoning! which, humbling the curiosity and the pride of man, opens his heart to the virtues that befit his feebleness, namely, humility and faith!

Then, addressing himself to Job, from the midst of a dark cloud, the Lord says: "Gird thy loins, like a warrior. I will question thee; do thou answer me. Where wast thou when I laid the foundations of the earth? Who placed its measures, if thou knowest? Who stretched out the line upon it? Upon what are its bases fixed? Who enclosed the sea in its bed, when it broke its bonds, as a child coming forth from the womb of its mother, and I wrapped it in mist as in a garment, and surrounded it with clouds as with the swathing-bands of infancy?

"Hast thou commanded the morning star? Who has shown the dawn the place where it should appear? Dost thou know the pathway of light or the abode of darkness? Didst thou know that thou shouldst be born. Wast thou acquainted with the number of thy days? How is the light spread, or the heat diffused over the earth? Who traced the furrows of the thunderbolt? Canst thou send the lightning, and it will go, and return to thee, saying: 'Here I am'? Dost thou furnish meat for the lioness, and satisfy the appetite of her whelps? Dost thou prepare food for the raven, when its little ones wander about hither and thither, and, pressed with hunger, cry to the Lord?"

The rain, the snow, the hail, the cold, the heat, thunders and storms, the peculiarities and the instincts of animals, the resources and the harmonies of providence in the government of the physical world, are so many subjects on which the Lord is pleased, so to speak, to lead the curiosity of Job about, and exhaust his knowledge. Job, humbled, acknowledges that he does not know enough to answer the Creator.

Such is the very acknowledgment to which all upright and sensible men are reduced, like Job, notwithstanding the discoveries that are daily made by our greatest scholars in the secrets of nature.

Job justified and rewarded. — God, satisfied with his servant, reproves the three princes for the rashness of their judgments and the bitterness of their words. He requires that they should offer a sacrifice of expiation to him. "Job," adds the Lord, "will pray for you:

for his sake, I will forgive you." The sacrifice was accordingly offered; Job accompanied it with his prayers. The Lord heard them; and the three kings, indebted to their friend for their reconciliation with God, returned home.

The time had arrived when the prodigy of Job's recovery and reestablishment should be wrought. The Lord restored him to health, gave him the same number of children as before, and doubled the amount of the riches of which the devil had deprived him. Abounding in wealth, and respected by all the East, Job lived for 140 years more. He saw his children and his children's children unto the fourth generation, and died in a good old age, full of days.

Thus ended the life of the holy man, affording edification to all just souls and an abundance of consolation to all patient sufferers.

PRAYER

O my God! who art all love, I thank thee for giving all men the grace necessary to know their Redeemer. Grant that all may profit by it, and that, after the example of Job, we may courageously endure the pains of life, looking forward with confidence to our resurrection and reward.

I am resolved to love God above all things, and my neighbor as myself for the love of God; and, in testimony of this love, I shall take part in the work for the propagation of the faith.

Lesson 19: Knowledge of Religion

When, after a toilsome journey, the traveler reaches the summit of a mountain, he delights to rest his weary limbs, and to cast a look over the distance which he has passed. Let us imitate him, and discontinue our studies for a moment to consider the lesson that we have learned.

We know God. On the wings of reason and faith we have soared to the highest heavens, and proved the existence of a being superior to all other beings. His adorable perfections, his eternity, his independence, his immensity, have appeared to us as the sparkling rays of an ever unclouded sun, which knows neither rising nor setting. From the heavens we have descended to the earth, and contemplated God in his works. We have beheld in all creatures, as in a splendid mirror, the existence, the power, the wisdom, the liberty, and the goodness of the great Creator. The harmony of the universe, and the government of the moral world, have made providence palpable to us. We know God.

We also know man. Our ears have heard the creating words, "Let us make man"; and our eyes have seen him rise before us, in his regal majesty, the image and the viceroy of God among creatures. The body of man, with its wondrous organs, and his soul, with its still more wondrous powers and faculties, have revealed their secrets to us. Entering the terrestrial paradise, we have visited the palace of man, and assisted at his coronation. The charter, which established him the king and the high priest of the universe, has been read to us: his rights and his duties have been laid open before us. Our hand has turned over the first leaf of his history, so grand on one page, so sorrowful on the next. We know man.

After having studied God and man in themselves, what have we next to do but to examine whether there exist any relations between God and man, and what are those relations, the sum of which constitutes what the language of every people terms *religion*.

Hence arise the following questions, whose development will now engage our attention: 1) Is there a religion? 2) What is religion? 3) Can there be many religions? 4) Whence does religion come? 5) Which is the true religion? 6) Can the true religion change? We shall enter separately into each of these questions, which ought to interest us much more than all the political, scientific, literary, and social questions to which the great majority of men do not hesitate to devote a very considerable portion of that precious time which makes up their life on earth.

I. *Is there a religion?*—I summon around me, in a great circle, all the people that have ever appeared on and passed away from the earth, all the fathers and mothers, all the children, all the rich and poor; I place myself in the midst of this immense circle and, turning toward every point of it, interrogate my countless auditors: "Is it necessary that there should be relations of superiority and inferiority, of love and respect, of protection and gratitude, between father and son, between mother and daughter, between parents and children?" And I see all heads bending forward, all lips opening to answer me: "Yes, it is necessary that there should be relations between father and son, between mother and daughter, between parents and children."

I put a second question: "Is man born of himself?" The answer is: "Man is not born of himself; he has been created by God."

I continue to ask: "If there exist necessary relations of superiority and inferiority between a father and a son, because one is the author of the life of the other, is it not evident that relations even of a higher order must also exist between God, the Creator and Father of man, and man, the creature and child of God?" And my whole audience, rising, reply: "It is evident, as evident as is the light of day." What is better, the relations between God and man are much more intimate, much more sacred, much more noble, than those between parents and children; because parents are not the creators, nor the preservers, nor the last end of their children: these titles belong to God, and to God alone.

These answers received, I dismiss the vast assembly, and say to myself: "Let me see whether all these persons, whom I have been questioning, have told me the truth, and whether facts confirm their words: I shall make a tour round the world." Now, everywhere and always, I find nations believing in a religion, professing a religion; having temples, altars, priests, festivals, sacrifices. I do not meet a single tribe, however savage it may be, without some kind of worship; and I repeat, at the end of my journey, the words of a pagan philosopher: "If you travel the world, you may find cities without walls, without literature, without laws, without palaces, without riches, without money, without schools, without theatres; but, as for a city which has no temples or gods, which makes use of no prayers or oaths, which consults no oracles, which offers no sacrifices to obtain the blessings of heaven or to avert the evils with which it is threatened, this is what no one has ever seen; it would be easier to find a city built in the air than a people without some religion."[442]

Thus, religion exists; moreover, it has always and everywhere existed. This is a universal fact: consequently, a fact which is the work, not of man, but of God; a fact as necessary as the relations of superiority and inferiority which exist between God and man, and of which it is the direct manifestation. Religion is, therefore, necessary.

II. *What is religion?*—We have seen that between God the Creator, and man the creature, there exist natural and necessary relations, just as they exist between a father and a son. To these relations, already so noble, God gratuitously added others, still more perfect, by making himself the last end of man. Thenceforward, man was no longer destined to a mediate, but to an immediate possession and vision of the supreme being. The immediate possession and vision of God constitute supernatural happiness, that is, a happiness to which man had no claim, and which the conditions of his simple nature did not require. These additional relations, and the sublime union which was their consequence, existed from the first moment of man's creation; for man was at his creation established in a state of grace or supernatural justice.[443]

From all these natural and supernatural relations there arises between God and man a union or society, which is properly termed *religion*, that is, "a new bond."

If the word *religion* is admirably adapted to express the union which exists between God and man in the state of innocence, with much greater reason does it suit for the description of that union which exists between God and man after original sin. In effect, the fault of our first parents having broken the supernatural bond that existed before their revolt, the Son of God, as you know, volunteered to reestablish this sublime union, to withdraw man from the punishments due to his sin, to restore him his lost goods, and with advantage too, and thus to form again the alliance between God and man.

Hence, this new alliance, or restoration of the old, is called religion, that is, a "new bond," a "second bond," from a Latin word signifying "to bind again, to bind a second time." Such is the meaning of the word *religion*. To anyone knowing the world at the present day, and considering how many persons there are who speak of religion without understanding it, or ever reflecting on what it is in its essence, nothing will appear less surprising than the detailed explanations that we have just given.

These things being so, if now we are asked the question, *What is religion?* we answer with the incomparable St. Augustine, "Religion is the bond that unites man with God!"[444] From this definition, we derive the following: "Religion is the intercourse between man and God," or rather: "Religion is the sum of the relations that exist between man and God." All these definitions equally express the new bond, which, in virtue of the merits of the Redeemer, unites man with God, after the breaking of the first bond by original sin.

III. *Can there be many religions?*—Suppose I ask you, "Can it be true at Constantinople that two and two make four, and also true at Paris that two and two do not make four? Can it be true at Constantinople that there is one God, and also true at Paris that there is no God? Can it be true at Constantinople that God created man, and also true at Paris that God did not create man? Can it be true at Constantinople that between God, the Creator of man, and man, the creature of God, there are relations of superiority on the one hand and inferiority on the other, and that these relations impose certain duties on the part of man, and also true at Paris, that between God, the Creator of man, and man, the creature of God, there are no relations of superiority on the one hand and inferiority on the other, nor any duties resulting from these relations?

"Can it be true at Constantinople that man is obliged to believe in God, to hope in him, to love him, and to serve him as God desires that man should serve him, and also true at Paris that man is not obliged to believe in God, to hope in him, to love him, or to serve him, either as he wishes to be served or even in any manner whatsoever? Can it be true at Constantinople that man has an immortal soul, that there is a judgment after death, that heaven and hell are eternal, and also true at Paris that man has not an immortal soul, that there is no judgment after death, that heaven and hell are not eternal?" If I put all these questions, and others like them to you, what will you answer me? You will say: "Truth is one, and cannot change with the degree of longitude; whatever is true at Constantinople, cannot be false at Paris, and vice versa."

If it were otherwise, we should be obliged to say that *yes* and *no* are one and the selfsame thing; and that God employs, with respect to man, the following revolting language in his intercourse: "Let truth exist or not exist, what business is it of thine? It does not exist for thee. Thy duty is to obey blindly all the impostors who tell thee that they are sent from God: whatever error they teach thee, thou shalt admit it; whatever worship they establish, thou shalt practice it. Is it thy lot to be born in a pagan country? Adore the gods of thy country. Sacrifice to Jupiter, to Mars, to Priapus, to Venus. Piously initiate thy daughters in the mysteries of the good goddess. In Egypt, thou shalt render divine homage to crocodiles; among the Phoenicians, thou shalt offer thy children to Moloch; at the city of Mexico, thou shalt slay human victims to appease the wrath of the idol that has been overthrown; through the wilds of the earth, thou shalt humbly prostrate thyself before the trunks of trees, before stones, before plants, before the refuse of animals, before the remains of the impure dead. Hast thou seen the light at Constantinople? Repeat from the bottom of thy heart: 'God is God, and Mahomet is his prophet.' At Rome, thou shalt despise the same Mahomet as an impostor."

Suppose I ask you again: "Can that which is true today be false tomorrow, the day after tomorrow, a hundred years hence, a thousand years hence? Or, rather, can that which was true yesterday have been false the day before yesterday, a hundred years ago, a thousand years ago?" You will answer me anew: "Truth is one; it does not change with the year. That which was true on the first day of the world, will be true on the last."

Such would be your answer; such would be the answer of every child sufficiently educated to put two ideas together; and this answer is unassailable. You see, then, clearly, that there cannot be many true religions. In point of fact, either these religions teach all of them the same thing, neither more nor less—in this case, they are all one and the same religion—or, again, these religions do not teach the same thing—then, they cannot all be true; they must all, with one exception, be false in some respect. You see, therefore, that all religions cannot be good, and that those who say the contrary do not know what they say.

Before concluding this point, I ought to meet a difficulty that may have occurred to your minds. Persons often speak of the primitive, or natural religion, of the Mosaic religion, and of the Christian religion, and remark, with reason, that God has been their author: here, then, they say, are three religions equally true! The consequence is false; for these three names designate only one and the same religion in three different states: the more simple under the patriarchs, the more developed under Moses, and the perfected under the gospel, as we shall see in the following lessons.

IV. *Whence does religion come?*—Evidently it comes either from God or from man: there is no middle course. Let us see whether it comes from man. Religion is founded on the necessary relations which, by the single fact of creation, exist between God, the Creator of man, and man, the creature of God: it comprises truths to be believed, duties to be fulfilled, a worship to be rendered. To suppose that man is the author of religion is therefore to presume that he is the author of the relations which exist between the Creator and the creature; the author of the truths to be believed, of the duties to be fulfilled, of the worship to be rendered. There was then a time when the rights of the Creator over his creature, of the father over his child, of the workman over his work, did not exist, or were not known; and it was thou, O man! who didst discover them, and didst determine their nature and their extent! There was a time when good, evil, immortality, heaven, hell, prayer, sacrifice, worship, virtue, did not exist, or were not known; and it was thou, O man! who didst invent them.

There is only one thing wanting to this fine hypothesis: it is to acquaint us with the period, the country, and the name of the illustrious inventor. Verily, it would be worth all the gold in the world to know what man invented God! in what century the soul was invented! in what region of the earth virtue was invented! On all these important matters there is not one word in history: ungrateful history!

To say, then, that man invented religion is to maintain an absurdity, in comparison with which every other absurdity disappears; even that of the fool, who accused his neighbor of having stolen the two towers belonging to the church of Notre-Dame in Paris, and hidden them in his pockets.

But it was not sufficient to have invented religion; to impose it on men, it should be preserved and interpreted. Now, by what means did the inventor of religion succeed in making the whole world adopt his views? In what country or century was such a wonderful work accomplished? After this man's death, who perpetuated the work, despite all the passions leagued for its destruction? How is it that no one discovered any fraud in it? Who preserved the dogmas, the morality, the worship, from error? Truly all these suppositions can be considered but as dreams! Man is so incapable of imposing a religion of his own invention on others, that Plato, the wisest as well as the most eloquent of pagan philosophers, could never make a single village in Greece adopt even one article of his divine doctrine. Man is so incapable of preserving intact the religion which he has fabricated that he cannot even preserve from innumerable errors the religion which God has given him.

A little after the deluge idolatry began; it so defiled the whole world that all truths became a vast mass of confusion, and, according to the saying of Bossuet, everything was God, except God himself. In our days, again, irreligious sages and philosophers are so far from being unanimous, that Rousseau, who knew them well, said, with the applause of the whole world: "To understand philosophers, should they not be regarded as a company of charlatans, who cry out in the public marketplace, each one from his stand: 'Come to me; I am the only one that will not deceive you'? This man pretends that there are no bodies, and that all visible things are mere representations; that man asserts that there is no other substance than matter. One declares that there is neither vice nor virtue, and that good and evil are chimeras; another proclaims that all men are wolves, and that they may devour one another with a safe conscience."[445]

In fine, man is so incapable of infallibly interpreting religion that, without revelation, he cannot give any certain answer to the most elementary religious questions; for example: Should I render to the supreme being, who has created me, a worship of respect and submission? In what manner and with what ceremonies can I acquit myself of this duty? Who will assure me that my homage is agreeable to him? What sacrifice does he prefer? If I become guilty, can I hope for pardon? What means must I employ to appease his justice? If, having been once pardoned, I should offend him anew, will there be any mercy left for me, or must I abandon myself to despair? What do I owe to beings like myself? What do I owe to myself? If I am just, what have I to hope for? If I die guilty, what have I to fear? From these simple questions, we see that God owed it to his goodness, to make known to man the manner in which he desired to be served. Accordingly, history is at hand to teach us that, in his infinite goodness, God gave this precious knowledge to man.

This knowledge was communicated to man by revelation. We thus term the external and supernatural manifestation made by God himself of any truth relating to religion. We have just seen that revelation is necessary. To ask now whether it is possible is to ask whether God can speak to men, and manifest to them the truths of which he judges the knowledge useful for their perfection and happiness; it is to ask if God enjoys, with regard to men, the power which men hold, even from God, with regard to one another—the power of communication. What! We can, in whatever manner pleases us, manifest our thoughts and our wishes to beings like ourselves, and cannot the Creator manifest his, in any manner whatsoever, to his creatures! To think it is madness, to say it is blasphemy; for it is to deny the power, the wisdom, the will of God—it is even to deny the belief entertained by all nations.[446]

"Travel over and take a survey of all countries; ascend to the most remote antiquity: Where will you find a nation which has not had some positive religion; which has not believed in communications with the divinity; which has not also believed itself to hold directly from God a doctrine to be professed, practices to be observed, and rules to be followed? The necessity of revelation must have been very deeply and generally felt indeed, thus to unite the whole human race in one belief. People have varied among themselves on revelation; they have agreed on its necessity. They have altered, obscured, and disfigured the positive teachings of religion; but the conviction of a positive teaching has remained firm among them. This agreement, so prevalent, at all times and in all countries, is a solemn acknowledgment, pronounced by the whole human race, of the inability of reason to fathom religion in its entirety. Does our age not join in an attestation as formal, as constant, and as general as that of all the ages that have preceded it?"[447]

In truth, it is to deny history, which tells us positively, and proves to us convincingly, that God has spoken to men: pointing out to us the time, the place, and the object of these communications, and giving us the names of the persons to whom they were made. Thus, the greatest of books, not only because of the perfection of its doctrine and its high antiquity, but also because of its divine origin and its incontestable authenticity, the Bible, teaches us that the parents of the human race received from God not only the knowledge and sentiment of good and evil, but, moreover, instructions, lessons, and rules of conduct—that he taught them his law—that they heard his voice and beheld the majesty of his countenance; that this religion, thus primitively revealed, was perpetuated in the families of the patriarchs; that, later on, when the Jews were collected together into one nation, God spoke anew to Moses, developed the primitive teachings, added new ordinances, and regulated the details of the worship which he required of them; finally, that, in the fullness of time, the Son of God himself came to speak to men, to complete the teachings given to Adam and Moses, and to place the whole human race in possession of all the religious truths which they should know, in order to serve God, as he wished to be served, and to obtain the recompense attached to their fidelity. Hence, three principal revelations: the primitive, made to Adam; the Jewish, made to Moses; and the Christian, made to all nations, by the Son of God in Person.

V. *Which is the true religion?*—The true religion is that religion which comes from God. Now, from the very first ages of the world, many pretended religions have appeared in it; and each one has exclaimed: "I come from God." Evidently all, with one sole exception, have lied. Which speaks the truth? How are we to know it among such a variety of sects? The thing is not difficult; for truth bears characteristics which error can never usurp. These characteristics are numerous; we shall only cite three: miracles, prophecies, antiquity.

1. *Miracles.* God can, and he alone can perform miracles; God, being truth itself, cannot perform miracles in testimony of falsehood; therefore, the religion in favor of which miracles are performed is the true religion. "To ask whether God can perform miracles," said Rosseau—"ah! it would be doing too much honor to him who should propose such a question, to answer him: it is enough to be silent." "Let a man," continues the same philosopher, "employ this language with us: 'Mortals! I announce the will of the Most High to you; recognize in my voice that of him who sends me. I command the sun to change its course, the stars to form new combinations, the mountains to become level, the waves to rise, the earth to assume a new appearance.' At these wonders, who will not instantly recognize the master of nature? It does not obey impostors."[448]

2. *Prophecies.* God alone knows the future; the future, which depends on the free will of intelligent beings; the distant future, which escapes all calculations. God alone, then, can reveal it to man; and, many ages beforehand announce to him, with certainty, events perfectly free in their causes. This act, by which God raises the intelligence of man to a participation in his infinite intelligence, is itself a great miracle. God, being truth itself, cannot perform such a miracle, cannot inspire prophets, to sanction falsehood.

3. *Antiquity.* Religion was made for man. When man appeared on earth, religion also came into existence; for, from that moment, there were necessary relations of superiority and inferiority, of love and gratitude, between God and man. It clearly follows hence that the true religion is that which ascends, without interruption, to the origin of the world, and that we must look upon every later religion as false.

Now, the catechism will show us Christianity, and Christianity alone, sparkling with miracles and prophecies, and reaching back, without interruption, to the terrestrial paradise.

VI. *Can the true religion change?*—We have seen that religion is founded on the nature of God and the nature of man. On God's side, on his qualities of Creator, Father, and last end of man; and, on man's side, on his qualities of creature, of child, and of a being in utter indigence, yet ever thirsting after the infinite, and that cannot find its contentment, except in the enjoyment of the being of beings: the source of all truth, of all love, and of all goodness. Religion is therefore unchangeable, notwithstanding its successive developments.

Who, indeed, could change it? God or man? On the one hand, God is the same forever and ever; he does not change.[449] Now, to change religion in its essence, God should change his own nature, that is, should cease to be truth itself, the infinite good, the Creator of man, and thereby the necessary term of man's homages and prayers, the supreme object of man's aspirations; on the other, even though he could, he would not do so, considering that he has a thousand times declared with an oath that religion will be always the same—that heaven and earth may pass away, but it will not pass away—and that all his cares, from the beginning of the world, have had no other object than to preserve it intact.

Can man change religion? But religion is not his work. He can no more change it than he can change his own nature or that of God, to cause that God should not be the truth and the infinite good, or that he himself should not be made to know the one and love the other. He can no more withdraw himself from religion, than he can cause God to be no longer his superior, his Creator, his Father, his last end, or himself the inferior, the creature, the child, and the dependent of God. These relations, we repeat, are necessary and unchangeable.

True, the laws of this admirable society had not always been as clearly known as since the time of the gospel; nevertheless, religion has not ceased to be always the same. It has had, so to speak, various ages: infancy, from Adam to Moses; youth, from Moses to the coming of the Messias; and maturity, from the coming of the Messias to the end of ages, without ceasing to be the same religion.

Remarks of Bossuet and St. Augustine.—Like man, who is first a child, then a boy, and then a full-grown man, and who, passing through these different stages, does not cease to be the same individual; or again, like the sun, whose rays increase in brightness from dawn to rising and from rising to noon, and which, nevertheless, always remains the same sun: "Religion," says Bossuet, "is always the same. Placed between the two testaments, Jesus Christ is their center. 'Jesus Christ was yesterday, is today, and will be forever.'[450] Religion, of which he is the great object, was under the law, appears next under the gospel, and will continue throughout eternity, when Jesus Christ, reunited to his elect, will subject all things to his Father, with whom he shall be praised, honored, and glorified forever. Thus, it is by Jesus Christ, and for Jesus Christ, that all ages have been made: those of the old law to prepare for those of the law of grace, and those of the latter to be lost in an eternity of glory."

It follows, hence, that the old and the new testaments have both had the same design and the same issue: one prepares the perfection, which the other displays openly; one lays the foundation, the other completes the building: in short, one predicts that which the other points out as fully accomplished. Henceforward, all times are united; the tradition of the Jewish and that of the Christian people will make only one continuous chain of the same religion, and the scriptures of the two testaments will make only one book. Our faith is, therefore, the faith of the prophets. The dogmas, which are its object, were not only prefigured in the ancient scriptures, but even those scriptures contained express promises of them. It is, then, not to know Christianity, to look upon it as a new religion, in the sense that it has no root in the ages prior to the Messias.

The religion that we profess has always existed, since, from the beginning of the world, the expectation of Jesus Christ has been its soul. "One light," says Bossuet again, "appears everywhere from the beginning of the world. It rises in the time of the patriarchs; it increases in the times of Moses and the prophets. Jesus Christ, greater than the patriarchs, with an authority more absolute than Moses, and more enlightened than all the prophets, causes it to shine before our eyes in its utmost plenitude. Jesus Christ reaches to all times: he is the center in which all things, viz., the law, the prophets, the gospel, and the apostles, meet. Faith in Jesus Christ has been the faith of all ages. From the birth of the world, the faithful were obliged to believe in Jesus Christ promised, as the faithful now believe in Jesus Christ who has come."

In one word, the ancient patriarchs had no other religion than ours, since they relied on the same promises as we do, and sighed for the coming of the same Savior that we have received. There were evangelical men before the gospel, Christians in spirit before they bore the name.

Thus, those among the Jews who recognized Jesus Christ as the Messias did not change their religion in becoming Christians;[451] they only believed in the arrival of him whom they had expected, and the promise of whom had previously been the object of their faith. On the contrary, those who disowned him then truly changed their religion; for they renounced the law of Moses, which commanded them to receive and to hear him—they renounced the oracles of the prophets, who clearly pointed him out—in a word, they renounced the ancient hope of Israel.

"Although the times have changed," says St. Augustine, in his turn, "although the mystery of the redemption was formerly announced as future, which is now preached as accomplished, yet faith has not changed on that account. Although, before the coming of the Messias, the true religion was practiced under other names and with other signs than since his coming; although it was then proposed in a veiled and is now exposed in a clear manner, nevertheless, there has always been but one religion, ever the same. That which we do today call the Christian religion existed among the ancients, and has never ceased to exist in the world from the beginning of human existence until the incarnation of Jesus Christ, when it began to bear the name of *Christian*."[452] How venerable does this remote antiquity render religion! What a testimony to the divinity of its origin, to see it beginning with the world!

But if, on this account, it deserves all our respect, does not its perpetuity, that is to say, its uninterrupted continuance during so many ages, in spite of so many unexpected obstacles, manifestly show that God supports it? If, to the first period of religion before Jesus Christ, we join the next period, which is only its continuance (I mean the succession of the Christian Church), what authority does not such a lapse of time, embracing as it does the whole extent of ages, thus give to religion? Should we not recognize herein a design steadily maintained and gradually developed, an order in the counsel of God, which prepares from the beginning of the world that which it completes at the end of time, and which, through various stages, but with an ever constant succession, perpetuates before the eyes of the world the holy society in which the Almighty desires to be served?[453]

Certainly, a religion, which ascends even to the first man, and which survives without change the lapse of centuries; which explains everything, and without which nothing can be explained, can have no other author than the infinite wisdom and no other support than the infinite power of him, who, holding it in the hollow of his hand, can alone commence, continue, and complete a design embracing all times.

What we have said on the existence, necessity, and nature of religion, will be made plainer by the following story.

A worldly woman, who, like many others, did not know very well what religion was, and who even made little account of it, as of a mere conventionality, complained bitterly, in the presence of a missionary, regarding the conduct of her daughter. "But, Madam," said the missionary, "are there any relations between a mother and a daughter, that a daughter should be obliged to respect and obey her mother?" "How so, sir," she replied, "am I not her mother? Whatever age she may be, is she not still my daughter? Is she not indebted to me for whatever she is? Is she not always bound to respect and love me?" "But, Madam, perhaps these relations of superiority on your part, and dependence on the part of your daughter, are conventionalities, that may be changed?" "Changed, sir! so that I should not be her mother, nor she my daughter: the rights of a mother are unchangeable, because they are founded on the character of mother." "You are quite convinced then, Madam, that between you and your daughter there exist the closest relations; that you have a right to command her, and that she is bound to obey, respect, and love you; that if she fails in doing so, she is culpable; and that this is no conventional affair, but a sacred matter founded on your title of mother and her character of daughter: Do you believe this?" "Certainly, I believe it." "Very well, Madam; change the names: in your place put God, and in your daughter's place put *yourself*, and you shall have religion."

PRAYER

O my God! who art all love, I thank thee for having given us religion, which teaches us to know and love thee; grant us ever to conform our lives to our belief.

I am resolved to love God above all things, and my neighbor as myself for the love of God; and, in testimony of this love, I will make a short meditation every day.

Lesson 20: Antiquity of the Christian Religion

When we consider society as it is, we are witnesses of a strange spectacle! The greater part of men no longer practice religion, do not pray, do not hear Mass, do not observe the Sunday, do not confess, do not communicate, do not give any sign of Christianity; a great number of women imitate the men; and among both classes who call themselves Christians, we observe a recklessness, a contempt, a facility in committing sin, that grieves and sickens the heart. At this spectacle, is not one tempted to say that religion must be an unimportant affair; that each person is allowed to practice or not practice it, to take it up or lay it down, to accept it in its entirety or to divide it according to circumstances; in one word, that religion imposes no obligation on us, or only binds us as far as we choose, in the manner we choose, and simply because we choose to be bound by it, without having anything to fear from its violation, or anything to hope from its observance?

To dissipate this error, unexampled in the history of any people, we now proceed to show that religion is a law, the most sacred of all laws; a universal law, from which no man can dispense himself; a law, which has no substitute: and, to promote its observance, we shall also show that it is one of the most magnificent presents that God could make to man.

I. *Religion is a law.*—If we inquire of jurisconsults and theologians the definition of law, they will tell us: a law is a general, just, and permanent command, promulgated in the interests of society by him who has the right to rule.[454] Now, all the qualities here mentioned pertain to religion a thousand times better than to the most respectable or the most respected law among men.

First, religion is a precept, a command, a rule of conduct, more general than all human laws taken together. Human laws are necessarily incomplete: they only regard external acts. Religion, on the contrary, is a complete law: it not only regulates external acts, but, taking possession of the conscience, directs the thoughts, the desires, the least movements of the soul—encouraging some, condemning others, and defining good and evil at the moment of their appearance in the heart.

Human laws only regulate the relations of men among themselves. Religion regulates not only the relations of men among themselves, but also the relations of men with God. It alone teaches them whence they come, whither they go, why they are on the earth at all; what they owe to their superiors, to their inferiors, to their equals, and to themselves; what they have to do, and what they have to avoid; and the lot which awaits them beyond the grave.

Human laws are found only in certain places; they vary with nations; they wear out with time. Religion has no other limits than those of the world: every clime belongs to it. To the Chinese and the Japanese, to the Hottentot and the Tartar, to the European and the American, as to the savages of Polynesia, it teaches, commands, forbids the same things: it does not vary with races. They may change their language, their customs, their laws, their forms of government; it remains always the same: the same in its dogmas, in its morals, in its sacraments, in its hierarchy. It does not wear out with time. Born with the world, it embraces all times; ever fruitful and ever young, it has never lost one of its dogmas, not one of its precepts, not one of its essential rites: like the sun, which, during six thousand years, has poured its torrents of light on the world without wasting itself or growing old.

Religion is therefore a law, since it is a general and permanent precept: it is the most venerable law, since it is the most ancient, the most general, and the most enduring.

Again, law, say the jurisconsults, is a just command, published in the interests of society. Here, again, behold the vast preeminence of religion over all human laws! When one searches through the immense collection of human laws—the laws of the ancient Egyptians, the laws of the ancient Greeks, the laws of the ancient Romans, the laws of the Gauls, the laws of the Lombards, the laws of the Tartars, the laws of the Chinese—is he sure to find all these human precepts without a single exception stamped with the seal of justice and equity? Too often, alas! will he not find that cruelty, immorality, falsehood, and violence, transformed into rules of conduct, have usurped and profaned the sacred name of law? What nation is there that does not blush at some of the articles in its statute-books?

It is far otherwise with religion, which, as the prophet says, is an "immaculate law."[455] All that it teaches is true; all that it commands is good, just, amiable, and moral; all that it forbids is evil. There is not a virtue that it does not encourage; there is not a vice that it does not condemn. It is all comprised in these two precepts: you shall love God above all things, and your neighbor, that is, all the rest of mankind, even your enemies, as you love yourselves, for God's sake. If you only love those who love you, what reward shall you have? Pagans do as much. And if you only salute those who salute you, what reward shall you have? Publicans do as much. You shall love, therefore, those who do you evil; you shall pray for those who persecute you, that you may be the children of your heavenly Father, who maketh his sun to shine on the good and the bad.[456]

After this simple explanation, let me ask: Do you know anything more just than religion, or more capable of improving man and securing his happiness in this world? It is then a law, the most august of all laws.

Finally, law is a rule of conduct given to society by him who has the right to rule it. The just and wise laws that emanate from human legislators are undoubtedly worthy of respect, and ought to be obeyed. Every day you say so; every day you act in accordance with your conviction. Every day your courts are open to judge any infractions of the law. How often do the prison doors close on the violators of the law! Nay, how often is the scaffold erected to make atonement to the majesty of the law by the death of its transgressors! You recognize, therefore, in human legislators, who are the rulers of the people, the right to make laws, and in subjects, the duty to obey them.

But that legislative authority which you justly concede to a few men, will you refuse to God? If the child is obliged to obey its father, the subject his king, has man a right to disobey God? Are the orders of God less formal, the rights of God less sacred than yours? This is not all. Whence do human laws themselves derive their authority? From the legislator himself? No. Whether the laws are made by an emperor, a king, a parliament, or a senate, the human legislator is always but a man; and, from this title, he obtains no right to impose his will on other men; for one man is as good as another.

In virtue of what right, then, is the legislator to be obeyed? Whence does his law derive its authority? Should I scandalize you if I were to say it—for nowadays it is quite the fashion to ridicule the divine right of kings? Well, the truth is that every right is divine, in the sense that God alone can impose on one man a conscientious obligation to obey another man. Hence, in the nation, the king or other leader of the state commands in the name of God, by whom kings rule; and in the family, the father commands in the name of God, from whom all paternity proceeds. As often as a man in authority raises his voice to command an inferior, the latter must hear within himself another voice, saying: "Obey; it is God who commands thee."

From the day in which this heavenly voice will no longer be heard, from the day in which the belief in the divinity of right will be effaced from the human heart, there will no longer be left standing a single power, a single authority on earth. There is no middle course. From the day in which man ceases to command in the name of God, he must command in his own name. What then is power, authority, law, but a yoke, which might imposes, which reason disowns, and which strength throws off? The very idea of right is banished: the will of the strongest becomes the rule of duty, and the habits of wolves become the morals of men. It is, therefore, fully established that, in the highest sense of the word, religion is a law. Consequently, it is also fully established that the men of our days who continually harp on law, who push respect for law even to excess, and who, at the same time, despise the laws of religion, are among the most inconsistent, as well as the most dangerous, not to say the most guilty of men, though they pretend to wisdom.

II. *Religion is the most sacred of all laws.*—The sanctity of a law is derived from the person of the legislator who makes it, from the importance of the duties which it imposes, and from the sanction which confirms it. Now, these three conditions unite to form the most incontestable proof of the proposition that religion is the most sacred of all laws.

First, the person of the legislator. I travel the world, and, at the head of the various codes which have served as a rule for nations, I read the names of Minos, Rhadamanthus, Lycurgus, Solon, Numa, Confucius, Mahomet, the founders of kingdoms, the founders of empires, the founders of modern republics. I bow before many of these names, which millions of my fellow men have respected and still respect. But, at the head of the sacred code I behold an emblazoned name, which is not that of a man, nor that of an angel, nor that of an archangel—a name above all names—a name before which every knee bends in heaven, on earth, and in hell: the name of God. Now, if the laws, elaborated by celebrated men, have a right, by reason of their origin, to our respect and submission, how much more respectable, how much more sacred should we consider that law which emanates from God himself, the supreme legislator, and the source of all justice, of all wisdom, and of all power?

Next, the importance of the duties which it imposes. Without doubt, the duties imposed by human laws are important. On men's fidelity to them, depend, at least in part, the order, peace, and prosperity of nations, and the health and welfare of individuals: their material well-being. All these advantages, however, relate only to time, and must end with time: the body alone is a gainer by them, the soul has no share in them. But what shall we say of the importance of the duties prescribed by religion? They embrace both body and soul, time and eternity, man and society. If they are not observed, happiness, intelligence, and virtue, society, the family, and the individual, are all degraded: all perish, if they are not observed.

Now, the first duty that religion imposes on us is to believe; for it is written: "He that believeth not shall be condemned."[457] Yes, condemned, both in this world and in the world to come. In truth, violate this first article of the sacred code, take away the Creed; what have you left? For the individual, a hell of doubt; for society, chaos. Enter into that mind which has extinguished the lamp of faith. The indisputable truths which constituted its happiness fall one after another, like the pictures of a sanctuary that has been delivered over to pillage. Then, behold the uncertainties, the contradictions, the vain phantoms that continually succeed one another. All these reveries of a disordered brain pursue, combat, destroy one another, and the incessant struggles weary out the human reason, until at length it flings itself on the couch of a gross materialism or tries to end its furious career in the grave of a miserable suicide. All this is matter of history. We can today name among us, in England, in Germany, in France, such deserters from the faith, who have propounded theories on God, religion, society, and the family, not less extravagant than the incoherent systems and shapeless fancies of the wildest savages.

See what becomes of the mind of the man that has been unfaithful to faith. Is his heart less to be pitied? The second duty that religion imposes on us is to act; in other terms, to conform our thoughts, our words, and our deeds, to the great rule of conduct called the decalogue. What becomes of the man that dares to trample under his feet this second article of the sacred code? In the depths of his heart, live three great passions: pride, avarice, luxury. Night and day they solicit, impel, force him to yield to their yoke. The only voice capable of breaking the bewitching charm of these fatal sirens is the majestic voice of religion, with its eternity of rewards and punishments. The only chain capable of holding these furious hyenas is the majestic will of God. Stifle the voice; break the chain: What do you see? On the moment, the human heart becomes the slave of its cruel passions. Man no longer knows himself. He must have enjoyment, much enjoyment, enjoyment at any cost: such is his law. Honor, probity, health, fortune, conscience, all must be sacrificed to his gratification. Self, and nothing else: such is his motto. And, if opportunity offers, he will be faithful to it, you may be sure, even though it should cost him his life. The meannesses of every kind, the corruptions, the frauds, the outrageous and unheard-of crimes, that sully the face of the earth, are unfortunately but too conclusive a proof of this humiliating truth. So much for the heart of man.

Society, in its turn, soon experiences a reaction from the contempt of religion. There can be no society without respect for authority. Now, when men come to such a pass as no longer to respect the first of all authorities, that from which all others flow—when they no longer make any account of God or his laws, they are not slow to despise inferior authorities and to violate human laws: the ideas of right and duty, of authority and submission, are effaced; the social bonds are relaxed. It has been said with reason: "Where God has no altar, kings have no throne." By kings we must understand authority, whatever may be the person's name or rank in the general hierarchy: pontiff, king, magistrate, father, or venerable old age. A sullen hatred, a turbulent spirit of insubordination, ferments in the minds of subjects. Threatened in their power and their person, the heads of society are obliged to make the burden heavier, and soon a rebellion breaks out.

There can be no society without common beliefs, admitted as the immutable rules of the thoughts and actions of all the citizens. Take away religion: no more divine beliefs; consequently, no more common and sacred beliefs. Everything becomes problematical among men. The truths we know henceforward are only relative; consequently, changeable and uncertain; and, although reverenced today, they must be prepared to bear the shaft of ridicule tomorrow. By the force of knavery and falsehood, society comes at last to doubt of all things, even of itself. This fatal doubt undermines it, enervates it, degrades it, renders it incapable of anything great, and by turns casts it from a state of dejection into one of feverish excitement, which delivers it at length, vilified and degraded, to the sanguinary fury of anarchy, or the iron yoke of a brutal despotism.

There can be no society without the spirit of sacrifice. The whole world will tell you that society cannot exist without the sacrifice of particular to general interests. Now, this sacrifice, which costs the passions so much—this sacrifice, which we must continually begin anew—cannot be accomplished except by the fear of God and the hope of a future recompense. Let man waver in his belief regarding God, or cease to believe in him altogether—let him doubt his rewards and his punishments, and you may hold for certain that, in the same proportion, selfishness—cold, cruel, barbarous selfishness—becomes, under one form or another, the universal law. Society then no longer exists: the something that bears its name is only an aggregation of individuals, who vie, the most cunning with the most powerful, to satiate, at one another's expense, their ignoble thirst for riches, honors, and pleasures.

Evident as they are of themselves, these truths are confirmed by an experience so ancient and yet so new that the leading axiom of all sensible men is this: Without religion there can be no society. "That," says Plato, "which overthrows religion, overthrows the foundation of all human society."[458] "Cities and nations," adds Xenophon, "most attached to the divine worship, have always been the wisest and the most lasting."[459]

"The laws of Minos and Numa," says a modern jurisconsult, "rest entirely on the fear of the gods. Cicero, in his *Treatise on Laws*, places providence as the basis of all legislation. Numa made Rome the sacred city, in order to make it the eternal city…The laws of morality do not suffice. The laws regulate only certain actions; religion embraces them all. The laws arrest only the arm; religion guides the heart. The laws have reference principally to one's conduct toward his fellow citizens; religion takes possession of the whole man. What would morality be, if it were exiled to the lofty region of the sciences, and if religious institutions did not bring it down to the level of the multitude? A morality without positive precepts would leave reason without a rule; a morality without religious dogmas would be only justice without tribunals. Dogmas and morals would only be abstractions, without the rites, the ceremonies, and the practices that give them a body, and serve them for a support. In the matter of religion, it is less a question to know than to do. Now, good actions can only be secured by good habits. It is by practicing the things that lead to virtue, or at least that recall the idea of it to the mind, that one learns to love and to practice virtue itself.

"True philosophy respects forms as much as pride despises them. Discipline is as necessary in manners as order in ideas. To deny the utility of religious rites and practices, in regard to morality, would be to deny the influence of sensible considerations on beings that are not pure spirits…A religion without public worship would soon languish, and assuredly lead back the populace to idolatry…If there were nothing to unite those who profess the same belief, would there not in a few years be as many religious systems as individuals?…

"To assert that religion arrests no disorder in the countries where it is most honored, because it does not prevent the crimes and scandals of which we are witnesses, is to propose an objection that strikes at the root of all morality and law, since morality and law have not strength to prevent all crimes and scandals from being committed…We behold the crimes that religion cannot prevent, but do we behold those that it does prevent? Can we scrutinize consciences, and see there all the dark proposals that religion stifles and all the salutary thoughts that it inspires? How does it happen that men who appear to us so wicked in detail are as a mass such honest people? Is it not because inspirations, which the thoroughly corrupt resist, and to which the good do not always yield, are sufficient to direct the generality of men in the greatest number of cases, and to secure in the ordinary course of life that uniform and universal progress without which any durable society would be impossible?…

"We believe in controlling laws; and everywhere there are manners. Manners are the slow result of circumstances, usages, and institutions. Now, of all things that exist among men, there is nothing that so fully embraces the whole man as religion, nothing more capable of giving him good habits…Take away religion from the mass of men; by what will you replace it? If one is not engaged with good, he will be with evil; the mind and the heart cannot remain idle. When religion is no more, country and society are no more in regard to men, who, resuming their independence, have strength only to abuse it. It is particularly in free states that religion is necessary. For it is there, says Polybius, that, in order not to place a dangerous power in the hands of a few men, the greatest fear ought to be that of the gods."[460]

We have considered the sanctity of the religious law, both in regard to the person who establishes it and the importance of the duties which it imposes; it only remains for us to study it in regard to the sanction which confirms it.

The sanction of a law consists in the advantages or rewards promised to him who observes it, and the penalties or punishments threatened against him who violates it. From this new point of view, how great is the sanctity of the religious law! Scarcely ever do human laws stipulate for a reward in favor of those who observe them. Thus, our codes offer no reward to him who does not steal, who does not kill, who does not injure his neighbor's reputation, who does not cheat the tax collector. The only reward promised him is protection against injustice; in other words, the tranquil enjoyment of his liberty, his property, and other such advantages, which make up an outward, transitory, and necessarily imperfect happiness.

It is quite otherwise with religion. On earth, peace of conscience is secured to him who observes its precepts: an inward happiness, which cannot be disturbed or destroyed—a uniform happiness, which, according to the scriptural expression, makes life a continual feast—a happiness, therefore, as perfect as can be expected in this valley of tears. And, while the promises of human laws are confined to the short years of time, those of religion are realized throughout eternity. So much for rewards, as a sanction of law.

As for the punishments threatened against the violators of human laws, what are they? Heavy as they may be considered, they only touch a part of man, namely, his body, his liberty, his property, his character, his life: they always end with time. Not so with the punishments sanctioned by the divine law. They touch man both in body and soul. Hence, the saying of the divine legislator himself: "Fear not them who can kill only the body; but fear him who can kill both body and soul: yea, verily, fear him."[461] A second difference: while the penalties, like the rewards, that cause human laws to be respected, end with time, the punishments decreed against the violators of the divine law affect man throughout the whole extent of his present and future existence: eternity even will not see their termination.

In fine, that which often lessens the penal sanction of human laws is the possibility of escaping the stroke of justice. You have conspired against a king: you are condemned to death. It is not always impossible for you to leave his kingdom and secure yourself from punishment; but would you then depart from the jurisdiction of God? You have made an attack on the life, the property, the character of another; it is not always impossible for you to deny the fact, to annihilate the material proofs of your guilt, and to be acquitted as innocent; but will your denials be of any avail before the tribunal of him who knows all things? Brought before some human tribunal, you may even be able to bribe your judges, and to purchase your deliverance; but do you know any means of corrupting God, so that he should connive at your disorders, and permit you to escape with impunity?

By these arguments, it is therefore demonstrated that religion is the most sacred of all laws.

III. *Religion is a universal law, from which no man can dispense himself.* — "Go, teach all nations," said the divine legislator, "tell them to observe all my commandments."[462] "Whoever violates a single one of them is a violator of the whole law."[463] Thus, religion embraces all times, all places, all men; it is confined by no mountains, no seas, no rivers, no boundaries; it makes no distinction of sex or race. Henceforward, religion is no more national than the sun is national. Henceforward, there is no exception or privilege for anyone: kings and subjects, rich and poor, learned and ignorant, Greeks and Barbarians, the men of today and the men of tomorrow, all must be the subjects of the divine law. For all, the same gospel, the same Creed, the same decalogue, the same sacraments, the same rewards, the same punishments, without any other difference than that of merit or demerit.

Any development of this truth would be superfluous, if it were not necessary to show how culpable is an indifference toward religion, and how impious is the maxim, too often repeated in our days, that: religion is fit only for common people, women, and children.

Religious indifference is the height of crime and folly. — We distinguish two sorts of indifferentists: the speculative and the practical. The speculative indifferentist is he who does not believe in any religion, and who neglects to examine whether or not there is a true religion. To confound him, it is enough to exhibit his mode of reasoning:

"I do not know," he says, "who has placed me in the world, nor what the world is, nor what I am myself. I am in a state of frightful ignorance concerning all things. I do not know what my body is, what my senses are, what my soul is; and that portion of me which thinks what I say, and which reflects on itself and on everything else, understands itself no better than the rest of me.

"I behold the bewildering magnitude of the universe that surrounds me, and find myself located in one little corner of its vast extent, without knowing why I am placed here rather than elsewhere, or why the short space of time that is assigned me for my life is fixed in one period rather than another of that eternity which has preceded and will succeed me. I see the infinity of things in which I am engulfed as an atom, or lost as the passing shadow of a moment. All that I know is that I must soon die; but that of which I am most ignorant is the very death which I cannot shun. As I know not whence I came, so I know not whither I am going. I am conscious only that, on leaving this world, I shall fall forever either into nothingness or into the hands of an angry God, without having any assurance as to which of these two conditions shall be my lot.

"How full, then, am I of wretchedness, helplessness, and darkness! And the conclusion to which I come is that I must pass all the days of my life without ever thinking on what will yet happen to me, and that I have only to follow my inclinations without uneasiness, doing everything that will bring me into eternal misery, in case what we are told about matters is true. Perhaps I might be able to find some light in my doubts; but I do not wish to go to any trouble, or to make one step, for that purpose; and treating with contempt those who concern themselves about me, I desire to walk on without foresight and without apprehension, to have an experimental knowledge of the great event, and to let myself meet death tamely, utterly uncertain of what is likely to be my eternal condition."

"Truly," says Pascal, "it is an honor to religion, to have such unreasonable enemies."[464]

The practical indifferentist is he who believes in religion, but does not fulfill its duties. To confound him also, it is only necessary to exhibit his mode of reasoning:

"I believe," he says, "that there is a God, the Creator and absolute master of man and the world. I believe that this God has manifested his adorable will toward men, directing their actions in the various circumstances of life, all which orders together form religion, which I ought to accept, such as it is, without adding to or taking from it. I believe that this religion requires from me not only internal acts of faith and adoration, but also certain external acts of private and public worship. I am acquainted with these acts, and I know that in disdaining to perform them I place myself in a state of permanent rebellion against God. I know that, to punish my contemptuous insolence, an abyss of eternal fire is prepared beneath my feet. I know that I am only withheld from it by my life. I know that my life is only a thread, a thread which is held in the hands of God, which he can cut when he pleases, which he will cut without warning me, perhaps this very night. And the conclusion at which I arrive is that I should continue to live tranquilly in my indifference, with the certainty of falling sooner or later into the depths of eternal misery."

Truly, we may say again, it is an honor for religion to have such unreasonable enemies.

As for the maxim, "Religion is fit only for common people, women, and children," it is in the mouths of those who utter it an impiety, a folly, a lie, and a cruelty.

An impiety. — In fact, you say thereby that there is no religion for the educated and the wealthy; that God leaves them free to act according to their caprices and passions, imposing on the poor and the weak the obligation of laboring for their advantage; or you say that there is one religion for the educated and the wealthy, and another for common people, women, and children; or, in fine, you say that religion is a nice toy for the amusement of common people, women, and children, but unworthy of engaging the attention of sensible men — a brilliant system, good for supplying excitement to ardent imaginations and idle minds, but whose emptiness and falsehood are perfectly well known to business men — a good leading-string for keeping common people, women, and children to their duty, condemned to a state of everlasting pupilage, but which becomes perfectly useless when one is dressed in broadcloth or is adorned with a little hair on his chin. Remember what has been demonstrated, namely, that there is one and only one religion, that it comes from God, and that it imposes its obligations on all men without exception; and say, is there a more impious maxim than that which we have just explained?

A folly. — Either religion is true, or it is not. If it is true, it is good and necessary for the whole world, as well for the educated and the wealthy as for common people, women, and children. If it is not true, it is not good for any person; since error is never useful. Moreover, if, as you say, religion is good, it is much more so for the rich than for the poor, much more so for men than for women and children. Religion, you know, is a bridle to restrain the passions. Now, which of the two has more need of a rein: he who has many means of gratifying his passions with impunity, or he who can calculate neither on means nor on impunity? Evidently, the first man, the rich, the strong, the powerful. Hence, that true saying of Montesquieu: "Though it were useless for subjects to have a religion, yet it would not be useless for princes to have one, and to be tightly curbed by the only reins which those who do not fear human laws can be held by."[465] "I would not like," adds Voltaire, "to have anything to do with an atheistical prince that might find it his interest to pound me in a mortar: indeed I should be pretty sure to be pounded."[466]

In fine, all you who imagine yourselves superior to the populace by your position, your fortune, or your learning, and who wish to find in the religion of the populace the guarantee of its respect and obedience toward you, do you think that the populace does not also wish to find in the religion of its masters the guarantee of their justice, their moderation, and their equity toward it? Because a man has an income, has he no longer any passions to subdue? Does the heart of an angel invariably beat under the laced uniform of an officer or the ermined robes of a judge? Are the better-bred class, the burgesses, far beyond their inferiors, at the present day, as accomplished models of probity, loyalty, disinterestedness, and all other public and private virtues? Are not the motives of the common people in requiring you to be religious, a thousand times better founded than yours in requiring them to be so?

"Is it not in the midst of the most exalted conditions that voluptuousness is most refined, ambition most eager, revenge most implacable, all the passions most imperious, on account of the means which they have to gratify themselves? And you would tear away from these classes of society the salutary bridle of religion! That is, you would break the embankment on the side where the waters rage with the greatest violence, you would banish the remedy from places where the epidemic rages with the most dreadful mortality: in other words, you would take away religious sentiments from those to whom they are most necessary. Rather begin by tearing away pride from the heart of the scholar, self-interest from the heart of the rich, covetousness from the heart of the trader and of the manufacturer, pusillanimity from the heart of the magistrate, ambition from the heart of the great, and then perhaps it may be allowed you to leave religion to the populace."[467]

A *lie.* — In the eyes of the propagators of this maxim, "Religion is not good even for common people, women, and children": the proof of which is that they do all they can to take it from them. To what, I ask, do the railleries and satires tend, with which, in their books, in their theatrical exhibitions, in their newspapers, in their clubs, in their studios, in their manufactories, in their saloons, in their restaurants, they themselves assail or suffer others to assail, with sacred things, and sacred ceremonies, the practicers of religion? What can be the effect of the tyranny which they exercise over the commonalty, over the workman, over the servant, by obliging them to labor on Sundays, and by depriving them of the liberty to fulfill their religious obligations? What can be the effect on the minds of their inferiors, of that absolute indifference which they openly profess, and which they seem to glory in? The sure result of it all is the complete destruction of religion.

Yes, if religion is for the people alone, there will soon be no religion at all. The people have a pride and a dignity of their own: if they perceive that religion is thrown to them as a contemptible thing, they will despise it in their turn. Religion is nothing to him who does not believe in it. What value forsooth is set on its threats and promises, by those who only see in it the chimeras of a disordered imagination? And how can you expect that the people will continue to believe in it, when they see that it is an object of derision or indifference to those who, by their birth, their intelligence, and their occupations, are placed above them?

But when the people have no longer any religion, reflect on what must sooner or later follow. When there is no religion, the people will say that there is no heaven or hell: that everything passes with time. As for paradise, it consists in wealth, pleasure, and power. Hell means poverty, labor, and subjection. The wealthy citizens are in paradise; I am in hell! But each has his turn, and in the day of its strength the unchained mob will rush upon your lands, your houses, and your iron safes; it will do so in virtue of the principles that you have taught it, and what can you say in reply?

A *cruelty.* — Will they say that, while remaining strangers to religion themselves, they believe it good for the populace? Let us take them at their word: they shall only escape from falsehood by cruelty. What! they are convinced that religion is good for the common people; yet they do not fear to rob them of their precious patrimony! To sweeten the pains of life, they themselves have their social position, their independent fortune, their feast days, their balls, their exhibitions, their travels, their numerous friends. The common people spend their days in labor, sorrow, misery, and abandonment. And they have the barbarity to snatch from the needy the only consolation that remains to them, the hope of happiness in a better world! Truly, it is quite clear, as we have shown, that their indifference to religion destroys religion in the heart of the people. O cruel men! what evil has religion done you? Evidently, therefore, they are only enemies of the people, anxious to degrade and oppress them who advocate this guilty maxim: "Religion is good only for the populace."

"Flee then from those who, by their indifference and their impious doctrines, sow such desolating doctrines in the hearts of men. Overthrowing, wasting, trampling under their feet, all that men respect, they deprive the afflicted of the last consolation in their misery, they take away from the rich and powerful the only restraint that checks their passions, they snatch from hearts the salutary remorse for crime or the hope of virtue, and, after all, they boast that they are the benefactors of the human race. Never, they say, is truth hurtful to men; I believe so, as well as they; and, in my opinion, it is a great proof that they do not teach the truth."[468]

IV. *Religion is a law which has no substitute.* — Destroy religion, what will you set in its place to render man virtuous? Honor and interest: there remains no other motive for human actions.

Of all the foundations whereon persons endeavor to build virtue, honor is unquestionably the weakest. "What is honor? A sentiment of personal dignity, which, outside of religion, degenerates into pride and self-conceit; an ever-shifting principle, which by turns inspires the most contrary and immoral acts: devotedness to the priest, integrity to the magistrate, audacity to the assassin, cunning to the robber, the spirit of revenge to the soldier, suicide to the coward; a disguised selfishness, good for show and ostentation, but which indemnifies itself in solitude, by giving free course to the most shameful inclinations; an empty smoke, which lifts the head without purifying the heart; an empty sound, which the wise man scorns, and which cannot soothe a single affliction in life; a nameless thing, which varies with the caprice of the multitude; a helpless divinity, which some adore without gain, and others despise without loss, for it often exalts vice, and as often pursues virtue with hatred, contempt, and persecution. Should I be the first mortal to gather this bitter fruit of my fidelity to painful duties? As a compensation, I find offered to me the joy that accompanies a good opinion of oneself. What mockery! the joy of poverty, of hunger, of thirst, of diseases, of anguish in body and soul, of prisons and scaffolds, of misery without hope!"[469]

Powerless for those who believe in it, honor is of no use at all to those who do not believe in it. How can it become a principle of virtue for the latter? Is it by forcing themselves to believe in it? By what means then? Is it by the fear of contempt? "But what is this contempt, with which I am threatened, if, to obey my inclinations, I trample underfoot that which you are pleased to call honor, but which I call prejudice? Of what real good can it deprive me? How will the opinion of another affect my well-being? Will it take away my health, my riches, my pleasure, or my liberty? I say contempt is nothing, if I despise it; and, even were I so weak as to be moved by it, what would hinder me from avoiding it like so many others, by hiding my enjoyments under the thick veil of mystery? But, hiding them from other men, I could not hide them from myself; I should purchase them at the expense of remorse.

"This is a rather serious matter: let us then consider it. I mean that, outside religion, conscience is not a prejudice, or, if it is a prejudice, I have not been able to conquer it: it is always certain that, placed between a pleasure which I desire to enjoy and a remorse which I fear in yielding to it, the choice of vice or virtue is an affair of pure sensation. If the desire carries me away, I fall; on the contrary, if fear is stronger, I resist. Now, let anyone tell me the passion, which, without having any other chastisement to dread, will be restrained by the simple feeling of regret for having violated the abstract laws of order."[470]

Interest. What interest is meant? Public interest or private interest? With regard to the former, I shall reply that sophisms do not destroy the reality of things. One will in vain endeavor to confound general with particular interests; there will always exist an irreconcilable opposition between them. On a thousand occasions, the common interest will require that I should languish in want; that I should employ my health and strength in painful labors, of which others will gather the fruit; that I should stifle my desires, inclinations, and affections; that I should suffer; and, in fine, that I should die. Until it has been shown that miseries, sufferings, and death are in themselves preferable to riches, pleasures, and life, it will be false, evidently false, that self-interest, apart from the consideration of future rewards and punishments, should be the rule of duty and the foundation of morality. "Let all men do me good at their own expense, let everything in the world be referred to me alone, let the whole human race die if necessary in pain and misery, to spare me a single moment of sorrow or hunger: such is the interior language of every unbeliever that reasons."[471]

Would you speak of private interest? I shall again reply that the man who expects no future life has only one interest—that of making himself happy, at any cost, in this life.

Now, what a strange kind of happiness to propose to man, that he should incessantly combat his desires, his inclinations, and even the wants of nature, without any hope of reward! What! the interest of the poor man is to suffer indigence, when he can take possession of some of the superfluities of the rich! But he will be hanged, if he steal. Very well; then the interest of living ought to prevail over the interest of appeasing his hunger. Therefore, if he were sure to avoid execution, the second interest would determine a contrary line of action or duty. Take away the hangman, and a new system of ethics appears. The hangman is the father of all virtues. Nevertheless, whatever may be done, this influential moralist cannot reach to everything. Many of the vices that insensibly undermine society or disturb its repose, such as avarice, selfishness, ingratitude, hard-heartedness, envy, hatred, calumny, licentiousness, are not within his domain at all. And even of the crimes that he has to take cognizance of, how many elude his vigilance! Thanks to the progress of science, have we not a thousand means of robbing, deceiving, living at the expense of others, and of escaping the law? At the present time more than at any former, may we not say with truth, in the words of an ancient, that human laws are but cobwebs, fit only for holding flies?

Let us then conclude with Rousseau: "I do not know how anyone can be virtuous without religion; I was deceived with the contrary opinion for a long time, but I have been thoroughly disabused of it."[472]

PRAYER

O my God! who art all love, inspire us with a profound respect for thy holy law: enlighten those who know it; move to amendment those who neglect and violate it; grant that we may be the docile children of the wisest and best of fathers.

I am resolved to love God above all things, and my neighbor as myself for the love of God; and, in testimony of this love, I will pray for the indifferent.

Lesson 21: Religion; Messias Foreshadowed: Adam and Abel

Religion is a great grace, the sum of all graces.—Religion is a law, a supreme, universal law, and the basis of all other laws: as we have seen in the preceding lesson. At the name of *law*, nature has perhaps shuddered; and we have felt a strange emotion of fear and repugnance rise in the depths of our soul. Let us hasten to repress it. If religion is a yoke, it is a very sweet yoke and a very light burden;[473] it is, moreover, a magnificent benefit, a grace, a favor, an immense glory for man: I speak amiss, it is the only source of all happiness and all glory in this world and in the next.

Such is the point of view, so perfectly just besides, from which we ought always to regard religion. The ignorance, and more especially the passions or vicious inclinations, of man too often persuade him that religion is a heavy yoke and an undesirable present that God has given us. Victims of this deplorable error, a great number of men submit to its salutary prescriptions only by constraint and through fear; others abandon it openly, or remain in a state of criminal indifference toward it. O men! my brethren, my brethren so unfortunate and so blind, what a strange perversity and delusion! You do not see, then, that religion is the most beautiful present that God has ever made to us! You do not know, then, that, if religion imposes its amiable yoke upon you, it is to deliver you from the crushing and shameful yoke of your passions and vices! You do not feel, then, that religion is the light of your mind, the guarantee of all your rights, the consoler of your many sorrows, the principle of all that which is beautiful, good, grand, and sublime on earth! You do not understand, then, that without it we are only animals, like those which graze in our meadows and chew the cud in our stalls: whilst with it we are the children of the

Most High, the gods of the earth, the candidates for heaven, the emulators of the angels, the heirs of an empire whose magnificence eclipses all the splendors of the firmament, and whose exquisite delights are to earthly pleasures what the honeycomb is to vinegar!

But, in a still more elevated sense, religion must be called a benefit, a magnificent alms. We have said that man at his creation was constituted in a supernatural state of grace and justice, destined to lead him to the intuitive vision of God in heaven. Now, this happiness was not due to us. Religion, which is the sum or aggregate of the supernatural relations gratuitously established between God and man, is therefore an immense favor. It is the grace of graces—a grace diversified in a thousand ways. In point of fact, Catholic theology defines grace a succor, or rather the sum of supernatural succors, which God grants gratuitously to men in consideration of the merits of Jesus Christ, that they may be able to work out their salvation.[474] It recognizes two principal kinds of graces: external graces, and internal graces.[475]

External graces.—External graces are all the supernatural means,[476] visible or sensible, by which God assists us to work out our salvation. Since it is religion that conducts us to salvation, the first kind of grace contains all that which forms the exterior of religion. Hence, it comprises, under the old testament, all the revelations made to the patriarchs; all the promises, figures, and predictions of the Messias; the law given on Mount Sinai; all the sacrifices, observances, ceremonies, feasts, hymns, and prayers of the Jewish worship; all the teachings of the prophets to recall the Hebrews to virtue; all the good examples given by the holy personages of those times: in a word, all the external helps that could lead men to do good of a supernatural order—consequently, all the Mosaic religion, as far as it was sensible. It is then true that, before the coming of the Messias, religion, considered outwardly, is only one great grace, diversified in a thousand ways, to conduct man to supernatural happiness.

The case is the same after the coming of the Messias. Considered outwardly, the Christian religion, that is, religion developed by the Redeemer in person—the admirable teachings, miracles, and examples of our divine Savior, the preachings of the apostles and their successors, spread during the last eighteen hundred years over the whole world; the Creed, the decalogue, the festivals and fasts, all the laws of the Church; the examples of an innumerable multitude of martyrs, virgins, and solitaries; in a word, all the external helps that, since the coming of Jesus Christ, could lead men to do good of a supernatural order, are so many external graces—consequently religion, as far as it is sensible, in this happy epoch, is only one great grace, diversified also in a thousand ways, to conduct man to supernatural happiness.[477]

Such is the first kind of graces—external graces.

Internal graces.—Let us come to the internal graces. This second kind comprises the virtues infused into our soul by baptism, namely, the theological virtues of faith, hope, and charity: all that moves our heart, all that enlightens our mind, all that disposes us inwardly to good of a supernatural order and gives us strength to accomplish it. Good thoughts, salutary inspirations, pious emotions, holy resolutions, chaste desires, are so many internal graces. Who can count them? Ah! it would be much easier to count the hairs of one's head.

Like external grace, internal grace is also diversified in a thousand different ways. It takes every color; it assumes every form; it utters every voice—the voice of faith, the voice of hope, the voice of love, the voice of remorse, the voice of fear, the voice of sadness, the voice of joy; the voice of a tender mother, who weeps and beseeches; the voice of an angry father, who warns and threatens; the voice of a kind friend, who addresses us with mild reproaches. Night and day, from the first dawn of reason to our last sigh, the Redeemer stands at the door of our heart, continually repeating these words: "My child, open to me; give me thy heart."[478]

What we have said suffices to make us forever bless the mercy of God, who was pleased to restore the sacred bond of religion, after it had been broken by the sin of the first man. But he was not content with restoring it. To worthily glorify his adorable Son, to make his infinite mercy shine forth in all its splendor, to punish the jealousy of the infernal author of our ruin, he made grace superabound where sin had abounded,[479] by contracting with fallen man a second union, no less intimate than the first, and even more advantageous than it. This new wonder justifies the astonishing expression of the Church, which calls the fault of Adam "a happy fault," and gives a last touch to the demonstration of this grand leading truth, that religion is a magnificent alms.

You ask wherein consists the superabundance of the good things that we owe to Christianity, that is, to the union reestablished between God and man by the Redeemer? We shall endeavor to show you. "Would you wish to know," asks St. Chrysostom, "the superabundance of the grace of our Lord? Listen! A servant contracted a debt of ten pieces of silver. Not being able to pay it he was arrested by his master, and cast into prison with his wife and children. A rich man hearing the news sought for the creditor, and counted out to him not merely ten pieces of silver but ten thousand pieces of gold. Then, entering the prison, he set the debtor free, conducted him to a magnificent palace, placed him on a throne, and crowned him with honor and glory. This, and much more, is what our Lord did for us. He paid infinitely more than was due, and replaced by more precious treasures the advantages of which we were deprived by the sin of Adam."[480]

Thus, created in the friendship of God, Adam made us children of wrath, liable to the punishment of damnation for all eternity, and deprived us of grace, in virtue of which alone man can persevere: our Lord makes us children of adoption, delivers us from both the pain of loss and the pain of sense, and communicates to us at the same time a stronger grace, in virtue of which, notwithstanding our frailty, and the terrible enemies that make war on us, we really persevere.

Created in innocence, Adam defiled us by transmitting a single sin to us: our Lord purifies us by effacing not only original sin, but even all the sins committed by our own personal will. Stronger than the sin of Adam, the grace of our Lord erects a barrier around the august Mary, and preserves her from all contamination. It makes her an inexhaustible ocean of graces for the world, and a miracle of sanctity, far surpassing anything imaginable in the state of primitive innocence. More penetrating than the sin of Adam, with which the human race alone is infected, the grace of our Lord extends not only to all men born, or to be born, but moreover to the angels.

Created free from the attacks of a rebellious flesh, Adam bequeathed us concupiscence: our Lord makes it the occasion of a generous warfare and noble victory for us, until it is completely extinguished in the joys of heaven.

Created free from death, Adam abandoned us all to its empire, and deprived us of the fruits of the tree of life: our Lord breaks the scepter of death, becomes himself our tree of life, by giving us his adorable flesh for our nourishment, and secures us a glorious and immortal life in eternity.

Created in grace, Adam precipitated us with himself from the heights of the supernatural order, and reduced us, little as it was wanted, to a state of simple nature: our Lord takes us by the hand, and raises us to a more perfect and sublime state than that in which Adam was formed.

Created to the image of God, Adam in his own person caused us to lose this august resemblance, and we became like to the beasts: our Lord restores to us our resemblance with God, and in himself and in Mary our nature is elevated above all the hierarchies of heaven.

Created in original justice, Adam despoiled us of it: our Lord gives us in exchange a plentiful supply of graces and virtues. In the first place he gives us virtues which would never have existed in the state of innocence: patience, penance, martyrdom, virginity, apostleship, and a crowd of others that make human nature an object worthy of the admiration of angels. Then, he gives us graces that elevate these virtues to a degree which they never would have attained in the state of innocence.[481]

What is demanded of us by religion. — Religion, then, is the most beautiful present and the most magnificent alms that God could bestow upon us. Need we be surprised that the saints of all times have preferred it to everything else in the world, and suffered with joy the most frightful torments rather than renounce this precious treasure? At the very moment while we write these lines, there exists so heroic an example of this love of religion, that we should have reason to reproach ourselves with our neglect if we did not endeavor to give it all the publicity in our power.

A missionary of China writes thus: "During the persecution of 1805, sixteen persons, among whom were three women, three Tartars of the imperial family, and a mandarin, were sent into exile. All have generously supported the weight of this persecution, and remained steadfast in their faith. Three others were condemned to carry the *kang*, and had the cross burned on the soles of their feet with a hot iron, to oblige them to trample on it. Two of them have now been dead for a long time — real martyrs; the third still lives. He has been carrying the *kang* for the last thirty years! His name is Peter Tsay — a name well worthy of being preserved, for I feel assured that it will yet be the name of a martyr. The single expression, 'I renounce my religion,' which his persecutors have a thousand times in vain endeavored to extort from him, would suffice to deliver him from the instrument of his pain and to set him at liberty, but, by the grace of God, he has always been immovable in the faith, and will continue so, as we hope, to his last breath.

"He has been placed in a prison near one of the gates of the city of Pekin, so that all passersby may be able to contemplate in him an example of that rigor which all those must expect who desire to embrace the faith of Jesus Christ. This venerable champion of religion remains indifferent to the promises and the threats of his persecutors. Nothing is more edifying than to witness the contentment which he feels in his cruel position. Pious souls often visit him to be edified, and to afford him all the encouragement and consolation that he can receive. This long and sorrowful punishment, considering the facility with which he might deliver himself from it by apostasy, renders him a thousand times greater before God than if he laid down his head on the block. What a glorious crown the Lord reserves for him in heaven! This confessor of the faith is a true treasure to Christianity: his example speaks powerfully to the consciences of all, strengthening the fainthearted, encouraging the fervent, and making us all clearly understand how glorious a thing it is to suffer for the name of Jesus Christ."[482]

This example, heroic as it is, is not surprising in the eyes of a Christian; nor would it be, though it were a thousand times more heroic. What is surprising is to see the little account that the generality of men make of religion, that is, to see how they outrage their benefactor and lose their right to heaven rather than part for a moment with their pleasures: this is indeed surprising! Yet, in comparison with religion and the eternal possession of God, what is the transitory enjoyment of all existing or possible creatures? Nothing at all. Do we think of this?

There is nothing even in a profound knowledge of religion and of the duties imposed on us by it that ought not to excite our gratitude and to determine our fidelity. Religion, in effect, on God's side, consists of the truths which he reveals to us, and of the duties which he imposes on us: these are the laws and the conditions of our future enjoyment of him in heaven. On man's side, this happiness depends on the fulfillment of the duties which he owes to God, to his neighbor, and to himself. Such is the nature of religion. Its means are the helps or graces which God gives to man; and the cooperation which man, assisted by God, gives to grace. Its end is, for God, glory; for man, happiness — that is, the entire satisfaction of all his faculties. Its sanction, the punishments and rewards of time and eternity. How glorious, how pleasant, and how advantageous is this divine society or association with God!

The Christian religion is as old as the world.—But it is time to study it in its history. We have seen that the Son of God, our Lord Jesus Christ, by becoming our mediator, restored the supernatural bond which had been broken by the revolt of our first parents. Hence, it evidently follows that there is only one religion, the religion of Jesus Christ; consequently, that the Christian religion is as old as the world, and that Christianity is like a magnificent chain, whose last ring is in our hands, and whose first is attached to the throne of the eternal.

This consoling truth is the object of all our instructions, namely, that the salvation of man has been, from the origin of time, the only thought of God, the term of all his counsels, and the end of the world and of all events!

Wisdom of God in the gradual development of religion.—Since the only thought of God has been to save man, it will be asked, doubtless, why he did not send the Savior sooner after the fall. Whether one regards this delay on God's side or on man's side, it is an admirable proof of the wisdom of God and of his love for us.

1. As for the reasons taken on the side of God to explain the delay of the Redeemer, the principal one is this: God wished, during the long interval of four thousand years, to have the great event of the coming of the Messias predicted with all its circumstances, and to impress upon him with so much splendor the seal of the divinity, that it would be impossible not to recognize in our Lord Jesus Christ the liberator of the human race. With this view, the whole economy of our salvation, all the mysteries of the Redeemer, were promised, prefigured, predicted, and prepared for by a multitude of signs and events, centuries before their accomplishment, with such degree of light or evidence as suited each particular age. This conduct not only reveals the wisdom of God, but also displays his tender solicitude for man. He saw our first parents, those noble creatures whom he had loved, deprived of their innocence and happiness; he saw in their posterity the rulers of the world condemned to painful labors, like the vilest slaves, and dragging toward the grave a long chain of infirmities and sorrows. His tenderness could not endure the sight of so many misfortunes however well-deserved.

"Courage!" he seemed to say in each promise and in each figure, to the generations as they passed on earth, undergoing their painful trial, "your evils will end; I am your Father—you are always my children; a day of happiness will yet be your portion." And these figures, and promises, and prophecies of the liberator, he scattered in the ancient world at the feet of exiled man; as, in the modern world, the Church has planted the cross, that affecting memorial of our deliverer, on highways, in public squares, in deserts, on the roofs of houses and the tops of mountains, that the exile of heaven, on whatever side he looks, may perceive the sign of hope. Thus, God never ceased to remind man of the Redeemer, who was to restore him to his original throne.

2. As for the reasons taken on the side of man, it was necessary that man should have a long experience of his misery in order that he might better understand the necessity and the cost of the remedy. It was necessary that man should be for a long time profoundly humbled in order to be cured of his pride, the original cause of his fall. It was necessary that man should ardently desire the Messias; for he would then be better disposed to profit of the example and the teaching of his Savior. In fine, it was necessary that man should be well convinced that God alone could save him, since all the efforts of the philosophers and sages of the earth were unavailing to deliver him from the deep abyss of ignorance and corruption into which he had fallen. At the same time, man experienced, from the moment of his fall, the benefits of the future incarnation, and was able to avail himself of it.

Another no less admirable mark of the goodness of God toward man is that he only made the Savior known to him little by little: the divine Wisdom thus proportioned itself to human weakness. In the order of grace as in that of nature, everything is done sweetly and gradually: our Lord Jesus Christ is the sun of the spiritual world. Now, the sun does not appear suddenly above the horizon, with all the splendor of its sparkling rays. It is preceded by the gentle gleams of the dawn, followed by the soft, golden hues of the morning. This gradual increase of light prepares our eyes for the dazzling brightness of the daystar.

It is the same in the spiritual world. In the beginning, men were just like persons awaking: too great a light would have blinded them.[483] God accommodated himself to the weakness of their vision. He only allowed to appear at first the soft gray of daybreak, that is, he only gave men such a knowledge of the great mystery of the incarnation as they were capable of receiving. It was thus from Adam to Moses; this was religion under the patriarchs, or the law of nature—a law simple in its dogmas, in its morality, and in its worship: it was the outline or first sketch of the picture.

Then came the stronger light of the aurora, that is, religion from Moses to the Messias, or religion under the law. More developed in its dogmas and precepts, accompanied with a more majestic worship, and surrounded by a more complicated ceremonial, it gave men a fuller knowledge of the liberator: it was the rough draught of the picture.

Finally, in the plenitude of time, when men were sufficiently prepared to support the glorious manifestation of the great mystery of the redemption, God displayed the sun, our Lord Jesus Christ, beaming in all the splendor and magnificence of the brightest day: it was the perfection of the picture.

Thus it was decided in the counsels of the eternal Wisdom, that the Messias should not come immediately after original sin. Let us seek, henceforward, what God, of his own goodness, should do for man in order to console him during a delay of four thousand years.

We easily imagine what God should do: 1) promise the Redeemer to man; 2) give man a sign by which he might know the Redeemer on his arrival, and attach himself to him; and 3) prepare the world for the coming of the Redeemer and the establishment of his reign.

Behold, then, what God did in a manner worthy of his infinite goodness and his infinite wisdom. Let us enter with profound respect into the sanctuary of his counsels, and examine the uninterrupted series of promises, figures, prophecies, and preparations which will lead us step by step during the long space of four thousand years, that is, from the commencement of the world to the great event of the incarnation of the Word.

But, in the first place, how do we know that the patriarchs, and the extraordinary men whom God raised up from time to time among the Jewish people, together with the sacrifices and a thousand events and circumstances in the life of this people, were so many figures of the Messias?

We know it a) by the authority of the sacred writers of the new testament. Besides a great number of formal testimonies given by our Lord himself and the evangelists, which show that all the old testament was a figure of Jesus Christ and his Church, St. Paul says, in express terms, that what happened to the Jews was a figure of what is fulfilled among Christians.[484]

We know it b) by the authority of tradition. The holy fathers are unanimous in regarding Jesus Christ and his Church as the great objects veiled under the shadows of the old testament. They look upon the old testament as a rose in bud—upon the new, as a rose in full bloom. "The old testament," says St Augustine, "is hidden in the new; the patriarchs, their alliances, their words, their actions, their children, their whole lives, were a continual prophecy of Jesus Christ and the Church; the whole Jewish nation and its government were a great prophecy of Jesus Christ and the Christian kingdom."[485]

Let us hear another of the most eloquent expounders of tradition. Eusebius, a historian of the Church, speaks thus: "All the prophecies, all the ancient scriptures, all the revolutions of political states, all the laws, all the ceremonies of the first covenant, only led to Jesus Christ. They announced him alone; they prefigured him alone. He was in Adam the father of a posterity of saints; an innocent, virginal martyr in Abel; the restorer of the world in Noe; blessed in Abraham; a high priest in Melchisedech; a voluntary oblation in Isaac; chief of the elect in Jacob; sold by his brethren in Joseph; a traveler, a fugitive, a wonder-worker, and a legislator in Moses; an abandoned sufferer in Job; hated and persecuted in most of the prophets; a conqueror in David, and King of nations; a pacific ruler and the consecrator of a new temple in Solomon; swallowed up and restored to life in Jonas. The tables of the law, the manna of the desert, the luminous pillar, the brazen serpent, were all emblems of his gifts and his glory."[486]

We know it c) by the perfect conformity between these figures and our Lord. If anyone should assert that the resemblance which is found between the figures of Jesus Christ and Jesus Christ himself is only the effect of chance, or of an arbitrary arrangement, he would show as little sense as the man who, seeing numerous portraits of a king, taken by different artists, and very much alike, should maintain that one of the artists intended, indeed, to represent the monarch, but all the others only succeeded in giving his likeness by chance.

But there is no such thing as chance where we see a design, a sequence, a combination, as wise as it is well sustained. Of this nature are the figures of the Redeemer. The succession of mysterious figures, beginning with the world, and continuing uninterruptedly to Jesus Christ, is an incontestable proof of the unvarying design of providence. Like the prophecies, they reflect light on one another; this figure completes what that begins; and, all together depict to perfection our Lord, his labors for the salvation of the world, his death, his resurrection, his glory, and his Church.

In these figures the just of the old law found their consolation. All were acquainted to a certain extent with their meaning, as all understood, to a proper degree, the oracles of the prophets concerning the Messias. While the better instructed had a more intimate knowledge of them, the rest had as clear a knowledge as was necessary to preserve that which was indispensable for salvation, an implicit faith in the mystery of the redemption.[487]

It was also for us that God exhibited this long line of pictures. He would hereby confirm our belief by showing us that the Christian religion stretches its roots back even to the most remote times, and that it is the completion of a design which has its origin with the commencement of the world, and which was regularly developed during four thousand years: the promises have the same end always in view. It is time, however, to enter into details.

First promise of the Messias. — The first promise of the Redeemer was made in the terrestrial paradise. The guilty parents of the human race had not yet heard the sentence which was to be so justly pronounced upon them when they were already assured that they would have an expiator for their crime and a repairer of their evils. The condemnation pronounced against the devil, and his instrument, the serpent, contained this consoling hope. "The woman shall crush thy head,"[488] says the Lord to the serpent, that is, there will be born of the woman a Son, who shall destroy the empire of evil, the empire of Satan. Our first parents understood the meaning of this figurative language: it sufficed to uphold their courage, and to render their works meritorious by faith in the merits of the future Redeemer.

Still, consoling as it is, this first promise is very general. No doubt, it announces a Savior. But when will he come? In what place, in what country will he be born? By what characteristics shall he be known? By what means shall he save the human race? On all these matters there is absolute uncertainty. He will come; he will be a child of Eve and Adam, an heir of their blood, but exempt from their sin: this is the sum of their information. It was a faint ray from that sun of justice which was one day to rise upon the world; the languid eyes of sinful man could not bear the brightness of a greater light. In this very obscurity, his faith found an occasion of greater merit, and his fault a first expiation.

Adam, the first figure of the Messias. — To prevent man from losing, even for a moment, the consoling remembrance of his liberator, God hastened to confirm the first promise, or rather he translated the figurative language into other language no less eloquent. Adam himself became the first figure of his Redeemer: by understanding the one, he could also understand the other. Let us see the striking relations that exist between these two stems or roots of humanity. Adam is the father of all men, according to the flesh; our Lord is the father of all men, according to the spirit — he is the Son of God by whom we have been both created and regenerated. Adam is the king of the universe — for him all creatures have been made; our Lord is the King of the universe — by him and for him all creatures have been made. Adam is the high priest of the universe — he should offer to God the homage of all creatures; our Lord is the supreme pontiff of the universe, the Catholic priest of the eternal Father — he should offer to God our homage and that of all creatures.[489] Adam is at first only surrounded with animals which cannot form his society; our Lord is at first alone on the earth, surrounded with men immersed in sensual affections, and resembling by their inclinations the vilest animals.

Adam sleeps — the Lord takes from his side a rib, of which he forms a companion; our Lord sleeps the sleep of death on the tree of the cross — during his sleep his side is opened, and from the wound comes forth the Church, his spouse, figured by the blood and water. Eve, the spouse of Adam, is his living image — she will be his associate, and will bear him many children; the Church, the spouse of our Lord, is his living image — she will be his associate, and will bear him many children. Between Adam and Eve there exists an indissoluble bond; between our Lord and his Church there exists a bond that will never end — he will be with it all days, even to the consummation of the world, and throughout all eternity.

Adam sins — he is driven from paradise; our Lord charges himself with the sins of the world[490] — he descends from heaven. Adam is condemned to labors, sufferings, and death; our Lord condemns himself to the same punishments. Adam involves all men in his own misfortune; our Lord saves all men by his redemption — for, says St. Paul, as death entered into the world by one man, in whom all sinned, so life has entered into it by one man, in whom all are saved.[491]

Such are the principal traits of resemblance that reason and faith discover to us between the two Adams.[492]

The patriarchs. — With the father of the human race begins the long line of living prophecies — the patriarchs — who give us in their actions a perfect picture of the Redeemer.[493]

Before opening our eyes on this magnificent gallery of living pictures, we must know something of the patriarchs who compose it. And what noble and tender recollections are attached to their names! Which of us can read at any time their history without being carried away in fancy to the happy days of childhood, when, a pious mother opening her *Pictorial Bible* on her knees, we listened to her explanations with so much eagerness, and our eyes melted into tears at the story of Isaac about to be sacrificed by his father, or of little Joseph sold by his brethren?

Patriarch signifies father, or head of a family: the name is given to the first ancestors of the Savior — we count thirty-four of them. The patriarchs are divided into three classes:

1. Those who flourished before the deluge: namely, Adam, Seth, Enos, Cainan, Malaleel, Jared, Enoch, Mathusalem, Lamech, and Noe.

2 Those who lived after the deluge, and before the vocation of Abraham: namely, Sem, Arphaxad, Sale, Heber, Phaleg, Rehu, Sarug, Nacher, Thare, Abraham.

3. Those who appeared after the vocation of Abraham, and before the Egyptian bondage: namely, Isaac, Jacob, and the twelve sons of Jacob, who were the roots of the twelve tribes of the people of Israel.

Let us say a word of their lives. The patriarchs were perfectly free, and their family formed a little state, of which the father was a kind of king. It was the great number of their flocks that made them value wells and cisterns so much, in a country which had no rivers but the Jordan, and where it rained but rarely. With all their riches they were very industrious, always in the country, dwelling under tents, changing their place of abode according to the convenience of pasturage—consequently, often engaged with camping and decamping; for they could only make short journeys with so numerous a train.

This manner of life was always regarded as the most perfect, since it attached men least to the earth. Hence, it expressed better the condition of the patriarchs, who only dwelt on the earth as travelers, awaiting the promises of God, which should be fulfilled after their death. The most ancient cities of which there is mention were built by the wicked, by Cain and Nemrod. The wicked are surrounded with fortifications, to defend them from the punishments due to their past crimes, and to afford them impunity in the commission of new ones: the good live openly on the hills and plains without any fear.

The principal employment of the patriarchs was the care of their flocks. Though the agricultural life is innocent, yet the pastoral is more perfect. There is something in it more simple and more noble; it is less painful; it attaches one less to the earth, and, at the same time, it is more profitable. We may judge of the labor of the men by that of the women. Rebecca came a considerable distance to draw water from the well, and carried the pitcher on her shoulder, and Rachel led her father's flock: neither their beauty nor their nobility made them too delicate. It was, without doubt, in a great measure, the simple, laborious, and frugal life of the patriarchs that enabled them to reach such an advanced age, and to die so tranquilly. Abraham and Isaac lived nearly two hundred years each; the other patriarchs whom we know spent at least a hundred years on the earth; and there is no mention that they were sick during the whole time.[494]

Such was, in general, the life of the patriarchs: a great degree of liberty, with no other government than that of a father, who held absolute sway in his family; an easy and natural existence, in an abundance of things necessary, and a contempt of things superfluous, in honest labor, with careful industry, without anxiety or ambition.[495]

Scarcely had our first parents departed from the terrestrial paradise, when they learned, by sad experience, the evil which they had done themselves, and the melancholy change which their fault had wrought in all nature. Condemned to rude labors, and eating their bread in the sweat of their brow, how much need they had of being consoled and encouraged by new marks of the divine mercy! The Lord, ever good and ever attentive to their wants, came to their asistance.

Two children were given them. The elder received the name of Cain, and the younger that of Abel. Cain applied himself to tilling the earth, Abel occupied himself with pastoral cares. Instructed by their father, both were in the habit of rendering their homage to God by the oblation of a part of the goods which they had received from his bounty. One day Cain offered the firstfruits of his harvest, and Abel sacrificed the firstlings of his flocks, with the fat of victims. But the piety of Cain was as cold, and his offering as miserly, as those of Abel were sincere and generous. The Lord testified in a sensible manner the difference which he noticed between the two sacrifices. He accepted that of Abel and rejected that of Cain.

Jealousy cannot be just. Instead of entering into himself and reflecting on the cause of his disgrace, Cain preferred to avenge himself on his innocent brother. At the moment the crime was conceived in his heart, it manifested itself on his countenance. The Lord, who wished to save Cain, by recalling him to himself, spoke to him thus: "Why art thou angry? Why has thy countenance lost its serenity? If thou do good, shalt thou not receive reward? If thou do evil, shall not thy sin instantly provoke my vengeance? But there is still time for thee to save thyself; however violent thy passion may be, thou canst resist it."

The divine remonstrances of a master, who seeks to prevent the faults of his servants, made no impression on the envenomed heart of Cain. Listening only to his cruel jealousy, he said to his brother: "Let us go out into the fields." Abel thereupon willingly consented; perhaps he even tried to remove the vexation which seemed to gnaw the heart of Cain. Without any warning, Cain fell upon his brother and killed him.

Immediately the Lord addressed himself to the murderer, with a gentleness which the fratricide did not deserve and of which he did not profit. The Lord only said a few words at first: "Cain! where is thy brother Abel? " "I do not know," replied the wretch, "am I my brother's keeper?" You will admit that such an insolent answer deserved a thunderbolt on the spot; but the Lord, who, by his remonstrances, had endeavored to stay the crime, wished now to excite the criminal to repentance for it. "What hast thou done, Cain?" He continued: "The voice of thy brother's blood cries from the earth, and demands vengeance against thee. Thou shalt be cursed on the earth, which thou hast forced to drink thy brother's blood. Thou shalt cultivate it with great labor, and it shall not correspond to thy cares or thy hopes. Thou shalt wander over its surface, a vagabond, a miserable fugitive."

The culprit, alarmed at the sentence, exclaimed with more despair than contrition: "My crime is too great to hope for pardon. Thou dost condemn me to wander in different countries, without being able to settle in any. Whosoever meets me will believe that he has a right to kill me." "No," answered the Lord, "I wish to leave thee time to expiate thy crime, and to repair thy offense. If anyone dares to touch thy life, he shall be punished seven times more rigorously than thou."

God ceased to speak. To preserve the fratricide from that assassination which he dreaded, God impressed on his appearance something wild and terrible, which would frighten anyone from attacking him. Cain had abused the preventing graces that would have dissuaded him from his crime; he profited no better of the means of salvation, which the patience of the Lord supplied to him. In this matter, as in everything else, he was a model often copied by the impenitent, who, always inexcusable, fall into the abyss only by withdrawing from the charitable hand that is extended to support them, and remain buried therein only because they will not make use of the helps which it offers them to rise therefrom.

We see in Cain and Abel a figure of that which was to happen throughout the lapse of ages, the church of Satan rising against the Church of Jesus Christ. From this date begins the long persecution that the wicked shall wage against the just till the end of time. But the chastisement of Cain reminds the just that providence watches over them, to reward and to avenge them. The conscience of the first fratricide, abandoned to continual fears, induced him to build the first city, that he might find therein an asylum against the hatred and the horror of the human race.

This history of the first Cain and the first Abel is the anticipated history of another Cain and another Abel. Four thousand years after the former, the latter history should be written in letters of blood, almost in the same place, for Abel is the second figure of the Messias.

Abel, the second figure of the Messias. — Abel is a shepherd; our Lord calls himself a shepherd — the Church is his fold, Christians are his lambs. Abel offers a sacrifice, which God receives favorably, while that of Cain is rejected; our Lord offers himself as a sacrifice, which is received favorably, while all those of the old law are rejected. Abel becomes an object of jealousy to Cain, his brother; our Lord becomes an object of jealousy to the Jews, his brethren. Abel is enticed into the fields, and falls under the blows of his brother; our Lord is led out from Jerusalem, and put to death by the Jews, his brethren. The blood of Abel invokes vengeance on Cain; the blood of our Lord invokes mercy on his executioners.

In punishment of his fratricide, Cain is condemned to be a wanderer and a vagabond on the earth; in punishment of their deicide, the Jews are condemned to be wanderers and vagabonds over the whole earth. For eighteen hundred years the world has seen them roaming everywhere, without priest, without king, without sacrifice; wandering everywhere, without a place they can call their own. Cain was an object of dislike and fear to all who met him; the Jewish people are an object of dislike and contempt to all who meet them. God placed a mark on the brow of Cain, to prevent anyone from killing him; he has also placed a mark of reprobation on the brow of the Jewish people, to prevent anyone from exterminating them — they alone have survived all ancient peoples — they exist alone and distinct in the midst of all, without being confounded with other nations. Adam is consoled for the death of Abel by the birth of Seth, a child of benediction, who perpetuates the race of the just; God is, so to speak, consoled for the death of our Lord, by the birth of an innumerable multitude of Christians, who have been made by him the adopted children of God.

PRAYER

O my God! who art all love, I thank thee for having multiplied the promises and the figures of the Messias; grant that they may more and more excite in my heart a desire of knowing and loving thee; grant me the innocence of Abel, his zeal for thy glory, and his charity for my brethren.

I am resolved to love God above all things, and my neighbor as myself for the love of God; and, in testimony of this love, I will salute those who injure me and will pray for them.

Lesson 22: Messias Foreshadowed: Noe

Birth of Seth; Enoch taken up to heaven. — To replace the just Abel, God gave Adam a third son, who was named Seth. It was he that should perpetuate on earth the race of the children of God. The scripture calls "children of God" those who lived according to the spirit of religion, and "children of men" those who followed only the depraved inclinations of the flesh and of concupiscence. Cain was the father of the latter. Enoch, one of the descendants of Seth, particularly distinguished himself by his fidelity in observing the law of the Lord. While he was among men he never ceased exhorting them to penance, announcing to them the judgments of God that were to fall on the wicked.

When he had spent 365 years on the earth, God took him away, exempting him from death; and he appeared no more, having been translated to heaven, whence he shall come again on earth, toward the end of the world, to convert the Jews, and make sinners enter into the way of penance.[496] Thus, God always preserved in the posterity of Seth some faithful servants, and the anticipated effect of the redemption was felt from the beginning of the world.

Corruption of the human race. — As long as the race of Seth lived apart from that of Cain, it retained its primitive innocence. In the course of time the two families drew nearer, and were united by marriage; and to them were born the giants, that is, men of extraordinary height and strength. These men, whose name has long been celebrated, spread disorder and impiety[497] everywhere.

We see hereby that the cause of evil was then what it has been ever since, a mixture of the good with the bad. Soon the corruption became general, and the earth was filled with crimes. Iniquity arrived at such an excess that it obliged God, who is goodness itself, to repent, so to speak, of having created man. The expression which the scripture employs is astonishing: "God, being touched inwardly with sorrow of heart, said: 'I will destroy man, whom I have created.'"[498]

Noe.—But, amid the general depravation, he met with one just man, who remained free from the contagion: this was Noe, then aged 480 years. The Lord called him, and said to him: "Man hath corrupted all his ways; I repent of having created him, and I am resolved to destroy him—and, with him, the animals, the reptiles, the birds, and all the other creatures, infected by the crimes of the human race. I will destroy the world by a deluge. As for thee, thou hast found favor before me. Make, then, an ark of solid planed wood, divide it into several compartments, and cover it with pitch inside and outside. Thou shalt make it three hundred cubits long, fifty cubits wide, and thirty cubits high. Thou shalt make an opening to serve as a window; thou shalt place a door in one of the sides; and the whole interior of the vessel shall consist of three stories. When the ark is finished, thou shalt enter into it, thou and thy children. Thou shall take with thee animals of every species, that they may be again renewed on the earth. Thou shalt gather into the ark all the provisions necessary to preserve the lives of its inhabitants."

The dimensions appointed by the Lord were just, and though we might not be able, by the most exact calculations, to discover their fitness, yet we might well expect them to come correct from the experience of the great master, who vouchsafed himself to be the architect of this wonderful building.[499]

Noe obeyed the Lord, and employed a hundred years in the construction of the ark. Let us here admire the patience of God. He caused the ark to be built before the eyes of guilty men, expressly with a view that it should be a continual warning to them of the punishment with which they were threatened. Noe ceased not to recall them to penance, but they closed their ears against his salutary warnings and laughed at the fears with which he sought to inspire them. When the ark was finished, the Lord deferred yet seven days the exercise of his justice, affording sinners this last delay to think upon themselves. He could not, so to speak, make up his mind to strike the blow. We have seen, besides, that the prophecy of Enoch preceded that of Noe. Thus God was uttering his warnings and threats for nearly a thousand years. It was all useless. At length came the punishment so long threatened, but always despised, and it proved as terrible on its arrival as it had been previously deemed contemptible.

In the year of the world, 1656, the Lord caused Noe, his wife, and his three sons, and their wives, together with animals of every kind, to enter into the ark. After which, seeing in the ark the eight persons from whom a new world should spring, and the animals that should replace those of the old world, God closed the door of the ark on the outside, so that water could not penetrate into it. Free henceforth to punish the guilty, without injuring the innocent, he abandons the world to the effects of his indignation.

The deluge.—Suddenly the sea overflows; all the fountains of the earth, all the reservoirs of heaven, are opened. Rain, more frightful in its violence than in its duration, falls continually during forty days and forty nights. The surface of the globe is inundated, and the waters rise fifteen cubits above the highest mountains. Nothing escapes them; men, beasts, birds, all perish alike. The ark alone floats tranquilly over the waters, which lift it up toward heaven, as it bears on its bosom the firstfruits of a new world.

The earth remained covered with the waters of the deluge for the space of 140 days. Then God sent a wind, which cleared them away little by little. To acquire a knowledge of what was happening, Noe opened the window of the ark, and gave a raven its liberty.

This carnivorous bird, finding among innumerable carcasses an abundance on which to live, never returned. Noe accordingly judged that the waters were now much diminished. Seven days afterward, he sent forth a dove, with the same object as he had in view when despatching the raven; but it, not finding any dry ground on which to rest its foot, returned to the ark. It presented itself to Noe, who stretched forth his hand, and brought it in. The patriarch waited yet seven days more, and again sent forth the dove. The dove returned in the evening, bearing in its bill an olive branch, with green leaves. At this sign, Noe judged that the waters were completely subsided. But he preferred to have patience yet seven days more, and then sent forth the dove for the third time. It never came back. Noe still waited for the orders of the Lord. These orders were given him on the 393rd day after he had gone into the ark.

The rainbow. — Scarcely was Noe at liberty, when his first impulse led him to an act of gratitude. He offered a sacrifice to the Lord, and the Lord promised never to destroy the world again by a deluge, saying: "This is the sign of the alliance which I establish forever between thee and me: when I shall cover the sky with clouds, my bow shall appear in the clouds, and I will remember, on seeing it, the promise that I have made never more to destroy the world by a general inundation." Accordingly, as often as we see the rainbow, it ought to encourage us, and to remind us that God will never sweep away the human race in a flood again. From this divine promise, perpetuated by tradition, came undoubtedly the veneration, which the Peruvians appear to have long entertained for the rainbow, a manifest sign to them of the entire cessation of those terrible inundations which resulted in the deluge.[500]

If the remembrance of this particular circumstance is found among all pagan nations, with much greater reason ought we to find among them a remembrance of that awful catastrophe which almost annihilated the human race. Indeed, the reality of the deluge is chronicled with indelible letters in two great books open to all, the memory of mankind and the surface of the globe. To be convinced of this, let us rapidly question the nations that have appeared at different epochs and in different climes. Commencing with Asia, the cradle of the human race, we learn (after the Jews, whose belief is known) from the ancient Persians, that the deluge, in which the human race perished, was occasioned by a flood that lasted ten days and ten nights.

See in what manner the Hindus relate the history of this dreadful event. Vishnu one day addressed a king of Dravadam, named Satievaraden, a very religious prince. The god said to him: "Thy piety toward me and thy charity toward men are pleasing to me. Accordingly, hear my words: I announce to thee that in seven days the sea will submerge the world. I intend to save thee from this deluge, thee and the seven patriarchs. Wherefore, prepare for the event. I will send you a ship, into which you shall collect all sorts of provisions, seeds, fruits, and roots. You shall then ascend into it, and be borne away on the waters." The prince made provision of seeds and roots, as well for his nourishment, as for reproduction in the renovation of the world. At the end of the seventh day, the cataracts of heaven were let loose, and the clouds discharged such copious streams of rain that the sea covered the whole earth. But, under the safekeeping of Vishnu, the ship floated along on the waters, and all that which he had predicted came to pass. The deluge being ended, the eight persons descended safe from the vessel, and adored Vishnu.[501] These same people attribute the deluge to the corruption of the human race.

The Chinese, as different from us in their institutions and customs as perhaps in their appearance and temperament, also admit a deluge; they date it almost at the same epoch as ourselves. Their Chouking, or most ancient book, commences the history of China with an emperor named Yao, whom it represents as engaged in sending forth the waters that covered the greater portion of the earth. The Chinese even instituted a festival in memory of the men who perished at the time of the deluge. This festival, likewise celebrated by the Japanese toward the end of August, had the same object and the same origin.[502]

Similar beliefs prevailed as much among the Arabians, the Turks, the Mongols, and the Babylonians. Berosa, who wrote at Babylon under Alexander, speaks of the deluge in terms very closely resembling those of Moses; and the period at which he places it, immediately before Belus, the father of Ninus, agrees with that given it in Genesis.[503]

If we pass from Asia to Africa, the Egyptians will tell us that at the time when Osiris was engaged in instructing the men of Ethiopia, the Nile overflowed its banks and desolated the immense plains through which it flows. All men would have perished in this deluge had it not been for the powerful hand of Hercules, who alone was able to raise dikes, and thus defend a portion of the human race.[504]

Advancing farther into Africa, you will find the same traditions among the Abyssinians.

In Europe, the Scandinavians tell us that the giant Ymir having been slain, there flowed from his wide and deep wounds so great an abundance of blood that the human race was drowned in it. A man, whom they name Belgémer, and his family, were the only persons saved; and their good fortune arose from the kindness of the divinity, which directed them to take refuge in a large boat. The traditions of the Celts seem even more explicit on this great historical event. According to them, as according to the most ancient nations, the deluge destroyed the whole human race, excepting, however, Dwvan and Dwivach. These alone escaped the danger, having built beforehand a vessel without sails, and placed in it a couple of animals, male and female, of every species that existed. Even the poor Laplanders have their traditions about the deluge.[505]

To complete our tour of the world, let us now pass to America. The ancient Incas, from the time of their conquest of Peru, sought to persuade the people, whose absolute masters they had become, that since the universal deluge, of which a tradition was preserved among the Indians, the world had been repeopled by their ancestors. According to their account, their ancestors, to the number of seven, coming forth from the cave of Pacaritambo, had alone perpetuated the human race. Thenceforward all men owed them homage and obedience; and these ideas, in no small degree, favored the establishment of their empire.

The remembrance of the deluge was so deeply imprinted on the minds of the various tribes of the New World, that one of the Indians of Cuba thus addressed Gabriel de Cabrera: "Why do you scold me? Are we not all brothers? Do not you, as well as I, descend from him who constructed the great vessel that saved our race?" The same ideas prevailed among the savages of North America.[506]

Thus, we may say that the record of the deluge, and of the crimes that occasioned it, is familiar to every people. The memory of mankind is accordingly a new book, in which appears a sketch of the great events related by Moses.

The other book is the surface of our globe. Indeed, we everywhere find on mountains, as well as in the bowels of the earth, even at a considerable distance from the sea, a vast quantity of shells, fishes' teeth, and the remains of marine animals quite foreign to our countries. It is evident that these bodies came from the sea, and that they were transported so far inland by a sudden inundation and by a violent motion of the waters over the whole surface of the earth.[507] It is only to the period of the deluge indicated by Moses that all our geological facts bear homage. If we examine in the Alps the results of the action which must have begun when these mountains assumed their present shape, such as the formation of debris or slopes of mountains or glaciers; if we study the alluvial deposits formed by our present rivers; and if we take into consideration that the slopes and deposits ought to have been made much more rapidly when the falls were much more abrupt than they are today, we shall be inclined to conclude with Deluc, Cuvier, Buckland, and others, that the revolutions which gave our mountains their present form, and our rivers their present course, do not ascend to periods exceedingly remote. Hence, the distance of four thousand years from the present time, as assigned by Genesis to the deluge, may very well agree with all the results that are announced to us by nature's chronometers.[508]

Noe, the third figure of the Messias.—Meanwhile, the Lord was not content with saving Noe; he made the holy patriarch the third figure of the Messias. *Noe* signifies "consoler"; *Jesus* means "Savior." Of all men, Noe alone found grace before God; of all men, our Lord alone found grace before God his Father. Noe was chosen to people the earth a second time; our Lord was chosen to people the earth with the just, and heaven with saints. Noe received an order to construct a vessel; our Lord received an order to establish the Church. During 120 years, Noe labored at the construction of the ark, and preached penance to men, though they would not hear him; our Lord labored during his whole life to construct the Church, and preached penance by himself, by his apostles, and by their successors, but wicked men would not listen to them. Noe, by building the ark, prepared a means of escape from the general destruction; our Lord, by establishing the Church, prepared for men a means of salvation from the deluge of fire that will eternally consume sinners.

Noe and the others who entered with him into the ark were saved; out of the Church of Jesus Christ, there is no salvation for those who, knowing it, refuse to enter into it, or leave it to join some strange sect. The ark was full of creatures of every kind; the Church encloses in her bosom the inhabitants of every nation. The higher the waters of the deluge rose, the nearer the ark reached heaven; the more severely the Church is tried by afflictions, the more perfect she becomes, and the more dear to Almighty God. The ark, which bore Noe and his children, was the only hope of the human race; the Church, which possesses Jesus Christ and his children, is now the only hope of the human race. On leaving the ark, Noe offered a sacrifice, with which the Lord was well pleased; on the cross, our Lord offers a sacrifice a thousand times more pleasing to God than that of Noe. God made a covenant with Noe; God makes an eternal covenant with our Lord, and through him with all men. Noe received full power over the earth and over animals; our Lord receives from God his Father all power in heaven and on earth. By Noe, God restored the world, which he had destroyed; by our Lord, God restores to the world the good things of which sin had robbed it.

PRAYER

O my God! who art all love, I thank thee for the patience with which thou dost await the return of sinners. I thank thee for having so long waited for me to do penance. I return to thee; receive me in thy mercy. I thank thee for having given me birth in the bosom of thy Church, out of which there is no salvation. Grant me the grace to observe and practice to the end whatever it teaches me.

I am resolved to love God above all things, and my neighbor as myself for the love of God; and, in testimony of this love, I shall every month renew my baptismal vows.

Lesson 23: Messias Foreshadowed: Melchisedech

Shortening of human life.—After the deluge, there appeared a new world, a new earth, so to speak; but this earth, already stricken with malediction after the sin of the first man, lost again, by the natural consequence of a long inundation, a portion of its vitality and fruitfulness. Before the deluge, nature was very fertile and vigorous. By the immense quantity of water that covered the surface of the earth for such a long period, plants, deprived of light and saturated with rain and vapor, lost much of their energy. The air, overcharged with heavy moisture, the eating of the flesh of animals, and the drinking of wine to excess, gradually strengthened the principles of corruption; and human life, which previously had lasted for almost a thousand years, declined little by little to the term of a hundred years or even less. Thus was executed the decree of the divine justice against man, who had so often offended.[509]

Noe transmitted to his three sons, Sem, Cham, and Japhet, the holy truths of religion, and particularly the tradition of the divine promise of a future liberator.[510] The holy patriarch also planted the vine, which was undoubtedly known before that time; but, instead of being content as previously with eating its fruit, he discovered the use that could be made of grapes by pressing out and preserving their juice. Wine was a benefit intended to give a little joy to the heart of man, saddened by the shortening of his days and the enfeeblement of all nature. Why is it that so great a number abuse this new present of their heavenly Father?

Curse of Chanaan.—One day Noe, having drunk of the liquor, the effects of which he was not yet acquainted with, fell involuntarily into a state of inebriety, and lay asleep in his tent. During his sleep, he chanced to be very negligently covered, which Cham perceived. Despite what filial respect or shame would suggest on such an occasion, he immediately went to tell his brothers of it. Sem and Japhet were more mindful of their duty. Taking a cloak, they carried it, walking backwards, and threw it over the venerable old man. Noe, on awaking, learned in what manner he had been treated by Cham. Suddenly inspired, he uttered his curse, not against Cham, through respect for the blessing which God had given him on quitting the ark, but against Chanaan, the son of Cham. "Let Chanaan be cursed on the earth; let him become the slave of the slaves of his brethren," said the holy patriarch. A terrible malediction, which is verified later on, when the Chanaanites are exterminated and reduced to slavery by the Israelites, the descendants of Sem. A malediction ever subsisting in the race of Cham, and teaching children the respect which they ought to have for their parents.

By an admirable counsel of providence, Noe lived yet 350 years after the deluge. God prolonged his days and was pleased that his descendants should remain during this long period under the eyes of their common father that they might learn in detail and preserve among mankind the chief truths of religion, as well as the account of ancient facts, regarding which Noe alone was well instructed.

Tower of Babel.—The children of the patriarch were now so numerous that they eagerly desired to separate. But before doing so, they wished to execute a project which clearly manifested their folly and their vanity. "Come," they said to one another, "let us build a city and a tower whose top may reach even to heaven." This extravagant design had two equally ridiculous motives: one, to immortalize their name by a splendid building; the other, to defend themselves against God in case he should again desire to punish the world by a deluge. Herein, they rendered themselves guilty not only of folly but of unbelief; for the Lord had promised never again to submerge the earth by a general inundation. They immediately set to work. But, at the moment when they urged the work forward with the greatest eagerness, God raised among the workmen such a confusion of languages that they no longer understood one another. Being unable thenceforward either to command or to obey, they were obliged to abandon their enterprise. The city and the tower remaining unfinished were called Babel, that is, "confusion," because God confounded there the language of men, who previously had spoken but one and the same language, and thence he scattered them abroad into all the countries of the world.[511]

In their dispersion, the children of Noe carried with them the remembrance of the principal truths of religion, which they had learned from their common father. This is the reason why a knowledge of the greatest events, such as the creation of man, his innocence, his fall, the promise of a Redeemer, the deluge, etc., has been preserved more or less distinctly among every people in the world. But what has happened since the time of the dispersion of men, no matter how wonderful or extraordinary it may have been, is not so generally known: a manifest proof that the bond of communication, which had previously existed among all mankind, was then broken.

Beginning of idolatry. — Meanwhile the devil, the father of lies, was not slow to resume his sway over the human race. The primitive traditions were soon altered by fables, and men abandoned themselves to excesses still more frightful than those which had formerly raised the avenging arm of the Almighty. In vain did the world still wet with the waters of the deluge, in vain did the striking decline of human life, in vain did the general revolution throughout all nature present to the eyes of all the sad monuments of the Creator's justice: the knowledge of the true God was effaced from the memory of mankind. Corruption became universal, and idolatry, at once the daughter and the mother of the passions, began her dismal reign.

Lamentable blindness! The Almighty is refused the tribute of adoration which all things that breathe owe him, and a sacrilegious incense is offered to demons, who render themselves actually present in creatures. Gold, silver, stone, wood, the vilest animals, lifeless statues behold man, the high priest of the universe, prostrate before them, and addressing to them his timid prayers. After this shameful act, the guilty prodigal son squanders away, one by one, the valuables that form his rich patrimony, and walks with incredible folly in the path of shame and disorder, which stretches out broader and broader each day before him. He has been adorned by the Lord with an exquisite crown of knowledge and innocence, but he now takes delight in snatching from his brow its diamonds and its flowers, in tarnishing and sullying them. Let him do so, and very soon you will see him degraded, overwhelmed with weariness and disgust at the sad effects of debauchery, and believing in nothing but fate, annihilation, and despair. Great and terrible lesson! of which Christian nations have not always known how to profit.

There was scarcely a family remaining faithful to the God of Adam and Noe; and it was necessary that the Most High, weary of threatening, waiting, and punishing, should reject anew the human race and abandon it to its perversity. In the midst of this deluge of crimes, what will become of the true religion? Has God resolved to deprive men of it? No; the word of the Eternal is irrevocable. If he had only consulted the misdeeds of our forefathers, he would undoubtedly have destroyed our criminal race; but, even at the moment when he punishes, his mercy tempers the strokes of his justice: God never forgets that he is a Father. The sight of the future merits of the expiatory victim, whom he had announced to the human race, moved him to clemency. Thus, without entirely abandoning the nations, which could only attribute their blindness to their own fault, God resolved to choose one people, appointed to preserve intact the deposit of primitive revelation, and particularly the great promise of the Redeemer.

Vocation of Abraham. — Abraham, a descendant of Sem, was chosen to be the father of this new people, from whom the Messias should spring. Now, from all eternity, God had decided that the Messias should be born in Judea, at that time called the Land of Chanaan. Hence, he drew into this country the holy man, of whom the Messias should be the Son according to the flesh. Abraham dwelt far from the Land of Chanaan, in a country called Chaldea: it was thence the Lord brought him. "Leave the country in which thou dwellest," said God to him, "and come into the land which I will show thee. I will give the country to thy descendants, whom I will multiply as the stars of heaven and as the sands by the seashore." To this magnificent promise God added another, much more magnificent: the promise of the Messias. "I will bless thee," said the Lord to him, "and all the nations of the earth shall be blessed in thee," that is, in him who shall be born of thee, as God himself explained afterward.

Second promise of the Messias.—The second promise of a Redeemer made to Abraham is a great deal clearer than the first. The first did not say among what people the Messias should be born; the second affords us this information in precise terms: he shall be born in the family of Abraham. All other nations are set aside; it is no longer among them that we are to seek the Redeemer. The first promise told us that he would crush the serpent's head; the second explains the meaning of these words: it tells us that the Messias shall overthrow the empire of the devil, by recalling all nations to the knowledge of the true God, in which alone a true blessing is to be found. Hence, a) the blessed germ promised to Eve will also be the germ and offspring of Abraham; b) the victory, which the Messias must gain over the devil, will consist in recalling men to the knowledge and worship of the Creator; and c) the son of Eve and of Abraham will overthrow the empire of the devil throughout the universe by destroying idolatry, which is nothing else than the reign of the devil, and by restoring the worship of the true God. The conversion of the Gentiles, that is, of pagans, is always indicated in the divine scriptures as the special work of the Messias.

Full of faith in the words of God, Abraham quitted his country, accompanied by Sara his wife and Lot his nephew, and arrived in the Land of Chanaan. His flocks and those of Lot were so numerous that the district in which they were residing at the time could not contain them. The holy man proposed to his nephew that they should separate. Lot accordingly withdrew to Sodom. This separation did not cool Abraham's charity, of which he soon gave a remarkable proof.

The king of Sodom, and four other kings, his allies, were attacked and vanquished by a prince to whom they had been tributary: in the affray Lot was taken prisoner. Abraham quickly learned it. At the head of 318 of his bravest servants, and full of confidence in God who protected him, the patriarch fell with this handful of warriors on the victorious troops, put them to flight, recovered the booty, and delivered his nephew and all the other captives out of the hands of their oppressors. Transported with gratitude, the king of Sodom came to his liberator, and, as a slight reward for the kindness he had displayed, besought him to accept the whole of the riches taken from the enemy. Abraham would not accept anything. Only, he gave a tithe of the spoils to Melchisedech, king of Salem, priest of the Lord, who blessed Abraham, after having offered to the Lord bread and wine.

Abraham honored in the person of this royal priest the future Messias, whom this great priest represented; for, of the Messias it is written: "Thou art a priest for ever according to the order of Melchisedech."[512]

Melchisedech, the fourth figure of the Messias.—Thus Melchisedech is the fourth figure of the Messias. In effect, Melchisedech means "king of justice"; our Lord is justice itself. Melchisedech is both a king and a high priest; our Lord is both a King and a high priest. Melchisedech is a priest of the Most High; our Lord is the priest of priests. Melchisedech appears alone—we have no account of his father, or mother, or genealogy, or predecessor, or successor; our Lord has no father on earth or mother in heaven, no predecessor or successor in the priesthood—for priests are only his ministers. Melchisedech blesses Abraham; our Lord blesses the Church, represented by Abraham. Melchisedech offers a sacrifice of bread and wine; our Lord offers himself as a sacrifice every day under the appearances of bread and wine.

This figure adds some new touches to the portrait of the Messias. The preceding ones represent him to us a) as the father of a new world, b) as a just man suffering and persecuted, c) as the Savior of the world from the deluge. Here, he appears to us as an eternal priest, offering bread and wine in sacrifice. The succeeding figures will add other strokes to the picture; for, with these living prophecies, as with the promises and predictions, their development is continual.

PRAYER

O my God! who art all love, I thank thee for not having abandoned men after the deluge, and for having preserved to them the benefit of religion, notwithstanding so much ingratitude. I thank thee for having chosen a particular people, among whom to preserve the remembrance of the great promise of the liberator. Preserve me from pride. Grant me, in regard to my parents, the respect of Sem and Japhet, and in regard to thee, the faith of Abraham and the piety of Melchisedech.

I am resolved to love God above all things, and my neighbor as myself for the love of God; and, in testimony of this love, I will on all occasions respect my father and mother.

Lesson 24: Messias Foreshadowed: Isaac

Visit of the angels; birth of Isaac promised.—Abraham had no children who might be the heirs of his great possessions, and still more of his exalted virtues. God therefore appeared to him anew; and, after having entered into a closer alliance with him, prescribed for him and all his posterity the law of circumcision. God also declared to him plainly that Sara, his wife, should soon give him a son, one who would be the object of heaven's choicest blessings and the heir of all the divine promises.

The matter happened thus. One day as Abraham was seated at the door of his tent about noon, he saw approaching him three young men, whom he took to be travelers. It was the Lord, who appeared to him under the figure of three angels, a symbol of the most Holy Trinity. Charity is ever on the alert, and the very appearance of want suffices to excite its tender sympathies. Abraham arose on the moment, and advanced to meet the three strangers. Then, bowing to the ground: "Whoever you are," he said, "do not pain me so much as to pass by, without condescending to stay a moment and receive the kind offices of your servant. I will bring water that you may wash your feet. Rest yourselves here, under the shadow of these trees; you will eat a morsel with me, and then you may continue your journey." The travelers accepted the invitation.

After having shared the generous hospitality of Abraham, one of them said to him: "In a year's time from this date, I will return to see you; and Sara, your wife, will then have given you a son." Humanly speaking, the promise of the traveler was outside the limits of all probability. Sara was very old, and Abraham was at that time ninety-nine years of age. Yet the holy patriarch did not entertain the least doubt on the matter.

Thus did God prepare men to one day believe both in the maternity of a Virgin, by making fruitful a woman who was ninety years of age and barren, and in the dogma of the Holy Trinity, by giving an image of it in this apparition to Abraham. Three angels present themselves before the holy patriarch, and the scripture gives them, in the singular number, the great, the incommunicable name of *Jehovah*. Abraham, who sees three of them, adores only one, speaks only to one. This great mystery, which has since been manifested in the gospel, was only shown under veils in the old testament, and could only be known by those who had, at that time, the spirit of Christianity.

The three travelers took leave of their host. Abraham desired, as an act of respect, to accompany and guide them on a part of their way. This new display of charity procured him a new favor, in which the Lord, his God, speaking to him with incredible familiarity, made him the confidant of the most secret designs of providence. They walked in company along the road to Sodom, when the Lord, under the figure of one of the three angels, said to Abraham: "The cry of the sins of Sodom and Gomorrha has been heard by me, and demands vengeance of me. I am going to see whether the measure of their iniquities is full, and if it is time to strike."

Abraham's interview with the Lord.—Abraham drew near to him respectfully, such courage does charity and zeal sometimes inspire, and said: "But what! Lord, wouldst thou confound the innocent and the guilty in the same punishment? If one of these wicked cities should contain fifty just men, mixed up among the crowd of sinners, wouldst thou destroy them altogether, or wouldst thou not rather forgive the multitude of sinners for the sake of the fifty just men?" The candor and simplicity of this touching prayer won the heart of God. "If Sodom present fifty just men to mine eyes," said the Lord, "I will not destroy the city: the fifty just men shall obtain pardon for all the guilty." "Since I have begun to speak to thee," rejoined Abraham, "I, who am but dust and ashes, I will add another word: if there should be forty-five just men in it, wouldst thou destroy a city for which forty-five of thy servants asked forgiveness?" "I do not wish to afflict thee," answered the Lord; "I will forgive all for the sake of the forty-five." "But, my God," continued Abraham, "if unfortunately there should be only forty found, what wouldst thou do?" "I would still forgive them," said the Lord.

Abraham had already done much; but the innocence of the friends of God gives them rights, with which other men are unacquainted. Accordingly, Abraham, who at first made his petitions only from five to five, next passed on to ten, and, taking this number at once from forty, said: "I beseech thee, O Lord! be not angry if I speak again; what if there should be only thirty?" "I will not strike," answered the Lord. "Since I have done so much," rejoined the holy patriarch, "I will go a little further still; what if there should be only twenty?" "These twenty would disarm my wrath," answered the Lord. "I conjure thee, O Lord!" added Abraham, "be not angry if I speak once more; if there should be only ten just men found in the city, what wouldst thou do? " "For the sake of these ten just men I would pardon all," replied the Lord.

Destruction of Sodom. — Here ended this admirable conversation, which reveals to us at the same time the infinite goodness of God, who punishes only with regret, and the extraordinary power of prayer, the power of the intercession of the saints. The ten just men were not found, and five whole cities were consumed by fire from heaven. At the place there may be seen today an unclean pool, called the Dead Sea. Lot and his family were the only persons saved from the disaster; yet Lot's wife, turning round to behold the conflagration, was changed into a pillar of salt, which was still seen in the times of the apostles.[513]

Abraham's sacrifice. — Meanwhile, Abraham returned to his tent. At the time fixed by the Lord, Isaac was born. The holy patriarch had nothing more to desire; but God had resolved to subject the faith of his servant to a last and terrible trial. Not content with having promised him that the Redeemer of the world should spring from his race, God wished to place before his eyes an image of the manner in which the redemption should be accomplished. In the middle of the night, the holy patriarch heard a voice: "Abraham! Abraham!" "Here I am," answered the venerable old man. "Take," said the Lord to him, "take thy only son Isaac, who is so dear to thee, and go and offer him to me as a holocaust on a mountain that I will show thee."

The only answer that Abraham returned to an order so likely to make nature rebel was prompt obedience. During three days, he prepared everything for the great sacrifice and traveled with his dear son to fulfill the command of the Lord. After a wearisome journey, he reached the foot of the mountain of sacrifice: this mountain was Calvary.[514] "Remain here," my children, he said to his servants, "my son and I will go up to yon height to offer a sacrifice to the Lord." There did not appear the slightest change in the ordinary manner of the holy patriarch. With the same calmness, he laid the wood for the holocaust on his son's shoulders, took a sword with which to pierce Isaac's heart, and carried the fire that should consume his beloved victim.

The father and the son went on thus together, engaged in very different thoughts, but both resigned to accomplish cheerfully the divine will, when God, who arranged the various degrees of merit for his servant, permitted the occurrence of one of those little incidents which, not being considered worth any notice in such great trials, often disconcert even the best regulated affection, unless supported with a heroic courage. "My father!" said Isaac, with amiable simplicity. "What dost thou desire, my son?" replied Abraham. "I see in thy hands," continued Isaac, "fire for a holocaust, and I myself carry the wood; but where is the victim?" "My son," answered Abraham, without uttering a word that in the least betrayed him, "the Lord will provide one." Isaac asked no more questions.

Arrived at the top of the mountain, Abraham fitted out the altar, arranged the wood, prepared the sword: it was at length necessary to explain. A glance, a turn, a sigh sufficed to show Isaac the victim: he perceived it without being astonished. He adored the will of God, ascended the funeral pile, and allowed himself to be fastened there by his father's hand. Abraham, always full of faith and obedience, seized the sword, raised his arm above his victim's head, and was ready to strike the fatal blow. The time of trial was ended: that of reward began. "Stay, Abraham," said the Lord, "it is enough; I now know thy faith. Because thou hast obeyed my voice, I will bless thee; I will multiply thy race: it will triumph over its enemies; and all the nations of the earth will be blessed in him who shall spring from thee." At the same time, the holy patriarch observed a ram caught by the horns in a neighboring bush; he took it, and immolated it instead of his son. O Jesus! crowned with thorns, how easily I recognize thee here!

Isaac, the fifth figure of the Messias.—In effect, the sacrifice of Isaac was a lively figure of the future sacrifice of Jesus Christ. The figure and the reality have such a close resemblance that we cannot consider the one without remembering the other. Accordingly, Isaac is the fifth figure of the Messias. Isaac is the well-beloved son of his father; our Lord is the well-beloved Son of God the Father, whose delights are placed in him. Isaac, all innocence, is condemned to die; our Lord, innocence itself, is condemned to die. It is Abraham, the father of Isaac, who must execute the sentence; it is God the Father, who, by the hand of the Jews, must himself execute the sentence of death against his Son. Isaac, laden with the wood on which he shall be consumed, ascends the hill of Calvary; our Lord, laden with the wood of the cross, ascends the same hill of Calvary. Isaac allows himself to be laid on the pile, and meekly bows his head to the sword that is to sacrifice him; our Lord suffers himself to be fastened to the cross, and, as a tender lamb, to be pitilessly slaughtered. Isaac is not put to death, because he is only a figure; our Lord is put to death, because he is the reality. Isaac descends from the mountain full of life, and laden with benedictions—a numerous posterity is promised him; our Lord issues from the tomb full of life, and laden with glory—as a reward for his obedience, he receives all nations for an inheritance.

This figure adds two particulars to the preceding ones: it tells us the place on which the Savior shall be immolated, and that he shall die by the command of his Father. Thus, the great portrait of the Redeemer is drawn little by little. Have not these two scenes, so touching and so similar, the sacrifice of Isaac and the sacrifice of our Lord, a manifest relation to each other? Can one doubt, in reading them, that the first was appointed to prepare for the second? Can one reject the striking truth that the old testament is only a prediction of the new? The first is undoubtedly veiled in the beginning; but the veil rises gradually, and at length allows the object to be seen openly, when the time of its appearance has come.

PRAYER

O my God! who art all love. I thank thee for the graces thou didst grant to thy faithful servant Abraham, as a reward for his faith and charity. Grant me charity toward my neighbor, confidence in prayer, and perfect obedience to the will of my superiors.

I am resolved to love God above all things, and my neighbor as myself for the love of God; and, in testimony of this love, I will resign myself entirely to the disposal of providence.

Lesson 25: Messias Foreshadowed: Jacob

Marriage of Isaac.—Isaac had now attained his fortieth year. Abraham, his father, thought of giving him a wife; but he wished to receive her from the hand of God. He comported himself in this affair with that faith, piety, and trust in providence which merited for him, even to the end of his days, the happiest success in all his undertakings: giving a precious example, which parents ought always to imitate, when there is question of providing for their children.

The holy patriarch called his old servant, the faithful Eliezer, and said to him: "Go into Mesopotamia, where I left my brother Nachor; there, in my own country, among my own kindred, thou shalt seek a wife for my son Isaac." Eliezer chose ten camels from his master's herd; he loaded them with magnificent presents, with specimens of all the riches that filled to superabundance the opulent house of his master. He was accompanied by a number of slaves, in keeping with the importance of his embassy. The splendor of this equipage would do honor to the holy patriarch, and gain credit for his envoy. The journey was happy, and the troop arrived in Mesopotamia, within sight of the city where Nachor dwelt.

Eliezer unloaded his camels, and made them lie down in the neighborhood of a well, where it was customary to water flocks and beasts of burden. It was in the evening, when the women of the city, without distinction of birth, came forth to draw water from the well. Eliezer then addressed this humble and fervent prayer to the God of his master: "O Lord, the God of my master Abraham, come, I beseech thee, to mine aid this day, and let thy mercy shine forth over Abraham, my lord! Behold I stand near the well, when the daughters of the city come out to draw water; I cannot discern in the multitude her whom thou dost destine for Isaac. I will regard, as the object of thy choice, her to whom I shall say: 'Lower thy pitcher, and allow me to drink'; and she shall answer: 'Drink, and I will also give thy camels to drink.'"

In a man less replenished with that simple faith which works miracles, and less accustomed to prodigies, such a course of procedure might have appeared rash: But what cannot the confidence of the saints obtain from the heart of God?

Eliezer had not finished his prayer when he saw a young maiden approaching, whose modesty added new charms to her natural beauty: this was Rebecca, the daughter of Bathuel and grandniece of Abraham. She drew up the water, filled the pitcher which she had brought on her shoulder, and was returning with it. The old servant beheld her with attention. Charmed with her manners and her air of innocence, he respectfully said to her: "Wouldst thou give me a little water from thy pitcher to relieve my thirst?" "Drink, my lord," said she; and, immediately resting her pitcher on her arm, she held it in this convenient position and allowed him to drink as much as he desired. Then she added: "I will also draw water for thy camels, until they all drink." Without waiting for a reply, she cast into the troughs what water remained in her pitcher, returned to the well, and began to draw more water, with which to refresh the camels.

The servant of Abraham admired her in silence, and, when the camels had done drinking, addressed himself to the young unknown, presenting bracelets and earrings to her, and saying: "Whose daughter art thou? Are there any lodgings in thy father's house?" She answered: "I am the daughter of Bathuel, the son of Nachor; we have plenty of hay and straw, and room to lodge in." Eliezer bowed profoundly, and adored the Lord. Rebecca, on her side, ran to tell her mother all that had happened to her. Laban, Rebecca's brother, came to invite the stranger to a lodging in his father's house. The envoy of Abraham did not require to be entreated. But, before accepting the repast which was placed before him, he sought Rebecca in marriage for Isaac: his request was granted. Then Eliezer made magnificent presents to all the family, and next morning begged leave to depart.

Having set out with his numerous train, he reached home in safety. The accomplished spouse, Rebecca, could alone alleviate the sorrow which Isaac felt for the loss of Sara, his mother, whom he had been mourning for three years.

Death of Abraham; his burial. — Abraham, full of days and merits, had reached a glorious old age: he had now seen 175 years. The time had come for terminating this long life, rendered remarkable by the constant exercise of all the virtues that should adorn a man chosen by heaven to be the head of a new people, the founder of a holy nation, and the ancestor of the Messias; worthy by his faith to be called "the father of the faithful," and so esteemed by the Almighty, that the sovereign of all men gloried in being known as the God of Abraham.

His two eldest sons, Isaac and Ismael, rendered him the last services. According to his own wish he was buried beside Sara, his wife, in a double cave, in the field of Ephron, the son of Seor, the Hethite. Abraham had purchased it thirty-eight years previously: he had chosen it for the place of his burial, because it was in a valley at the foot of a mountain, where he had raised an altar to the Lord his God, and where he awaits a glorious resurrection and the consummation of felicity as the crown of all his hopes in the Lord his God. He had received, as we have seen, a promise from the Lord that the Messias should be born of his posterity, and that one day they should possess the Land of Chanaan, in which country the Messias was to be born. This promise dispenses us from the necessity of seeking for the Messias in any other country than Chanaan, or among any other people than the descendants of Abraham. Still this light appears to be obscure — or rather this promise requires a new explanation.

Third promise of the Messias made to Isaac. — Abraham has seven children, of whom the eldest are Isaac and Ismael. Which of them will be the father of the Messias? A new illumination becomes necessary: we are not kept long in suspense waiting for it. A general famine takes place in the Land of Chanaan, where Isaac dwells. He has a mind, therefore, to go into another country. At this moment he is visited by the Lord, and informed that he is the heir of the great promise, and that the Messias shall be born of him. "Go no farther, Isaac," said the God of Abraham to him, "remain in the country that I will show thee. Thou shalt abide in this land, and I will be with thee. All these vast and beautiful regions I give thee, and I will put thy descendants in possession of them. I will make thy posterity as numerous as the stars of heaven. All the nations of the earth shall be blessed in him who shall be born of thee."

The preceding promise informed us that the Messias should be born in the family of Abraham. Among all the children of the holy patriarch, Isaac is now designated by this third promise as the father of the future deliverer. Accordingly, the descendants of Ismael and of the other children of Abraham are set aside: this is a new light. But fresh clouds will soon require a further explanation. For Isaac has two sons, Esau and Jacob. Which of the two shall be the father of the Messias? The sequel will let us know.

Birth of Jacob and Esau. — After twenty years of barrenness, Rebecca, Isaac's wife, brings forth two sons into the world. While she was still bearing them, the children struggled with each other in her womb. Affrighted, she consulted the Lord, who answered her: "Thou carriest in thy womb two children, of whom one shall be the head of a great people. They will be enemies to each other: the elder will be subject to the younger, and the posterity of the latter will be over that of the former." By this answer, God made known to Rebecca that Abraham's blessing, to which the promise of the Messias was attached, should rest on the younger in preference to the elder.

When the twins were grown, Esau became an expert hunter: he was always in the field. Jacob, on the contrary, a mild and gentle character, remained at home. Esau was the elder. Now, among the rights of his primogeniture might be regarded that of a spiritual alliance with God and that of transmitting to his descendants the blessing promised to Abraham and Isaac: this blessing chiefly regarded the Messias. But the Lord, who is the master of his gifts, had resolved to bestow this honor on the younger. Jacob was informed of these matters by his mother. Full of gratitude, he neglected no occasion to correspond with the will of the first of fathers, and to secure for himself the possession of a title which already belonged to him.

Esau sells his birthright.—One day, Esau having gone a-hunting, Jacob had prepared a mess of pottage for his evening meal. Late in the day Esau arrived exceedingly faint, at the moment when the food was ready. "I am worn out," he said to his brother, "give me speedily this dish which thou hast prepared." "I will not give it to thee," said Jacob, "but, if thou art willing, I will sell it to thee for thy birthright."

There appeared little proportion between a dish of lentils and a right of this kind; but Jacob sought to promote his own welfare by it. He did not think it was taking an advantage of the necessities of his brother, but seizing an occasion of executing the designs of God. The bargain was made, however unexpectedly. "I shall die," replied Esau, "if I do not this moment obtain what I ask, and what will my birthright avail me?" And he sold it, ate his dish of lentils, and went his way, thinking little of what he had done. And I, who read these lines, have not I sometimes like another new Esau sold my right to heaven for less than a dish of lentils, and, after this shameful sale, have I not slept tranquilly, thinking little of what I have done?

God had promised to Abraham that the Redeemer should be born of the descendants of Isaac; and it was supposed, as we have seen, that this honor was reserved for the eldest of the family. Accordingly, in selling his birthright, Esau renounced the inestimable happiness of giving the Messias to the world. Hence it happens that St. Paul terms him profane, for having sold, and at such a vile price, a thing so holy as the privilege peculiar to the firstborn.

Isaac blesses Jacob.—Meanwhile Isaac attained the age of 137 years. His great age, and the almost total loss of his sight, admonished him that the day of his death was not far distant. He desired, in accordance with the practice observed in families where God was known, to give his last blessing to his children.

Rebecca was not ignorant of the importance of this action: she took care not to let the moment of rendering it favorable to Jacob escape. She knew, moreover, the will of God, who was pleased that the privileges of the elder should fall to the younger. The matter was begun by the voluntary renunciation of Esau himself; but it should be confirmed by the blessing of Isaac.

Isaac then commanded Esau to go a-hunting, and to bring him something to eat, that, having taken his repast, he might bless his firstborn son. Esau set out. Unfortunately for him there was one person too many present at the conversation: Rebecca heard it, and profited of it without loss of time. She called Jacob. "Run, my son," she said, "to the flock, and bring me two of the best kids; I will prepare them for thy father as I know that he likes them; and thou wilt present them to him, in order that having eaten of them he may bless thee." The matter seemed to present no difficulty to Rebecca; not so with Jacob. "Dost thou forget," he said to his mother, "that my brother is covered with hair, and I am not so? If my father, to make sure who is near him, should chance to touch me, he will not fail to know me; he will imagine that I have been mocking him, and, instead of his blessing, I shall draw his curse upon me." "No, my son," answered Rebecca, "thou hast nothing to fear; I will take all the danger on myself." Jacob obeyed her.

When all was ready, she put the garments of Esau on Jacob, and covered his hands and neck with the skins of the kids, so that, with the exception of the voice, he was the image of his brother. In this condition, Jacob carried what had been prepared to his father. Disguising himself at first as well as he could, he said only these two words: "My father." "I hear," said Isaac, "it is one of my sons, but which of the two?" "It is thine elder son Esau," said Jacob, "eat of my venison." Isaac appeared not to be fully satisfied about the matter. "Come near," he said, "that I may touch thee, and be certain that thou art my son Esau." This was a critical moment; and, if the Lord had not shortened the time of trial, Jacob could not have escaped. He drew nigh, and Isaac touched him. "As for the voice," said the holy old man, "it is indeed the voice of Jacob, but the hands are the hands of Esau. Art thou truly my son Esau?" "Yes, I am," replied Jacob. Then the holy old man embraced him, and blessed him. Jacob immediately withdrew.[515]

Scarcely had he gone out from his father's presence, when Esau arrived. Learning what had passed, he became furious, and swore to take his brother's life. Isaac adored the designs of God, and did not revoke his blessing. Rebecca made Jacob set out for Mesopotamia, in order to be secure from his brother's vengeance. Isaac gave him the same advice as Rebecca, with a renewal of the blessing, and recommended him to choose a wife in the country to which he was going.

Jacob goes into Mesopotamia. — Jacob departed at once. He walked alone. One day, as he advanced with all speed, darkness overtook him. The weather was beautiful: he resolved to pass the night in the open air. The son of Isaac was not delicate. The bare earth served him for a bed; he placed a stone under his head for a pillow, and slept tranquilly. This was the moment which the Lord had selected to invest him in a certain manner with the dignity of patriarch, as his father Isaac and grandfather Abraham had been invested before him.

Fourth promise of the Messias made to Jacob. — Suddenly he was visited by a mysterious dream and the most consoling revelation. He saw a ladder, the foot of which rested on the earth, while its top reached to heaven. Angels ascended and descended on it; the God of angels and of men was seen leaning on its top. "Jacob," said the Lord, "I am the God of thy fathers, the God of Abraham and Isaac. The land on which thou restest I will give to thee and to thy descendants."

In order to show the immutability of his word, it is always at the moment when the patriarchs are leaving the Land of Chanaan that God promises to fix them and their posterity in it. It is necessary that in this land the forefathers of the Messias should dwell, for it is here that the Messias shall be born. "The number of thy descendants," adds the Lord, "shall be as countless as the sands of the earth. All nations shall be blessed in thee, and in the son who shall be born of thee. Thou art traveling toward a strange country; but I will bring thee back into this land which I have promised to thy fathers, and which I reserve for thy children."

Such was the fourth promise of the Messias. It teaches us that we must look for him in the family of Jacob. Esau and his descendants are put aside: the search, accordingly, becomes easier and easier. The veil, which hides the great mystery, rises little by little, and we walk confidently toward the term whither God conducts us.

Jacob awakes, and, full of fear and gratitude, prostrates himself on the earth. "How terrible," he says, "is this place! This is no other than the house of God and the gate of heaven." Then, taking his staff, he continues his journey.

Jacob marries Rachel and returns to Isaac. — Arrived in Mesopotamia, he drew near the city of Haran, the abode of his uncle Laban. The manners of the inhabitants of Haran had not changed during the hundred years since Rebecca left it to become the wife of Isaac. The young maidens of the most respectable families in the place still guided the flocks. The condition of a shepherd or shepherdess presenting nothing but innocence to these people, it was regarded as exceedingly honorable. Jacob, having reached the neighborhood of Haran, saw a well, near which three flocks of sheep rested themselves during the great heat of the day. This well was a kind of chief reservoir, from which the water was distributed by little canals; it was carefully covered with a large stone. Jacob approached some shepherds, and said to them: "Brethren, whence are you?" "We are of Haran," they answered. "Do you know Laban, the son of Nachor?" "We do indeed." "Is he well?" "Yes, he is well; and here is Rachel, his daughter, coming with his flock."

The conversation continued, till Rachel arrived with her father's flocks. Jacob, who knew that she was his cousin, hastened to remove the stone from the well. When the sheep had drunk, Jacob saluted Rachel, and tears flowed from his eyes. "I am," said he to her, "the son of Rebecca, thy father's sister." Rachel wished to hear nothing more. She ran home, and, almost out of breath, told her father of the meeting that had taken place. Laban, at the name of Jacob, his sister's son, came out to meet the traveler. Embracing him tenderly, he held him a long time in his arms, and then led him into his house.

In accordance with the directions of Isaac, Jacob asked his cousin in marriage. The proposal was accepted: Rachel was promised. But it cost Jacob fourteen years of painful labor, spent in the service of Laban, to obtain her. He then returned to Isaac, bringing with him his numerous and wealthy family. It was during this journey that, in a mysterious conflict with an angel, Jacob received the name of Israel, which means "prevailing with God." Hence, his descendants are termed Israelites, or the children of Israel. Isaac died soon afterward; and his two sons, Jacob and Esau, buried him in the double cave in the valley of Mambre, beside his wife Rebecca, his mother Sara, and his father Abraham.

Jacob, the sixth figure of the Messias. —God led Jacob through many adventures, in order to represent to us in ample detail the life of the Messias, of whom this patriarch is a most admirable figure. Thus, by the order of his father, Jacob goes into a distant country to seek a spouse; our Lord, by the order of his Father, passes over the immense distance that separates heaven from earth, to form the Church, his spouse. Jacob, the son of a most wealthy father, and most wealthy himself, takes the road alone and on foot; our Lord, the Son of God, and God himself, and Lord of all things, descends from heaven with no other companion than the most perfect poverty. Jacob, surprised by nightfall, is obliged to sleep in the open air in a desert place, with a stone for his pillow; our Lord is so poor that he has not whereon to rest his head. The land, nevertheless, belongs to Jacob; so also the whole world belongs to our Lord. Jacob, having arrived among his friends, must undergo many painful labors to obtain his spouse; our Lord comes unto his own, and they know him not—he must pass his life in lowly toil to form the Church, his spouse. Jacob sees his union blessed by the Lord—Rachel gives him children, the future fathers of a great people; our Lord sees his union with the Church blessed by God the Father—the Church gives him innumerable children. Jacob, overcoming all difficulties, returns to his country and his father, bringing with him his riches and his children; our Lord, conquering all his enemies, and laden with their spoils, returns to his Father in heaven, leading with him the saints of the old law, and opening his kingdom to all Christians—his children. Jacob, on reaching Isaac, receives again his father's blessing; our Lord, on his arrival in heaven, is welcomed by his Father with every tribute of honor and glory.

PRAYER

O my God! who art all love, I thank thee for having given me in the patriarchs such perfect models of all virtues. I thank thee for the promises and the figures by which thou didst announce so long beforehand the Redeemer of the world. Happier than Isaac and Jacob, we possess that which they expected. Grant that we may be, if possible, more grateful and faithful than they; but we especially beseech thee to revive among Christians the amiable simplicity of manners which characterized those early times.

I am resolved to love God above all things, and my neighbor as myself for the love of God; and, in testimony of this love, I shall often say, "God is here."

Lesson 26: Messias Foreshadowed: Joseph

The twelve children of Jacob. — Jacob had twelve sons, who were the fathers of the twelve tribes of the Hebrew people. The following are their names: Ruben, Simeon, Levi, Juda, Issachar, Zabulon, Gad, Aser, Dan, Nephtali, Joseph, and Benjamin. Jacob, like his fathers, led a pastoral life. In order to complete the preceding explanations, let us add another word on a life so beautiful, the account of which has so many charms for the young. The patriarchs were free from all subjection; and we may regard each of their families as a little state, of which the father was the sovereign, or as a little church, of which the father was the high priest. We see, in effect, the patriarchs offering sacrifices to the Lord. Their riches consisted chiefly of flocks; that is, goats, sheep, camels, oxen, and asses; they kept neither horses nor swine. Their wealth was very great. But, in the midst of all their opulence, they led a most laborious life.

As they were still strangers in the Land of Chanaan, which God reserved for their descendants, they built no houses there. They dwelt in tents, which they raised in whatever locality they selected to feed their flocks; on quitting the place, they took down their tents to set them up again in some other quarter. They could undoubtedly have built cities like other people, but they preferred a pastoral life as the most simple, and the most proper to detach men from earth and make them look forward to a more perfect country. Thus did God vouchsafe to teach us that the life of a Christian in this world is only a pilgrimage.

Their repast was frugal: witness the pottage which Jacob had prepared, and which so strongly tempted Esau; also, the repast which Abraham served up to the angels, and which consisted of roast kid, fresh bread (baked under the ashes), milk, and butter. One of their leading virtues was hospitality toward strangers. Sometimes their generous persistence amounted to importunity; it became necessary to yield to their invitations. Then the whole family hastened to do honor to their guests, whom they looked upon as visitors from heaven. The master washed their feet, gave his orders, selected meats, and waited on the strangers himself.

The women did not appear on these occasions, or were only seen with a veil, so great was the modesty that existed in those happy times. What were the fruits of a life so little conformable to the manners of the voluptuous and effeminate age in which we live? Detachment from the earth, fraternal charity, exemption from infirmities, old age, and a peaceful death. Such were the lives of Jacob and his family: we see the same more fully exemplified in the history of Joseph.

Joseph sold by his brothers and taken to Egypt. — This most deservedly beloved son, was, with the exception of Benjamin, the youngest of Jacob's children. Modesty, candor, sincerity, and innocence seemed born with him. It was impossible for Jacob not to give the preference in his heart to a child so amiable. But, however attentive a father is to conceal his feelings, the eyes of many brothers are too sharp not to discover the favorite. Without intending it, Jacob roused the jealousy of his elder sons against Joseph. A great and terrible lesson, which parents ought never to forget! A coat of various colors, which he had procured for Joseph, sufficed to put them all into ill humor.

The conscientious obligation which Joseph felt of acquainting his father with a great crime they had committed further embittered their feelings. At length, what crowned their envy against him was the narration of two dreams that indicated his future greatness. "It seemed to me," he said to them, "that we were binding sheaves in a field, and that my sheaf arose and stood, while yours bowed down before it." "What!" said his brothers, "dost thou mean to be one day our king, and to have us subject to thy dominion?" Joseph made no reply.

A little while afterward, he said to them again with the same simplicity: "I saw in a dream the sun, the moon, and eleven stars worshipping me." Jacob was a wise old man;

foreseeing the consequences of such language, he reprimanded Joseph, and said: "What is the meaning of this dream? Is it that thy mother, thy brothers, and I shall worship thee on the earth?" Joseph's brothers were out of themselves with envy; but Jacob, who could not fail to perceive something mysterious in these dreams, considered the affair in silence.

In a short time, the sons of the holy patriarch led their flocks to the pasture-lands around Sichem. Joseph was not one of the company. But, in a few days, Jacob called him, and said: "Go, and see whether thy brothers conduct themselves well, and whether the flocks are in good condition, and return and let me know." Joseph immediately prepared for the journey, embraced his father—taking farewell of each other for a much longer time than either imagined—and safely arrived at his destination. His brothers observed him coming; the sight of him aroused their hatred. "This is the dreamer coming," they said to one another, "let us kill him, and cast him into an old well: we can say that a wild beast devoured him, and we shall see what will become of his dreams."

It would be very strange if, among so many sons of a saint, this criminal project should pass without opposition. Ruben, the eldest, undertook to save the innocent victim. "No, do not kill him," he said, "cast him if you will into this well, but do not stain your hands with his blood." He made this remark with a view to deliver him out of their hands, and to restore him to his father. The advice of Ruben was accepted. While they thus disposed of the innocent Joseph's life, the amiable youth, full of joy to see his brothers again, came forward with haste, running to cast himself, without knowing it, into the arms of his murderers. He had no sooner arrived than they seized him, pitilessly stripped him of his long and beautiful coat, the old object of their jealousy, and lowered him into a dry well, where he might perish of hunger.

Then having coolly seated themselves to eat, they beheld a caravan of Ismaelite merchants approaching them on the way from Galaad:[516] the travelers had their camels laden with aromatic spices to sell in Egypt. Juda said to his brothers: "What shall we gain by destroying this child? After all, he is our brother, and our own blood. Let us rather sell him to these merchants." The others relished the proposal. Joseph was drawn up from the well, and delivered for twenty pieces of silver to the Ismaelites, who led him off with them into Egypt. The brothers now took his coat, and, having dipped it in the blood of a kid, sent it to Jacob, with the following message: "This is a coat we found; see whether it is thy son's."

Jacob, on seeing it, exclaimed with tears: "It is my son's coat, a cruel beast hath devoured him, a wild beast hath eaten Joseph." He rent his garments, put on sackcloth, and for a long time bewailed his dear Joseph. His children were not ignorant that they had wounded their father in his tenderest affections. They gathered around him to soothe his sorrow; but he would admit no consolation. "I will continue to deplore his loss," he said, "until I go to rejoin my son in the grave."

Meanwhile, the Ismaelites, having arrived in Egypt, sold Joseph to a lord of the country, named Putiphar, the general of Pharao's army. The modesty and comely appearance of the young slave rendered him very pleasing to his master. God was with him and prospered all things in his hands. Putiphar, who was not slow to perceive it, placed the utmost confidence in him, and surrendered to him the superintendance of his household.

Yet these were only a sample of the favors which the God of Abraham, Isaac, and Jacob was preparing for Joseph, who had still to be exposed to many trials, in which his virtue should always triumph. The wife of Putiphar wished to make him offend God; but he had a horror of doing so. One day she took hold of his mantle. Joseph, to be rid of her solicitations, fled, leaving the garment in her hands. Mad with rage, this guilty woman accused the innocent Joseph to her husband. Putiphar, too credulous, had him cast into the prison destined for state criminals. The Lord accompanied Joseph into this dark abode, and made him find grace with the governor, who placed him over all the other prisoners.

Among these were the king's chief butler and chief baker. Both had similar dreams one night, with which they were much troubled. Joseph interpreted the dreams for them: informing the first that in three days he should be restored to his office, when, it was fondly to be hoped, he would not forget his friend; and the second, that in three days he should be put to death. Everything came to pass as Joseph had foretold.

If gratitude were a virtue common among the favorites of fortune and the great ones of the world, Joseph might have flattered himself with the prospect of a speedy deliverance from his bondage; but the chief butler, elated with prosperity, forgot the benefactor who had inspired him with hope in his abandonment. The virtuous prisoner had yet to wait two years for the end of his disgrace. At length, the moment of his delivery arrived.

Joseph raised to glory.—The king of Egypt saw in a dream seven lean kine consume seven fat kine, and seven thin and blasted ears of corn consume seven full and fair ears. This vision disturbed the mind of the monarch. When morning was come, he ordered all the seers of Egypt to be brought into his palace. He detailed to them his dreams, but the diviners were utterly unable to give him any explanation. Then it was that the chief butler remembered Joseph, and told Pharao of him. The king sent for him immediately. The young interpreter listened to the narrative of the dreams. "The two dreams," answered Joseph, "mean the same thing. The seven fat kine and the seven full ears denote seven years of plenty; the seven lean kine and the seven thin ears denote, on the contrary, seven years of scarcity that are to follow. Let the king, then, choose a wise and able man, to whom he may confide his authority for the general welfare of the country during the approaching crisis. Let this principal minister have other officers under him, who may establish granaries in all the cities of the kingdom. Let them purchase and store, for the benefit and by the authority of the king, the fifth part of all the corn that may be gathered in abundance. This will be a safe resource during the seven years of famine that will afterward desolate the country. If thou neglectest these precautions, the corn will be sold to thy neighbors, and wasted, and thy subjects will die of starvation."

"Where can we find a man wiser or more skillful than thyself?" exclaimed Pharao. "I appoint thee therefore over my kingdom: all my subjects shall be subject to thee: I alone shall be above thee." Saying these words, the king took his ring from his finger and placed it on Joseph's. He also ordered a robe of fine linen to be brought to him; put a chain of gold round his neck; and made him occupy the chariot that immediately followed his own. A herald went before, exclaiming with a loud voice: "Let every one bend the knee to Joseph, and know that Pharao has made him governor throughout the whole land of Egypt!" Pharao also changed Joseph's name to another, which meant "savior of the world." Joseph was only thirty years of age when he was presented to Pharao, and, from being an unfortunate captive, he became the favorite of the king and the ruler of the kingdom. No sooner was he in possession of his dignities than with a suitable equipage he traveled through the provinces, and established granaries in every city. Thanks to his prudent economy, Egypt became the nurse of innumerable unfortunates, who, otherwise, must have perished of hunger and misery.

Joseph found again by his brothers. — Among the number of families who suffered from the general dearth was that of Jacob particularly. They still dwelt in the Land of Chanaan, where the famine began to be severely felt even from the very first year. Jacob called his children and told them to go into Egypt and buy corn. They all set out except Benjamin, the youngest, whom Jacob kept near himself.

Arrived at the capital, it was necessary to present themselves before the viceroy, who desired to be informed of everything. They were admitted in their turn to an audience with him. The ten strangers humbly prostrated themselves at his feet; Joseph recognized them. He was then thirty-eight years old; and, during the twenty-two years that had elapsed since his separation from his family, he had changed very much in his appearance. His brothers, therefore, did not know him. Joseph assumed a stern look of authority, and, addressing them as suspicious characters, put two questions to them: "Whence do you come and what do you want?" "We come," they said, "from the Land of Chanaan to buy corn." As Joseph mused on them in the most submissive posture at his feet, he remembered the dreams that he had had long ago, and interiorly adored the wondrous ways of providence. "You are far from being what you pretend to be," he said to them. "You are spies, sent out to view the unprotected parts of the kingdom." "No, my lord," they answered, trembling, "it is not so. Thy servants are come hither to buy corn; we are all the children of one father; we have no evil intention."

Joseph, who wished to know whether his father Jacob and his young brother Benjamin were still alive, continued to exhibit toward them the same suspicions. "You are deceiving me," he said. "You are spies." The suspicion of the minister threw the brothers into a state of strange embarrassment: they did not know how to act in order to satisfy him. One among them, taking up the word, said, with every appearance of candor: "We thy servants are twelve brothers, all the children of one man, who dwells in the Land of Chanaan; the youngest is at home with our father, another is dead, and thou beholdest the remaining ten at thy feet."

Joseph was satisfied; but he had his mind made up not to appear so. "That is just what I say," he answered. "You are spies. I wish to be quite sure of the matter; so, by the health of Pharao, you shall not depart hence until I see the young brother of whom you have told me, and who, if he were here, as he is assuredly more sincere, would acquaint me with the intrigues of your journey. Choose one of yourselves to go for this boy. As for the rest, they can remain in chains until I am fully enlightened as to the truth or falsehood of your assertions." Joseph, however, was content with detaining one of the ten as a hostage: this was Simeon. He allowed the other nine to depart.

For the first time, perhaps, during twenty years they made serious reflections on the cause of their misfortune. "We well deserve," they said, "the evils that have befallen us. They are the just punishment of the cruelty that we exercised toward our brother. He wept at our feet; he besought our compassion; we would not hear him, and now heaven takes vengeance on us." "I warned you of it," added Ruben, "did I not say to you: do no evil to the boy? You would not listen to me; and now God demands his blood."

This conversation took place in the presence of Joseph. As he had previously spoken to them by an interpreter, they did not suppose that he understood them. They set out at length and returned to Jacob. They informed him of all that had taken place. "The chief minister," they added, "commanded us to bring Benjamin to him; if we do not, he will regard us all as traitors, put Simeon to death, and give us no more corn." "I am truly unfortunate," said the holy old man, "if I am to believe you, I shall soon see myself without any children. I have already lost Joseph; Simeon is a prisoner in Egypt; and now you wish me to abandon Benjamin to you."

Still the famine continued; it was therefore necessary, unless they were to perish of starvation, to let Benjamin go. But Juda promised to answer for his life. They started on their journey with the boy and arrived in Egypt. Their first care was to visit the minister and to request an audience. Joseph granted it in due course, and brought forth Simeon from prison, that all might be witnesses of the scene that should ensue. At the appointed hour, Joseph entered the hall, and the strangers were admitted. He saluted them, saying: "How is your father, of whom you told me? Is he still alive and well?" They answered him: "Our father is still alive and well."

Uttering these words, they made a profound bow, and awaited a new question. Joseph sought out Benjamin, for this was the beloved child, a son of Rachel like himself, who held the first place in his affections. Having singled him out among the rest: "Is not this," he said, pointing to him, "the young brother of whom you told me?" Without waiting for an answer, he added: "May God bless thee, my son!" He could no longer refrain from an expression of his feelings; his whole soul was moved; his tears began to flow and in a little while his secret should escape with them. He retired quickly into another apartment and allowed his tears to flow abundantly.

His heart being relieved thus, he washed his face and reappeared with so much ease of manner that no one observed his emotion: he then ordered dinner to be served up. But his brothers had not yet reached the end of the trials to which he had resolved to subject them. He directed his steward to fill their sacks with corn, and to place in the mouth of each sack the money which they had brought for it. "Another thing thou shalt do," he added, "is this: thou shalt hide in the sack of the youngest, along with the price of the corn, the silver cup which I am accustomed to use." Joseph's order was executed.

Next morning the travelers set out joyfully on their way home to Jacob. Already they were out of the city when Joseph called his steward, and said to him: "Go quickly after the strangers; stop them, and ask: 'Why have you returned good for evil? The cup which you have stolen is that which is specially used by my master.'" The messenger speedily overtook the travelers. Their surprise was extraordinary when they heard him accusing them of stealing a silver cup. "If anyone among us," they exclaimed, "be found guilty of such a crime, we agree that he shall be put to death, and that the others shall remain thy slaves for the rest of their days." With these words, everyone opened his sack. The officer inspected them all, beginning with that of the eldest; and he found the cup in Benjamin's sack.

Hereupon, they rent their garments, and reloading their beasts of burden, determined to return and cast themselves at the feet of the viceroy. He awaited them in the same apartment where they had bidden him farewell. They prostrated themselves, with their faces to the ground, to hear in this humble posture the sentence which their judge should pass upon them. Joseph appeared with an air of authority calculated to terrify the guilty and even to disconcert the innocent. He addressed them some severe reproaches, and concluded by resolving to hold Benjamin in prison. Juda, speaking in the name of the brothers, besought him to let the youth go; otherwise, their father should die of sorrow.

This was too much for the heart of Joseph. He directed all the Egyptians to withdraw. When he found himself alone with his brothers, he allowed his tears to flow freely. Then, raising his voice, he said: "I am Joseph your brother; is my father yet living?"

Arrival of Jacob in Egypt. — At these words, Joseph's brothers, struck with terror, remained dumb. With a gentleness that might calm their fears, Joseph added: "Come nearer to me. I am Joseph, your brother, whom you sold, and who was led into Egypt; fear nothing. It was for your sake that the Lord sent me before you into Egypt. Return in all haste to my father, and say to him: Thus saith thy son Joseph: 'The Lord hath made me master of all Egypt: come down to me, linger not.'" With these words, Joseph cast his arms round Benjamin's neck. They remained a long time in each other's embraces, shedding sweet tears. Joseph next embraced his other brothers. He presented them with wagons and provisions for their journey, adding rich presents for themselves and Jacob.

They reached the holy old man in safety. "Thy son Joseph is not dead," they said to him. "It is he who governs the whole land of Egypt." At these words, Jacob appeared like a man suddenly awaking from a profound sleep: he could hardly believe what he had heard. However, when he saw the wagons that had arrived, and the magnificent presents that his son had sent to him, he exclaimed: "It is enough! Since Joseph my son is still alive, I will go and see him before I die."

Joseph, the seventh figure of the Messias. — Joseph has always been regarded, and with much reason, as one of the most beautiful figures of the Messias. In effect, Joseph is the well-beloved son of his father; our Lord is the well-beloved Son of God, his Father. Joseph is clad with a garment of various colors: he has dreams which prefigure his future greatness, and on this account becomes an object of jealousy to his brethren; our Lord is adorned with all kinds of virtues: to the Jews, his brethren, he announces his future greatness, and on this account he becomes the object of their hatred and persecution. Joseph is sent to his brethren; our Lord is sent to men, his brethren. Joseph, having reached his brethren, is ill-treated by them—they resolve to put him to death—they sell him to foreign merchants; our Lord having come to the Jews, his brethren, is ill-treated by them—is sold by Judas—is delivered to the Romans, who put him to death. Joseph, being sold, is led into Egypt, and becomes the master of the kingdom; our Lord, being sold and humiliated, receives as a reward all power in heaven and on earth. Joseph, condemned for a crime which he has not committed, is cast into prison; our Lord, condemned for crimes which he has not committed, is cast into chains and led away to death. The imprisoned Joseph is found in company with two state criminals—he announces deliverance to one and death to the other; our Lord is found on the cross between two malefactors—he promises the glory of paradise to one and leaves the other in a state of damnation. Joseph passes from the depths of a prison to the height of glory, even to the steps of Pharao's throne; our Lord passes from the cross to the summit of the highest heavens. Joseph saves Egypt from a great famine; our Lord saves the world dying from ignorance of the truth. Joseph is proclaimed the savior of Egypt, and received with the utmost honor from one end of the kingdom to the other; our Lord is proclaimed the Savior of the world, and adored, blessed, and glorified from one end of the earth to the other. Joseph is called savior of the world by strangers, before being acknowledged such by his own brethren; our Lord is acknowledged Savior of the world by the Gentiles, before being so by the Jews, his own brethren. As long as Joseph's brethren do not come to ask him for corn, they are exposed to the danger of perishing of hunger; while the Jews delay to be converted to Jesus Christ, they must endure a famine of truth, they must remain the slaves of error. Joseph's brethren at length decide on visiting Egypt; toward the end of time the Jews will decide on returning to Jesus Christ, by embracing Christianity. In fine, Joseph recognized by his brethren, pardons them, embraces them, and makes them happy; our Lord, acknowledged by the Jews as their Savior, will forgive them, and load them with blessings.

This figure confirms a preceding one in which we saw that the Savior should be persecuted by his brethren. It tells us, besides, that he will be condemned for a crime which he has not committed; it traces for us the order in which nations will be converted—first the Gentiles, and then the Jews—and it shows us the goodness with which the Savior will pardon his enemies.

PRAYER

O my God! who art all love, I thank thee with my whole heart for having revealed to the world its Redeemer under so touching a figure. I adore that infinite wisdom which, according to the necessities of times, added some touches to the divine picture of the Savior. Grant me, O my God! the innocence, the meekness, and the humility of Joseph, and a charity like his for those who injure me.

I am resolved to love God above all things, and my neighbor as myself for the love of God; and, in testimony of this love, I will banish every sentiment of jealousy from my heart.

Lesson 27: Messias Foreshadowed: Paschal Lamb

Jacob goes to Egypt.—The family of Jacob, consisting of thirty persons, assembled under the command of the holy patriarch, and departed from the Valley of Mambre for Bethsabee, or the Well of the Oath, situated not far from the river that separated Egypt from the Land of Chanaan. Jacob rested here to consult the Lord. A touching example! which shows us how we ought never to undertake anything of importance without invoking the light of heaven. "Fear not," said the God of his fathers to him, "go down into Egypt; I will multiply thy posterity there, and I will recall them thence to establish them with glory in the land which I have promised thee!" Strengthened by this revelation, the patriarch advanced toward the capital of Egypt. When he was within a few leagues of it, he directed his son Juda to go before, and acquaint Joseph of his arrival. Joseph was no sooner informed of his father's arrival, than he procured his chariot and went forth to meet him. He cast his arms round the holy old man's neck, and bedewed him with his tears. He then conducted him with all his brothers, to Pharao.

Jacob honored the kings of the earth as men invested with the authority of God, though his single title of patriarch and head of the holy family placed him far above them. The holy man, having therefore saluted the king, said to him with a dignity becoming his advanced age and his glorious destiny: "May the Lord my God enrich thee with his blessings and grant thee many happy years!" The king, in his turn, inquired the old man's age. "The days of my pilgrimage on the earth are 130 years," said Jacob, "short and evil days, which are little in comparison with the long lives of my forefathers." After this brief interview Joseph took leave of the king, who presented to Jacob and his family the rich province of Gessen, one of the most fertile in Egypt. It was here that the children of Israel dwelt, and multiplied so rapidly.

Jacob lived for seventeen years more. Having nothing further to desire on earth since his discovery of Joseph, he beheld the approach of his last hour with tranquility. When he could no longer move from his bed he was visited by Joseph, from whom he obtained a promise that he should not be buried in Egypt but be carried to the Land of Chanaan and laid in the tomb of Isaac and Abraham. Joseph besought him to rest assured of the fulfillment of his last wishes.

Fifth promise of the Messias made to Juda. — Jacob, seeing the end of his life at hand, did not delay to consecrate his last moments with one of the most memorable prophecies that ever the Lord inspired. Having assembled his twelve sons around his bed, he announced to them what should happen to their descendants, the different conditions in which they should find themselves after their establishment in the promised land, and the peculiar characteristics that should distinguish each of the twelve tribes of which they were to be the roots.

He soon came to Juda. Suddenly the holy patriarch appeared quite changed. Congratulating Juda with a holy delight on the future greatness of his tribe, he spoke to him in this manner: "Juda! thy brethren shall praise thee; thy hand shall be on the necks of thine enemies; the children of thy father shall prostrate themselves before thee! The scepter shall not depart from Juda until he comes, who is to be sent, and who shall be called the expectation of nations."

a) This prophetical promise confirms what preceding ones told us of the Redeemer, foreshadowed from the beginning of the world. It informs us that he shall be the expectation and the salvation of all nations: the conversion of the Gentiles is the grand characteristic by which he shall be especially recognized. b) This celebrated oracle of Jacob is not limited, like preceding ones, to a mere prediction of the Savior, the expectation of nations: it also determines the time in which he shall appear. It will be when the sovereign power, denoted by the scepter, shall have ceased in the house of Juda.[517] Precious words! which enable us to see so clearly at the present day that Jesus, the Son of Mary, is the divine Messias promised by the dying Jacob. c) This promise delivers us from another matter of considerable embarrassment. We know according to the preceding promises that the Messias should be born of Jacob; but Jacob has twelve sons: which of them shall be the ancestor of the Redeemer? The prophecy of the good old man removes our doubts: it sets eleven of the tribes aside and instructs us to look for the Messias in the tribe of Juda.

Jacob does not stop here. To prove to his children the truth of this wonderful prophecy, he adds a second regarding Juda, that should be accomplished a long time before the first. "O Juda, my son!" he says, "how fertile and well chosen will be thy portion in the promised land! Vines will be its riches, and wine, as common as water, may be used for the washing of thy garments!" All is verified to the letter. Henceforward, the tribe of Juda is always, even before it gives kings to its people, the richest, the most numerous, and the most powerful of all the tribes.

Burial of Jacob in the sepulchre of Abraham.—Having given these excellent instructions to his children, Jacob died peacefully in their midst, absorbed in the thought and the desire of that Redeemer whom God had promised to him, and of whom he was both a figure and a prophet. Accordingly, he exclaimed in his last moments: "I will expect, O Lord, the Messias, whom thou art to send!" Joseph had the body of the holy patriarch embalmed, and conveyed with great pomp into the Land of Chanaan, where it was buried by the side of Abraham and Isaac.

Death of Joseph.—Joseph himself did not long survive his father. The eminent services that he had rendered to Egypt were quickly forgotten: so little can we rely on the gratitude of men! A new king ascended the throne. Alarmed on beholding the rapid multiplication of Jacob's children, and the formation of a distinct people within his realm, he resolved to enfeeble them by laying upon them the heaviest burdens. This means did not succeed to a degree commensurate with his desires. He then formed a resolution well worthy of a tyrant. He ordered all the sons of the Hebrews to be put to death immediately after their birth. But what can the malice of men accomplish against the Lord or against those whom he protects? We shall see by-and-by that this cruelty shall turn to Pharao's ruin.

Birth of Moses; he is saved and educated by the daughter of Pharao.—One day, the daughter of this king went down to the banks of the river to bathe. She noticed among the sedges a basket covered with pitch and carefully concealed. She told one of her waiting-maids to bring it to her. On opening it, she found a little infant weeping. She had compassion on it. "This," said she, "is one of the babes of the Hebrews." Mary, the infant's sister, who had remained at some distance awaiting the result, heard the words of the princess. "If thou desirest it," said she, drawing nigh, "I will go and call one of the Hebrew women to come and take care of this child." "Go," answered the princess. The little girl ran and called her mother. The daughter of Pharao said to her: "Nurse this child for me, and I will reward thee." She thus adopted him and named him Moses, that is, "saved from the waters." When well grown, he was sent to the princess, and brought up even in the midst of Pharao's court.

Moses retires into the desert of Madian.—After a time, Moses, who was not ignorant of the circumstances of his birth, began to groan within himself on beholding his brethren in a state of slavery: he resolved to deliver them. The Lord himself, who had chosen Moses for the accomplishment of this memorable deliverance, inspired him with the design of quitting the court of Pharao and retiring into the land of Madian.

Moses spent here forty years, employed, like the patriarchs, in the care of numerous flocks, which belonged to Gethro, his father-in-law. One day, having advanced a considerable distance into the desert, he came to the foot of a high but fertile mountain, named Horeb. Here the Lord suddenly appeared to him in the midst of a burning bush. The Almighty assumed the figure of a bright flame, shining with a soft brilliancy, and apparently not consuming either the branches or the leaves. Moses, astonished, said to himself: "I will go and see this wonder; I will examine how it is that the bush, all on fire as it seems, is not consumed."

Moses is ordered by God to deliver his people. — He was drawing nigh, when the Lord, who wished to make him regard this apparition with all that profound respect which his awful Majesty demands, began to speak: "Moses, Moses," he said, "beware of approaching too near this bush! Take off thy shoes from thy feet, for the ground on which thou treadest is holy. I am the God of Abraham and of Jacob." Moses, trembling, covered his face. "I have beheld the affliction of my people," continued the Lord, "the time to deliver them from slavery and to lead them into the rich land which I promised to their fathers is come. Prepare thyself, for thou art the man whom I have chosen to set my people free from the slavery of Egypt."

Moses excused himself for a long time: modesty and humility are always the virtues that distinguish the greatest men as well as the greatest saints. "The Hebrews will not believe me," he observed, "but will say it is not true: 'The Lord hath not appeared to thee.'" "Well, I," said the Lord, "I will give thee something to convince the incredulous. What is it that thou holdest in thy hand?" "It is a rod," answered Moses. "Throw it on the ground," said the Lord. Moses obeyed, and immediately the rod was changed into a frightful serpent, from which he fled alarmed. "Fear not," said God to his servant, "take hold of it by the end of the tail." Moses did so, and found that he held in his hand the rod now in its natural state which he had just let fall. "That which has been wrought before thee," added the Lord, "thou shalt work again in presence of the Hebrews, and they shall know by this sign that the God who hath appeared to thee is the God of their fathers, the God of Abraham, Isaac, and Jacob. If this miracle be not sufficient, here is another that will convince them. Thou shalt take before them the water of the river, and they shall see it forthwith changed into blood. Aaron, thy brother, will assist thee in the ministry which I have confided to thee."

Vocation of Aaron. — The Lord also spoke to Aaron, who was in Egypt. "Depart," he said, "from this country without delay; go into the desert and meet thy brother Moses: he will acquaint thee with my designs over both thee and him." Aaron set out immediately, and reached his brother. The meeting of these two great men was the salvation of Israel. They came into the land of Gessen, where the Israelites dwelt. Moses performed in the presence of the people the miracles that confirmed his mission. The people acknowledged the truth, and blessed the Lord for being mindful of Israel. Thence the brothers went together to Pharao, to whom they said with an air of authority becoming their dignity: "This is the message of the Lord, the God of Israel, to thee: 'Grant my people liberty to offer me a sacrifice in the desert.'" The tyrant, enraged at the utterance of language to which his ears were unaccustomed, refused their petition with scorn, but he became the victim of his obstinacy.

Plagues of Egypt. — The Lord struck Egypt with ten great plagues.[518] At each new calamity, Pharao promised to grant liberty to the children of Israel. But no sooner had Moses caused the punishment to cease, than the stiff-necked prince withdrew his promise. At length the tenth plague was so severe that Pharao hastened to implore the Hebrews to depart as speedily as possible. The tenth plague was this: at midnight, when nature was calm and silent, the Almighty sent his exterminating angel, who put to death all the firstborn of the Egyptians, from the eldest son of the monarch on the throne to the eldest son of the slave whose days were spent in the toils of the field and his nights in the miseries of a prison. The firstborn of beasts perished in like manner. When morning came, there was nothing but one cry of desolation throughout the land of Egypt: not a house but contained a corpse. Pharao sent immediately for Moses and Aaron. "Depart," he said, "from my kingdom, you and the children of Israel!"

Some days before this bloody execution, Moses had warned the Hebrews of it. "To protect yourselves from the scourge of the destroying angel," he said, "hear what the Lord the God of our fathers commands you. On the tenth day of this month, every father of a family shall put aside a lamb without blemish, a male of one year old. Should the family not be sufficiently numerous to consume the lamb at one meal, some of the neighbors shall be called in. The lamb, put thus aside on the tenth, shall be kept till the fourteenth day. On the evening of this day, all the children of Israel shall sacrifice the lamb. The blood of the victim is to be preserved; and with it you shall sprinkle the posts and the lintel of the door of each house, in which the repast is made. The lamb must be roasted, and eaten with unleavened bread and wild lettuces.

"As for the manner in which you shall make this repast, you shall have your loins girt, shoes on your feet, and staves in your hands; you shall eat it standing, and in haste, like travelers: for it is the Pasch, that is, the passage of the Lord. The blood that you will place on the doors of the houses shall be a preservative for the children of Israel. I shall behold this blood, saith the Lord, and I will not enter with my avenging sword into the houses that shall be marked with it."

Still further, God forbade, and not without a mysterious reason, that any of the bones of the lamb should be broken: for the paschal lamb is the eighth figure of the Messias.

The paschal lamb, the eighth figure of the Messias. — We shall now illustrate this point. The paschal lamb should be without blemish; our Lord is the Lamb of God, a Lamb without spot, purity itself. The paschal lamb should be eaten in one house; our Lord cannot be received in any house but the Catholic Church. None of the bones of the paschal lamb should be broken; on the cross, none of our Lord's bones were broken, though the case was different with the two thieves. The paschal lamb should be eaten with azymes or unleavened bread; our Lord must be received with the greatest purity of heart and without the leaven of sin. The paschal lamb should be eaten with bitter lettuces; the Blessed Eucharist must be received with the bitter lettuces of mortification and penance. Those who partook of the paschal lamb should have their loins girt, a staff in their hand, and shoes on their feet, like travelers ready for a journey; those who eat the flesh of our Lord must have their loins girt, which is an emblem of chastity, have a staff in their hand, that is, be armed against the attacks of the devil, and have shoes on their feet, that is, be careful to avoid the defilements of the earth and to appear in all respects as travelers who seek a heavenly country.

It was at the moment of quitting Egypt, on their way to the promised land, that the Hebrews ate the paschal lamb; it is when we have decided on quitting sin, and are traveling toward heaven, the true land of promise, that we are permitted to receive the body of our Lord. The blood of the paschal lamb was sprinkled on the doors of the houses, and every house marked with it was spared by the destroying angel; the blood of our Lord is shed on our souls, and every soul devoutly marked with it will be spared by the Lord when he shall come to punish the wicked.

This figure adds considerably to our knowledge: a) it shows us one of the most brilliant characteristics of the Messias, his wonderful meekness — he will be as meek as a lamb; b) it reveals to us that the Messias will unite himself to men as food is united to the body; and c) it teaches us that none will be saved except those who unite themselves to the new Adam in the manner appointed by him.

PRAYER

O my God! who art all love, I thank thee for having delivered me from the slavery of sin, as thou didst deliver thy people from the slavery of Egypt; I thank thee especially for having nourished my soul with the adorable flesh of thy Son, the true Lamb prefigured by that of the Hebrews. Grant me the dispositions of purity, fervor, and detachment, always necessary to receive him worthily.

I am resolved to love God above all things, and my neighbor as myself for the love of God; and, in testimony of this love, I will neglect nothing to be able to communicate frequently.

Lesson 28: Messias Foreshadowed: Manna

Departure of the Israelites. — We approach that solemn moment in which the people of God should quit the scenes of their long and bitter slavery. At the beginning of the account of this miraculous journey, let us remember that the train of prodigies, of which we shall be witnesses, entered into the general designs of providence, whether to confirm the faith of the Hebrews, or to enlighten idolatrous nations, by giving them innumerable and splendid proofs that the God of Israel was the only true God, the supreme Lord of nature and of the elements, as well as of kings and nations.

The pillar of cloud. — While the Egyptians were engaged in burying their dead, Moses issued the order of departure. To the number of about 600,000 men, not counting women and children, the descendants of Jacob directed their steps toward the Red Sea. From the very commencement, the Lord displayed his special protection over his new people. To instruct them as to the direction which they should take, the time to move and to halt, and the places of their encampment during their sojourn, he formed a great pillar, whose base corresponded to the size of the future tabernacle, and whose top reached very high. During the day, it had the appearance of a beautiful cloud, but during the night, it seemed all on fire and luminous like the sun. An angel was placed in charge of this pillar, which was designed to serve as a guide to the Hebrews.

When it was time to move from any place, the pillar arose, and settled over the tents of the tribe that was to depart first. The march continued as long as the pillar advanced, being regulated by its movements. When it was time to stop, the pillar rested at the place appointed by the Lord. Here it remained until the will of heaven directed a new change. Its top was inclined in such a manner that it overshadowed the people, and served as a great veil protecting them from the scorching rays of the sun, which would otherwise have been wholly unsupportable in the burning sands of the desert.

Passage of the Red Sea. — After a few encampments, they reached the shores of the Red Sea. The Israelites found themselves enclosed on all sides: before them, the sea; behind them, their enemies. For Pharao, repenting of his permission to the Hebrews to depart, had assembled his army and pursued them. But Moses, full of confidence in the Lord, reassured them, saying: "Fear not, but patiently await the miracle which the Lord shall work in your favor." Immediately the pillar, which was at the head of the Israelite multitude, changed its place. It took up a position between their camp and that of the Egyptians. On the side toward the Israelites, the cloud was luminous; on the other, it presented nothing but darkness, which hindered the enemy from advancing. Moses now stretched forth his hand over the sea, which opened, and the Israelites marched through with dry foot, having the waters on their right hand and their left, like high walls. This miraculous passage was effected during the night.[519]

At break of day, the Egyptians noticed the escape of their prey. They rushed precipitately into the extraordinary road that had not been opened for them. The Lord awaited them in it. Suddenly a horrible confusion takes place in the army. The chariots are broken. A shout of alarm is heard above the din: "Let us flee from the Hebrews: the Lord fights for them against us!" But it was too late. The Lord said to Moses: "Stretch forth thy hand over the sea, that the waters may resume their wonted course and engulf the Egyptians, chariots and horsemen." Moses stretched forth his hand; the depths closed in, and the pursuing host disappeared among the waters. There did not escape a single man to carry to Egypt the news of this terrible disaster. At the sight of the miracle, Moses and all the people gave expression to their joy and gratitude in a canticle of thanksgiving. Never was there a miracle better attested, since it took place under the very eyes of far more than 600,000 witnesses.

Having crossed the Red Sea, the Israelites entered an immense desert, which lay on their way to the promised land. Soon the provisions began to fail, and the people began to murmur against Moses and Aaron. The holy leader had recourse to God, who ordered him to inform the people that they should be furnished with food from heaven. They were to go out in the morning, and everyone to gather as much as would suffice for the nourishment of one day. On the sixth day they were to gather twice the usual complement, that they might sanctify the seventh or sabbath day. Moses hastened to communicate this intelligence to the children of Israel. "From tomorrow morning," he said to them, "the Lord will send you out of heaven a food that henceforward shall never fail you." In point of fact, the manna never ceased to fall daily, except on the sabbath, during the forty years that the Israelites spent in the desert.

Next morning, at an early hour, the promise of the Lord was fulfilled. The neighborhood of the camp was covered with a dew, on which appeared a multitude of little white grains, so closely fastened to one another that they resembled a hoarfrost extending over the plains. Never had such a sight been seen before. The Israelites, astounded, asked one another in their own language, *Man-hu?* that is, "What is this?" Whence comes the name of *manna*. No one dared at first to touch it: they went to consult Moses. "This," said he, "is the bread which the Lord promised you." Being once informed of the matter, they set to work. Every Israelite gathered in his harvest. Some among them wished to amass a supply for many days, but that which was not used the first day corrupted; God desiring that henceforward men should learn to be solicitous only about the present, and to leave the care of the morrow—that is the future—to providence. In preparing the grains for nourishment, they were pounded under a stone. Being thus reduced to the form of a white paste or dough, they were baked into bread of exquisite taste. Still more, those who, by their faith, were particularly pleasing to God, found in them something unusually delicious. The manna assumed every variety of sweetness in accordance with their desires. The manna should be gathered at daybreak, for it melted with the rays of the sun.

The manna, the ninth figure of the Messias.—This was one of the most signal miracles that the Lord wrought in favor of his people, and, as we shall just see, was one of the most admirable figures of the Messias. The manna was a food that fell from heaven; our Lord, in the Holy Eucharist, is the living bread that came down from heaven. The manna fell every day; the Holy Eucharist is our daily bread. The manna was only for the Israelites; the Holy Eucharist is only for Christians. The manna was given to the Israelites only after their passage through the Red Sea; the Holy Eucharist is given to Christians only after baptism, which is signified by the passage through the Red Sea. The manna was a substitute for every other kind of aliment; the Holy Eucharist is the bread by excellence, the bread that suffices for all our wants.

The manna had every kind of agreeable taste; the Holy Eucharist has the same—it strengthens the weak and comforts the afflicted, enlightens the mind and inflames the heart. Nevertheless, the manna did not ward off death; the Holy Eucharist is a pledge of eternal life. The manna fell as long as the people remained in the desert; the Holy Eucharist will be given to the human race as long as men remain in the desert of this world. The manna ceased as soon as the Hebrews entered the promised land; the Holy Eucharist will cease when we enter heaven, that is, when we behold without a cloud that God whom we receive under the sacramental veils.

This figure adds several new touches to the picture: a) while the paschal lamb was to be eaten only once a year, the manna, a figure of the Holy Eucharist, should be eaten every day; b) the food that the Savior reserves for our souls will be a heavenly food; and c) this food will be given us as long as we shall remain pilgrims on earth.

The rock of Horeb.—The Israelites, supported by a heavenly food, continue their journey through the desert. Very soon the supply of water is exhausted: the people, according to their custom, begin to murmur. The Lord, out of the depths of his inexhaustible goodness, only answers their complaints with a new prodigy. He says to Moses: "Take the rod with which you struck the river of Egypt, strike the rock of Horeb, and you shall see a stream of water spring forth in such abundance that all the men and beasts may drink plentifully of it, and so quench their thirst." Moses obeyed: at the first stroke of the miraculous rod, there sprang from the hard rock such a rich and rapid stream that the whole valley was watered by it as by a beautiful river.

Victory gained over the Amalekites. — In a short time another danger threatened the pilgrim multitude. The Amalekites, a brave and numerous people, attacked them. While the children of Israel fought in the plain, Moses was stationed on the summit of a neighboring mountain. His hands were raised toward heaven. While his hands were lifted up, Israel had the advantage, but when they fell, the Amalekites recovered their lost ground. On perceiving this change of fortune, Aaron and another Israelite, who were in the company of Moses, supported his arms till sunset, and the victory was won. A striking example of the efficacy of prayer when animated by faith!

Arrival at the foot of Mount Sinai. — After this new wonder, the Israelites continued their journey toward the interior of the desert. On the forty-sixth day after the passage of the Red Sea, the pillar rested at the foot of Mount Sinai. Of all the halting places made by the Hebrew people in the desert, this was assuredly the most celebrated, on account of the promulgation of the law. Let us speak of the cause and the manner of this occurrence.

Promulgation of the law. — The truths which God had taught to Adam, and of which a knowledge had descended from parents to children by tradition, had become corrupted: it was to be feared that these truths should soon disappear altogether from the memory of man. To preserve them, and especially to preserve the great promise of the Messias, God resolved to give them in writing. He called Moses up to the mountain, and told him to say in his name to the Israelites: "You have seen the manner in which I have brought you out of Egypt, and how I have chosen you to be my people. If you hear my voice, and observe my covenant, I myself will govern you: you shall be the holy nation." Moses came down from the mountain and faithfully repeated to the Israelites what he had heard from the Lord. He required a precise answer from them. The whole nation replied as with one voice: "We will do all that the Lord commands."

Moses returned with this answer to his God, who said to him: "Go and purify your Hebrews, and let them be ready on the third day; I will then descend on Mount Sinai before all the people. Place a barrier round the mountain: no one shall pass it under penalty of death." These preparations were necessary in order to give solemnity to the promulgation of the law, and to move the hearts of the multitude to receive it with sentiments of religious veneration.

As the morning of the third day broke, thunder began to roll and lightning to flash. A thick cloud overspread the mountain. From the midst of the cloud rang out the piercing sound of a trumpet, which summoned the people to attend; but the people, terrified, shrank back into their tents. Moses, however, encouraged them, and, having induced them to come forth, arranged them in a space that lay unoccupied between the camp and the boundary at the foot of the mountain. Then was heard the voice of God from the midst of the flaming cloud, publishing the ten commandments of the law, which were likewise written on two tables of stone: this is what is called the decalogue.

When the Lord had ceased to speak, the sounds of the thunder and the trumpet began again with the same dreadful grandeur as before. The mountain, all the while smoking, covered with a cloud, and sparkling with flames, shook. The Hebrews, in a state of indescribable alarm, fled to their tents, whither Moses followed them. The ancients said to Moses: "Speak for us thyself henceforward; if the Lord speak to us, we shall die. How can a mortal man hear the voice of the living God, speaking from the midst of flames?" Moses returned, and, lost in the awful darkness that enveloped the mountain, represented to the Lord the alarm of his people. "I know their petition," answered the Lord, "it has not displeased me."

Of his infinite goodness the Lord chose this moment to renew to the whole nation, and in the most affecting manner, the great promise of the Messias. "Return to the people," he said to Moses, "and say to them: 'The Lord promises to give you a prophet of your own nation, taken from among your brethren, one like to me, who am commissioned to make the announcement to you. Your God shall place words in his mouth: you shall be submissive to his orders. If any one will not hear that prophet, let him expect the avenging stroke of God.'"

These words indicate the Messias. St. Peter, speaking to the Jews, applies them to our Lord, of whom he preaches. This promise acquaints us with a new characteristic of the Redeemer. It teaches us that he will one day accomplish, in an easy and familiar manner, that which has been wrought in the midst of such awful splendor. It will not be with a display of formidable power, but with mildness and gentleness, that he will manifest to us the will of God. It also teaches us that he will be, like Moses, a mediator between God and man, a leader, a liberator, and a legislator, though in a more perfect manner. Now, all this has been literally fulfilled in our Lord, the true and only Son of God; born of the royal blood of Juda; the mediator, the leader, the legislator, and the Savior of a new people.

PRAYER

O my God! who art all love, I thank thee for having confirmed the truths of my holy faith by so many resplendent miracles. May thy light conduct me during life, as the pillar conducted thy people during their pilgrimage in the desert! I thank thee for having so often nourished me with the true bread that descended from heaven, and for having given me, through our Lord Jesus Christ, the law of grace, so much superior to the old law. Grant that I may say with more sincerity than the Israelites: "I will do all that the Lord commands."

I am resolved to love God above all things, and my neighbor as myself for the love of God; and, in testimony of this love, I will seek an opportunity of instructing the ignorant.

Lesson 29: Messias Foreshadowed: Sacrifices and the Brazen Serpent

Confirmation of the covenant blood of victims sprinkled on the people. — Besides the two tables of stone, on which the decalogue was written, the Lord gave Moses a great many other infinitely wise laws, relating to the ceremonies of religion as well as to the ordinary duties of everyday life.[520] Moses wrote them out, and next morning had an altar made at the foot of the mountain that seemed to be the very throne of God. Around the altar were twelve pillars, which represented the twelve tribes of Israel. This work being finished, Moses summoned the multitude to the ceremony of confirming the covenant.

All came forth, and ranged themselves around the altar. Victims were offered. Moses read the book of the law. The people answered: "We will do all that the Lord commands." Then Moses, standing near the altar, and taking a bunch of hyssop, with some scarlet wool, mixed a little pure water with the blood of the victims, and sprinkled the book of the law with the mysterious fluid. He next sprinkled each of the twelve tribes in succession, saying: "This is the blood of the covenant, which the Lord hath made with you."

Sacrifices, the tenth figure of the Messias. — By this aspersion the Lord, in the person of Moses, ratified the alliance, and engaged to fulfill his part of it. The people, wet with the blood of victims, renewed their oaths, and submitted themselves to punishment if they should transgress. In virtue of this contract, the children of Israel from that very time acquired a particular title to the denomination of the "people of God;" and God declared himself to be in a special manner the God, the Father, and the King of the children of Israel. Never had a more august or imposing ceremony been witnessed. Nevertheless, it was only the shadow of that which, more than fifteen centuries later on, should confirm the new alliance of the Lord with mankind in general, when the Messias, the Son of God, and God himself, would ratify it by the effusion of his own blood, and become at once the victim and the mediator of the covenant. Moses on this occasion was a figure of our Lord.

To confirm the old alliance, Moses erected an altar, surrounded with twelve pillars; our Lord, to confirm the new alliance, also prepared an altar, surrounded by his twelve apostles. The twelve pillars represented all the people of Israel; the twelve apostles represented the whole Church. It was after descending from the mountain, whence he bore to the Israelites the law of God, that Moses offered his sacrifice; it was after descending from heaven, whence he brought us a divine law, that our Lord offered his sacrifice. Moses immolated victims and poured out the blood on the people; our Lord immolated himself and gave his blood to his apostles to drink. Moses, when pouring out the blood of victims, said: "This is the blood of the alliance which the Lord makes with you"; our Lord, when giving his blood to his apostles, said: "This is the blood of the new alliance which the Lord makes with mankind."

The people, sprinkled with the blood of victims, became the people of God, who promised to protect them in the desert and to lead them into the promised land; in like manner, we, being washed and purified with the blood of our Lord, became the true people of God, who promises to protect us in the desert of this life and to lead us to the joys of heaven. From the time of the confirmation of the alliance there existed among the Hebrews two kinds of sacrifices, bloody and unbloody;[521] since our Lord confirmed the new alliance, we observe among Christians the bloody sacrifice of Calvary and the unbloody sacrifice of our altars. In the bloody sacrifices of the old law the victim was put to death; in the bloody sacrifice of the new law the victim is also put to death.

In the unbloody sacrifice of the old law the victim was not put to death; in the unbloody sacrifice of the new law the victim is not put to death as on Calvary: it is mystically immolated. For our Lord, having once risen from the dead, dieth now no more. The matter of the unbloody sacrifices of the old law was flour and wine; the matter of the unbloody sacrifice of the new law is bread and wine, which are changed into the body and blood of our Lord. The various sacrifices of the old law were offered for four principal ends: to adore, to thank, to impetrate, and to expiate; the sacrifice of the new law includes in itself alone all these excellences: it is a sacrifice of adoration, of thanksgiving, of impetration, and of expiation. In the old law a lamb, without blemish, was sacrificed every morning and evening, as a substitute for all other kinds of sacrifices; to perpetuate the sacrifice of Calvary, which has taken the place of all the ancient sacrifices, the Lamb of God is sacrificed every day, nay, at every hour of the day and the night, on our altars—for during eighteen centuries there have always been priests in some part of the world celebrating the Holy Mass.

Thus you see that every sacrifice of the old law was only a figure of the sacrifice of our Lord, as the old law itself was only a figure of the new. Hence, we reckon the ancient sacrifices as the tenth figure of our Lord.

Idolatry of the Israelites; the golden calf; the Lord appeased by Moses. — In dictating his law to the Israelite people and entering into an alliance with them, the Lord had given them a wonderful proof of his goodness. Perhaps he gave them a still greater one in pardoning them the horrible crime of which they shortly afterward became guilty, even at the very foot of Mount Sinai. After the confirmation of the alliance, Moses had gone up into the mountain, which was still covered with a thick cloud. The people supposed that his absence would continue only for a few days, or a few weeks at most; but a month having passed away, without receiving any intelligence of him, they began to murmur. "The Lord hath undoubtedly abandoned us," they said. "Let us make gods to go before us and lead us out of these deserts in which we are lost!" Who would believe it, if he did not know the inconstancy of the human heart? This mad language found a response. The Israelites made a golden calf, and worshipped it with abominable sacrifices. Having done so, they began to eat, and drink, and dance round the idol.

At this sight, the Lord said to Moses: "Get thee down; thy people, whom thou hast brought out of Egypt, have sinned against me. They have made a golden calf, which they adore in my stead. Leave me, that mine anger may rise against this people and that I may destroy them." Moses was too well acquainted with the heart of his master to abandon his opportunity. He fell on his knees before the Lord, and besought him thus: "No, Lord! thou wilt not strike thy people, whom thou hast delivered from the slavery of Egypt. Wouldst thou have the Egyptians insult thy holy name, saying that thou hadst cruelly led thy people into this desert in order to destroy them? Remember the promises that thou didst make to Abraham, Isaac, and Jacob. Thou didst swear to multiply their descendants as the stars of heaven, and to establish them in the Land of Chanaan."

O wonderful power of prayer! At the voice of Moses, the anger of the Lord is appeased, and the sentence, which condemned the Israelites to total ruin, is revoked. The most guilty alone were punished as they deserved.

Description of the ark and the tabernacle.—The Lord next ordered Moses to construct the ark of the covenant. It was a chest intended to receive, besides some other things, the book of the law, and the two tables of stone on which the decalogue was written. The ark was made of incorruptible wood, covered inside and outside with the purest gold, decorated round about with a golden cornice, shut with a lid covered with gold, and surmounted with two cherubs of massive gold. It was from the ark that the Lord desired henceforward to make known his will, and to hear the petitions of his people. The ark was two and a half cubits long, one and a half broad, and one and a half deep: it was to be placed in the tabernacle.

The tabernacle was a tent of rich and elegantly embroidered stuffs: it was thirty cubits long and ten broad. This portable temple was a figure of the Church in its state of instability and motion on earth, as later on the Temple of Solomon should be a figure of the Church in its state of stability and rest in heaven. The tabernacle was borne by the tribe of Levi, who were all consecrated to the service of the Lord. Aaron, who belonged to this tribe, was chosen to be the high priest.

The Lord appointed three great feasts, in memory of the three great favors which he had granted to his people: first, the feast of the Pasch, to commemorate their deliverance from Egypt by passing through the Red Sea; secondly, the feast of Pentecost, to commemorate the promulgation of the law on Mount Sinai—it was celebrated seven weeks after that of the Pasch; and thirdly, the feast of Tabernacles or Tents, to commemorate their miraculous journey in the desert, during the period they had dwelt under tents.

Each of these solemnities continued for seven days. During the celebration of the last-mentioned, the Israelites dwelt under tents, or huts constructed of twigs. When they entered into possession of the promised land, they were obliged to visit Jerusalem on these three great occasions: women were permitted to come thither also.

The Israelites assisted at the prayers and sacrifices, which were always accompanied with music. Then followed some innocent pleasures. Those were considered fortunate who were able to be present; but those who were hindered from attending were looked upon as very unfortunate. Such ought to be the conduct and the sentiments of Christians on those solemn days when they celebrate the far higher spiritual benefits which they have received from God.

Journey of the people through the desert.—At length, these various matters being regulated, the pillar arose, and the people departed from the ever-celebrated mountain of

Sinai. The following was the order of their march. The multitude divided themselves into four great bodies, each composed of three tribes, and all forming a square, in the midst of which was the tabernacle, borne by the Levites. These four great bodies, as well as the particular tribes, were never allowed to intermix, either during a time of rest or when on the march. Accordingly, the people were always prepared to meet their enemies on whatever side they should be threatened. Every tribe had a chief and a standard. In the center of each tribe were placed the women, the children, the old men, the wagons, and the flocks. Thus, the journey was made not only without confusion but in the most admirable order that we can imagine.

The journey toward the promised land was therefore begun in this heavenly order, presenting to the world a spectacle the most magnificent and most formidable ever seen. It was an army of more than 600,000 fighting men, not to mention a vast multitude of women, children, and old men, guided by the Lord their God, ranged under their banners and leaders, advancing to the conquest of a beautiful country, which had been promised to their forefathers, and in which they might establish, on the ruins of the ancient occupants, their homes, their religion, and their authority. This grand project was yet to be accomplished; but its success depended on the fidelity of those very men who had, it might be supposed, the deepest interest in it.

About two months after their departure from Sinai, the Israelites arrived within sight of the Land of Chanaan. The pillar stood; and the multitude encamped at a place called Cadesbarnè. This pause was intended by Almighty God to afford them an opportunity of taking their final resolution to attack the enemies whom they had come to engage, and thus to enter into the long-promised land. Moses, therefore, assembled the children of Israel. "This land," he said, "on whose border you stand, is that into which the Lord promised your fathers to lead you; the time has come to undertake its conquest, with his protection; fear not, but be assured of a success which the promise and the assistance of the Almighty render certain!"

Nevertheless, before passing the frontiers, it was decided to send a number of men to reconnoiter the country. Twelve deputies were chosen: one for each tribe. Among the number were Caleb and Josue. The deputies set out, and acquitted themselves successfully of their commission. On their way back, they brought with them some samples of fruit, including figs, pomegranates, and grapes. The grapes were of such extraordinary size that it was found necessary to hang a branch of them on a pole, which was carried by two men.[522] The tour was one of forty days, at the end of which the deputies reached again the camp of Cadesbarnè.

Revolt at Cadesbarnè. — As soon as they made their appearance, there was a general gathering round Moses and Aaron, to whom the twelve travelers rendered publicly an account of their commission. First of all, they allowed the beautiful fruits that they had brought with them to speak for them. "Judge," they said to the people, "by the enormous size of these fruits, what is the fertility of the country that we have explored. It was no deception to tell you that it was a land flowing with milk and honey." Moses was delighted at these words. But what was his surprise, what was his grief, when he heard the spies continue their story? "The country, however," they said, "abounds in large, well-walled cities. It is inhabited by men of extraordinary strength and stature. We saw some giants there, by the side of whom we should be only grasshoppers. The land itself, fertile as it is, devours its inhabitants. It would be impossible for us to live there."

You may imagine the strange impressions that such an account, supported by the authority of numerous envoys, made on the minds of a people generally ill-disposed, and at present on the verge of rebellion. Discouragement was pictured on every countenance, and murmurs began to spread forth through every rank. Still there were two faithful deputies, Caleb and Josue. These endeavored immediately to undeceive the people. "You are being grossly deceived," they exclaimed, "only let us have courage to move forward and every difficulty will vanish!"

Night drew on. The people retired to their tents. But time only increased the evil. Next morning, there was a frightful tumult throughout the camp. All the blame was thrown on Moses and Aaron. "Would that we had died in Egypt," said the people openly, "or that we might perish in this desert! No, we will not enter into that land to be sacrificed by the swords of our enemies!" Moses, afflicted beyond anything that can be expressed, exhorted, wept, and entreated. But no one would listen to him; his words were lost upon the excited multitude: the sedition spread wider and wider.

It was time that the Lord should take in hand the cause of his servants. Just as the multitude were ready to stone them, the pillar of cloud, which had rested on the roof of the tabernacle, was changed into a dreadful fire, and the furious crowds were enabled to perceive clearly that their outrageous conduct had awakened the just indignation of God. Moses, trembling for their danger, ran to implore pardon for them.

The Lord answered Moses with a goodness beyond all expectation. "I pardon them," he said, "as thou dost desire: they shall not all perish in one day by a pestilence, as I had resolved on; but, as I am the living God, I swear by myself that my glory shall not suffer by the pardon which I grant them. This is the sentence which thou shalt announce to them: 'You shall be treated as you have desired; all of you, from the age of twenty upwards, who have murmured against me, shall die in this desert—here shall your carcasses rot—you shall not enter into the land which I swore to your forefathers to give in possession to their descendants. I except only Caleb and Josue. The children shall wander in the desert for forty years, until the carcasses of their fathers are consumed.'"

At the very same time the ten unfaithful deputies fell dead, stricken by the hand of God, in presence of the multitude. The Lord remained inflexible; and the multitude were obliged to wander about through the desert, there to see a million of doomed men perish, there to fulfill during more than eight-and-thirty years the irrevocable decree pronounced by a just judge, in the day of his wrath, against his rebellious people.

The brazen serpent, the eleventh figure of the Messias.—Many years afterward, the Israelites revolted again. To punish their continual murmurs, the Lord sent against them some serpents, whose bite, burning like a fire, caused death. In this extremity, they ran to the tent of Moses. "We have sinned," they said, "by speaking against the Lord and against thee. Pray for us, that we may be delivered from these serpents."

God chose this occasion to exhibit to mankind a new figure of the Messias. Moses prayed for them; and the Lord said to him: "Make thee a brazen serpent, and place it on an eminence; whosoever looks upon it shall be cured of his wounds." Moses obeyed; and, as soon as anyone turned his ghastly eyes toward the serpent, fastened to the saving wood, he was restored to health. This is the eleventh figure of the Messias. The Hebrews are bitten by serpents, whose wound is mortal; the human race, in the person of Adam, is bitten by the infernal serpent, whose wound brings death into the world. The Lord is touched by the miseries which the serpents bring upon his people; the Lord is touched by the evils which the infernal serpent brings upon mankind. God orders a brazen serpent to be made, and placed on an eminence; our Lord, by the appointment of his Father, becomes man, and is raised on the cross.

All those who looked on the brazen serpent were healed of their corporal wounds; all those who turn their eyes with faith and love to our Lord on the cross are healed of their spiritual wounds. The brazen serpent was shown only to one people; our Lord is shown to the whole world. The brazen serpent did not remain long exposed to the view of the people; our Lord will continue to appear exposed on the cross even to the end of the world, to heal the wounds inflicted by the infernal serpent on mankind. The wounds could not be cured but by looking on the brazen serpent; it is only by faith in our Lord that the wounds inflicted on our soul by the devil can be cured.

This figure adds to our preceding knowledge of the Messias. It teaches us: a) that he will cure the diseases of our souls; b) that, to be cured, we must look upon him, that is, believe in him and love him; and c) that he will be the only physician of mankind.

PRAYER

O my God ! who art all love, I thank thee for the innumerable prodigies which thou didst work in favor of thy people. Make me grateful for those which thou hast wrought in my favor, especially that of immolating thyself upon the cross as a tender Lamb. Grant me the faith and charity which are necessary in order that I may profit of thy death.

I am resolved to love God above all things, and my neighbor as myself for the love of God; and, in testimony of this love, I will always carry a crucifix about with me.

Lesson 30: Messias Foreshadowed: Moses

New murmurs of the Israelites.—During more than thirty-nine years, the Israelites had now wandered in the desert. After many journeys and encampments, the Lord led them back again to the borders of the promised land: the moment of entering it drew nigh. But the want of water to allay their thirst at present caused the ungrateful Israelites to renew their murmurs once more. Accordingly, the people gathered in a tumult around Moses and Aaron. It was nothing short of a rebellion. They sighed for death to take them—lamenting that they themselves had not perished in the desert like so many others. To the shame of the human heart, we must acknowledge that this was the ordinary language of Israel. Their usual manner of asking a favor was to insult those from whom they expected it. Moses and Aaron hastened to the tabernacle. There, prostrate on the ground, they exclaimed: "O Lord, the God of Israel, hear the cries of thy people; grant them a plentiful stream of fresh water, that they may appease their thirst."

God was moved by the earnest prayer of his servants. "Take thy rod," he said to Moses, "assemble the multitude; thou and thy brother shall approach the rock, and do nothing else than simply command it, in my name, to yield water. The rock will obey, the water will flow, and the multitude will have an abundance with which to satisfy their thirst and that of their flocks." Moses did as the Lord commanded.

He assembled the multitude around the rock; but a slight feeling of distrust came over him. He did not doubt that the Lord could perform a miracle; but he doubted whether he would perform it on this occasion. Aaron shared the uneasiness of his brother. Both trembled for their success; and, in the moment of their alarm, Moses struck the rock. It did not obey at first—Moses perceived his fault. He struck it a second time with that lively faith and humble repentance by which so many wonders are wrought. The water flowed plentifully, and men and animals were speedily refreshed.

The Waters of Contradiction.—The Lord was offended at the hesitation of Moses and Aaron. Such is the nature of our God that he cannot endure the appearance of any distrust in his goodness from those on whom he has bestowed signal favors. Before this sad event, Moses and Aaron had not been condemned, like the murmurers, to end their days in the desert. Their fault, though pardonable in men of less exalted position, drew them now into the general proscription list: and the Lord their God did not wish that they should be ignorant of the sentence which they had incurred. "You have not believed in me," he said to them, "you have hesitated; you have dishonored me before the children of Israel: you shall not lead my people into the land which I reserve for them."

This wonderful exclusion conceals a mystery. It shows us that Moses and his law should not lead anything to perfection—that, unable to bring us the fulfillment of the promises, they could only show us our reward from afar off, or conduct us at most to the gate of our inheritance.

The mournful spot was soon quitted, but not before it had received the name of "Waters of Contradiction"; and an encampment was formed at the foot of Mount Hor. It was during this encampment that Moses was called by the Lord to receive the most painful order that had ever fallen to his lot since his investment with the leadership of God's chosen people. "Let thy brother Aaron," said the Lord, "prepare to die; thou shalt inform him that this is his last day. He shall not enter into the land whither I am about to conduct the children of Israel. Thou shalt arrange the matter thus: take Aaron and his eldest son Eleazar to Mount Hor; divest the father there of his pontifical garments and of all other emblems of his sacerdotal dignity, and place them on his son, to initiate him in the high priesthood. After this ceremony, Aaron shall pass away in thy arms and be gathered to his fathers."

Such a commission may well have appeared painful to a brother. We are not informed in what manner Moses acquitted himself of it; but we may easily imagine the courage with which these two great men, so closely united together and so dear to God, assured moreover of meeting each other again before the close of the year in the bosom of Abraham, submitted to the orders of the Lord.

Death of Aaron.—Accompanied by Eleazar, they ascended the mountain, in sight of all the children of Israel. Moses, with his own hands, took away the pontifical robes from his brother and clothed Eleazar with them. Aaron, meanwhile, without illness, without weakness, without any other indication of approaching death than his simple belief in the word of God, prepared himself in peace for his last moment. Scarcely was the sad ceremony over, when he tranquilly expired in the arms of his brother and his son.

Thus died, in punishment of a momentary sin, and for the instruction of all succeeding pontiffs, the first high priest of the holy nation, after a period of 33 years spent in a glorious but difficult ministry. He was 123 years old. The people sincerely lamented his loss, and the mourning continued for thirty days.

Election of Josue.—This death was the prelude to another, much more sorrowful: Moses should follow his brother. The holy man was not unaware of it. Humbly submissive to the will of God, and always full of tenderness for the people committed to his care, he addressed himself thus to the Lord: "O Lord God! who knowest the hearts of all men, vouchsafe to give a leader to the children of Israel, that they may not be like sheep without a shepherd, but may have a guide to lead them into the lands of their enemies and to command them in the day of battle." "Take," said the Lord to him, "Josue, the son of Nun; to him I have communicated, as to you, the plentitude of my Spirit; present him to the high priest Eleazar, before all the multitude; and lay thy hands upon him, as a sign of the choice which I have made of him."

No choice could have been more in accordance with the views of Moses, nor any man better suited to the holy nation. During forty years, Josue had been the disciple and the friend of the holy legislator. Being now ninety-three years of age, he had had ample opportunities of studying in the school of his great master. His uprightness, his bravery, his advanced years, all recommended his selection to the approval of the children of Israel. Moses fulfilled the orders of the Lord, laid his hands upon Josue, and began to share those duties of government with him which he should soon surrender entirely to him.

Last farewell and death of Moses.—Like a father who is about to die, and whose heart overflows with tenderness for the beloved family whom he must soon leave forever, Moses desired, as a last consolation, to secure for the children of Israel a long and prosperous future. Accordingly, he made them renew the oft-repeated promise of being faithful to the Lord. He then assembled the multitude around him, and addressed them thus: "Hear me,

O children of Israel! and choose one of the two portions which the Lord directs me to lay before you. If you observe the law of your God, you shall be the greatest, the happiest, the most illustrious of all the nations of the earth—you shall be laden with the choicest blessings; the rest of the world shall tremble before you; the treasures of heaven shall be open to you; gentle dews and abundant rains shall fertilize your fields in their season; and all mankind shall learn from your prosperity that you are the dearly beloved of the Most High.

"If, on the other hand, you fail in your promises, you shall be the disgrace and the mocking-stock of the world; the heavens above you shall be turned into brass, the earth beneath you into iron; instead of the dew and the rain, you shall behold your lands covered with a dry and scorching sand; you shall be exiled, banished, scattered through every region of the world. You would not choose to serve the God of your fathers in joy and abundance: you shall serve both his and your enemies. But you shall serve them in hunger, and thirst, and nakedness; having cast away a light yoke that was your honor, you shall bear a yoke of iron that shall crush you. I call heaven and earth to witness what occurs this day: I have concealed nothing, I have dissembled nothing from you; I have placed life and death before you. Ah! choose, then, blessings for yourselves, your children, and your children's children." Such were the parting words of Moses to his people.

While the assembled Israelites remained as they were in silence and consternation, the holy old man withdrew from the multitude, and, taking with him Eleazar and Josue, whom he wished to be witnesses of his death, as he himself had been a witness of his brother's, he ascended the mountain of Nebo. There, from the highest point, called Phasga, the Lord ordered him to cast his eyes over the Land of Chanaan. He considered it all, on each side of the Jordan. "This," said the Lord to him, "is the beautiful country which I swore to Abraham, to Isaac, and to Jacob, to bestow on their posterity: I am about to fulfill my promises. Thou hast seen the land with thine eyes, but thou shalt not enter into it."

When the Lord had concluded these words, Moses, 120 years old, but still so strong and healthy that he felt none of the infirmities of age—his eyes were not dimmed and his teeth were not loosened—yielded up his soul to God, and delivered over his body to his two faithful friends, Eleazar and Josue.

Moses, the twelfth figure of the Messias.—This great man is one of the most perfect figures of the Messias. Thus, when Moses was born, a cruel king was causing all the children of the Hebrews to be put to death; when our Lord was born, Herod ordered all the children in Bethlehem and its neighborhood to be put to death. Moses escaped the fury of Pharao; our Lord escaped the fury of Herod. Moses was brought from his family to the court of the king of Egypt; our Lord was reared for a time in Egypt, a foreign land. Moses, having attained man's estate, returned to the Israelites, his brethren; our Lord returned to the Jews, his brethren, in Palestine. Moses was chosen by God to deliver the Israelites from the slavery of Pharao; our Lord was chosen by God, his Father, to deliver all men from the slavery of the devil. Before making himself known to his brethren, Moses passed forty years in the desert; before manifesting himself to the world, our Lord spent thirty years of his life in obscurity and forty days in the desert.

Moses wrought great miracles, to prove that he was the envoy of God; our Lord wrought great miracles, to show that he was not only the envoy, but the true Son of God. Moses commanded the sacrifice of the paschal lamb; our Lord, the true Paschal Lamb, sacrificed himself, and commanded his apostles and their successors to continue this sacrifice to the end of time. Moses leads the Hebrews through the Red Sea, and thus separates them from the Egyptians; our Lord leads his people through the salutary waters of baptism, which separates Christians from infidels. Moses leads the Hebrews through an immense desert toward a country flowing with milk and honey; our Lord leads Christians through the desert of this life toward the true land of promise—heaven.

Moses supplies his people with food from heaven; our Lord nourishes Christians with a living bread come down from heaven. Moses gives his people a law; our Lord gives Christians a more perfect law. Prodigies of power, which strike fear into the hearts of the people, accompany the publication of the Mosaic law; prodigies of sweetness and mercy, strongly inviting the heart to love so good a Redeemer, accompany the publication of the Christian law. Moses frequently appeases the anger of God raised against the Jews; our Lord continually appeases the anger of his Father raised against mankind. Moses offers the blood of victims, to ratify the old covenant; our Lord offers his own blood, to ratify the new covenant The law of Moses is intended only for a time; the law of our Lord shall endure to the end of ages. Moses has not the happiness of leading the Hebrews into the promised land; our Lord, greater than Moses, opens heaven for mankind, leading thither with him all the just of the old law, and preparing places for all the just who shall live after him till the end of time.

This twelfth figure of the Messias leaves us nothing to desire; it reveals our Lord to us in the clearest manner.

PRAYER

O my God! who art all love, I thank thee for having so often pardoned my disobedience to thy holy law—and pardoned me, too, with a mercy greater than that with which thou didst formerly pardon the transgressions of the Israelites. Grant me henceforward a more steadfast fidelity in the observance of thy holy commandments!

I am resolved to love God above all things, and my neighbor as myself for the love of God; and, in testimony of this love, I will never deliberately commit a venial sin.

Lesson 31: Messias Foreshadowed: Josue

The promised land: Various names given to it.—Moses being dead, the people mourned for him thirty days. At the end of this time, Josue, the successor of Moses, undertook, by the order of God, that wonderful invasion which should make the Jews masters of a land promised to Abraham and his posterity, five hundred years before. But it will be useful, before entering into the history of this remarkable event, to say a few words on the country itself, a country so celebrated in the annals of the world.

The territory which the Israelites were about to enter is situated in Asia, and has borne many names. It was called a) "the Land of Chanaan," because it was occupied by the descendants of Chanaan, grandson of Noe—we count seven different tribes in it, who were vanquished by the Hebrews under the command of Josue; b) "the promised land," because Almighty God had promised Abraham, Isaac, and Jacob, to bestow it on their posterity; c) "Judea," after the captivity of Babylon, because the greater number of those who returned to settle in it belonged to the tribe of Juda; d) "Palestine," from the Palestines or Philistines, with whom, through commerce, the Greeks and Romans were acquainted before they knew the Jews; e) finally, "the Holy Land," a name given it by Christians, and which it bears to the present day, on account of the mysteries wrought there by our Lord for the salvation of the human race. Its extent is about 180 miles from north to south, and 240 from East to West. The only river that flows through it is the Jordan.

The Israelites, to the number of nearly 600,000 fighting men, had encamped on the banks of this river. From their position they could see the walls of Jericho, the first of their enemy's cities that lay in their way. Josue selected from among his bravest men two of especial ability and devotedness, and directed them to cross the Jordan secretly, to approach Jericho, to examine the whole neighborhood, and to return as soon as possible with a full account of the situation. The envoys found a fording-place, and reached the gates of the city at evening. They entered: but the difficulty was to find a place to pass the night. They spoke to a woman, whose name was Rahab: she received them. Important as was their secret, they thought that they might safely confide it to her. Their confidence was not misplaced. Rahab answered all their questions, and supplied them with all the information that they could desire. But lo! during their conversation, the gates of the city were shut.

In a short time, the noise of a tumultuous crowd approaching Rahab's house was heard. These were messengers, whom the king had sent to arrest the two Israelites. The latter could not enter the city so quietly, nor retire to their lodgings so cautiously, but the news soon reached the ears of the king. Rahab hastened to make them ascend to the roof of her house, where she covered them with stalks of flax. The king's messengers having entered, she answered them that there had, indeed, been two strangers in the house, but that they merely paid a passing visit.[523] Her words were believed.

Next morning, she went up to them, and asked, as a reward for her services, that when the Israelites should take Jericho, they would spare her and her family. The envoys promised it. She then fastened some long ropes to one of the windows of her house that looked out on the country, and the two Israelites descended with but little trouble to the foot of the wall. A couple of days afterward they reached the camp. They gave an accurate account of their adventures to Josue, and an order was immediately issued to the people to be in readiness to move the camp next morning. "Sanctify yourselves," said Josue, "for, tomorrow, the Lord will do wonderful things for you."

Passage of the Jordan.—At break of day the people advanced. The priests, bearing the ark of the covenant, marched first. The army, ranged in two columns, followed in admirable order. Having reached the banks of the Jordan, the priests, though alarmed at the depth of the river, advanced until their feet were dipped in the water. But God had spoken. At this moment the upper waters of the river stopped in their course, and began to swell up like a great mountain, while the lower waters swept off out of sight. An immense passage was thus made free. The ark was kept in the midst of the bed of the river, and the multitude passed over to the opposite bank.

Then the Lord said to Josue: "Choose twelve men out of the twelve tribes of Israel, and say to them: 'Go to the place where the feet of the priest stand in the bed of the river, and take twelve large stones, which you shall carry to your first place of encampment. There you shall pile them in a heap; and, when your children shall one day ask you: What is the meaning of this monument in your fields? You shall answer them: When we were passing the Jordan to take possession of the land that we now inhabit, the ark of the Lord, borne on the shoulders of the priests, stood in the river; and the waters, stopped by its presence, gave us an open way.'"

Taking of Jericho.—The order of the Lord was executed, and the river, on the departure of the ark, at once resumed its ordinary course. Soon the multitude came in sight of Jericho. It was one of the largest and best fortified cities in Chanaan. The Lord said to Josue: "I have delivered Jericho, its king, and all its inhabitants to you. To gain the victory will cost you nothing but obedience. This is what you shall do. Place your soldiers in battle array: let them march before the ark of my covenant, which shall be borne by four priests of the tribe of Levi. Seven other priests, each with a trumpet, shall also precede the ark; and the multitude shall follow it. In this order, you shall march for seven successive days around the walls of Jericho: every one shall observe strict silence—no other sound shall be heard but that of the trumpets; the seventh and last time that you shall make the circuit of the city, the whole multitude of the children of Israel, when they hear the trumpets sounding with a longer and shriller tone, shall raise a loud shout; at that moment, the walls of the city shall fall, even to their foundations, and every one shall enter opposite the place where he stands."

Josue acquainted the army with the orders of the Almighty. "Remember," he added, "that the city is anathematized. No person must take anything for himself. The least prevarication on this point will bring misfortune on us all." These precautions having been taken, the people began their task; and, on the seventh day, as the Lord had announced, the walls of Jericho fell with a frightful crash. The city was sacked, burnt, and wasted to its very foundations. There was no one spared except the hospitable Rahab and her family.

Punishment of Achan. — After a few days' rest, Josue resolved to proceed to a new conquest. He sent three thousand men to lay siege to a little city, named Hai. The Israelites were defeated. The holy general understood that the Lord was displeased with them. Immediately he hastened to prostrate himself before the ark of the covenant, and there he remained during the whole day. At length the Lord heard his prayer, and said to him: "Israel hath sinned. The conditions of my covenant have been violated. Some of the spoils of Jericho have been carried away and hidden in the baggage. Assemble the people: casting lots will acquaint thee with the guilty. Thou shalt condemn him to the stake, and all that belongs to him shall be cast into the fire along with him." The lot fell upon Achan, of the tribe of Juda. "My son," said Josue, in the mildest manner, "what hast thou done?" "I have sinned," answered Achan, "among the spoils that came in my way I noticed a scarlet cloak that looked very fine, and I found two hundred sides of silver, and a bar of gold weighing fifty sides: these riches tempted me; I took them away secretly, and, having dug a hole in the midst of my tent, hid them there."

Josue informed him of the sentence that the Lord had pronounced against him; and, on the spot, it was executed. This is an example which teaches us that we are all sharers in the same responsibility — that if the good works of the just are most powerful in drawing upon their brethren the benedictions of heaven, the crimes of the wicked are no less so in provoking its chastisements. The glory of the Lord having been repaired, Josue did not hesitate to advance against the enemy. The little city of Hai was taken, and treated as Jericho had been: it was then that this holy leader renewed the covenant of his people with God. This renovation was accompanied with ceremonies that were well calculated to strike the multitude with awe, and to render them steadfast ever afterward in their allegiance.

Renewal of the covenant. — The nation was divided into two equal parts. One occupied the mountain of Garizim; the other, the mountain of Hebal. In the valley that separated them, stood the priests, with the ark of the covenant. The tribes that were placed on one of the mountains pronounced, in a loud tone of voice, twelve formulas of blessing in favor of the faithful observers of the law, and as many formulas of cursing against its violators. The tribes placed on the opposite mountain answered, "Amen" — that is to say, "May those who are devoted to the law be rewarded! May those who are rebellious to the Lord be punished!" Thus, the first six tribes, raising their voice, exclaimed: "Cursed is the man who shall make idols, and adore them in his tent!" And the six other tribes raising their voice, replied: "Amen, so be it!" The same order was observed to the end of the twelve formulas of blessing and cursing. The Lord, represented by the ark, which was placed between the two camps, attended to receive and to confirm these terrible oaths.

Stratagem of the Gabaonites. — Meanwhile, the kings and the people of Chanaan, alarmed at the progress of the Israelites, had made a league to engage them with their united forces. The only persons that took a different resolution were the inhabitants of the city of Gabaon. Feeling no confidence in their strength, they had recourse to a stratagem, to defend themselves from the arms of the Israelites. They sent ambassadors to Josue in an equipage that might well make it supposed that such wayworn travelers came from a very distant country. They gave these messengers asses to carry provisions; enclosed some hard and broken loaves for them in sacks that were old and torn; and added a few leather wine bottles that were rent and sewed up again, and shoes that were covered with patches. In this condition the ambassadors set out. After a few hours, they reached the Israelite camp, and were admitted to an audience with the general and his officers.

"We come," said they, with every appearance of sincerity, "from a country that is very remote, to enter into an alliance with you. It is in the name of your God that we come. The account of the wonders of his omnipotence, of the great things that he did for you in Egypt, has reached even to us, notwithstanding the distance. Our ancients have commissioned us to come to you. They said to us: 'Take abundance of provisions, for the way is long.' You may judge of the length of the journey by the state in which you behold us. When we left home, the loaves that we brought were just baked and still warm. See! what remain to us today are broken into little pieces as hard as stones. These bottles, in which we placed our wine, were then quite new, and now, as you perceive, they are useless. Our clothes, our shoes, are so very much worn by the journey that we are ashamed to appear in your presence."

There was such an appearance of candor in the language of the Gabaonites that it seemed a cruelty to suspect them of the least fraud. The Lord was not consulted. The matter was not even thought worthy of deliberation. The general granted them peace. The treaty of alliance expressly declared that they should not be put to death. This was all that the Gabaonites desired. Congratulating themselves on their success, they returned to acquaint their fellow citizens with the news of their happy negotiation.

Victory of Josue. — The petition of the inhabitants of Gabaon displeased the kings of Chanaan. It was resolved that they should be made to repent of their singularity. Accordingly, their city was besieged. Josue, though he had discovered the fraud that had been practiced on him, hastened to assist his allies, and gained a brilliant victory over the five attacking kings: the Lord fought for him, by casting on the enemy a shower of hailstones, which killed an immense number. Meanwhile night approached; and it grieved Josue exceedingly to see so many of his opponents escaping. Seized with a sudden inspiration, he addressed himself to the Lord, in the presence of his soldiers; then, turning his eyes toward the sun, he exclaimed: "Move not, O sun, toward Gabaon!" The sun, or rather God, was pleased to obey the voice of a man, whom he had invested with his own authority. However wonderful such a miracle may appear, it need not disturb our faith. Nothing is difficult to the Almighty. It costs no more to him who launched the heavenly bodies into the wide ocean of space to stop them than to move them. All creatures are in the divine hands like playthings in the hands of a child. The sun stood still for twelve hours. Josue profited of these precious moments, and completed the defeat of his enemies.

Death of Josue. — After six years of conflict, the illustrious general saw himself master of the Land of Chanaan, which he divided among the twelve tribes of Israel. The holy old man had now accomplished his mission. Feeling himself about to die, he caused the covenant with the Lord to be renewed, gave the wisest advice to his people, and slept in peace, being 110 years old.

This great man, the worthy successor of Moses, deserved the praise of the Lord; but his chief glory, as indicated by his name, was to have been a figure of him who should one day be the Savior of mankind.

Josue, the thirteenth figure of the Messias. — Josue is the thirteenth figure of the Messias. The word *Josue* means "Savior"; the word *Jesus* means "Savior." Josue succeeds Moses, who cannot lead the Hebrews into the promised land; our Lord also succeeds Moses—his new law replaces the old law—he alone can lead men into heaven. Josue triumphs in a miraculous manner over the enemies of his people; our Lord, by his miracles, triumphs over the world, which is opposed to the establishment of Christianity. Josue arrests the sun on the point of setting; our Lord arrests the torch of truth on the point of being extinguished, and illumines the world with the bright rays of the gospel. Josue is obliged to contend for several years against idolaters, the enemies of his people; our Lord is obliged to contend for several years against paganism, the enemy of his doctrine.

After six years of struggles, of battles, and of victories, Josue establishes his people in the promised land; after three years of struggles, our Lord establishes his Church, which reigns over the world. Josue dies after having given the wisest counsels to the Hebrews; our Lord ascends to heaven after having given the most admirable lessons of wisdom to his disciples and the world. As long as the children of Israel are faithful to the words of Josue, they are happy; while Christians are faithful to the words of our Lord, they are happy. As soon as the Israelites abandon the directions of Josue, they become the slaves of their enemies; when we renounce the precepts of our Lord, we become the slaves of the devil and of our own passions.

This figure unveils a new characteristic of the Messias. It teaches us that he will lead the human race into heaven, represented by the promised land.

PRAYER

O my God! who art all love, I thank thee for having established thy people in the Land of Chanaan, and for having caused me to be born in the bosom of the Catholic Church. Lead me to heaven, the true promised land, where I may praise and love thee, without fear of ever losing thee, for all eternity!

I am resolved to love God above all things, and my neighbor as myself for the love of God; and, in testimony of this love, I will never do anything from a merely human motive.

Lesson 32: Messias Foreshadowed: Gedeon

Division of the promised land; government of the judges.—After a war of six years, nearly the whole of the promised land was taken from its ancient inhabitants. Possessed by the Israelites under a title of absolute sovereignty, it was divided into twelve little provinces or counties, which formed henceforward the patrimony of the people of God. Each tribe had its own portion, the tribe of Levi excepted. This tribe, being consecrated to the service of the altar, had no share in the division. God was pleased that the Levites should be scattered through all the districts, in order that, by their example and discourse, they might move their brethren to the worship of the Most High, and preserve among all classes the knowledge of the true religion, together with a remembrance of its benefits.

Caleb and the ancients governed after Josue; but neither the wisdom of their administration nor the lustre of their example could prevent the disorders into which the ungrateful Israelites soon plunged. Forgetful of the benefits of the Lord, the chosen people made alliances with the neighboring nations, and joined in their idolatry. The Lord speedily avenged this violation of a covenant so frequently ratified.

When we reflect on the astounding miracles of which the Israelites had been witnesses, on the wonderful benefits with which they had been favored, and on their oft-renewed promises of fidelity to God and his holy law, their reiterated revolts against the Lord seem almost incredible. But let us reflect a while on our own resistance to the lights of faith and the strongest inspirations of grace—let us consider the scenes of stubbornness or weakness, sometimes whimsical, sometimes scandalous, that even in the present day are continually repeated before our own eyes—and we shall learn not to be surprised at the obduracy of the human heart.

Josue had not destroyed all the Chanaanites. A very large number of them still dwelt in various parts of the promised land. God was pleased that it should be so, in order to keep the Israelites exercised; to make them, by their fidelity in the midst of idolaters, deserve the favors which he desired to bestow upon them; and, also, that he might employ these same Chanaanites as a scourge to punish his people in case they should prevaricate. This is the manner in which God allows us to struggle with temptations, that our virtue may be proved, and that we may meet with opportunities of increasing our merits.

Israel falls into idolatry.—The Israelites did not long resist the trial to which the Lord subjected them. They fell into idolatry: and one of the chief persons in setting them the example was a woman. She belonged to the tribe of Ephraim, and was advanced in years, a widow, and apparently of comfortable circumstances, but superstitious. She had put aside a considerable sum to supply herself with false gods, after the manner of the Chanaanites. She had a son called Michas, as superstitious as herself. They both had recourse to a skillful artificer, and he made them idols, which they placed in one of their rooms. It only remained to find a priest somewhere, who should burn incense and offer sacrifice before these idols. Michas was not long in finding one out. The artificer that could make good could well supply a minister for them: his eldest son became the priest.

It was indeed a great misfortune for Israel that a single family should dare to raise the standard of idolatry; for, though it was but a spark, it gradually enkindled a flame, which, in the course of a few years, spread over, and included in its range, the greater portion of the nation. Idolatry soon led the way to new crimes. To punish a people so frequently rebellious, the Lord summoned against them a number of Chanaanite kings, who still existed in the promised land: Israel became their slave. Misfortune opened the hearts of the Israelites to repentance, and the Lord, ever merciful, raised up some eminent personages, whom he invested with a divine commission to break the fetters of his wayward people. Such is the history, in a few words, of the Hebrews under the government of the judges, that is to say, from the death of Josue till the appointment of Saul, their first king. One of these extraordinary men, whom God raised up for the deliverance of his people, was Gedeon.

During seven years, the Israelites had been oppressed, in punishment of their idolatry, by the Madianites and Amalekites. These people plundered and desolated the country, so that the misery which ensued was extreme. The Israelites then returned to the Lord. He was moved by their tears, and despatched one of his angels to choose a liberator for them. The angel assumed the appearance of a traveler, and took his seat under an oak tree, not far from the place where Gedeon, a man of mature age, was working.

Gedeon is raised up by God for the deliverance of Israel from the Madianites.—In expectation of an approaching irruption of the enemy, he was arranging, like every one else, for flight, and preparing provisions for his family. He was at the moment engaged in thrashing and cleaning wheat. The angel saluted him, saying: "The Lord is with thee, O most valiant of the children of Israel!" "If, my lord," answered Gedeon, "the Lord is with us, why are we a prey to all the evils that overwhelm us?"

The angel, with a very sweet look, then said: "No, the Lord hath not abandoned you; he hath chosen thee to deliver his people from the persecution of Madian." "If that is the case," replied Gedeon, "grant me, O my God! some sign by which I may know that it is thou that speakest to me. Whoever thou art, my lord, wait here until I bring thee something to eat." Gedeon soon returned with a kid and some loaves of unleavened bread. "Take the flesh and the bread," said the angel of the Lord, "and lay them on the rock before thee." Gedeon obeyed. The angel, with the tip of the rod that he held in his hand, touched the flesh and the bread; and a fire sprang forth from the rock and consumed the holocaust. At the same time, the angel vanished. Gedeon no longer doubted of his vocation.

Double miracle of the fleece.—Meanwhile a host of Madianites and Amalekites were ready to burst in upon the territories of the Israelites. More than 135,000 men, accompanied with innumerable flocks, had passed the Jordan, and were quietly settled in the beautiful valley of Jezrael. The Spirit of God took possession of Gedeon. This man summoned around his person all the heroes of Israel. He was instantly obeyed; and, in a few days, found himself at the head of 32,000 men. To fill them with confidence, he besought the Lord to favor him with some miraculous signs, which might prove to his army that he was a general commissioned by heaven. "O Lord!" said he, in a loud voice, before his officers and soldiers, "if it is true that thou hast resolved by my means to save Israel, grant me the proof that I have chosen regarding the source of my mission! I will stretch out here a fleece of wool. If the fleece alone be wet with dew, and the ground around it remain dry, I shall know that thou hast selected me."

The thing was done. The fleece was stretched out; and, next morning, Gedeon, rising before day, found the ground perfectly dry, but the wool so wet that he wrung a large quantity of water out of it. Gedeon was not content with this first miracle. "O Lord! " he said, "let not thine anger be enkindled against me if I ask of thee another prodigy, the reverse of the first, in regard to the fleece: I desire that the earth should be covered with dew and the fleece remain dry." The Lord again complied with the wishes of his general: the fleece remained dry, while the earth around it was covered with dew.

Victory of Gedeon. — The Lord, who had honored Gedeon with such evidences of almighty power, presently required of him some similar prodigies of confidence, and was satisfied. By the divine command, Gedeon set out during the night to encamp at the head of his 32,000 men near the valley of Jezrael. The Madianites were scattered through the valley, to the number of 135,000, as already stated. Even thus there was a very great disproportion between the two armies; but God considered that Gedeon had still too many men.

"Thou hast too numerous an army," said the Lord to him, "Madian shall not be delivered into thy hands; Israel would attribute to itself the honor of its deliverance, and my glory would suffer in consequence. Assemble thine army, and, according to the ordinance of the law,[524] proclaim aloud, through all the ranks, that thou dost not only permit, but command, every man who feels afraid to return to his house." More than two-thirds of the men quitted the army; in other words, there remained only 10,000 troops with Gedeon.

"There are still too many," said the Lord to him; "lead thy 10,000 men to the banks of a stream: I wish to try them there." The general obeyed. The soldiers marched for a portion of the day; and all were at length weary with the trouble of the journey, and especially with thirst. When they had reached the river, the Lord said to Gedeon: "Among thy soldiers, there are some who will go down on their knees to drink the water at their ease, and others who will only carry a few drops of it to their mouths in the hollow of their hands: separate these two classes from each other."

Of the 10,000 men on whom the general had counted, there were only 300 who did not stoop to drink, and who contented themselves with swallowing, as they marched along, the small quantity of water that they could lap up in their hands. Gedeon put them aside. "By these 300 men," said the Lord, "I will deliver my people: send the others away." The 9,700 disbanded men departed under the shadow of night.

Gedeon, with the 300 brave men who remained to him, encamped on a rising-ground near the stream, and above the army of Madian, which occupied the valley. In the middle of the night, the Lord called the general, and said to him: "I wish to inform thee that thy enemies look upon themselves as men already conquered, whom I have delivered into thy hands. Go down quietly with one of thy servants, and thou shalt hear their discourse." Gedeon, accompanied by Phara, crept along, without being perceived, as far as the advanced guard of the enemy, where he could hear the conversation of the sentinels. One of them addressed his comrade thus: "I dreamt that I saw a barley loaf baked under ashes: it seemed to me to roll from the top of the hill into our camp; I saw it pass even to the general's camp, which it threw to the ground." "That is a serious dream," answered the Madianite soldier, "this is undoubtedly its meaning: the barley loaf is Gedeon, the Israelite; the God, whom he adores, hath delivered Madian to him: we are lost men."

Gedeon, having heard this dream and its explanation, thanked the Lord, and took his way back to the camp. "Arise," he said to the soldiers, "it is time to act; the Madianites are ours! Let every man take in one hand a trumpet, and in the other a pitcher, with a lighted lamp inside. The sound of my trumpet shall be your signal. When you hear me sound it, you shall all sound your trumpets too; we shall then strike, with a loud noise, our earthen pitchers one against another; afterward, holding the lamps aloft in our left hands, we shall keep steadily sounding the trumpets held in our right, and from time to time shout together: 'The sword of the Lord and the sword of Gedeon!'"

Thereupon they set out and reached the enemy's camp from three different points. On the signal being given, all the trumpets sounded, the pitchers were broken, and the lamps were held up high. Loud above the confusion was heard at intervals the war cry: "The sword of the Lord and the sword of Gedeon!" They did not move; they merely continued to sound their trumpets and to cry out alternately.

A panic spread through the enemy's camp. All was tumult and disorder; every one fled whithersoever he could; in the darkness of the night they encountered and slew one another, without knowing what they did; and, in a few hours, the valley of Jezrael was red with the blood of Madian, of which Israel had not shed a single drop. Whoever escaped the slaughter made haste to recross the Jordan.

After having delivered his people from their enemies, Gedeon thought of uprooting idolatry, which had drawn so many calamities on Israel. If he did not entirely succeed, he at least made crime hide its head, and deprived it during the rest of his days of that scandalous liberty which so surely provokes the vengeance of God. Gedeon ruled over the people for forty years, after which he slept in peace, full of days and merits. Though glorious in his exploits, he was still more glorious in his resemblance to the Messias, of whom he is the fourteenth figure.

Gedeon, the fourteenth figure of the Messias. — Thus, Gedeon is the youngest brother of the family; our Lord is pleased to become the last of men. Gedeon, notwithstanding his weakness, is chosen by God to deliver the Hebrews from the tyranny of the Madianites; our Lord, notwithstanding his apparent weakness, is chosen by God to deliver the world from the slavery of the devil. Gedeon, before delivering his people, offers a sacrifice; it is only after having offered himself in sacrifice on the cross that our Lord delivers mankind. Two great miracles prove that the Lord has chosen Gedeon; more stupendous miracles prove that our Lord is the liberator of the human race. By the first miracle performed in favor of Gedeon, the fleece alone is wet with dew, while the ground around it remains dry; the Jewish people alone are bedewed by our Lord with the special benedictions of heaven. By the second miracle performed in favor of Gedeon, the fleece alone remains dry, while all the ground about it is wet with dew; in punishment of their ingratitude, the Jews are deprived of the heavenly dew, while all other nations receive it, through the ministry of the apostles, commissioned by our Lord.

Gedeon marches with three hundred men against a host of enemies; our Lord marches with twelve poor fishermen to the conquest of the world. The soldiers of Gedeon do not stop to drink; the apostles of our Lord, desirous to convert the world, forget even the ordinary wants of life, and despise all earthly comforts. The soldiers of Gedeon advance without arms; the soldiers of our Lord are unacquainted with weapons. The soldiers of Gedeon carry only trumpets and torches; the apostles of our Lord carry the trumpet of preaching and the torch of charity. The soldiers of Gedeon triumph over the Madianites; the apostles of our Lord triumph over all men. Idolatry is much weakened by Gedeon; it is destroyed by our Lord.

This figure, adding to our previous knowledge, teaches us that our Lord shall employ the weakest instruments for the salvation of the world, and that the Gentiles shall take the place of the Jews.

PRAYER

O my God! who art all love, I thank thee for the great mercy which thou didst so many times display toward thy people, notwithstanding their infidelities! I owe thee no less gratitude for the great mercy which thou hast displayed toward myself. How many times hast thou forgiven me! I purpose henceforward to be faithful to thee at all costs, as the soldiers of Gedeon remained faithful to their leader in spite of thirst and fatigue.

I am resolved to love God above all things, and my neighbor as myself for the love of God; and, in testimony of this love, I will every day deprive myself of something or other in expiation of my sins.

Lesson 33: Messias Foreshadowed: Samson

The Israelites relapse into idolatry.—The faithful Israelites bewailed the death of Gedeon when he was taken from amongst them. They did not feel the greatness of their loss until their miserable relapse into idolatry awakened them to a lively sense thereof, by the calamities that were its just consequences. They offered incense to their idols. They renounced their alliance with the God of Abraham and Isaac and Jacob, to make sacrilegious treaties with Baal, whom they swore to recognize as their God. The revolution was so sudden and rapid that we could scarcely believe it possible, if our acquaintance with the previous inconstancy of the Hebrews did not teach us that we should never again be astonished at their perfidy.

They are reduced to slavery by the Philistines; they have recourse to the Lord.—The punishment of their prevarications was not long delayed. The Philistines, an idolatrous nation, who occupied a little canton of the promised land, reduced them to a state of the most humiliating dependence. The Hebrews were deprived of arms. Not an iron or steel tool was left in their possession. If any one desired to have his ploughshare sharpened, he should have recourse to the Philistines, no matter in what part of Israel he dwelt. Such was the new kind of slavery that the Israelites had to endure for twenty years. They then cried to the Lord. But their past fickleness required a long proof; the Lord should put their sincerity to a severe test: accordingly, their slavery continued for twenty years longer. Yet, during this period a new judge, whom God gave them for their comfort, greatly sweetened the bitterness of their sufferings, and, toward the close of his days, so terrified the enemies of his people that the yoke of the Philistines seemed entirely broken and the liberty of Israel restored.

Samson is sent to deliver them.—This new judge—so different from all preceding saviors of Israel—this powerful warrior, who, without companions, and without arms or soldiers, could alone engage in deadly struggle with a whole people, was the celebrated Samson, so famous in the history of the people of God. He was miraculously granted to the prayers of his father and mother. The Lord blessed the child, by giving him prodigious strength of body, and by revealing to him the great deeds that he should afterward perform as liberator of the Israelites from the yoke of the Philistines. Samson knew that he was born to be their scourge, that he possessed over them all the rights of the great master who sent him, that he was in no ways bound to follow the usual formalities of a declaration of war against these people, and that whatever he should do for the ruin of such idolaters would be acceptable to the Lord. Full of these high thoughts, he had no sooner attained the age of twenty years than he set himself earnestly to work.

He made a journey to the Philistines, and, that he might have an opportunity of inflicting on them the injuries which they deserved, he resolved to marry among them. His father and mother gave their consent, for they were not ignorant that it was the Lord who brought this matter about. Yet they accompanied their son to regulate the terms of the contract. As they approached the city, they entered a vineyard, where Samson wandered a little out of his way. It was here that the first trial of his prodigious strength took place.

He perceived a young lion, which came bounding toward him with fury in its eyes, raging and roaring. Samson had no weapons, not even a staff, at hand; but, animated by the Spirit of God, he seized the animal, and tore it to pieces with as much ease as if it were only a kid. He did not say one word afterward regarding this affair to his father or mother.

The marriage arrangements having been concluded, Samson was returning to his own country; and, passing by the vineyard, he was anxious to see the carcass of the lion that he had slain. What was his surprise to find in the dead lion's mouth a swarm of bees and a honeycomb! The day of his nuptials soon came round: thirty young Philistines attended him on the occasion. "I wish," said he to them, according to the custom of the time,[525] "to propose a riddle to you, and I will allow you seven days to answer it. If you succeed, I will give you thirty suits of clothes; but if you fail, you will give me the same number." The spirit of the young Philistines would not allow them to decline the challenge: they agreed to the wager. "This, then," said Samson, "is the riddle: 'He who hath eaten hath supplied meat; and sweetness hath come forth from strength.'" The riddle would have been easy to anyone who knew of Samson's encounter with the lion, and of the honey found afterward in its mouth; but no person had heard of this occurrence.

The Philistines put themselves in a fret; but it was to no purpose, for they could not make out the riddle. They then had recourse to Samson's wife. She could not at first overcome her husband's silence. At length, however, on the seventh day, she so wearied Samson by her importunities that he allowed himself to be conquered. Having explained the riddle to her, she, contrary to good faith, hastened to inform her countrymen of it. They immediately came to Samson, and, with an air of triumph, told him the secret of the riddle. "You are right," he said. "I have lost the wager; I will pay you." At that moment the Spirit of God came upon him: he rushed out of the city, slew thirty Philistines, and returned with their garments. After this frightful slaughter, he indignantly left his wife without bidding her farewell, and withdrew to his father's house. Some time afterward he learned that the woman, thinking herself despised, had married one of the young Philistines who had assisted at her nuptials. Samson felt that the insult was too keen to be allowed to pass unpunished; he therefore declared war against the Philistines in general.

He burns the crops of their enemies. — It was then harvesttime; and the ripened grain only awaited the hand of the reaper. Samson was musing on a species of revenge the like of which, perhaps, no one before had ever thought of. The land of Israel was infested with foxes; and travelers attest that, even at the present day, the inhabitants are often obliged to assemble in multitudes for the destruction of these ravenous creatures: otherwise the country would be ruined. Samson pursued the foxes, and captured three hundred of them. He fastened them in pairs by the tail, and placed a lighted torch in the knot. Thus arrayed, he set them free over the beautiful fields of the Philistines, which were ready to shed their grain. The maddened foxes ran everywhere, and set fire to such a variety of things in different places that it was impossible to extinguish the flames. The grainfields were completely burnt; and the fire spread through the vineyards and olive-fields. The loss could not be repaired, and famine was its consequence.

After this, Samson retired into a rocky cavern, in the territory of the tribe of Juda. The Philistines were not slow to suspect the author of their misfortune, or to discover the place of his retreat. They assembled an army, and encamped at a short distance from the cavern. Many of the tribe of Juda joined them. Three thousand men belonging to this tribe were despatched with an order to seize Samson. They found him in the cavern, and reproached him bitterly with the rashness of his revenge. "Of what do the Philistines complain?" he answered, coldly. "I treated them as they deserved." "Be that as it may," answered the soldiers, "we have come to arrest thee, and to deliver thee into their hands." "Swear to me," said Samson, "that you will not kill me, and I will at once surrender to you." The assurance that Samson asked was given him. They bound him with two new cords, brought him out from his fortress, and led him along to the camp of the enemy.

As soon as the Philistines saw him coming, they set up shouts of joy. They ran to seize their prisoner; but, although he was bound, he was by no means captured. The Spirit of the Lord seized on him; he burst his bonds, and, snatching up the jawbone of an ass, which was on the ground near him, he attacked the Philistines with such strength that in a short time he killed a thousand of them. The others took to flight, and their only trouble was to see who should first reach a place of safety.

Samson, the conqueror of his enemies, rested himself tranquilly under the shadow of the wings of the Lord. He had no sooner recovered his strength than he thought of continuing his exploits against the enemies of his people. It is believed that during the twenty years which saw him a judge in Israel, he performed many valorous deeds that are not now known, and thereby rendered the Philistines much more tractable. What is certain is that the very sound of his name made them tremble.

He carries away the gates of Gaza. — One day he entered a city of the Philistines called Gaza; he was recognized and betrayed by the person into whose house he had retired. She gave notice to the citizens that she had captured the prey which they had so long endeavored in vain to destroy. The Philistines turned their information to account. They did not, however, dare to attack him, fearing lest, at the first sound they should make, the lion would awake and fill their city with bloodshed before they could lay hands on him. They contented themselves with closing fast the gates of the city, at which they placed guards during the night, with instructions to kill him, as he should be departing in the morning. Samson slept till midnight; he then arose and went to the gate of the city. It was on this occasion more than on any previous one that the superhuman strength of the hero of Israel appeared: he took the two sides of the gate, with its bolts and locks, laid them on his shoulders, and carried them away to the summit of a neighboring hill. Awakened by the noise, the sentinels did not feel any inclination to pursue him.

These actions appear very extraordinary to us; but they should necessarily be so, to strike the minds of a sensual, stupid people. In order to confound the pride of the Madianites, God had vanquished their army of 135,000 men with Gedeon's little band of 300, armed only with trumpets and torches; now, in order to punish the pride of the Philistines, he judges it proper to oppose against the whole nation only a single man; at a later period, the prodigy will be still more astounding, when he shall bring about the conquest of the world by twelve poor fishermen.

Moreover, if we examine the matter minutely, we shall find that these prodigies entered admirably into the general plan of divine providence. To preserve from idolatry a people living in the midst of idolatrous nations, inclined as that people was, from its own corrupt feelings, to join in the seductive worship of idols; and, to recall pagan nations to the knowledge of the one only God: such was, from the time of Noe to that of Moses, the great object and aim of God, the Creator and Father, who watches over all the children of men. Now, to attain this end, what means could be more efficacious than that of miracles? And what miracles could be better calculated to strike a gross ignorant people—mere children, in fact, who lived only by the senses—than prodigies that were wrought in the natural order, and that proved so clearly that the creatures which were adored as gods were only playthings in the hand of the one true God, and that that one only God was to be found in Israel?

His capture and death. — The Philistines, in despair of overcoming Samson by open force, had recourse to stratagem. They engaged a woman of their nation called Dalila, at whose house Samson frequently stayed, to draw the secret from him, and to find out from him whence his wonderful strength proceeded. "If thou discover it," they said to her, "we will give thee every one of us eleven hundred sides of silver." Dalila agreed. The next time she saw Samson she said very earnestly to him, "Tell me, I pray, whence does thy amazing strength come, and what are the fetters that would hold thee captive?" Such a question coming from a Philistine woman was not likely to surprise a sensible man. Samson was sufficiently wise not to betray himself. "If I should be bound," he said, "with seven good cords made of sinews not yet dry, my strength would vanish, and I could no more defend myself than other men could."

He had no sooner departed than she acquainted the Philistines with her discovery. A considerable number of them came to her house, bringing the cords that she had asked, for she had concealed her friends in a room adjoining that in which she received Samson. He came on the expected day, and had the condescension to permit the woman to bind him with the cords that he had mentioned. Immediately she began to cry out: "Save thyself, Samson; the Philistines are upon thee."

At the words of Dalila, the hero of Israel broke his bonds with the same ease as fire consumes a thread of tow. Dalila complained that he had deceived her. "Today, at least," she said to him, "tell me thy secret." Samson again set her astray. Dalila, however, continued to importune, without allowing him a moment's rest. Overcome by the entreaties and the tears of this perfidious woman, Samson at length yielded to the deplorable indiscretion that ruined him. "I am a Nazarite," he said, "consecrated to God from my youth. One of the engagements of my consecration is never to have my hair cut; a razor hath never touched my head. If my head were once shaved, my strength would forsake me."

Dalila immediately conveyed this important news to the princes of the Philistines. They assembled on an appointed day in the apartment adjoining that of Samson. He was asleep. Dalila had the seven locks of hair, in which his strength lay, removed. The operation having been performed, the wretch cried out: "Awake, Samson; the Philistines are upon thee!" Samson awoke; but, alas! the Spirit of the Lord had abandoned him: his strength was gone. The Philistines came forth from their hiding-place, loaded him with strong chains, tore out his eyes, and led him away to Gaza. There they cast him into a prison, where he was forced to turn a millstone.

After some time, the princes of the Philistines ordered a solemn feast in thanksgiving to their god, whose name was Dagon, for having delivered them from the scourge of the nation. All the great lords of the country came to Gaza. The temple was crowded for the sacrifice. The victims were very numerous. When the idolatrous rites had terminated, all classes set to work in preparing a banquet in the temple, which rang with the praises of Dagon. There was only one thing wanting to the feast to end it with general satisfaction. This was the presence of Samson, bound in chains and abandoned to insults. An order was immediately issued for his appearance.

A child led the poor blind man in his chains, and placed him between two pillars in the middle of the building. There he served as a pastime for the multitude. Samson, whose hair had begun to grow, felt his strength return; he did not appear to be offended at anything; the amusement, which delighted the spectators, continued for a long time; it even attracted new visitors, who occupied the recesses and the roof of the building, to share in the barbarous sport that was going on below. The number of newcomers alone, independently of the nobility and citizens that were at the tables in the temple of the idol, amounted to about three thousand persons, male and female.

It was a grand occasion to deliver Israel from its persecutors, and to strike such a mighty blow that all Palestine would be terrified. The Lord inspired Samson with this design, after having given him the strength to accomplish it. The generous hero was not dismayed at the thought of sacrificing his own life. Two principal pillars supported the roof of the temple. Samson, who was acquainted with the nature of the structure, said to the little boy appointed to guide him: "Allow me to touch the two large pillars upholding the temple, that I may lean against them and rest myself a little." Here he invoked the Lord his God. "Remember me, O my God!" he said. "Grant me strength that I may requite with one blow the twofold injury that they have inflicted on me, in tearing out my eyes; it is time that, avenging thy glory, I should punish their cruelty." Then, seizing the two pillars, he exclaimed: "Let me die with the Philistines."

At that moment he vigorously shook the pillars; and the temple, with a fearful noise, tumbled to the ground, crushing to pieces the princes of the Philistines and the rest of the multitude assembled in it. Samson perished beneath the ruins; but he had slain a greater number of the enemies of God at his death than during his whole life. His death completed the great work of the deliverance of Israel; and the day on which he buried with himself the tyrants of his people was properly that on which he merited the beautiful title of savior of his brethren and avenger of their wrongs. Accordingly, Samson has ever been regarded as a figure of the Messias.

Samson, the fifteenth figure of the Messias. —Samson was born in a miraculous manner; our Lord is born in a miraculous manner. Samson spends twenty years with his father and mother, without making himself known as the savior of his people; our Lord spends thirty years with Mary his Mother and Joseph his foster-father, without making himself known as the Savior of mankind. Samson takes a wife among the Philistines; our Lord chooses the Church, his spouse, among the pagan nations. Samson kills a lion which draws near to devour him; our Lord destroys the pagan world, which, like a lion, seeks for three centuries to devour the infant Church. Samson finds a honeycomb in the lion's mouth; our Lord now finds men of a charity and sweetness wholly celestial among pagans who were formerly the enemies of Christianity. Samson slays a thousand Philistines with the jawbone of an ass; our Lord overthrows the world with an instrument the weakest in appearance, namely, his cross.

Samson is imprisoned by his enemies in the city of Gaza; our Lord is imprisoned by his enemies in the tomb. Samson awakes at midnight, tears up the gate with its fixtures, and, in spite of the guards, marches away a conqueror out of the city in which he has been a captive; our Lord, after descending into limbo, where he breaks the gates of hell and death, comes forth full of life from the tomb in spite of the guards that surround it. Samson when dying overthrows the temple of Dagon; our Lord when dying overthrows the temple of the devil, that is, idolatry. Samson in his death does more harm to the Philistines than he has previously done them during his whole life; our Lord when dying does more harm to the wicked spirits and draws to himself a greater number of disciples than he has previously done during his whole life.

This figure adds three new touches to the picture of the Messias. It reveals to us a) that the Messias will be born in a miraculous manner; b) that he will choose the Church, his spouse, from among the Gentiles; and c) that by his death he will gain so complete a victory over the devil as thereby to crown all his works.

PRAYER

O my God, who art all love, I thank thee for having bestowed thy spirit of strength on Samson to effect the overthrow of the enemies of thy people; grant me the same spirit of strength to effect the overthrow of the enemies of my salvation.

I am resolved to love God above all things, and my neighbor as myself for the love of God; and, in testimony of this love, I will carefully avoid the occasions of sin.

Lesson 34: Messias Foreshadowed: David

Heli, judge of Israel. — After the death of Samson, the high priest Heli was judge over Israel. Heli was a man of irreproachable manners: but, by neglecting to correct the disorders of his two sons, Ophni and Phinees, he drew down upon himself, upon his family, and upon the people the most terrible vengeance of the Lord. In a battle with the Philistines, the Israelites were defeated; thirty thousand men were left dead upon the field; the holy ark of the covenant was taken by the enemy; the two sons of Heli were numbered among the slain, and their unfortunate father on hearing the sad intelligence fell back from his seat, broke his neck, and died.

Succeeded by Samuel; choice of kings. — Samuel was called by God to succeed Heli. After having gained a bloody victory over the Philistines, this great man restored the divine worship to its original purity, banishing out of Israel all the dumb divinities of the nations. We find in the government of the Israelites at this period an occurrence that furnishes us with a new proof of the ingratitude of this inconstant people. As we have already said, the judges were magistrates only in a republic of which the Lord was the head; but Samuel becoming old, the Israelites were dissatisfied with his mode of administration, and desired, after the example of the neighboring nations, to have a king to rule over them.

Saul, the first king of Israel, proves himself unworthy; David, a young shepherd, is selected in his stead. — The first was Saul. Two years after ascending the throne, he had the audacity to disobey God and to despise the laws of religion. For this conduct he was rejected and his crown placed on a more worthy brow. In the lifetime of Saul, David, a young shepherd of the tribe of Juda, was secretly elected his successor by Samuel, and, though only sixteen years of age, was consecrated king. The event took place in this wise:

One day the Lord spoke to Samuel: "Take," he said, "thy vessel of oil, and go to the old man Jesse at Bethlehem; it is for one of his sons that I intend the crown." Samuel went to Bethlehem, and there invited Jesse and his family to eat with him. "Bring thy sons before me," said he to Jesse. Jesse presented seven of them. "Are there no others?" said Samuel. "There is one more," said Jesse, "but he is a boy of fifteen or sixteen years, whom I have employed in guarding the flocks." "Send for him immediately," said the prophet, "we will not sit down to table till he comes." The little David arrived.

He was a handsome boy, of ruddy countenance and graceful figure. Scarcely had he appeared, when the Lord said to Samuel: "This is the king of Israel; consecrate him without delay." Immediately Samuel poured out on David's head the little vessel of oil that he had brought. From that day forth the Spirit of the Lord rested on David, having abandoned the unhappy Saul. The latter was about the same time attacked by a wicked spirit, which, by God's permission, violently tormented him. David's consecration remained a secret throughout the kingdom. Assured of a crown, which he should not wear till he was thirty years of age, David awaited it for fourteen years from the hands of God, without giving during that long period the least sign that he aspired to it.

David appeases Saul's anger. — Meanwhile, some of the officers in Saul's service, seeing their master cruelly troubled by the evil spirit, advised him to try the effect of music, as a solace for his melancholy. An order was issued to procure the finest harper in the kingdom. Saul quickly learned that David, one of the sons of Jesse, understood perfectly how to play the harp. He thereupon commanded the youth to be sent for. David arrived at court. The moment Saul beheld him, he felt a lively affection for him, and made him his armor-bearer. As often as the evil spirit molested Saul, David took his harp, and woke from its strings such exquisite sounds that the sufferer immediately grew better.

A few months after this, the Philistines declared war against the Israelites. The two armies came within sight of each other, and encamped on opposite mountains, which were separated by a deep valley. They spent a considerable time in preparations and threats of defiance. At length an event occurred that engaged the attention of both camps.

Combat between David and Goliath. — A man, belonging to the Philistines, came forth toward the Israelites and made a sign that he desired to speak to them: his name was Goliath. He was a giant of great height, and enormous strength, in proportion to his size. His very appearance might well strike terror into a whole army. He wore a helmet of brass and a breastplate of the same material. His legs were covered with brazen greaves, and on his shoulders lay a buckler of brass. The lance that he carried was of almost incredible weight: the iron alone in it weighed about three hundred pounds.

Thus arrayed, the giant, preceded by his armor-bearer, came within earshot of the troops of Israel, drawn up in battle array on the opposite mountain, and addressed his challenge to them. "Choose out among you a champion," he said, "and let him come down and fight me: if I be overcome, the Philistines shall be the slaves of the Israelites; but if I gain the victory, the Israelites shall be the slaves of the Philistines." Saul's army trembled with fear. They had to endure these insults for forty days, during which, every morning and evening, the hideous giant continued to hurl his defiant challenge amongst them.

David had not accompanied the army, having returned to the care of his father's flocks. He came, however, at last; and, on hearing of Goliath's insults, was indignant. "What reward will be given to him, who shall slay the Philistine?" asked the young shepherd. He was told that Saul had promised a magnificent reward. Full of confidence in the Lord, David appeared before Saul, and said, "I am ready to go and fight this Philistine." "Thou knowest not what thou sayest," answered Saul, "thou couldst do nothing against this monster: thou art only a boy, fit for tending the flocks, and he is a giant, who has had no other study from his youth than the use of arms." David insisted, saying, "I do not rely on my own strength or valor, but on the protection of the Lord."

So much courage and piety in a boy moved Saul. "Go, my son," said he, "and may the Lord be with thee! " He then placed his own helmet on David's head, clothed him with a coat of mail, and girded on him his own sword. David made a few steps to see whether he might not be too much embarrassed by his armor. "I cannot walk in this coat of mail," he said to Saul, "I am not accustomed to it." Hereupon, he laid aside his clumsy dress, lifted his crook, picked up five smooth pebbles out of the bed of the stream, secured his sling, took leave of the king, and marched to an encounter with the Philistine.

Goliath saw him advancing; but, when he perceived that his adversary was a mere boy, a youth of delicate complexion, remarkable, not for his soldier like appearance, but for his great beauty, he imagined himself insulted. Provoked at the sight of such a feeble opponent, he cried out in a voice of thunder: "Am I a dog, that thou comest forth to attack me with a staff? Draw nigh then, till I give thy body for food to the birds of the air and the beasts of the earth."

"I come in the name of the Lord of hosts," answered David, "in the name of the God of the armies of Israel, whom thou hast not been afraid to insult: it is he who will deliver thee into my hands, that all the earth may know that there is a God in Israel." David was still speaking, when the giant advanced to the combat. David, on his side, went forward to meet him. The two armies awaited in silence the issue of this wonderful engagement.

Instantly, David put his hand into his scrip, took out a pebble, placed it in his sling, and sent it flying against his enemy. It struck the giant in the middle of the forehead. The whirl was so vigorously made, that the stone went far into Goliath's head: the monster fell without a struggle on the ground. David ran up to him, pulled out his sword, and cut off his head.

Death of Saul. — The Philistines, terrified at the result of the conflict, took to flight; the Israelites pursued them with loud cries and made a frightful slaughter of them. David, on his return, was presented to Saul. He carried Goliath's head in his hand, as a trophy of his victory. Saul, accompanied by David and the army, returned to the interior of the kingdom. In all the cities through which they passed, the women came forth before the conqueror, and, dancing to the sound of musical instruments, exclaimed: "Saul has slain a thousand, but David has slain ten thousand Philistines!" This praise so much excited the jealousy of Saul that he endeavored to put David to death; but David escaped by flight. Some years afterward, Saul perished in battle. David was acknowledged king, first by the tribe of Juda, and afterward by the other eleven tribes of Israel. He began his reign by a glorious expedition.

David captures the fortress of Sion. — Jerusalem, the most beautiful, extensive, and powerful city in the promised land, had long been in the hands of the children of Israel. They had exterminated its inhabitants; but a portion of the latter had taken refuge in the "upper city," as it might be termed, situated on Mount Sion, of which mention is so frequently made in scripture. There they occupied a fortress so strong that their position was deemed impregnable. For nearly four hundred years, the Hebrews had in vain endeavored to obtain possession of it. David now laid siege to it, and summoned its inhabitants to surrender.

They answered him with raillery: "No, David, thou shalt not enter the citadel of Sion; we are so little afraid of thine efforts that we shall only oppose to thee the blind and the lame." David was not surprised at this insolent reply. He announced to his army that whosoever should be the first to scale the wall of Sion and slay those blind and lame men that were opposed to him, would be rewarded with the dignity of general of the whole army. Joab, a nephew of David, was the hero that merited this honor. The fortress was carried by storm; and David converted it into his palace. Accordingly, Jerusalem became the capital of the kingdom, the abode of royalty, and shortly afterward the seat of religion, the ark of the covenant having been solemnly removed to it.

Removal of the ark; Oza is struck dead. — David, who was still more remarkable for his piety than for his bravery, formed a design of placing the ark of the Lord in the citadel that he had just captured. When he made the proposal to his people, it was received with the utmost applause. He speedily caused a magnificent pavilion to be erected in his palace for the reception of the sacred deposit. Through every quarter of Palestine the people were invited to the ceremony at Jerusalem. The various tribes of Israel deputed thirty thousand chosen men to represent them on the occasion. David placed himself at their head, and was followed by almost the whole tribe of Juda. They ascended the hill on which was built the house of Abinadab, to whom the care of the ark had been confided. A new chariot, drawn by oxen that had never yet been yoked, was brought, and the holy ark was placed on it.

An immense concourse accompanied the procession. The king himself, surrounded by musicians, who played on various kinds of instruments, marched at their head, and from time to time caused the most beautiful canticles, composed by himself, to be sung. In this manner they drew nigh to Jerusalem, filled with such sentiments of joyous and devout enthusiasm as cannot well be expressed. But their happiness was soon disturbed by a very painful occurrence. The oxen yoked in the car became restless and pulled with violence; the ark leaned over to one side and appeared in danger of falling: a Levite named Oza stretched out his hand to support it. Now the law forbade simple Levites, under pain of death, to touch the ark of the Lord. To inspire the vast assembly with a due sense of the respect that the divine presence merits, Almighty God struck the rash man dead.

Seized with fear at the sight of this punishment, the king did not dare to bring the ark into his palace, according to his first intention. He resolved to leave it at the house of a virtuous man named Obededom. It remained there for three months, and was a source of many blessings to the good Israelite. David, encouraged by the account of the favors that accompanied the ark, resumed his former resolution of conveying it to his palace. But he took care that no precaution should be forgotten to render suitable honor to the holy deposit left in his charge.

David dances before the ark. — On an appointed day, the king arrived at the house of Obededom, with the ancients of Israel and the officers of the army. The priests took the ark on their shoulders, and, at every six steps, a victim was immolated. The king had laid aside his royal ornaments. He was clothed, like the Levites, in an ephod of fine linen. Leading the procession as before, and carrying his harp in his hand, he gladdened the multitude by his songs, in which he was assisted by seven choirs of musicians. All the voices and instruments joined in the responses. He himself danced before the ark, to express the joy of his heart. When at length it was deposited in the place prepared for it, the king terminated the event with costly sacrifices to the Lord. He likewise made presents to all the people.

These lively demonstrations of David's piety were not according to the taste of Michol, his wife. This princess had witnessed the procession from the window of her room. She considered that the royal dignity was degraded by the singing, playing, and dancing of the king, her husband, and especially by his laying aside the royal robes. David had believed that there should be no display of luxury in a religious assembly. She said to him sarcastically: "The king of Israel has done himself much honor today, by dancing like a buffoon before his subjects." David answered her: "Yes, I have danced before the Lord, who chose me to be the leader of his people; I will abase myself still more, and I will become contemptible in my own eyes, to honor him who is the sovereign master of kings and subjects." Such was the language of this great man, who understood better than any other earthly king how to unite the humility of a saint with the nobility of a monarch. For having mocked him, Michol was deprived of children the rest of her days.

So many honors, rendered to the ark of the covenant, did not yet satisfy the piety of the holy king. "I have a splendid palace," he said, "I dwell under ceilings of cedar, and the ark of the Lord is lodged under skins!" He then formed a resolution to build a temple worthy of the majesty of the God of Israel.

The sixth promise of the Messias is made to David. — As he was one day profoundly occupied with this design, the Lord spoke to him by the mouth of the prophet Nathan. It was the moment selected by the God of Abraham, Isaac, and Jacob, to renew the promise of the Messias. "Thou knowest," he said to David, "that since the day on which I delivered the children of Israel out of their captivity in Egypt, I have been a pilgrim like my people. I have accompanied them everywhere, and I have had no other abode than a tabernacle and a tent. Yet it will not be by thee that a temple shall be built for me: I reserve that honor for thy son. I will place upon thy throne a son that shall come forth from thee. I will establish his throne forever. I will be his Father, and he shall be my Son. Thy house shall subsist forever, and thy throne shall be eternal."

Who is this Son, promised by the Lord in such magnificent terms? Is it Solomon? No, since Solomon is not the son of God and the son of David at the same time; nor does eternity coincide with a mortal man or a temporal kingdom. Who, then, is the Son of David, here promised by the Lord? Evidently the Messias, our Lord. Our Lord alone is the Son of God and the Son of David at the same time. He alone is eternal. He alone is to sit forever on the throne of David, since it is as a God-man, the Son of God and the Son of Man, that he reigns, and shall forever reign, in heaven and on earth.

This promise assists us very much in discovering the Messias. The first promise, made to Adam, announces a Redeemer, without mentioning the time or place of his birth, or the people from whom he shall spring; the second, made to Abraham, informs us that he shall be born of the race of Abraham; the third, made to Isaac, teaches us that he shall be born of Isaac; the fourth tells us that he shall be born, not of Esau, but of Jacob; the fifth, uttered by the dying Jacob, warns us that he shall come of the tribe of Juda; and the sixth reveals to us that he shall belong to the family of David. Henceforward, all the nations of the world but the Jewish, all the tribes of Israel, and even all the families of the tribe of Juda, with the single exception of the family of David, are set aside: we need no longer seek the Savior of the human race anywhere but in the family of the holy king. This is the manner in which we gradually advance, until we lay our hand, so to speak, on the babe of Bethlehem.

PRAYER

O my God! who art all love, I thank thee for the graces with which thou didst load the holy king David, and especially for the promise which thou didst make to him regarding the Messias. Grant that I may resemble him in humility, in devotion, in gratitude for thy benefits, and in zeal against the enemies of my salvation!

I am resolved to love God above all things, and my neighbor as myself for the love of God; and, in testimony of this love, I will bend my knee when passing before the Blessed Sacrament.

Lesson 35: Messias Foreshadowed: David (Continued)

David sins; Nathan is sent to him. — Whilst David was rendering himself illustrious by his exploits and his virtues, this wise and virtuous ruler forgot himself for some time, and showed by his example how much reason all men have to distrust their own weakness, and how carefully they should guard against the occasion of offending God to which they are exposed. David committed two enormous crimes. He remained at enmity with God for the space of a year, so profound is the darkness that sin casts over even the holiest soul. But, while living in forgetfulness of God and of his duty, the Lord had compassion on him, and sent him the prophet Nathan to admonish him, that he might at length open his eyes and enter into himself.

The prophet discharged his commission fearlessly. "In punishment of thy double crime," he said to David, "the sword shall never depart from thy house; it is from thine own family that the Lord will choose the instruments of his vengeance: innumerable evils await thee."

David, struck by the words of the prophet, entered into himself and acknowledged his offense. Forgetting that he was a king, to remember only that he was a sinner, he condemned himself without any excuse. "I have sinned against the Lord," he exclaimed in sentiments of bitter and heartrending sorrow. He humbly accepted the misfortunes that Nathan foretold him should fall upon his family. The Lord, who never rejects a humble and contrite heart, informed him, by the mouth of the same prophet, that he had received him again to his friendship; but still, in the interests of the divine glory, and even in those of the penitent's salvation, David should make atonement for the crimes that had been pardoned him.

Absalom rebels. — Absalom, one of David's sons, rebelled against his father. By his efforts to render himself popular, he had succeeded in gaining the affection of a considerable number of his father's subjects. Every morning he was to be found at the gate of the palace, and when any Israelite made his appearance, to lay some business affairs before David, Absalom drew nigh to him and tendered him a thousand civilities. "Tell me," he would say, "what hath brought thee to the court?" Having satisfied his curiosity, he would continue: "Indeed, there is nothing in the world more just or reasonable than what thou art seeking. But what means hast thou of obtaining justice? The king hath not appointed anyone to hear the petitions of his subjects. If I had any authority in Israel to judge the cases of the king's subjects, all persons should have free access to me. I would listen to everyone. I would sacrifice my own ease for the general welfare. I would deliver just judgments." If any one saluted Absalom, the latter would give him his hand and embrace him. In short, he conversed so familiarly with all classes that no one left his presence without being charmed by the affability of his manners.

By this deceitful conduct, Absalom gained many partisans. When he thought that a favorable moment had arrived, he withdrew from Jerusalem, under pretext of making a journey to fulfill a vow: his followers accompanied him, and he had himself proclaimed king. When the news spread, a multitude of persons rallied to his standard, and he immediately marched on Jerusalem.

David quits Jerusalem. — To avoid greater evils, David resolved to seek safety in flight. Surrounded by his bravest soldiers, he bade adieu to his capital. He was then more than sixty years of age. He crossed the brook Cedron, and ascended the Mountain of Olives, his head veiled and his eyes bathed in tears. Meanwhile Absalom entered Jerusalem in triumph: nothing opposed his progress. David traveled on farther and farther. In this mournful journey, he drank the chalice of humiliation to the very dregs. One of Saul's descendants, a man named Semei, beholding the miserable condition to which the king was reduced by the Lord, wished to enjoy the cowardly pleasure of insulting him with impunity. He came out after David, and, as he followed, step by step, hurled the basest insults against him; he even had the audacity to fling stones at the king and his attendants. An officer in the service of David begged permission to return for a little to chastise such impudence. The holy king was content with this answer, "Let the man curse the poor culprit that the Lord punishes; it is God that employs Semei's malice against me; and who are we, that we should call the sovereign master to account for what he does?"

Defeat and death of Absalom. — Meanwhile, the sojourn of Absalom at Jerusalem gave David time to recover from his surprise and to recruit his strength. The rebels began at length to move and encamped at a short distance from the royal troops. Both sides prepared for the conflict. David intended to command in person, but the necessity of providing for the security of his life was strongly represented to him. A piece of intelligence that had arrived in David's camp served to raise his hopes of success. Achitophel, the very soul of the conspiracy, the counselor of Absalom, the man that had delivered to the son the father's crown, seeing himself despised, had gone and hanged himself in his own house.

Before sending his army to battle, David called his three generals together and said to them publicly: "Above all things, spare my son Absalom." The combatants immediately engaged. The army of the rebels was routed. Absalom, himself urged on by the fugitives, took refuge in a neighboring forest. He was met by the soldiers of David's army, who, remembering the injunctions of the king, deliberately allowed him to escape. He was mounted on a splendid mule, and rushed along at full speed. As he was passing under a large thick oak, his head caught in one of the spreading branches: either his neck fastened between two of the branches, or his hair, exceedingly strong, became so entwined among them as to attach him to the tree. The mule went on, and left its master hanging between heaven and earth.

He was seen in this condition by one of David's soldiers. The man ran quickly to Joab. "I have seen," said he to the general, "the king's son hanging from an oak in the forest." "Thou hast seen him," answered Joab, "and thou hast not run thy sword through his body! I would have given thee ten sides of silver and a belt." "Though thou shouldst have given me a thousand," replied the soldier, "I would not raise my hand against the king's son. We were all present when the king gave the order, above all things to save his son Absalom." "Since thou wilt not do it," said Joab, "I will do it myself." With these words, he took up three lances, and ran toward the place pointed out. There he found the miserable Absalom, drove the three lances into his heart, and, before the victim had yet expired or fallen from the oak, ten young men, armor-bearers of Joab, rushed to the scene, and completed the task with their swords. A terrible but just punishment on a son that had rebelled against his father!

The general immediately despatched a courier to David with the news of the victory. On his arrival, the courier cast himself on his knees before the king and exclaimed: "Blessed be the Lord God of David, who hath confounded all the rebels!" "But my son, Absalom," answered the king, "is my son alive?" While the first messenger awaited a reply, a second arrived confirming the news of the victory. "But thou sayest nothing of Absalom," remarked the king, "hath any evil befallen him?" "May all the enemies of the king, my lord," answered the courier, "be treated like that rebellious son!"

David understood the meaning of these expressive words. Heedless of victory, and thinking only of the death of his son, he made no inquiry as to the circumstances or the authors of the sad occurrence, but retired alone to his apartment. "My son, Absalom," he cried out, "Absalom, my son, would that I could die for thee!" Not a word fell from his lips but the name of his son. Distracted in mind, and with hood drawn over his head, he continued to repeat: "Absalom, my son; my son, Absalom!" O my soul! these touching words of David ought to remind thee of the much more tender lamentations of thy Savior, when thou hadst had the misfortune to lose the life of grace by sin. Canst thou again consent to sadden the heart of so good a Father?

Joab, offended at the little share that the king took in the joy of the recent victory, entered David's house, and dared to reproach him with loving those who hated him, and hating those who loved him. He obliged him to show himself in public, in order to receive the congratulations of his people on the victory that had just been won. David was merciful: but mercy has its limits. He forgave those who had taken part with his son. As for Joab, who had so insolently violated his commands, he gave an order, when dying, to Solomon, to put him to death. This order was duly executed.

A new fault committed by David. — David, having regained his throne, restored subordination throughout the districts that had been the scene of the rebellion. The peace that he now enjoyed made him fall into a new fault, less grievous, indeed, than those which God had so severely punished, but such, nevertheless, as drew upon his people a very great scourge. This memorable example teaches us that man, however just or penitent he may be, is always man, always exposed to temptation, always liable to fall. From a motive of vanity, David now wished to number his people. It was represented to him that this pompous numbering of the people would assuredly offend the Lord, and draw down new chastisements on Israel. The vanity of the great rarely permits them to give ear to counsel. David gave his orders, and the census was made. His vanity was scarcely satisfied, when he recognized his fault. The Lord forgave him, but upon conditions that he directed one of his prophets to announce to him.

"O king!" said the prophet, "these are the words of the Lord to thee: 'Thou shalt not escape the chastisement which thou deservest, but of the three scourges which I present to thee, thou mayst choose whichever thou pleasest. For three years thy kingdom shall be afflicted with a famine, or for three months thou shalt flee before thine enemies, or for three days a pestilence shall reign throughout Israel.'"

"I am cruelly perplexed," answered David, "but since necessity compels us, let us select that scourge with which the malice of men shall have least to do, for it is better to fall into the hands of God than into the hands of men." And David chose the pestilence. Immediately this terrible calamity burst out over the whole kingdom. Before the end of the third day, seventy thousand men had already perished. David, pierced with sorrow, lay prostrate on the ground, saying to the Lord: "It is I, O Lord, that have sinned; it is I that have done the evil. What mischief hath been done by these innocent sheep? Let thy blows fall upon me and upon my father's house; but, I beseech thee, spare thy people."

David's prayer was sincere: God could not resist it. The destroying angel was commanded to restore his sword to its sheath. Thus, for the fault of one man a whole nation was punished: so true it is, as we have already said, that if the just are all-powerful to draw upon their brethren the blessings of heaven, the wicked are no less so to provoke its punishments.

Death of David.—David was now approaching his seventieth year. His great labors had exhausted his strength; and his weakness warned him that his end drew nigh. He sent for Solomon, his son and successor, to give him his last instructions. "I am about to die, my son," he said, "take courage, and act as becomes a generous prince. Observe the commandments of the Lord thy God, that thou mayst deserve his blessings and strengthen thy throne."

After some further advice respecting the manner of government, David slept his last sleep, and was gathered to his fathers. He died full of days and merits, honored and beloved by his people, whom he had governed more as a father than as a king; and cherished by his God, whom he had had the misfortune to offend in the most prosperous periods of his life, notwithstanding a youth spent in toil and innocence, but with whom he had the happiness to be reconciled by the fervor of his repentance and the humility of his submission. He was a king according to God's own heart. He was not only an ancestor, but a prophet and a figure of the Messias.

David, the sixteenth figure of the Messias.—David was born at Bethlehem; our Lord was also born at Bethlehem. David pleased God, who chose him to be the king and the liberator of his people; our Lord was well pleasing to his heavenly Father, who chose him to be the King and the liberator of mankind. David was appointed to calm the fury of Saul, when the evil spirit took possession of him; our Lord was appointed to banish the evil spirits and to destroy their empire. David, armed with only a staff and a sling, marches against the giant Goliath, who for forty days has been insulting the army of Israel; our Lord, armed with his cross, marches against Satan, who, for four thousand years, has been insulting the human race. Goliath receives David with ridicule and scorn; the world and the devil contemn the apparent weakness of Jesus Christ, whose cross they regard as folly. Notwithstanding the disproportion between the physical powers of the combatants, David kills Goliath; notwithstanding the apparent disparity of forces, our Lord overcomes the world and the devil.

David is persecuted by Saul, to whom he nevertheless returns only good; our Lord is persecuted by the Jews and the world, to whom he likewise returns nothing but good. David opposes to Saul only meekness and patience; our Lord opposes to those who persecute him only meekness and patience. David twice spares Saul; our Lord continually spares his enemies. After more than thirty years of struggle and persecution, David is at length acknowledged king by all the children of Jacob; after thirty-three years of humiliation, labor, and pain, our Lord is at length acknowledged King of kings—after three centuries of suffering, his Church triumphs over the world—and, to the end of time, the Jews themselves will be gradually embracing his holy law.

David sins, and, to expiate his crime, he is obliged to flee from Jerusalem; our Lord is innocent, but, to expiate the crimes of the world, with which he charges himself, he is led out of Jerusalem. David, with tears flowing from his eyes, passes the brook Cedron; our Lord, with a heart brimful of sorrow, passes over the same brook. David ascends the Mountain of Olives barefooted; our Lord ascends the Mountain of Calvary as a criminal.

CATECHISM OF PERSEVERANCE (1 OF 4)

David is accompanied by a small band of faithful servants; our Lord is accompanied by his holy Mother, St. John, and a few other pious persons. David, in his affliction, is insulted by Semei; our Lord, on the cross, is insulted by the Jews. David forbids any evil to be done to the man that curses him; our Lord implores forgiveness for his murderers. Achitophel, who betrays David, hangs himself in despair, because he is despised; Judas, who betrays our Lord, hangs himself in despair, because he is despised by the priests of Jerusalem. David is inconsolable for the death of his son Absalom; our Lord is full of compassion for the sinner. David returns victorious, and receives the homage of his subjects; our Lord arises victorious from the tomb, and receives the worship of the whole world.

This figure supplies us with two new characteristics of the Messias: a) he shall be a King, but a King full of meekness; and b) it will only be through many tribulations, that he shall finally establish his kingdom.

PRAYER

O my God! who art all love, I thank thee for having with so much goodness pardoned the holy king David; vouchsafe to pardon me in like manner, and to grant me, with a heart ever contrite and humble, a great sincerity in the acknowledgment of my faults.

I am resolved to love God above all things, and my neighbor as myself for the love of God; and, in testimony of this love, I will never indulge in idleness.

Lesson 36: Messias Foreshadowed: Solomon

Solomon, king.—When David died, the first care of Solomon was to render, with all magnificence, the last tribute of respect to a father who had left him as an inheritance one of the fairest kingdoms on the earth. He buried him in the city of Sion, which has ever since borne the name of the city of David. Instructed by the lessons and the example of his virtuous father, Solomon began his reign with the faithful fulfillment of all the duties of a prince. Clemency toward his subjects, piety toward God, a wise distrust of himself, and an ardent love of justice raised the highest hopes regarding his administration. After the example of David, he considered it his glory to do honor to the Lord, from whom he held both his crown and his life.

His prayer to the Lord; he obtains wisdom.—He one day went to Mount Gabaon, where the tent, which Moses had made in the desert to cover the ark of the covenant, was still preserved. After a solemn sacrifice, offered in presence of all his court, Solomon withdrew to take a little repose. The Lord, moved by the tender piety of the young king, was not slow to recompense him. Appearing to him that night in a dream, he said: "What dost thou desire of me? Ask, and thou shalt be heard." "Ah, Lord!" answered Solomon, "Thou hast seated me on the throne of David, my father; but I am only a child, without experience, one that understands not how to guide or govern a great people: I ask of thee a docile heart, an upright mind, in a word, the wisdom necessary for government."

Desires so pure could not fail to be very pleasing. "Because thou hast asked this thing of me," said the Lord, "and not the goods that flatter the ambition and cupidity of kings, such as long life, riches, and glory, I grant thee what thou hast solicited, namely, wisdom, the like of which no one hath ever had before thee, and no one shall ever have after thee. To this favor, I will add what thou hast not asked, riches and glory."

At these words Solomon awoke. Animated with new fervor, he returned to Jerusalem, where he offered many sacrifices to testify his lively gratitude to the Lord. After a short time, he married the daughter of the king of Egypt, and built a magnificent palace.

In the meantime, abundance and peace reigned throughout the kingdom. While the neighboring nations purchased the friendship of the king by their embassies, tributes, and presents, the Israelites, protected from insults, enjoyed a happy tranquility. Every family assembled without fear under its own vine or fig tree, to celebrate its innocent feasts with joy. From one end of the kingdom to the other not a word was to be heard of troubles, of quarrels, of sterility, of indigence. The king had found sown the seeds of so many fruits of benediction on his elevation to the throne; it only remained for him to cultivate them in peace, to increase the splendor of a rich inheritance, and especially to carry into execution the great idea of the erection of a temple.

He begins the erection of the Temple.—He knew that it was to accomplish this mighty work, the Lord had placed the crown upon his head: he was, therefore, careful not to lose sight of it for a moment. One of his first acts was to address himself to the king of Tyre, whose name was Hiram, an old friend and ally of David's. "Thou knowest," he wrote, "that the king, my father, had formed the design of building a temple to the glory of his God, and that the continual wars in which he was engaged, during his reign, prevented him from carrying out his intention. I have taken up my father's resolution; but I stand in need of thy assistance in this great enterprise. I shall require excellent workmen, as well as a large quantity of cedar wood from Mount Libanus. I rely upon thee to furnish me with the same. For the rest, I do not at all mean that thou shouldst oblige me at thine own cost. Arrange the terms according to thine own desire: I will pay thee whatsoever thou pleasest." Hiram received the letter with much delight, and hastened to offer Solomon as many cedars and workmen as might be required. Solomon immediately put his hand to the work.

He employed 30,000 men to cut down trees, and prepare them for the carpenter. He sent them in turns of 10,000 men a month to Mount Libanus. Eighty thousand men were employed to hew stones, 70,000 to carry burdens, and 3,600 to superintend the works. All the stones were cut and polished before being removed from the quarries: there was nothing afterward to be done but to set them in their places, so that the sound of a hammer was never heard in the Temple during the time of its erection.

The foundations of this magnificent building were laid in the fourth year of Solomon's reign, 480 years after the departure from Egypt, and 1,000 years before the birth of our Lord. The Temple was constructed on the model of the tabernacle, which Moses had raised in the desert, and whose plan had been supplied by the Lord himself. But the various parts of which it was composed were much larger and richer.

Description of the Temple.—The Temple consisted of four parts:

1. *The court of Israel.* This was a vast court, surrounded with galleries and buildings, which, besides affording lodgings to the priests, contained the treasures of the Temple and the vessels intended for the divine worship. All Israelites were allowed to enter this first enclosure.

2. *The interior court.* This was smaller than the first, but surrounded in like manner with galleries and buildings. Admission was usually allowed to none but priests. In the middle stood the altar of holocausts, and a large brazen basin, in which the priests purified themselves before performing their sacred functions. Here, the flesh and fat of victims were consumed by fire.

3. *The sanctuary.* Within the interior court was the part called the "sanctuary," or "holy place." In the middle of this new enclosure was a golden altar, or, as it was termed, the "altar of perfumes," on which the sweetest perfumes were burnt every morning and evening. This altar bore ten golden candlesticks with several branches, having golden lamps, which the high priest himself should keep continually lighted. There were also in this place ten golden tables, to receive the "loaves of proposition." The twelve loaves of proposition were made of unleavened bread, and renewed weekly. It was not permitted any persons but the priests to eat of those which were removed.

4. *The holy of holies.* This part of the Temple, the most venerable of all, contained the ark of the covenant. It was all covered inside and outside with the purest gold. No one

dare enter it but the high priest, and he but once a year. All these vast structures, forming together one great citadel, as it were, bore the name of the Temple.

Its dedication. — The erection of this august pile, one of the wonders of the world, occupied a period of seven years. Its dedication was celebrated with unparalleled magnificence. Let us collect our thoughts and listen to the interesting history thereof. All the ancients of Israel, all the chiefs of tribes, and an innumerable multitude of people came to Jerusalem on a day appointed by the king. The first thing done was to convey the ark of the covenant from the place where it had been deposited. It was borne by priests. At their head moved the high priest Sadoc, preceded by 150 other priests, the children of Aaron, who, to the sound of their sacred trumpets, led the procession, and announced the triumph of the God of Israel. The king followed, accompanied by all the chief members of his court. Then came, but arranged in the most admirable order, the countless multitude of the common people.

This triumphal procession made regular halts, during which the air reechoed with the sounds of the trumpets and all other kinds of musical instruments, to which the singing choirs answered together: "How great, how adorable, how amiable, how good is the God of Israel! His mercy endureth from age to age, and continueth even to the end of time!" Whenever the ark stopped, which occurred at intervals, according to a certain number of steps, victims were immolated.

Miraculous cloud. — At length, having reached the Temple, where the harmony of the instruments, the chant of the psalms, and the immolation of victims were renewed, the ark was placed in the holy of holies, and the priests came forth. Then appeared one of those prodigies by which the God of Israel was pleased to manifest not only his power, but the pleasure that his people had afforded him. A miraculous cloud issued from the holy of holies, in which it had been formed and filled all parts of the Temple, so that the priests could not continue their functions. It was the Lord, who filled this new dwelling-place with his glory and consecrated it by his presence.

On beholding this wonderful manifestation of the divine favor, Solomon cast himself on his knees, blessed his people after the example of Moses and David, and, addressing himself to the Lord, prayed thus: "O Lord, the God of Israel, there is no other God in heaven nor on earth besides thee! And is it credible, then, that thou shouldst deign to dwell amongst men? If the whole extent of the heavens cannot contain thee, how much less can this house, which I have built, receive Thy Majesty? Ah! it is destined only to be the place where thou shalt favorably hear the prayers of thy servant and thy people. Let thine eyes be open, O Lord, let thine ears be attentive to the most humble supplications that we shall address to thee in this place! Hear them from thy throne in the highest heavens, and grant us thy mercy."

Fire descends from heaven. — The Lord did not delay to show how agreeable this prayer was to him. Victims were on all sides prepared and laid upon the altar to be immolated, when, on a sudden, a sacred fire descended from heaven and consumed in an instant the holocausts. The most evident testimony that could be desired was now given, that God was well pleased with the solemn services of this day. Another prodigy followed shortly afterward, which crowned the joy and gratitude of Israel. The majesty of the Lord, symbolized by a luminous cloud, filled the different portions of the Temple a second time. Struck by this twofold prodigy, the children of Israel prostrated themselves with their faces on the ground. They then began to praise and bless the God of their fathers, singing canticles in honor of his infinite goodness and eternal mercy.

The solemnity of the dedication continued for seven days, to which seven others were added, on account of the feast of Tabernacles. On the fifteenth day, the people returned home, full of joy and fervor.

The queen of Saba.—Solomon's renown soon spread through all the East. A famous princess, delighted at the wonderful things that rumor announced to the world, desired to satisfy herself of their truth: this was the queen of Saba. She visited Jerusalem, with a suite worthy of her royal dignity, as well as of the majesty of the king whom she had come to see. Solomon received the distinguished lady with a splendor that astounded and enchanted her. But she was particularly anxious to know something of the mental qualities of the king of Israel. She proposed a number of most difficult questions to him. The king solved them for her with the utmost ease. So many wonders and so much wisdom had such an effect on the queen's mind, that she was out of herself with admiration and could not say a word.

Solomon's fall.—The height of glory to which Solomon saw himself elevated by the pomp of this flattering visit appeared to be the term of his wisdom and the shipwreck of his innocence. Flattered on all sides, at peace with the ancient enemies of his people, respected by other nations, venerated by his own subjects, and without any special occupation at home, since he had completed all his great undertakings, he gradually approached the precipice where he at length perished by the seduction of pleasure, from which a youth spent in virtue and chastity does not always secure the closing years of old age. Solomon, the king of kings, the sage of sages, the beloved of heaven, is overcome by shameful passions! After having built the first Temple to the true God, he adores as many false gods as strange women make known to him! Astounding fall, which freezes the very blood in our veins!

Justly provoked by the disorders of the king, the Lord sent a prophet to him with the following message: "Because thou hast not observed the fidelity which thou owest to me, I will divide thy kingdom, and I will give a portion of it to one of thy servants. In consideration of David, however, I will not do so during thy lifetime. But, under the reign of thy son, I will accomplish my threat; I will not take away the whole kingdom; I will reserve one tribe for the sake of David, my servant, and of Jerusalem, which I have chosen, that my holy name may be adored therein. I reserve one tribe, that there may always remain to my servant David a lamp to shine before him, that is, a child of his race."

Solomon died after a reign of forty years, whose wise and glorious beginning had promised the happiest end. We do not know whether he repented of his faults before appearing at the dread tribunal of God. Be that as it may, Solomon, like his father David, was an illustrious figure of the Messias, but the Messias glorious and triumphant.

Solomon, the seventeenth figure of the Messias.—Thus, Solomon, rejoicing in the victories of David, his father, ascends the throne, and reigns in peace over his vanquished enemies; our Lord, rejoicing in his own labors and victories, ascends in the highest heavens the throne of his Father, and reigns in peace over his vanquished enemies. Solomon espouses the daughter of a foreign king; our Lord chooses the Church, his spouse, among the Gentiles, who are strangers to the Jews and to the true religion. Solomon, by this alliance, associates a foreign princess to his people, and crowns her with honors; our Lord, by his alliance with the Church sanctifies it, associates it to his angels, and loads it with graces on earth and with crowns of glory in heaven. Solomon builds a magnificent Temple to the true God; our Lord changes the world, which was previously but a vast temple of idols, into a temple of the true God. The Jews and Tyrians unite for the construction of the Temple of Solomon; the Jews and Gentiles unite for the establishment of the Church, the temple of the true God.

It is Solomon that invites strangers to take part with his people in this great work; it is our Lord that calls the Gentiles to form with the Jews the grand edifice of the Church. It is Solomon that communicates to the workmen the plan of the work; it is our Lord that reveals to the Jews and the Gentiles the plan of his Church. Solomon employs far more strangers than Jews in the erection of the Temple; our Lord employs far more strangers than Jews in the formation of his Church.

Solomon lays large stones of great value in the foundations of the Temple; our Lord is himself called the cornerstone, the foundation-stone of the Church. Solomon has all the stones that should enter into the construction of the Temple prepared at a considerable distance from it; our Lord has all the stones that must one day enter as spiritual stones into the construction of the heavenly Jerusalem prepared for it on earth, where the faithful are purified by sufferings. The chisel and mallet take away from stones whatever is rough and superfluous; mortification and penance take away from our souls, here on earth, whatever is rough and superfluous, that is to say, all irregular affections.

At the fame of the wisdom of Solomon, the queen of Saba leaves her kingdom; at the name of our Lord, the nations quit the empire of the devil. The queen of Saba admires the wisdom of Solomon and the happiness of his people; the world admires the wisdom of our Lord and of his gospel, and acknowledges the happiness of those who live as Christians, though it has not always the courage to imitate them. The queen of Saba makes rich presents to Solomon; the nations offer, as a present to our Lord, their hearts as well as their riches.

All the preceding figures showed us the Redeemer persecuted, struggling with his enemies, or dying as a sacrifice; in this, he appears glorious and triumphant. So that the figures, in their entirety, present us with a complete life of the Redeemer: a life of labor on earth, and a life of glory and happiness in heaven.

PRAYER

O my God! who art all love, I thank thee for having chosen an abode among men: inspire me with a profound reverence for thy Church, and also for myself, who am thy living temple!

I am resolved to love God above all things, and my neighbor as myself for the love of God; and, in testimony of this love, I will contribute according to my power for the ornamentation of our churches.

Lesson 37: Messias Foreshadowed: Jonas

In the preceding figures we have seen the Savior, after a series of persecutions, humiliations, and other sufferings, elevated to the summit of glory, and reigning tranquilly over his defeated enemies. To complete our magnificent picture, it only remains for us to show how the Savior should thus pass from the depth of humiliation and shame to the height of glory. Providence has been careful to instruct us regarding this matter by the eighteenth figure, the last in our catechism.

Schism of the ten tribes. — Solomon had burdened his subjects with many taxes in the latter years of his reign. After his death they endeavored to lighten the yoke under which they groaned. For this purpose they addressed themselves to Roboam, the son and successor of Solomon. Their petition ran thus: "Thy father laid an exceeding heavy burden upon us; we beseech thee to relent somewhat from the severity with which he treated us, and we will not only submit willingly to thy authority, but thou shalt always find in us the most perfect obedience."

Roboam first consulted the old men that had been members of Solomon's council: they were of opinion that the people's request should be granted. Roboam did not relish such an advice: he summoned around him a number of young men that had been brought up with him in the gaieties and delicacies of the court, and proposed the same question to them. They counseled him to establish his authority in the beginning by one vigorous and telling stroke. He accordingly determined to answer the people with a stern refusal. "My father," he said, "laid a heavy burden upon you, but I will make it much heavier; my father beat you with whips, but I will beat you with scorpions." God permitted that the evil advice should prevail.

The king's answer excited general discontent among the people. Ten tribes withdrew from Roboam; and there only remained under his obedience the two tribes of Juda and Benjamin. Thus was accomplished the threat which the Lord had made to Solomon.

The Jewish nation became thus divided into two portions. That of the ten tribes took the name of the Kingdom of Israel; the other was called the Kingdom of Juda. Jeroboam, the head of the former, established his abode in a city named Sichem. Amri, one of his successors, built the city of Samaria, which became the capital of the kingdom of Israel, as Jerusalem was the capital of the kingdom of Juda.

Their idolatry.—Afraid lest the ten tribes should unite again with their brethren of Juda, Jeroboam forbade his subjects to go to sacrifice at the Temple of Jerusalem. He raised two golden calves, which he named the gods of Israel, and commanded that they should be adored. He preserved, nevertheless, the law of Moses, which he interpreted according to his fancy. He caused nearly all its external regulations to be observed, so that the Pentateuch ever remained in veneration among the separated tribes. It was in the midst of this schismatical kingdom that the Lord, whose mercy is infinite, raised up one of the most admirable figures of the Messias: we mean Jonas. At once a prophet and a figure, Jonas forms the transition, so to speak, from figures to prophecies.

Jonas exhorts them to be converted; he is sent to preach penance to the Ninivites.—After having for a long time exhorted the kingdom of Israel to renounce its false gods, he was sent by the Lord to preach penance to the inhabitants of the city of Ninive. "Go, O prophet," said the Lord, "and speak to the great city of Ninive; announce to its inhabitants that the voice of their iniquities has come up even to my throne, and cries out for vengeance."

He wishes to avoid this commission.—The commission appeared dangerous to Jonas. Knowing the infinite goodness of his master, it came unto his mind that the inhabitants of Ninive, touched by his discourses, as well as by the evils with which he should threaten them, would have recourse to penance; that the Lord, naturally inclined to mercy, would not decide on their destruction; that his own language and character would consequently become contemptible; and that he should, perhaps, run the risk of his life. Instead of going to Ninive he went to Joppe, a seaport on the Philistine coast; there, having found a ship ready to set sail for the city of Tharsis, he paid his passage and embarked.

Jonas is cast into the sea.—It is in vain, O prophet, that thou callest the sea and the winds to thine aid: no one can avoid the presence of God by flight! Scarcely had the voyagers left port, when the Lord raised a violent wind: the storm raged with such fury that the vessel was well nigh swallowed up by the waves. Every one imagined her on the point of foundering. The alarm was so great, even among the sailors, that they cast out the merchandise on board into the sea, in order to lighten the vessel.

During this danger Jonas was fast asleep in the hold of the ship. The pilot went down to find him, and said: "How canst thou sleep in the midst of the dangers that surround us? Arise, invoke thy God, and perhaps he will have pity on us." Jonas set himself to prayer, but the Lord was inflexible. There seemed hardly any resource left, when the passengers began to say to one another: "There must be among us some person whose crime provokes the anger of heaven; let us have recourse to lots, and discover who is the guilty one." The lot fell on Jonas. He was asked whence he came, whither he went, what was his nation, and particularly what he had done that could be the cause of such a fearful storm. "I am a Hebrew," answered Jonas, "I serve the God of heaven, who made both the sea and the land; I am guilty before him, because I fled from his presence, not to execute the orders that he had given me."

These words terrified all on board. "What shall we do with thee," they said to the prophet, "to appease the wrath of heaven, and to calm the fury of the storm?" For the waves continued to rise. "Take me," said Jonas, "and cast me into the sea; and the Lord will still the storm." The counsel of the prophet did not please them. On the point, as they were, of perishing all together, the passengers could not determine on the death of a stranger who had entrusted his life to them. They endeavored to regain the land with the help of oars; but they could not succeed. They then took the resolution which the culprit himself continued to recommend to them. Jonas was cast into the sea, and immediately the storm ceased.

He is swallowed up by a fish.—The Lord did not forget his prophet: he brought near the vessel a fish of monstrous size, which swallowed up Jonas, and preserved him from being drowned. Jonas remained safe in the whale's belly for three days and three nights.[526] This was a miracle like that of the preservation of the three children in the furnace of Babylon; but miracles cost nothing to him who created the universe, and who disposes of all creatures according to his good pleasure.[527]

Although it is not permitted us to scrutinize the deep counsels of the Most High, and although good sense teaches us that God does nothing without reasons worthy of his infinite wisdom, even when we least understand them, still it is only natural that we should behold two principal motives in the miracle of Jonas. The Lord sends his prophet among a pagan people, into a city of great extent, abandoned to the abominations of voluptuousness. But how will the pleasure-seeking inhabitants receive a stranger, who appears in their midst without character or mission? How will they listen to the severe sermons of a mourning prophet, who commands them the most painful of all mortifications, that of their passions? Will they not have a right to ask for his credentials; and, as long as he cannot show them, will they be guilty, if they look upon him as an impostor?

On the other hand, when they see in Jonas the man whose miraculous history has been made known to them by fame—the prophet who, to evade the declaration of approaching ruin to their city, wishes to escape by flight from the all-powerful will of the God that sends him, but whom tempests and sea monsters force to a fulfillment of duty; what, I ask, ought to be the impressions made on their minds by the preaching of such a man, a man preserved miraculously during three days and three nights in the belly of a sea monster, and delivered by God from this dreadful prison, only to preach penance to Ninive? Thus, it appears to us that to authorize or confirm the divine mission of Jonas by a splendid act of supernatural power was the first motive of the miracle.

To give all succeeding ages a striking prophecy in regard to a fundamental article of our faith, the resurrection of Jesus Christ, was the second motive. This new motive, by attaching the deliverance of Jonas to the general plan of providence, which arranged that all the circumstances of the life and death of the Messias should be prefigured and predicted, gives it a high degree of importance, and points out, so to speak, its necessity.

Jonas is cast out by the fish onto the shore.—Meanwhile, from the depths of his living tomb, Jonas addressed a fervent prayer to the Lord, who heard him, and commanded the fish to deliver up the deposit that was confided to it. The obedient animal accordingly cast up the prophet on the shore. "Go," said the Lord immediately to him, "go to the great city of Ninive, and announce to its inhabitants their approaching ruin in punishment of their iniquities."

He preaches at Ninive; penance of the Ninivites.—Jonas set out without reply, and entered Ninive. It was a city of three days' journey.[528] Invested with authority from God, Jonas appeared in the streets and public places, crying out with a loud voice: "Yet forty days and Ninive shall be destroyed!" These few words, uttered by a stranger whom no one knew, but whose commission every one knew to be ratified by a splendid miracle, made a deep impression on the minds of the idolaters. They believed in God; their hearts were moved to penance; and, from the highest to the lowest, they clothed themselves in garments of mourning. The king himself descended from his throne, laid aside the emblems of his royalty, covered himself with sackcloth, seated himself in ashes, and commanded a general fast. "Let us forsake our iniquities," he said to his subjects, "let us humble ourselves; let us do penance; let us cry to the Lord! Who knows but, touched by our repentance, he may again sheathe the sword, which he holds drawn over our heads?" Every one obeyed. The conversion was sincere. The Lord, being appeased, revoked his sentence.

Such is the character of the great master, or rather of the tender Father, whom we serve: he punishes only with regret. It is by the traits of his clemency, much more than by those of his justice, that he delights to make himself known. Men, who cannot fathom the abyss of his charity, sometimes grow angry at his patience.

Jonas was one of those men who are a little too severe, who have no great compassion for the guilty. He was troubled, and even displeased, to see that to all appearance his prediction was not likely to be fulfilled. He withdrew to the country, on the east of the city, and took up his abode for the time under a tent of foliage, to await the result. When the forty days had rolled by, and he saw nothing of what he had foretold accomplished, he felt much chagrin, and could not refrain from expressing his disappointment. Addressing himself to the Lord, he spoke thus: "Is not this exactly what I foresaw, while yet in my own country? I was acquainted with thy goodness, thy mercy, thy clemency. I knew that thy patience is not easily exhausted, that thou canst not resolve to punish until after long delays. At the least sign of repentance given by the guilty, thine anger is disarmed. This is what induced me to seek a retreat at Tharsis: I did not wish to be constrained to make, in thy name, prophecies which thou wouldst not verify. After this disgrace, I ask death of thee as a favor."

"Dost thou think," answered the Lord mildly, "that thou hast reason to complain?" Jonas made no reply. Piqued at the turn of events, he was not in a condition to profit of the remonstrances of his God. This, however, was only the first salve that the Lord applied to his wound; after a few moments allowed for grief, he prepared a more efficacious remedy.

Jonas complains of some withered ivy; remonstrances of the Lord. — The foliage that covered Jonas was almost entirely withered, and the prophet suffered much from the heat. God caused a thick ivy plant to spring up over his head in a single night: this defended him from the scorching rays of the sun. Jonas, perceiving in the morning the paternal attention of the Lord, was full of joy and gratitude. Next day, about dawn, God ordered a worm to cut the root of the little bush. In a little while, it dried up, and its leaves fell off.

With the morning the Lord sent a burning wind. In addition, the rays of the sun fell right on Jonas's head. The heat that the prophet had to endure seemed insupportable. "O Lord!" he cried out, "Thou art always loading me with new afflictions; I have already besought thee to send me death, and I ask it of thee again."

"What!" answered the Lord, "dost thou think that thou hast reason to be angry because thou hast lost the shade of the ivy?" "Yes, I have reason," answered the prophet, with a degree of brusqueness, "I do not know what will become of me: I am longing for death."

"Hear me," said the Lord, "and learn to profit of thy faults. Thou art angry, thou art impatient, thou murmurest for the loss of an ivy bush, which thou didst not plant, which cost thee neither care nor labor, which grew up over thy head without thine interference, and which one night saw born, as another night saw it die. I ought, according to thee, to have preserved this plant as a shade against the heat that broils thee: and, because thou didst foretell the destruction of Ninive, thou art unwilling that I should pardon that great city, in which there are more than 120,000 children that cannot distinguish their right hand from their left! Thou wishest that I should sweep them all away, men, women, children; even the beasts of the field and the birds of the air!"

At these words of the Lord, Jonas awoke as it were from a deep sleep, and recognized his fault. The Lord, who only desired to instruct him, kindly forgave him, when he saw him confounded. Jonas directed his course again to Israel, and, convinced by this sensible proof that God threatens only to be appeased, he made public an account of the recent events at Ninive, and did not forget a single circumstance that could rouse the hopes of sinners or encourage them to conversion.

On the day of judgment, the example of the Ninivites will be set forth in condemnation of a great many Christians, because the former were converted from their errors at the voice of Jonas, who was only a prophet, while the latter look with disdain on the advances and warnings of the master of the prophets.

Jonas, the eighteenth figure of the Messias.—For the rest, Jonas was not only a prophet, but has always been regarded as one of the most striking figures of the Messias. Jonas, in effect, was a prophet appointed to recall men to penance; our Lord is more than a prophet, and is sent by his Father to recall men to penance. Jonas is not listened to by the Israelites, his brethren; our Lord is not attended to by the Jews, his brethren. Jonas receives a command to preach penance to the Ninivites, who are idolaters, and the Ninivites are converted; our Lord, by the instrumentality of his apostles, preaches penance to the idolatrous nations, and those idolatrous nations are converted. The guilty disobedience of Jonas causes a violent storm, and he is cast into the sea; our Lord, innocent, but laden with the crimes of the world, provokes against himself all the justice of his Father, and is put to death. Jonas is no sooner cast into the sea, than heaven is appeased and the storm ceases; our Lord is no sooner put to death, than the divine anger is appeased and justice is turned into mercy.

Jonas remains three days and three nights in the belly of a whale, and comes forth full of life; our Lord remains part of three days and three nights in the tomb, and comes forth full of life. Jonas, after his deliverance, preaches penance to the Ninivites; our Lord, after his resurrection, commissions his apostles to preach the gospel to all nations. Our Lord said several times: "I am sent only to bring back the lost sheep of the house of Israel," that is, the Jews; and, accordingly, it was only to the Jews that he preached the gospel during his mortal life. But as he was the Savior of all mankind. He commanded his apostles, after his resurrection, to scatter themselves over the earth, and to announce to all mankind the glad tidings of salvation.

This figure teaches us a) that the Jews will refuse to be converted and that the Gentiles will be called in their stead; b) that the Messias will be put to death; c) that the Messias will remain some three days and three nights in the grave; and d) that the Messias will rise again and, after his resurrection, convert the nations.

PRAYER

O my God! who art all love, I thank thee for having given us in the pardon granted to the Ninivites such a touching proof of thine infinite mercy: bestow on me the grace ever to hope in thee, no matter what may be the number or the enormity of my faults!

I am resolved to love God above all things, and my neighbor as myself for the love of God; and, in testimony of this love, I will never be discouraged, whatever my faults may be.

Lesson 38: Messias Prophesied by David

Jesus Christ, the object of prophecy.—From the time of the fall of our first parents, God never ceased, as we have seen, to promise a Redeemer to mankind. He showed him from afar in numerous figures, which became clearer and clearer with the progress of ages. As images and figures are only the books of children, God did not heretofore present the most sublime truth of faith under any other forms than those of emblems and symbols. He spoke to the human family in language suitable to children, in order to prepare them for the understanding of the language of men.[529]

Accordingly, we must admit that the different traits of the Messias which we have just studied, do not suffice: the rough draught is not the portrait, and it is the portrait that we want. Scattered here and there, and obscured by clouds more or less dense, these rays of light form only a sort of twilight: they convey, after all, but a faint knowledge of the future liberator. Now, God desires that the description should be so full and circumstantial, that it should be impossible for man, unless voluntarily blind, to mistake his Redeemer.

He proceeds, therefore, to scatter the dark clouds, to give the finishing touches to the portrait, and to put an end to all uncertainties. How, then, does he act? In his infinite wisdom, he raises up the prophets. Associating their intelligence to his infinite intelligence, he communicates to them the secrets of the future. Before their eyes he places the Desired of Nations, and commands them to depict him with so much accuracy that nothing can be easier than to distinguish from all others that Son of David who is to save the world. What, then, are the prophecies? They are the complete description of the Redeemer, promised from the beginning of time, and prefigured in a thousand different ways.

"Thus," says one of our most celebrated orientalists, "we clearly see, by an attentive examination of the sacred text, that all the prophecies during the four thousand years which precede the coming of the Messias form, if I may venture so to express myself, only one great circle, whose radii meet in a common center, which is and can be no other than our Lord Jesus Christ himself, the Redeemer of the human race involved in guilt since the sin of Adam. Such is the object and the only object of all the prophecies, which agree in describing him to us in such a manner that we cannot be deceived. They form altogether a most perfect picture. The more ancient prophets trace the outline. As others follow, they complete the parts left unfinished by their predecessors. The nearer we approach the term, the brighter the colors glow; and, when the picture is finished, the artists disappear. The last, as he retires, is careful to announce the personage that will lift the veil. 'Behold, I send you,' he says,[530] in the name of the Eternal, 'Elias the prophet (John the Baptist) before the great and terrible day of the Lord.'"[531]

The prophecies, then, are the description of the Redeemer: their end is to acquaint us with his various characteristics. What one begins, another finishes, and, taken altogether, they form a complete portrait of the Redeemer, a portrait that corresponds perfectly and solely with the babe of Bethlehem. Whence it follows that the Messias predicted by the prophets is truly our Lord Jesus Christ.

What the prophecies prove.—Yes, all the circumstances of the birth, life, death, and triumphant resurrection and ascension of our Lord were manifested in predictions clearer than the sun. A full and precise history of the Son of Mary was given to the world by men that lived a thousand years, seven hundred years, four hundred years, before his appearance in it.

Now, it is certain 1) that all these prophecies preceded the coming of the Messias, since we find them in the hands of the Jews, a nation existing long anterior to the coming of the Messias; a nation the sworn enemy of Christianity; a nation that, far from receiving these prophecies from us, had the greatest interest in suppressing them, because they contain its condemnation and bear invincible testimony to our faith.

It is certain 2) that the prophecies prove unanswerably the truth of that religion in whose favor they were made. God alone knows the future—that future which, depending on the free concurrence of human wills and passions, escapes all our calculations. God alone then can give a knowledge of it to man. The gift of this knowledge, which makes the created intelligence participate in the lights of the infinite intelligence of God, is one of the greatest miracles that God can work. But God cannot work miracles in favor of deceit. Our Lord is therefore truly the Son of God. His religion is, therefore, the true religion: since Jesus Christ and his religion are announced long beforehand by prophecies that cannot be called in question.

It is certain 3) that all the prophecies that announce the Messias relate to our Lord Jesus Christ, for they agree perfectly with him and with no other. Accordingly, our choice lies between two extremes: either the prophecies of the Redeemer mean nothing, or they describe Jesus Christ; for in him alone they are all fulfilled to the letter. Before showing the admirable conformity between the prophecies and our Lord, let us say a few words on the number and the lives of the prophets.

Details regarding the prophets. — We call a man that foretells the future by divine inspiration a "prophet." God, who knows all things, past, present, and future, can communicate to whomsoever he pleases a knowledge of certain future events, which all the ingenuity of man can never discover. He has given this knowledge of the future to many persons, under both the old and the new testament. We speak here only of the prophets of the old covenant. They are divided into two classes: those who did not write their prophecies, as Nathan, Gad, Elias, and Eliseus; and those who wrote their prophecies.

Among the latter, there are some termed the "greater prophets," because we have a greater number of their writings; such are David, Isaias, Jeremias, Ezechiel, and Daniel. Others are termed the "minor prophets," because we have a less number of their writings; they are twelve in number: Osee, Joel, Amos, Abdias, Micheas, Jonas, Nahum, Habacuc, Sophonias, Aggeus, Zacharias, and Malachias.

Let us speak of the manner of life adopted in general by these inspired men. They usually lived like religious, apart from the people, in some country retreat. With their disciples they formed communities, and occupied themselves in labor, instruction, and study. They built their own cells, cutting down whatever wood they required for this purpose. Their habit was sackcloth or haircloth, that is, a mourning dress, in order to show that they continually did penance for the sins of all the people. Their whole life was spent in the hardships of poverty. They received presents of bread and firstfruits of the harvest like the poor.

They were not always prophesying. But when the Spirit of the Lord descended on them, they came forth from their retirement, and announced to kings and peoples the will of heaven. They spoke with great freedom, as became men that were inspired and sent by God. As the preachers of the truth have always had the same lot, they were often exposed to the violence of princes whose impiety they reproved, and to the insults and railleries of multitudes whose irregularities they condemned. Several of the prophets, as we shall see later on, died by a violent death.

The prophets are numbered among those holy men, whose sufferings and virtues the apostle St. Paul so highly praises. "Some among them," he says, "were racked, not wishing to save their present life, that they might find a better in the resurrection. Others suffered mockeries and stripes, chains and prisons: they were stoned, they were cut asunder, they were tried in every manner. They were put to death by the sword, they wandered about in sheepskins, abandoned, persecuted, afflicted: of whom the world was not worthy. They passed their lives in deserts, and in mountains, and in dens, and in the caves of the earth."[532]

In the midst of these opprobriums and persecutions we always see them despising, with a holy liberty, every danger, every torment, and even death itself; attacking, with wonderful courage, whatever was opposed to God; and contemning riches, favors, and honors, with a disinterestedness that astonished those who endeavored to shake their constancy or to tempt their ambition. The houses of the prophets and their communities were so many asylums against impiety. Persons went thither to consult the Lord, or to hear the reading of the law. They were schools of virtue and homes of innocence.

Although prophecy was not a thing which depended on the industry, study, or will of men, the Lord usually communicated his Spirit to the children or disciples of the prophets, either on account of the purity of their manners and the sanctity of their lives, or because the vocation to the study of wisdom and the company of the prophets was a preliminary step, in the designs of God, to the grace of prophecy.

When the Spirit of the Lord descended on them, they were not so much transported out of themselves with enthusiasm that they could not resist it: they were very different men, indeed, from the priests of the false gods, who, possessed by the evil spirit, lost the use of their senses and reason, and could not control their agitations. The Spirit which animated the prophets was subject to the prophets, says St. Paul,[533] and the Church condemned the error of the Montanists, who attributed to the prophets of the old and the new testament that which pertained only to the priests of the idols, who spoke in spite of themselves by the inspiration of the evil spirit. Our prophets were calm and recollected; they possessed their souls in peace, and spoke only from a desire to obey the command of the Lord. They always knew what they were saying: they understood perfectly well the meaning of their discourses.

To give authority to their words, the prophets were accustomed to foretell two classes of events: one, near; the other, remote. The accomplishment of the first prophecy was an excellent guarantee of the accomplishment of the second.[534] Thus, Isaias predicted to Achaz, king of Juda, that he should be delivered from the kings of Samaria and Damascus, his enemies: the realization of these words was a proof that other words uttered by Isaias at the same time—namely, that the Messias should be born of a Virgin Mother—would be realized too. The first object is clear and near; the second is obscure and remote. The latter has a kind of dependence on the former. In a word, by this twofold prediction, the prophets seemed to say: "We announce to you distant events, whose accomplishment you will never see; but, to prove to you that we speak the truth, here is something close at hand, and within reach of your senses, that you will see fulfilled to the letter before your eyes."

As if I myself should say: "In a hundred years there shall be born in this city, in such a family, on such a day, of such a month, a child, who shall bear such a name, who shall perform such an act, who shall live such a number of years, and who shall die in such a manner; yes, everything shall happen precisely as I say; and, to prove to you that I speak the truth, I will now inform you of an event which shall take place one month hence, and which no person in the world except myself foresees. It is this: in one month from this date, on such a day of the week, we shall have rain in this place, from such a minute of such an hour till such a minute of such another hour, not a second more or less. The rain shall be preceded and followed by thunder, and shall fall only within such and such limits." It is quite certain that, after having seen the fulfillment of the latter prophecy in a manner that no amount of human knowledge could ever forecast, one would be obliged to believe unhesitatingly in the birth to occur a hundred years afterward.

At other times, to prove a distant and less striking fact, the prophets announced along with it another which should happen sooner and be so evident that all the world might see it, and could no more doubt it than doubt the existence of the sun. For example, Isaias announces, seven hundred years before the coming of our Lord, that the Jews shall despise the Messias, that they shall load him with injuries and spittle; this is the distant and less striking fact. As a proof of it, Isaias announces another fact, which no man has ever dared or can ever dare to deny: this fact is the destruction of the city of Tyre.

At the time of Isaias, the city of Tyre was one of the most beautiful, powerful, and opulent cities in the world: Isaias foretold that it should one day be no more than a miserable village. And behold! haughty Tyre, which afforded an anchorage to the mariners of every nation, and which sent its vessels, laden with beautiful stuffs, precious stones, and riches of every other description, to all parts of the world; haughty Tyre, ruined by Alexander, is today no more than a miserable village, inhabited by fifty or sixty poor families, barely sheltered under their mean cabins, and living by the culture of a few fields and a little fishing. This is a fact which every one can verify for himself. Not long since, a celebrated infidel visited the ruins of Tyre, and, seeing what Isaias had predicted, could not avoid exclaiming: "The oracle is fulfilled!"

David, a prophet of the Messias.—Let us now show how the prophecies that announce the Redeemer correspond with the babe of Bethlehem. David is the first prophet that describes at length the characteristics of the Messias.[535] As a proof of his predictions regarding the liberator of the world, the holy king informs the Jews of approaching events, whose occurrence should lead them to entertain no doubt that his other predictions would also be fulfilled. Among the events predicted by David are the captivity of Babylon, which should not happen for four hundred years later, and the magnificent reign of Solomon, which should be witnessed by the Jews within a very brief period. It is in the psalms that David anticipates for us the history of our Lord.

The royal prophet begins with the grand characteristic of the Messias, that he should convert the nations and bring them back to the knowledge of the true God. "All peoples," he says, "shall know the Lord and shall glorify him";[536] "all the kings of the earth shall adore him; all nations shall be submissive to him";[537] "no country shall withdraw itself from his power." It was by our Lord and his apostles that the world was converted. Our Lord is therefore the Messias announced by David.

He predicts that foreign kings should come to adore the Messias, and to offer him presents. "The kings of Tharsis, as well as those of Arabia and Saba, shall bring him precious gifts."[538] Our Lord was adored by the Magi, who, as a constant tradition informs us, were kings; and they offered him presents of gold, frankincense, and myrrh. Our Lord is therefore the Messias announced by David.

He predicts that the Jews should despise the Messias, that they should cease to be his beloved people, and that the Gentiles should be chosen in their stead. He makes the Messias express himself to his Father thus: "Thou wilt deliver me from the contradictions of the people: thou wilt make me the head of the Gentiles. A people whom I knew not hath served me: at the hearing of the ear they hath obeyed me."[539] "The children that are strangers have adhered to me; my own children, on the contrary, have ceased to follow me." Our Lord was despised by the Jews. From the moment of their treating him in this manner, the Jews lost the knowledge of the true religion, and the Gentiles received the light of the gospel. Our Lord is therefore the Messias announced by David.

He predicts that the Messias should be a priest according to the order of Melchisedech. This means that the Messias should have neither predecessor nor successor in the priesthood, and that he should offer a sacrifice of bread and wine. "The Lord," he says, "hath sworn it, and will not repent: Thou art a priest forever, according to the order of Melchisedech."[540] Our Lord had neither predecessor nor successor in the priesthood. He is an eternal priest, and offers, like Melchisedech, a sacrifice of bread and wine. Our Lord is therefore the Messias announced by David.

He sees kings and peoples form leagues against the Messias. "The nations raged," he says, "the peoples devised vain things; the kings of the earth stood up, and the princes met together, against the Lord, and against his Christ."[541] But the Lord "shall laugh at them...For I am appointed king by him over Sion."[542] It is only against our Lord that kings and peoples have formed such leagues; but their efforts have been vain. Our Lord has triumphed over them; and they have been obliged to submit to his law. Our Lord is therefore the Messias announced by David.

He describes, more than a thousand years beforehand, the kind of death, and all the particulars of the punishments, to which the Messias should be condemned. Listen to the complaints which he makes our Savior utter: "He that used to sit at my table hath shown his perfidy toward me."[543] "I looked for one that would grieve together with me, but there was none."[544] "Mine enemies have insulted me."[545] "They have wagged their heads at me, and said: 'Since he places his confidence in God, let God come and deliver him.'...They have dug my hands and my feet...They have divided my garments amongst them, and upon my vesture they have cast lots."[546] "In my thirst they gave me vinegar to drink."[547] Our Lord was betrayed by Judas, who used to sit at his table. He was abandoned by all his disciples. His countenance was covered with spittle. The Jews, on Calvary, wagged their heads, saying: "Since he hoped in God, let God come and deliver him." His hands and feet were pierced. The soldiers divided his garments amongst them, cast lots for his robe, and gave him vinegar to drink. All these things have been accomplished only in regard to our Lord. Our Lord is therefore the Messias announced by David.

In fine, he predicts that the Messias should arise again after death, without experiencing the corruption of the tomb. Here are the terms in which the Messias is supposed to express himself: "My flesh shall rest in hope; thou wilt not leave my soul in hell; thou wilt not permit thy holy one to see corruption."[548] Our Lord died; he descended into limbo; but he did not experience corruption, for he arose again triumphant from the tomb on the third day after his death. Our Lord is therefore the Messias announced by David.

PRAYER

O my God! who art all love, I thank thee for having caused the mysteries connected with the Messias to be foretold so long a time beforehand, and for having thus given me an infallible proof of the truth of my faith.

I am resolved to love God above all things, and my neighbor as myself for the love of God; and, in testimony of this love, I will read the gospel with the most profound respect.

Lesson 39: Messias Prophesied by Isaias

Whilst the ten rebellious and schismatical tribes abandoned their God and their king, the other two tribes, under the name of the kingdom of Juda, continued in the covenant and faith of Abraham. Faithful to God and to David, they observed the law of Moses in all its extent. Thus began the celebrated division in the empire of the Hebrews. The crime of a single prince caused the first schism that afflicted the bosom of the true Church. Hereby, God shows to fathers that he makes their rewards or punishments continue after their death, and that he desires to keep them submissive to his laws by the dearest of their interests, that of their families.

State of the kingdom of Israel.—The kingdom of Israel lasted 254 years. During this time the Lord sent a great many prophets, among whom were Elias and Eliseus, to recall the Israelites from their idolatry. A small number of persons had regard to their words. At length, the Lord, irritated by their perversity, summoned against them Salmanazar, king of Assyria, who took Samaria, after a siege of 3 years, and led away the ten tribes captive to Ninive. So ended the kingdom of Israel.

State of the kingdom of Juda.—As for the kingdom of Juda, the Lord neglected no means to maintain it in the practice of the true religion. But the example of the ten schismatical tribes soon made it fall into idolatry. Roboam was the first to lead the way. The Lord, to avenge the insults offered his holy name, brought against Jerusalem Sesac, king of Egypt, who carried away the treasures of the Temple. Instructed by this misfortune, the Jews renounced the worship of those stone and wood divinities which could afford them no protection. But, after a few years of fidelity, this inconstant people again returned to their idols. New chastisements recalled them to their duty. This alternation of conversions to the Lord and relapses to the service of strange gods forms the chief part of the history of the kingdom of Juda till the time of its fall, that is, till the captivity of Babylon.

Still, warnings were not wanting to the unfaithful Jews. A long succession of prophets, sent by God during the space of two hundred years, continually predicted to them the evils that awaited them if they persevered in their idolatry, as well as the blessings that should be the reward of those who should remain faithful to the God of Abraham and of David. It was not the only object of the prophets to maintain the true religion in the kingdom of Juda; they were also charged with the duty of announcing the Messias, and of describing gradually the great traits by which he should be known. The first and most admirable of these extraordinary men was Isaias.

Isaias, a prophet. — This prophet was the son of Amos, of the royal family of David. He prophesied during the reigns of four kings of Juda, namely, Ozias, Joathan, Achaz, and Ezechias, who flourished about seven hundred years before Christ. The Lord chose him from his childhood to recall the Jews to penance, and to announce anew the great mystery of the Messias. A seraph took a burning coal from an altar, and touched his lips with it to purify them. Isaias spoke, not only with incomparable eloquence, but with all the authority of a divine mission. Manasses, the successor of Ezechias, was offended at the reproaches which the holy prophet addressed to him on account of his impieties. This heartless and wicked king, to avenge himself, ordered Isaias, then about 130 years old, to be cut in two with a wooden saw. The prophet's writings were deposited in the Temple of Jerusalem, and preserved with religious care.

Approaching events, which he foretells as a proof of his mission. To show the Jews that he was really the messenger of God, and that everything he announced regarding the Messias would certainly come to pass, Isaias foretold three important events, of which the Jews were witnesses.

He announced to them 1) that Phacee, king of Israel, and Rasin, king of Syria, who were leagued together for the destruction of the kingdom of Juda, should not succeed.[549] Yet everything at the time seemed to promise victory to these allies. With a formidable army, they were already seated before the very walls of Jerusalem. The king and the people were exceedingly alarmed. This was the critical moment which Isaias chose to come and say to the king, on the part of God: "Be in peace, fear nothing, the project of thine enemies shall not succeed, the house of David shall subsist. On the other hand, the kingdom of Israel shall in a few years be destroyed, and Israel shall no longer be a people." The word of the prophet was fulfilled: the hostile kings could not take Jerusalem, and a few years afterward the kingdom of Israel was destroyed.

He announced 2) that Sennacherib should fail in his projects against Jerusalem. Sennacherib was a king of Assyria, who sent a declaration of war to Ezechias, king of Juda, and marched against him at the head of an army of 200,000 men. Every one fled before him. Ezechias was in no condition to meet him. It was in this extremity that Isaias came and said to Ezechias, in opposition to all human foresight: "Have confidence; the king of Assyria shall not enter the city nor take it;…he shall be obliged to return home disgracefully by the way he came."[550] A few days afterward the oracle of the prophet was fulfilled. The Lord sent an angel, who, during the night, slew 185,000 men in Sennacherib's camp. This prince, on awaking in the morning, was wonderfully struck to behold so great a carnage. He thought of nothing but of fleeing to his capital, where he was murdered by his two sons.

He announced 3) that Jerusalem should be taken by Nabuchodonosor, and that the Jews, led captive to Babylon, should afterward return to the land of their fathers. We shall see, at a later period, the fulfillment of this prophecy.

Let us now examine what Isaias predicted regarding the Messias.

What he announces concerning the Messias. Like David and the other prophets, he predicts that the grand characteristic of the Messias, the distinctive mark by which he shall be known, is the conversion of the Gentiles. "There shall come forth a rod out of the root of Jesse, the father of David. This rod shall be exhibited as a standard to the view of all peoples. The Gentiles shall come to offer him their prayers: he shall be the leader and the teacher of the Gentiles. The Gentiles shall see this just man: all the kings of the earth shall know him, who is so celebrated in the prophecies of Sion. He shall teach justice to the

Gentiles. Men shall then cast far from them their idols of gold and silver, and shall adore the Lord alone."[551] Who converted the nations, and destroyed the worship of idols? Was it not our Lord, and our Lord alone? Our Lord is therefore the Messias predicted by Isaias.

He says that the Messias shall be born of a mother who will remain ever a virgin. "Behold a virgin shall conceive and bear a son, and his name shall be called Emmanuel,"[552] that is, a God-man, or "God with us." Our Lord was born of the ever glorious Virgin Mary. No other than he has been born of a virgin. Our Lord is therefore the Redeemer predicted by Isaias.[553]

He sees the various characteristics of this sacred child, who shall be adored by kings, and who shall have a precursor. "A child is born to us," he says, "a son is given to us, and the government is upon his shoulder, and his name shall be called Wonderful, Counselor, God the Mighty, the Father of the world to come, the Prince of Peace."[554] The incommunicable name of God shall be his name. "He shall sit upon the throne of David":[555] kings shall come to honor his cradle, and to offer him presents. "A voice shall be heard crying in the desert: 'Prepare ye the ways of the Lord!'"[556] Our Lord bore on his shoulders the instrument of his power—his cross—for by it he overcame the world; our Lord was adored in his cradle by the Magi, who also offered him presents; our Lord had St. John the Baptist as a precursor, who repeated the very words of Isaias: "The voice of one crying in the desert—Prepare ye the ways of the Lord!"[557] To no other than our Lord can all these circumstances be applied. Our Lord is therefore the Messias predicted by Isaias.

He foretells that the Messias shall be meekness itself, and shall perform a multitude of miracles in favor of mankind. "The Messias shall be full of meekness," says the prophet. "He shall feed his flocks like a shepherd. He shall gather together the little lambs, and shall take them up in his bosom."[558] "He shall not be troublesome."[559] "The bruised reed he shall not break, and smoking flax he shall not quench."[560] His power shall equal his goodness. "The eyes of the blind shall see the light; the ears of the deaf shall be unstopped; the lame shall bound like the roe; and the tongue of the dumb shall be set free."[561] Our Lord was meekness itself. He was the good shepherd. He healed all the sick that had recourse to his goodness. No other person has borne such characteristics or wrought such miracles. Our Lord is therefore the Messias predicted by Isaias.

He beholds the Messias establishing a new priesthood, and taking priests, not from the race of Aaron, but from among the Gentiles. I will select, says the Messias, by the mouth of the prophet, among those who shall escape from the general unbelief of the Jews, men whom I will mark with a particular sign; I will send them to the nations, from whom they shall draw others, who will become your brethren. They shall offer those whom they convert as a holy oblation to God; and among these converts I will choose priests and Levites.[562] Our Lord alone established a new priesthood. He selected priests who were not of the race of Aaron; he sent them to the Gentiles; and, from among the Gentiles converted to the gospel, he chose priests. All the Jewish doctors who preceded the birth of Jesus Christ apply to the Messias, as we do, the texts just quoted. Now, all these texts were verified in our Lord. Our Lord is therefore the Messias predicted by Isaias.

He describes the ignominies and death of the Messias so minutely that we might imagine we were reading one of the evangelists rather than one of the prophets. Let us hear him: "And he shall grow up before him as a tender plant, and as a root out of a thirsty ground. There is no beauty in him, nor comeliness. We have seen him, and there was no sightliness in him...He was despised, and the most object of men—a man of sorrows, and acquainted with infirmity; and his look was, as it were, hidden and despised: whereupon we esteemed him not. Surely he hath borne our infirmities and carried our sorrows; and we have thought him, as it were, a leper, and as one struck by God and afflicted."[563] "He was offered because it was his own will...He shall be led as a sheep to the slaughter, and shall be dumb as a lamb before his shearer; and he shall not open his mouth. He was taken away from distress and from judgment."[564]

Our Lord, on the day of his passion, lost all his comeliness. His beautiful countenance could hardly be recognized. He was a man of sorrows. He was set up in comparison with the criminal Barabbas; and was crucified between two thieves, after having been condemned by Pilate. He died in the midst of torments. He did not open his mouth to complain; but he prayed for his murderers. He was innocent; but he was charged with the expiation of the sins of all men. He delivered himself voluntarily to death, and the prodigies which accompanied his last breath proved that it depended on himself alone to surrender himself into the hands of his enemies. Our Lord is therefore the Messias predicted by Isaias.

He informs us that the Messias, in recompense for his sufferings and death, shall become the conqueror of the devil and the world, and that his sepulchre shall be glorious. "But because he suffered death," continues the prophet, "a long posterity shall be born to him." "His sepulchre shall be glorious."[565] "He hath acquired dominion." "He shall divide the spoils of the strong."[566] "He shall gather the fruits for which his soul suffered; he shall be satisfied with them, and shall sanctify, by his doctrine, an immense number of men." Our Lord saw all peoples flock to him after his death. For eighteen centuries his tomb has been an object of veneration to the whole world. The East and the West have contended for its possession; they have sent rich offerings to it; their deputies watch day and night over its preservation. The doctrine of our Lord has procured the salvation of millions of men in every age and clime. Our Lord is therefore the Messias predicted by Isaias.

Finally, he witnesses the astounding fruitfulness of the Church. This Church, formed originally in the terrestial paradise, had been a long time barren, giving only a few adorers to God. But, become fruitful by the blood of the Savior, it begins, says the prophet Isaias, to extend itself over all nations, and to people the earth with believers and saints. Nothing can surpass the magnificent picture that he draws of the propagation of the gospel. "Rejoice, thou barren one! that didst not bear: sing canticles of gladness; raise shouts of joy!...For she that was forsaken," that is, the world of Gentiles, "hath now a greater number of children than she that had a husband,"[567] that is, the Jewish nation, united to the Lord by the covenant of Abraham. "Raise thine eyes, and behold the immense multitude that come to join my people": all these new children "shall be to thee as a beautiful garment, with which thou shalt be clothed...Thy deserts and solitudes will be too narrow"[568] to receive the multitude coming to thee. "I will stretch out my hand toward the nations; and I will raise my standard before all peoples. They shall bring thee sons and daughters";[569] and "all flesh shall then know that I am the Lord."[570]

Our Lord established his Church. This holy spouse gave him speedily such an immense number of Christians, his faithful children, that, ten years after the death of the Savior, St. Paul wrote that the gospel was preached and believed throughout the whole world; and, a century later, Tertullian said to the pagans: "We are but of yesterday, and yet we fill your cities, your villages, your armies, the senate, the forum, the palace; we leave you only the temples and the theatres."[571]

Thus all the traits of the Redeemer, alluded to by the prophet Isaias, agree with our Lord, and with none but him. Our Lord is therefore the Messias predicted by Isaias.

PRAYER

O my God! who art all love, I thank thee for having sent so many prophets to thy people, in order to recall them to penance, and to instruct them regarding the Messias. Render me docile to the voice of the prophets of the new law, thy ministers, who recall me on thy behalf to penance, and who promise me heaven as the reward of my docility.

I am resolved to love God above all things, and my neighbor as myself for the love of God; and, in testimony of this love, I will attend respectfully to the catechism.

Lesson 40: Messias Prophesied by Micheas, Jeremias, and Joel

The two kingdoms of Israel and Juda fell, after their division, into strange disorders. Never had such a number of crimes, or such a propensity to idolatry, been witnessed. God, on his side, as he never ceases to love men, never showed himself more attentive in watching over the sacred deposit of religion, in preserving the tradition of the great promise, and in proclaiming solemnly the coming of the Messias. These evil times were an epoch of numerous and detailed prophecies.

Osee, a prophet; he foretells approaching events. — Isaias was still living when the voice of a new prophet was heard in Juda: this new envoy of God was Osee, the son of Beeri, born about seven hundred years before our Lord. We have no particulars concerning his life or his death. To prove to the Jews that his prophecies regarding the Redeemer, and the times subsequent to the incarnation, are true, he announces to them two events which should be accomplished in a very short time: the first, the ruin of Samaria; the second, the ruin of the kingdom of Juda.

What he announces concerning the Messias. He predicts that the Messias, while yet a child, shall go into Egypt, and that his Father shall recall him from it. The Lord himself, speaking figuratively by the mouth of his prophet, thus expresses himself: "Israel was but a child when I loved him, and I called my son out of Egypt."[572] Our Lord, while yet a child, was led into Egypt, along with his Mother, by St. Joseph, who had received an order to this effect from heaven; "and he remained there until the death of Herod, that the word," says St Matthew, "which the Lord had uttered by the mouth of his prophet, 'Out of Egypt I have called my son,' might be fulfilled."[573] Our Lord is therefore the Messias predicted by Osee.

The grand characteristic of the Messias, the conversion of the idolatrous nations, who were not the people of God, astonishes the prophet, and he exclaims: "I will say to that which is not my people: 'Thou are my people'; and they shall say: 'Thou art my God.'"[574] "And it shall happen that where it was said, 'You are not my people,' it shall be said, 'You are the sons of the living God.'"[575]

It was our Lord that converted the nations, and made idolaters his well-beloved people and the children of God. He is therefore the Messias predicted by Osee.[576]

The same prophet also beholds the reprobation of the Jews, the state of desolation in which they are plunged at the present day, and their conversion toward the end of the world: "The children of Israel shall sit many days without king, and without prince, and without sacrifice, and without altar, and without ephod, and without theraphim. And after this the children of Israel shall return, and they shall seek the Lord their God…and they shall fear the Lord and experience his goodness in the last days."[577]

Our Lord was despised by the Jews; they are today wanderers without an altar or a sacrifice. This first part of the prophecy, whose accomplishment we behold before our eyes, assures us that the second part shall be accomplished in like manner, and that the Jews shall be converted toward the end of time. Accordingly, it is with our Lord alone that all the traits of this prophecy agree: they suit no other. Our Lord is therefore the Messias predicted by Osee.

Micheas, a prophet; approaching events. — About the same period there appeared another prophet, who left us one of the most striking predictions regarding the Redeemer: this prophet was Micheas. He first announces two events close at hand: the woes and the destruction of the kingdom of Israel, and the woes and the destruction of the kingdom of Juda. Then, passing on to the Messias, he expresses himself thus: "And thou, Bethlehem

Ephrata (Ephrata was the ancient name of Bethlehem) thou art a little one among the thousands of Juda; out of thee shall he come forth unto me who is to be the ruler of Israel, and his going forth is from the beginning, from the days of eternity."[578]

In consequence of this prophecy, the Jews were perfectly aware that the Messias should be born in Bethlehem. When the Magi afterward arrived at Jerusalem, Herod assembled all the chief priests and the doctors of the law, and asked them where Christ, the Messias, should be born. They answered him without hesitation: "In Bethlehem of Juda, according to the prediction of the prophet." And they cited for him the words of Micheas. The Messias, therefore, should be born in Bethlehem. Now, it was at Bethlehem that Jesus Christ was born, when the time and the circumstances marked out for the coming of the Messias had arrived. Our Lord is therefore the Redeemer predicted by Micheas.

What he announces concerninig the Messias. The prophet announces that the generation of the Redeemer is eternal; that he shall convert the nations; that his empire shall have no end; and that he shall be our peace. His empire shall subsist. "He shall stand and feed his flock in the strength of the Lord, in the height of the name of the Lord his God; and they shall be converted, for now shall he be magnified even to the ends of the earth. And this man shall be our peace."[579] Our Lord, who is both God and man, is begotten in the bosom of his Father from eternity; he is born in Bethlehem, in time, of the purest of virgins; he alone possesses an eternal empire; he alone has converted the nations; he alone enjoys a sovereign power; he alone is our peace, our reconciliation by the blood which he shed for us on the cross. You see, then, that it is to our Lord alone that all the lines drawn in this prophecy exactly refer. Our Lord is therefore the Messias predicted by Micheas.

Joel, a prophet. — Joel, another prophet, and a contemporary of the preceding one, gives two great traits in connection with the Redeemer: the descent of the Holy Ghost, and the last judgment. To confirm his words, Joel announces a fact, of which the Jews then living should behold the accomplishment, namely, a dreadful famine, which should desolate the whole country. These are the terms in which he expresses himself: "Hear this, ye old men; and all ye inhabitants of the land, give ear. Did this ever happen in your days, or in the days of your fathers?...That which the palmer-worm hath left, the locust hath eaten; that which the locust hath left, the bruchus hath eaten; that which the bruchus hath left, the mildew hath destroyed...The whole country is desolate: the ground hath mourned, for the corn is wasted; the wine is confóunded; the oil hath languished...Why did the beasts groan? Why did the herds of cattle low but because there is no pasture for them? Yea, and the flocks of sheep are perished."[580]

Passing then to the Messias, the prophet shows him to us pouring out his Spirit on the Church, and coming in the most formidable manner to judge the world. "And it shall come to pass after this, that I will pour out my spirit upon all flesh; your sons and your daughters shall prophesy, and your old men shall dream dreams; your young men shall have visions. In those days I will pour out my spirit on my servants and my handmaids."[581] Our Lord, according to his promise, sent his Holy Spirit on the apostles, and they prophesied; and this divine Spirit bestowed the gift of prophecy on many of the faithful in succeeding ages. St. Peter himself gives the explanation of this prediction.

The occupants of the upper chamber are filled with the Holy Ghost, and the Jews of Jerusalem, struck with astonishment, say to one another: "'What is the meaning of this?' But others, mocking, say: 'These persons are full of new wine.' Then Peter, presenting himself with the eleven, says to them: 'These persons are not drunk, as you suppose;... but this is that which was spoken by the prophet Joel:...I will pour out my spirit,'"[582] etc., relating the prophecy of Joel, as we have quoted it.

The prophet announces, secondly, that the Messias shall come in a most formidable manner to judge the world. It is the Messias himself who speaks: "I will show prodigies in heaven and on earth, blood, fire, and whirlwinds of smoke. The sun and the moon are darkened, and the stars have withdrawn their shining, and the heavens and the earth shall be moved before the great and terrible day of the Lord...I will gather together all nations, and will bring them down into the valley of Josaphat,...for there I will sit to judge all nations round about."[583]

Our Lord shall come to judge the world. He announces it himself in the gospel, and he pictures for us the signs going before this terrible day in language like that of the prophet. Our Lord sent the Holy Ghost on his apostles, as Joel had predicted; our Lord, then, shall also come to judge the world at the end of time. The accomplishment of the first prophecy assures us of the accomplishment of the second. Our Lord is therefore the Messias predicted by Joel.

Jeremias, a prophet; his life. — About fifty years after the time of the inspired men concerning whom we have just spoken, God raised up Jeremias — the prophet of sorrows. He excused himself a long time from accepting the sad mission that the Lord wished to entrust to him. "Ah! ah! ah!" he said, "my Lord God! I know not how to speak: I am only a child. The Lord answered him: Do not say 'I am only a child'; but go wherever I shall send thee, and whatever I command thee thou shalt speak. Be not afraid at their presence, for I am with thee to deliver thee, saith the Lord." The Lord put forth his hand and touched the mouth of Jeremias, saying: "Behold, I have given my words in thy mouth; I have set thee this day over the nations,"[584] etc., Jeremias at length obeyed.

The misfortunes with which he threatened the Jews, and the holy liberty with which he rebuked them on account of their disorders, irritated them to such a degree against him that they cast him into a deep, miry dungeon, from which an officer belonging to the court of king Sedecias extricated him. After the capture of Jerusalem, a number of the Jews remaining in Judea took refuge in Egypt, being afraid of the king of Babylon. Jeremias did everything in his power to oppose this project; but he was obliged to follow them with his disciple Baruch. There he continued with his accustomed zeal to reproach them for their crimes. He prophesied against them, and against the Egyptians. The scripture does not inform us of his death; but it is believed that the Jews, provoked by his repeated threats, stoned him in the year 590 before Jesus Christ.

His prophecies. To accredit his prophecies regarding the Redeemer and remote events, he announced to the Jews some facts that should happen in a very short time, that should be seen by every one, and that no amount of human foresight could discover. Let us here cite, from among their number, the terrible destruction of Jerusalem by Nabuchodonosor and the captivity of Babylon. Consider the manner in which he foretells these catastrophes. "Go," says the Lord to him, "and take an earthen vessel, made by a potter." The prophet takes the vessel, and departs from the city.

Coming to the ancients of the people and the ancients among the priests, he pauses in a valley not far from the gates of Jerusalem. "King of Juda and inhabitants of Jerusalem!" he says to them, "thus saith the Lord of hosts: 'I will bring an affliction upon this place, so that whosoever shall hear of it, his ears shall tingle.'" Then, raising his earthen vessel before all the people, he adds: "Thus saith the Lord of hosts: 'I will break this people and this city, even as this potter's vessel is broken.'"[585] At these words, he dashes the vessel to pieces. A few years afterward the proud Nabuchodonosor comes to fulfill this prophecy to the letter: he destroys the city from end to end, and leads away the people captive to Babylon.

Passing then to remote events, Jeremias announces that at the time of the birth of the Messias all the little children in the neighborhood of Bethlehem shall be put to death, and that their mothers shall be inconsolable. "A loud voice," he exclaims, "was heard of lamentation, of mourning and weeping, of Rachel bewailing her children, and refusing to be comforted because they are not."[586]

Our Lord was born at Bethlehem; Herod, to have him put to death, ordered a general massacre of the children of Bethlehem and its environs, from the age of two years downwards. Then were heard the sorrowful shrieks of mothers; and St. Matthew tells us that this was the accomplishment of the words of Jeremias, which we have just quoted. Our Lord is therefore the Redeemer predicted by Jeremias.

The prophet is careful not to forget the grand characteristic of the liberator, who, he says, will teach the truth to the nations, and make with men a new alliance, more perfect than the old. "I have made thee a prophet unto the nations,"[587] says the Lord to him; and the Messias himself adds, by the mouth of Jeremias: "Behold, the days shall come, when I will make a new covenant with the house of Israel, and with the house of Juda...I will give my law in their bowels, and I will write it in their hearts...and they shall all know me, from the least of them even to the greatest."[588] Our Lord alone has taught the truth to idolatrous nations; he has converted the world; he has made with men a new alliance, more perfect than the old. Our Lord is therefore the Messias predicted by Jeremias. St. Paul expressly states that it is our Lord who is referred to in this prophecy of Jeremias.[589]

PRAYER

O my God! who art all love, I thank thee for sending us the Messias, so often predicted by the prophets. Grant that we may listen to him with the same docility as sheep to their shepherd; and that, on the day of his terrible judgment, we may deserve to hear these consoling words: "Come, ye blessed of my Father, possess the kingdom prepared for you from the beginning of the world."

I am resolved to love God above all things, and my neighbor as myself for the love of God; and, in testimony of this love, I will often say to myself: "God will judge what I am now saying, what I am now reading, what I am now doing."

Lesson 41: Messias Prophesied by Ezechiel and Daniel

Ezechiel, a prophet. — The terrible predictions of Isaias, Jeremias, and the other prophets against Jerusalem were at length verified. This opulent city was utterly destroyed; its noble Temple, one of the wonders of the world, was left a heap of smoking ruins; and its inhabitants, led away captive by Nabuchodonosor to Babylon, groaned there under the chains of their slavery. It was then that a new prophet appeared. He was raised up by God to chide and to console the unfortunate exiles, and especially to announce to them the Messias, the liberator of all mankind.

Ezechiel, the great prophet to whom we refer, was himself led away in captivity to Babylon, where he uttered a number of his predictions. In order, like his predecessors, to prove to the Jews the truth of that which he announced concerning the Messias, he informed them of several approaching events which they should see with their own eyes, and of others whose accomplishment is borne witness to by the whole world at the present day.

Approaching events, which he foretells. The first thing he predicts to his brethren is their return to Judea, with the rebuilding of the Temple of Jerusalem.[590] These two facts are accomplished about forty years afterward. The second, which proves with what divine penetration Ezechiel reads even the most distant future, is that from the time of Nabuchodonosor, a contemporary of the prophet, Egypt should no longer have a native king. Here are the words of this astonishing prediction: "I will make the multitude of Egypt to cease by the hand of Nabuchodonosor, king of Babylon: he...shall be brought to destroy the land... and there shall no more be a prince of the land of Egypt."[591] Who would have thought that Egypt, the mother of sciences, the foundress of nations, should be deprived of a king of her own race, and should bow her head throughout all future ages to a foreign scepter? And, nevertheless, during the last twenty-three centuries, the oracle of Ezechiel has been fulfilled. As an infidel writer of our day remarks,[592] "Egypt, taken away from its natural owners, has been subjected without interruption to the yoke of strangers."

What he announces concerning the Messias. Coming to the Messias, Ezechiel announces that he shall spring from the race of David, that he shall be a shepherd who shall save his flock and gather all his sheep into one fold. Let us hear the Lord himself announcing this consoling event by the mouth of the prophet: "I will save my flock: it shall no more be a spoil; I will judge between sheep and sheep; I will set up one shepherd, David my servant, over them, to feed them. And I, the Lord, will be their God, and my servant David the prince in the midst of them."[593]

Our Lord himself acquaints us with the meaning of this prediction, when, speaking to the Jews, he says: "I am the good shepherd. The good shepherd giveth his life for his sheep...I have yet other sheep that are not of this fold; them also I must bring,...and there shall be one fold and one shepherd."[594] Our Lord guided these other sheep, that is, the idolatrous nations; he associated them to the sheep of the house of Israel: and today there is but one fold, which is the Church, and one shepherd, who is our Lord. Moreover, that nothing might be wanting to the accomplishment of the prophecy, this shepherd should belong to the race of David, or rather be the true David: now, our Lord belonged to the race of David, and, if we may so speak, was the real David, that is, the "well-beloved."

Ezechiel adds that the Messias shall establish a new covenant more perfect than the old. "I will make with my sheep a covenant of peace," says the Messias, by the mouth of the prophet. "It shall be an everlasting covenant. I will multiply them, and establish forever my sanctuary in the midst of them. My tabernacle shall be with them; I will be their God: they shall be my people, and the nations shall know that I am the Lord and the sanctifier of Israel, when my sanctuary shall be in the midst of them forever."[595] It was our Lord that established a new covenant more perfect than the old—an eternal covenant. It was he that assembled the Jews and the Gentiles in one fold. He was, moreover, of the race of David, and truly the well-beloved. Our Lord is therefore the Messias predicted by Ezechiel.

About the same time, and in the same city of Babylon, prophesied the last of the greater prophets: this was Daniel, whose interesting history we shall now consider.

Daniel, a prophet; his history.—Nabuchodonosor desired to have at his court some children belonging to the Jewish nation, whom he had led into captivity. His intention was to have them taught the language and the sciences of the Babylonians. He accordingly gave orders on the matter to the master of his palace. The choice of this officer, guided by the Lord, fell on Daniel and his three companions, Ananias, Misael, and Azarias. They were lodged in apartments suited for their studies. The king directed, as a mark of his favor, that they should be fed with the same meats as those served up at his own table, and should be offered no other description of wine than that which he himself used. They were to be brought up thus for three years, at the end of which time the king should rank them among his attendants, and they should always appear in his presence.

One thing alone disturbed the minds of these virtuous children: the sort of food and drink ordered them from the king's table. It might easily happen that among the dishes presented to them, there would be something forbidden to the Jews or that had even been offered to idols: they resolved not to touch any of them. Daniel spoke to the master of the palace, appointed to provide for their nourishment. This man replied that the king, desiring none but beautiful youths, well formed, and of good mien, for his service, had given express directions on the manner in which they should be treated. He added that if, by not using the wine and meats from the king's table, they should grow sickly in their appearance, the cause would soon be known, and it would cost him his position, perhaps his life.

Daniel was not discouraged. He addressed himself to Malassar, an inferior officer, specially appointed over him and his three companions. "Give us," he said, "as we desire, some pulse to eat and water to drink. We only ask thee for a ten days' trial. Examine then our looks; compare us with the other young persons that eat of the king's table. If thou have any reason to repent of thy kindness, we will submit to whatever thou shalt say." Malassar agreed to this proposal. Daniel and his companions lived for ten days on simple pulse, and, at the end of this time, they looked fairer and stronger than those who were nourished from the king's table. Malasser then continued to treat them in the same manner, and with the same happy results.

The three years of their instruction drawing to a close, the day of presenting the four young Israelites to the king arrived. Nabuchodonosor was delighted with their charming manners and healthy appearance. He was much more so with their intelligence. "I have not in all my kingdom," he exclaimed, "any wise men to be compared with the four young Hebrews." He did not hesitate to retain them near himself: he gave them employments in his court, and desired that they should always serve in his presence. Such was the beginning of the great elevation of the prophet Daniel. The Lord, ever infinitely good, was thus preparing a resource for the captive Israelites.

Daniel explains Nabuchodonosor's dream. — After a few years, Nabuchodonosor had a dream that troubled him very much. On awaking, he sent for all the sorcerers, diviners, and magicians of Babylon. "Last night," said the king to them, "I had a dream that terrified me; but the anxiety that followed it has made me quite forget it. If you recall the dream to my mind, and give me its explanation, I promise you a reward worthy of me; but, if you disappoint my expectations, I will put you all to death, even to the last man."

"That which thou demandest, O king!" they answered, "is an impossibility to mortals." The king, in a fury, ordered them to be put to death. This order was being pitilessly executed, when Daniel, full of confidence in God, and suddenly inspired, ran to the apartment of the king, whom he found plunged in the deepest melancholy. He begged a short respite, that he might be fully able to explain the dream. "Be it so, Daniel," said the king to him, "take the time of which thou hast need."

Daniel withdrew, and spent the night in prayer. Morning having come, one of the court officers accompanied him into the presence of the king, saying: "Here, my lord, is one of the captives from Jerusalem, who will give the king, my lord, the information that he desires." "Art thou able," says the king to Daniel, "to remind me of my dream, and to give me its explanation?" "The dream that thou hast had," answers Daniel modestly, "surpasses the comprehension of all the magicians. But there is a God in heaven, the one only God, whom I adore, from whom nothing is concealed, and who reveals, whensoever and to whomsoever he pleases, the most hidden things. It was he, O great prince, that showed thee in the darkness of the night the events that will happen in the last times."

The king and all his court had their eyes fixed on the young prophet, who continued thus: "This, my lord, is the dream that thou hadst. There was presented before thee a great statue. This great statue stood before thine eyes, and its looks were terrible. Its head was of fine gold, the breast and the arms of silver, the belly and the thighs of brass, the legs of iron, and the feet partly of iron and partly of clay. Thou wast very attentive to the vision, when a stone, detaching itself from a mountain, struck the feet of the statue, and broke them. Then did the statue itself fall to pieces, as small as the dust that the wind blows about in summer. But the stone that struck the statue became a great mountain, and filled the whole earth. This was thy dream, O great king!

"And this is its explanation: Thou, O king, art the greatest of kings; thou art represented by the head of gold. After thine empire, there shall arise another, figured by the silver, less than thine. Then shall follow a third, figured by the brass, and extending over all the earth. The fourth empire, like iron, which breaks all other metals, shall break and overthrow everything opposed to its establishment. Yet, this fourth empire shall be weakened by its divisions, represented by the mixture of iron and clay in the feet of the statue. In fine, at a time when these empires are still subsisting, the God of heaven shall raise up a new empire that shall never be destroyed, and that shall overthrow all the others: it was signified to thee by the stone, which, detaching itself from a mountain, reduced to dust the clay, the iron, the brass, the silver, and the gold."

As for us, who live after the event, it is easy to distinguish the empires whose succession is announced by Daniel. The first, represented by the gold, is the empire of the Babylonians. The second, represented by the silver, is that of the Medes and Persians. The third, represented by the brass, is that of the Greeks, under Alexander the Great. This empire, the prophet tells us, should extend over the whole earth. As a matter of fact, Alexander carried his conquests to every quarter of the world. The fourth empire, represented by the iron, is evidently that of the Romans. As iron breaks all other metals, so this empire reduced to powder all the kingdoms that existed before it in the known world.

As for the stone which detaches itself from the mountain without the aid of any human being, which breaks the statue, which becomes so large, which covers the whole extent of the earth, and which forms an empire whose duration shall be eternal, it clearly denotes the spiritual empire of our Lord, an empire formed without the help of any man, an empire overcoming all others, an empire which shall not pass to another people, an empire as extensive as the world and whose duration shall be eternal. To what other empire than that of Jesus Christ do these characteristics agree?

At the conclusion of the prophet's discourse, Nabuchodonosor, seized with an astonishment beyond anything that can be expressed, and regarding Daniel as a god hidden under the form of a man, fell on his face to the ground, in sentiments of the most profound adoration. He also commanded that incense should be forthwith offered, and victims sacrificed to Daniel. Daniel prevented all this impious worship, and hastened to refer the praise to God, who had inspired him. Nabuchodonosor acknowledged that the God of Daniel was the God of gods, and the master of kings. He then raised Daniel and his companions to the highest dignities in the empire.

The children in the furnace.—The young Hebrews soon found, as so many others have done, that to be hated, it is not necessary to be wicked: it suffices to be happy. The kindness with which they were treated drew around them some jealous enemies, who resolved on their destruction. These zealots persuaded Nabuchodonosor to forbid his subjects to adore any god that was not ranked among the gods of Babylon. The king then commanded that a great statue of gold, sixty cubits high, should be made, and placed in the center of a vast plain, near Babylon. At the same time an order was issued to the officers of the army, the magistrates, the judges, the rulers, the governors of provinces, and all the chief men of the realm, to appear on a certain day in the plain: there to offer to the statue that religious worship which the king intended for it, under pain of being instantly cast into a burning furnace.

Ananias, Misael, and Azarias, the three companions of Daniel, came with every one else to the plain. But, at the moment when the signal was given to all present to cast themselves on their faces to the ground, the three Israelites remained standing, without showing the least sign of adoration. Their enemies ran to inform the king of it. Fired with wrath, Nabuchodonosor ordered that they should be immediately cast into the furnace, heated seven times more than usual. The generous youths were seized by some of the strongest of his guards, and, their hands and feet having been tied, were cast into the midst of the flames. But the God of Israel accompanied them: the fire, respecting their persons, consumed their fetters; and they walked about undisturbed in the flaming gulf. After a little while, they began to sing the praises of the Lord.

At the sight of this miracle, Nabuchodonsor drew nigh to the furnace, and, calling them, said: "Ye servants of the Most High God, come to me." He proclaimed that the God of Israel was the only true God, and published an edict by which he forbade anyone, under pain of death, to blaspheme the living God. This solemn homage is a new proof of that merciful watchfulness of our heavenly Father which only permits the persecution of his servants and the mixture of his people with the infidel nations in order to display his glory, to confirm the Israelites in the faith of their fathers, and to prepare the Gentiles gradually for the worship of the true God.

PRAYER

O my God! who art all love, I thank thee for preserving thy servants in the midst of flames. Grant me an inviolable fidelity to thy holy law, and courage to brave all human respect, in order that I may save myself from eternal flames.

I am resolved to love God above all things, and my neighbor as myself for the love of God; and, in testimony of this love, I will never violate the fasts and abstinences prescribed by the Church.

Lesson 42: Messias Prophesied by Daniel (Continued)

Continuation of the history of Daniel.—We can easily understand that the miracle wrought in the fiery furnace confirmed the reputation of Daniel's three young companions. These virtuous Israelites profited of their authority only to make known that powerful God who had preserved them, and to sweeten the lot of their captive brethren throughout the whole extent of the empire.

Meanwhile, Nabuchodonosor died, and, under the reign of his successor, Daniel was forgotten. Advanced in age, he thought only of serving the Lord his God in silence, and of praying for his poor captives; but the master had very different views from those of the servant. It was this Daniel, aged and forgotten as he was, that providence chose to employ for the consummation of the great work of the deliverance of the Jews, his chosen people.

Baltassar's vision.—Baltassar, the grandson of Nabuchodonosor, had ascended the throne of his grandfather. Much more devoted to his pleasures than to the care of his kingdom, he one day decided on giving a most sumptuous feast, to which he invited a thousand of the greatest lords in his kingdom. Abandoned without restraint to a foolish mirth, the king drank freely, and in his carouse commanded the officers to bring into the festive hall the gold and silver vessels which Nabuchodonosor had carried away from the Temple of Jerusalem, in order that the lords and ladies present might drink out of them with him. The king gave the example, and everyone gloried in following it. Their only concern was to see who should profane with the greatest insolence the sacred vessels. They drank their flowing cups, and sang hymns in honor of their false divinities. The unfortunate Baltassar, coming thus to the height of his crimes, filled up the fatal measure for which God was waiting in order to destroy his monarchy.

Suddenly there appeared, as it were, the fingers of a man on the wall, opposite the chandelier that illumined the banquet hall, and the king could see distinctly the motion of the hand that wrote. Then he changed color, his spirit was troubled, his strength forsook him, and his knees struck against each other; and he was only able to exclaim: "Let the diviners, the soothsayers, the magicians, be called immediately!"

He was promptly obeyed. " If there is anyone among you," said the king to them, "who shall read this writing, and explain its meaning for me, I will order him to be clothed with purple, I will give him a collar of gold, and I will make him the third person in my kingdom." All his impostors set to work; but their efforts were vain. The king's despair increased: he relapsed into his first dejection, and his terrified court knew not whom to have recourse to: this was the moment for which the Lord was waiting.

Daniel explains the dream. — The queen, informed of what had taken place, descended to the hall of the feast. "My lord," said she to the king, "reassure thyself. There is a man in thy kingdom to whom the holy gods communicate their spirit: he is named Daniel. Send for him, and he will relieve thee of thy anxiety." The king ordered Daniel to be called, and, when he saw him coming, said: "Art thou Daniel, one of the children of Juda, whom my father led away into captivity? If thou wilt explain this writing, traced on the wall by an unknown hand, thou shalt be clothed with purple, thou shalt wear a collar of gold, and thou shalt be, after the queen and me, the first person in my kingdom."

Daniel perceived the danger of the commission; but it was now nearly eighty years since he had learned not to tremble before the princes of the earth. "O great king," he said to Baltassar, "I will not accept thy presents, but I will read for thee the words written on the wall, and give thee their explanation. This writing consisteth of three words: *Mane, Thecel, Phares.* And this is their meaning: *Mane,* the Lord hath counted the days of thy reign, and they draw to a close; *Thecel,* thou hast been weighed in the balance, and found too light; *Phares,* thy kingdom hath been divided between the Medes and Persians." Notwithstanding the trouble and terror that such an explanation must have cast into his soul, the king obliged the prophet to accept the honors that he had promised.

Baltassar is slain. — The execution of this terrible sentence was nearer than Baltassar imagined. That very night, Cyrus, the king of the Medes and Persians, entered Babylon. His troops penetrated even to the palace of the king, where Baltassar was slain in the midst of a general carnage — on a night made ever memorable by a sacrilegious feast, by a miracle from the hand of God, by the death of a powerful ruler, by the end of a great monarchy, and by the fulfillment of the prophecies of three prophets: of Daniel, who had announced, a few years beforehand, the destruction of the empire of the Assyrians; and of Isaias and Jeremias, who had — one, two hundred years, the other, seventy years, previously — predicted, with the fullest details, the taking of Babylon by the Medes and Persians.[596]

Daniel in the lions' den. — Under the new dynasty Daniel enjoyed the same favor as under the Babylonian kings. Jealous of his merit and his fortune, the lords of the court resolved on his destruction. They persuaded the king to forbid, by a solemn edict, any petitions or prayers to be offered during the space of thirty days to any man or divinity, throughout the whole extent of the kingdom: this under pain, if any person should be found violating it, of being cast headlong into the lions' den, there to be devoured.

Nothing could be more unjust or absurd than this proposal. But the king feared the great ones of his court: he considered them necessary to him, and the decree was published. Daniel might have eluded the prince's edict: it would have sufficed for him not to appear publicly to offer his petitions to God; but he knew that, on an occasion of this kind, to keep secret the worship which he rendered to the Lord would be to disown it. He therefore changed none of his practices. Three times a day he opened, according to his custom, the windows of his chamber on the side that turned toward Jerusalem; he fell on his knees, he prayed, he adored his God. There were spies in watch for him, and he was not ignorant of it. When they had found him actually in prayer, his triumphant enemies ran to give an account to the king of the contempt that he had shown for the royal orders. "Daniel," they said, "that Jewish slave, become thy dearest favorite, is the first to violate thy command."

At the name of Daniel, the king was inwardly grieved. He loved the great man, respected his virtue, honored his old age, and understood the full value of his services. He made no reply to the accusers beyond desiring them to leave him alone, until he should declare his intentions.

His design was to save Daniel: the informers suspected it. They returned boldly to the king, and said to him in a very threatening manner: "We know not, O king, what stayeth thy justice; but know thou that thou art not above the laws, and that it is a fundamental law among the Medes and Persians that no prince can revoke his own edicts." The king, alarmed, sent for the prophet. Moved by the presence of the venerable old man, he said only these few words: "Go, Daniel, whither thine enemies lead thee; thy God, whom thou hast never ceased to adore, will deliver thee." He was so convinced of it, that he chose to follow closely the men that had taken on themselves the execution of the sentence. Accompanied by all his court, he advanced to the brink of the pit; and, Daniel having been precipitated into it, he caused its mouth to be covered with a stone, which he sealed with his own seal and with the seal of the nobles of his suite, that the malice of men might add nothing to the ferocity of the beasts.

The king returned to his palace a prey to deadly fears: he could take neither food nor rest. At break of day he arose to visit the den of the lions. He drew nigh, trembling; and, his eyes wet with tears, he cried out in a sorrowful voice: "Daniel, faithful servant of the living God, hath thy God been able to deliver thee from the fury of the lions?" "Yes, O king," answered Daniel, calmly, "my God sent his angel, who closed the mouths of the lions, and they have not done me any harm."

His heart full of joy, the king ordered that Daniel should be immediately drawn up from the den. There was not a single wound to be found on his body, and the infidel monarch, seeing most plainly what faith in the true God can do for the salvation of those who place their confidence in him, could no longer resist so striking a miracle. He adored the sovereign God with all the sincerity of his heart, and cast Daniel's accusers into the den. The wretches had scarcely reached the bottom of the pit before the lions had torn their flesh into pieces and broken their bones.

The idol of Bel. —Daniel, more powerful than ever, employed all the resources of his wisdom to draw from idolatry the new king that had just ascended the throne of Babylon: this was the great king Cyrus. On his arrival in the state, the prince had found an idol, named Bel, in great reverence among the Babylonians: he declared himself one of its adorers, and every day regularly went to offer it his homage. Nothing could induce Daniel to follow him into the temple of the false god. The king remarked the absence of his minister. "Why," he said to him, "dost thou not adore Bel?" "Because," answered the holy old man, "I do not adore idols made by the hands of men. There is one living God, who created heaven and earth, and who is the absolute master of all creatures. It is he whom I have adored from my childhood, and whom I will always adore." "What!" replied Cyrus, "is not Bel a living God? Dost thou not see how much he eats and drinks everyday?"

In effect, the idol of Bel was an enormous statue to which there were supplied every day, without fail, twelve great measures of most pure flour, forty sheep, and sixty vessels of the best wine. This was intended only for one of its repasts, and nothing was ever left the next day. "Sire," said Daniel, with a sigh, "do not deceive thyself. This pretended god is only a statue of clay, covered with brass. I assure thee that it never eats or drinks."

Cyrus, astonished, sent for the priests of Bel, and said to them with a tone of authority: "If you do not tell me who it is that consumes the meats and the wine every day supplied before Bel, I will put you all to death. But if you can show that it is the god that nourishes himself with these things, I will put Daniel to death, in order to avenge the blasphemies that he has uttered against Bel." "I am willing," said Daniel, "I accept the conditions."

The priests of the idol enjoyed an anticipated triumph, imagining that they already beheld the blood of their enemy flow. They numbered seventy altogether, without counting their wives, children, and grandchildren. They had placed under the table of the altar a secret entrance, of which they never feared that anyone would form the least suspicion.

By this passage they were accustomed to visit the temple every night, and to carry off the meats, the flour, and the wine: their policy seemed infallible to them.

They besought the king to come, with Daniel, to their temple, adding: "We shall go out; and do thou, O prince, cause the ordinary meats, flour, and wine to be laid. Thou mayest close the door of the temple; thou mayest seal it with thy royal ring. If, returning next morning, thou find that Bel hath not consumed everything during the night, thou mayest put us all to death. If, on the contrary, he hath consumed everything, thou wilt put Daniel to death for having blasphemed our god and calumniated his ministers." When, therefore, they had gone out, the king caused the usual refreshments to be placed before Bel. Daniel, on his side, ordered some of his servants to bring him ashes and a sieve. He sprinkled the ashes over the pavement of the temple in presence of the king, who was much astonished at this strange manaeuvre, of he which did not penetrate the meaning. The king, accompanied by Daniel, then came forth from the temple, and, having closed the door, sealed it with his ring.

About midnight, the priests of Bel, with their wives and children, entered the temple, according to their custom, by the private passage that they had constructed. They carried away everything that the king had left there. They made a great feast together, and their joy seemed to outdo itself in evil railleries on the simplicity of the good king, and in bitter insults against the enterprises of his old minister; but they little knew what was prepared for them.

The king, rising at dawn, and taking Daniel with him, proceeded to the temple. When he drew nigh to it, he said to his minister: "Are the seals whole?" "O prince," answered Daniel, "they are whole." The door being opened, the king looked in, and, seeing that nothing remained on the table of the altar, exclaimed in a transport of delight: "How great art thou, O Bel! Thou justifiest in a glorious manner the sincerity of thy priests." Daniel began to laugh, and, holding the king to prevent him from entering, said: "Just examine the pavement of the temple, and tell me whose footsteps are these." "I have been deceived," exclaimed the prince, indignantly, "I perceive the marks of the feet of men, women, and children." He instantly commanded the priests of Bel and their families to be brought to him, and ordered them to tell him what were the prints that he perceived. Trembling with fear, they showed him the hidden openings by which they had entered, and carried off everything placed before the idol. The king put them all to death, and abandoned the idol to the discretion of Daniel, who overthrew it on the spot, broke it in pieces, and destroyed the temple that had been consecrated to it. It was thus that Daniel led Cyrus to know the God of Israel, and to restore liberty to the Jews.

Daniel is, as we have said, the last of the greater prophets. As a proof of the truth of his predictions regarding the Messias, he announced many events that were realized under the eyes of the Jews and the Babylonians themselves. The first was the succession of four great empires. He predicted that the empire of the Assyrians, of which Nabuchodonosor was king, should pass to the Medes and Persians; that the empire of the Medes and Persians should pass to the Greeks, under the command of Alexander; and, in fine, that the empire of the Greeks should pass to the Romans.[597] The second was the precise epoch at which Jerusalem, destroyed by Nabuchodonosor, should be rebuilt.[598] These things were accomplished to the very letter: even the Jews and profane historians admit it.[599]

Daniel predicts the epoch of the birth of the Messias. —Passing to the Redeemer, Daniel announces that the Messias, so much desired, shall come in 490 years; that he shall be put to death; that the Jews shall deny him, and cease to be his people; that the Temple and the city of Jerusalem shall be destroyed; that the Messias shall establish a new covenant; that the sacrifices of the old law shall cease; and that then shall begin that desolation in which we behold the deicide people at this day. To understand properly the words of Daniel, it must be remarked that, among the Jews, as among other people, there were two sorts of weeks:

weeks of days, like ours, and weeks of years, or periods of seven years. There is question of the latter only in the celebrated prophecy of Daniel, of which we shall now give the text.

The archangel Gabriel speaks to Daniel, and says to him: "Seventy weeks (that is 490 years) are shortened upon thy people and upon thy holy city, that transgression may be finished, and sin may have an end, and iniquity may be expiated, and eternal justice may be brought, and vision and prophecy may be fulfilled, and the saint of saints may be anointed...Christ shall be slain, and the people that will deny him shall no longer be his people. Another people, with their leader that shall come, shall utterly destroy the city and the sanctuary; and the end thereof shall be waste, and after the end of the war the appointed desolation. Christ shall confirm his covenant with the world...Sacrifices shall be abolished, and there shall be in the temple the abomination of desolation, and the desolation shall continue even to the end."[600]

By this prophecy it is made as clear as the sun 1) that the Messias has come. Daniel announces that the ruin of the temple and the city of Jerusalem should follow the death of Christ. "The Christ shall be put to death," he says, "and the city and the sanctuary shall be destroyed." Jerusalem was taken and destroyed, and its Temple burnt, by the Romans, in the year 70 of the Christian era. The Christ or Messias, foretold by Daniel, had therefore come, and had therefore been put to death, before this epoch. It is therein vain that the Jews still look for the coming of the Messias.

It is demonstrated by the same prophecy 2) that the Christ or Messias foretold by Daniel is our Lord Jesus Christ.

The Messias announced by Daniel should expiate the iniquities of the world. It was our Lord who expiated the iniquities of the world; it was he of whom St. John the Baptist said: "Behold the Lamb of God, behold him who taketh away the sins of the world!" The Messias predicted by Daniel should bring back to the earth the reign of all virtues. It was our Lord who brought back to the earth the reign of all virtues, by abolishing idolatry and recalling all people to the knowledge of the true God. The Messias foretold by Daniel should fulfill in himself all the prophecies. Our Lord literally fulfilled all the prophecies in his birth, his life, his death, and his resurrection.

The Messias should be the saint of saints—in a word, God. Our Lord was the saint of saints, so holy that he defied his mortal enemies to find any sin in him. To prove that he was God, he performed a multitude of miracles, which the Jews could never question—that, for example, of the resurrection of Lazarus. The Messias predicted by Daniel should establish a new covenant. Our Lord alone established a new covenant with the world. The Messias predicted by Daniel should be put to death, and, on account of this death, the Jewish people should cease to be the people of God, while Jerusalem and the Temple should be destroyed. Our Lord was put to death by the Jews, who refused to receive him; it was after this death, and on account of this death, even according to the prediction of our Lord, that the Jews fell into that state of desolation in which we today behold them, and that the city and the Temple of Jerusalem were utterly ruined. Our Lord united in himself all the characteristics of the Messias predicted by Daniel; these characteristics agree with no one else: our Lord is therefore the Messias predicted by Daniel.

PRAYER

O my God! who art all love, I thank thee for having announced with so much accuracy the characteristics and the time of the birth of the Messias: it is with a transport of delight that I recognize this divine Messias in our Lord Jesus Christ, who alone unites in himself all the characteristics of the Messias predicted by Daniel.

I am resolved to love God above all things, and my neighbor as myself for the love of God; and, in testimony of this love, I will pray for the conversion of the Jews.

Lesson 43: Messias Prophesied by Aggeus, Zacharias, and Malachias

Edict of Cyrus. — Daniel's efforts to promote the deliverance of the Jews and their return into their own country were at length crowned with the happiest success. Cyrus issued the famous edict in which he granted liberty to the Jews that were captives in the empire of Babylon to return to Judea, to rebuild the Temple, and to repeople the city of Jerusalem. Everyone immediately hastened to avail himself of the royal permission. As it was impossible for all the Jews to return at once into an uncultivated country, which had lain idle for nearly seventy years, a portion only of the captives set out under the guidance of the high priest, Josue, and of Zorobabel, a young prince of the family of David. Cyrus surrendered to them all the sacred vessels of the Temple of Jerusalem. He caused these vessels to be counted in his presence, and, between gold and silver ones, their number amounted to 5,400.

Return of the Jews to Judea. — The departure took place in the tenth month of the seventieth and last year of the captivity. The journey occupied a considerable time; for Jerusalem was about nine hundred miles distant from Babylon, and the pilgrims included whole families, aged men, women, and children. After a wearisome march of four months, they at length set foot on the soil of Judea. On their arrival, the party were numbered, and were found to consist of 42,360 persons. The first care of the exiles on returning to their country was to raise an altar to the Lord, which might serve until such times as their resources would permit them to build a temple to him. A year later, they laid the foundations of this Temple; but, great difficulties arising, in accordance with the prophecy of Daniel, the work was interrupted for several years.

While Josue, Zorobabel, and especially the old men that had seen the Temple of Solomon were very much downcast, and wept to think how far inferior the new Temple would be to the former one, the Lord was pleased to console some and to encourage others.

Aggeus, a prophet. — With this view he called the prophet Aggeus, and said to him: "Speak to Zorobabel, the chief of Juda, and to Josue, the high priest, and to all the people, saying: 'Who is left among you, that saw this house in its first glory? And how do you see it now? Is it not in comparison with that as nothing in your eyes? Yet now take courage, O Zorobabel, and take courage,' saith the Lord, 'O Josue, the son of Josedec the high priest, and take courage, all ye, O my people, take courage: and perform (for I am with you, saith the Lord of hosts) the word that I covenanted with you…: Yet a little while, and I will move heaven, earth, the sea, and the dry land: and I will move all nations: and the desired of all nations shall come; and I will fill this house with glory…Great shall be the glory of this last house, more than of the first; for, in this place, I will give peace.'"[601]

Both Jews and Christians have always maintained that this prediction regards the Messias. Now, it proves two things. The first is that the Messias has come. The prophet announces that the Messias shall come in person into the second Temple, and it is on this account that the glory of the second Temple shall infinitely surpass that of the first. As the second Temple was burned by the Romans, in the year 70 of the Christian era, the Messias had therefore come before this epoch, and it is in vain for the Jews to continue to expect him.

The second is that our Lord Jesus Christ is truly the Messias predicted by Aggeus. The prophet announces that, at the coming of the Messias, God shall move heaven, earth, the sea, the whole world. Now, at the coming of our Lord, heaven, earth, and sea were moved by prodigies. The concert of the angels who announced his birth; the star which pointed him out to the Magi; heaven opened at his baptism; the darkness which covered the earth at his death: all were so many prodigies wrought in the heavens. The earth was astonished at the splendor of his works. The sea felt the strength of his omnipotence: he calmed its angry billows, and obliged its troubled waves to serve as a solid support for the feet of St. Peter. The whole world was set in motion by the fall of the great monarchies of the Persians and the Greeks, overthrown by the Romans.

Moreover, the prophet designates the Messias as the Desired of Nations; it was thus that Jacob himself, when dying, pointed him out to his children. Now, it is certain that, at the time of the coming of our Lord, the various nations of the earth were in a state of anxious expectation regarding some mysterious personage, who was to appear in Judea, and was to become the master of the world. This expectation, say two pagan historians, Tacitus and Suetonius, was founded on ancient traditions scattered throughout all the East. Since the time of the coming of our Lord, the nations have ceased to expect this mysterious personage, who should appear in Judea, and become the master of the world. Our Lord was therefore truly the Desired of Nations; and since, as we have seen, the Desired of Nations is the Messias, it necessarily follows that our Lord is truly the Messias.

The prophet announces that it is in the second Temple the Lord "shall give peace." This peace is not a peace limited to a certain people or a certain time. It is peace, simply so-called—an eternal, constant peace—comprising all goods and embracing all peoples. It is the peace of heaven with earth—the reconciliation of all creatures with the Creator, of the human race with God. Such was the work reserved for the Messias predicted by Aggeus.

And now, who but our Lord ever gave peace to the world: the peace of God; a peace comprising all goods and embracing all peoples; that peace which is the reconciliation of heaven with earth? Was it not he whose coming the angels announced in the hymn: "Peace to men of good will?" Was it not he who bequeathed to the world, as his only legacy, peace? "My peace I give you," he said, "my peace I leave you: not the peace which the world giveth." Did not the divine Savior, the minister of that peace, announce it even in the Temple of Jerusalem? Was it not in the very Temple that this peace was concluded, when the Savior shed there the first drops of his blood under the knife of circumcision? Our Lord is therefore undoubtedly the Messias predicted by Aggeus.

To prove to the Jews the truth of his predictions regarding the Messias, the prophet at the same time announces to them some events of which they were to be the witnesses. The first was the cessation of that sterility which had now lasted for nearly ten years, and the return of abundance. The second was the fall of foreign kingdoms, such as the overthrow of the monarchy of the Persians by the Greeks, and of that of the Greeks by the Romans, and especially the preservation of the royal race of Juda until the birth of the Messias, who, by the descendants of Zorobabel, should come of David, Jacob, Isaac, and Abraham. These two events were verified. Aggeus prophesied about 520 years before the coming of our Lord.

Zacharias, a prophet.—Scarcely had Aggeus made these consoling promises to the people of God, when Zacharias, another prophet of the Lord, came to confirm them, and to add new ones. Following the unvarying course of the prophets, he begins to establish his divine mission by predicting events close at hand, whose accomplishment should prove the truth of his predictions regarding the Messias.

He announces: a) that Jerusalem, so often unfaithful, shall no more relapse into idolatry, and that she shall be called the city of truth: this prophecy was fulfilled to the letter—after the return from captivity Jerusalem no more abandoned herself to the worship of idols; b) that, notwithstanding all the appearances to the contrary, Jerusalem should be rebuilt and reinhabited: old men, says the prophet, shall yet be seen in the public places of Jerusalem, supporting themselves with staffs, on account of their great age, and the streets of the city shall be filled with little boys and girls, who shall play in the public places; c) that the land of the Philistines, those ancient enemies of the people of God, should be abandoned to desolation: this last prediction was accomplished under Alexander the Great,[602] as the preceding one had been accomplished under the king of Persia.

Passing on to the Messias, the prophet enters into the most interesting details, telling us that he shall blot out the iniquities of the world; that he shall be a King; that he shall be just; that he shall be the Savior; that he shall be meek and humble; that he shall enter Jerusalem on an ass, and the foal of an ass; that he shall be struck, and that, at this sight, his disciples shall abandon him; that he shall be sold for thirty pieces of silver—that this silver shall be brought into the Temple, and given to a potter; that he shall have his hands pierced; in fine, that he shall convert the nations, that those who put him to death shall end by recognizing him, and that there shall be great mourning in Jerusalem.[603]

Our Lord blotted out the iniquities of the world; our Lord was a King—he boldly declared it to Pilate, and he still reigns over the world, whose ideas and manners he has reformed; he was just—so just that his enemies could not make him the least reproach; he was the true Savior; he was meek and humble: "Learn of me," he said, "because I am meek and humble of heart";[604] he entered Jerusalem on an ass, followed by its foal; he was seized in the Garden of Olives, and abandoned by his apostles; he, and he alone, was sold for thirty pieces of silver, and this silver, the price of a God, Judas returned to the priests, who purchased with it a potter's field; he, and he alone, converted the nations; for him, and for him alone, the Jews wept bitterly when they found, after his resurrection, that they had crucified the Son of God. Our Lord is therefore truly the Messias predicted by Zacharias.

The city and the Temple of Jerusalem are rebuilt.—Encouraged by the words of Aggeus and Zacharias regarding the future greatness of the Temple, the Jews were disheartened no more. They labored with great earnestness at the erection of the edifice, without being discouraged by fatigues or by the evil designs of their enemies.

A few years afterward, Esdras, who was still in Babylon where he held a distinguished rank, obtained permission from the king to conduct into Palestine a second colony of the Jews that remained in his states. Having assembled all the travelers, he spoke to them in this manner: "We are alone, my brethren, without arms, without any means of defense in a vast country, which we are about to traverse, and where we are surrounded by enemies whose delight would be to ensnare us. I might have asked the king for troops to accompany us, but I confess to you that I was ashamed to do so. You know what I said to this prince before you on the powerful protection with which the Lord our God honors all those who seek him in the simplicity of their hearts, and who place their confidence in him. But, to render yourselves worthy of his protection, let us spend one day in fasting and prayer: let us ask of God, by fervent supplications, that he may vouchsafe to be our guide and our protector during our journey."

Esdras had the consolation of seeing all the travelers share his sentiments. There was not one among them who did not look on fasting and prayer as a far better means of defense than any escorts that might be given them: and their hope was not vain. Arrived happily in their country, they joined their brethren in removing the ruins of Jerusalem, and pushing forward to the completion of the Temple. Esdras had the happiness of finishing this august work; and the Lord chose Nehemias to rebuild the walls of Jerusalem, and to replace the Jewish nation in a state which might make it respected among the numerous and jealous enemies that surrounded it.

Malachias, the last of the prophets.—At this time appears Malachias, the last of the prophets, himself authorized by the other prophets, and having no need to announce approaching events as a proof of his mission.[605] God sent him to inform the Jews that the sacrifices which they were beginning to offer in the new Temple of Jerusalem should not be always agreeable to the Lord; that a holier sacrifice should succeed them; and that thus their religion was only a preparation for, and, as it were, an outline of, a more perfect covenant, which the Lord had resolved to make, no longer with a single people, but with the whole human race.

Transported into the future, he seems to behold the accomplishment of the great wonder whereof the world is today the witness: instead of the ancient sacrifices, the august victim of our altars offered up in every region of the globe. Addressing himself to the priests of the law, the prophet speaks thus: "These are the words of the Lord of hosts: I have no pleasure in you, saith the Lord of hosts: and I will not receive a gift of your hand. For from the rising of the sun even to the going down thereof my name is great among the Gentiles, and in every place there is sacrifice, and there is offered to me a clean oblation: for my name is great among the Gentiles, saith the Lord of hosts."[606]

Malachias also announces that the Messias shall have a precursor, who will prepare men to hear him. "Behold, I send my angel, saith the Lord, and he shall prepare the way before my face; and presently the Lord whom you seek, and the angel of the testament whom you desire, shall come into his temple."[607] To make this precursor known, the prophet says that he shall be another Elias, and that he shall turn the hearts of the fathers toward the children, and the hearts of the children toward the fathers.[608]

Our Lord had John the Baptist for a precursor. The angel that announced the birth of this miraculous child had said: "He shall walk before the Lord in the spirit and power of Elias, to unite the hearts of the fathers with those of the children,...and to prepare a perfect and well-disposed people for the Lord."[609] John the Baptist is therefore the precursor predicted by Malachias. Now, John the Baptist walked only before our Lord, whose ways he prepared. Our Lord is therefore the ruler, the angel of the covenant, the Messias desired by the Jews and announced by Malachias.

And what is the great sacrifice of which the same prophet speaks? Evidently the august sacrifice of the new covenant. In point of fact, Malachias announces that the Jewish sacrifices shall cease, that God will accept them no more. He announces in their stead a sacrifice which shall be offered from the rising to the setting of the sun: the one only sacrifice of the new law is offered from the rising to the setting of the sun. The prophet announces a pure sacrifice, which shall render the name of the Lord great among the nations: the one only sacrifice of the new covenant is a pure sacrifice, which renders the name of the Lord great, infinitely great, among the nations. The sacrifice of the new covenant is therefore the sacrifice predicted by Malachias. Therefore the old law was abolished from the day on which the new sacrifice, destined to replace all others and to seal the new covenant, was established. Therefore the Messias, the mediator of this new covenant, had come from the day on which the ancient sacrifices were abolished.

It only remains to inquire of the Jews how long it is since they lost the altar and the Temple, where their fathers were permitted to offer sacrifice. It is eighteen centuries ago: such is the answer of history. It is therefore eighteen centuries since the Messias came, and our Lord Jesus Christ is truly this Messias, since it was he alone that instituted the sacrifice of the new covenant. It must therefore necessarily follow that all things are accomplished, and that the hope of the Jews cannot be anything henceforward but blindness and illusion.

PRAYER

O my God! who art all love, I thank thee for having watched with so much solicitude over thy people during their abode in the midst of infidel nations, and for having drawn them out of their captivity and led them back to the land of their fathers. Watch also, I beseech thee, over me, while I dwell in the midst of a world that knows thee not. Deliver me from my exile, and guide me to thee in my heavenly country.

I am resolved to love God above all things, and my neighbor as myself for the love of God; and, in testimony of this love, I will assist piously at the Holy Sacrifice of the Mass.

Lesson 44: General Recapitulation: Application of the Promises, Figures, and Prophecies to Our Lord Jesus Christ

To have a correct idea of what we are about to say, represent to yourselves a powerful and happy monarch—occupying a palace radiant with gold and diamonds, and surrounded by a brilliant court—suddenly deprived of his throne, stripped of his purple robes and sparkling crown, torn with scourges, clothed in rags, and consigned to the recesses of some dark dungeon: such was Adam, such was man after the fall.

God, moved with compassion for the king of creation, for that being whom he so much loved, desired to draw him out of the abyss, and to restore him to his throne, giving back to him his lost goods: such was the end of the incarnation and redemption, such was the object of all religion.

A repairer, a Savior should therefore be sent to this fallen monarch. If this Redeemer should not come immediately, we can conceive that God owed it to his goodness to announce him to the human family in order to console them, to give them a description of him, and to prepare the world for his reception and for the success of his mission.

Promises of the Messias.—In fact, man has no sooner fallen, than God announces a Savior to him. This first promise is vague and general. "One shall be born of you that shall save you," he says to the father of the human race: But when shall this Savior be born? In what country shall he appear? From what people shall he spring? The promise does not mention any of these things: all that it announces is that he shall come.

Centuries roll on. A new promise comes to throw light on the first. This second promise is made to Abraham: God tells him that it is from his race the Messias shall be born. Thus, all peoples that are foreign to the race of Abraham are at once set aside. It is no longer among nations in the aggregate that we are to look for the Messias; it is only in the posterity of Abraham. Now, here arises a new difficulty. Abraham has seven children: Which among them shall be the father of the Messias? A third promise will inform us.

The third promise is made to Isaac. Hereby the other children of Abraham are set aside, and all the nations descending from them. Truth becomes clearer and clearer; but suddenly a new cloud appears to obscure it. Isaac has two sons: Esau and Jacob. Which of the two shall give birth to the Messias? The fourth promise teaches us: Jacob.

The fourth promise is made to Jacob: it dispenses us from henceforward concerning ourselves with the posterity of Esau, and fixes our attention exclusively on the descendants of his brother. This is another step made, but scarcely have we made it, when we encounter a new obstacle. Jacob has twelve sons, who shall be the fathers of the twelve tribes of Israel. Shall it be Ruben, the eldest, or shall it be the innocent and virtuous Joseph, who will behold the Messias spring from his race? A new promise becomes necessary; it is not delayed.

God makes this fifth promise to Juda by the lips of the dying Jacob. To one side, therefore, pass the eleven other children of the holy patriarch, and the eleven tribes of Israel, who should spring from their blood. But in the tribe of Juda there are many families. Now, which shall be the fortunate family that shall one day give birth to the Redeemer of the world? It shall be the family of Jesse.[610] But in the family of Jesse, which shall be the house appointed to give the Christ, the Savior, to the world? The last promise will inform us.

This last promise of the Messias is made to David. It is therefore in the house of David that we must seek the Savior so many times announced.

In parallel lines to the promises run the figures. While the former give us the genealogy of the Messias, and conduct us, step by step, from the whole human race to a particular people, from this people to one of its tribes, from this tribe to one family, from this family to one house, the latter give us the outlines of the portrait of that Son of David who shall save the world.

Figures of the Messias. — By them he is represented to us in Adam, the father of a lost world, giving existence during his sleep to a spouse, bone of his bone, flesh of his flesh; in the inncoent Abel, put to death by his own brother; in Noe saving the world from universal ruin, and repeopling the earth with the children of God; in Melchisedech without predecessor or successor in the priesthood, offering a sacrifice of bread and wine to the Most High. We see him in Isaac, offering a sacrifice on Mount Calvary, immolated by the hand of his father; in Jacob, laboring through long years to obtain a spouse worthy of him; in Joseph, sold by his brethren, delivered to foreigners, condemned for a crime of which he is innocent, placed between two criminals, to one of whom he announces life, to the other, death — finally, loading his cruel brethren with favors.

We find him in the paschal lamb offered as a sacrifice, and preserving the people from the destroying angel; in the manna, miraculously feeding the pilgrim nation with food from heaven; in the sacrifices, offering atonement, adoration, supplication, and thanksgiving to the Lord; in the brazen serpent, elevated on a cross, and healing by its presence the wounds of the fiery serpents. He appears to us in Moses delivering his people from captivity, and giving them a law that makes them the beloved people of God; in Josue, leading his people into a land of blessings; in Gedeon, triumphing over the enemies of his people with a handful of soldiers and the weakest weapons.

We behold him in Samson taking a spouse among the Gentiles, and waging war single-handed against a whole nation; in David, striking to the earth a huge giant notwithstanding the disproportion between the strength of the combatants, maltreated by a jealous prince, persecuted by an unnatural son, ascending barefooted and weeping the Mountain of Olives, insulted by a man to whom he forbids any injury to be returned; in Solomon, seated on a magnificent throne, surrounded with power and honor, endowed with a divine wisdom, and raising a wondrous Temple to the glory of God; finally, in Jonas, preaching penance to the Jews, who do not listen to him, and, after remaining three days and nights in the bowels of a whale, coming forth full of life and preaching penance to the Gentiles, who are converted at his words.

These various characters, as you perceive, agree so perfectly and exclusively with the Messias, that is, with our Lord Jesus Christ, that it is impossible not to recognize in him the type of so many figures, the model of so many sketches.

At the same time, these scattered indications, as we have remarked, do not suffice. Veiled under shadows more or less dense, they give but a hazy picture; they present only an imperfect description of the Redeemer. Now, it is the complete description that we require: God gives it to us by means of the prophets.

Prophecies of the Messias. — Let us read. The Messias, they say — some a thousand, some seven hundred, some five hundred, some four hundred years before the event — shall be both God and man, the Son of God and the Son of David; he shall be born at Bethlehem in Judea, of a Mother ever a Virgin: his birth shall take place when the scepter of David shall have passed into the hands of a stranger. He shall be adored in his cradle by kings, who shall offer him a present of gold and perfumes. On the occasion of his birth, the children of Bethlehem and its neighborhood shall be put to death: the weeping mothers shall make the hills resound with their cries. As for him, he shall retire into Egypt, whence, at a later period, God his Father shall cause him to return. He shall be poor. Humility, goodness, and justice shall be his characteristics. He shall be so meek that he shall not break the reed already bruised, or extinguish the yet smoking flax.

Before him shall go a precursor, who, raising his voice in the desert, shall preach penance, shall announce him as about to appear, and shall dispose men to recognize him and to attach themselves to him. This precursor shall have so much of the spirit and virtue of Elias, that he shall be himself another Elias. The Messias shall preach salvation to the poor and the little. Numerous prodigies in heaven, on earth, and on sea shall render testimony to him. He shall heal the lepers, deliver the possessed, and restore sight to the blind, hearing to the deaf, and life to the dead.

Yet his people shall despise him: he shall be persecuted, contradicted, slandered. Seated on an ass, followed by its foal, he shall enter Jerusalem in the midst of acclamations; he shall visit in person the new Temple, which shall thus become more glorious than the first; he shall announce the reconciliation of heaven with earth, of men with God. One of his disciples, accustomed to eat at his table, shall betray him, and sell him for thirty pieces of silver: this silver shall be brought back into the Temple, and given to a potter in exchange for a field. His enemies shall lay hands on his person; all his disciples shall forsake him; he shall be outraged, torn with scourges, covered with spittle, treated as a worm of the earth. His hands and feet shall be pierced: as a lamb that is led to the slaughter, he shall not open his mouth to complain. He shall be placed between two malefactors; vinegar shall be given him to drink, his garments shall be divided, lots shall be cast on his coat. Finally, he shall be put to death, and this, says Daniel, shall happen after the lapse of 490 years.

By his death he shall atone for all the iniquities of the world, with which he shall voluntarily charge himself. He shall remain three days in the tomb; he shall come forth from it full of life, shall ascend to heaven, and shall send down the Holy Ghost on his disciples. He shall make a new covenant, more perfect than that of Moses. He shall convert the nations, who shall hasten on all sides to abandon their idols and to attach themselves to him: from one end of the world to the other, peoples, the most dissimilar in language and in manners, shall come together to adore him. He shall establish a new sacrifice, which shall alone replace all the sacrifices of the old law, and which shall be offered, not in one country or in one temple, but in every region of the earth, from the East to the West: this sacrifice shall be holy, and shall magnify the name of the Lord.

As for his people, who shall deny him, they shall cease to be his people; and, to punish them for putting the Messias to death, the city and the Temple of Jerusalem shall be wrecked and burned by a strange people under the command of their prince, and the children of Israel, wandering and despised, shall remain without altars, without sacrifices, without priests, in a state of desolation that shall continue till toward the close of time.

Then shall Elias descend from heaven to convert them, and shortly afterward there shall be fearful signs in the sun, in the moon, and in the stars. The various elements shall be in confusion; and the Messias, assembling all the generations of mankind in the Valley of Josaphat, shall come with great power and majesty to judge them.[611]

This is the description of the Messias, such as it is traced by the prophets. The descendant of David, who shall unite in himself all these various characteristics, shall therefore be the Messias so often promised, so ardently desired, and so necessary to the human race that there cannot possibly be any salvation but in him and by him.

With this description at hand, search, among the children of David that lived before the destruction of Jerusalem and of the Temple, for him to whom this description corresponds in every particular: he is no other than the Messias. Thou oughtest, then, to attach thyself to him, and to do all that he shall say to thee, under penalty, O fallen king, of never being rescued from the abyss and restored to the heavenly throne which thou hast lost! Begin thy search. Ah! I hear thee: the search is neither long nor difficult. Thou knowest, we all know, a child of David to whom this description corresponds perfectly, corresponds exclusively; and, in the most profound sentiments of admiration, reverence, and love, we pronounce the adorable name of our Lord Jesus Christ.

The accuracy with which, so long a time beforehand, the prophets traced the portrait of the Messias, is therefore worthy of admiration. But that which is perhaps still more so is the means chosen by God to preserve, and to place before the eyes of all peoples, these astonishing prophecies. Who would ever imagine that it was precisely to the Jewish people, to the people most interested in vilifying and annihilating the prophecies, as branding them with dishonor and condemning them to infamy, that God confided their guardianship?

The Jews do not preserve them as a worthless thing: they preserve them religiously, love them, render testimony to them before and against all, and, in their wandering career, bear them throughout the earth and cause them to be read by all nations. Admirable providence! which makes the very incredulity of the Jews one of the strongest proofs of religion. If all the Jews were converted, impiety would not fail to say that we had only witnesses long suspected regarding their prophecies, and we should be less disposed to believe them. If all the Jews had been exterminated, we might have none of the prophecies at all. It is not so: and, during eighteen centuries, the people least suspected of favoring us have been seen giving evidence in our favor, carrying about everywhere and preserving with a jealous and incorruptible vigilance the proofs of their own condemnation and our justification.

Another miracle. To fulfill his providential mission, the Jew, unlike any other inhabitant of the globe, enjoys a double privilege: immortality and cosmopolitanism.

Immortal: all the ancient peoples have disappeared, have become by lapse of time completely changed, or, in fine, have been blended with other races—the Jew alone has everywhere remained what he was, guarding his traditions, his rites, his characteristics, his nationality, his type, like those rivers which, passing through lakes, mark their onward course, and preserve the original qualities of their waters.

A cosmopolitan: the Jew is to be found everywhere, and yet he can claim no country as his own. While other men cannot be acclimatized to certain zones, the Jew can accommodate himself to every region. Born in the valley of the Jordan, which by a singular phenomenon is more than a hundred feet below the level of the sea, the Jew lives on the summit of the highest mountains, and in the frozen countries of the North, as well as in the temperate regions of Central Europe, and under the scorching fires of the tropical zones, without any excess of deaths appearing over births against him in the mortuary tables.[612] So true it is that the Jewish people are visibly and expressly appointed to serve as everlasting witnesses to the Messias!

PRAYER

O my God! who art all love, I thank thee for having not only promised us a Savior, but given us his portrait in a long succession of figures and prophecies. I fall at thy knees, O my Lord Jesus! and recognize in thee the Son of David, the Redeemer of the world. I thank thee, moreover, O my God, for having chosen such admirable means of preserving thy holy scriptures, and of bringing them to the knowledge of all peoples.

I am resolved to love God above all things, and my neighbor as myself for the love of God; and, in testimony of this love, I will pronounce respectfully the adorable name of our Lord Jesus Christ.

Lesson 45: Messias Prepared For: Up to the Assyrians

We have seen in the preceding lessons that everything which God was pleased to reveal to men regarding the birth, the actions, and the characteristics of the Messias, was promised, prefigured, and predicted with the fullest particulars during a long course of ages. The books of Moses and the prophets, which contain these precious teachings, were preserved with care in the Temple of Jerusalem. Copies of them were to be found in the various families. They were the assiduous study of all Israelites, whether in private or in public, on the sabbath day, or at Jerusalem, where the whole nation congregated thrice a year, on the great feasts of the Pasch, Pentecost, and Tabernacles. Thus, it was impossible for these books to be lost or altered. Everything remarkable concerning the Messias, as well as the time and the place of his coming, was therefore fixed and known. Henceforth, what remains to be done by providence?

We shall see. When a great king, tenderly loved and impatiently expected, is about to make his entrance into a city, every person of importance hastens to prepare the way, to open the gates, to arouse the public attention for his reception. Thus, the Son of God, the eternal Word, the immortal King of ages, the Desired of Nations, being about to make his entrance into the world, God the Father smoothed the way for him, opened the gates for him, disposed men's minds to receive him, and made all events concur to the establishment of his eternal kingdom. These admirable preparations it is now time to develop.

What we are to understand by preparations for the Messias.—And, first, what is meant by the preparations for the Messias? The preparations for the Messias are the direction and concurrence of all events to the glory of the Messias. Some have for their end to preserve on earth the true religion, that is, the religion of the Messias; others to bring about the birth of the Messias in Bethlehem; others, in fine, to facilitate the propagation of the gospel, or the reign of the Messias, throughout the whole earth. So that all the events which took place among the Jews and among infidel nations before the coming of the Messias, the whole government of the world, may be summed up in three lines:

All for the Messias.
The Messias for man.
Man for God.

It is thus that religion is the center in which everything terminates, and that the whole creation returns to God, from whom it came.

All events prior to the coming of the Messias lead to the establishment of his kingdom.—Now, from all eternity, it was settled in the decrees of the Almighty: a) that the Jewish people should give birth to the Messias—that they should be the acknowledged depositary of the great promise—consequently the faithful guardian of the true religion; b) that the Messias should be born in Judea, of the family of David; c) that the kingdom of the Messias, or the gospel, should spread rapidly from one end of the world to the other; d) that the Messias should assemble under one scepter all the peoples of the East and the West, become, by a community of faith and love, one family of brethren; and e) that the Messias should be born at Bethlehem, when the sovereign power would have departed from the tribe of Juda. The proof of these truths is found in every page of the prophets, whose oracles we have just narrated. It therefore remains for us to show how all the events of the world, anterior to the Messias, concurred to the accomplishment of these eternal decrees of providence.

They first established the Jewish people as the depositary of the great promise of the Messias—consequently as the guardian of the true religion. It was therefore necessary that the Jewish people should know and preserve this sacred promise with much more fidelity than other peoples. Hence, the renewal of it, which was so frequently made to the prophets; hence, the endless variety of figures, which repeated it, according to their manner, during four thousand years; hence, in fine, the prophets, who, during more than a thousand years, never ceased to recall the idea and to depict the character of the Messias. It was especially necessary that the Jewish people should be surrounded with innumerable barriers that might prevent them from falling into idolatry. Hence, those countless laws, regulations, and practices, established by Moses, their legislator; hence those terrible threats, those magnificent promises, those grand ceremonies, which, isolating them from the nations, formed around them, as it were, an adamantine wall impassable to error. Hence, also, the ark of the covenant, the awful monument of the continual and sensible presence of God in the midst of Israel.[613]

It was necessary, moreover, that if, notwithstanding all these things, they should ever fall into idolatry, they should not persevere in it, but should be forcibly brought back by public chastisements, humiliations, and calamities to the worship of the true God. Hence, the long chain of bloody defeats and disgraceful slaveries which formed the great body of their history, which were renewed as often as they prevaricated, and which continued until such times as, recognizing their fault, they amended it, and returned to the true God. Hence, especially, the elevation and power of the empire of the Assyrians or Babylonians.

The four great monarchies predicted by Daniel.—This was, according to the prophecy of Daniel, the first of the four great empires, which should succeed one another till the coming of the Messias, and magnificently prepare the way for his eternal kingdom.[614] Now, this formidable monarchy was employed by God to chastise the Jewish people as often as they fell into idolatry, and by means of this salutary chastisement, to lead them back to the true religion. Such was the providential mission of the empire of the Assyrians. Isaias informs us of it in express terms. The Lord, says the prophet, shall call, by a whistle, for a swarm of Assyrians,[615] "because the Assyrian is the rod and the staff of my fury; I have made his hand the instrument of my wrath."[616] "But," adds the prophet, "when the Lord shall purify Jerusalem, he shall visit the insolence of the king of Assyria and the glory of the haughtiness of his eyes. For he hath said: 'By the strength of my own hand I have done it, and by my own wisdom I have understood.'"[617] "Shall the axe boast itself against him that cutteth with it?"[618]

O my God! how great thou art, and by how just a title art thou styled the King of kings and the Lord of lords! The king of Assyria, the haughty Nabuchodonosor, the terror of the East, was only a subordinate minister, a servant commanded by his master—he was only a rod and a staff in the hands of the Almighty.

To prevent the Jewish people from forgetting the great promise of the liberator, by abandoning themselves to the worship of idols, and to chastise them severely as often as they proved unfaithful to their noble duty, was, as we have just shown, the mission of the great monarchy of the Assyrians. History attests it. As soon as the Jews became prevaricators, the Assyrian, ever in readiness, ever in arms, passed the frontiers of Judea, and obliged the guilty inhabitants to have recourse to the God of their fathers, and to break their idols.

But the Assyrian wished to exceed the orders of the master that had sent him: not content merely to punish, he desired to exterminate the Jewish people. Still more, instead of preserving them faithful to the true God and to the great promise, he wished to one day render them prevaricators, and to abolish among them, together with the true religion, the remembrance of the promise, the only hope of the world. Thou dost not therefore know, O Assur! that there is no power or wisdom against the Lord! Wait a while: thou shalt soon see one that will teach thee and humble thy pride, making use of the feeblest means to do so.

The seat of the empire of Assyria, which was afterward fixed at Babylon, was yet at Ninive. Nabuchodonosor I, successor of the king that had done penance at the preaching of Jonas, intoxicated with his victories, resolved to subject the whole East to his sway. He even thought that it would be a small matter to acquire subjects for himself, if he did not make them his adorers. With this sacrilegious design he sent his ambassadors to all the neighboring peoples, and even to the nations established beyond the Jordan, as far as Jerusalem. They were ordered to require an absolute obedience to the commands of the king of Assyria. The astonished peoples received these ambassadors with the contempt that the pretensions of the monarch seemed to deserve; and the ambassadors returned to Ninive, laden, not with the submission that they had expected, but with the scorn of all reasonable men.

Nabuchodonsor, his pride being wounded to the quick, fell into a furious rage against all the countries in which his ambassadors had been so grossly insulted. He swore by his throne and by his empire that he would take a vengeance worthy of his majesty. He therefore held, in his palace at Ninive, a great council, in which he publicly declared his resolution of avenging himself. This council consisted of all the ancient nobles of his court, and all the generals and other officers of his army. "I wish," he distinctly announced to them, "to bring the whole earth under my dominion." His words were universally applauded, and his project, incensed by so many flatterers, was confirmed on the spot by a fixed and unalterable resolution.

History of Holofernes.—He called Holofernes, commander-in-chief of his troops, and said to him: "Go, Holofernes, and subject to me all the kingdoms of the West; punish those especially who have despised my orders." He then recommended the general to exterminate all the gods of the nations, and to abolish every species of worship, that no other god than himself might any longer be adored throughout the whole extent of his conquests.

Holofernes undertook the duty of accomplishing the commission which his master had just confided to him. In a short time his army numbered 120,000 men on foot, and 12,000 archers on horseback. He sent beforehand the baggage, whose appearance everywhere spread terror. What else could be expected from an innumerable multitude of camels, laden with all the provisions necessary, not only for the wants, but for the luxuries of the army? These were followed by countless herds of oxen and flocks of sheep, and by an immense number of chariots, filled with gold and silver, which the general had taken at discretion out of the coffers of his master. As for corn, he ordered that supplies of it should be raised in Syria, and delivered to his soldiers during their passage through the country.

Holofernes followed close to the commissariat. He marched at the head of his army, with his chariots, his horsemen, his archers. The face of the land was covered with this mighty host. They seemed like one of those clouds of locusts that darken the air. Whatever dared to resist them was annihilated; the strong cities were taken by assault, and the inhabitants put to the sword. Soon the terrible conqueror descended on the beautiful plains of Damascus. It was the harvesttime: he ordered the crops to be set on fire, and the vines and other trees to be cut down, so that the country should be wholly deprived of its means of subsistence. After having caused rivers of tears and blood to flow, and filled all the neighboring countries with terror, he paused for a few days to gather in repose the fruits of so many victories.

There was no delay in presenting them to him. The consternation was so general that the princes and governors of provinces sent ambassadors to him, asking his forgiveness, and offering him both their crowns and their services. Holofernes chose out of these various peoples such young persons as he found capable of bearing arms, and obliged them to follow him during the remainder of the expedition. In proportion as he advanced, his army increased like a torrent that overflows its banks and spreads its ravages far and wide.

The fear of the name of Holofernes was so deeply impressed on the minds of all the inhabitants of these countries that, when the conqueror drew nigh to any city, the princes, the magistrates, the whole population came forth to meet him. They gave him a magnificent ovation. They welcomed him with timbrels and flutes. They prepared illuminations for him. Everyone was crowned with flowers as a sign of joy. To see so much eagerness, it might be supposed that all these honors were tendered to the best of masters. But Holofernes had no sooner entered than the multitude learned from his most odious acts that they had greeted a tyrant. Nothing was capable of appeasing his ferocity. The cities were destroyed, and the altars especially were overthrown; for the impious man did not forget that it was against the gods, even more than against men, that he had been commanded to wage war.

Continuing his cruelties, and violently forcing the consciences of men, he at length reached the land of Gabaa, inhabited by Idumeans. Here, as elsewhere, every place was immediately carried. Holofernes now gave a rest of thirty days to his troops, sending threats from his unassailable position to Samaria and Judea.

At these tidings the Jews were greatly alarmed. They feared that the fate of other capitals was in store for Jerusalem, and that the Temple would be sacrilegiously profaned: all the people cried to the Lord. Men and women humbled their souls by a rigorous fast. The priests clothed themselves with sackcloth and haircloth. All persons, even the children—worthy objects by their innocence of the compassion of heaven—prostrated themselves before the Temple of the Lord. The altar of the living God was covered with haircloth. On all sides was heard the cry of humble and contrite hearts: "O Lord, deliver us not into the hands of our enemies!" The high priest Eliachim, delighted at the holy dispositions that he found in Jerusalem, visited the other cities to excite in them a similar fervor. Everywhere his exhortations produced their desired effect: prayer was incessant.

To so much piety the high priest joined vigilance. He sent directions that all the heights of the mountains should be occupied without delay, and that everyone should hold himself in readiness for a vigorous resistance. The children of Israel attended with docility to the orders of Eliachim, and, full of confidence in the Lord, prepared to defend themselves bravely at every point of attack.

Holofernes, having received information of these preparations, became furious: he sent for the princes of Moab and the chieftains of Ammon, whom he had brought to the war. "Who then are these people," he inquired, "that beset the mountains? What are their cities? What is their strength? Who is their leader? Why do they alone, among all the peoples of the East, dare to resist us?" Achior, the commander of the Ammonites, answered him: "My lord, I will tell you the truth. The people that prepare to resist you adore one only God, who is the God of heaven. This God protects the Jews while they are faithful to him. Before attacking them, inform yourself with care whether they have committed any fault against their God, which might draw down his anger upon them. In case they have, let us go forward: the Lord will deliver them into our hands. But if they are guiltless, if their God has not been offended, let us beware of measuring our strength with them: we cannot resist them."

The discourse of Achior was sensible, but it was not flattering. Scarcely had he done speaking, when a universal murmur rose against him throughout the camp of Holofernes, in which the great officers were assembled. Holofernes himself burst out into fierce threats against Achior and blasphemies against the God of the Jews. Still more, he ordered that Achior should be immediately delivered to the Israelites, so as to perish with them when they should all in a short time be undoubtedly slain by the Assyrians. The guards in waiting on Holofernes arrested the Ammonite general and led him away toward Bethulia. This was the first city to be sacked.

It was not so easy to approach the city as the Assyrian general imagined. His soldiers accompanied their prisoner along the plain; but, coming near the mountain, they met with a detachment of slingers, who soon made them change their ideas. They turned out of the way, and, passing along the side of the mountain, fastened Achior hand and foot to a tree. Here they left him, and fled precipitately. The Israelites, witnesses of the occurrence, came down from the city to the prisoner. Having released him, they brought him back with them. All the people of the place assembled around him, beseeching him to relate in detail the circumstances of his adventure.

PRAYER

O my God! who art all love, I thank thee for the innumerable miracles by which thine infinite power and wisdom made all the events of the world concur to the glory of the Messias, thy Son and my Redeemer, as thy prophets had predicted, and thou thyself hadst decided from all eternity.

I am resolved to love God above all things, and my neighbor as myself for the love of God; and, in testimony of this love, I will submit without a murmur to the decrees of providence.

Lesson 46: Messias Prepared For: Judith

Mission of the Assyrians; Holofernes besieges Bethulia. — On the morning of the day that followed the departure of Achior, Holofernes gave the command to his army to advance against Bethulia and to invest it on all sides. He was at the head of 120,000 infantry, and 22,000 cavalry — regular troops — without counting an innumerable multitude of strangers, whom he had chosen out of the newly subjected nations and compelled to follow him.

Bethulia was a small place, situated on a mountain, the natural defenses of which constituted its whole strength. For this very reason, however, it could easily be reduced by starvation, when one had a sufficient army to surround it completely. From an early hour the inhabitants of the city could perceive the grand army of Assyria deploying over the heights. It formed an immense circle around Bethulia. At this sight they redoubled their prayers and supplications; all the people, with their faces to the ground, besought the God of Israel to let his mercy shine forth.

It was indeed solely on the assistance of heaven that they calculated, and that they should calculate in a contest so unequal; but it was necessary that they should await the time of the Lord, without tempting him, and that they should make at least some efforts on their own part, until the time came which he had marked out for assisting their weakness. They armed themselves in his presence; they took possession of every pass in the mountain which could serve as a road to reach them; and, relieving one another, they kept guard continually day and night.

Before attempting an attack, Holofernes made a circuit of the mountain in the neighborhood of Bethulia; he perceived that the waters of a spring belonging to this mountain were conveyed into the city by an aqueduct; he ordered the aqueduct to be cut off immediately, in the hope that, after a few days, thirst would oblige the inhabitants to surrender at discretion. The conjectures of Holofernes were only too well founded: the city was soon brought to a state of extreme distress. The elders of the city were summoned to deliberate on what was to be done, and it was agreed that if, after five days, the Lord did not display his mercy, any further resistance would be useless: meanwhile, it was resolved to spend these five days in works of penance.

God, who had permitted the trial to proceed as far as it could go, at length allowed a ray of hope to shine on his servants. He was preparing a miracle, but, according to his custom, he desired to work it by a feeble hand, the more certain to attribute to his omnipotent arm the glory of its success. Accordingly, as there was question of humbling the proudest of men, he chose a woman to be the instrument of his wonders.

History of Judith; her connection with the preparations for the Messias. — This heroine was called Judith, of the tribe of Simeon. She had married, when a little more than twenty years of age, an Israelite of the tribe of Zabulon, named Manasses, dwelling like herself at Bethulia. Becoming a widow after three and a half years of married life, she had determined never again to form an alliance with man. She was young, rich, childless, and endowed with every quality of mind and body that could be desired in an accomplished lady.

Resolved to make public profession of the retirement and modesty becoming the state of widowhood, which she had promised never to quit, she occupied in the upper part of her house a private chamber, in which she remained shut up with the maids who served her. Notwithstanding the innocence and the regularity of her life, she condemned herself to the severities of penance. She was clothed with a rude haircloth, and she fasted every day except on feast days, which she solemnized by holy rejoicings. Her character for sanctity was so well known, that there was not a single person found to say an ill word of her. Such was the liberatrix whom the Lord had destined for his people.

Judith heard of the resolution that had been taken to surrender Bethulia after five days, in case the place should not be in the meanwhile succored by some extraordinary manifestation of divine power. She sent for two of the ancients of the people. "What is this I have just heard?" she said to them, "is it that you have resolved to deliver the city to the Assyrians, if the relief which you expect from heaven should not appear before the lapse of this time? Who are you, then, thus to tempt the Lord? You venture to give him laws, and to prescribe, according to your liking, the time for his mercies! This is not the way to merit his protection, but rather to provoke his just indignation. Nevertheless, since his patience is infinite, let us humble ourselves before him, let us do penance anew, and await with confidence his consolation."

The ancients and the priests, who had gathered round the virtuous widow, moved by her words, said to her: "Your words are true. Pray therefore to God for us, because you are a holy woman." "Since you recognize the Spirit of God in my words," replied Judith, "go and prostrate yourselves in his presence, to know whether it is he who has inspired me with the resolutions that I have taken, and to obtain for me the courage to execute them. Let all of you stand this night at the gate of the city, from which I will go forth with one of my maids. You shall pray to the Lord that, within the space of five days, he may vouchsafe to have compassion on his people. Ask me nothing more: I do not wish to make anyone the confidant of my secret." "Go in peace," answered Ozias, the commander of the city, "we repose in you the hope of our deliverance."

Judith's piety. — The grand preparation of Judith was prayer and penance. She entered her oratory, resumed her haircloth, covered her head with ashes, prostrated herself at the feet of the Lord, and poured out her soul before him. After her fervent prayer, she arose, and called one of her maids; they descended to the apartment that she had previously occupied. Here she laid aside her haircloth, put away her sad mourning garments, and perfumed herself with exquisite essences. She plaited her hair, put on a gorgeous head-dress, arrayed herself in her richest garments, and ornamented her feet with sparkling sandals; she took her bracelets, her necklaces, her earlets, and her rings: she wished that nothing should be wanting to her adornment.

This was not all. As the love of God and the purest virtue were the motives of these cares, which ordinarily are suggested to persons of her sex by vanity, the Lord was pleased to add new charms to the gifts of nature which his servant already possessed, so that she shone with incomparable beauty in the eyes of everyone who saw her. Her preparations being now complete, Judith said to the maid who was to accompany her: "Bring a bottle of wine, a vessel of oil, some bread, some figs, and some cheese; and follow me."

They soon arrived at the gate of the city. Ozias and the ancients were waiting there, as had been arranged. Without daring to propose any question to her, they contented themselves with saying: "May the God of our fathers accompany you, and support by the power of his arm the generosity of your heart; may your name, made illustrious by the deliverance of your people, be written forever with those of the just and the holy!"

Judith continued her course, accompanied by her servant; and, always united to the Lord by fervent prayer, she descended the mountain. At break of day she found herself close to the outposts of the Assyrians: the men perceived and arrested her. "Who are you," they said to her, "and where are you going?" "I am," she answered, without appearing in the least surprised, "a daughter of the Hebrews. I have fled from their city, because I foresee that they will not for long resist you; and I have said to myself, I will go and find the great Holofernes, and I will let him know a secret by means of which he may at once achieve his victory, without the loss of a single man."[619] "You have acted wisely," they said to her, "in providing for your safety by coming to our general; you shall find favor before him. Follow us with confidence: we will introduce you to him."

She arrives in the camp of Holofernes.—In a short time Judith was conducted to the tent of Holofernes. He was enchanted with her beauty. Judith, having cast a respectful look on the haughty general, prostrated herself on the ground, and remained in a state of profound abasement before him. Holofernes ordered his attendants to raise her up. "Fear nothing," he said to her, "only explain to us why you have quitted Bethulia, and what urged you to commit yourself to my discretion." Judith answered everything with confidence.

Holofernes was charmed with all the words that fell from the mouth of Judith; they were as so many oracles to him and his officers, who could not but admire their wisdom. Matters took the best direction possible for the execution of Judith's project. Holofernes ordered that an apartment should be prepared for her in the cabinet of his treasures, that she should be left at liberty, and that meats should be brought her every day from his own table. Judith accepted everything but the food destined for her. "I cannot," she said, "partake of dishes of your table; it is a point forbidden by my law; I have been careful to secure provisions for myself, and what I require has been brought."

Before entering the tent that had been prepared for her, Judith asked that she might be allowed to go out during the night, and before day, to make her accustomed prayer to the Lord. This freedom was essential to her project: she easily obtained it. Holofernes commanded the officers of his chamber not to contradict her in anything, but, at whatever hour she might please, to permit her to enter and depart, during three days, to adore her God.

The holy widow turned the permission to good account. Every night she descended into the valley of Bethulia, where she washed herself in a fountain, to purify herself from the contamination of infidel society. She returned immediately to her tent, where, thus purified, she spent the day in prayer and fasting until evening: taking then only a frugal repast. The evening of the fourth day, Holofernes prepared a great feast for all his officers: Judith was invited to it. Sure of the protection of her God, she accepted the invitation without reluctance. Arrayed in her most splendid ornaments, she appeared before Holofernes, who said to her: "Eat and drink, for you have found favor before me." "I will do so," answered Judith, "but you know, my lord, that all meats are not permitted to me: I have brought what suits me." She ate and drank in his presence that which her companion had prepared.

Death of Holofernes.—Holofernes, who was closely approaching the moment of his death, abandoned himself, like so many sinners, to a foolish and beastly joy. He drank so freely that, having carried the debauch further than he had ever done in his life before, and being overcome with drowsiness through the fumes of wine, he had to be carried away from the table, and laid in his bed, where he immediately fell into a most profound sleep. A few moments afterward his officers withdrew, every one by himself, in a condition little better than that of their general. Judith alone remained in the tent of Holofernes, but she had been careful to warn the maid that attended her not to be far distant, and to have an eye to everything that passed outside.

The decisive moment was come: she should either perish herself, or make her enemy perish. Judith, standing before the bed of Holofernes, addressed her petition with tears to the Lord, saying very gently: "O Lord, the God of Israel, assist me at this moment!" With these words she went up to the pillar that was at the head of the bed, and took down the general's sword, which was suspended from it. Then, seizing Holofernes by the hair, and exclaiming: "O Lord, my God, help me!" she struck him twice on the neck with all her strength, and cut off his head. She then unfastened the canopy from the pillars, and covered the mutilated body.

Immediately she went out, and handed to her servant the head of Holofernes, saying: "Put it in the bag that you have brought." They forthwith moved off, without any sign of agitation. The guards allowed them to pass, imagining that they went to pray according to their custom. They crossed the whole camp; and, walking along the valley, arrived safely at the gate of Bethulia.

It was time for them to arrive. The day destined for the surrender of the place was about to dawn, and the patience of the inhabitants was almost exhausted. From as great a distance as Judith was able to make herself heard by the watchmen on the walls, she cried out to them: "Open the gates: the Lord is with us; he hath extended the power of his arm over Israel!" The guards, recognizing her voice, hastened to let her in; soon all the people were assembled around her. Then Judith, ascending a little eminence, explained herself thus: "Praise ye the Lord our God, who hath not abandoned those that put their trust in him! Behold," she added, opening the bag, "the head of Holofernes!" When the multitude had gazed on it, they were intoxicated as it were with joy, and united their voices with that of Judith in blessing the Lord.

While this was passing in Bethulia, the camp of the Assyrians was buried in a profound sleep. Judith ordered that an attack should be made on them at break of day, and that the head of Holofernes should be placed on the highest part of the walls. The Assyrians, seeing the Israelites advance in battle order, ran to the tent of the general; but no one dared to enter it, for it was forbidden to disturb him in his sleep. At length a valet took the risk of going in. Hearing no noise, he turned aside the curtain, and found only a headless corpse. At this sight he raised a loud cry, and, returning to the officers, said to them: "Come and see!" A spirit of frenzy seized on the leaders, and soon on the whole army: no one thought of anything but flight. The Israelites arrived, and drove their swords into the backs of their enemies: the victory was complete. Thirty days scarcely sufficed to gather up the spoils. Judith, proclaimed the liberatrix of her people, a living figure of Mary, speedily returned to her obscurity, and continued until death her life of prayer and penance.

By this brilliant stroke the Assyrians learned to respect the people of God, a people whom it was their mission to correct, not to destroy. Thus, the history of Judith, so beautiful in itself, becomes magnificent when we see that it enters as an essential part into the general plan of providence for the preservation of the great promise of the liberator, confided to the keeping of the Jewish people. Moreover, attaching them by bonds so close to the preparations for the Messias, it is a splendid proof of this fundamental truth, that all occurrences previous to the birth of our Lord are explained in three lines:

All for Christ.
Christ for man.
Man for God.

PRAYER

O my God! who art all love, I thank thee for having preserved with so much care the thought of a Redeemer: grant us the grace to profit of his merits.

I am resolved to love God above all things, and my neighbor as myself for the love of God; and, in testimony of this love, I will recommend myself to God in every danger.

Lesson 47: Messias Prepared For: Tobias

Divine object of providence in the dispersion of the ten tribes, and in their sojourn among infidel nations. — "Assur," says the Lord, "is the rod of my anger." We have, as a matter of fact, seen that the great monarchy of the Assyrians was an instrument in the hand of the Lord to speedily chastise the kingdom of Juda, as often as it sought to forget the great promise of the Redeemer and to abandon itself to the worship of idols. To punish the kingdom of Israel, God employed the same power. Salmanasar led away into captivity the ten tribes guilty of idolatry; but the Lord, who knows how to draw good from evil, made their punishment contribute to the accomplishment of his great design.

True, it was not to the ten separated tribes that the guardianship of the promises had been confided. Nevertheless, they should concur in preparing the way for the reign of the Messias; and the Assyrians, without knowing it, should aid them in this providential mission. The latter thought only of leading to Ninive a host of captives, but they led thither a host of missionaries; for it was either to diffuse or to renew, among the nations of the East, the knowledge of the future liberator, that God permitted the dispersion of the ten tribes among the Assyrians.

This object of providence is expressly mentioned in the holy books. One of the captives of Ninive, inspired by God, says to his brethren: "Children of Israel! praise the Lord, and render glory to him in presence of the nations; he hath scattered you among infidels, who know him not, that you may relate his wonders, and make them know that there is no other God than he."[620]

Tobias.—The prophet that so clearly reveals the design of the Lord to us is the holy man Tobias; he was himself one of the most zealous preachers of the glory of God among the Assyrians. A kind of evangelist, he contributed by the splendor of his virtues, still more than by the eloquence of his words, to make known the true religion, of which the first article was the expectation of the Messias. Let us listen to his interesting history with a great desire to reap fruit therefrom.

Tobias was a descendant of the tribe of Nephthali, and a native of the city of the same name, situated in the north of Upper Galilee. He lost his virtuous parents at an early period of life; but, although the youngest head of a family in his whole tribe, he was the only one that the general infection could not corrupt. While his fellow countrymen rushed in crowds to adore the golden calves that Jeroboam had set up at Dan and Bethel, he went to Jerusalem to adore the God of his fathers. His boyhood and youth were passed in the constant exercise of all virtues. Having arrived at a mature age, he married a young maiden of his own tribe, named Anna. She bore him a son, to whom he gave his own name, and who, while becoming the object of his tender affection, became still more the object of his care and vigilance. He taught him from his infancy to fear God, and to avoid every kind of sin.

He is led away captive; manner of life in Ninive.—After some time, the army of Salmanasar, king of Assyria, attacked Israel, and laid waste the kingdom of Samaria. The holy man, involved in the misfortunes of his nation, was led away captive, with his wife and son, to Ninive. He was the same in Assyria as he had been in Israel. The example of his own brethren had not seduced him; that of strangers could not do it. The other Israelites, accustomed for a long time to violate the law of God, partook indifferently of all the meats that the Gentiles used. The faithful Tobias never wished to sully his soul with such a crime. As charitable toward his unhappy brethren as he was observant of his religious duties, he distributed among his fellow exiles the little property that he had been able to bring with him.

In reward for his fidelity, the Lord made him find favor before Salmanasar. Touched with the charity of his captive, this prince gave him ten talents of silver, and, what Tobias valued much more, permission to go whithersoever he desired, and to do whatsoever seemed good to him. Tobias availed himself of his liberty to visit his brethren, and to carry them assistance and consolation.

Having gone to Rages, a city of the Medes, whither a number of the captives had been conveyed, he performed there a heroic act of generosity, which became for him, if not the source, at least the occasion of the wonders by which the Lord chose to recompense his virtue. He found in this city a great many Israelites of his tribe—among others, a relative of his own, named Gabelus, poor and virtuous at the same time, having need of immediate help, and not knowing to whom to have recourse. Tobias lent him the ten talents that he had received from the king, and took an acknowledgment by which Gabelus engaged to repay the amount.

Meanwhile, Salmanasar died. His son, Sennacherib, the inheritor of his crown, had little kindness for the Hebrews. He hated them. Tobias regarded this disposition of the king as a new motive for redoubling his exertions and attentions. Every day he visited those of his kindred who languished in Ninive. He consoled them, shared with them whatever goods remained to him, and buried such of them as died or were slain; for Sennacherib, overcome in a bloody battle, had turned his fury against the Israelites, of whom he destroyed an immense multitude, with an order to leave their bodies unburied.

Tobias was acquainted with this prohibition. He foresaw all the danger that he should run. But nothing could daunt his pious courage; and he continued to inter the bodies of those who had been slaughtered. It was not long before Sennacherib was informed of this: the head of Tobias was marked out for death, and all his goods confiscated. The holy man was obliged to flee, and to conceal himself, with his wife and child. Meanwhile, the royal persecutor was slain. Tobias returned to Ninive, and received from the new king both his confiscated goods and his former liberty. Forthwith, his charities were resumed.

More than fifty years of a life spent in virtue and good works demanded, one would think, some great reward: but the views of the Lord over his saints are very different from those of men. After a thousand trials, generously supported, he destines for them, instead of the favors that we might expect, only new combats that will enrich their crown by perfecting their virtue. Tobias had been stricken in his goods and in his liberty; he had not been stricken in his person. There was a necessity for this last trait of resemblance with the ancient patriarchs, of whom he was the faithful imitator.

Tobias loses his sight.—It was the practice of the holy man, according to the spirit of the law, to have a feast at his house on great solemnities. The guests on these occasions testified their gratitude to the Lord with a joy wholly religious, and the poor of the nation always benefited most by them. It was on one of these days that Tobias, having prepared his table as usual, called his son, and said to him: "Go, my son, and invite some of our brethren that fear God to come and dine with us." The young Tobias executed his father's orders: on his return, he announced that one of the children of Israel had just been put to death.

Tobias, on hearing this news, rose from table, ran to the place where the body lay, lifted it on his shoulders, and carried it away as cautiously as possible to his house, that he might bury it when the sun had set. He then rejoined his friends, and ate a few morsels of bread, which were moistened with tears.

The dangers that he ran were represented to him; but the charitable Tobias, fearing God more than the king, still pursued his work of mercy. One day the venerable old man, being exceedingly tired after burying the bodies of Israelites, returned home so exhausted that he cast himself down for a little rest at the foot of a wall, where he soon fell asleep without the least protection. This was the place at which divine providence was waiting for him. From a swallow's nest there dropped upon him some fresh dung, whose heat and acidity deprived him almost instantly of sight. Tobias had been a model of piety from his childhood; he now became a model of patience in his adversity.

Like those kings, the friends of Job, who added insults to the miseries of the illustrious unfortunate, the kinsmen of Tobias were so cruel as to upbraid him with the regularity of his life and to declare that his hopes were vain. But, following the example of Job, Tobias sought consolation in the noble teachings of faith. He contented himself with saying to his relatives: "Speak not to me in this manner; for we are the children of saints, and expect that blessed life which the Lord hath promised to those who continue faithful to him."

Poor, forsaken, blind, he lived henceforward on the little that Anna, his wife, could earn by the labor of her hands. Once, as the price of her work, she received a kid, which she brought to her house. Tobias hearing the little creature bleat, and not knowing to whom it belonged, said to his wife: "See whether this kid has not come wrongfully into our house, and restore it to its owners." The wife of Tobias was indignant at the scrupulous delicacy of her husband. She burst out into a tirade of abuse, not only against Tobias, but against providence. After the example of Job, subjected to the same trial, the good man addressed himself with tears to the God of all consolation, saying: "Thou art just, O Lord, and thy judgments are right!"

Tobias, thinking himself at the point of death, gives advice to his son. — Tobias, imagining that he should no longer be of any use to his brethren, implored the Lord to call him to himself, and hoped to be heard. In anticipation of the event, he called his son, and spoke to him as all Christian parents should speak to their children before dying. "Hear, my son," he said, "the last words of your father: let them be the rule of your whole conduct. When God receives my soul, bury my body. Honor your mother all the days of your life. Never forget what pains and dangers you cost her. When she finishes her course on the earth, bury her beside me. Have God present to your mind all the days of your life; take care never to consent to sin. Give alms out of your goods; do not turn away your eyes from any poor person, and thereby you shall merit that the eyes of the Lord will never be turned away from you. If you have much, give much; if you have only a little, give willingly even of that little. To employ it thus is to lay up a treasure for the time of need, because almsgiving atones for sin and delivers from death. Watch over your heart: fear even the beginning of an inclination that leads to crime. Never suffer pride to reign in you, for it was the source of all perdition. Do not to another that which you would not wish another to do to you. Always take counsel of a wise man. Bless the Lord on every occasion, and beseech him to direct you in all your ways."

Thus the holy man placed in the front rank all the great duties, as being the great interests of his son. It was only at the end that he said: "When you were yet in your cradle, I lent ten talents of silver to Gabelus. He dwells in Rages, a city of the Medes: I have his receipt. Look about and see how you can make this journey, to receive the amount from him, and to return him his note. Fear nothing, my son; we are poor, but we shall always have enough if we fear God, avoid sin, and practice good works."

"Father," answered the young Tobias, "I will do all that you have commanded me; only I do not know how to recover this money. Gabelus does not know me; neither do I know him: I do not even know the way that leads to Rages." "My son," said the father, "I have his acknowledgment; when you show it to him, I am sure that he will give you the ten talents. Seek among your brethren for a faithful guide to accompany you, and we shall reward him for his trouble."

Journey of the young Tobias. — The son of the good old man went out immediately, and just at the moment met a handsome youth, with a noble, grave, mild air, dressed as a traveler, and ready to set forth. Not knowing that this was an angel of God, Tobias saluted him, and said: "Who are you, excellent young man?" "I am one of the children of Israel." "Do you know the way to Rages, a city of the Medes?" "I know it perfectly; I have stayed with Gabelus, our brother, who dwells at Rages." "Wait a moment till I tell this news to my father." Tobias, informed of all, told his son to make the young stranger come in. It was agreed that he should accompany the young Tobias, and that, on their return, he should be given his reward. The venerable patriarch invoked a blessing on the two travelers; and the son, having bidden adieu to his father and mother, set out with his guide.

Until the moment of separation, the constancy of the mother had been pretty well supported; but, immediately afterward, maternal love overcoming her, she began to weep, and to say to her husband: "You have taken away from us the staff of our old age; would to God that you had never possessed that money which you have sent him to obtain!"

The young Tobias, conducted by the angel, went on farther and farther: his dog followed him. At the close of the first day they reached the banks of the Tigris, in which Tobias desired to wash his feet; but suddenly a monstrous fish sprang up to devour him. The young traveler, terrified, exclaimed: "Sir, he is going to swallow me!" The angel reassured him, and told him to seize the fish by the gill, and to draw it out on the bank. Tobias drew the fish to land, and it lay palpitating at his feet. "Open it," said the angel, "and take out the heart, the gall, and the liver; they will one day serve you to work a cure." Then roasting a portion of the animal's flesh on coals, and salting the rest, they carried away as much food as sufficed them to the end of their journey.

After a long march they drew nigh to a city of Media. "Where do you wish," asked Tobias, "that we should go and lodge?" The angel answered: "Here is a near relative of your own, named Raguel. He has an only daughter, named Sara, whom the Lord destines for you, with all her fortune. Ask her of her father; she will not be refused you." Tobias said: "I have heard that she has been married seven times, and that all her husbands have been killed by the devil; I am afraid lest the same misfortune should befall me, and that my parents, whose only support I am, should die of grief." "Fear not," said the angel to him, "those husbands were killed by the devil because their sentiments were not holy. As for you, fear not. Live in innocence and prayer, and the devil will have no power over you."

The angel ceased to speak as they entered the house of Raguel. This man was an Israelite—the soul of honor, piety, and candor—and a near and dear friend of the elder Tobias, whom he had known intimately in his youth. He received his guests with joy, without yet knowing them otherwise than as travelers of his own nation. But, having fixed his eyes on Tobias, he said in a low tone to his wife: "How like this young man is to my cousin Tobias!" Then, turning to the travelers, he said: "Whence are you, my brethren?" "Of the tribe of Nephthali, of the number of the captives." "Do you know Tobias, my cousin?" "We know him." Raguel immediately began to praise him. "This is his only son," said the angel. Raguel cast himself on the neck of his young relation, bedewed him with his tears, and, holding him in a tender embrace, exclaimed: "May God bless you, my son, because you are the son of a good and most virtuous man!" On their side, Anna and Sara, witnesses of this sight, shed tears of tenderness in abundance.

Young Tobias marries Sara.—After these first transports of loving friendship, Raguel ordered a feast to be prepared. When all things were ready, he invited them to sit down to table. "I will accept nothing," said the young Tobias to him, "unless you first grant me in marriage your daughter Sara."

A marriage arranged in heaven, and brought about by an angel, is soon concluded on earth. Raguel, however, was seized with fear: he hesitated. The angel reassured him, and he gave his consent. The guests then took their places at table. It was an innocent feast, in which all continually blessed the mercies of the Lord, who bestowed on them so many sensible marks of his kindness.

Next day, Raguel signed a deed, by which he then and there transferred to the young Tobias one half of all his goods, stipulating moreover that, after his death and that of his wife, the remaining half should also revert to him, as his sole heir. So many evidences of affection and generosity seemed to place the young Tobias in a position of utter inability to resist the earnest solicitations of his father-in-law not to depart for a couple of weeks longer. But, on the other hand, if he owed much to Raguel, he owed still more to his father and mother, whom the least delay would cast into a state of the most painful uneasiness.

To obey their orders, it was necessary that he should pursue his journey as far as Rages of Media, in order to receive back the ten talents lent to Gabelus.

Uncertain of what was best to be done, he besought his guide to go himself to Rages, to hand the note to Gabelus, and to beg him to come and share in the rejoicings of his wedding. The angel departed, received the money, and brought Gabelus back with him. At the sight of the son of his benefactor, Gabelus, moved to tears, exclaimed: "May the God of Israel load you with his blessings, for you are the son of a most worthy man! May you see your children, and your children's children, to the third and fourth generations! May your race be specially favored by the God of Israel, who reigns forever and ever!" All those present answered, "Amen." Due honor was rendered to Gabelus. The joy of the marriage feast was renewed — a joy always regulated by the fear of God, of whom all the guests were faithful adorers.

He returns to his father. — At length, the moment of departure having arrived, the same desire as before was manifested to detain the young Tobias; but he answered: "I know that my father and mother count the days, and that they are in the greatest anxiety." Then Raguel delivered to him his daughter, and with her the half of all that he possessed in men-servants, women-servants, flocks, kine, and camels, besides a very large sum of money. The father and mother of Sara tenderly embraced her, and said to her: "Honor your father- and mother-in-law, love your husband, take care of your family, govern your house well, and behave yourself without fault."

The journey was long. The numerous beasts could only advance slowly. The angel then said to Tobias: "You know how you left your father and mother; if you choose, let us go on beforehand; your wife, the servants, the cattle, the baggage, will follow us, and we shall announce their approach. Bring with you what remains of the gall of the fish, for you shall have need of it." Tobias yielded without hesitation to the advice of his guide, and they set out.

The diligence of the two travelers could not prevent the repinings of old Tobias and his wife, who spoke of nothing but the absent object of their affections. According to their calculations, their son should now have returned. Ever submissive to the orders of providence, Tobias would say from time to time to Anna, his wife: "Why, do you think, does my son tarry so long?" And the old pair would begin to weep. But nothing could calm the solicitude of the mother of Tobias. "Alas! alas!" she would say, shedding tears, "why did we send you so far away from us — you, the light of our eyes, the staff of our old age, the consolation of our life?" Sad beyond measure, she went forth every day from her house, looked about on all sides, and visited all the ways by which there seemed any hope that he might return, so as, if possible, to see him coming from afar.

Meanwhile, the young Tobias was speeding onward with his companion, who pointed out to him the means that he should adopt to restore sight to his father. Anna was as usual making her search: she was on the top of a hill that overlooked the whole country. The eyes of a mother recognize a son at a greater distance than the eyes of another. She saw him, she knew him, and, running to the house, she said to her husband: "Your son is coming." Then the dog, which had followed them throughout the journey, ran before, and, as if it brought the news of their arrival, testified its joy by wagging its tail and fawning. The father of Tobias, though blind, arose and began to run, stumbling at every step; and, reaching his hand to a servant, hurried forward to meet his son. Receiving him into his arms, he embraced him affectionately, as did also his wife: and the two began to weep for joy.

After having adored and thanked the Lord, they sat down together. Then the young Tobias, taking the gall of the fish, rubbed it on his father's eyes. In the course of half an hour there fell from them a little white skin, and Tobias recovered his sight. He returned the liveliest thanks to the Lord. The young Tobias related to him, as well as to his mother, all the favors that he had received from the Lord during his journey.

Seven days afterward, Sara arrived in good health with all her troop. There was no fear that this virtuous family should ever fail in the sacred duty of gratitude. After the holy rejoicings by which so many happy events were celebrated, Tobias called his son to him, and said: "What can we offer this young man who has served you as a guide?" "All that we could give him," answered the young Tobias, "would be as nothing in comparison with the services that he has rendered to me; but I beg you, father, to ask him if he will condescend to accept the half of all the things that I have brought."

They took the angel aside, and made their proposal with a most generous heart. It was then that the angel made himself known to them, and said to the old Tobias: "When thou didst pray with tears, and didst bury the dead—when, for this purpose, thou didst leave thy repast, and didst hide the bodies during the day so as to inter them during the night, I offered thy prayer to the Lord; for I am the angel Raphael, one of the seven angels who always stand before the Lord." At these words, the father and son fell upon the ground on their face. "Peace be to you," said the angel, "fear not; it is time that I should return to him who sent me; as for you, bless the Lord, and publish all his wonderful works." Immediately he disappeared.

Death of the elder Tobias; blessings of God on the family.—Tobias lived yet a long time, and saw his children and his grandchildren walk in the way of justice. The young Tobias, after the death of his father and mother, returned to Raguel and Anna, and he was their comfort in their declining days. At the age of ninety, he went himself to rejoin his father, leaving after him a numerous posterity, beloved by God and man for the virtues of which they continually set the brightest example.

The history of Tobias, like that of Judith, is undoubtedly taken by itself—one of the most interesting episodes in our holy books. But if we regard it in its relations with the preparations for the Messias, it suddenly assumes a grander bearing; we understand it better, we admire it more, for we see that it occupies an important place in the general plan of providence. Such is the point of view from which we have considered it, as well as that of Judith: it will be the same with that of Esther, of which we shall next speak.

PRAYER

O my God! who art all love, I thank thee for having drawn good out of evil, by making the punishment of the Israelites, and their dispersion among the Gentiles, serve to prepare the way for the kingdom of the Messias.

I am resolved to love God above all things, and my neighbor as myself for the love of God; and, in testimony of this love, I will have the greatest respect for my father and mother.

Lesson 48: Messias Prepared For: Esther

We have alluded to four great decrees of providence in reference to the preparations for the Messias. The first establishes that the Jewish people, destined to give birth to the Redeemer of the world, should be the special depositary of the great promise—consequently, the faithful guardian of the true religion. The preceding lesson has rendered the literal execution of this first decree palpable to us.

The second establishes that the Messias should be born in Judea, and of the family of David. Let us again show providence making all events in the history of the Jews and other nations concur to the accomplishment of this new design. It is for this object that, two thousand years before the coming of the Messias, God calls Abraham from the distant regions of Mesopotamia, and directs him to fix his abode in Judea, then called the Land of Chanaan. It is for this that he engages with an oath to give the country to

Abraham and his posterity. It is for this that, four hundred years later on, he moves heaven and earth to deliver the descendants of the holy patriarch out of the land of Egypt, and to lead them into their own land.

It is for this that he exterminates the seven powerful nations who occupy it; that he steadily maintains his people in it during fifteen hundred years, notwithstanding the continual efforts of the neighboring nations to deprive them of it; that he wishes, if the Israelites are led into captivity, to retain a small number who may guard the sacred land, without ever permitting any strange people to succeed in establishing themselves in it. It is for this also that, in the midst of so many cities destroyed during these incessant wars, the little city of Bethlehem subsists. It is for this, in fine, that the little city of Bethlehem falls as a portion to the tribe of Juda, and becomes later on the inheritance of the family of David, from which the Messias should spring. So much for events having particular reference to the Jewish people.

Mission of the Persians.—Outside, we have the same design and the same concurrences. It is for the execution of this same decree that the powerful monarchy of the Persians, the second of the four great empires predicted by Daniel, takes the place of the empire of Babylon. In effect, according to the prophets, the Messias should be born in Judea, of the race of Abraham, and of the tribe of Juda. It was therefore necessary to preserve the Jews in Judea, or to lead them back into it in case they should be removed from it. Moreover, the Messias should be born not only in Judea, but in Bethlehem, of a Virgin of the family of David. His origin was one of the marks by which on a future day he should be recognized. It was therefore necessary to maintain among the Jews the various distinctions of tribes and families.

Now, as we have remarked, the Assyrians entertained quite opposite views; they desired nothing more earnestly than to exterminate a people who were odious to them. For seventy years they held them prisoners in Babylon. A longer captivity, if it should not have destroyed the Jews altogether, would have exposed them to the danger of being confounded with those among whom they lived. To preserve them, to prevent their being blended with a foreign nation, and to provide for their return into Judea, God raised them up a liberator. As he had employed the princes of Assyria for the execution of his vengeance, he rendered the kings of Persia the ministers of his bounty toward the holy nation, and destined Cyrus, the founder of this second empire, to set free the children of Israel.

It is Isaias that again instructs us regarding the designs of God over this second monarchy. How admirable!—the prophet mentions Cyrus by name, two hundred years before this prince's birth; represents the Almighty taking him by the hand, leading him from province to province, making the ramparts of cities fall at his approach, and abandoning to him the riches and treasures of every place. All these things were to happen in order to punish Babylon, and to liberate Juda.

Let us recollect ourselves, and hear these magnificent oracles, "Thus saith the Lord to my anointed Cyrus, whose right hand I have taken hold of, to subdue nations before his face, and to turn the backs of kings, and to open the doors before him, and the gates shall not be shut. I will go before thee, and will humble the great ones of the earth: I will break in pieces the gates of brass, and will burst the bars of iron. I will give thee hidden treasures, and the concealed riches of secret places: that thou mayest know that I am the Lord who call thee by thy name, the God of Israel. For the sake of my servant Jacob, and Israel my elect, I have even called thee by thy name: I have made a likeness of thee, and thou hast not known me. I am the Lord, and there is none else: there is no God besides me: I girded thee, and thou hast not known me…I have raised him up to do justice, and I will direct all his ways: he shall build my city, and let go my captives, not for ransom, nor for presents, saith the Lord the God of hosts."[621]

As we see, the mission of the Persians is one of protection and benevolence in regard to the Jews. The chiefs of this new monarchy, it must be said to their praise, acquitted themselves faithfully of their commission. Thanks to them, the city and the Temple of Jerusalem were rebuilt, and the Jews were removed to and maintained in Judea, with the distinctions of tribes and families, until the coming of the Messias. There were found at that time, nevertheless, some ambitious and shortsighted men, such as are found in every court, who leave not a stone unturned to direct their masters in a wrong course, and thus hasten the fall of their empires, by placing their leaders in opposition to the designs of the Most High. From being protectors of the Jews—the proper character of those powerful Eastern monarchs—some perverse courtiers endeavored to make them the most cruel persecutors, the most heartless exterminators: at the head of these imprudent and guilty men appears Aman, the favorite of Assuerus.

But the supreme ruler of the world, who holds in his hands the reins of empires, and who makes the wills and wickednesses of men serve for the accomplishment of his eternal purposes, turned to the advantage of his great design the machinations of this haughty minister. God had employed the services of a weak woman to break the power of the proud Holofernes; by similar means he is now about to overthrow the projects of Aman. The history of Esther, therefore, like that of Judith, is admirably connected with the general plan for the redemption of the human race: these two heroines, figures of her who was to crush the serpent's head, save the Jewish people, to whose keeping is confided the great promise of the liberator.

History of Esther.—Among the captive Jews at Babylon was Mardochai, of the tribe of Benjamin. He had a niece named Esther, who had lost in her childhood both her parents. Adopted by her uncle, the young orphan lived in innocence and in the faithful observance of the law of God. Assuerus, who was at that time reigning in Babylon, having gained some splendid victories, desired to hold, on his return to his capital, a succession of feasts that might seem worthy of the most powerful monarch in the East. He invited thither all the officers of the army, and all the satraps or governors of the 127 provinces into which his vast empire was divided.

On the seventh day of these feasts, he took a fancy to bring Queen Vasthi, his wife, before the eyes of all the court, that every one might render homage to her extraordinary beauty. Vasthi refused to present herself. Assuerus, enraged beyond measure, at once repudiated her. He immediately ordered that the most accomplished young virgins in his kingdom should be brought to him, that he might select a wife from amongst them. Esther was one of their number. The humble daughter of Juda asked little for her adornment; she was content with what it was judged proper to give her. She appeared before the king with that air of modesty and simplicity which never abandoned her. The king preferred her to all the others, placed the diadem on her head, and made her reign instead of Vasthi.

Having become a queen, an all-powerful queen, Esther did not swerve from the simplicity of her conduct or the innocence of her life. She was still the same in her palace, and in the midst of a crowded and pompous court, as she had been in the house of her uncle, and in the society of the other young Israelite maidens of her age. She spent her time in holy prayer and in meditation on the divine law. As docile as ever to the instructions of Mardochai, whom she honored as a father, she observed with fidelity whatever he directed her to do in the various circumstances in which she found herself. The principal care of this virtuous man was to make the young queen remember that it was not for herself but for her people that she had been raised to the throne.

All that passed at the court of the king of Persia entered into the plan of divine providence. There was nothing, even to the assiduity of Mardochai at the gates of the palace, which proceeded only from his tenderness for Esther, that did not tend directly toward the welfare of the Jewish people—consequently, toward the preservation of the great promise of the liberator: a matter of the first importance, in which the lordly Assuerus bore only an inferior part.

Mardochai discovers a conspiracy.—One day as Mardochai, according to his custom, was alone, he heard the two commandants of the gate whispering to each other of murdering the king. Having lent a more attentive ear, he discovered the whole plot of the conspiracy. When he was fully convinced of it, he found means of secretly informing Esther regarding the affair; and the queen, without delay, acquainted the king, her husband, with the danger that threatened him, adding that it was from Mardochai she had received the particulars of this cruel design. The officers were arrested: they acknowledged their crime, and were condemned to death.

Following the example of his royal predecessors, Assuerus had the record of this event laid up in the archives of his kingdom; but God permitted that he should forget his deliverer. Mardochai received a few trifling presents, with an invitation however to remain always within the precincts of the palace.

While Assuerus treated with so much indifference a faithful servant to whom he owed his life, the same prince, by a second permission of providence, placed his empire at the disposal of a man whom he discovered at a later period to be the most dangerous of his enemies.

Aman, the favorite of Assuerus, wishes to receive divine honors.—This traitor was called Aman. By his wily artifices, he managed little by little to become the favorite of the monarch and the master of the court: Assuerus had elevated him to a throne little inferior to his own. Whenever Aman appeared at the gates of the palace, it was necessary, by the express orders of the king, to bow before him, to bend the knee to the earth, to prostrate profoundly. He was the idol of the master: everyone was compelled to adore him.

Mardochai refuses Aman this tribute.—Aman pretended that these honors were rendered to him as a god. The creatures of the court and the people generally complied with whatever he desired; but their prevarication was no rule for Mardochai. Aman had frequent occasion to pass before this intrepid adorer of the true God, and, from the moment that he claimed such marks of respect as the Jews rendered to God alone, received no notice from him whatsoever. The officers and guards of the palace, surprised at the hardihood of Mardochai, often asked him whether he did not fear to draw upon himself the indignation of Aman. He told them in reply that he was a Jew, and that his religion forbade him to render to man the honors that were due to God alone.

Aman swears to destroy Mardochai, and all the other Jews along with him.—They represented the matter to the haughty minister, who did not delay to prove, by personal experience, the truth of their report. More than once he remarked that, as he passed, this Jew still stood upright, and did not bend the knee to him: stung to the quick, he resolved to be revenged. Mardochai was doubly guilty in the eyes of the traitor—for having refused him divine honors, and for having discovered the late conspiracy against the king. The sacrifice of his life would be too little to expiate this twofold crime: the whole Jewish nation should wash it away in their blood.

Aman went in search of the king, and, describing the Jews scattered through his kingdom as a turbulent race, enemies of the gods, censurers of immemorial practices, and rebels to the commands of their sovereign, he added that the public peace demanded that the land should be freed as soon as possible from such a hated race. He begged an order to exterminate them all in one day. Assuerus, jealous of his authority, signed the sentence of death. While couriers bore the proclamation to the governors of all the provinces, it was hung up publicly in the capital.

We may judge how great was the consternation of the Jews on receiving this news. They shed torrents of tears; they raised the most piteous cries. Happily they did not confine themselves to these fruitless lamentations: they had recourse with one accord to prayer, to fasting, to the most sincere repentance.

Mardochai gives information of Aman's design to Esther.—Mardochai himself, having seen the edict, rent his garments, put on sackcloth, and covered his head with ashes. In this melancholy costume he ran to the gates of the palace, where he was obliged to stop; for it was a crime to enter with mourning dress into the house of the prince. He desired, by his demonstrations, to make known to Esther something of what was occurring: God did not permit him to be disappointed. The waiting-maids of the queen, aware indeed that she took some interest in Mardochai, but not having the slightest suspicion that she was a Jewess, or a niece of the stranger, informed her of the condition in which he had appeared.

Esther immediately called one of her officers, and ordered him to go and ask Mardochai what was the meaning of his sorrow. Mardochai gave the officer a copy of the edict, and told him to deliver it to the queen, conjuring her in his name to see the king at once, and to implore its revocation. The officer returns to Esther, hands her the edict, and faithfully repeats all that Mardochai has charged him to say. "Does not Mardochai then know," exclaims Esther, "that no person, unless specially called by name, can appear in the king's chamber, under penalty of instant death? Return," she adds, "and acquaint Mardochai with the law of which he is not aware." "Tell the queen from me," says Mardochai to the officer, "to visit the king. Who knows whether the Lord has not crowned her in order to make her the instrument of his mercy?"

Esther, having received this answer, sent a message to Mardochai: "Assemble all the Jews that are in the capital, and pray ye for me." On her side, she had recourse to prayer, fasted three days, and, recommending herself with tears to God, offered herself up as a victim for the salvation of her people.

Esther goes to the king.—After three days she takes her most splendid apparel, and calls two of her maids: one follows her, bearing up her train; she leans on the arm of the other. Arrived in the hall adjoining the apartments of the king, she pauses. In a little while the door opens: Assuerus appears on his throne, clad in his royal robes, and radiant with gold and diamonds. At the approach of Esther, whom he beholds entering without his orders, his fiery eyes reveal the deep anger of his soul. Esther falls to the ground in a faint; the bright tints of her countenance are changed to a deathlike pallor, and her head, motionless, rests on one of her handmaids.

God permitted this accident to draw his glory from it: the master of the hearts of kings, he suddenly changed that of Assuerus. This prince, trembling with fear at the sight of the queen's sad condition, rose quickly from his throne, ran toward Esther, took her in his arms, and spared no pains to restore her. "What is the matter, Esther?" he said to her, "I am your brother, fear not. No, you shall not die; the law made for others does not concern you; come near, and touch the scepter." Esther not having yet quite come to herself, the king placed his golden scepter on her neck, and said to her: "Speak to me." The queen at these words recovered consciousness a little, drew near, and kissed the end of the golden scepter; then, raising her eyes to Assuerus, she said with difficulty: "My lord, you appeared to me as an angel of God; I was not able to endure your glance."

At these words, she fainted away again in the arms of her attendant. The king's trouble was excessive: he neglected nothing that could afford solace to his wife, until she had perfectly regained her senses. Assuerus, now at the summit of his desires, said to her: "Esther, what do you desire of me? Though it should be the half of my kingdom, I will give it to you." She contented herself with answering: "If it please the king, I beg him to come today, with Aman, to a banquet that I have prepared." The invitation was accepted willingly, and the king went with his minister. In the midst of the feast, which was magnificent, Assuerus asked the queen anew whether she had anything to desire of him. Esther answered him: "I beseech the king to come again tomorrow with Aman to take part in my banquet, and I will tell him what I desire."

Intoxicated with the honor that he had just received, Aman returned home; and, as he was passing through the gates of the palace, he again saw Mardochai sitting in his accustomed place, and not making the slightest motion. The minister of state hastened to inform his wife and friends of what had just happened to him. "The queen," he said, "has invited me alone, with the king, to her banquet, and tomorrow I must dine with them; but all these things are as nothing to me so long as I see Mardochai the Jew not taking the trouble even to rise when I pass." His wife and friends said to him: "Order a gibbet fifty cubits high to be prepared, and have him hanged upon it." The advice pleased Aman: the gibbet was prepared, and next day Mardochai was to be hanged upon it.

Triumph of Mardochai.—Meanwhile Assuerus, not being able to close an eye the whole night, occupied himself in the perusal of the annals of the latter years of his reign. He came to the place in which it was narrated how Mardochai the Jew had discovered the plot against the king's life: he inquired what reward this faithful stranger had received for such an important service. "Sire," answered his officers, "you made him a few little presents at the moment of the public alarm; but they were so trivial that it was not thought necessary to record them."

The officers had scarcely finished speaking when the king, hearing a noise, asked: "Is there not someone in the antechamber?" There was indeed someone: it was Aman, who had come to beg permission to hang Mardochai. "It is Aman," answer the officers. "Tell him to come in," says the king. On his entrance, Assuerus says to him: "What ought to be done for a man whom the king wishes to honor in a special manner?" Aman, quite certain that it is himself whom the king wishes to honor, answers: "My lord, the man whom the king wishes to honor should be clothed in your royal robes, should be set on the horse that the king himself rides on days of ceremony, should have the crown placed upon his head, and should be led thus through the city, the first of all the king's princes and nobles holding the horse's bridle, and crying out in a loud voice: 'Thus shall he be honored whom the king wishes to honor.'" "Very well," says Assuerus to him, "make haste: take my royal garments and my horse of state, and do these things for Mardochai the Jew, who sits at the gate of the palace. Omit nothing of what you have advised."

Death would have been less painful than such an order. It was necessary, however, to approve of it, to bury his vexation in the depths of his soul, and to obey without reply. Aman took the royal robe, clothed Mardochai with it in the public street, helped him on the king's horse, and, holding the bridle, marched along, proclaiming in a loud voice: "Thus shall he be honored whom the king wishes to honor." When Mardochai had returned to the gate of the palace, Aman hastened to reach his house with tears in his eyes and his head covered. He related to his wife and friends all that had just happened to him. His account was not ended, when the officers of the king came to request his immediate attendance at the feast that the queen had prepared. He arrived in all haste, and entered with the king into the banquet-hall of the queen.

Humiliation and death of Aman.—The entertainment, like that of the day before, was magnificent. At the close of the repast, Assuerus, addressing Esther, said: "What do you desire of me? Though it be the half of my kingdom, you shall obtain it." Esther answered: "If I have found favor before you, O king, I only ask of you my own life and the lives of my people. For we are, I and my people, given over to death, proscribed and condemned. Would to God that it were enough to sell us, men and women, as slaves! The evil would be endurable, and I should be content to mourn in silence. But so much cruelty on the part of our enemy reflects upon the king's name." "Who is this enemy," answered Assuerus, struck with astonishment, "and what is his power, that he should dare attempt such things?"

Esther answered: "This enemy is Aman!" At these words, Aman was stupefied. Assuerus, scarcely able to repress his indignation, went out for a moment. Aman fell at the feet of the queen, beseeching her to obtain his life. The king returned; and his officers cast a cloth over Aman's face to hide this odious object from the eyes of their master. One of them exclaimed aloud: "In the house of Aman there is a gibbet, fifty cubits high, which he had prepared for Mardochai, who saved the king's life." "Go and hang him upon it," said Assuerus. The order was executed, and the king's anger was appeased.

Behold the well-merited fate of an impious man, who had become so intoxicated with his greatness as to imagine himself a deity! The death of Aman is also a terrible example of the justice of God in regard to the persecutors of innocence, and an illustrious monument of his goodness toward his adorers, when, in the midst of dangers, they remember that he is their Father, and rely upon his protection.

Deliverance of the Jews. — This was only the beginning of the favors of God. The gratitude of his people, who publicly sang his praises in the midst of an idolatrous city, joined with the virtue of Esther, who referred all the glory of so many wonders to him, attributing nothing to herself, obliged him to put the finishing stroke to his work by the most signal benefits. Assuerus gave the queen all the possessions of Aman, and made Mardochai his favorite and his prime minister. Esther, on her side, confided to her uncle the superintendence of her house. Then, casting herself at the feet of the king, she besought him with tears to revoke the edict of proscription issued against the Jews: this favor was promised to her on the spot. Thanks to a new edict, published throughout all the provinces, the Jews were not only delivered from obloquy, but treated with the utmost respect, on account of Esther and Mardochai.

It was thus that providence watched over his chosen people, and conducted the monarchy of the Persians toward its true mission, which was to protect the Jewish nation. All these things were done in consideration of the Messias, who should be born of it. How often do events, apparently trivial, become of great importance, when viewed in their relations with the general plan of the Most High for the redemption of the human race!

Penetrated with gratitude for so many benefits, the Jews consecrated by a perpetual feast the remembrance of their deliverance. The eve of this feast was a day of general fasting, to remind them of the destruction with which they had been threatened. The feast itself was spent in psalmody, and in innocent rejoicings. On these occasions they sent to one another presents of dishes that they had prepared. They were especially careful not to forget the poor of their nation, that all might have a share in the general jubilation. A touching example of that charity which the Christians of the early ages followed to the letter, but which their children nowadays do not so often imitate!

PRAYER

O my God! who art all love, I thank thee for having miraculously preserved thy people, and thereby prepared the way for the kingdom of the Messias; grant us the grace to be, like Esther and Mardochai, full of confidence toward thee in adversity, and of gratitude toward thee in prosperity.

I am resolved to love God above all things, and my neighbor as myself for the love of God; and, in testimony of this love, I will often repeat this little prayer: "O Jesus, meek and humble of heart, have mercy on me!"

Lesson 49: Messias Prepared For: Greeks and Romans

The preceding lessons have enabled us to behold the accomplishment of the first two decrees of providence relative to the preparations for the Messias, namely, that the Jewish nation should be the privileged guardian of the great promise of the liberator, as well as of the true religion; and that the Messias should be born of this race in Judea, and of the family of David.

It was likewise decided in the counsels of the Most High that the kingdom of the Messias, that is, the gospel, should be spread with rapidity from one end of the world to the other. We now proceed to show in what manner events limited to the Jewish people, as well as the third empire predicted by Daniel, concurred to the accomplishment of this third decree of the Almighty.

Third monarchy predicted by Daniel, that of the Greeks. — God had raised up the empire of the Persians to deliver his people from the captivity of Babylon and to restore to them the possession of Judea. The kings of Persia had acquitted themselves faithfully, perhaps unwittingly, of the commission that they had received from the sovereign master. Judea was repeopled by its ancient inhabitants; the city and the Temple of Jerusalem were rebuilt. Under the protecting shadow of the monarchy of the Persians, the Jews had multiplied: they were now a compact people; they were become a strong, rich, and flourishing nation. The empire of the Persians having accomplished its mission, God allowed it to pass into the hands of the Greeks. This new revolution was intended to serve the future work of the Messias, and to make remote preparations for the promulgation of the gospel.

The proof of this is to be found in the prophecy of Daniel, and in the history of Alexander and his successors. The distinctive characteristics of the third monarchy are, in the eyes of the prophet, its rapid rise and its amazing extent. "After that," he says, "as I looked, I saw another beast like a leopard; and it had upon it four wings as of a fowl. And this beast had four heads, and power was given to it."[622] Further on, Daniel again describes Alexander, and expresses himself thus: "I was attentive to what I saw, and behold! a furious he-goat came from the West over the face of the whole earth, and he did not touch the ground…And this he-goat became exceeding great and grown, and his great horn was broken, and there came up four horns under it, toward the four winds of heaven."[623]

In this double characteristic of rapidity and extent is shown the nature of the providential mission assigned to the empire of the Greeks. History will explain the matter clearly to us, and confirm by facts the prediction of the prophet.

1. *Spread of the Greek language prepares way for the gospel.* — The monarchy of the Greeks prepared the way for the spread of the gospel by rendering the Greek language popular throughout the whole East, that is, the language in which the gospel should be announced. Thereby, God secured a free course for the preaching of the apostles and a rapid circulation for the doctrine of the Messias.

See how manifestly the action of providence appears here. The progress of Alexander in the East ought, according to human calculations, to overthrow the design of the Lord. But he who makes kings, who elevates and depresses empires at his pleasure, knew how to turn the power of this fierce conqueror to the glory of the great liberator and to the establishment of his eternal kingdom. Alexander, who, in his victorious career, scarcely touched the ground, so surprising was the rapidity of his conquests, had laid siege to Tyre. This powerful city held him at bay for seven months. From the foot of its walls, the terrible conqueror sent commissioners to summon the Jews to submit to his authority and to furnish him with supplies. The Jews excused themselves on the plea that they had already sworn fidelity to Darius, the king of Persia. Irritated at this answer, Alexander had no sooner reduced Tyre than he marched against Jerusalem, determined to make this city another example of his severity.

Visit of Alexander to the East: He swears to exterminate the Jews, then God changes his heart. — As he was advancing to exterminate the holy nation, the high priest, who was named Jaddus, had recourse to God. He commanded public prayers and offered sacrifices to implore the assistance of heaven. God watched over the preservation of his people, and the accomplishment of his promise regarding the Messias, who should be born of them. He appeared in a dream to the high priest, told him to scatter flowers through the city, to open all the gates, and to go himself, clad in his pontifical garments, to meet Alexander, without fearing anything from this prince, for he himself should protect him. Jaddus, full of joy, related to the people the vision with which he had been favored. Everything was prepared as had been prescribed in the revelation. The high priest, accompanied by various other ministers, robed in linen, proceeded out of the city to an elevated spot from which a distinct view might be had of the city and the Temple of Jerusalem. Here they awaited the arrival of Alexander.

When it was known that he was coming, the multitude went forward to meet him in the pompous manner that has been described. Alexander was struck at the sight of the high priest, clothed in his ephod, with his tiara on his head, and a plate of gold on his brow, having the name of God written on it. Seized with respect, he bowed before the pontiff, and saluted him with a religious veneration. The surprise of all present cannot be expressed: they scarcely believed their eyes; they could not imagine anything like a change so unexpected.

Parmenion, one of the confidential attendants on the prince, could not recover from his astonishment. He asked why the king adored the high priest—the king, who was himself adored by all the world. "It is not the high priest that I adore," answered Alexander, "but God, whose minister he is. When I was yet in Macedon, meditating the conquest of Persia, this same man, in the same dress, appeared to me in a dream, and assured me that his God would accompany me and make me victorious over the Persians. The moment I perceived this priest, I immediately recognized him by his garments and his features: it is impossible for me to doubt that this war has been begun by the command and under the guidance of the God whom he adores. It is on this account that I render homage to him in the person of his minister."

Alexander then embraced Jaddus and came to Jerusalem. He went up to the Temple, and there offered sacrifices to God in the manner pointed out to him by the high priest. He was shown the prophecies of Daniel, which announced that the empire of the Persians should be destroyed by a king of Greece. Alexander, transported with delight and admiration, granted the Jews whatever they desired.

The empire of Alexander, of which the devil made use to enlarge his city, but which, in the counsels of providence, was intended to facilitate the preaching of the gospel, by spreading far and wide a knowledge of the Greek tongue, extended itself much more than that of the Persians. Besides a great part of Africa, it comprised the vast territory lying between the River Ganges and the Adriatic Sea. Providence, which had chosen Alexander to be the instrument of its designs, withdrew him from the world when he had accomplished his task. It was predicted that his empire should be divided, and that four new monarchies should be formed of its ruins: all this was accomplished point by point.

2. *Jews are drawn into most parts of the world, thus preparing the way for the gospel.* — The monarchy of the Greeks prepared the way for the gospel by drawing the Jews into most parts of the known world. At first, there were some who enrolled themselves in the armies of Alexander, and followed him throughout his expeditions. Afterward, under the reign of his successors, that is, during a space of about two hundred years, the Jews spread themselves through all the East. Attracted by the promises, favors, and advantages that the Greek princes held out to them on all sides, on account of their inviolable fidelity to their sovereign, they came eventually to establish themselves in every region of the immense empire of Alexander.

It was not without a special design of providence that the Jews, isolated as they were in their own country, spread themselves over the other countries of the East. New missionaries, they made known the true God to these different peoples, and thereby prepared them remotely to one day receive the light of the gospel. What is very surprising is that this intercourse with the nations, which had previously been so dangerous to them, only rendered them henceforth more zealous for the worship of the one true God and more attached to his holy law. Thus, providence was arranging everything to facilitate the execution of the great work of the redemption.

3. *Sacred books of the Jews are made known throughout, thus preparing the way for the gospel.* — The monarchy of the Greeks prepared the way for the gospel by rendering celebrated and making known to distant regions the sacred books of the Jews, that is, Moses and the prophets. Let us give a history of this important fact. Ptolemy Philadelphus, ruler of one of the four kingdoms formed out of the vast empire of Alexander, had just ascendèd the throne. Among other provinces under his sway was that of Egypt, whose capital was Alexandria. This prince, a lover of science and literature, established in the city a splendid library; here were assembled, from all parts of the world, the rarest and most interesting books. This library soon became the resort of the learned both of East and West. Ptolemy having heard that the Jews had a book that contained the laws of Moses and the history of the Israelite nation, conceived the design of enriching his library by having it translated from Hebrew into Greek. For this purpose, he addressed himself to the high priest Eleazar, who had succeeded Jaddus. Ambassadors were despatched with a very courteous letter and magnificent presents. They were received with every demonstration of respect, and obtained without difficulty what the king asked.

Eleazar gave them an exact copy of the law of Moses, written in letters of gold, and appointed six old men of every tribe to accompany it, in order to translate it into Greek. Ptolemy loaded with tokens of his friendship these seventy-two interpreters. He prepared a house for them, and directed that they should be supplied with everything they might require. They began their work without loss of time, and it was speedily completed: this is what we term the Septuagint version. It was read in presence of the king, who highly approved of it, admired especially the profound wisdom of the laws of Moses, and sent back the interpreters with rich presents for themselves and for the Temple of Jerusalem.

4. *Further preparation for the gospel: Authenticity of books are certified.* — The monarchy of the Greeks prepared the way for the gospel by rendering unquestionable the antiquity and the authenticity of the prophecies and the other sacred books. The truth of this proposition appears from the very translation whose history we have just related. In point of fact, it is certain that, under the reign of Ptolemy, a long time before the birth of Jesus Christ, there was made in Egypt a Greek version of the holy books: this version we still have. All the prophecies that it contains and that we have quoted in reference to the Messias are therefore incontestably anterior to the gospel. Not only their existence, but their publicity itself, preceded by several centuries the events that are therein recorded. Moreover, this translation being found in the hands of pagan nations, it became impossible for the Jews to alter the old testament, or to expunge from it what referred to the Messias.

Thus, to render unassailable the authenticity and to popularize the knowledge of the divine book, every page of which announces the Desired of Nations, was the result of the Septuagint version, as well as the greatest benefit bestowed by the third monarchy foretold by Daniel. Who does not clearly see that such was the principal design of God in delivering the whole East over to the power of the Greeks, and in maintaining them there in spite of their divisions? Henceforward, we understand without difficulty why he caused the empire of the Persians to be succeeded by that of the Greeks, whose language was eagerly adopted by all the peoples whom they subjugated. Evidently he desired to prepare an easy way for the preaching of the gospel, which was now near at hand, and to facilitate by that universal language the reunion of so many distinct peoples in one and the same society, doctrine, and worship.[624]

Mission of the Romans. — When the monarchy of the Greeks had accomplished its mission, God allowed it to be absorbed into the vast ocean of the Roman Empire. Behold the last and most terrible of the four great empires, pointed out to Daniel in the vista of ages! What shall be its mission? To raise itself to the highest degree of power, so as to become invincible—to subject the whole earth to its authority in order that, at the command of Imperial Caesar, the blood of apostles and the blood of Christians may flow in every clime, and thus render humanly impossible the establishment of the gospel. Such was the desire of Satan. The views of the sovereign master were very different.

It was predicted that the kingdom of the Messias should be established with rapidity throughout the whole earth, and that he himself should be born in Bethlehem when the supreme power should have finally departed from the tribe of Juda. The Roman Empire is charged with the accomplishment of this decree in its two parts. It shall fulfill its duty; and all the efforts, and even all the success of Satan, shall be turned against himself.

As for the first part, it was not enough that the Jews, evangelical pioneers as they were, should, after the visit of Alexander, be scattered over the East and the West, and that Europe, Asia, and Africa, understanding the Greek language, might easily be instructed by one company of men; it was also necessary to facilitate for the bearers of good tidings their passage from one end of the world to the other, and in fine it was necessary that the whole human race should form only one body, so as to be promptly animated by one and the same spirit.

Now, to trace out on all sides immense roads, to sweep away nationalities, to overthrow the walls of separation that divided peoples, to level and cultivate the soil, to form out of so many countries one great compact society, united under a common scepter—finally, to establish a universal peace, which would reign over land and sea, from East to West: such were even in the eyes of reason the means most proper for the accomplishment of this wonderful and gigantic design. Are they not also the distinctive characteristics of the Roman Empire and the first objects of its mission?

Daniel had predicted these things with surprising energy, while Rome was yet in its cradle. "The fourth empire," says the prophet, "like iron, which breaks and subdues all other metals, shall overturn and crush all others."[625] And elsewhere he represents it as a ferocious beast, whose nature is a mixture of the wonderful and the terrible. It was armed, he tells us, "with iron teeth: eating and breaking in pieces, and treading down the rest with its feet."[626] The same prophet, who beheld in the future the formidable power of the Roman Empire, shows it also to us as preparing the way for the everlasting reign of our Lord Jesus Christ. It shall be replaced, he tells us, by another kingdom "that shall never be destroyed," which, formed without any human aid, "shall break in pieces and shall consume all these kingdoms: and itself shall stand forever."[627]

These few words of the prophet contain the whole philosophy of Roman history, as the preceding oracles explain to us the secret of the rise, progress, and decline of the other monarchies. We now know the reason why the Romans, acting differently from the other peoples of antiquity, made it a part of their glory to cover the earth with that immense network of roads whose solidity still excites the wonder of modern science; why they were always the conquerors of their enemies; why their empire, extending every day its limits during eight centuries, finished by absorbing nearly all other nations in its capacious bosom, and by admitting no other boundaries to its sway than those of the world; why, also, after the most protracted and sanguinary wars of which history has preserved a record, the triumphant Roman legions all at once stopped their march at every point of the globe, folded up their colors, and allowed their arms to rest; why, in fine, toward the year 4000 from the creation, the world enjoyed a universal peace. It was at this time that the Messias, the Prince of Peace, should make his entrance into the world at the little city of Bethlehem.

There remains the second part of the divine decree, in virtue of which the Messias should be born at Bethlehem, and should be authoritatively recognized as the Son of David. For the Roman Empire—the glory of procuring its accomplishment! We have not forgotten that Jacob, on his deathbed, announced that the Messias would come when a foreign king should be seated on the throne of Juda. Now, after the defeat of Pompey, Antony, the Roman consul, passed into Asia, and confirmed Herod, an Idumean by descent, in the government of Galilee. Behold the act that publicly took away the sovereign power from the house of Juda!

Antony was not content with this. Having returned to Rome, he was able to conciliate in regard to Herod the favor of Augustus, who shortly afterward became emperor. The new master of the world had no difficulty in moving the Roman Senate to bestow on Herod by a solemn decree the title of King of the Jews. In this character, Herod was conducted to the capitol and crowned with the usual ceremonies. Now this very epoch, at which the ancient scepter of David and Juda passed into the hands of a stranger, had been fixed by Jacob eighteen centuries before for the coming of the Messias. Then, in fact, the times assigned by the prophet being fulfilled, our Lord Jesus Christ did come into the world: it was on the fall of the kingdom of Juda, under the fourth monarchy, toward the end of the seventy weeks marked out by Daniel, before the destruction of the second Temple, which the Messias should honor with his presence, and at the moment when a general expectation prevailed in every region of the immediate arrival of a deliverer.

If Jacob announces that the Desired of Nations shall come when the scepter has departed from Juda, the prophet Micheas adds that he shall be born in Bethlehem. The Roman Empire shall also be charged with the verification of this latter circumstance. Joseph and Mary dwell at Nazareth. Their poverty, the severity of the season, the state of the holy Virgin, all these things forbid her to undertake a journey. Notwithstanding this, the Messias must be born at Bethlehem. God, who makes the passions of men serve for the accomplishment of his designs, avails himself of the caprice, the vanity, or the cupidity of Augustus, to verify the prophecies.

This prince issues the famous edict that obliges all the heads of families throughout the whole extent of the Empire to repair to their original family residence, here to be enrolled in the public registers. Joseph and Mary set out for Bethlehem, the city of David, to whose family they belong; the oracles are accomplished; and Augustus, without knowing it, has only been like Nabuchodonosor, like Cyrus, like Alexander, the servant of the Almighty. Behold in what manner God made events and empires concur to the glory of the Messias and to the establishment of his eternal kingdom![628]

Let us terminate this grand and majestic history of events that prepared the way for the promulgation of the gospel with a reflection very proper to fill our minds and hearts with religious sentiments. The old profane authors, and too great a number of modern writers, have attributed the rise and fall of these monarchies, the most powerful that the world ever knew, to the personal abilities or defects of their emperors. They have only perceived the apparent cause. The prophets extended their views much further. They beheld the great God, who dwells in the highest heavens holding in his hands the reins of empires, and making the virtues and vices of kings and peoples serve for the accomplishment of his great design, the salvation of the human race, by the establishment of the kingdom of his Christ. Now, God has not abdicated his throne. It is he who still directs all the events that bring joy or sorrow to the world, and who exalts or abases conquerors, for the accomplishment of his great design, the salvation of the human race, by the preservation and extension of the kingdom of his Christ.

PRAYER

O my God! who art all love, I thank thee for all that thou hast done for my salvation. It is therefore true, O my God! that, since the beginning of the world, everything has been for Jesus Christ, my Savior; but this Savior himself has been for me, and I am for thee.

I am resolved to love God above all things, and my neighbor as myself for the love of God; and, in testimony of this love, I will adore thy providence, O my God, in all events!

Lesson 50: Messias Prepared For: Heliodorus, Eleazar, and the Machabees

The preparations for the gospel were made in the East by various dispersions of the Jews from Ninive and Babylon; afterward, throughout the whole world by the conquests of Alexander. By means of these events, the knowledge of the expected Messias was become general. Lest it should grow weak among the nations, or rather that it might become clearer and more general, providence permitted that, during the last three centuries preceding the coming of the Messias, the Gentiles of all parts of the earth should come into perpetual contact with the Jews of Palestine. Hence the wars undertaken against the latter, first by the successors of Alexander and then by the Romans.

Trials purify the Jews, and makes them both desire and recognize the Messias. — In the views of providence, these wars had yet another end: they prepared the Jews themselves for the immediate coming of the Messias. These wars, so often renewed, and nearly always unjust, were severe trials destined to purify the Jewish people more and more, training them, by the practice of patience and other virtues, to the sanctity with which they should welcome the Messias, and affording them the light necessary to preserve them from failing to recognize the Desired of Nations. Pure hearts see the truth more clearly than others: this glorious privilege forms, even in this life, a portion of their reward.

Moreover, these uninterrupted vexations were marvelously well suited to excite in their hearts a lively desire of the liberator. The true Solomon, bringing truth and justice to the earth, should at length banish tyranny and make all men brethren. The misfortune was that the Pharisees, blinded by pride, gave a false interpretation to these prophecies according to the desires of their corrupt hearts, and could only understand the glory, the power, and the triumph of Christ in a gross and material sense. Providence had neglected nothing to prevent this fatal error, and humble and docile Jews were not the victims of it. Giving the proper meaning to the prophecies, they recognized the little babe of Bethlehem as the Messias promised to the human race: and the Lord was justified.

Not being able to relate fully the history of these last centuries of the ancient world, we shall confine ourselves to a few facts that render evident the continuance of the divine action over Jews and Gentiles, to prepare them for the approaching arrival of the Redeemer.

Heliodorus. — The first of these facts is that connected with Heliodorus. What could be more proper than the exemplary punishment inflicted on this sacrilegious profaner, as well as his own personal testimony, to remind the nations of the existence of the God of the Jews and of the truth of his religion, of which the belief in the Messias was a fundamental article.

Seleucus, king of Syria, had resolved to pillage the treasures of the Temple of Jerusalem. To execute this sacrilegious scheme, he chose Heliodorus, the comptroller of all his finances. Heliodorus, setting out to obey the orders of his master, seemed to have no other design than that of visiting the government of Judea. He arrives at Jerusalem, where the high priest Onias, no less respectful to his king than faithful to his God, receives him with all kinds of honor. The minister scarcely delays to explain himself on the commission with which he is charged: he declares that he is come in the king's name to take possession of the treasures of the Temple.

Onias represents to him that the money, kept in the house of the Lord, consists of sacred deposits left there for the support of widows and orphans. Heliodorus is little moved by the remarks of the pontiff, and, the will of the king taking the place of reason, selects a day to enter the Temple. The news of this sacrilegious attempt being spread throughout Jerusalem, the city is one scene of terrors and alarms. The priests, clothed in their sacerdotal robes, prostrate themselves at the foot of the altar, and, in this humble posture, implore the God of heaven to come to the assistance of his Temple.

The afflicted inhabitants, on their side, flock in crowds from their houses, and, animated by the same religious feelings, conjure the Lord not to permit his holy abode to be exposed to a sacrilegious contempt. The women, covered with rough haircloths, move in crowds along the streets. Even the virgins, retired within the precincts of the Temple, consider it their duty to come forth. Some rush to the high priest, others to the walls; a few, more timid than the rest, eagerly watch from the place of their retreat the issue of the event. All together, with hands raised toward heaven, address their prayers and sighs to the Lord. In the midst of the general confusion, the sovereign pontiff manifests such a degree of consternation that no one can behold him without being penetrated with the deepest sorrow.

Heliodorus beaten with rods. — Meanwhile, Heliodorus was earnestly urging forward his design. He was now at the gate of the treasury, surrounded by a troop of guards, who were ready to force an entrance; but, at the very moment when all seemed lost, the Lord gloriously manifested his omnipotence. Suddenly the wretched slaves, who had dared to lend their services to the enterprise of their leader, found themselves struck by the hand of God, thrown into disorder, and put to flight. They had seen a horse magnificently caparisoned, with a rider of terrible mien, whose armor seemed of gold, so refulgent was its brightness. This horse, rushing fiercely on Heliodorus, strikes him with his forefeet, and casts him to the ground. At the same time, two young men, full of majesty, radiant with glory, and elegantly attired, approach the profaner, and, being armed with rods, beat him severely and cover him with stripes. Heliodorus, chastised so roughly and wrapped in darkness, is laid half dead on a litter and carried outside the enclosure of the Temple, where he remains for a long time motionless, speechless, and almost lifeless.

An admirable effect of the justice of God, which ordains that a man, so rash as to dare to enter his holy house with all the pomp of a triumph, should be taken away from it covered with confusion, without any one being able to defend him from the avenging strokes of the almighty master whom he has sacrilegiously insulted; but, at the same time, a very important lesson for profaners and the favorites of princes, which teaches the former the reverence that is due to holy things, and the latter that it is always their bounden duty to resist iniquitous commands with an inflexible firmness and a respectful freedom!

While Heliodorus pined in the sad state to which his impiety had reduced him, the Jews passed suddenly from an excess of grief to joy: the Temple rang with canticles of thanksgiving. The friends of Heliodorus were engaged with very different cares. Not finding on earth any remedies for an evil that came from heaven, they had recourse to Onias himself, beseeching him to entreat the Lord to spare the life of the unfortunate culprit, who seemed ready to expire.

Onias, considering that if Heliodorus should die, the king would not fail to suspect some malice on the part of the Jews and to attribute to them the death of his envoy, offered a propitiatory sacrifice to the Lord for the recovery of the dying man. It was necessary, too, in the designs of providence, that the Gentiles should know more and more fully the God of Israel, the truth of his threats, and the certainty of his promises, of which the first was that of the great liberator. What could be more conformable to this divine plan than that Heliodorus himself should bear testimony to all these things and to the power of the God of Israel, after having experienced two unquestionable miracles in his chastisement and recovery?

Heliodorus announces the power of the true God. — The Lord heard the petitions of the high priest; but he did not wish that the guilty man should be ignorant of his benefactor.

"Thank the pontiff Onias," say the same angels to Heliodorus, " it is for his sake that the Lord has granted you the favor of life. As for you, punished by the command of a true God, be careful to announce his power, his truth, all his wonderful works, in the midst of idolatrous nations." Luminous words! which show us clearly that the judgments on Heliodorus entered into the general plan of the preparations for the future preaching of the gospel.

Having spoken thus, the angels disappeared. Heliodorus, on his side, profited of this terrible lesson. He offered a sacrifice of thanksgiving, accompanied with great vows, to the supreme God, of whose justice and mercy he had just had experience. After having thanked the sovereign pontiff, he hastened to return with his attendants to the king, his master. Not blushing to become an apostle of the true religion, he everywhere published the wonders of the great God, which he had seen with his own eyes, and which had been wrought in regard to his own person.

One day, the king said to him: "Who do you think might be a fit man to send on another expedition against Jerusalem?" "If," said he, "you have any enemy or traitor, charge him with the commission. I will engage that he shall return to you torn with stripes, if perchance he escape death. It is the simple truth: the Temple of the Jews is filled with the divine power. He who dwells in heaven makes his abode there: he declares himself its guardian and protector. And whosoever enters that holy place with the design of profaning it, must expect either a heavy chastisement or death."

If God took so much care to prepare the Gentiles for the kingdom of the Messias, by taking advantage of every occasion to give them a knowledge of the true religion, he was no less solicitous regarding the Jews. Nothing was omitted by him to purify them and to detach them from earthly things. Never had there been seen among them so many or such beautiful examples of a virtue already Christian. It seemed as if the sun of justice, about to rise on the world, made its powerful influence more deeply felt. Not only did Judea adore no idols: it even had its martyrs of every age and sex.

The holy man Eleazar.—Antiochus Epiphanius, king of Syria, was the instrument of which the Lord made use to prove his people. This impious and cruel prince undertook to abolish the worship of the true God in Judea. In a short time, the blood of the faithful flowed throughout the whole extent of Palestine. In the height of the persecution, there lived at Jerusalem a holy man named Eleazar, who occupied a leading rank among the doctors of the law. He was a venerable old man, whose appearance, full of gentleness and majesty, inspired confidence and commanded respect. He became the chief object of the furious rage of the persecutors. Having arrested him, they opened his mouth by force, and endeavored to make him eat, in spite of himself, some meats that were forbidden. His generous resistance immediately merited his condemnation. Preferring a glorious death to a dishonorable life, he took his place at the head of his executioners, and went forward of his own will to the tortures.

His martyrdom. — While he thus walked cheerfully to death, some of his friends, moved by a criminal pity, drew near to him and whispered: "Allow us to bring you some meats that may be lawfully eaten, and you can pretend to be tasting them, so that it may be believed that you have obeyed. This is a sure and, at the same time, a very innocent means of saving yourself from punishment." While Eleazar was listening to these base suggestions, a thousand noble and encouraging thoughts passed through his mind: he represented to himself the untarnished honor of his old age and his gray hairs, and the wise and virtuous life that he had led since he was a child, and the majesty and the justice of the holy laws promulgated by the Lord.

Full of these high ideas, he exclaimed: "Suffer me to be led to torments! It does not become our age to dissemble. It would be to deceive our young people, who might hence suppose that Eleazar, at the age of fourscore and ten years, had passed from the religion of his fathers to the superstition of foreigners, and so they, through my dissimulation, and out of love for a few additional days of a perishable life, would be seduced. I should hereby shamefully sully my name and merit for my old age the execration of centuries. Moreover, though I might save myself from the torments of men, could I hope to escape during my life or after my death from the hand of the Almighty? On the contrary, by quitting life courageously, I shall show myself worthy of my great age, and I shall leave an admirable example for the young."

These few words, pronounced with dignity, were received as the expression of arrogance and pride, and drew upon him an increase of cruelty. The venerable old man was stripped, laid on the ground, and bound; the executioners beat him unmercifully for a long time. In the midst of so many torments, the martyr, groaning, cried out: "Thou knowest well, O Lord, that being able to avoid such a cruel death, I have preferred the torments that I endure. Thou also knowest that I endure them most willingly, through fear of displeasing thee." These were the last words of the martyr. Leaving in his death a rare example of courage and fidelity, not only to the Jewish youth, but to the whole Jewish nation, he went to await in the bosom of Abraham the reward of his faith.

Sufferings of the Machabees.—The rumor of this death, far from causing the zeal of true Israelites to relent, only served to animate it the more: the blood of Eleazar became the seed of martyrs. After the struggle of the venerable old man, there might be seen entering the lists, on one side a mother, with her seven sons, in the flower of their youth; and on the other, Antiochus himself, with all the pomp of the persecutors of the faith. What a worthy employment for a great prince, to try the hardness of his heart against a woman and her children! He causes to be brought to them, and commands them to eat upon the spot and without reply, some meats forbidden by the law. On their refusal, he causes them to be stripped before him and to be torn with whips and scourges. The eldest of the seven brothers, without being astonished at this treatment, says to the tyrant: "What do you desire of us, or what answer do you expect? We are ready to die rather than violate the laws that God gave our fathers."

This intrepidity set Antiochus in a rage. He commanded that frying pans and brazen caldrons should be made red-hot: he was promptly obeyed. In the meantime he directs the tongue of the young martyr to be cut out, the skin to be torn from his head, and the extremities of his hands and feet to be chopped off, in presence of his mother and his brothers. Thus mutilated, he causes the fire to be applied to him; and, after this cruel trial, has him cast alive into the burning frying pan, where he pitilessly beholds him fried. The mother and brothers of the martyr, instead of bewailing his lot, think only of encouraging one another. "The Lord," they say, "will have regard to the justice of the cause that we defend; he will console us according to his promises."

While they fortified themselves in this manner, the eldest brother died, without mollifying by his death the cruel heart of the tyrant. On the contrary, he attacks the second, and brings him forward to insult him bitterly. The executioners tear away the skin with the hair from the young man's head, and ask him whether he will obey before they deprive him of all the members of his body. "I will not obey," the youthful martyr replies; and he is condemned to the same punishment as his brother. Before expiring, he says to the king with a strength that God alone could give: "Wicked prince! you torment us now; but the King of the world will restore us to life with everlasting glory."

This one being dead, they came to the third brother. The executioners ask him for his tongue—he puts it forth; for his hands—he presents them without hesitation. "It was from heaven that I received these members," he says confidently, "I surrender them with pleasure, for my God knows well how to restore them to me hereafter." The tyrant and his satellites cannot contain their surprise, on beholding in one so young so much contempt for the most frightful torments. Nevertheless, more irritated than surprised, Antiochus continues the barbarous execution. The fourth, the fifth, the sixth of these generous children, worthy imitators of their brothers, expire with courage in the midst of the same dreadful torments.

During their martyrdom, the mother, infinitely above all praise, and worthy of being eternally remembered by all virtuous persons, beheld, without emotion, her seven children pass away one after another by the most horrible tortures. Instead of shedding tears over their fate, which might have endangered their faith, she lavished on them the encouragements most proper to secure their victory; her anxieties, however, were not all calmed yet.

There still remained the last and youngest. The tyrant endeavored to seduce him, promising even with an oath to make him rich and happy, and to take him for his own friend. These base flatteries were ill-becoming in the mouth of a barbarian by whose orders the child had just seen his six brothers burned to death. The youthful martyr repaid them with a just contempt, not condescending so much as to answer them. Seeing his promises unheeded, Antiochus had recourse to the mother, and recommended her to save her son from death: she promised to advise him. In effect, she began to exhort with all her strength this last precious fruit of her blood, but in a very different manner from that which the king had intended. Mocking the tyrant, and bending toward her son, she spoke to him in her own language, that Antiochus might not be able to understand it: "My son have pity on me, who bore you nine months in my womb. Look, I beseech you, upon heaven and earth—they are the works of the God whom you adore. He created them all out of nothing, and mankind also. Let this sight encourage you, and teach you not to fear our cruel tormentor. Worthy of your brothers, receive death with constancy, that I may meet you all again in everlasting rest."

The mother had scarcely finished, when the courageous child exclaimed: "Why do you wait? I will not obey the orders of the king, but the law that God gave us by Moses." At these words, the tyrant is beside himself. Ashamed to see himself thus vanquished by a child, he pours out on his innocent victim all the vials of his wrath. The young martyr experiences more than his brothers the ingenious cruelty of his tormentors; but, as faithful as his elders, he preserves to the end the purity of his faith and confidence in the promises of the Almighty.

The mother, left alone in the midst of the lacerated remains of her children, was triumphant. She also aspired to the palm of martyrdom and expected a share in the glory of her sons. Antiochus, always the same, unwilling to yield, unable to pardon, ordered that the mother should be numbered with the children; after which he retired, covered with disgrace and abandoned to despair.

Thus became extinct in their own blood an illustrious family, destined by the Lord to reconcile him with Israel, and to prepare the Gentiles for the near approach of the Messias, by making known to them the truth and the power of the God of Abraham: a family whose members, by devoting themselves to death, left a name that has been more honorably enshrined in the memory of men than if they had all borne scepters and crowns.

PRAYER

O my God! who art all love, I thank thee for having by so many admirable means prepared the world for the coming of the Messias; grant us the grace to suffer everything rather than lose thy grace.

I am resolved to love God above all things, and my neighbor as myself for the love of God; and, in testimony of this love, I will have the greatest respect for holy things.

Lesson 51: Unity of Religion and of the Church

On the eve of quitting the ancient world, let us pause a moment to sketch in a few plain simple strokes the history of religion before Jesus Christ and of that society which was its depositary. You behold on the immortal brow of each, shining like two bright rubies, its unity and perpetuity; two grand characteristics, which distinguish the religion and the Church of God from the thousand religions and the thousand sects begotten by the passions of men and swept away by the breath of time. Religion is like a magnificent picture, which God began with the origin of the world, filled in under the patriarchs, toned down under Moses, and completed under Jesus Christ. Thus, though religion has not always had the same degree of clearness and development, it has always been one and the same in itself.[629]

I. *Religion: One and the same in its author.*—Revealed by God on the first day of the world, and founded on the necessary and unchangeable relations that exist between God, the Creator, Father, and last end of man, and man, the creature and child of God, destined to behold him face to face in heaven, religion, in the old testament, referred entirely to Jesus Christ to come—the mysterious and indispensable bond of alliance between God and man—as, in the new testament, it refers entirely to Jesus Christ already come.[630] Faith in Jesus Christ has been the foundation of religion in all ages. The Jew, to be justified, should believe in Jesus Christ promised, as the Christian must believe in Jesus Christ now come. The only difference is that, in the order of religion, the Jew was a child, acquainted with mere elements and taught but the first principles on account of the weakness of his age, while the Christian is a grownup man, who penetrates the substance and possesses a full knowledge of what the Jews believed without a clear comprehension thereof, as the saints in heaven see what we believe.[631]

II. *Religion: One and the same in its dogmas.*—It has believed and taught from the origin of time what it believes and teaches at the present day, and what it will believe and teach to the consummation of ages. Under the patriarchs and Moses it believed:

Regarding God.—1. In the existence of one eternal, omnipotent God, who created the world by his will and governs it by his wisdom. It believed confusedly what it knows today in a clear manner, viz., that in God there are three Persons equally adorable. This profound mystery of the Trinity had begun to be declared by the ancient expression of the divinity, "Let us make man"; in which God speaks to some one like himself, to another self. The Trinity was shown to Abraham under the figure of three angels, to whom the scripture applies the great name of God, and to whom the patriarch, although he sees three, speaks as to one alone, and renders adoration in the singular number.[632]

2. It believed in the mystery of the incarnation, signified to the patriarchs in the different apparitions of God under human form. By these, the Son of God preluded, if we may be allowed so to speak, his future incarnation. This same mystery was afterward announced more clearly by the prophets. They tell us in express terms that the Messias shall be called Emmanuel, that is, God-with-us, a God-man; that he shall be at once the Son of God and the Son of David.[633]

3. It believed in the mystery of the redemption. This was shown to Abraham in the sacrifice of Isaac, a touching figure of the Son of God, delivered up by his Father, and immolated for us on the same mountain. This mystery was indicated by all the different sacrifices of the old law, which were only representations of the one great sacrifice of the new law. The prophets afterward proclaimed it aloud, saying that the Messias should efface by his death the sins of the world.

4. It believed in the Spirit of the Lord: an omnipotent Spirit; the searcher of the secrets of the future and of hearts; the Spirit of light, of charity, of truth, and of life. The proofs of this belief are written in every page of our holy books. We must remember, however, that these mysteries have been revealed to us with a complete evidence by Jesus Christ alone, for whom alone it was reserved to raise the veil that hid them before his coming. It was he who, in the institution of baptism, taught us clearly that the true God, one and indivisible by his essence, is nevertheless Father, Son, and Holy Ghost. Thus, the mystery of the Father, the Son, and the Holy Ghost, one only God in three Persons,

shown obscurely to the patriarchs and to the disciples of Moses, is revealed clearly under the gospel: such, under this head, is the whole difference between the old and the new testament. The one places in broad daylight that which the other hides under veils.

Regarding man. — 1. It believed that he is made to the image and likeness of God; that he is composed of a body and a soul; that his soul is spiritual, like a breath from the mouth of God, and free to do either good or evil: the threats and the promises, the punishments and the rewards, of which the holy books speak continually, are so many proofs of the liberty of the soul. It believed that the soul is immortal. The ancient patriarchs called death a sleep. Now, sleep is not annihilation: it supposes an awaking. "Bury me," says Jacob when dying, "in the tomb of Abraham and Isaac"; then, addressing himself to God, he adds: "I will expect, O Lord, the Messias whom thou shalt send."[634] Thus, the dogma of immortality is stamped on the tomb of the patriarchs. We find it written in every page of the books of the prophets. "Remember thy Creator in the days of thy youth," says Solomon, "before the dust returns to the earth from which it was taken, and the spirit returns to God who gave it."[635] Elias, wishing to restore life to a child, says to God: "O Lord, grant that the soul of this child may return into its body." The scripture adds that the soul of the child did return, and the child was restored to life.[636]

2. It taught that man, created in a state of innocence and happiness, lost himself through disobedience to God; hence came all the evils that afflict humanity: for the first man transmitted his sin to his posterity, and we are all born guilty. "Who is pure before thee, O Lord?" asks the holy man Job—and he answers: "No one, not even the child of a day old."[637] Religion also taught that God had not abandoned man, but had promised him a Redeemer: this promise, and this expectation, pervaded all the ancient covenant. It added that man had need of grace to work out his salvation; that grace was to be obtained by prayer, sacrifice, and good works; and that this heavenly succor did not destroy but perfected free will. There is not a book of the old testament that does not bear testimony to these truths.

3. It taught that man should rise again after his death. "I know," says the patriarch of sorrow, "that my Redeemer liveth, and that on the last day I shall come forth from the tomb. I shall take back my flesh, and in this state I shall behold my God…This, my hope, is laid up in my bosom."[638]

4. It taught that, at the end of time, God would come to judge all mankind, and that there should be eternal rewards for the good and eternal punishments for the wicked. "I will gather together all peoples…in the valley of Josaphat,"[639] says the Lord, by the mouth of the prophet Joel, "and there I will sit upon my throne to judge the assembled nations."[640] He speaks of the signs that shall be the forerunners of this last day in the same terms as our Lord himself. After the judgment, what shall become of the wicked? "I have kindled," says the Lord to Moses, "a fire in my wrath: it shall burn even to the lowest hell."[641] To that place of torments shall be consigned "the sinners that rebel against me: their worm shall never die, their fire shall never be extinguished."[642] The Savior, speaking in the gospel of the reprobate, applies the same words to them. What shall become of the just? "They shall live eternally; their reward shall be with God."[643] They shall be inebriated with a torrent of delights and enlightened with the light of God himself.[644] Such was the answer of religion before the coming of Jesus Christ.

Regarding the world.—Religion taught that the world was drawn from nothingness by the power of the Lord, that it is governed by the divine wisdom, that it has been given to men that they may derive benefit from creatures and may learn to recognize their God in the wonders that surround them; moreover, that this world shall pass away, and that then there shall be "a new heaven and a new earth."[645] Such were the dogmas of religion before Jesus Christ: such are also the dogmas of religion after Jesus Christ. Religion, therefore, has always been one and the same in its creed or in its dogmas.

III. *Religion: One and the same in its morality.* — It commanded the same virtues: toward God — faith, hope, charity, adoration; toward the neighbor — justice, charity, truth; toward ourselves — humility, detachment, chastity. The old testament is full of passages in which these virtues are prescribed. But, to show by one solitary stroke that religion before was the same as religion after Jesus Christ, it suffices to say that the decalogue given to Moses is that which religion teaches today, and this decalogue is only a development of the law given to the father of the human race.[646]

IV. *Religion: One and the same in its worship.* — Acts of faith, hope, and charity, adoration, prayer, ceremonies, rites, sacrifices, public festivals: such were the fundamental works of the internal and the external worship of religion before Jesus Christ. All the patriarchs believed, hoped, loved, prayed, and sacrificed. From Moses to Jesus Christ, prayers and sacrifices, feasts, sacred rites, holy ceremonies, were not interrupted for a single moment.

Now, all these things, but especially a prayer and a sacrifice infinitely more perfect than the former, are still the fundamental works of the internal and the external worship of religion. For the figurative and feeble rites of the old law, our Lord has substituted the sacraments, august signs, full of efficacy: and this is what gives the worship of the Catholic Church an immense superiority over the worship of the Judaic Church.

This superiority of the Catholic Church is manifested everywhere, as well in dogmas as in morality and worship. Hence, when saying that religion has always been the same, we did not mean to convey that it was as perfect under the law as under the gospel, but only that it did not teach one thing under the law and another under the gospel. It could well teach us truths unknown to the ancients: but it never could teach us contradictory dogmas.

V. *Religion: One and the same in its object.* — What was the object of religion before Jesus Christ? To unite man with God in time, so as to do so still more closely in eternity; to reestablish the primitive order, which had been disturbed by original sin; to liberate man from the consequences of sin. And all this by means of the Redeemer, the mysterious mediator, who should be of the nature of God on the one hand and of the nature of man on the other: in such a way that God and man should meet in him, and that he should form forever a new and indissoluble society. Now, is not this still the object of religion after Jesus Christ? Is not its only end to unite us in such a manner with our Redeemer, that we may be new embodiments of him, as it were? Does it not continually repeat to us, and to all generations, with the apostle: "My little children, I continually feel for you the pains of childbirth, until Christ is formed in you."[647]

Hence, to summarize all the preceding remarks, religion has always been, since the fall of man, one and the same in its author, in its mediator, in its dogmas, in its morality, in its worship, and in its object. Therefore, there never has been any but one religion. Therefore, the Christian religion goes back to the first days of the world, as it will continue to the end of ages. Like a magnificent tree, planted at the beginning of time by the hand of God himself, it has gradually developed its mighty trunk and stretched out its protecting branches: nourishing with its salutary fruit and sheltering with its immortal foliage all the generations that have passed, that are now passing, and that shall ever pass over the face of the earth.

Since religion has always been one and the same from the beginning of the world, it necessarily follows that the society or the Church which is the guardian, interpreter, and embodiment of religion has always been one and the same; so that there never has been, and there never shall be, any but one true Church, as there never has been, and there never shall be, any but one true religion. Like religion, the Church is catholic, embracing all times and places: this is one of the marks of her divinity. Hence, religion and the Church are two sisters, who have been born, who have grown, who have lived together, and who have experienced the same vicissitudes on all occasions. Let us trace a hurried outline of the admirable relations that exist between the Church before and the Church after Jesus Christ.

I. *The Church before Christ: One in its foundation and destiny.*—Perpetuated before the deluge in the posterity of Seth, represented after the deluge by the patriarchal families of Abraham, Isaac, and Jacob, she travels as a stranger into a country, the possession of which is promised to her, and in which she shall secure a permanent establishment. A tender and enlightened mother, she then offers only milk to her children, in order to prepare them for a more substantial nourishment at a later period. Her teaching is veiled under the forms of images and symbols: the simple language of mothers to their children. Cruelly persecuted in Egypt during several centuries, she departs at length triumphant after her long trial. Under the direction of Moses, and proceeding onward in the midst of prodigies, she destroys pagan nations, with their temples and their idols, as she advances, until at length she rests in the land that she conquers. Then she develops her magnificent constitution.

II. *The Church before Christ: One in its constitution.*—She has her books, in which are contained her laws given from heaven, and written by the hand of God himself. She has a sovereign pontiff and a council of elders, or the synagogue, charged with the duty of explaining them: all her children are obliged to submit to the decision of this august tribunal. She has her sacerdotal hierarchy—a high priest, invested with supreme power; then, her priests, Levites, and inferior ministers. Scattered through every tribe, these priests are like salt, destined to preserve the whole body from corruption; or like torches, which, placed at regular distances, should dissipate the darkness of error and ignorance. In the midst of all is her God, almost visible in the ark of the covenant. She has her sacrifices, which she presents exclusively to the Lord, to adore, to thank, to appease, and to impetrate. She has her holy day every week; she has her great solemnities, that of the Pasch, that of Pentecost, that of Tabernacles, on which all her children come with gladness to Jerusalem to offer up prayer and praise.

III. *The Church before Christ: One in its trials and victories.*—Though mistress of the promised land after the destruction of the idolatrous nations, yet she only enjoys short intervals of peace and tranquility. Sometimes it is strangers who attack her; sometimes it is her own children who, by their scandals, force her to shed bitter tears, or, by their divisions, pierce her maternal heart with the sword of sorrow. Finally, a great schism comes to overwhelm her with grief: ten tribes abandon her, and renounce her authority. But, if the Lord afflicts her, he does not forsake her: though she be ever assailed, she shall never be destroyed. Great prophets are sent to her, whose office it is to console her and to preserve the truth in her bosom. All the events that occur around her, powerful empires rising and falling in turn, contribute to her welfare, to her glory, and to the accomplishment of the great design for which she has been raised up, namely, the establishment of the kingdom of Christ, which should repair the sad consequences of sin, reconcile man with God, and restore primeval order in the full vigor of its perfection.

Such are the leading traits in the historical picture of the Church or that society to whose care the true religion was confided before our Lord Jesus Christ came on earth. Now, all these traits, but shining with far more splendor, we shall find again in the Church to which is confided the true religion after Jesus Christ has come.

I. *The Church after Christ: One in its foundation and destiny.*—After the ascension of Jesus Christ, we find the Christian Church, represented by the apostles and a small number of the faithful, coming forth from the upper chamber. She is at first a stranger and a traveler on earth, the possession of which is, nevertheless, promised to her, and in which she shall enjoy a never-ending establishment. The world becomes for her another

Egypt, in which, during several centuries, she is the object of the most cruel persecution. She comes forth at length triumphant from the catacombs, and, under the guidance of her divine leader, ascends through struggles and miracles to the throne of the Caesars.

II. *The Church after Christ: One in its constitution.* — Then, victorious over an idolatrous world, she rests tranquilly in the land that she has conquered, and develops in the sight of the world her magnificent constitution. To the ancient books, written by the hand of God himself on the summit of Sinai, she adds another, more perfect, written in the blood of the Messias on the summit of Calvary. Her pontiffs, as well as her councils, are charged with the duty of explaining the divine code, and constitute an august tribunal to whose decisions all her children are bound to submit.

She has her sacerdotal hierarchy — a high priest, invested with supreme power; then her bishops, priests, and inferior ministers. Scattered everywhere among her children, these priests are like salt, destined to preserve the whole body from corruption; or like torches, which, placed at regular distances, should dissipate the darkness of error and ignorance; or like vigilant shepherds, who should feed the flock and drive the wolves far away from the fold.

In the midst of all is her God, really present in the tabernacle. She has her sacrifice, which, from the rising to the setting sun, she is continually offering up, to adore, to thank, to appease, and to impetrate. Every week she has her holy day; she has her great solemnities — Christmas, Easter, Pentecost, and others — on which her children flock with gladness to the temple to offer up prayer and praise.

III. *The Church after Christ: One in its trials and victories.* — Though mistress of the world after the overthrow of idolatry, yet she only enjoys short intervals of peace and tranquility. Sometimes it is strangers who attack her; sometimes it is her own children who, by their scandals, force her to shed bitter tears, or, by their divisions, pierce her maternal heart with the sword of sorrow. Finally, a great schism comes to wrap her in mourning-weeds: the East withdraws from her, and refuses to recognize her authority, and, like the ten schismatical tribes, the haughty East falls under a yoke of iron.

If the Lord afflicts the Church, he does not forsake her; though constantly assailed, she shall never be destroyed. Great saints, powerful intellects, are sent to her, to console her and to preserve the truth in her bosom. All the events that occur around her, mighty empires rising and falling, contribute to her welfare, to her glory, and to the accomplishment of the great design in consideration of which she has been formed, namely, the preservation and extension of the kingdom of Christ, which should repair the consequences of sin, reconcile man with God, and restore primeval order in the full vigor of its perfection.

Such are the leading strokes in the historical picture of the Church or that society to which the true religion was confided after Jesus Christ. Such are the striking congruities that cause the Church to be recognized throughout the course of ages as the immortal and immutable guardian of religion from the origin of the world.

Thus, the daughter of heaven, the well-beloved spouse of Christ, uniting to the incorruptible modesty of a virgin the courageous tenderness of a mother, the Church has seated herself, from the beginning of time, under the venerable tree of religion. A faithful guardian, with one hand she presents her fruit of life to all the generations of men that march onward to death; with the other, she wields a terrible sword against all the rash adventurers that would dare to strike the majestic trunk or to cut off any of the spreading branches of her tree. A guardian unchanging in her conduct, she has seen the centuries glide by her feet, she herself remaining still the same; and when the last hour of the world is tolled, this salutary tree raising its head toward heaven, the immortal virgin shall rise like it, and the chaste spouse of Christ, accompanied by all the generations that have been vivified by her tender cares, shall ascend, never more to leave, the eternal throne of her celestial bridegroom.

What admirable characteristics of unity, perpetuity, and divinity shine everywhere in the Church and in the Christian religion! What a majesty appears in this holy religion, whose children we have the happiness to be! As old as the world, all that precedes, accompanies, and follows the coming of its divine author, tends to demonstrate its excellence. Its history is found written beforehand in a book open to all eyes, a book revered equally by two inimical peoples, among whom there could not be the slightest collusion.

No, O my God, the best of fathers—whom all languages name the good God—it is not possible that thou shouldst leave to error all the characteristics of truth! If that which we believe, after so many convincing proofs, were an error, ah! thou wouldst no longer be the good God, since we might justly say that it was by thee we had been deceived.

PRAYER

O my God! who art all love, I thank thee with my whole heart for having given us religion, and for having caused us to be born in the bosom of the true Church. Grant us the grace ever to be docile and faithful children.

I am resolved to love God above all things, and my neighbor as myself for the love of God; and, in testimony of this love, I will often pray for the wants of the Church.

Lesson 52: Influence of Religion

We might justly be reproached if, after presenting religion to the mind, by sketching the grand characteristics of truth that distinguish it, we did not also present it to the heart, by showing its salutary influence on the nation that lived according to its teachings. Moreover, the benefits of religion are by no means the least proof of its truth. It is therefore our duty to explain the beneficent action of religion on the ancient people of God.

There can be no society without religion. We must add that society is so much the more tranquil, flourishing, and content, as religion is better known and observed by it: the Jewish nation offers a memorable example of this truth.

If, since the coming of the Messias, Christians have been the model people, the Israelites were also, among the nations of antiquity, the model people, that is, the most moral and enlightened people, and, taking them altogether, the happiest. Now, this glorious privilege they owed to religion. As a matter of fact, the greater number of the ancient nations were more considerable, more opulent, more powerful than the Jewish nation. Nevertheless, these nations were much less moral; their legislation was much less wise and less complete; their ideas were much less noble; their manners were much less pure. With them, children, women, slaves, the poor, in other words, three-fourths of the population were buried in deep abjection. Why this depth of inferiority? Because one thing was wanting to them, the knowledge of the true religion. These people enjoyed only some faint glimmers of the primitive truths, and the happiness of a people is always proportioned to the number of the truths that it believes.

The Jews, who possessed a more complete revelation of the truth, ought to be, and really were, superior to the idolatrous nations; a few simple details will suffice to prove it. To observe order in this examination, let us consider the Jews with reference to their domestic society, their political society, and their religious society.

I. *In the family.*—The family is the basis of states, which are only a collection of families. But there can be no family without parental authority. Now, it is necessary that this authority should be firm, wise, and prudent. Such was parental authority among the Jews. Among the pagans, parents arrogated to themselves the right of life and death over their children, and they exercised it without pity or control. According to their caprices or their interests, they killed, sold, or abandoned their sons and daughters; and their barbarity was not regarded as a crime in the eyes of their civil or religious laws. This was despotism exalted into a principle.

Among the Jews, fathers and mothers had not the right either to abandon or to sell their children. Truly, they could put them to death, but it was only for just reasons, and never without the interference of the magistrate. After having tried every kind of domestic correction in vain, the father and mother went to the senate of the city, and denounced to it their disobedient and debauched son. On this complaint, he was sentenced to death and stoned. Thus, on the one hand, the necessity of having recourse to the public authorities moderated the parental authority, while, on other, the fear of incurring the anger of parents kept a child in perfect submission. This excellent constitution of the family helped powerfully to consolidate society.

We could scarcely believe the number of evils that the enfeeblement, or rather the annihilation, of parental authority has produced in states. See what happens among us! However young a son may be, as soon as he is married or is able to subsist without the aid of his father, he pretends that he fulfills all his filial obligations by merely showing his parents some little respect. Hence, that multitude of little families who lead an isolated life, or who are bound to one another only by the weakest ties, which the slightest discord suffices to break. Besides, the depravity of manners that this independence fosters is likewise very dangerous to the state itself, as half a century of revolutions has but too clearly proved.

From the paternal power is derived the influence of the aged: it was great among the Israelites. It was especially from among the old that the judges and counselors of state were chosen. When the Hebrews first began to form themselves into a people, they were governed by old men. Throughout the whole course of the scripture, as often as there is mention made of assemblies and public affairs, the ancients are placed in the front rank: sometimes they are even named alone.

Nothing more useful than this power of venerable old age to maintain peace in families and order in the state. Youth is fit only for action and motion; age is able to counsel, to instruct, and to command. Youth has neither patience nor foresight; it is unwilling to submit to rule and is eager for change. Age takes advantage of times and occasions, considers things well beforehand, walks with caution, acts on sound principles, and avoids every rash innovation.

Accordingly, the Lord takes special care to ensure respect for old men: it is one of those things that he recommends most frequently in scripture. Severe punishments avenged any injury offered to age: witness the two-and-forty children torn in pieces by two bears, for having mocked the prophet Eliseus because he was bald.

Far from fearing the care of a large number of children, fathers and mothers asked them with earnestness of the Lord: they regarded them as a signal honor. He was considered happy who saw himself surrounded by a crowd of children and grandchildren, ever ready to execute his orders and to receive his instructions. The education of children was regarded as the first and most agreeable of the duties imposed on man. It began in some manner with the birth of the child, since mothers did not dispense themselves, as with us, from the duty of nourishing the fruit of their own womb.

As soon as the child could walk and articulate some words, its body was developed by labor and sports, and its mind by letters and music. The father accustomed his growing son to run, to lift burdens, to draw the bow, to whirl the sling; he joined military exercises to all these. He also taught him everything connected with agriculture, illustrating his lessons by continual practice; so that a young man, on quitting the paternal roof, knew how to procure for himself all things necessary to life.

The mother taught her daughter to fulfill all the duties of housekeeping, to knead the dough with skill, to do everything connected with cookery, to spin, to use the needle, to manufacture stuffs on the loom. While training her body to labor, she formed her heart to virtue, by lessons to which we find nothing comparable among pagan nations. When we recollect that it is on the good education of the young that the happiness of the family depends, how can we doubt of the peace that must have reigned in innumerable Israelite families?

"A wise woman," the mother would say to her daughter, "given to labor, and attentive to the care of her household, is the joy of her husband; she is more precious than gold and diamonds that are brought from the ends of the earth. The heart of her husband places confidence in her, and her house shall be blessed with abundance.

"She seeks for wool and flax, and sets them in motion with her quick hands. She rises before day, and distributes food to her domestics. She puts a hand to the heaviest undertakings, and, when she leaves them, her fingers return to the spindle.

"She opens her hand to the needy, and stretches it out to assist the poor. She fears neither cold nor snow for her house, because all her domestics are well clothed. She makes herself excellent tapestry, and she is covered with linen and purple. She utters only words of wisdom: her tongue is guided by the law of sweetness and clemency.

"She has her eyes on everything that passes in her house, and she does not eat her bread in idleness. Her children declare that she is happy, and her husband never ceases to praise her."

Such were the wise maxims by which the mothers formed the minds and hearts of their daughters, and these lessons had so much the more weight as they themselves gave an example of them to their cherished pupils.

The maxims that the fathers repeated continually to their sons were no less solid. "My son," they would say, "love from your youth to be instructed, and you shall acquire a wisdom that will preserve you even to the grave. The fear of the Lord is the beginning of wisdom. Fear, therefore, the Lord with your whole soul, and venerate his priests. Do not say: 'I have sinned, and what evil hath befallen me?' My son, the Most High is slow to punish.

"When you enter the house of the Lord, consider where you place your foot, and draw nigh to hear that which God commands you; for obedience is worth more than sacrifice. Remember always that the blessing of the Lord is on the head of the just man.

"Let your mouth never be accustomed to oaths, for by swearing, God is offended in many ways.

"If you know a wise man, go in search of him from the break of day, and let your foot often mark the threshold of his door. Do not consult an irreligious man on what relates to piety; an unjust man, on what relates to justice; a timorous man, on what relates to war; a merchant, on what concerns his business; but address yourself to a good man, whose views are in accordance with your own. Consult your own conscience; for you have no more faithful counselor.

"Do not say: 'I will treat this man as he has treated me'; and beware of ever doing to others that which you would not wish them to do to you. If your enemy be hungry, give him to eat; if thirsty, give him to drink.

"Dispense alms according to your power. If you have much, give much; if you have little, give with a generous heart out of the little that you have. He who has pity on the poor lends at interest to the Lord. Do not turn away your eyes from the poor, though they importune you; and do not give occasion to those who ask of you, to curse you behind your back. Lend an ear willingly to the poor man; answer him kindly and mildly.

"Be not like a lion in your house, by rendering yourself terrible to your servants and ill-treating those who are subject to you.

"Listen to your father, who gave you life, and despise not your mother when she is old. He who honors his father and his mother shall receive consolation from his own children. Comfort your father in his old age; do not grieve him during his life. If his mind become weak, bear with him, and do not despise him on account of the advantages that you shall have over him. For the charity that you exercise toward your father will not be forgotten; and God will reward you for enduring patiently the defects and failings of your mother."

Such was the morality of the Israelites. Let any one search as much as he pleases among the other nations of the time, never—we delight in repeating it—never shall he find anything so sublime.

Besides these instructions, fathers and mothers were obliged to give their children lessons on the great things that God had done for them and their ancestors; and the law commanded that they should explain to the young the origin of the different feasts that were celebrated and the different ceremonies that were observed.

The Israelites had no public schools: instruction was derived for the most part from the wise conversations of parents and aged persons. The better to make themselves understood by their pupils, they employed not only the simplest stories, but also proverbs, riddles, and parables. The chief use of this figurative discourse was to convey the maxims of morality under natural and agreeable forms, so that children might more easily remember them. The soul of education consisted in learning by heart the canticles of Moses and the other prophets, as well as the psalms of David. In these admirable writings, youth found a national history, poetry, eloquence, and as much knowledge as it required, without ever having recourse to foreign authors. As the national poems were sung, everyone acquired some tincture of music as a matter of course.

Thus, while among the pagans, mothers and nurses taught children from their cradles the fables of the gods, that is, obscene and ridiculous adventures, which tended only to a contempt of the divinity and a corruption of morals,[648] the Israelites alone taught their children such truths as were proper to inspire them with the fear and love of God and to excite them to virtue. All their traditions were true, noble, and useful. On which side, then, was the superiority?

II. *In civil and political society.*—This superiority of the Jews over other nations is no less marked in their civil and political society. On opening the books of Moses, we find there a code of laws that tend, not only to preserve religion and the worship of the true God, but also to form the manners of the people and to maintain a happy and tranquil state. Idolatry, luxury, intemperance, debauchery, in a word, all the vices that disturb social order, are severely proscribed. The duties of fathers and mothers, of masters and servants, are wisely laid down. We behold many sumptuary regulations in favor of modesty and frugality. All is foreseen, all is adjusted by the supreme legislator, of whom Moses was only the minister and interpreter.

In this admirable code are found, among others, two laws so touching that it would be a pity not to make them known: we refer to the law of the sabbatical year and the law of the jubilee. Every Israelite had his own land to cultivate: the same land that had been allotted to his ancestors in the time of Josue. He could not change his place; neither could he ruin or enrich himself exclusively. The law of the sabbatical year and the law of the jubilee provided for it.

By the first, it was ordained that the land should be allowed to rest every seventh year, in honor of the Lord. During this year, no one could sow his field or prune his vineyard or orchard. There was no mowing or reaping; there was no vintage; there was no gathering of fruits or grains: everything that the land produced of itself was abandoned to the poor and to strangers. The proprietor made provision for themselves during the sixth year; and, if they stood in need of any new fruits, they could take some of the spontaneous productions of their lands, but with moderation, and without doing injury to those who, by the right of indigence, were entitled to them.

By the law of the jubilee, every fiftieth year was sanctified in the same manner. A general liberty was then proclaimed, in virtue of which those Hebrews whom misery had compelled to become the slaves of their brethren recovered all the privileges of citizens. Everyone came again, by a full right, into possession of the property that he had alienated. During the year of the jubilee, as during all the sabbatical years, it was forbidden to require the payment of debts, and often they were entirely remitted in favor of the poor. This difficulty of securing payment, joined with the impossibility of making permanent acquisitions, rendered loans very objectionable and sales rather infrequent, and consequently cut away the root of ambition, while it diminished the occasions of impoverishment: this was the object of the law. Everyone limited himself to his inheritance, and endeavored to make it as valuable as possible, knowing that it should never depart from his family.

When a man desired to sell his property, a valuation was made according to the number of years that remained till the next jubilee. The greater the number was, the higher the price. No one ever sold without the condition of ransom. The seller could recover his property two, three, or four years after alienating it, by returning to the purchaser the money that he had received for it; if he had not the means to do so, he waited for the year of the jubilee.

Thus, the Hebrews were only the usufructuaries of their lands: they were the farmers of God, who was the true proprietor of them. Hence it came to pass that, before the period of the election of kings, they were not burdened with any rent, except the tithes and firstfruits reserved by the Lord.

Another law, no less admirable, was the law of hospitality: Did any other nation observe it so religiously? While among the old Romans, of whose civilization we hear so many boasts, every stranger was an enemy, a suspected man, who was often immolated to the gods of the country,[649] the Jews received their guests with the utmost eagerness; they rendered to them all the good offices in their power; in a word, they fulfilled with joy, in regard to their unknown friends, all the duties of humanity.

Accordingly, no matter what the pretended sages of the last century have said, there never was a people more humane. Let them be judged by this law of Deuteronomy: "If when walking along a road, says the Lord, you find a bird's nest in a tree or on the ground, and the dam sitting upon her young or upon her eggs, you shall not take away the dam with her young; but, taking the young, you shall let her go, that you may be happy, and may live a long time."[650] If they comported themselves thus in regard to weak, irrational creatures, how then did they act in regard to human beings?

But, says someone, the Israelites slaughtered the Chanaanites. First, the people of God are not the only people in whose history we see the vanquished immolated without mercy by the victors. Open the annals of the Greeks and Romans, those nations so much lauded, and what a scene of carnage and ferocity will meet your eyes! Besides, if the Israelites slaughtered the Chanaanites, it was to obey the formal command of the Most High, who had reprobated these idolaters. Why had he reprobated them? Because they had not profited by the severe chastisement of the Sodomites nor by the exemplary conduct of the patriarchs; because they had not opened their eyes to the wonders wrought on their frontiers, during the space of forty years, in favor of the children of Jacob; because, in fine, they had defied and wearied the divine justice, for nearly ten centuries, by the unheard-of crimes and disorders in which they lived. Who has a right to say to God: "Thou hast not the power to punish the guilty?" Now, the people of Israel were the instruments of his vengeance.

If we experience a feeling of regret at this moment, it is on account of our inability to enter into a more extensive examination of the legislation of the Hebrews. It would have been as agreeable as easy to us to show the evident superiority of the people of

God over all other nations. But this attentive examination has been already made by learned men,[651] and their labor fills us with the highest admiration for the Mosaic code, on which the blind and senseless impiety of the last century dared to make such unbecoming criticisms.

III. *In religious society.*—Who would venture without blushing to place the religion of the Jews on a level with the idolatry that formerly reigned everywhere? As well might one compare day with night, virtue with crime, God with the devil. In this fundamental point, the superiority of the Jews over the pagans was never a subject of any difficulty: for whatever truth or goodness existed in paganism was only a slight reflex of the revelation that the Jews possessed in all its plenitude.

They had only one Temple and one altar at which it was permitted to offer sacrifices to God: this was a sensible mark of the unity of God. To represent his sovereign Majesty, the sacred edifice was not only the most magnificent in the whole country, but it was one of the wonders of the world.

Besides the Temple of Jerusalem, there were in the other cities places consecrated to the divine service and called "synagogues," that is, houses of assembly. The service in the synagogue consisted of prayers, readings from the holy scripture, and sermons. The people met there three times a week, without counting feast or fast days. In every synagogue there was a certain number of ministers appointed to take charge of the religious exercises performed there: the majority were priests or Levites. In default of them, the old men most venerable by their years and virtues were chosen.

Three times a year, on the solemnities of the Pasch, Pentecost, and Tabernacles, all the men were obliged to visit Jerusalem, and it was permitted the women to go thither also. We speak elsewhere of these feasts and of the manner in which they were celebrated;[652] let us here add only a few details. These great solemnities continued for seven days. On the second day of the feast of the Pasch, a sheaf of new corn, the firstfruits of the harvest, was brought to the Temple.

The ceremonies that accompanied this offering were full of mystery. The judges deputed three men to go and gather the sheaf in the neighborhood of Jerusalem. The deputies asked the multitude present three times if the sun had set, and three times they were answered that it had. Then they three times asked permission to cut the sheaf, and three times it was granted them. They cut it down at length in three different fields, with three different sickles, and placed the ears in three little caskets to carry them to the Temple. When the sheaf was come, it was threshed in front of the porch; and of the grain that it yielded, about three pints were taken. After having winnowed, roasted, and ground this quantity well, some oil was poured over it, and a handful of incense added. The priest that received this offering shook it before the Lord toward the four ends of the world: he cast a portion of it on the altar, and the remainder belonged to himself. After this, everyone might begin the harvest.

We see in the offering of the sheaf a striking picture of the unbloody Sacrifice of the Altar, a sacrifice that sanctifies the four quarters of the world. This salutary offering began only when the sun of justice had set, that is, after the death of the Savior, and its object is to preserve a holy remembrance thereof. In fine, the number three, a mysterious number, so often repeated, visibly indicates the operation of the three Persons of the Holy Trinity in the great work of the redemption of the human race.

Seven weeks after the offering of the new sheaf, the festival of Pentecost was celebrated, on which occasion two loaves, firstfruits of the loaves of the new harvest, were offered to the Lord.

On the fifteenth day of the seventh month, after the gathering in of all the fruits of the year, the festival of Tabernacles was celebrated, continuing for seven days, like the two preceding ones. Five days before this festival, that of Expiations was celebrated by a general fast. This was the only day of the year on which the high priest could enter the sanctuary, to make atonement for the sins of the people. Here are the details of the ceremony.

The high priest, after immolating a calf for his own sins and those of his family, entered the sanctuary, carrying a censer, perfumes, and the blood of the calf. He placed the perfumes on the fire of the censer, so that the smoke rising from them might hide the sight of the ark of the covenant from him; then, dipping the end of his finger into the blood of the calf, he seven times made an aspersion with it toward the propitiatory that covered the ark.

He next sacrificed for the sins of the people one of the two goats that had been brought to him in the name of the whole nation. The selection of the goat was made by lot: the one on which the lot fell was immolated. The pontiff took the blood of this goat and made an aspersion with it in the sanctuary, through all the tabernacle, and on the altar of holocausts, to purify the holy place and the altar from all the impurities of the children of Israel. He presented the other goat alive to God; and, placing his hands on its head, he confessed the people's sins, which he laid with a curse on the mysterious animal. After this, he caused it to be driven out into the desert, so that it should never more reappear: it was called the scapegoat.

These two goats represented the one sacrifice of the Savior, who, like the emissary goat laden with the sins of the people, was led out of Jerusalem, and, like the other goat, was immolated, to purify us by the sprinkling of his blood.

The Israelites, as we have seen, were only the tenants of God: he alone was the real Lord of Palestine. To acknowledge his sovereign dominion, they were obliged to offer him a portion of their crops. These offerings were made in the name of the whole people, before they gathered in the harvests. The offering consisted of the sheaf and the loaf already mentioned. After the harvests, these same offerings were repeated by individuals, before beginning to use the new fruits, and were termed "firstfruits."

There was no special time marked out for the presentation of the firstfruits by individuals; neither was the quantity precisely determined. Troops of eighty persons would gather together to bear in pomp their offerings to the Temple of the Lord. Each troop was preceded by an ox destined for sacrifice: the animal was crowned with olives and its horns were gilt. Every person bore in a basket the firstfruits of his lands: the rich had gold or silver baskets; the poor, osier ones. They advanced in ceremonial order to the Temple, singing canticles. As soon as they reached the mount of the Temple, all, not excepting even the king, if he was present, took their baskets on their shoulders, and bore them to the enclosure of the priests, who, on receiving them, offered up prayers in keeping with this pious act.

He who made an offering said: "I acknowledge this day before the Lord that I have entered into the land that he promised to our forefathers...On this account, I offer the firstfruits of the land that the Lord has given me."[653]

The law also ordained that the Hebrews should consecrate to the Lord the firstborn of their sons and the firstborn among their animals. The firstborn children were redeemed with silver. The firstborn of unclean animals could also be redeemed. As for clean animals, they were sacrificed, and their blood was poured out around the altar. Their fat was burned, and the flesh belonged to the priests, as well as all the other offerings. So the Lord had ordained.

If the Israelites had feast days, they had also fast days. The law had appointed only one day of general fasting: it was the tenth of the seventh month, the festival of Expiations; but there were extraordinary ones, some in times of public calamity, others in times of private affliction. There was also fasting through simple devotion.

Their fast did not consist merely in eating at a later hour, but in afflicting themselves in every manner. They passed the whole day without eating or drinking anything until night.

This has been the practice, not only among the Jews, but among the Mahometans, who on this matter imitate both the Jews and the early Christians. Public fasts were announced with sound of trumpet, like feasts. All the people at Jerusalem assembled in the Temple; elsewhere, in the public places. Readings were made from the law, and the most venerable old men exhorted the people to acknowledge their sins and to do penance for them. No nuptials were celebrated on this day. All remained in silence under ashes and haircloth.

They wore dirty and torn garments, or sacks, that is, garments narrow and unplaited, and consequently disagreeable. They also called them haircloths, on account of their being made from coarse camlet or some similar stuff, rough and heavy. They had their feet as well as their head bare, but the face was covered: sometimes it was so wrapped in a cloak that they could not see the light. The prophets were very careful to remind them that all these external marks of repentance would not suffice unless accompanied with a true conversion of heart.

Compare now the cruel, ridiculous, and obscene festivals of the Greeks and Romans with this worship of the Hebrews, at once so touching, so varied, and so magnificent; contrast the teachings of the mysteries of Ceres or the good goddess with the lessons given by the great solemnities of the Pasch, Pentecost, and Tabernacles; remember that it is religion which communicates to nations their lights and their manners; and then, with your hand on your breast, say whether you know in antiquity a people comparable to the Jewish people. Yet this people had nothing in its character, in its instruction, in its riches, or in its power, to place it in the front rank of nations.

Render homage, therefore, to religion, and say: "Thanks to it, the Jews were of all ancient peoples the most enlightened, the most moral, the most happy. But religion procured all these advantages only because it was good; it was good only because it was true; it was true only because it came from God. Let the homage, therefore, of my love and my faith be given to this Judaic religion, the most beautiful present that heaven ever made to earth, except the Christian religion, of which I have the happiness to be a child; or rather, let the whole homage of my soul be given to the one only religion, which existed under the patriarchs, which existed under Moses, which exists under the gospel, and which shall exist forever and ever!"[654]

PRAYER

O my God! who art all love, I thank thee for having given religion to the world, and for all the benefits of which it has been the continual source: grant us the grace to be ever faithful to its salutary laws.

I am resolved to love God above all things, and my neighbor as myself for the love of God; and, in testimony of this love, I will have the greatest respect for all the ceremonies of the Church.

ENDNOTES

1 Vatican I, Dogmatic Constitution *Dei Filius de fide catholica*, Ch. 4

2 Pope Benedict XIV, Apostolic Constitution *Etsi minime*, n. 13

3 Cf. Pope St. Pius X, Encyclical *Acerbo nimis*, n. 27

4 Translator's note: The French work is published in eight vols.

5 See the rescripts of Pius VIII, dated 10th May, 1830; of Gregory XVI, dated 13th September, 1831; and of Pius IX, to the *Catechism of Perseverance* at Nevers, dated 11th December, 1846.

6 See *Histoire des Catéchismes de Saint-Sulpice*. On the discipline of the "Catechisms of Perseverance," see *Méthode de Saint-Sulpice*.

7 Cf. Tertullian, *Apology*, Ch. 17

8 Manner of teaching religion to the ignorant.

9 Narratio plena est cum quisque primo catechizatur ab eo quod scriptum est, in principio fecit Deus coelum et terram, usque ad presentia tempora Ecclesiae. Non tamen debemus totum Pentateuchum totosque Judicum et Regum et Esdrae libros,…narrando evolvere et explicare: quod nec tempus capit, nec ulla necessitas postulat; sed cuncta summatim generatimque complecti, etc. (Augustine, *On the Catechizing of the Uninstructed*, Ch. 3, n. 5ff).

   Quapropter in Veteri Testamento est occultatio Novi, in Novo Testamento est manifestatio Veteris (Augustine, *On the Catechizing of the Uninstructed*, Ch. 4, n. 8).

   Denique universa ipsa gens totumque regnum prophetia Christi christianique regni (*Contra Faustum*, Bk. 22 et passim).

10 Hac ergo dilectione tibi tanquam fine proposito quò referas omnia quae dicis, quidquid narras ita narra, ut ille cui loqueris audiendo credat, credendo speret, sperando amet (Augustine, *On the Catechizing of the Uninstructed*, Ch. 4, n. 8).

11 Ubi eras quando ponebam fundamenta terrae?...cum me laudarent simul astra matutina, et jubilarent omnes filii Dei? (Jb 38:4, 7).

12 Interroga jumenta, et docebunt te; et volatilia coeli, et indicabunt tibi. Loquere terrae, et narrabunt pisces maris. Quis ignorat quod omnia haec manus Domini fecerit? (Jb 12:7-9).

13 See their *Hexaemeron*, and their sermons on Genesis.

14 Chrysostom, *Sermon 1 on Genesis*

15 Chrysostom, *Homily 11, to the People of Antioch*

16 Chrysostom, *Homily 7 on Genesis; Sermon 2; Homily 8*

17 Leo the Great, *Sermon 2, De Nativ.*

18 Gn 3:3

19 Cum Adam peccaverit, manifestum est quod Deum per essentiam non videbat. Cognoscebat tamen Deum quadam altiori cognitione quam nos nunc cognoscamus, et sic quodammodo ejus cognitio media erat inter cognitionem praesentis status et cognitionem patriae, qua Deus per essentiam videtur. "Deus fecit hominem rectum" (Eccles 7:30). Haec autem fecit reetitudo hominis divinitus instituti, ut inferiora superioribus subderentur, et superiora ab inferioribus non impedirentur. Unde homo primus non impediebatur per res exteriores a clara et firma contemplatione intelligibilium effectuum quos irradiatione primae veritatis percipiebat sive naturali cognitione, sive gratuita. Unde dicit Augustinus (*De Genesi ad Litteram*, Bk. 11, Ch. 33, n. 43), quod "fortassis Deus primus hominibus antea loquebatur, sicut cum angelis loquitur; ipsa incommutabili veritate illustrans mentes eorum, et si non tanta participatione divinae essentiae quantum capiunt angeli" (*Summa Theologiae*, I, q. 94, a. 1, c.).

   The "Angel of the Schools" then describes at considerable length the prerogatives of man in a state of innocence; what we say here and elsewhere is only an abridgment of his doctrine.

20 Lk 2:14

21 "Where sin abounded, grace did more abound" (Rom 5:20).

22 This is the explanation given by St. Augustine in his *Retractationes*.

23 According to some grave theologians, Christianity reaches still further back. They teach that man was created in a supernatural state only in consideration of the merits of the Word, whose incarnation would have taken place, even on the supposition that man had not sinned. Benedict XIV formally authorizes this

opinion. Here are his words: *Merito Sixtus Papa IV animadvertit in nonnullos theologos qui censura afficiebant opinionem in his versiculis contentam: Peccatores non abhorres sine quibus nunquam fores digna tanto Filio, teste Diago*, (Bk. 1, Annal, Ch. 33), *ubi sensum dicti Pontificis exponit his verbis: Cum duplex sit opinio Catholicorum doctorum circa causas praecisas Incarnationis; altera quod si Adam non peccasset, Dei Filius carnem non sumpsisset; altera quod etiam si humana natura in Adam non fuisset lapsa adhuc divinum Verbum factum fuisset homo, et utraque opinio pietati, fidei, auctoritatibus et rationibus subsistat, atque priori opinioni versus innitantur: dicimus quidquid contra ipsos attentatum fuerit, temerarium, presumptuosum et poena dignum fuisso (De Canonizat. et Beatif. Sanct.*, Bk. 2, Ch. 28, n. 10). Everyone knows that Benedict XIV was one of the most learned popes that ever ascended the chair of St. Peter, and that he himself approved his *Treatise on the Canonization of the Saints*, composed while he was yet archbishop of Bologna.

24 "For there is no other name under heaven given to men, whereby we must be saved" (Acts 4:12). "For there is one God, and one mediator of God and men, the man Christ Jesus" (1 Tm 2:5).

25 Sicut revera homines, nisi ex seminae Adae propagati nascerentur non nascerentur injusti; cum ea propagatione, per ipsum dum concipiuntur, propriam injustitiam contrahunt: ita, nisi in Christo renascerentur, nunquam justificarentur (Council of Trent, Session 5, Can. 3).

26 Omnis Scriptura Christum narrat et charitatem docet...Tota lex gravida erat Christo (Augustine, *Contra Faustum*).

27 The meaning of this expression is easily understood.

28 Cf. Gn 3:15

29 *Quorum quidem sacrificiorum significationem explicite majores* (the more enlightened) *cognoscebant: minores autem* (the less enlightened); this is the meaning attached by St. Thomas himself to the word, (a. 4) *sub velamine illorum sacrificiorum credentes ea divinitus esse disposita, de Christo venturo quodammodo habebant velatam cognitionem (Summa Theologiae*, II-II, q. 2, a. 7, c.).

30 See Augustine, *On the Catechizing of the Uninstructed* and *Contra Faustum*, Bk. 22; *Contra Felicem Manichaeum*; Eusebius, *Demonstratio Evangelica*, Bk. 4.; *Catechism of the Council of Trent*, p. 63; Bossuet, *Sur les caractères des deux alliances*; and the general preface to the Bible of Vence.

31 Mal 4:5. M. Drach, *Première lettre aux Israélites*, p. 41.

32 It has been remarked by Pascal, who expresses himself thus: "The words of the prophets are blended with particular prophecies and with prophecies of the Messias, in order that the prophecies of the Messias should not be without their proof, nor the particular prophecies without their fruit" (*Pensées*, Ch. 15, n. 13).

33 *Dispersi, palabundi, et coeli et soli sui extorres, vagantur per orbem, sine nomine, sine Deo et rege, quibus nec advenarum jure terram patriam saltem vestigio salutare conceditur*, says Tertullian (*Apology*, Ch. 16). Science has proved that the Jewish people, different from all others, are acclimatized everywhere, that is, that they live and multiply in the warmest as well as the coldest climates. The reason is to be found in the mission that is appointed them. See *Geog. medic.*, by Dr. Bondin, Vol. 11, Ch. 4.

34 Mt 22:42

35 Ibid.

36 Mt 26:63

37 Cf. Jn 12:34. "Ce Messie, la Synagogue l'attendait comme une des trois personnes de l'essence divine de Jehova hypostatiquement unie à la nature humaine formée miraculeusement dans le sein pur, immaculé de la Vierge royale, cette Vierge signalée six cents ans d'avance par le prophete Isaïe." Such are the words of Chevalier Drach, a converted rabbi, and the librarian of the Propaganda, in his learned work, printed at Rome in 1840, by order of Pope Gregory XVI, *Du Divorce dans la Synagogue*, p. 15. See also, *Preuves de la divinité du Messie*, drawn from ancient traditions, p. 385ff, by the same author.

38 *Summa Theologiae*, II-II, q. 2, a. 7, c.

39 Cf. Acts 10:43

40 Cf. Augustine, *On the Catechizing of the Uninstructed*, Ch. 27

41 *Tota lex gravida erat Christo.* St. Jerome uses the same language. Here are his remarkable words: "The whole economy of the visible and the invisible world, before and after the creation, refers to the coming of Jesus Christ on earth. The cross of Jesus Christ is the center in which all things meet, the summary of the history of the world" (*Commentary on the Epistles of St. Paul*).

42 Heb 1:2

43 Let us add that all this was done without the intention of the founder, *praeter intentionem fundatoris*. Satan was, in one sense, the founder of those great empires, which formed his city, or the city of evil. It was on this account that God showed them to Daniel under the figures of unclean and cruel beasts. Being the work of the beast, they performed the works of the beast. To exalt Rome was, during all antiquity, the great thought of Satan and the constant aim of his policy. God allowed him to succeed. When Rome had reached the zenith of its power and Satan imagined his empire indestructible, St. Peter came to overthrow it. We hereby see, in all its splendor, the miracle of the establishment of Christianity. (See our *Traité du Saint Esprit*, t. 1, Ch. 26.)

44 Quapropter in Veteri Testamento est occultatio Novi, in Novo Testamento est manifestatio Veteris (Augustine, *On the Catechizing of the Uninstructed*, Ch. 4, n. 8).

45 Illa nobis expectanda sunt, in quibus perfectio, in quibus veritas est. Hic umbra, hic imago, illic veritas. Umbra in lege, imago in Evangelio, veritas in coelestibus (Ambrose, *On the Duties of the Clergy*, Bk. 1, Ch. 48).—Status novae legis medius est inter statum veteris legis...et inter statum gloriae (*Summa Theologiae*, III, q. 61, a. 4, rep. 1; *Sentences*, IV, d. 1, q. 1, a. 1, qa. 5, rep. 1)—Lex vetus est via ad legem novam, sicut lex nova ad coelestem Ecclesiam, seu ad coelestem hierarchiam (Aquinas, passim).

46 Et ea quae ad mysteria Christi pertinent, tanto distinctius cognoverunt, quanto Christo propinquiores fuerunt (*Summa Theologiae*, II-II, q. 2, a. 7, c.).

47 Mt 5:17

48 Cf. Eph 2:20

49 Ps 87:6

50 Cf. Dn 9:26

51 Jn 1:29

52 Cf. Gn 3:15

53 Cf. Gal 5:2

54 "The whole science of religion," says St. Augustine, "the whole Christian faith, consists properly in a knowledge of the two Adams—what we have inherited from the first, what we have received gratuitously from the second. Nature fallen in Adam, nature repaired in Jesus Christ: behold the sum of religion!" (*On Original Sin*).

55 Cf. Rom 5; 1 Cor 15; Eph 4. See also the Council of Trent, cited above.

56 Omnes erant unus Adam (Cf. Augustine, *Against Two Letters of the Pelagians*, Bk. 4, Ch. 4, n. 7; *On Marriage and Concupiscence*, Bk. 2, Ch. 5, n. 15).

57 Cf. 2 Pt 1:4; 1 Cor 15:49; Heb 2:14; Heb 3:14

58 Sicut fuit vetus Adam effusus per totum hominem et totum occupavit; ita modo totum obtineat Christus qui totum creavit, totum redimit, totum et glorificabit (Bernard, *Sermon 4, De Advent.*, n. 2-3).

59 Per virtutem perficitur homo ad actus quibus in beatitudinem ordinatur. Est autem duplex hominis beatitudo, sive felicitas. Una quidem proportionata humanae naturae, ad quam scilicet homo pervenire potest per principia suae naturae. Alia autem est beatitudo naturam hominis excedens, ad quam homo sola divina virtute pervenire potest, secundam quamdam Divinitatis participationem secundum quod dicitur (2 Pt 1) quod per Christum facti sumus consortes divinae nature.

Et quia hujusmodi beatitudo proportionem humanae naturae excedit, principia naturalia hominis, ex quibus procedit ad bene agendum, secundum suam proportionem, non sufficiunt ad ordinandum hominem in beatitudinem praedictam; unde oportet quod superaddantur hominis divinitus aliqua principia, per quae ita ordinetur ad beatitudinem supernaturalem, sicut per principia naturalia ordinatur ad finem conaturalem; non tamen absque adjutorio divino: et hujusmodi principia virtutes dicuntur theologicae: tum quia habent Deum pro objecto, in quantum per eas recte ordinamur in Deum; tum quia a solo Deo nobis infunduntur; tum quia sola divina revelatione in sacra Scriptura hujusmodi virtutes traduntur...

Unde oportuit quod aliquid homini supernaturaliter adderetur ad ordinandum ipsum ad finem supernaturalem. Et primo quidem quantum ad intellectum adduntur homini quaedam principia supernaturalia, quae divino lumine, capiuntur; et haec sunt, credibilia, do quibus est fides. Secundo vero est voluntas, quae ordinatur in illum finem et quantum ad motum intentionis in ipsum tendentem, sicut in quod est possibile consequi, quod pertinet ad spem; et quantum ad unionem quamdam spiritualem, per quam quodammodo transformatur in illum finem, quod fit per charitatem (*Summa Theologiae*, q. 62, a. 1; a. 3).

60 Domus Dei credendo fundatur, sperando erigitur, diligendo perficitur (Augustine, *Sermon 27*, n. 1.).

61 Among others, Clement VIII, 15th July, 1595; and Benedict XIII, 17th Aug. 1728.

62 *Quidquid narras, ita narra ut ille cui loqueris audiendo credat, credendo speret, sperando amet...divinam coelestemque rempublicam, cui nos cives adsciscit, fides, spes, charitas. Quando omnis terra cantat canticum novum, domus Dei est. Cantando aedificatur, credendo fundatur, sperando erigitur, diligendo perficitur. Modo ergo aedificatur; sed in fine saeculi dedicatur* (Augustine, On the Catechizing of the Uninstructed, Epist., clas. iii., t. 11, p. 622; Sermon 27, t. 5, p. 206, Ch. 1).

Bellarmine founds his plan on our last quotation from St. Augustine; but he slightly modifies the idea of the holy doctor, which we have followed in all its sublime simplicity. Thus, Bellarmine places the sacraments under their own special title; he makes them a separate part, which St. Augustine does not do. The means of obtaining grace we arrange under the heading of hope, where Bellarmine himself places one of the means of obtaining grace, namely, prayer. But let us give the original words of the illustrious prince of the Church:

"De parti principali più necessarie di questa dottrina sono quattro; civè il Credo, il Pater noster, i dieci Commandamenti, ed i sette Sacramenti.

"Perchè sono quattro nè più nè meno?

"Perchè tre sono le virtù principali, fede, speranza, e carità. Il credo è necessario per la fede, perche c'insegna quello che abbiamo da credere. Il Pater noster é necessario per la speranza, perche c'insegna quello che abbiamo da sperare. Li dieci Commandamenti sono necessari, per la carita, perche c'insegnano quello che abbiamo da fare per piacere a Dio. I Sacramenti sono necessari, perche sono gli istrumenti con i quali si ricevono e conservano le virtù, le quali abbiamo detto esser necessarie per salvarsi.

"Santo Agostino *Serm. 20, De Verbis Apostolis* (vetus edit.), ci dà la similitudine della casa: perche, siccome per fare una casa è necessario mettere primo il fondamento, e poi alzare le mura, ed alla fine coprirla con il tetto, e per fare queste cose ci bisognano alcuni istrumenti; cosi per fare nella anima l'edificio della salute, ci bisognano il fondamento della fede, le mura della speranza, il tetto della carità, e gli' istrumenti che sono i santissimi sacramenti (*Dottrina Crist.*, Ch. 1, p. 7, 8, 9).

We see here that the learned cardinal adds to St. Augustine's idea, and that he makes four parts, while St. Augustine counts only three. We also see, however, that this modification does not affect the fundamental division.

63 Cf. Acts 1:3.— Such is also the sentiment of St. Leo: *Non ergo ii dies qui inter resurrectionem Domini ascensionemque fluxerunt, otioso transiere decursu, sed magna in his confirmata sacramenta, magna sunt revelata mysteria* (Sermon 1, De Ascens.).

64 Mk 16:16

65 Lex tua veritas (Ps 118:142). Non minus est verbum Dei quam corpus Christi (Augustine, *in Gen.*).

66 Cf. Gal 2:20

67 *Et autem fides sperandarum substantia rerum, argumentum non apparentium* (Heb 11:1). St. Thomas explains these words thus: *Re sperandae sunt sicut arbor in semine virtute latens, ac per fidem quodammodo jam existunt in nobis.* (See also Cornelius a Lapide, On Hebrews, Ch. 11, v. 1.)

68 Participes enim Christi effecti sumus, si tamen initium substantiae ejus...retineamus (Heb 3:14). Initium substantiae vocat fidem, per quam primo coepimus quasi subsistere in substantia spirituali et divina, factique sumus divinae consortes naturae (Cf. Heb 3:14).

69 Merito apostolus fidem sperandarum rerum substantiam esse definit, quod videlicet non credita nemo sperare plusquam super inane pingere possit. Dicit ergo fides: Parata sunt magna et inexcogitabilia bona a Deo fidelibus suis. Dicit spes: Mihi illa servantur. Nam tertia quidem charitas: Curro, mihi ait, ad illa (Bernard, *Sermon on Psalm 90*).

70 Gratia nihil aliud est quam quaedam inchoatio gloriae in nobis (*Summa Theologiae*, I, q. 4, a. 8, rep. 2).

71 Dicendum quod homo post peccatum ad plura indiget gratia, quam ante peccatum, sed non magis; quia homo etiam ante peccatum indigebat gratia ad vitam aeternam consequendam, quae est principalis necessitas gratiae. Sed homo post peccatum super hoc indiget gratia, etiam ad peccati remissionem, et infirmitatis sustentationem (*Summa Theologiae*, I, q. 95, a. 4, rep. 1). Quia et divina gratia Dei sit et largitio quodammodo ipsius divinitatis (Cassian, *De Incarn. Chr.*, Bk. 2, Ch. 6). Sic igitur per hoc, quod dicitur homo gratiam Dei habere, significatur quidam supernaturale in homine a Deo proveniens (*Summa Theologiae*, I, q. 110, a. 1).

72 Cf. Lk 18:1; 1 Thes 5:17

73 "To pray always," says St. Augustine, "is to seek always to please God." *In ipsa ergo fide, et spe, et caritate continuato desiderio semper oramus. Ac per hoc, et quod ait Apostolus: Sine intermissione orate; quid est aliud quam beatam vitam, quae nulla nisi aeterna est, ab eo qui eam solus dare potest, sine intermissione desiderare? Semper ergo hanc a Domino Deo desideremus, et oremus semper* (Augustine, Epistle 130, n. 16).

74 Ecce enim orat (Acts 9:11).

75 Eucharistia est quasi consummatio spiritualis vitae, et omnium sacramentorum finis. Per sanctificationes enim omnium sacramentorum fit praeparatio ad suspiciendam vel consecrandam Eucharistiam (*Summa Theologiae*, III, q. 73, a. 3, c.).

Sacramentum Eucharistiae est potissimum inter alia sacramenta,…nam in sacramento Eucharistiae continetur ipse Christus substantialiter. In aliis autem sacramentis continetur quaedam virtus instrumentalis participata a Christo…Semper autem quod est per essentiam potius est quam quod est per participationem. Insuper omnia alia sacramenta ordinari videntur ad hoc sacramentum sicut ad finem. Manifestum est enim quod sacramentum ordinis ordinatur ad Eucharistiae consecrationem; sacramentum vero baptismi ordinatur ad Eucharistiae receptionem; in quo etiam perficitur aliquis per confirmationem, ut non vereatur se subtrahere a tali sacramento; per poenitentiam etiam et extremam unctionem praeparatur homo ad digne sumendum corpus Christi; matrimonium etiam saltem sua significatione attingit hoc sacramentum, in quantum significat conjunctionem Christi et Ecclesiae, cujus unitas per sacramentum Ecclesiae signatur. Tandem hoc apparet ex ritu sacramentorum; nam fere omnia sacramenta in Eucharistia consummantur, ut Dionys. dicit, (*Coelest. hierarch*, Ch. 3) est sacramentum sacramentorum, quia sacramentis omnibus consummatam perfectionem confert (*Summa Theologiae*, III, q. 65, a. 3, c.).

76 Communion is to be found among all peoples, with the great idea of expiation attached to the sacrificing and eating of victims. "No doubt is entertained amongst us," says Pelisson, "that all false religions have come from the true, and the sacrifices of paganism, from the sacrifices instituted by the first men, of which Abel and Cain give us an example—sacrifices that were only a figure and a shadow of a great sacrifice, in which God himself should be immolated for us. Throughout the whole earth, the flesh of victims was eaten; in all nations, the sacrifice that ended thus was regarded as a solemn feast between man and God: whence it happens that, among the ancient pagan poets, we find mention so frequently of the feast of Jupiter, the viands of Neptune, etc., referring to the victims that were eaten after being immolated to these false divinities; and, if among the Jews there were holocausts, that is, sacrifices in which the victim was wholly consumed by fire, they were accompanied with oblations of cakes, in order that, even in these sacrifices, there should be something for man to eat" (*Traité de l'Eucharistie*, p. 182).

Whence did the strange idea come to the human race, that man communicated with the divinity by the aid of substances sacrificed to it? What relation could there be between the immolation or the eating of an animal and the remission of sins or the sanctification of souls? Did the vile blood of victims that fell under the sacred knife possess the virtue of purifying the conscience? Never did such a foolish notion prevail in the world. But the whole world had faith in that which was represented by these sacrifices. All that was known was that they figured a divine mystery of justice and grace; and, from the depths of this mystery, which the future should reveal, four thousand years heard ascending the voice of hope (See *Eclaircissements sur les sacrifices*, by De Maistre).

Ainsi, une communion à la grace, à Dieu, à la foi spirituelle et corporelle, invisible dans son essence et visiblement manifestée: tel etait le centre auquel aboutissaient, dans ce que elles avaient do commun, les liturgies de tous les peuples, tel etait le foyer vital du culte universel (Mgr. Gerbet, *Dogma générateur*, etc.).

77 In order to remain here within the limits of Catholic faith, on the necessity of communion, relatively to salvation, it is well to remember the doctrine of St. Thomas. This angel of theology expresses himself thus: Conclusio *Quanquam non quoad realem perceptionem, sicut Baptismus, Eucharistiae sacramentum est necessarium ad salutem. In hoc sacramento duo est considerare: scilicet ipsum sacramentum et rem sacramenti. Dictum est autem quod res hujus sacramenti est unitas corporis mystici sine qua non potest esse salus: nulli enim patet aditus salutis extra Ecclesiam, sicut nec in diluvio absque arca Noe, quae significat Ecclesiam. Dictum est autem quod res alicujus sacramenti haberi potest ante perceptionem sacramenti, ex ipso voto sacramenti percipiendi. Unde ante perceptionem hujus sacramenti potest homo habere salutem ex voto percipiendi hoc sacramentum: sicut et ante Baptismum ex voto Baptismi. Est tamen differentia quantum ad duo: primo quidem quia Baptismus est principium spiritalis vitae et janua sacramentorum; Eucharistia vero est quasi consummatio spiritalis vitae et omnium sacramentorum finis. Per sanctificationes enim omnium sacramentorum fit praeparatio ad suscipiendam vel consecrandam Eucharistiam, et ideo perceptio Baptismi est necessaria ad inchoandam sip-ri talem vitam; perceptio autem Eucharistiae est necessaria ad consummandam ipsam: non ad hoc quod simpliciter habeatur, sed sufficit eam habere in voto sicut et finis habetur in desiderio et intentione. Alia differentia est, quia per Baptismum ordinatur homo ad Eucharistiam, et ideo ex hoc ipso quod pueri baptizantur, ordinantur per Ecclesiam ad Eucharistiam. Et sicut ex fide Ecclesiae credunt, sic ex intentione Ecclesiae desiderant Eucharistiam, et per consequens recipiunt rem ipsius; sed ad Baptismum non ordinantur per aliud praecedens sacramentum, et ideo ante susceptionem Baptismi non habent pueri aliquo modo Baptismum in voto, sed soli adulti. Unde rem sacramenti non possunt percipere sine perceptione sacramenti. Et ideo hoc sacramentum non hoc modo est de necessitate salutis sicut Baptismus* (*Summa Theologiae*, III, q. 73, a. 3, c.).

78 Heb 11:1

79 Already cited. The same saint adds: *Conformitas cum Verbo in charitate maritat animam Verbo* (*Sermon 83, On the Canticle of Canticles*).

80 1 Jn 5:3

81 Perfectus amor docet veritatem, quia in dilectione tota lex pendet et prophetae. Quidquid latet, et quid-quid patet in divinis sermonibus et in tota sacra Scriptura, dilectio ipsa comprehendit; quia scriptum est: Plenitudo legis est dilectio. Nam tota lex, imo tota scriptura, aut praecipit et consulit ea quae faciunt ad tuam et proximi dilectionem, sicut patet in praeceptis affirmativis; aut inhibet et dissuadet illa, quae impe-diunt et dirimunt dilectionem, ut liquet in praeceptis negativis (*Idiot. Contempl.*, Ch. 26, n. 1).

82 Tollite jugum meum super vos...jugum enim meum suave est, et onus meum leve...et invenietis requiem animabus vestris (Mt 11:29-30).

83 Lucerna pedibus meis verbum tuum (Ps 118:105).

84 Jn 10:10

85 Cf. Jn 17

86 Cf. Rom 8:29

87 Mk 7:37

88 Lk 2:51

89 Acts 10:38

90 Mt 11:26

91 Ex 25:40

92 "Entretiens sur la vie cachée de Jésus-Christ dans l'Eucharistie," par le P. Lallemant, p. 6-7.

93 Jn 21

94 Mt 28:18-19

95 Cyprian, *On the Unity of the Church*, n. 6

96 Narratio plena est cum quisque primo catechizatur ab eo quod scriptum est, "In principo creavit Deus coelum et terram," usque ad praesentia tempora Ecclesiae (*On the Catechizing of the Uninstructed*, Ch. 3, n. 5).

97 A Domino factum est istud, et est mirabile in oculis nostris (Ps 117:23).

98 Cf. M. Raoul Rochette, "Tableau des Catacombes," p. 93

99 See our little work entitled "Credo."

100 We outline only this grand picture in the catechism; we complete it in "l'Histoire de la Famille," 2 vols. 8 vo.

101 1 Cor 11:19

102 Mt 18:7

103 Acts 14:21

104 Cf. Jb 7:1

105 Lk 22:19

106 Heb 5:1

107 Mt 5:14; 28:19

108 Mt 5:13, 16

109 Mt 10:8

110 Mt 28:20

111 See Bergier "Dict. Theol.," art. *Eglise*.

112 Ws 11:21

113 Cf. 2 Cor 5:15

114 Cf. Gn 22:18

115 Mt 5:18

116 Mk 13:31

117 These remarks refer to ceremonies in use in many churches in France.

118 "Tableau Poétique des Fetes Chrétiennes," par Viscomte Walsh.

119 There is no omission here. Formerly Advent occupied six weeks, beginning on St. Martin's day, immedi-ately after the octave of All Saints. The Church of Milan, adhering to its ancient practice, still observes

the six weeks of the primitive Advent. The same course is followed in the East, among the united Greeks ("Annal. de la Prop. de la Foi," n. 47, p. 537).

120 The harmony here alluded to is more apparent in our hemisphere; and in this hemisphere it is that Rome, the mother, the mistress, and model of all the Churches, is found. This is as it should be.

121 Cf. Augustine, *On the Catechizing of the Uninstructed*, Ch. 4, n. 8

122 Cf. 1 Tm 3:16

123 Cf. Jn 3:14

124 Cf. Mt 22:37

125 Augustine, *Of the Morals of the Catholic Church*, Ch. 15, n. 25 et passim

126 1 Jn 4:8, 16

127 Gn 1:27

128 Apoc 22:17

129 Mt 6:10

130 Cf. Rom 8:19-22

131 Ps 16:15

132 Cf. Rom 8:18

133 The reader will do us sufficient justice to believe that we do not condemn discussion in the teaching of religion, but we are convinced that the exposition recommended by St Augustine is preferable, and much better suited to the object of this work. Such is also the opinion of Tertullian, St. Cyprian, and St. Frances de Sales. See the "Spirit" of the last-mentioned, § xvi., Pt. 3, Ch. 1, p. 169.

134 Ps 18:2

135 Ex 8:19

136 Noverimus quia non sine magno discrimine de Religionis veritate disputamus, quam tantorum sanguine confirmatam videmus. Magni periculi res si post prophetarum oracula, post apostolorum testimonia, post martyrum vulnera, veterem fidem quasi novellam discutere praesumas (*Sermon, Des SS. Martyrs*).

137 Lk 19:14

138 Qui propter nos homines et propter nostram salutem, etc.

139 1 Jn 4:8, 16

140 Editor's note: For the sake of brevity, these summary questions have been omitted in this edition.

141 This assemblage of catechisms comprises: 1) le *Petit Catéchisme des mères*, 1 vol. in 22; 2) le *Catéchisme des mères*, 1 vol. in 18; 3) l'*Abrégé de Catéchisme de persévérances*, 30 edition, 1 vol. in 18.

142 Jn 1:9

143 2 Pt 1:19

144 Cyril of Jerusalem, *Catechetical Lecutres*; Cf. Ducange, *Dict.* au mot *Catechisare*.

145 Cf. Gn 28:48

146 Cf. Gn 31:48

147 Cf. Gn 26:18. See Fleury, *Manners of the Israelites*, p. 8.

148 Mt 7:6

149 Cyril of Jerusalem, *Catechetical Lectures*

150 Editor's note: See Volume XII of the Tradivox series.

151 Cf. Augustine, *Sermon 213*

152 Cf. Voyez, sur la Discipline du Secret, *Discussion Amicale*, t. 1, p. 344

153 The Jews do not count David among the prophets, properly so called, because he was a king, lived in the midst of the world, and did not lead a life like that of the prophets; but there is no reason why his books should not be regarded as prophetical. See Bible de Vence, *Préf. sur les Psaumes*.

154 Dt 32:7

155 One well acquainted with the doctrines and the traditions of the synagogue speaks thus to the Jews, his former brethren: "Si vous vous appliquez à étudier les monuments de notre peuple fidèle…vous trouverez que nos ancêtres adoraient Jéhova subsistant en trois personnes unies dans une seule et indivisible

essence; qu'ils espéraient avec une ferme foi que *Jêsus*, c'est-à-dire le *Sauveur*, que le *Verbe* de Jéhova, que le seconde personne de la suprême Trinité viendrait, à l'heure fixée par les décrets du Très-Haut, prendre un corps semblable au nôtre dans les chastes flancs de l'auguste fille de David, désignée d'avance, toujours Vierge avant et après sa glorieuse maternité;…en un mot, que la naissance miraculeuse, la vie, la mort, la résurrection et l'ascension de Notre-Seigneur Jésus Christ au Ciel, où il est assis avec ses deux natures à la droite de son Père, pour être continuellement notre avocat, ne sont que l'accomplissement des prophéties tant écrites que *traditionelles* qui avaient vieilli avec l'antique race de Jacob, leur fidéle gardienne" (Drach, *Harmonie entre l'Eglise et la Synagogue*, t. 2, p. 484).

156 Cf. Jn 2:30; 2 Thes 2:14; 1 Cor 11:2; 2 Tm 1:13. See Bergier, article, *Tradition*.

157 See Bible de Vence, t. 1.; Bergier, art. *Inspiration*.

158 Cf. Augustine, *Epistle 71*; *Epistle 82*. See also Tassoni, Bk. 1, 181.

159 Modern philology has carried to the highest degree of evidence the proof regarding the perfect genuineness of the new testament.

160 Cf. Council of Trent, Session 4

161 2 Tm 3:16-17

162 2 Thes 2:14

163 Gregory Nazianzen

164 Ps 13:1; 52:1

165 Ps 99:3

166 See their testimonies in Jacquelot, *Traité de l'existence de Dieu*, etc.

167 Tertullian, *Apology*, Ch. 17

168 *Sent. de Napolèon sur le Christ*, p. 75 et suiv.

169 Cf. Ex 3:14

170 Mt 5:48

171 3 Kgs 17:1

172 Ps 15:8

173 See Fenelon, *De l'existence de Dieu*; Bergier, art. *Dieu*; Aquinas, q. 1, 11

174 Cf. Mt 10:29-30

175 Ps 18:2

176 Nec ideo credant iniqui Deum non esse omnipotentem quia multa contra ejus faciunt voluntatem; quia et cum faciunt quod non vult, hoc de eis facit quod ipse vult. Nullomodo igitur Omnipotentis vel mutant vel superant voluntatem: sive homo juste damnetur, sive misericorditer liberetur, voluntas Omnipotentis impletur (Augustine, *Sermon 214*).

177 Ws 8:1

178 Ws 12:13

179 Mt 6:26

180 Justitia elevat gentem, miseros autem facit populos peccatum (Prv 14:34).

181 While we write these lines at Nevers, on Saturday, December 19, 1849, a woman is being led to the scaffold for poisoning her husband!

182 See the whole of St. Matthew, Chapters 6 and 7.

183 Bergiér, "Traité de la Vraie Religion," t. 2, 224. Tertullien cité plus haut, p. 35.

184 The thought is St. Chrysostom's.

185 Ps 32:9

186 In order to satisfy the legitimate curiosity of a certain class of our readers we shall add to the work of the six days some notes on geology. The most advanced scholars shall be our guides, and thus the catechism shall be found, so to say, in the most advanced post of science. Geology is a science which has for its object the knowledge of the terrestrial globe. It studies the interior structure of the earth, and the organic remains found therein, together with the laws regulating the formation of these things. Not to deprive geological solutions of the merit which is due to them, it is well to remember that this science is only yet in its infancy, that geologists are not acquainted with a sufficient portion of the globe to form a system absolutely perfect. The deepest mines are only, in regard to our planet, like the punctures of a pin in the skin of an elephant.

We must also remember that geology was, for a long time, the arsenal in which impiety sought for weapons against the faith. Like all other sciences, it was enrolled by philosophers under the standard of incredulity, to make war open the Bible. But it has grown; in growing, it has become enlightened; and today it renders homage to religion. It asks the hand of religion to support it, as a delicate girl asks her mother's arm to support her tottering steps. "Surely it must be gratifying," says Cardinal Wiseman on this subject, "to see a science, formerly classed, and not, perhaps, unjustly, among the most pernicious to faith, once more become her handmaid; to see her now, after so many years of wandering from theory to theory, or rather from vision to vision, return once more to the home where she was born, and to the altar at which she made her first simple offerings; no longer, as she first went forth, a wayward child, but with a matronly dignity, and a priest-like step, and a bosom full of well-earned gifts to pile upon its sacred hearth" (*Lectures on Science and Revealed Religion*, Vol. 1, p. 307).

On the duration of the days of the creation there exist among geologists two opinions. The first maintains that these days were periods of indeterminate length, and considers this explanation necessary in order to account for geological phenomena; the second holds that they were only ordinary revolutions of twenty-four hours, and denies the need of any other explanation.

The first is supported by several reasons, of which we shall now present an abridgment:

1. The word *day* in Hebrew, as in Latin, French, and other languages, is often used to denote a long period of time, an epoch. Even in Genesis, Moses himself employs it thus. For having detailed the successive works of the creation, he makes a kind of recapitulation of them, saying: "These are the generations of creatures, in the day that the Lord God made the heaven and the earth" (Gn 2:4). Now, the word *day*, in this passage, evidently does not mean a space of twenty-four hours, but rather the six days or six epochs of the creation, and corresponds to the word *time* or *period*. It has the same sense in a great many other passages of scripture.

2. Our days of twenty-four hours are regulated by the revolution of the earth in presence of the sun. Now, asks M. Deluc, how could Moses, when speaking of the first day or epoch, have known how to assimilate it to our days of twenty-four hours, since these days are measured by the revolution of the earth on its axis, in presence of the sun, and the sun was not brought forth until the fourth day, or epoch, to shed its light on the earth? Moses, therefore, did not refer to a day of twenty-four hours, but rather to a period of indeterminate length.

3. St. Augustine says that the days of Genesis cannot be assimilated to spaces of time, as easily conceived, as are days like ours, of twenty-four hours (*De Genesi ad Litteram*, Bk. 4, n. 16, 44). And elsewhere he expresses himself thus: *Qui dies cujus modo sint aut perdifficile nobis, aut etiam impossible est cogitare, quanto magis dicerè?* (*City of God*, Bk. 11, Ch. 6). Bossuet asserts in his *Elevations sur les mysteres*, that the six days were six different progressions (111, Serm., VeElévat.). M. Frayssinous, in his *Conferences*, says that it is allowed us to behold in these six days so many indefinite periods. To these authorities might be added the names of many illustrious geologists, as Burnet, Whiston, Deluc, Kirwan, Cuvier, etc.

4. Physical facts announce that between the time of the creation of the first organic beings on the surface of the globe, and that of man, numerous modifications, or, if we choose, several cataclysms took place, and annihilated species primarily created, to which at a later period our present races succeeded. In the vegetable kingdom, the primitive species, to which nothing analogous can now be found, are, among others, the *horse-tail* or *shave-grass*, and *gigantic ferns*; and, in the animal kingdom, *mammoths*, buried, like the vegetables of which we have spoken, in the lowest strata of the earth, where the action of the deluge could never have disarranged anything.

Now, as it is demonstrated that the creation was not the instantaneous product of a blind, impetuous force, but the gradual work of a free, enlightened will, the succession of these ancient generations, of which we no longer find a living trace on the surface of the globe, cannot have occurred in an interval of time so short as six days. On the contrary, it is plain that those revolutions, which witnessed the birth, life, and death of such gigantic creatures, must have extended over a long course of ages; and as to each of them corresponds a class of species totally different from those which had at first been destroyed, as well as from those which should afterward be destroyed, the creation of organic beings must have been gradual and not instantaneous (Marcel de Serres, *Cosmogonie de Moise*, p. 18ff).

Such are the principal reasons with the authorities that support the first opinion. Let us now present those that favor the second:

1. The Hebrew word *day* in scripture often signifies an epoch, but then the context easily determines the sense in which it must be taken. Now, in the first chapter of the Bible, where this term is repeated even six times, there is nothing to indicate that it should receive any other signification than that which is most natural and common to it. "During six days you shall labor," says Moses to the Israelites, "and on the seventh you shall rest;...for in six days the Lord made heaven and earth,...and on the seventh he rested." (Ex 20:9-11). Moses here employs the same term to express the days of creation and ordinary days; would not language persistently equivocal have inevitably cast minds into an error, which Moses could have so

easily prevented? Besides the constant tradition of the Jews is that the Mosaic days were only periods of twenty-four hours (See a learned article by M. Drach in *Annales de philosophie chrétienne*).

2. Geologists, who are partisans of the indefinite periods, pretend that *morning, mane*, means the beginning, the aurora of a period or creation, and *evening, vespere*, a revolution, a catastrophe, a destruction of this same creation; and thus they explain the origin of fossils in the various geological formations. But, at the outset, this is a confusion of languages, and an excessively bold, arbitrary interpretation. Again, on the first day, God makes the light; on the second, he makes the firmament. Moses, to denote the end of these days, avails himself of the word *vespere, evening*: if this word means a "catastrophe," a "ruin," a "destruction," of what destruction was there question at the end of the two supposed periods? Was it the annihilation of the light or the firmament? Will any one dare to maintain one or the other?

Moreover, for what purpose would God destroy at the end of each day the work which he had created at its beginning, and which he had found good? And if he thus destroyed successively, at the end of each period, the productions of each preceding one, he therefore created them anew on the morning of the following periods. Moses acquaints us clearly enough with the special work of each day; but where does he speak of the restoration of a work previously destroyed? Do not all things, on the contrary, in his account, manifestly concur to make us believe that the work of each day continued to subsist entire and perfectly good, such as it came from the hands of an omnipotent and supremely wise Creator?

3. The partisans of the "periodic days," in order to be consistent, are obliged to admit that the most ancient rocks, those of transition, should contain only the remains of vegetables, and not the remains of animals, since the latter were not created till after the fourth day; and yet the lowest transition layers, such as the coal group, contain the remains of marine and land animals, and many kinds of air-breathing insects, mixed together with fossil plants. The system is, therefore, in direct contradiction with geological facts. The very impossibility of reconciling the convulsive action of those revolutions, which should have destroyed every creation, with the arrangement of rocks in regular stratification, proves the evident result of a gentle and gradual deposit.

4. Our modern geologists, struck by the foregoing difficulties, which appear inexplicable to them, place all those convulsions, of which the interior of the globe everywhere offers us undoubted traces, in the period which elapsed between the first and third verses of Genesis, and they say that the opinion of a period of time of indefinite duration, preceding the organization of the Adamic world, is at once founded on the most natural interpretation of the first verse of Genesis, and the irresistible conclusions to which the study of geological phenomena leads us.

Let us mention a few of the authors who uphold this opinion. M. Desdouits requires that the Mosaic account should be excluded from every geological discussion on the origin of our planet, or the history of the stratified formations which compose its crust. "No," says this learned gentleman, "geological facts are not contained in Genesis. The six days of the creation are manifestly natural days, or times of equivalent duration. Now, geological facts, however they may have been brought about, cannot enter into such an exceedingly narrow scheme. Therefore they do not belong to the work of the six days. But they are not posterior to it, since they suppose many convulsions of the earth. Therefore they are anterior to the six days of Genesis. Moses does not mention these facts to us, because they are foreign to the history of man, and to the organization of the earth, such as at length God prepared it for us" (*Universit. Cath.*, t. 111, p. 457).

"It is clear," says M. Jehan, "that the expression, *In the beginning*, means an unlimited space of time between the first act, which brought forth from nothingness the elements of the material world, and the chaos, or last revolution, which is referred to in the second verse, and which was the evening of the first day in the Mosiac narrative. It was during this interval, whose extent may have been immense, that occurred that long successsion of events, which settled the mineral structure of our globe, such as by the investigations of science it is found to be, and which accordingly placed our planet in perfect harmony with the wants of the human species, for whose habitation it was ultimately destined.

"The sacred narrator commences by proclaiming briefly that heaven and earth received their existence at an unassigned period—consequently, that they are not eternal; then, without pausing to satisfy a vain curiosity with the description of a state of things intermediate and altogether foreign to man, to whom the sacred narrator is to teach moral not scientific truths, Moses comes to the particular history of an order of events immediately connected with the origin and the destiny of that creature whom God is about to form to his own likeness" (*Nouveau Traité des Sciences Geol.*, p. 313ff).

Cardinal Wiseman is of the same opinion, and says that the theory of indefinite epochs, "however laudable in its object, is not certainly satisfactory in its results." He adds: "And what objection can there be in supposing that, from the first creation of the rude embryo of this beautiful world to the dressing out thereof, with its comeliness and furniture proportioned to the wants and habits of man, providence may have also chosen to keep a similar ratio and scale, through which life should have progressively advanced to perfection, both in its inward power and in its outward development? If the appearances discovered by geology shall manifest the existence of any such plan, who will venture to say that it agrees not, by strictest analogy, with the ways of God, in the physical and moral law of this world? Or who will assert that it clashes with his sacred word, seeing that in this indefinite period, wherein this work of gradual development is placed, we are left entirely in the dark?" (*Lectures on Science and Revealed Religion*, Vol. 1, p. 309).

Buckland, the Cuvier of England, maintains the same opinion, and his partisans declare that the early fathers of the Church were not opposed to it, since they likewise supposed an indefinite period between the creation and the first regular arrangement (They quote Gregory Nazianzen, *Oration 11*, t. 1; Basil, *Hexaemeron, Homily 11*; Caesarius, *Dialogue 1*; Origen, *De Principiis*, Bk. 4, Ch. 16, etc.). From the preceding remarks it follows:

1. That there are two geological systems in existence, and that they assemble all modern scholars under their respective standards. The first system places the interior revolutions of the globe between the first and third verses of Genesis, so that they should have occurred before the appearance of man on the earth, and before the arrangement of our planet to serve him as a habitation. The partisans of this system make no difficulty in admitting the Mosiac days as periods of twenty-four hours. The second system places the periods between the close of the third verse of Genesis and the sixth day of the creation, such as it is related by Moses. In this system, the Mosaic days are not revolutions of twenty-four hours, but much longer periods of time, even of an indefinite duration.

2. That geologists do not agree on one of the fundamental points of their science.

3. That the most approved theories of the present day are not at all opposed to the Mosaic account.

4. That these theories are rather by the side, than in the sense, of Genesis.

It is, therefore, not for the pleasure of breaking a lance with them that I venture to make a few observations on the scientific value of the two systems. To make geology a more Christian, and, consequently, a more solid and useful science, is the object of the doubts which, with all respect, I am about to suggest.

First doubt: *Is it quite certain that the great diversified irregularities found in the interior arrangement of our globe are the effect of revolutions successively accomplished during a long course of ages?* You admit the fact of creation. Creation is a miracle of the first order. Now, it is said that God separated the waters from the land, previously blended together. How can it be proved that, under the action of this omnipotent Word, the land did not instantaneously become dry and solid; that it did not receive in the twinkling of an eye both its interior and exterior configuration; that the rocks, the granites, the caverns, the mountains, did not assume, on the very moment, the situation and the dimensions required of them by the law of gravity, or by the sudden disintegration of the elements of terrestrial matter? You admit the instantaneous creation of light, such as it is at present; is it more difficult to admit the instantaneous configuration of our planet?

Second doubt: *Is it quite certain that those revolutions took place at the epoch assigned them, that is, before or during the Mosaic creation?* God acts outwardly only to reveal his glory. Every revelation supposes a being capable of understanding it. A rational being is alone capable of acquiring this knowledge. Outside of God, we know of only two classses of intelligent beings: angels and men. There can be no question about man, since, according to both systems, he did not exist. The angels remain. Where is the proof that they existed previously to the revolutions in question? Even supposing their preexistence, where is the proof that the knowledge of the revolutions of our planet was either necessary or useful to make them acquainted with the existence and the perfections of God?

Third doubt: *Is it quite certain that the deluge alone is insufficient to explain the geological revolutions of our globe?* The universality of the deluge, denied by the philosophers of the last century, is today acknowledged by all geologists. They merely contend that this dreadful cataclysm was only felt on the surface of our planet, and that the interior convulsions of the globe are due to other causes. But who has informed man of the precise measure which the avenging element observed, and which has caused such terrible effects? And then, how can any one speak of the interior of the globe, when science hardly knows its surface? Who has said to our *savants*: "This phenomenon is due to the deluge; that phenomenon had nothing to do with it"? Do not such distinctions appear founded less on solid reasoning than on the apprehension of a miracle, or rather on the dread of the extent of the action of a miracle? Having admitted the existence of convulsions in the bowels of the earth, they cannot explain them, either by the historical fact of the deluge, or by the historical fact of the creation. They prefer to have recourse to gigantic revolutions, of which no one can explain the duration, the motive, or the end — whose epoch is unknown, and whose occurrence there is nothing whatever to justify.

Fourth doubt: *If the deluge is insufficient to account for all geological revolutions, would not the curse, with which the earth was struck at the fall of man, afford some explanation of them?* Man, in his fall, drew with him the whole creation, which had been previously subject to his empire. The earth was specially cursed: *maledicta terra.* Who can measure the extent of this malediction? Who can explain its nature or effects? When, during the days of creation, God told the sea to enter its bed, that word of command, to us so gentle, was like a fearful thunderclap, which drove the waters tumultuously into their profound abysses; we may hence infer what terrible effects must have followed the awful word of *anathema!* Who will dare maintain that it only affected the surface, without carrying any perturbation into the depths of our planet? But, once more, why speak of the bowels of the earth, when we know nothing about them? All that we know is that the earth underwent instantaneously material change, and instead of bearing flowers and fruits alone, it bore thorns and briars, while a great number of the animals abandoned their allegiance to man, and became his enemies.

Would it be contrary to good sense to refer to these two historical facts, viz., the deluge and the curse, rather than to revolutions more or less hypothetical, the convulsions of which our globe has preserved so faithful a remembrance? Would it not be to give a rational explanation to phenomena, that have heretofore remained an enigma for science? Here, indeed, is a justification for everything. The geological convulsions, the destruction of the great creations in the vegetable and animal kingdoms, all have their reasonable explanations. As for every outward work of God, its reason is the manifestation of the glory of God, that is, of his perfections, especially his justice, his mercy, and his wisdom.

His justice: in destroying certain species of vegetables and animals, whose gigantic remains astonish the mind. God was pleased to show us the magnificence of the primitive world, and the majesty of man, who, in his state of innocence, was its pacific monarch; consequently, the utter degradation of man's fall, and the incomprehensible enormity of sin, which could produce such awful results.

His mercy: man, in his fall, lost much of his power, and the inferior animals became hostile to him. If the wonderful species of vegetables and animals, of which our globe contains the remains, had continued to exist, how would man, so greatly enfeebled, have been able to live in the midst of them? Would they not have perpetually menaced his existence? How would man have been able to defend himself against the mammoths, for example, and other such powerful giants, which had become his enemies? How would he have been able to live in the midst of such vegetables as certain ferns and shave-grass, which attained the height of seventy-two feet? How walk, breathe, cultivate the soil, seek for his nourishment, in a land covered with productions like to these? In destroying these great creations, the magnificent ornaments of a world which had been intended as the abode of innocence, God, therefore, showed his mercy toward fallen man, watched over his days, and rendered habitable his place of exile.

His wisdom: God, to whom all things are present, beheld that impiety which, in the course of ages, was to plunge into the bowels of the earth, to shake, if it were possible, the very foundations of faith, by denying the truth of the Mosaic account of man's early history. Now, by concealing in the interior of the earth itself, as in an inaccessible treasury, the magnificent remains of a world which no longer exists, he preserved incontestable proofs of the truths that are the basis of religion: the original greatness, and the subsequent fall of man, followed by a universal degradation. How worthy of our admiration is not this wonderful economy! At the very moment when impiety most insolently denies these essential dogmas, Almighty God opens his storehouse, and draws from it arms, which have been held in reserve for six thousand years, that he may confound his enemies.

Such are, with their consequences favorable to religion, the doubts which I have ventured to propose. In order to depreciate their value, persons may say: "Your explanation is not a scientific one." And what are yours? Is it indispensable that an explanation should exclude every intervention of divine science? "Your explanation rests on a direct and sovereign action of the Creator." True, but what conclusion do you draw from this? Is it that facts do not enter as elements into a scientific explanation? In the whole work of the creation, the destruction, and the rearrangement of our planet, is not this the direct action of God, and is it not a fact upon which I rely? Is not the curse of the earth a fact? Is not the degradation of all creatures, on the fall of man, a fact? Is not the universal deluge a fact? For two miracles, which I admit on good proofs, your two geological systems are compelled to admit twenty, without any proofs. Are not those successive creations, during a long lapse of ages, so many miracles? Are not those violent destructions and those terrible convulsions, which figure as essential elements in your theories, so many miracles, and, what is worse, miracles whose very existence or necessity there is not a single solid proof to demonstrate?

187 Cf. Gregory of Nyssa, *Hexaemeron*; Cyril of Alexandria, *Contra Julian*, Bk. 11; Augustine, *De Genesi ad Litteram*, Bk. 1, Ch. 3

188 Cf. Prv 8:30-31

189 According to the Hebrew text, the earth was without shape and aeriform, *informis et aeriformis*: the Samaritan text gives us to understand that it was in a fluid state; and the Septuagint version represents it to us as invisible (or gaseous) and uncompounded, *invisibilis et incomposita*. These words are the last expressions, as it were, of actual science.

"In effect," says M. Marcel de Serres, "the most positive data that astronomy, natural philosophy, and geology afford us, lead us to admit that the earth, like other planetary bodies, was first in a gaseous state, that is, that all the solid substances which compose it at the present day were scattered about in a space much more extended than that which they now occupy.

"This primitive condition of the earth probably approached very near to that under which comets appear to us at present. These luminaries would seem to be only in the first epoch of their formation; accordingly, they cease to be visible when, their vapors condensing, they form a sort of solid nucleus, which, by reason of its extreme littleness, is lost to sight in the immensity of the universe. The comets acquire this solidity by means of the radiation of the heat which maintains them in an aeriform state, and which becomes gradually dispersed throughout the celestial regions.

"In the same manner, the earth lost its primitive condition, and its surface assumed a certain degree of solidity, by the same effect of the radiation which singularly moderated its temperature. Of this mass of vapors that originally composed it there remained nothing but the vast aeriform stratum which now surrounds it, and which protects it against the icy coldness of interplanetary space" (*Cosmog. de Moise*, p. 54-55).

190 Cf. Jer 4:23. See on this matter our *Traité de l'eau bénite*.

191 The primitive submersion of the globe is averred by geologists. In the first period, say the authors of *l'Encyclopédic moderne*, the ocean would appear to have extended over the globe. This is a new act of homage rendered by science to the Mosaic account.

192 Jb 38:8-9

193 Jn 3:5-7

194 See the prayers used in blessing baptismal fonts.

195 Gn 1:3-5. "The scripture does not say that God created or made the light, but only that it should be, and the light was. If, then, the light is not a particular, distinct body, but simply the vibrations or undulations of ether, excited by certain causes, the sacred writer could not describe its appearance in clearer terms, or in a manner more conformable to truth. The scripture would thus have anticipated the most recent discoveries, and these discoveries should find support in an account which a false philosophy had regarded as contrary to what they asserted to be the known laws of physics" (*Cosmog. de Moise*, p. 58).

It follows hence: 1) That, in the conflict between the two hypotheses which still divide natural philosophers with regard to the nature of light, Moses seems to decide the question in favor of the modern school. More deeply acquainted, in some sense, with physics than Newton, the Hebrew legislator had more exact ideas in reference to light than that great scholar, who, by his discoveries, is perhaps the chief among the most illustrious of modern times. And it follows 2) that, according to Moses and a great number of natural philosophers, we can maintain that light and heat may be only one and the same thing, whether they are considered as distinct fluids or bodies, or, on the contrary are likened or compared to undulations or vibrations, produced in substances by some cause. Indeed, the Hebrew expression *or* or *aor*, would mean a fluid issuing by a kind of emanation or flux, from bodies which have the power to diffuse or communicate it.

This interpretation, the simplest, and the most conformable to the text of scripture, appears to us well-founded. At least, it is a matter of ordinary experience that no considerable combustion or development of heat takes place without being accompanied with the production of light. Hence, many philosophers, witnessing the constant repetition of these phenomena, have assimilated the radiating caloric to the luminous fluid. Moreover, experience itself proves to us that there exist a heat and a light quite independent of the sun. Does not a slight blow cause them to spring forth in sparks, even from flints which have been taken out of the most hidden places of the earth, where the solar rays had never penetrated? Do not phosphoric phenomena show us light in all the bodies of nature, as well in living beings as in minerals buried in the depths of the globe, which have never received one beam of the beneficent light of the sun?

It is evident, then, that this latent light does not derive its origin from the sun. It appears when an exciting cause produces the undulations necessary to its manifestation. Now, this cause, before the appearance of the sun, is recognized by modern geology in the elevated temperature of the globe on its issuing from nothingness. Experience, indeed, leads us to conclude that, in the beginning of things, all the materials that at present compose the solid mass of the globe formed only a vast liquid basin, in which the densest and most sedimentary matters everywhere boiled. How could such a conflagration have taken place without producing the bright scintillations of light on the surface of bodies rendered incandescent by so considerable a heat? This light ought, indeed, to be of the most resplendent nature, almost like that which we produce when bringing pieces of lime to a state of ignition in certain gaseous mixtures, and the brilliancy of which can hardly be endured by the eye. Actual science, then, has found a light independent of that of the sun, a thing at which impiety used to scoff. It is, therefore, true, here as everywhere else, that a superficial or half knowledge withdraws us from religion, and a profound knowledge enroots us in it (*Cosmog. de Moise*, p. 109, 114).

196 Cf. Desdouit's *Livre de la Nature*, t. 3, p. 369. We reason here according to the opinion of learned men, who say that light comes to us by radiation, and not by vibration. In the latter theory, the sun would not be the furnace of our light, nor even a luminous body, but simply a star, whose property it would be to set in motion the molecules of light, scattered through the expanse of interplanetary space.

197 It would appear that light is not a particular and distinct fluid, but rather, like sound, the result of the vibrations and undulations of ethereal matter, or of atmospheric air set in motion by the sun, etc. (Marcel de Serres, p. 111).

198 Cf. Rom 1:20

199 Gn 1:6-8

200 Dico firmamentum esse coelum stellatum, omnesque orbes coelestes illi vicinos, tam inferiores quam superiores usque ad empyraeum (Cornelius a Lapide, *On Genesis*, Ch. 1, v. 6).

201 Cf. Desdouits, *Livre de la Nature*, t. 4, 6.

202 Whatever instrument we may use, the stars, and especially the fixed stars, always appear as small as before, and thus demonstrate their astounding distance from us. If an inhabitant of our globe could, by ascending in the air, reach a height of 234,000,000 miles, these masses of fire would still appear to him as only radiant points. However incredible this calculation may appear, it is a fact of which we are every year the witnesses. Toward the 10th December, we are about 234,000,000 miles nearer the stars which adorn the northern portion of the heavens, than we are on the 10th June; and, for all that, we do not perceive any increase of size in the stars (Desdouits, *Livre de la Nature*, Vol. 4, 215).

203 The only reason, said the celebrated Huyghens, which leads us to believe that a rational animal may exist in the planets is that otherwise our earth would have too many advantages, and be too much elevated in dignity above the rest of the planets. What an admirable reason is this only reason! The opinion that the universe was made for man, says Viscount de Bonald, cannot astonish a high philosophy which teaches us that the material universe is only the least of the gifts that God has bestowed on man. When we reflect that the Creator of so many worlds has given himself to us, why should we refuse to believe that he has given us his creatures? Is the work of more value than the workman?

204 Firmamentum complectitur etiam aerem vicinum a coelo in terram expansum et suo loco quasi firmatum (Cornelius, *ubi supra*).

205 We comprehend under the name of *heaven* or *firmament*, not only the ethereal matter and the heavenly bodies scattered through it, but also the atmosphere which, according to Moses, was destined to separate the waters from the waters. As for the rest, there was not at all, in the ideas of the great legislator, any reference here to a hollow sea in the form of a vault over the earth, but to water in its gaseous state, which the air separates from water in its liquid or concrete state, a separation which is most real (*Cosmog.*, p. 64).

206 Gn 1:9-11

207 According to this account, it is evident that the formation of the ocean preceded the appearance of the continents—a fact which is alike confirmed by geological observations (*Cosmog.*, p. 67).

208 Cf. Ps 103:6-7

209 Jb 38:8-11

210 Hence, on the authority of Moses, as on the authority of geological facts, life began on earth with vegetable productions, and in the first place with herbaceous plants. At least, this great writer always places the word *herbam* before *lignum*, although trees attract our attention much more than herbs, properly so called. He therefore admitted, as a matter of fact, the truth, which has only been demonstrated after centuries of observation, that living creatures succeeded one another in an inverse ratio to the complexity of their organization (*Cosmog.*, p. 69, Paris edition, 1838).

211 Some naturalists assert that all the juices of the earth are homogeneous, and that the plant modifies them in the act of assimilation.

212 Mt 6:29-30; Lk 12:27-28

213 Gn 1:11

214 By these words we see that, at this moment, God appointed the sun to continually enlighten the earth. The works of the third and fifth days make us understand why our planet, which by the effect of radiation had lost a great portion of that primitive light which had been formed in the beginning of time, required a new source of light. This source, as necessary to the vegetables which adorned it, as to the animals which it was about to receive, should be no less constant than the wants that demanded it.

  We see that Moses only speaks of these great celestial luminaries in reference to their importance relatively to the earth, and to man, who should soon inhabit the earth, and not in reference to their real importance in the general system of the universe; the proof of which is that he scarcely mentions the stars. He just names them in a few words, in a passing way, and in order to announce that they were scattered through the heavens by the same power that had placed there the sun and moon, luminous bodies much more important and necessary for us than the countless multitude of twinkling worlds, whose immensity perhaps in many cases far surpasses that of our sun (*Cosmog.*, p. 116-117).

215 Gn 1:14-19

216 Analysis of the six days' work, St. Ambrose: Bk. 3, Ch. 6, 27; Bk. 2, Ch. 1, n. 2-4, etc.

217 Gn 15:5

218 Astronomers have divided all the stars that can be seen with the naked eye, into eighty-four constellations or groups, twelve of which form the zodiac, or the course through which the sun appears to pass annually in the heavens.

219 Thus, according to Moses, and also according to the examination of fossil-bearing strata, the creatures that live in the midst of water, whether fishes or aquatic reptiles, preceded the animals and reptiles that live on dry, uncovered, land, as these preceded man, who crowned the work of creation (*Cosmog. de Moise*, p. 442).

220 Gn 1:20-23

221 See note 224, below.

222 See *Hist. Univ. de l'Eglise*, by M. Rohrbacher, Vol. 1, p. 41, 3rd edit.

223 This occurred at Ostend a few years ago.

224 The whale nourishes itself with molluscous, crustaceous, and other very small fishes, which it absorbs in immense quantities; the very narrow opening in its gullet does not allow the creature to swallow animals of any considerable size. It is rather a mistake to attribute the celebrated fact in the history of Jonas to the whale. The Greek and Latin translations of the name of the animal that swallowed the prophet are *Κῆτος* and Cete, which, with the ancients, meant fishes of a very great size, and not whales in particular. Presumption naturally leads one to suppose that it was an animal of the dogfish species, a shark, for example, which can swallow a man or a horse without bruising them. Though this circumstance does not in any way detract from the character of the miracle, it seems reasonable that the creature ought to be a fish with a large throat, and the one which we have mentioned appears to be the fittest to serve as an instrument for the divine power in an occurrence of this kind (Desdouits, *Livre de la Nature*, Vol. 11, p. 113).

225 We speak here of the common whale; another species, the rorqual, or razor-backed whale considerably exceeds the dimensions just given.

226 For a detailed account of whale-fishing, see Pluche, Vol. 1, p. 404.

227 The octopus, being a mollusk, has no skeleton.

228 The croupion.

229 Mt 23:37. The departure of birds at seasons of migration gives occasion sometimes to very affecting scenes. We read in a Paris journal, under date, September, 1845, the following anecdote:
"This morning, at half-past seven o'clock, a crowd collected before the chief gate of the old metropolitan church of Paris, though the great bell, motionless and silent, had given no notice of any public solemnity; but there occurred under the arch of the ancient portico, a scene full of interest to lovers of ornithology, a fact well calculated to throw some light upon the habits of migratory birds.
"Thousands of swallows flew beneath the Gallery of the Kings, perched upon the projections of the columns, then flew off, and then returned again. Doubtless the antique edifice had been selected as the point of departure before emigrating.
"The spectators were not a little surprised at the delay of departure when they perceived that one of the little intended emigrants was hanging by the leg to a ribbon which was fastened to one of the old statues. It was an affecting spectacle to behold these little wayfarers expressing their uneasiness by little shrill notes, and by the flapping of their wings. They all flew round the little captive, and each pecked with its beak the string that held it fast. At last, after two hours of suffering, of effort, and of cruel anguish, a last pluck of the beak cut the ill-omened ribbon. A thousand joyous cries, joined with the shouts of applause from the assembled crowd, reverberated through the arched colonnade; and the poor little swallow, wounded doubtless more or less in the spot, where it had been held fast, encouraged by the greetings of its companions, flew off with them into distant lands, mingling in their joyous songs some such sounds as Phaedrus gave expression to in one of his fables:
"'Quam dulcis sit libertas breviter proloquar.'
"'How sweet is liberty I will briefly tell.'"

230 Cf. Mt 13:31-32

231 See *Bulletin de la Société d'Acclimatation*, 1865; article by Dr. Turrel.
Thanks to conscientious feeling, America appreciates, as well as Europe, the services that are rendered to agriculture by insectivorous birds. Thus, in the state of Virginia, there is a special law forbidding any one to kill vultures, because it has been found that they contribute to purify the air, by consuming, before putrefaction sets in, the dead bodies of buffalo and other wild animals.
Another bird, seen at a distance, might appear engaged in devouring the grains of an ear of corn, because forsooth it works very earnestly with its beak through the awn of the ear. It is not the grain that it seeks, but, on the contrary, the insect that destroys the grain. A superficial observation might induce one to believe that it ruins the harvests, at the very moment when it defends them against their real enemies.

Singing and prattling birds pass for enemies of our cherries and other red fruits, of which they doubtless eat a little. But caterpillars and spiders are their chief nourishment. The robins that frequent our vine-bowers do not seek the grape, but the gnats and little worms. Let the tender red-breasts live then: they do not carry away the fruits of our labor. Nor do they charge us anything for coming morning and evening to enliven our abodes by warbling under our windows among the vine-stalks that adorn our houses.

The greater number of small birds, belonging to the sparrow order, claim by every title the protection of man. Many are exclusively insectivorous; a few eat both grains and insects; nearly all contribute to our amusement by the melody of their song. The injury that they cause us is very trifling indeed, when compared with the services they render us.

One of the most useful of all birds for the destruction of insects is the wren; this little bird, far from shunning the presence of man, delights in his society. The benefits conferred by the wren are so well appreciated in many of the states of North America, that persons in the country usually place near their dwelling a wooden box on the end of a rod, so that the little king and queen may find a home, which they never fail to do, after some time. When the young are batched, the parents are all solicitude in finding insects for the support of their frail progeny.

An attentive observer counted the number of trips made by a pair of wrens lodged in one of these boxes. He found an average of fifty trips an hour. The minimum was forty; the maximum seemed to be about sixty—once only the number reached seventy-one. This pursuit continued, without any time for rest, during the whole day. Thus every pair of wrens, during the time in which they had to nourish their little ones, cleared the orchard and the kitchen-garden of six hundred caterpillars or other insects daily. This calculation only supposes one insect carried away at each journey, during twelve hours of the day; but, in fact, they often carry away two or three at a time, which increases the destruction to twelve or eighteen hundred a day.

In districts where tobacco is cultivated, how many times have we seen the negroes—men, women, and children—engaged under a burning sun in plucking away from the plantations large quantities of tobacco to preserve the precious leaves from the injuries of the caterpillar! Yet, a few wrens would have sufficed for the same service. And do we set no value on their joyous company and their pretty song? If, after these things they venture to peck a few cherries or raspberries, the sensible farmer ought not to regret it. It is little enough that they should have some share in the productions which they know so well how to defend (*Journal of Agriculture*, and *Natural History of Pensylvania*, by M. Baxton).

232 Translator's note: A play on the Latin term, *alaudae*, "larks."

233 Wadding, *Annal, Min., an. Christ*, 226, n. 39

234 Gn 1:24-25

235 Cf. Jb 39:12

236 *Magnus in magnis, non parvus in minimis* (Augustine, *Sermon 213*, n. 2).

237 *Vade ad formicam, o piger*, etc. (Prv 6:6).

238 See Basil, *Hexaemeron, Homily 7*, p. 73. Those among moderns, who have treated of the work of the six days and of natural history, have only copied St. Basil and St. Chrysostom, or have said nothing more interesting or more ingenious. This matter is deserving of notice, just now especially, when so much account is made of modern, and so little of ancient science. In the eyes of literary men, our fathers incontestably had the advantage of eloquence over modern authors; and in the eyes of Christians, the far more precious advantage of faith and piety, which saw and pointed out God in all his works.

239 It is calculated that every year about five percent of the animals perish. Would the earth not become a dreadful pesthouse, if all these carcasses, large and small, were left to corrupt on its surface?

240 Eccles 3:11

241 Linnaeus.

242 Cf. Rom 2

243 Chrysostom, *Homily on Genesis, to the People of Antioch*

244 Gn 1:26-27

245 Gn 2:7

246 Chrysostom, *Homily II, to the People of Antioch*

247 Even, according to the chronology of the Septuagint, the most extended of our sacred chronologies, the creation of man cannot be placed farther back than seven thousand years ago. Like the teachings of Genesis, this date was attacked with blind fury by the philosophers of the last century. The chronicles of the Egyptians, of the Chinese, of the Indians, were summoned, as well as geological facts, to give evidence against the Mosaic narrative. On this, as on every other point, impiety, for a moment triumphant,

has been beaten to the ground. Modern science, becoming more enlightened, has done justice to the pretended antiquity of the peoples mentioned above. In reference to the Egyptians, for example, those monuments, about which so much noise used to be made, have been estimated at their true value. "All the efforts of genius and of science that were made," says the celebrated Cuvier, "to demonstrate the high antiquity of the zodiacs of Denderah and Esneb, became useless, from the moment that, finishing where the beginning should have been made, had not prejudice blinded the first observers, one took the trouble to copy and to restore the Greek inscriptions cut on these monuments...It is now certain that those Egyptian temples, in which zodiacs were sculptured, were erected under the sway of the Romans" (*Disc. sur les révôl.*, etc., p. 269).

"The Chinese chronicle agrees perfectly with that of Moses, if we separate from it those fables which no one would wish to defend. The founder of the Chinese empire, according to Confucius, was Yao, who took the scepter 2337 before Christ" (*Livre de la Nature*, t. 1, p. 24; *Soirées de Montlhéry*, p. 237 et suiv.; Champollion, *Elém. de chronologie*, p. 246).

William John, president of the academy of Calcutta, after having passed twenty-five years on the spot, studying the monuments of India, concludes a long dissertation on the chronicles of the Indians thus: "We may conclude, with full security, that the chronology of Moses and that of the Indians are in perfect harmony" (*Asiatic Researches*, Vol. 2, p. 441).

The recent origin of the arts and sciences comes to the support of the documents of history. We are enabled frequently to assist at their birth; and we hear so much about their novelty, that sometimes we can tax the report with exaggeration. If the arts and sciences had prevailed on the earth from a time more remote than that indicated by Moses, they would have left us some monuments of their cultivation and their age; yet no such monuments exist anywhere. The circle of biblical chronology, which appears too limited for the makers of systems, is sufficiently large for historians. We can not only place within it heroic and historic Greece, but even the great empires of the East, whose coarse and enormous monuments took centuries to complete. We can also place within it the civilization of the Indians and Chinese, as well as the ancient migrations of the Kelts and the Scandinavians, whose epochs have been so judiciously determined by Suhm, the Varron of the Danes (See the proofs of these statements developed in the *Cosmographie de Moïse*, p. 295-319).

In fine, geology itself bears testimony to the veracity of Moses: first, in a negative manner, inasmuch as none of nature's monuments lead us back to a period anterior to the Mosaic dates; and, then, in a positive manner, inasmuch as all physical observations demonstrate the comparative modernness of man and the continents. The chief aids which nature affords us in the computation of time are bogs, the increase of glaciers, the crumbling of mountains, the alluvial deposits, and the like: all present the same result (Marcel de Serres, *Cosmog.*, p. 252 et suiv.; *Soirées de Montlhéry*, p. 159 et suiv.).

All the results of modern science lead us, therefore, to repeat, with Benjamin Constant: "The authors of the eighteenth century, who treated the holy books of the Hebrews with a contempt mixed with fury, judge antiquity in a miserably superficial manner; and, of all nations, it was the Jews, whose genius, character, and religious institutions, they were least acquainted with. To scoff with Voltaire at the expense of Ezechiel or Genesis, it was necessary to unite two qualifications, which added a sufficiently sad tinge to their merriment, namely, a most profound ignorance and a most deplorable levity" (Vol. 4, Ch. 11).

248 Cf. Basil, *Hexaemeron*, sixth day

249 Galen, *De usu part.*, Bk. 3, Ch. 10

250 *Sentiments de Napolèon sur le Christianisms*, p. 77

251 Cf. Mt 25:46

252 The image, says St. Thomas, consists in the knowledge of the truth; the likeness, in the love of virtue: *Imago consideratur in cognitione veritatis; similitudo in amore vertutis* (*Corp.*). The gloss, quoted by St. Thomas (*Summa Theologiae*, I, q. 93, a. 4), distinguishes three kinds of images: *Scilicet creationis, et recreationis, et similitudinis; prima imago invenitur in omnibus hominibus — secunda in justis tantum — tertia vero solum in beatis* (See the whole of question 93 in St. Thomas).

253 There are some who extend this divine resemblance still further. Our body also, they say, has been formed to the image of God; for, at the moment when he formed the body of the first man, God, to whom all things were present, foresaw his divine Son clothed with a human body, and it was on the model of this adorable body of the second Adam, that the body of the first was formed. It is in this sense that the bodies of Adam and all other men have been made to the image and likeness of God. God did not say: "Let us make the soul of man to our image and likeness"; but he said: "Let us make man to our image and likeness." Now, man is not simply a soul, but a soul and a body. That man may be called the image of God, he must, therefore, bear the divine resemblance and characteristics in each part of his being. Such is the reasoning of some philosophers (See *Work of the six days*, and Tertullian, *On the Resurrection of the Flesh*).

The same doctrine is expressed in a pious book, which ought to be in the hands of every Christian family: *Pensées sur les vérités de la Religion*, by M. Humbert. This venerable and learned missionary speaks thus in the third chapter: "...the Creator having, from all eternity, resolved to send his Son on earth, and to give him a body capable of the noblest operations. He formed our body to the image of the adorable body of the man-God, who is, as it were, our eldest brother, our prototype, our original. How great, then, is the dignity of our origin, according to the body! Do we understand the nobility of the body? You ought to treat it with honor and respect: Why should you degrade it by a conduct unworthy of you?"

Whatever there may be in this explanation, the following are the terms in which St. Thomas shows that our body has been made to the image of God: *Quia hominis solum inter terrenorum animalium corpora non pronum in alveum prostratum est; sed tale est ut ad contemplandum coelum sit aptius, magis hoc ad imaginem et similitudinem Dei, quam caetera corpora animalium factum jure videri potest. Quod tamen non sic intelligendum quasi in corpore hominis sit imago Dei, sed quia ipsa figura humani corporis repraesentat imaginem Dei in anima per modum vestigii* (Summa Theologiae, I, q. 93, a. 6, rep. 3).

254 Cf. Chrysostom, *Homily 11 on Genesis*

255 Leontius of Neapolis, *Life of St. John Almoner*

256 Universa propter semetipsum operatus est Dominus (Prv 16:4).

257 Cf. Gregory Nazianzen, *Oration 88*

258 In paradiso omnia erant avicularum genera, quae pulchritudine coelorum, et dulcedine concentus incredibiliter oblectabant hominem; erant illic variorum etiam animalium spectacula. Sed erant omnia mansueta, obedientia homini, inter se concorditer et pacificè viventia...Serpens autem non erat tune horridus sed mitis et mansuetus (Basil, *ap, Cor. a Lap., in Gen.*, 2:8).

259 Cf. Chrysostom, *Homily 15, to the People of Antioch*

260 Cf. Rom 8:22

261 Cf. Rom 8:20; Augustine, *City of God*, Bk. 20, Ch. 16. See the general rèsumè of the catechism at the end of Volume IV [i.e., Volume XIII of the Tradivox series], where this matter is fully explained according to the fathers and theologians.

262 Cf. 2 Pt 3:12-13

263 *Cum igitur gratia non tollat naturam, sed perficiat, oportet, etc.* (Summa Theologiae, I, q. 1, a. 8, rep. 2). Such would also appear to be the profound meaning of the seventeenth chapter of Ecclesiasticus.

264 See the passages from Benedict XIV in endnote 23, above.

265 *In statu innocentiae homo fuisset incorruptibilis et immortalis* (Summa Theologiae, I, q. 97, a. 1, c.). This immortality was a grace. Hence the condemnation of the proposition of Baius: *Immortalitas primi hominis non erat gratiae beneficium, sed naturalis conditio.*

266 Such is the doctrine of St. Thomas (*Summa Theologiae*, I, q. 95, a. 1, c.); of St. Augustine, *De Corrept et Gratia, Epistle 41, ad Irenaeum*, etc., etc. *Homo et angelus*, says St. Thomas, *aequaliter ordinantur ad Gratiam. Sed angelus creatus est in gratia. Dicit enim Augustinus* (City of God, Bk. 12, Ch. 9, n. 2) *quod, "Deus simili erat in eis condens naturam et largiens gratiam." Ergo et homo creatus fuit in gratia.* (Summa Theologiae, I, q. 95, a. 1, s.c.)—*Alii vero dicunt quod primus homo non fuit creatus in gratia; sed tamen postmodum gratia fuit ei collata antequam peccasset. Haec sententia non reprobatur ut erronea. Nam Concilium Tridentinum dicendo,* (Session 5, Can. 1), *"in qua constitutus fuerat," non vero in quo creatus, ita decretum attemperavit ut in fide catholica tradenda, nullis scholarum sententiis aut favere aut distrahere videatur, ut observat Pallav.* (Hist. Conc. Trid.)—*Quidquid sit, fide certum est primos parentes in statu justitiae et sanctitatis constitutos a Deo fuisse, quod constat ex Scriptura, SS. Patribus, et decreto Conc. Trid.*

267 Eccles 7:30

268 Cf. *Summa Theologiae*, I, q. 95

269 Gn 2:23-24

270 Gn 1:28. The unity of the human race is a fact for which modern sciences have avenged the attacks of encyclopedian ignorance and impiety. 1) The traditions of the different peoples are unanimous on this point (See *Cosmog, de Moïse; Soirées de Montlhéry*, etc., etc.). 2) Calculations of great simplicity have demonstrated that a single couple has sufficed for the propagation of the human race (*Soirées de Montlhéry*, p. 204). 3) The varieties of color and conformation are only accidental, and are very well explained by the difference of climates and habits (*Cosmog.*, p. 332 et suiv.). 4) Independently of the Mosaic account, science at present believes that it has a right to conclude from its researches that men were not simultaneously placed on the earth at different points, but that they radiated from one man over the globe, the vast extent of which should, at a later period, be peopled by their descendants; and, also, that Asia was the primitive country,

the cradle of the human race. This division of land, one of the chief of the old world, presents both the highest plains and peaks on the surface of the earth (*Cosmog.*, p. 33, et suiv. *Livre de la Nature*, t. 3, 105).

271 See *Du Divorce dans la Synagogue*, by M. Drach.

272 Gn 1:28-30

273 Cf. Ps 103

274 Ps 103:27-28

275 Cf. Augustine, *City of God*, Bk. 2, 438, 474

276 Quia ergo contemptus est Deus jubens, qui creaverat, qui ad suam imaginem fecerat, qui caeteris animalibus praeposuerat, qui in pandiso constituerat, qui rerum omnium copiam salutisque praestiterat, qui praeceptis nec pluribus, nec grandibus, nec difficilibus oneraverat, sed uno brevissimo atque levissimo ad obedientiae salubritatem adminiculaverat, quo eam creaturam, cui libera servitus expediret, se esse Dominum commonebat; justa damnatio subsecuta est (Augustine, *City of God*, Bk. 14, Ch. 15, n. 1).

277 *In resurrection...erunt sicut angeli Dei* (Mt 22:30). *Ineamus amicitiam cum angelis* (Leo the Great).
     Differently from our usual mode, we give the texts of the councils and the fathers here entire; the reason is easily understood.

278 *Summa Theologiae*, I, q. 50, a. 1

279 Angelos pene omnes sacri eloqii paginae testantur (Gregory the Great, *Homily 24 on the Gospels*).

280 Non acquirit intelligibilem veritatem ex varietate rerum compositarum; non intelliget veritatem intelligibilium discursive, sed simplici intuitu (*Summa Theologiae*, II-II, q. 180, a. 6, rep. 2).

281 Igitur per se non potest esse falsitas, aut error, aut deceptio in intellectu alicujus angeli (*Summa Theologiae*, I, q. 58, a. 5, c.).

282 Cf. *Summa Theologiae*, I, q. 106, a. 4

283 Cf. *Summa Theologiae*, I, q. 106, a. 4, rep. 3

284 Praescius rerum et cordium cognitor est solus Deus: nec enim vel angeli cordis abscondita aut futura videre possunt (Ath., q. 23, *Ad Antiochenos*).
     Daemones possunt miracula simulare et apparenter facere; praescientiam autem futurorum at praedictionem evidentem nullus habet, neque angelus, et quanto minus daemones (Theophylactus, *On John*, Ch. 1).

285 Non debemus opinari daemones occulta cordis rimari, sed ex corporis habitu et gestibus aestimare quid versemus interius (Jerome, *On Matthew*, Ch. 13).

286 Et sic angelus in uno instanti potest esse in uno loco, et in alio instanti in alio loco, nullo tempore intermedio existente (*Summa Theologiae*, I, q. 53, a. 3, rep. 3; q. 62, a. 6, c.).

287 Cf. *Summa Theologiae*, I, q. 110, a. 3

288 Cf. Viguier, *Inst., Theol.*, p. 81

289 Revelationes divinorum perveniunt ad homines mediantibus angelis (Dionysius, *Coelest. Hierarch.*, Ch. 4).

290 Cf. *Summa Theologiae*, I, q. 106, a. 2, c.; q. 3, a. 3-4, c., etc.

291 Cf. Mt 22:30

292 Illud evidenter divinus sermo declarat, neque post sidera productos angelos, neque ante coelum terramque constitutos. Est enim certa illa et immutabilis sententia, ante coelum et terram nihil omnino conditarum rerum exstitisse, quoniam in principio creavit Deus coelum et terram, ut illud sit creandi principium, ante quod creatis ex rebus omnino nulla fuerat (Epiphanius, *Adversus Haeresus*, n. 65).

293 See the Third Council of Lateran.

294 Ne populo rudi cui lex proponebatur idolatriae daretur occasio, si plures-spirituales substantias super omnes corporeas introduceret sermo divinus (Aquinas, *On Separate Substances*, Ch. 18, n. 11).

295 Cf. Jerome, *Epistle 139*

296 Si quis dicit diabolum non fuisse primo angelum bonum a Deo creatum, anathema sit (Council of Braga, Can. 7).

297 Is 14:13-14

298 Et factum est praelium magnum in coelo: Michael et angeli ejus praeliabantur cum dracone; et draco pugnabat, et angeli ejus (Apoc 12:7).

299 *Simul fuit peccatum angeli persuasio et consensus; sicut est accensio candelae, illuminatio aeris et visio, quae omnis sunt instantanea* (Cf. Aquinas, *Sentences*, II, d. 6, a. 2; 2 Pt 2:4). On the trial of the angels, and everything that concerns the angelic world, see proofs and details in our *Traité du Saint-Esprit*, t. 1, Ch. 1-14.

300 Cf. 2 Pt 2. Solus homo inter creaturas intellectuales potuit poenitentiam agendo venia dignus effici posse (Gregory of Nyssa, Bk. 1, *Phil.*, Ch. 5). Quod hominibus mors est, angelus est casus (John Damascene, Bk. 2, Ch. 4).

301 Mt 25:41

302 Aliqui dixerunt ad diem judicii differri poenam sensibilem tam daemonum quam animarum, et similiter beatitudinem sanctorum, quod est erroneum (*Summa Theologiae*, I, q. 64, a. 4, rep. 3).

303 Ideirco enim insectus est puerum masculum quem peperit mulier, puta Christum, ob eumque in coelo cum Michaele dimicavit, volens eum morti tradere, quia invidit ei hanc unionem. Omne enim ejus bellum est contra puerum hunc, adeoque duellum quod cum eo inchoavit in coelo, illud ipsum continuat jugiter in terra (Cornelius a Lapide, *On Apocalypse*, Ch. 12, v. 14).

304 Draco ille magnus, serpens antiquus, qui vocatur diabolus et Satanas, qui seducit universum orbem (Apoc 12:9).

305 Adversarius vester diabolus, tamquam leo rugiens circuit, quaerens quem devoret (1 Pt 5:8).

306 Chrysostom, *Homily, De Lazar.*

307 Cf. Gn 3:15

308 Ps 95:5

309 Eusebius, *Praeparatio Evanglica*, Bk. 7, Ch. 16

310 Quamvis enim internae felicitatis beatitudinem perditet, naturae tamen suae magnitudinem non amisit, cujus adhuc viribus omnia humana superat (Gregory the Great, *Moralia in Job*, Bk. 34, Ch. 17).

311 Dionysius dicit (*On the Divine Names*, Ch. 4) quod, "data sunt daemonibus aliqua dona, quae nequaquam mutata esse dicimus; sed sunt integra et splendidissima." Propter simplicitatem autem suae substantiae a natura ejus aliquid subtrahi non potest; ut sic per subtractionem naturalium puniatur, sicut homo punitur per subtractionem manus aut pedis, aut alicujus hujusmodi. Et ideo dicit Dionysius (ut supra) quod dona naturalia in eis integra manent (*Summa Theologiae*, I, q. 64, a. 1, c.).

312 Daemones in his quae naturaliter ad rem pertinent, non decipiuntur; sed decipi possunt quantum ad ea quae supernaturalia sunt (*Summa Theologiae*, I, q. 58, a. 5, c.).

313 Cf. *Summa Theologiae*, I, q. 57, a. 3, c.

314 Sciet diaboli nequitiam pertinacem usque ad aquam salutarem valere, in baptismo vero omnes nequitiae suae vires amittere (Cyprian, *Epistle 4*).

315 *Magnetismus animalis, somnambulismus ac spiritismus in suo complexu nil aliud sunt quam paganae superstitionis atque imperii daemonis instauratio* (Perrone, *De Virt., Relig.*, 351, n. 825, Romae, 1866. — See also the late *Decrees of the Index*). We consider it a duty to insist on these points of doctrine, as well on account of the spread of spiritism, as to warn the faithful against the inaccuracies into which, assuredly, without intending it, the esteemed M. Guillois has fallen, in the catechism which bears his name. See the refutation in *Moeurs et pratiques des démons*, by M. G. des Mousseaux, préf., xviii. et suiv. edit de 1865.

316 Rudentibus inferni detractos in tartarum tradidit cruciandos, in judicium reservari (2 Pt 2:4).

317 Vigilate quia adversarius vester diabolus tamquam leo rugiens circuit, quaerens quem devoret (1 Pt 5:8).

318 Secundum principem potestatis aeris hujus (Eph 2:2). Induite vos armaturam Dei, ut possitis stare adversus insidias diaboli, quoniam non est nobis colluctatio adversus carnem et sanguinem; sed adversus principes et potestates, adversus mundi rectores tenebrarum harum, contra spiritualia nequitiae, in coelestibus (Eph 6:11-12).

319 Haec omnium doctorum opinio est, quod aer iste qui coelum et terram medius dividit et inane appellatur, plenus est contrariis fortitudinibus (Jerome, *On Ephesians*, Ch. 6).

320 *Apud* Eusebius, *Praeparatio Evangelica*, Bk. 4, 123

321 *Summa Theologiae*, I, q. 64, a. 4, c.

322 Bonorum longe major numerus, in coelestibus suae naturae ordinem juvans. (Augustine, *City of God*, Bk. 11, Ch. 23, n. 1).

323 Non quod tanta solum esset multitudo, sed quia majorem dicere non poterat (Cyril of Jerusalem, *Catechetical Lecture 15*).

324 Hierarchia est sacer principatus (*Summa Theologiae*, I, q. 108, a. 1, c.).

325 *Summa Theologiae*, I, q. 108, a. 1, c.

326 Dionysius, *On the Divine Names*, Ch. 5

327 Ordo Angelorum dicitur multitudo coelestium Spirituum qui inter se aliquo munere gratiae similantur, sicut et naturalium datorum participatione conveniunt (Peter Lombard, sent. *distinct. 9, sent, i*).

328 *Summa Theologiae*, I, q. 108, a. 2, c.

329 Ordo Thronorum habet excellentiam prae inferioribus ordinibus, in hoc quod immediate in Deo rationes divinorum operum cognoscere possunt. Sed Cherubim habent excellentiam scientiae; Seraphim vero excellentiam ardoris (*Summa Theologiae*, I, q. 108, a. 5, rep. 6).

330 Cf. Mt 18; Apoc 7

331 Is 6:3

332 Apoc 4:8

333 Omnibus rebus angeli praesident, tam terrae et aquae, quam aeri et igni id est praecipuis elementis, et hoc ordine perveniunt ad omnia animalia, ad omne german, ad ipsa quoque astra coeli (Origen, *Homily 8 on Jeremiah*). Virtutes coelestes hujus mundi ministeria ita suscepisse, ut illae terrae, vel arborum germinationibus, illae fluminibus ac fontibus, aliae ventis, aliae marinis, aliae terrenis animalbus praesint (Origen, *Homily 22 on Josue*). Divinas ille virtutes, quae summi Patris numine orbi universo praesident, honorum divisioni accommodat (Eusebius, *Praeparatio Evanglica*, Bk. 7). Pronaque ad obsequium pars altera sustinet orbem auxilioque suo servat (Gregory Nazianzen, *Carmen vii*). Nonnulli eos angelos esse arbitrantur qui quatuor elementis praesident, videlicet, terrae aquae, igni, aeri (Jerome, *On Galatians*, Bk. 21). Unaquaeque res visibilis in hoc mundo habet angelicam potestatem sibi praepositam, sicut aliquot locis Scriptura divina testatur (Augustine, *De Diversis Quaestionibus Octoginta Tribus*, q. 79).

334 *De Mundo*, Bk. 1, p. 148

335 *De Mundo*, Bk. 1, p. 148

336 Cf. Gn 18, 19, 22, 28, 31, 32; Ex 3:19

337 Cf. Nm 20

338 Cf. Nm 20

339 Cf. Jgs 6:12-14

340 Cf. Jgs 13

341 Cf. Dn 3

342 Cf. Dn 6

343 Cf. 1 Mc 7

344 Cf. Is 63

345 Cf. Lk 1:11-25

346 Cf. Lk 1:26-38

347 Cf. Lk 2:8-15

348 Cf. Mt 2:13

349 Cf. Mt 2:19-20

350 Cf. Lk 4

351 Cf. Mt 26

352 Cf. Jn 1:51

353 Cf. Acts 5:19

354 Cf. Acts 8:26

355 Cf. Acts 10

356 Misit Deus angelos suos ad tutelam cultumque generis humanis (Lactantius, *The Divine Institutes*, Bk. 2, Ch. 14).

357 Angelis tanquam providis tutoribus humani generis curam demandavit Deus, ad custodiam salutemque humanam (Basil, *On Isaiah*, Ch. 8). Ad tutelam nostram constituit exercitus angelorum (Chrysostom). Salus in ministerio angelorum qui ad protectionem hominum deputantur (Ambrose, *On Psalm 43*).

358 Angeli omnes, ut appellationem unam, ita etiam eamdem omnnio inter se habent naturam; sed ex iis quidam praefecti sunt gentibus, alii vero unicuique fidelium adjuncti sunt comites (Basil, *Contra Eunom.*,

Bk. 3). Regna et gentes sub angelis posita sunt (Epiphanius, *Adversus Haeresus*, Bk. 51, n. 1). Angeli singulis prae sunt gentibus (Jerome, *On Isaiah*, Bk. 11, Ch. 15).

359 Quin etiam cuique genti proprium angelum praeesse affirmat Scriptura (Theodoret, *On Genesis*, q. 3).

360 Cf. Origen, *Homily 12 On Ezechiel; On Luke*, Ch. 25

361 Vult Deus angelos singulos ecclesiarum singularum sibi commissarum custodes esse (Eusebius, *On Psalm 47*).

362 Angelus hujus urbis cura commissa est. Nec enim mihi dubium est quin alii aliarum ecclesiarum praesides et patroni sint, quemadmodum in Apocalypsi Joannes me docet (Gregory Nazianzen, *Oration 32*).

363 Non solum ad eumdem gregem Dominus episcopos ordinavit, sed etiam angelos ordinavit (Ambrose, *On Luke*, Bk. 2; *On Repentance*, Bk. 1, Ch. 20).

364 Divinis potestatibus quae Ecclesiam Dei ejusque religiosum institutum custodiunt (Eusebius, *On Psalm 47*).

365 Ac ne leve praesidium in angelis, qui Ecclesiam quadem custodia circumsepiunt, esse putaremus (Hilary, *On Psalm 24*).

366 Existimo autem eam turrim multitudine clypeorum significare angelicum praesidium, quo circumsepti sumus.

367 *Assertio Catholica est: quamvis enim non sit expressa in Scripturis, vel ab Ecclesia definita, tanto consensu Ecclesiae universalis recepta est, et in Scriptura prout a Patribus intellecta est, tam magnum habet fundamentum, ut sine ingenti temeritate ac fere errore negari non possit* (Suarez, *De Angelis*).

These are the words of Suarez, who remarks, moreover, that Calvin was the first that dared to call this truth in question and then to reject it. The catechist will, therefore, say simply and absolutely: "We have each a guardian angel."

368 Angeli tenent curam animarum nostrarum, et eis ab infantia tanquam tutoribus et curatoribus committuntur (Origen, *Homily 8 On Genesis*).

369 Angelum unicuique ad custodiam divinitus datum ex Scriptura didicimus (Eusebius, *Praeparatio Evanglica*, Bk. 13, Ch. 7).

370 Magna dignitas animarum ut unaquaeque ab ortu nativitatis habeat in custodiam sui angelum delegatum (Jerome, *On Matthew*, Ch. 18).

371 Unaquaeque anima, dum in corpus mittitur, angelo committur (Anselm, *In Elucid.*).

372 Cf. Ps 90:12; 33:8

373 Cf. Augustine, *Soliloquies*, Ch. 17

374 Tutores piis addit suos angelos uc nec contrarii angeli. nec eorum princeps qui et hujus saeculi princeps dicitur, quidquam valeat contra Deo dicatos homines (Origen, *Contra Celsum*).

375 Neque enim infirmitas nostra nisi datis ad custodiam angelis tot tantisque spiritualium coelestium nequitiis resisteret (Hilary, *On Psalm 134*).

376 Deo omnipotente auxiliante, quod contra nos irascantur montes, id est principatus et potestates rectores tenebrarum harum nihil est; scriptum est enim: Castrametabuntur angeli circa timentes eum, et eruet eos (Cyril, *On Isaiah*, Bk. 1, Oration 4).

377 Angelicae virtutes nobis ad optima quaeque adjumento sunt (Gregory Nazianzen, *Oration 40*).

378 Tb 12:12

379 Cf. Apoc 8

380 Angelus christiani perpetuo faciem coelestis Patris aspiciens semper preces ejus in coelum offert per unicum Pontificem summo Deo, ipse quoque pro sibi commisso deprecans (Origen, *Contra Celsum*, Bk. 8).

381 Fidelium orationibus praeesse angelos absoluta auctoritas est (Hilary, *On Matthew*, Ch. 18).

382 Annuntiant angeli non solum beneficia Dei, sed etiam ipsi preces nostras (Augustine, *Epistle 120, De Gratia Novi Testamenti*). Gemitus nostrus atque suspiria referentes ad te, non quidem quod Deus illa ignoret, sed ut impetrent nobis facilem tuae benignitatis propitiationem, et referant ad nos tuae gratiae benedictionem (Augustine, *Soliloquies*, Ch. 7).

383 Assidet angelus cuilibet in Domino credenti, nisi operibus pravis abigatur (Basil, *On Psalm 33*).

384 Vitae nostras custodes angeli diligentius adsunt iis qui jejunio purgatam habent animam (Basil, *Homily 2, De Jejunio*).

385 And the catechist will say the same thing: *Cum custodia angelorum sit quaedam exsecutio divinae providentiae quae nunquam hominem ex toto derelinquit, nec angelus custos nunquam ex toto hominem deserit, licet permittat*

quandoque secundum ordinationem divinorum judiciorum, vel poene vel culpae defectum pati (Summa Theologiae, I, q. 108, a. 6).

386 See Volume IV [i.e., Volume XIII of the Tradivox series].

387 Cum magna reverentia disponis nos (Ws 12:18).

388 O homo, tantam nomen, si intelligas te (Tertullian, *Apology*, Ch. 48).

389 According to the Hebrew, *septénisa*; so that the words *to rest oneself* and *septéniser* have the same meaning: a permanent proof of the primal origin of the week, the memory of which is preserved amongst all nations.

390 Jn 5:17

391 On the work of the six days, see St. Thomas, *Summa Theologiae*, I, q. 65, and the following: Sturm, *Reflections on the Works of God*; Pluche, *Spectacle of Nature*; Duguet, *Work of the Six Days*; Charles Bonnet, *Contemplation of Nature*; St. Chrysostom, *Homilies in Genesis*; St. Augustine, *Genesis in its Literal Sense*; St. Gregory Nazianzen, *Discourses*, 38 and 40; St. Gregory of Nyssa, *Mechanism of Man*; St. Ambrose, *Hexaemeron*; St. Basil, *Hexaemeron*. This last work especially, of which St. Gergory Nazianzen used to say: "When I read it, I am transported to the throne of the Creator, and understand the economy of his works; I learn to admire the sublime author of all things, more than I had done by contemplating him." On the angels, in particular, see the learned *Pastoral Instruction* of Monsignore de la Bastie, Bishop of St. Malo; and the Bible de Vence, t. 7, 260, and Bk. 12, p. 1. Our endeavors only present a rapid analysis of these works and many others.

392 Cum homo in primo statu secundum intellectum sic a Deo fuerit institutus, quod nullum malum in ipso inerat, et omnia inferiora superioribus subdebantur, millo modo decipi potuit, nec quoad ea quae scivit, nec quoad ea quae nescivit (*Summa Theologiae*, I, q. 94, a. 4).

393 Adam non est seductus; mulier autem seducta in praevaricatione fuit (1 Tm 2:14).

394 Cf. Chrysostom, *Homily 17 on Genesis*

395 Gn 2:17

396 Marvelous as it is, the history of the tempting serpent is unassailable. The object of the following note is neither to explain nor to justify the words of Moses, but rather to show the utter impotence of human reason to convict of falsehood the account recorded in Genesis. To do so it would be necessary to show that a spiritual being, the devil, enjoying a power the extent of which is far from limited, could not move the organs of a serpent in such a manner as to draw articulate sounds from them, while another spiritual being, our own soul, inferior in power to the angels, avails itself with marvelous facility of that portion of matter to which it is united, to articulate sounds, and to enter into sensible relations with the persons that surround it. As for the curse of the serpent, expressed in these words: "Thou shalt crawl upon thy belly," to deny its effect it would be necessary to show that, before the commission of sin, all kinds of serpents moved on their breast, or at least that the species that had been cursed used to move as they move today. Now, this can never be shown because there exist, even at the present day, some kinds of serpents that fly; and because it is impossible to know the species the devil made use of, and upon which the malediction fell.

"Thou shalt eat the dust all the days of thy life"; to deny this second part of the curse, it would be necessary to show that before the commission of sin all kinds of serpents used to eat the dust, or that, since its commission, there has been no class of serpents that continually make the dust their nourishment. A twofold subterfuge baffled by science! The expression, "to eat the dust," can be understood, as Bullet and Bergier observe, to indicate in the scripture language, that as the serpent trails itself along the ground in search of food, its meats are generally covered with clay and dust. Moreover, we may say with commentators that, before the commission of sin, the serpent crawled on its breast and ate the dust; but that these habits, which were before natural to it, became painful to it after it had served as an instrument to the devil, and that this manner of living rendered it hateful and contemptible, so that man holds it in horror. And it was man especially whom God desired to instruct in the punishment of the serpent. Thus, to bear wood and water for the sacrifice in the Temple of the Lord was an honorable thing; and yet it was a penalty inflicted on the Gabaonites, which continually reminded them of their guilty stratagem, and rendered them more or less contemptible.

"I will put enmities between thee and the woman, between thy race and her race"; to deny this third part of the curse it would be necessary to show 1) that there does not exist among all peoples a sentiment of horror in regard to the serpent, and that it is not as a malicious creature, an enemy of man, that it has received, and still receives, the worship of certain nations. Now, the contrary is denied by facts. It would also be necessary to show 2) that the Son by excellence of the woman has not crushed the serpent's head, in other words, that our Lord Jesus Christ has not destroyed the empire of the devil, by overthrowing, even to this day, the temples and altars erected in his honor; and 3) that the serpent does not "lay snares for her feet"; in other words, that, on the day of our Lord's Passion, the devil did not let loose against his humanity all the powers of darkness, did not employ every stratagem and wickedness to put him to death, and that every day still he does not fight against him in his Church, and in each of his disciples. Now, the victory of the Son of the woman over the serpent, and this incessant war of the serpent against the Son of the woman, are facts as evident as the sun; and since this last part of the curse is accomplished we must conclude that the other parts continually receive their accomplishment too (See what is said on the worship of the serpent in our *Traité du Saint Esprit*, t. 1).

397 *Mulier*, says St. Thomas, *est gravius punita quam vir, ut patet* (Gn 3:16). *Ergo gravius peccavit quam vir...Si consideremus conditionem personae, peccatum viri est gravius, quia erat perfectior muliere. Sed quantum ad ipsum genus peccati, utriusque peccatum aequaliter dicitur, quia utriusque peccatum fuit superbia. Sed quantum ad speciem superbiae, gravius peccavit mulier, triplici ratione; 1) quia major elatio fuit mulleris quam viri: 2) quia non solum ipsa peccavit, sed etiam viro peccatum suggessit; 3) in hoc quod peccatum viri diminutum est, ex hoc quod in peccatum consensit amicabili quadam benevolentia* (Summa Theologiae, II-II, q. 163, a. 4, c.).

398 Gn 3:16

399 Tradition teaches that after wandering about for some time in the neighborhood of the terrestrial paradise, Adam settled in Judea, of which he was the first inhabitant, and where he was buried (See our *Histoire du bon Larron*).

400 *Eduxit illum a delicto suo* (Ws 10:2). Eve had the same happiness (See Cornelius a Lapide, *in hunc loc.*).

401 Gn 3:19

402 Eph 5:14

403 On the burial of Adam, let us hear the fathers of the Church:
   "The place where the cross of Jesus Christ was raised answers exactly to the grave of Adam, as the Jews assure us; and indeed it was very fitting that the first fruit of our life should be placed where the origin of our death had been laid." Thus speaks St. Ambrose.
   This is not a mere opinion of the illustrious bishop of Milan, since he first calls to witness the Jews, among whom the sentiment has prevailed from time immemorial. And he has read it in Origen, who rested it on ancient and undisputed tradition. "The place of Calvary," says the latter, "received a particular privilege, having been chosen for the death of him who should die for all men; for a tradition, which has descended even to our time, informs us that the body of the first man, formed by the hands of God, was buried in the same place where Jesus Christ should be crucified." He immediately gives the reason, which is also accepted by our holy bishop: "In order that," he says, "as all men died in Adam, so all should live in Jesus Christ, and that the chief of the human race should there find, for himself and his posterity, resurrection and life through the resurrection of the Savior, who there died and rose again" (Origen, *Tractate on Matthew*).
   Tertullian is no less precise. "Calvary," he says, "is the place of the chief; the first man was buried there; tradition preserves the remembrance of it: and it was at this same place that Jesus Christ erected the standard of his victory."
   St. Athanasius is still more positive. In a discourse on the passion and crucifixion of our Lord, he expresses himself thus: "Jesus Christ chose no other place in which to suffer and be crucified than that of Calvary, which, according to the opinion of the most learned among the Jews, was the place of Adam's burial. For they assure us that Adam, after his curse and condemnation, died there, and was buried there. If this is the case, the connection of such a place with the cross of Jesus Christ appears to me admirable; for it was most proper that our Lord, coming to seek and recall the first Adam, should choose to suffer in the place where he had been buried, and, while expiating his sin, should also expiate that of his race. It had been said to Adam: 'Thou art dust, and into dust thou shalt return'; and, on this very account, Jesus Christ comes to find him in the place where the sentence was executed, to deliver him from the curse, and instead of the words, 'Thou art dust, and into dust thou shalt return,' to say to him: 'Arise thou that sleepest; come forth from the tomb, thou that art dead, Jesus Christ will enlighten thee.'"
   In the time of St. Basil, this tradition was universally believed among Christians, though preserved rather in the memory of men than in their writings: still, Epiphanius assures us that he had seen books attesting it.
   An opinion resting on such respectable evidence ought to delight all Christian hearts; and it is surprising that St. Jerome should venture to refute it. For the rest, it is after having ably discussed his objections that a modern writer concludes, with St. Cyril of Jerusalem, and with Grotius, commenting on the Gospel of St. Matthew, that the name *Calvary* (in Syriac *Golgotha*), which means "Chief," united in one prophecy the sepulchre of Adam with the tomb of our Lord, the sacrifices and mysteries of the old law with those of the new (*Bibliothèque des Pères*, by M. Guillon, Vol. 9, p. 183). See these and other testimonies, as well as the passages of St. Jerome explained in our *Histoire du bon Larron*, dedicated to the nineteenth century.

404 Without original sin, let us remark that we should have been born in the same state as our first father was created, not in a better state. Like him, we should have had our trial; like him, we might lose grace and fall into a state of sin and death. St. Thomas, examining *ex professo* the question whether infants, born in the state of innocence, would have been confirmed in justice, answers formally, "No." Besides a text of St. Augustine to the same effect, he gives the reason: because it is evident that children could not have in their birth a greater perfection than their parents in the state of generation. Now, while they should be coming into existence, their parents would not have been confirmed in justice. The proof of which is that man is only confirmed in justice by the clear vision of God, which cannot coexist with an animal life, in which alone generation takes place. "Thou canst not see my face," said the Lord to Moses, "for no man shall see me and live" (Ex 33:20). Children, therefore, would not be born with this confirmation. *Pueri in sua nativitate non habuissent plus perfectionem quam eorum parentes in statu generationis. Parentes autem quamdiu generassent, non fuissent confirmati in justitia. Unde manifestum est quod parvuli non nascerentur in justitia confirmati* (Summa Theologiae, I-II, q. 100, a. 2, c.).

    It is well this matter should be remembered; for persons too often imagine that if our first father had been faithful, we should have nothing to fear or to do. The truth is that had this common ancestor been faithful, our particular ancestors might not have been so, and consequently have begotten us in an original sin. Finally, though all our forefathers had been faithful, we might not be so, and might fall into a state of sin and death. And, in this case, could we calculate on that mercy which followed the fall of our first father? Let us think well on this, and, instead of murmuring, we shall find reason to bless God. *Si aliquis ex posteris Adam peccasset, eo non peccante, moreretur quidem propter suum peccatum actuale, sicut Adam mortuus fuit, sed posteri ejus morerentur propter peccatum originale* (Aquinas, *Quaestiones Disputatae De Malo*, q. 5, a. 4, rep. 8. See M. Rohrbacher, *Grace and Nature*).

405 Council of Trent, Session 5, Can. 1

406 Council of Trent, Session 5, Can. 2

407 Cf. Bergier, *Traité de la Religion*, Bk. 3, 105; Augustine, *De Libero Arbitrio*, Bk. 3, Ch. 20; *Retractions*, Bk. 1, Ch. 9; *On the Gift of Perseverance*, Ch. 11-12; Baius, *Propositions* 24, 55, 78

    Primus creatus est homo immortalis, quod ei praestabatur de ligno vitae, non de conditione naturae...mortalis ergo erat conditione corporis animalis, immortalis a beneficio Creatoris (Augustine, *De Genesi ad Litteram*, Bk. 6, Ch. 25).

    Manifestum est quod illa subjectio corporis ad animam et inferiorum virium ad rationem, non erat naturalis; alioquin post peccatum mansisset, cum etiam in daemonibus dona naturalia post peccatum permanserint. Unde manifestum est quod et illa prima subjectio qua ratio Deo subdebatur, non erat solum secundum naturam, sed secundum supernaturale donum gratiae (Summa Theologiae, I, q. 95, a. 1).

    The same truth is established by the condemnation of many of the propositions of Baius (See 2, 5, 26, 34, 55, 78, and 79).

408 Jn 3:5

409 See Monsignor Bouvier, Bishop of Mans, t. 4, 519; and what we say in explaining the tenth article of the Creed.

410 *Peccato originali in futura retributione non debetur poena sensus* (Summa Theologiae, III, q. 1, a. 4, rep. 2). Such is also the opinion of the most grave theologians; and of Ferraris in particular, who expresses himself thus: *Pueri decedentes cum solo originali peccato nullam patiuntur poenam sensus, nec post diem judicii passuri sunt alias corporis afflictiones; sed tantum patiuntur, et patiuntur solam poenam damni sine ullo dolore interno et externo, seu sine ullo prorsus dolore, vel tristitia de omissione beatitudinis* (Biblioth., etc., art. Peccatum, n. 69).

411 *Traité de la Relig.*, 54, 3, 104. See also *Pieux souvenire des âmes du Purgatoire*, by Monsignor Devie, Bishop of Belley, p. 14.

412 Jb 14:4, Septuagint

413 Ps 50:7

414 Rom 5:12, 18

415 Clement of Alexandria, *The Stromata*, Bk. 3, Ch. 16

416 Origen, *Homily 14 on Luke*

417 Cf. Council of Trent, Session 5, Can. 2

418 Vendidad-Sade, p. 305-428

419 Cf. Humboldt, *Vue des Cordill.*, t. 1, p. 237

420 Cf. Macrob., *Satur.*, Bk. 1

421 Cf. Festus, *Do Verb. Signif.*

422 Voltaire, *Remarq. sur l'hist. gén.*, s. 9, p. 41

423 Voltaire, *Question sur l'Encyclop.* See also the *Zend-Avesta*, 14, 2; Virgil, *Aeneid*, Bk. 6, 5, 426-529; Creutzer, *Relig. de l'antiquité.*

424 Cf. Plutarch, *Delay of the Divine Justice*, p. 48-50

425 Cf. Rom 5; 1 Cor 15; Eph 4

426 Augustine, *On Merit and the Forgiveness of Sins, and the Baptism of Infants*, Bk. 3, Ch. 4, n. 7

427 *Office of Holy Saturday*

428 Rom 5:18

429 M. de Bonald, *Théorie de pouvoir*, p. 147, etc.

430 Ibid.

431 Leo the Great, *De Nativ.*, Sermon 20

432 *Summa Theologiae*, II-II, q. 2, a. 7

433 Non est aliud nomen sub coelo datum hominibus in quo oporteat nos salvos fieri (Acts 4:12), et ideo mysterium incarnationis Christi aliqualiter oportuit omni tempore esse ereditum apud omnes: diversimodo tamen secundum diversitatem temporum et personarum. Nam ante statum peccati, homo habuit explicitam fidem de Christi incarnatione, secundum quod ordinabatur ad consummationem gloriae; non autem secundum quod ordinabatur ad liberationem a peccato per passionem et resurrectionem...Post peccatum autem, fuit explicite creditum mysterium Incarnationis Christi, non solum quantum ad Incarnationem, sed etiam quantum ad passionem et resurrectionem, quibus humanum genus a peccato et morte liberatur; aliter enim non praefigurassent Christi passionem quibusdam sacrificiis et ante legem et sub lege. Quorum quidem sacrificiorum significationem explicite majores cognoscebant, minores autem sub velamino illorum sacrificiorum, credentes ea divinitius esse disposita, de Christo venture quodammodo habebant velatam cognitionem; et sicut supra dictum est, ea quae ad mysteria Christi pertinent, tanto distinctius cognoverunt, quanto Christo propinquiores fuerunt (*Summa Theologiae*, II-II, q. 2, a. 7, c.; Cf. Augustine, *On Rebuke and Grace*).

434 Everyone knows the famous testimonies of Tacitus and Suetonius: we shall repeat them in the beginning of the next volume.

435 With regard to the Sibyls, and the number and authenticity of their books, see Lactantius, *The Divine Institutes*; Augustine, *City of God*; Justin Martyr, *First Apology*; the learned Father Grisel, a Jesuit, in his work entitled *Le Mystère de l'Bomme-Dieu*; and the recent work of M. Alexandre on the *Sibyls*.

436 Cf. Augustine, *City of God*, Bk. 3, Ch. 47

437 Dicendum quod multis Gentilium facta fuerit revelatio de Christo, ut patet per ea quae praedixerunt; nam, Job 19, dicitur: "Scio quod Redemptor meus vivit." Sibylla etiam praenuntiavit quaedam de Christo, ut Augustine dicit (*Contra Faustum*, Bk. 13, Ch. 15). Invenitur etiam in historiis Romanorum quod tempore Constantini Augusti et Irenae matris ejus* fuit quoddam sepulcrum, in quo jacebat homo auream laminam habens in pectore, in qua scriptum erat: "Christus nascetur ex Virgine, et ego credo in eum. O sol! sub Irenae et Constantini temporibus iterum me videbis." Si qui tamen salvati fuerunt quibus revelatio non fuit facta, non fuerunt salvati absque fide Mediatoris; quia, etsi non habuerunt fidem explicitam, habuerunt tamen fidem implicitam in divina. Providentia; credentes Deum esse liberatorem hominum secundum modos sibi placitos, et secundum quod aliquibus veritatem cognoscentibus Spiritus revelasset (*Summa Theologiae*, II-II, q. 2, a. 7, c.; rep. 3).

   * This was not Constantine the Great, but the fifth or sixth emperor of the name, whose mother was called Irene. See Baronins, t. 9, ad annum 780, where the same fact is related.

438 Bergier, art. *Infidélité*. See also the excellent dissertation of St. Liguori on *Jansenism*, in his refutation of heresies, *Dissert. 14*.

439 People of Arabia (the district at present called Yemen), robbers and vagabonds, urged on by Satan.

440 People of Babylonia, between the Tigris and Euphrates.

441 Ubi non est mulier ingemiscit egens (Ecclus 36:27).

442 Plutarch, *Cont. Colotes*

443 *Si quis non confitetur primum hominem Adam, cum mandatum Dei in Paradiso fuisset transgressus, statim sanctitatem et justitiam in qua constitutus fuerit, amisisse...anathema sit* (Council of Trent, Session 6, Can. 1). Hence, the condemned proposition of Baius: *Humanae naturae sublimatio et exaltatio in consortium divinae naturae debita fuit integritati primae creationis, ac proinde naturalis dicenda est, et non supernaturalis (Prop. 21).*

444 *Religet ergo nos Religio uni omnipotenti Deo* (Augustine, *De Vera Religione*, Ch. 55, n. 113). And elsewhere: *Ad unum Deum tendentes, inquam, et ei uni religantes animas nostras, unde Religio dicta creditur, omni superstitione careamus. In his verbis meis ratio quae reddita est, unde sit dicta Religio, plus mihi placuit* (Augustine, *Retractions*, Bk. 1, Ch. 13, n. 9). *Vinculo pietatis obstricti Deo et religati sumus: unde ipsa Religio nomen aocepit* (Lactantius, *The Divine Institutes*, Bk. 4).

445 Rousseau, *Answer to the King of Poland*

446 Cf. Bergier, art. *Révél.*

447 De la Luzerne, *Diss. sur Rev.*, Ch. 2, n. 4

448 Rousseau, *Aemile*, Bk. 4

449 Ego Dominus et non mutor (Mal 3:6).

450 Heb 13:8

451 As [inculpable] protestants who become Catholics do not change their religion, but perfect it by sincerely admitting the consequences of the truths which they profess.

452 Augustine, *Retractions*, Bk. 1, Ch. 13. See the ideas expressed in this lesson and the last one, proved and developed in the learned work of M. Drach, *Du Divorce dans la Synagogue.*

453 Cf. *Hist. abrégés de la Relig.*

454 Lex nihil aliud est quam quaedam rationis ordinatio ad bonum commune, abeo qui curam communitatis habet, promulgata (*Summa Theologiae*, I-II, q. 92, a. 1, c.).

455 Lex Domini immaculata (Ps 18:8).

456 Cf. Mt 5:10ff

457 Qui non crediderit condemnabitur (Mk 16:16).

458 Plato, *De Legibus*, Bk. 10

459 On Socrates.

460 Portalis, *Discours sur l'organisation des cultes*, 15 germinal an X

461 Mt 10:28

462 Mt 28:19

463 Jas 2:10

464 Pascal, *Pensées*, Pt. 2, a. 2

465 *Esprit des Lois*, 54, 24, Ch. 2

466 *Dict. Phil.*, art. *Athéisme.*

467 Frayssinous, *Défens. du Christ Conf. sur les principes religieux*, etc.

468 Rousseau, *Aemile*

469 *Essai sur l'indiff.*, t. 1, Ch. 11, 475

470 *Essai sur l'indiff.*, t. 1, Ch. 11, 474

471 Rousseau, *Aemile*

472 Rosseau, *Lettre sur les spectacles*, 479

473 Jugum meum suave est, et onus meum leve (Mt 11:30).

474 Consider the manner in which the Angelic Doctor distinguishes between the need that man had of grace before and after his fall: man, after the commission of sin, did not require the grace of God differently from before, but for a greater number of purposes. He required it to heal and to merit: previously he had only required it for one of the two, the latter. Before his fall into sin, he could, without the supernatural gift of grace, understand natural truths, perform natural good works, and love God naturally above all things; but he could not without it merit eternal life, which is a thing above the natural reach of man. After his fall into sin, without grace he could only understand a few natural truths, and do a few good works of the same order. That he might be able to do everything as before, it was necessary that grace should heal the infirmity or corruption of his nature. In fine, both before and after, he had need of grace to merit eternal life, to believe in God, to hope in God, and to love God supernaturally as the object of the intuitive vision (Cf. *Summa Theologiae*, I, q. 95, a. 4, rep. 1; I-II, q. 109, a. 2-4). Thus, according to the Angelic Doctor, man before his fall had need of grace to rise above himself, even to God; but after his fall he had need of grace to rise, in the first place, even to a level with his former self.

475 We only speak here of grace generally: we shall treat of it particularly in the second part of the catechism [i.e., Volume XI of the Tradivox series].

476 The important word is *supernatural*—or that which is above nature. According to the explanation of St. Thomas, which is the Catholic explanation, grace is a supernatural gift, not only to man deprived of the perfection of his nature, but to man in the fullness of his nature; not only to man, but to every creature. For grace conducts us to the intuitive vision. Now, between God and the creature, there is an infinite distance. It is, therefore, naturally impossible for a creature, whatever it may be, to see God such as he is, such as he beholds himself. *Cum vita aeterna omnem facultatem excedat, non potest homo, neque in statu naturae integrae, neque in statu naturae corruptae, ipsam absque gratia et divina reconciliatione a Deo promereri. — Et inde est quod nulla natura creata est sufficiens principium actus meritorii vitae aeternae, nisi superaddatur aliquod supernaturale donum quod gratis dicitur (Summa Theologiae, I-II, q. 114, a. 2).*

477 See Bergier, art. *Grace*.

478 Prv 23:26

479 Cf. Rom 5:20

480 Chrysostom, *Homily 9 on Romans*, t. 10, p. 573, etc.

481 The preceding remarks may be found in Cornelius a Lapide (*On Romans*, t. 5). The learned interpreter concludes thus: *Longe majora bona et dona nobis contulit gratia Christi, quam Adam abstulerit, scilicet tot gratias et dona Spiritus Sancti, quas Christus contulit apostolis, martyribus, doctoribus, eremitis, episcopis, virginibus, aliisque filiis Novi Testamenti, quibus caruit Adam, ac tandem ipsam gloriam et immortalitatem ejusque dotes maximas, plurimas et diversissimas* (t. 9, p. 84).

482 *Annales de la Propag. de la Foi*, Nov. 1837, p. 112

483 Our Lord himself, having come to dissipate all shadows, conformed to this law; and he revealed to his apostles only by degrees the truths in which he wished to instruct them. If he acted in this manner, it was to accommodate himself to their weakness, finding them incapable of enduring the brighter lights. "I have yet many things to say to you," he said, "but you cannot bear them now" (Jn 16:12).

484 *Haec autem omnia in figura facta sunt nostri* (1 Cor 10:6). *Haec autem omnia in figura contingebant illis* (1 Cor 10:11). As it would be too long to quote the passages of the inspired writers, see the Bible de Vence, *Préface générale sur l'Ancien Testament*, t. 1, p. 248.

485 Augustine, *On the Catechizing of the Uninstructed*—The holy doctor returns a hundred times to this idea in his various works: see, particularly, his books against Faustus the Manichean. In the Select Library of the Fathers of the Church, see Origen, t. 2, p. 54; Tertullian, t. 2, p. 474; Chrysostom, t. 13, 129, etc.

486 Eusebius, *Demonstratio Evangelica*, Bk. 4, n. 174. See also Bossuet, drawing a similar picture in a sermon on the *Characteristics of the Two Testaments*, t. 3, p. 237.

487 *Quorum quidem sacrificiorum significationem explicite majores* (the more enlightened) *cognoscebant; minores autem* (the less enlightened: this is the meaning which St. Thomas himself gives to the word, art. 4) *sub velamine illorum sacrificiorum credentes ea divinitus esse deposita, de Christo venturo, quodammodo habebant velatam cognitionem (Summa Theologiae, II-II, q. 2, a. 7, c.).*

488 Gn 3:15

489 Sacerdos Patris Catholicus (Tertullian).

490 Cf. 2 Cor 5:21

491 Cf. Rom 5:12ff

492 See in the Select Library of the Fathers, Tertullian, t. 3, p. 20; Chrysostom, t. 13, p. 408, 509.

493 Cf. Augustine, *On the Catechizing of the Uninstructed*

494 On the longevity of the first men, let us give the teachings of modern science:
  1. The fact is not impossible. Is there really anything in the constitution of the human race that should limit its existence to a certain period? In the osseous, nervous, muscular, visceral systems—in the digestive, sanguineous, respiratory organs—are there 20 rather than 30, 60, 100, or 200 years of life? Assuredly not. And not only is it impossible to prove *a priori* that there are, but the solution in accordance with observations and facts would be quite the reverse: for there are some populations whose existence is confined to this side of 40 years; others, whose average is double that period. Long ago, Plutarch, in astonishment, asked himself this question: Why are the Ethiopians old at 30 years, while the Bretons live to 120 years of age? (*De Placid. phil.*, t. 5, Ch. 30). The first lived amid physical causes that rapidly exhausted life; the second were favored with circumstances of a contrary nature. Thus, even in our own day, in some countries, woman arrives at maturity at 10 or 12 years of age, and becomes decrepit at 25; while it is quite the

contrary in other countries. Frequently even in these opposite systems of longevity and decay, the elements of life remain, and by their resistance to dissolution protest against the accidental causes of destruction.

Now, can you not imagine material circumstances still more unfavorable than those in which men become old at 40 years; and, on the other hand, others still more favorable to the principles of life than those in which men live to 80 years? Assuredly no one has a right to say, "No." Well, behold us now placed face to face with the early patriarchs, and remark that Genesis acquaints us accurately with the reason for the alteration in the duration of human life, namely, that the original physical condition of the world was completely altered by the deluge! (Cf. Gn 6:3). This alteration could strike not only at external agencies, but also at the secondary powers of human organization.

2. The fact is supported by natural proofs. Since long life in man is a thing which of itself presents nothing impossible or improbable, we must ask then: Has the fact occurred? We have now to deal with a question of evidence, a matter of history. If there is evidence of a fact of this kind, giving life such or such a duration, we must either believe the evidence, or prove that it is false. The question, thus put, recoils on our adversaries. We are in possession of the field. According to every rule of law, it is the business of the objector to prove his assertion. We might content ourselves with this view of the question; but we will go further and adduce the authorities on which the facts of primitive longevity rest. The first is that of Moses. Now, putting aside both the inspiration and the high character of the witness, it must be remembered that, by general consent, he is admitted to be the most ancient historian, and consequently of greater weight than all later historians, whose negative testimony cannot suffice to counterbalance his positive declarations. Moreover, it must be borne in mind that if other historians lost the thread or link of the successive generations of the human family, they are not able in their inquiry as to the origin of man to ascend beyond the deluge, a period after which, according to the Bible, God curtailed the duration of human life, their testimony, in this case, is of very little value. Still, as even the years of the postdiluvian patriarchs extended considerably beyond a century, it would be very natural to find some traces of this fact in profane traditions.

Accordingly, the testimony of pagans is our second authority. Homer complains that the life of mortals in his time was much shortened. Josephus cites for the Greeks their historians Hesiod, Hecataeus, Hellanicus, Arcesilatiis, Ephorus, and Nicholas of Damas, affirming that the first men lived several centuries. The same belief is found among the Egyptians, the Indians, and the Chinese.

What can be said in reply to these things? Actual facts are brought forward. One says: men do not live today more than 70 or 80 years. And thence concludes: therefore it has been the same during more than 50 centuries. Man very rarely attains to 100 years; therefore there never existed a human constitution that could bear the weight of 700 or 800 years. Here, as in all other objections to religious facts, we meet with the same stupid pretensions of the would-be strong mind: "That which I have not seen, has not been, and can never have been!" See *Soirées de Montlhéry*, by M. Desdouits, third Soiree.

495 See Fleury, *Manners of the Israelites*, p. 3 and 14.

496 See *Dissertation upon Enoch*, Bible of Vence, Vol. 1, p. 350.

497 Voltairian impiety denied the existence of giants, and more than once the worldly levity of our age has reechoed that denial. Now, let us give a few scientific and historical proofs in support of the fact recorded in Genesis:

1. Commentators admit that the scripture word, which is translated *gigantes*, may simply mean strong and violent men, such, for example, as a population of athletes might well be. The context harmonizes perfectly with this interpretation, and somewhat indifferently with the reverse of it. We could take our stand here, and incredulity should have nothing to say.

2. Let us suppose that we must understand by the word *giants* men of extraordinary height and strength: we say that the existence of a gigantic race is credible, if we meet with analogous facts that one ought to consider as the result of circumstances physically favorable, yet most natural. Well, our vegetables are dwarfs in comparison with their like as seen on the soil of America. Every one knows that the fern, which is not even a bush with us, rises in the Western climate to the height of an immense tree; hence it is fitly styled the gigantic fern. Before the discovery of America, the gigantic fern would have been treated as a fable altogether worthy of the giants of the Bible. Let us now descend into the depths of the earth; we shall find giants here in the remains of the two kingdoms that sleep beneath the rocks. The monocotyledons, which are the deepest buried specimens of the organic creation found here, are gigantic ferns and palms, according to the testimony of all geologists. Among the fossil animals are monstrous lizards, attaining a length of seventy feet; and, what are better known, enormous mastodons, the huge mammoths. Now, these were really giants in the first ages of the world. If giants existed among vegetables and animals, why should not nature have been able to form them among men?

3. Since there is only question of the possibility of the existence of giants in the human race, we say that a few isolated facts of the kind are sufficient to justify us in pronouncing the general rule. Now, history has given us the names and heights of several men, who may well be termed giants. Not to speak of Goliath,

we may mention individuals of six, seven, eight, or nine feet, whose existence is unquestioned. Thus, Augustus had at his court a giant and a giantess named Pusio and Secundilla, whose skeletons, preserved in the gardens of Sallust, measured, according to Pliny (Bk. 8, Ch. 16), ten feet three inches, or about nine French feet. The giant Gabbara, sent from Arabia to the emperor Claudius, was half a foot less, according to the same author. The giant Eleazar, sent to Tiberius by Artabanus, king of Parthia, measured five cubits, according to Josephus, or somewhat more than seven feet. The emperor Maximinus (the Thracian) was still taller; Capitolinus describes him as eight Roman feet seven inches.

Now, remark that the position of all these personages at Rome, at the very court, placed them so much in view that it was impossible for the witnesses whose accounts we have given either to be deceived themselves or to deceive others. This suffices, independently of any other proof, to render credible the account of the Goliath of the Bible, and the whole gigantic family of the children of Enac, to which belonged the king of Basan, whose bed measured nine cubits, allowing, we may suppose, not more than eight, and perhaps less, for the individual that occupied it.

4. In favor of the existence of antediluvian giants, we might also cite the traditions preserved among the pagans. But to quote the testimony of the authors would lead us too much out of our way; you may consult them or read them in the dissertation on the matter in the Bible de Vence, t. 1, p. 371.

5. Against the existence of giants, therefore, nothing but absurd reasoning can be opposed. "There are no giants; therefore, there never have been any; therefore, it is impossible that there should ever have been any." Now, by what right do you determine thus the limits of the possible? But let us conclude with one important remark.

If you deny the existence of giants, at least you cannot deny the existence of dwarfs. If God made a certain number of them, you cannot deny that he might have made them larger, or even that he might have made dwarfs alone. Suppose, then, that for a long period the Creator had formed dwarfs alone, and that one among them three feet high, reasoning like our philosophers, should have said: "It is pretended that, during a former epoch, there existed giants of the height of five or six feet. Such a thing is certainly impossible; for neither I, nor any one else, within the memory of man, has ever beheld the like." In denying that at a certain epoch there could have existed men like us, the dwarf would have uttered a foolery; would he not? Well, our philosophers do the very same thing; for if God can produce men three feet high and men six feet high, he can as easily produce at the same time men six feet high and men twelve feet high. We have a proportion here in which three of the terms are certain; the fourth is quite fair.

See Bible de Vence, t. 1, p. 371; and *Soirées de Montlhéry*: third Soiree, p. 112.

498 Gn 6:6-7

499 See the *Dissertation on the Ark* in the Bible de Vence, t. 1, 404.

500 Cf. *Comogonie de Moise*, by M. Marcel de Serres, p. 182

501 Cf. Bagavadám, Bk. 8, p. 213 et suiv.

502 Cf. *Cosmogonie de Moise*, p. 183

503 Cf. *Cosmogonie de Moise*, p. 180

504 Cf. *Cosmogonie de Moise*, p. 187

505 Cf. *Cosmogonie de Moise*, p. 184-191

506 *Cosmogonie de Moise*, p. 186-188; Cf. Bible de Vence, t. 1, p. 420; Jehan, *Nouveau traité des sciences géologiques*, p. 293

507 See Cuvier, *Discours sur les révolutions de la surface du globe.* — In the following remarks, we present an abridgment of the physical proofs of the deluge, such as they are found in the most advanced treatises of modern geologists. Let us first remark that if the surface of the globe was ever subjected to a cataclysm, as Genesis and the traditions of peoples say, there must exist on the earth some traces of this tremendous inundation. For the ancient world should have scattered here and there its relics over the whole extent disturbed by the waters. Moreover, according to Genesis, the waters of the sea and of the rain united in producing the flood. There is nothing further wanted to explain certain facts, which reciprocally serve as a standpoint for the inductions by which we find their causes.

So much being settled, we say that the first diluvian fact, or, according to the beautiful expression of Buckland, the Cuvier of England, the *First Medal of the Deluge*, is the existence of sea sand and shells in the alluvia of our present continents. These immense beds of sea sand and shells exist even on the summits of mountains. If the sand and the shells were found in stony beds, this would not indicate a connection with the deluge; but it is in movable soils, in alluvial clays, in precisely what geologists term diluvian formation, that we find this sand and these shells. Although, according to some geologists, the diluvian deposits are not found on the ridges of the highest mountains; their absence, if it is real, does not militate against the universality of the deluge. Indeed the deposits, resulting from the impetuous action of running waters might perhaps not appear toward the points of their departure, and might only cover the lowest accidental points of the surface of the globe; very much as at the present time we often observe hardly a trace of the most violent inundations on the very mountains from which they took their rise.

Second Medal of the Deluge: the valleys of denudation. In the absence of sea sand and shells on the tops of the highest mountains, the valleys of denudation come to attest the passage of the terrible scourge over these lofty summits. We term "valleys of denudation" those valleys which have been scooped through the solid mass of the loftiest plains. They are easily recognized, inasmuch as, on the declivities of the hills, we may observe, as on the sides of a railway-cutting, the exact correspondence of the layers, which, before the separation, were evidently continuous, since they are today of the same height and structure, and in the same order of position on both sides of the valley. We cannot attribute the formation of these valleys to currents of water now actually flowing, for the greater number of them are dry valleys; some of them may even be seen, in which the strata composing the soil are vertical, and thus carry off in their seams all pluvial waters. De Saussure refers also to a violent action of the waters, the denudation of enormous masses of granite, 3,200 feet higher than the highest Alps.

Third Medal of the Deluge, which, like the two preceding ones, is found on the surface of the globe: erratic blocks or boulders. These scattered fragments of rocks, measuring over 2,500 cubic feet, and weighing as much as three hundred tons, are found lying on sand or buried in movable deposits, sometimes isolated, more frequently accumulated on extensive plains or spread out in long rows over the declivities, and even along the crests of mountains, to whose material they are quite foreign. What is very remarkable is that they are generally found at an immense distance from the chains of mountains which alone could furnish them, and from which they are separated by deep valleys, and even by extensive bays or arms of the sea.

Such are the blocks that may be seen in Denmark, in Prussia, in the North of European Russia, and that belong to the mountains of Norway, Sweden, Finland, etc., from which they have been transported across the Baltic Sea. Blocks of this kind may be met with in nearly all parts of Europe, and in North and South America. The transport of these enormous blocks is inexplicable without the deluge, whose prodigious violence alone could detach granite masses of many tons weight from the summits of mountains, and hurl them over the crests of other mountains.

Fourth Medal of the Deluge: the existence of the remains of many land animals, heaped together into light soil formations, with sand and other sea productions. This indisputable fact is repeated in every quarter of the globe, even in Australia, so recently discovered. On which phenomenon it is necessary to remark: a) That the species, whose remains are contained in these formations, are like species still extant; only a small number show a slight variation; for the rest, the dimensions are generally larger. b) These remains are found in climates very different from those in which species much the same now live. c) These races, fossilized in one mass, are very frequently races of strong antipathies, incapable of dwelling together; and, nevertheless, the state of the formations proves that they were mixed into one company by the general catastrophe which befell them, and, moreover, that they were crushed into a very narrow space. From the observation of these facts, admitted by all geologists, we ought to conclude:

1. That since there is a mixture of terrestrial and marine productions, the marine deposits cannot have resulted from a sediment gradually formed in the water, while it tranquilly covered the surface of our present continents. The carcasses of the animals belonging to the land cannot have mingled with those of the inhabitants of the sea, except in consequence of the sudden irruption of the latter on their domain. This precisely corresponds with the account given in the Bible.

2. That the vast proportions of some of the buried species agree very well with the ideas which Moses gives us of the vigor of organic nature at the epoch of the deluge.

3. That the difference between the climates where the fossilized species live and where their remains are now found can only be explained by an accidental, but powerful, cause, which must have transported these animals from their ordinary latitudes to very remote places, where the species subsequently perished. Ask Cuvier how it is that he could meet the reindeer and the rhinoceros together in our climates. Perfectly in accord with us, the great naturalist will tell you that, on the hypothesis of the deluge, this phenomenon is explained either by the efforts of the animals to flee toward points still unvisited by the inundation, or by the violent removal of their carcasses tossed about on the waves. Without our deluge, any attempt at an explanation utterly fails.

4. That from the assemblage of the remains of races that are averse one to another, such as tigers and hyenas with horses, it follows that many individuals of the different inimical species found themselves driven forcibly into very confined limits, where all perished alike. This forced assemblage would be the natural consequence of a gradual invasion of the waters, such as Moses pictures the deluge. Without this cause, everything is inexplicable. It is the same with bone caverns, in which are found mingled together the remains of a great number of animals remarkable for their antipathies, and which, it is easy to imagine, became, according to the instincts of the beasts themselves, their common shelter before the danger that threatened them.

The deluge being established, there remains only one question yet to solve: it is asked why we do not find among the abundance of diluvian remains anything to prove that man existed during the period immediately anterior, any human bones, any articles of human industry, any manufactured metals, any cut stones, any monuments whatever of the civilization natural to man. Before returning an answer, we shall make some observations:

1. The account in Genesis is so well supported by itself, that it may dispense with any proof drawn from the scientific order. Accordingly, when one only exercises a negative criticism in regard to geological facts, showing that none of them oppose insoluble difficulties to the Mosaic narrative, one does all that an intelligent man can require to reconcile faith and reason in a satisfactory manner.

2. Geology is a science yet in its cradle: as even the most learned geologists admit. Sixty years ago, the science did not exist. Now, the onward march of the sciences, and especially of geology, is only accomplished gradually, laboriously, with repeated, often ineffectual attempts; and therefore we ought at present to be content that, after so much labor and so many vicissitudes, geology has come to an agreement on a few points with Genesis, that divine book, which, according to the testimony of an illustrious geologist, is the most magnificent summary of geological systems, the fountain of eternal truth, the center of unity in which the various branches of human knowledge shall one day meet.

Answering the question directly, we say:

1. It is false that no fossil of man or of human civilization has been met with in the diluvian deposits. In the grotto of Bèze, near Narbonne, M. Tournai discovered human bones mixed with remains of pottery and bones of animals whose species no longer exist; and the materials that covered them are regarded by all geologists as belonging to the deluge (*Bulletin de la Soc. géol. de France*, 1830).

Another geologist, M. Schmerling, who took the greatest care in examining the caverns of Maëstricht, found some heads there, which recalled to his mind the African shaves. These skulls were mixed with fragments of pottery, bone needles, etc. Some years ago, the remarkable discovery of human bones and flint hatchets seemed to solve the difficulty.

2. Though we might find no human remains in our Western regions, yet we could draw no adverse conclusion hence. As a matter of fact, it is most reasonable to suppose that the human species was not widely diffused at the period of the deluge, and consequently, that its remains should hardly be found in more than one country. Now, this country, where every tradition places the cradle of the human race — Central Asia — is still geologically unknown.

3. Even though in this country we should not discover any vestige of antediluvian man, yet we could not hence conclude that the Mosaic narrative is false. On the contrary, we may well admit the hypothesis of Cuvier, that the places which man used to occupy were swallowed up, and his bones lost in the depths of our present seas, with the exception of the few individuals who continued the species.

4. Another cause, which ought to make the finding of the remains of antediluvian humanity very rare, is the universal and instinctive custom that exists even among the most savage tribes, of burning or burying the dead: and everyone knows how much the latter practice accelerates decomposition. (See Cuvier, *Discours*, etc.; Marcel de Serres, *Cosmogonie de Moise*; Desdouits, *Soirées de Montlhéry*; Jehan, *Nouveau traité des sciences géologiques*; Forichon, *Examen des questions scientifiques*.)

508 See also Biot, Beudant, Elie de Beaumont. — To these authorities, let us add the testimony of a man whose word is a proof in these matters: "None of the ancient monuments of profane history still subsisting," says M. Champollion, "and reaching back to a certain epoch, dispute the date assigned to the deluge according to the Greek text of the Septuagint Bible" (*Résumé complet de chronologie*, n. 60).

509 Cf. Gn 6:3

510 During our stay at Rome, we had the advantage of coming frequently into contact with Cardinal Mezzofanti. This man, unique in the annals of the world, speaks thirty-three languages and fifteen dialects, without counting *patois*. One day, we asked him whether philology could assist in demonstrating the unity of species, and the trinity of race, in humanity. "It not only assists," he said, "but it gives this demonstration. The human language, one in its essence, is divided into three branches, of which all other known languages are the boughs. These three branches are the Japhetic language, the Semitic language, and the Chamite language." What can be placed in opposition to such a testimony? [...]

511 All these biblical facta have been confirmed by the recent discovery of the ruins of the Tower of Babel (See *Annales de phil. chrét.* an 1862 et suiv., and our *Traité du Saint-Esprit*, t. 1).

512 Ps 109:4

513 See Muzarelli's dissertation on the destruction of Pentapolis.

514 See our *Histoire du bon Larron*.

515 St. Augustine shows in an admirable manner that the conduct of Jacob is altogether mysterious, and exempt from lying. The saint further observes that Isaac knew what he was doing, because he acted under the inspiration of the Holy Ghost, who revealed to him the mysterious figure of which he was the instrument.

"If he had been deceived," says the great doctor, "why would he not, recovering from his error, have cursed the disrespectful son who had sported with him? And yet he confirms the blessing which he has given."

He adds: "That no one might accuse Jacob of a lie, the scripture is careful to inform us of his simplicity and artlessness. Moreover, he could say in all truth that he was Esau, that is, the elder son, since he had the rights of the firstborn, both by the election of God and the contract made between him and his brother. Finally, we must take the word *dolus* in the sense of "figure." *Dolus in proprietate fraus; in figura, ipsa figura. Omnis enim figurata et allegorica lectio vel locutio, aliud videtur sonare carnaliter, aliud insinuare spiritualiter. Hanc ergo figuram doli nomine, appellavit. Quid est ergo: "Venit cum dolo et abstulit benedictionem tuam?" Quia figuratum erat quod agebatur, ideo dictum est: "Venit cum dolo." Nam ille doloso homini benedictionem non confirmaret, cui debebatur justa maledictio. Non ergo erat verus ille dolus? maxime quia non est mentitus dicendo, "ego sum filius tuus major Esau." Jam enim pactus erat ille cum fratre suo, et vendiderat primogenita tua. Hoc se dixit habere patri quod emerat a fratre: quod ille perdiderat, in istum transierat. Ideo sciens hoc in mysterio Isaac, confirmavit benedictionem* (Augustine, *Sermon 4*, n. 23; Cf. *City of God*, Bk. 16, Ch. 37; *Quaestiones in Genesim*, n. 74).

516 A neighboring district of Arabia, remarkable for its spices.

517 The *Chaldaic Paraphrases*, the most ancient Jewish doctors, the most learned rabbis of every period, have always applied and still unanimously apply this oracle of Jacob to the Messias (See *Munimen Fidei*, Pt. 1, Ch. 14). It is the same with all the fathers of the Church in both the East and the West. To comprehend well its meaning and to remove thereby all the difficulties of unbelievers, it is necessary to remark that the word *scepter* does not always refer to royalty in the strict sense of the term. It only expresses a preeminence, an authority corresponding to that of the various states of the nation. All interpreters agree on this point.

Consequently, Jacob predicts to Juda: a) a superiority of strength over his brethren, comparing him to a lion; b) a larger and richer share in the promised land than any of his brethren, denoted by the abundance of milk and wine; c) authority, represented by the scepter or baton of command; d) the privilege of giving birth to the Messias; e) the supplying of chiefs or magistrates from his tribe, until the envoy of God should come to gather the peoples together again.

The Jews do not deny any one of these circumstances, and all have been exactly fulfilled.

1. The tribe of Juda was always the most numerous: we see it by the enumerations that were made in the desert, and by the preeminence that was assigned to this tribe at various epochs (Cf. Nm 1:26-27; 26:22; Dt 33:7; Jo 15; Jgs 1:1).

2. In the division of the promised land, it had the largest share, and was placed in the middle; it contained in its portion, the city of Jerusalem, the capital of the nation — the vineyards of whose environs were celebrated.

3. Always the most powerful, even under Saul, it took, after his death, David for its king and formed a separate state. Under Roboam, it continued a kingdom apart under its own name of Juda; it often coped with the ten tribes. During the captivity of Babylon it preserved its own government, its own administration; as is proved by the histories of Susanna and Daniel, and the book of Esther (Ch. 16) where it is expressly stated that the Jews had retained their own laws. After the captivity it continued to uphold in the body of the nation its own laws and magistrates; its authority is so well established and clearly admitted that the residue of the tribes Levi and Benjamin are incorporated with it, and all become so amalgamated that henceforward the name of Jews, or children of Juda, becomes the common title of the whole race of Jacob.

4. Still later, under the Machabees or Asmonean kings, so called from Asmoneus, their grandfather, of the tribe of Levi, the tribe of Juda still preserved its authority and preeminence. For this tribe included with itself alone nearly the whole Jewish nation; and the nation willingly selected chiefs from it, and from it issued all acts of authority. The government next rested in the hands of the Jewish senate and people, in whose name the kings acted. This is proved by the first book of Machabees (12:16); the writings of Josephus, the Jewish historian (Bk. 11, Ch. 4); and the letter of Antiochus to the Jews: "King Antiochus to the senate of the Jews, and to the rest of the Jews, greeting" (2 Mc 11:27ff).

5. Under the Romans the power of Juda was greatly shaken; it received an additional check on the nomination of Herod; finally, it was annihilated at the destruction of Jerusalem. Therefore, at this epoch, the Messias was come. Up to this point the tribe had preserved its genealogies, its possessions, its preeminence; but now the Messias was come, and his gospel gathered the peoples of Juda together again into a new Church, of which the tribe of Juda was only a figure.

Therefore, the oracle of Jacob has been fulfilled to the letter (See Libermann, t. 1; Bergier, art. *Juda*; Cornel. a Lap., *On Genesis*, Ch. 49).

518 Here are some of the plagues or scourges with which the Lord struck Egypt by the ministry of Moses: a) the water of the Nile changed into blood; b) a countless multitude of frogs, coming forth from marshy places, and wandering about everywhere, even into the houses and over meats; c) a cloud of flies, whose stings were painful in the highest degree to men and beasts; d) tumors and ulcers, with which men and beasts were equally tormented.

The scripture says that the magicians of Pharao did the same things, *fecerunt similiter*. On which it will be well to make a few remarks. a) God undoubtedly permitted these wonderful performances of the magicians to punish Pharao and his people, by hardening the king in his obstinacy in not letting the Hebrews depart, in spite of the express command of the Lord. These enchantments, which seemed to equal the miracles of Moses, and to make the power of the gods of Egypt keep pace with that of the God of Israel, entered into the terrible counsels of the justice of God, and served for the accomplishment of this word: "I will harden Pharao's heart"—*Indurabo cor Pharaonis*. b) Yet God, who always leaves sufficient light to sinners to enable them to recover themselves, knew how to impress on the miracles of Moses such a character as would render it impossible not to behold in them the work of the Almighty. In effect, the magicians could not do that which Moses did; they could not even protect their own persons from the plagues with which Moses struck the Egyptians. While Moses extended the scourges to all the Egyptians and to everything belonging to them, the magicians were powerless to do any injury to the Israelites or to their cattle. In fine, there was such a difference between the wonders of the magicians and the miracles of Moses, that Pharao himself was obliged to exclaim in reference to the latter: "The finger of God is really here!" It has been the same at all times, and is the same today. Despite all the subtleties of incredulity, the true miracle has characteristics so exclusive and so evident that every man of earnestness knows and shall always know how to recognize it.

For the rest, if we go back to the remote times in which Moses lived, and consider the state of the nations, the state of Egypt in particular, buried in the darkness of idolatry, and in that materialism which is its consequence, we shall readily conceive the reason for the numerous prodigies narrated in the old testament. God, unknown, would cause himself to be recognized as the sole master of nature. There was a necessity for astounding prodigies, to strike those people who were yet but children, and who were ever disposed to adore the creature instead of the Creator. It is thus that providence always proportions the remedy to the disease, opposes the light of truth to the darkness of falsehood, and justifies himself in the eyes of the learned as well as of the simple.

519 On the passage of the Red Sea and the journey in the desert, see the letters of the learned Father Sicard, Egyptian missionary, in the *Recueil des Lettres édifiantes*.

520 See, on the laws of the Hebrews, the work of M. Frere, *l'Homme connu par la révélation*; the excellent *Critique des législations païennes et Defense de la législation mosaïque*, by J. Brunati, Professor in the Seminary of Brescia; *Dissertation sur le Deutéronome*, Bible deVence, t. 4, p. 8; and the admirable work of M. Tripart, Barrister, Besancon.

521 We do not mean to say that they did not exist previously.

522 The amazing fertility and the vigorous vegetation of the promised land are facts too well established and too generally known to require a proof (See the *Lettres de quelques guifs*, etc, by the Abbé Guéné). We shall only add a single incident, related by a learned archbishop, a missionary in Syria. "Being at Aleppo," he says, "such a prodigious bunch of grapes was brought to us from the neighborhood that my companions and I, in all seven persons, partook abundantly of them, and yet were unable to finish our supply. I was curious enough to have the remainder pressed, and it produced a bottle of wine."

523 Observe that the scripture records the falsehood of Rahab without approving of it. If this woman and her family were saved in the destruction of Jericho, it was on account of the generous hospitality that she had displayed toward the messengers of the Israelite general.

524 Cf. Dt 20:1-9

525 Profane history offers us many examples of this custom. See Life of Aesop.

526 It is believed that this fish was not a whale properly so called, but one of those large cetaceous animals whose esophagus would permit the passage of a living man.

527 From the moment you attack one scripture miracle, you must attack them all, and attack the scripture itself. Otherwise you must receive them all, with the books that contain them. *Aut omnia divina miracula credenda sunt, aut hoc cur credatur, causa nulla est* (Augustine, *Epistle 102*, q. 6, n. 31). Will you say that the miracle of Jonas is more extraordinary than the others? I will answer you, first, that one ought not to deny a fact because it is extraordinary, but because it is not well proved. I will ask you, next, is the preservation of Jonas in the belly of a sea monster more extraordinary than the resurrection of Lazarus four days after his death, or that of Jesus Christ three days after his crucifixion? And yet you cannot deny these facts, a thousand times better proved than those relating to Socrates, of which no person doubts, or can doubt, without destroying all historical certainty. No longer say that the miracle of Jonas is impossible, for I will ask you: Who has given you the right to fix the limits of the power of the Creator, and to say to the Most High: "Thus far shalt thou come, but no farther"? Modern science denies all those pretended impossibilities, and defies you to prove anything impossible in the occurrence with regard to Jonas.

528 That is, about 60 miles in diameter, and 180 in circumference. The recent excavations made by Mr. Layard have led to the discovery of the ruins of Ninive, and demonstrated the perfect accuracy of the dimensions given to the city by the sacred text.

529 See M. Drach, *Du divorce*, etc., p. 17.

530 Mal 4:4

531 Drach, *Première lettre aux Israélites*, p. 41

532 Heb 11:35

533 Cf. 1 Cor 14

534 "The words of the prophets," says Pascal, "are intermingled with private prophecies and with prophecies of the Messias, in order that the prophecies of the Messias should not be without proof, and that the private prophecies should not be without fruit" (*Pensées*, Ch. 15, n. 13).

535 See Bible de Vence, *Dissertation on the Prophets*, t. 13, p. 12.

536 Ps 85:9

537 Ps 71:11

538 Ps 71:10

539 Ps 17:44-45

540 Ps 109:4

541 Ps 2:1-2

542 Ps 2:4, 6

543 Ps 40:10

544 Ps 68:21

545 Ps 101:9

546 Ps 21:8-9, 17, 19

547 Ps 68:22

548 Ps 15:9-10

549 It seems necessary that we should give a few details on this fundamental prophecy. We abridge the dissertation of M. Drach, cited before.

Achaz, king of Juda, a cruel and unbelieving prince, had much to suffer from the arms of Rasin and Phacee, kings of the schismatical tribes of Israel. These two princes were at the foot of the ramparts of Jerusalem, with the intention, not only of ravaging the country and the capital of their common enemy, but even of annihilating the royal race of David, to substitute a new dynasty in its place. It was then that the Lord sent the prophet Isaias to say to the king of Juda: "Fear not; the design of thine enemies shall come to naught" (Cf. Is 7:4-7). A skeptical silence was the only reply given to the consoling words of the prophet. To overcome the obstinacy of Achaz, Isaias said to him: "As a proof of that which I announce to thee, do thou thyself ask a sign of the Lord thy God" (Cf. Is 7:11). "I will not ask a sign," answered Achaz, with a sacrilegious disdain; "I do not wish to tempt the Lord" (Is 7:12).

At these words, the man of God, filled with a holy indignation, turned aside from the incredulous king, and, addressing himself to all the princes of the royal family, said: "Since it is so, hear then you, O house of David! The Lord himself shall give you a sign, which will be a certain pledge of the preservation of the royal line, namely, a Virgin conceiving and bearing a Son, whom she shall name Emmanuel, *God with us*. This *God with us* shall be at the same time true man, for he shall be nourished, as other children, with butter and honey, until he arrives at the age when one knows how to choose the good and to reject the evil."

As this event was remote, the prophet took care to establish its certainty, by the announcement of an approaching occurrence. He had brought with him his young son, named Scheer-Yaschub. Then, addressing Achaz himself, he said: "This little child will not yet know how to distinguish good from evil, when the two kings, thine enemies, shall disappear from their own lands." It is at the age of seven years that one can hardly distinguish between good and evil. The son of Isaias being yet probably very young, the term indicated might appear too distant to the incredulous monarch. Isaias again takes care to reassure him. He says to the king: "I am about to be the father of a son, whom I shall name *Hasten to take away the spoils*. Well, before this future child is able to say *father* or *mother* (which children can generally do about the age of two years), thine enemies shall be no more" (Cf. Is 8:4).

In fact, about two years after this prediction, Theglathphalasar put Rasin to death. At the same time, Phacee perished by the hands of Osee, son of Ela, who had conspired against him (Cf. 4 Kgs 15:30; 16:9).

550 Is 37:33-34

551 Cf. Is 2, 11

552 Is 7:14

553 See the magnificent explanation of this prophecy by M. Drach, *Troisième Lettre aux Israélites*, Ch. 1, p. 45 et suiv. How remarkable!—the expectation of a Virgin, who should bring forth a God, was spread throughout the whole pagan world. See *Christ devant le siecle*, and *Harmonie entre l'Eglise et la Synagogue*, t. 2, p. 259 et suiv. A few years ago there was an ancient stone found at Châlons, with this inscription: *Virgini Deum pariturae Druides* (The Druids, to the Virgin who shall bear a God).

554 Is 9:6

555 Is 9:7

556 Is 40:3

557 Mk 1:3

558 Is 40:11

559 Is 42:4

560 Is 42:3

561 Is 35:5-6

562 Cf. Is 66:18-21

563 Is 53:2-4

564 Is 53:7-8

565 Is 11:10

566 Is 53:12

567 Is 54:1

568 Is 49:18-19

569 Is 49:22

570 Is 49:26

571 Tertullian, *Apology*, Ch. 38

572 Os 11:1

573 Mt 2:14-15

574 Os 2:24

575 Os 1:10

576 St. Paul himself applies to our Lord the words of this prophecy in his epistle to the Romans (9:25).

577 Os 3:4-5

578 Mi 5:2

579 Mi 5:4-5

580 Jl 1:2, 4, 10, 18

581 Jl 2:28-29

582 Acts 2:12-17

583 Jl 2:29-31; 3:2, 12. The Valley of Josaphat means simply, according to the Hebrew, the Valley of Judgment. Some persons have amused themselves with the following calculation: Suppose the world to have existed for six thousand years, as densely populated as at the present day, it would require, allowing one square foot for each individual, about fifty square leagues in France, or twenty-five in Germany, to contain all the generations of mankind (See *Catéch. Phil. de Feller*, p. 562).

584 Jer 1:6-10

585 Cf. Jer 19

586 Jer 31:15

587 Jer 1:5

588 Jer 31:31, 33-34

589 Cf. Heb 10:14ff

590 Cf. Ez 39, 42

591 Ez 30:10-11, 13

592 Volney, *Voyage en Syrie*, t. 1, Ch. 6

593 Ez 34:22-24

594 Jn 10:11, 16

595 Ez 37:26-28

596 Cf. Is 13, 14, 21; Jer 27:6-7; 50; 51

597 Cf. Dn 2:36ff

598 Cf. Dn 9:25ff

599 Cf. Bossuet, *Hist. Univ.*, Pt. 1

600 Dn 9:24, 26-27

601 Agg 2:3-8, 10

602 Cf. Zac 8-9

603 Cf. Zac 3, 8-9, 12-13

604 Mt 11:29

605 See Bible de Vence, *Dissertation sur les Prophètes* and *Préface sur Malachie*.

606 Mal 1:10-11

607 Mal 3:1

608 Cf. Mal 4

609 Lk 1:17

610 Cf. 2 Kgs 7:12ff; 3 Kgs 11:34, 36

611 Cf. Gn 44:8ff; 2 Kgs 7:12; Ps 21, 71, 109; Is 7:14; 11:1; Jer 23, 32; Ez 34, 37; Dn 2:44; 7:13-14; 9:24ff; Os 3:5; Jl 2:24; Am 19:11; Mi 5:2; Agg 2:8; Zac 3:8; 6:12; Mal 3; etc.

612 See the learned *Traité de géographie et de statistique medicales*, by Dr. Boudin, t. 2, p. 128.

613 To preserve the great promise of the Messias: this is the idea which explains and justifies the legislation of Moses; this is what bestows, on observances which to shallow minds appear mere trifles, the highest importance.

614 The four great monarchies of which we are about to speak composed the city of evil, of which Satan was the king. His constant endeavor was to raise these monarchies to such a degree of power that Our Lord should not be able to destroy them, should not be able to establish the kingdom of the gospel on their ruins. God permitted him to act; and, when Rome had become the mistress of the world, the capital of Satan, God sent thither St. Peter, armed with a wooden cross, which overthrew the citadel of the wicked one, destroyed his power, and made the miracle of the establishment of Christianity shine forth with incomparable splendor. In the meanwhile, God, who always draws good from evil, employed the four great monarchies to prepare the way for this immortal victory. See our *Traité du Saint-Esprit*, t. 1.

615 Cf. Is 7:18

616 Is 10:5

617 Is 10:12-13

618 Is 10:15

619 We know by the scripture that Judith was a most virtuous woman, and that, before executing her perilous design, she consulted the Lord by fervent prayer. We see that her action is praised by the Holy Ghost; that a solemn feast was established among the Jews to perpetuate the remembrance of it, and to render glory to God for it; that all the fathers of the Church have emulated one another in exalting her courage and her virtue to the highest. We know only imperfectly the customs of ancient nations: on which account we consider strange the ruses and stratagems that might be admitted among them as lawful. Finally, we have only the substance of the fact: if the details had reached us, they might have justified, even in our eyes, and without any additional proof, that which it would seem difficult to explain. These remarks suffice to defend against unreasonable criticism the conduct of the holy widow of Bethulia.

620 Tb 13:3-4

621 Is 45:1-5, 13

622 Dn 7:6

623 Dn 8:5, 8. We should see in the fathers and interpreters with what admirable precision all these characteristics agree with Alexander and the empire of the Greeks, of which he was the founder (Cornelius a
Lapide, *On Daniel*).

624 St. John Chrysostom (Cf. *Homily 4 on Genesis*) regards it as one of the greatest miracles of divine providence
that a barbarous king, a stranger to the true religion, an enemy of the truth and of the people of God,
should have had the scripture translated into Greek, and should by this means have spread a knowledge
of the truth among all the nations of the world. St. Augustine expresses himself to the same effect (Cf. *On
Christian Doctrine*, Bk. 2, Ch. 15, n. 22; *Sermon 48 on John*). "The Jews," he says, "whether from jealousy or
from scrupulosity, did not wish to acquaint strangers with the holy books. God employed an idolatrous
king to procure this advantage for the Gentiles." *Libri quos gens judaea caeteris populis vel religione, vel invidia,
prodere nolebat credituris per Dominum gentibus, ministra regis Ptolemaei potestate tanto ante prodita sunt.* "What
can be wanting to the authority of this version," says St. Hilary, "which was made before the coming of
Jesus Christ, and at a time when no one could suspect those who accomplished the work of desiring to
flatter him who is announced therein, or accuse them of ignorance, since they were the leaders and doctors
of the synagogue, instructed in the most secret doctrines of the Messias, and invested with all the authority
that pertained to the doctors of Israel?" *Non potuerunt non probabiles esse arbitri interpretandi, qui certiesimi et
gravissimi erant auctores docendi* (Hilary, *On Psalm 2*; Cf. Eusebius, *Praeparatio Evanglica*, Bk. 13, Ch. 1).

625 Dn 2:40

626 Dn 7:7

627 Dn 2:44

628 On the formation and mission of the four great monarchies, see much more complete details in our *Traité
du Saint-Esprit*, t. 1.

629 See the texts cited [above] in the Introduction, and at Lessons 19 and 20 of this first part.

630 Nec inter Judaeos et Christianos, ullum aliud esse certamen nisi hoc: ut eum illi nosque credamus Christum
Dei Filium repromissum, et ea quae sunt futura sub Christo, a nobis *expleta*, ab illis *explenda*, dicantur
(Jerome, *On Jeremiah*, "Preface," Bk. 6).

631 Status novae legis medius est inter statum veteris legis…et inter statum gloriae (*Summa Theologiae*, III, q.
61, a. 4, rep. 1; *Sentences*, IV, d. 1, q. 1, a. 1, qa. 5, rep. 1). Lex vetus est via ad legem novam, sicut lex nova
ad coelestem Ecclesiam, seu ad coelestem hierarchiam (Aquinas, passim).

632 The doctrine of the Trinity was already an article of belief in the ancient synagogue, which named God the
Mysterious Unity. Some rabbis express themselves in so orthodox a manner regarding this great religious
truth, that the most scrupulous Catholic theologian can find nothing to reprehend in their terms. Others
speak of it less clearly and less precisely; yet it finds its way through their obscure and perplexing language
(*Du Divorce dans la Synag.*, by M. Drach, p. 12). The fathers of the Church speak to the same effect. These
are the words, for example, of St. Epiphanius: *Una Trinitas semper nuntiata, creditaque ab illis est qui caeteris
antecelluerunt, cujusmodi Prophetae atque eximia sanctitate praediti homines fuere* (*Adversus Haeresus*, Bk. 1, n. 5).

633 See the Introduction, p. 19–20.

634 Cf. Gn 49

635 Eccles 12:1, 7

636 Cf. 3 Kgs 17:21ff

637 Cf. Jb 14

638 Jb 19:25-27. The ancient synagogue, like the modern, did that which the Church does; it not only prayed
for the dead, but it begged the intercession of those among them whom it regarded as saints. It sought
favors too from the angels (M. Drach, *Dissert. sur l'Invoc des Saints dans la Synag.*; *Annales de phil.chrét.*, t. 14,
p. 422).

639 Jl 3:2

640 Jl 3:12

641 Dt 32:22

642 Is 66:24

643 Ws 5:16

644 Cf. Ps 35:9

645 Ps 65:17

646 Hence these words of Tertullian: *In hac lege Adae data, omnia praecepta condita recognoscimus, quae postea pullulaverunt data per Moysen. Primordialis lex est enim data Adae et Evae in Paradiso, quasi matrix omnium praeceptorum Dei* (*Against the Jews*, Ch. 2. See also *Du Divorce dans la Synag.*, p. 11).

647 Gal 4:19

648 Cf. Fleury, *Manners of the Israelites*

649 Hostis apud majores dicitur quem nunc peregrinum vocamus (Cicero, *De Officiis*, Bk. 1, n. 37).

650 Dt 22:6-7

651 See the *Défense de la législation mosaïque*, by Professor Brunati of Brescia; *l'Homme connu par la révélat.*, by M. Frère; *Préf. du Deutér.*, in the Bible de Vence.

652 [See above] first part, Lesson 29.

653 Dt 26:3, 10

654 See Fleury, *Manners of the Israelites*, and Filassier, *Eraste*, t. 1.

ABOUT THIS SERIES

Tradivox was first conceived as an international research endeavor to recover lost and otherwise little-known Catholic catechetical texts. As the research progressed over several years, the vision began to grow, along with the number of project contributors and a general desire to share these works with a broader audience.

Legally incorporated in 2019, Tradivox has begun the work of carefully remastering and republishing dozens of these catechisms which were once in common and official use in the Church around the world. That effort is embodied in this *Tradivox Catholic Catechism Index,* a multi-volume series restoring artifacts of traditional faith and praxis for a contemporary readership. More about this series and the work of Tradivox can be learned at www.Tradivox.com.

SOPHIA INSTITUTE

Sophia Institute is a nonprofit institution that seeks to nurture the spiritual, moral, and cultural life of souls and to spread the Gospel of Christ in conformity with the authentic teachings of the Roman Catholic Church.

Sophia Institute Press fulfills this mission by offering translations, reprints, and new publications that afford readers a rich source of the enduring wisdom of mankind.

Sophia Institute also operates the popular online resource Catholic Exchange.com. *Catholic Exchange* provides world news from a Catholic perspective as well as daily devotionals and articles that will help readers to grow in holiness and live a life consistent with the teachings of the Church.

In 2013, Sophia Institute launched Sophia Institute for Teachers to renew and rebuild Catholic culture through service to Catholic education. With the goal of nurturing the spiritual, moral, and cultural life of souls, and an abiding respect for the role and work of teachers, we strive to provide materials and programs that are at once enlightening to the mind and ennobling to the heart; faithful and complete, as well as useful and practical.

Sophia Institute gratefully recognizes the Solidarity Association for preserving and encouraging the growth of our apostolate over the course of many years. Without their generous and timely support, this book would not be in your hands.

www.SophiaInstitute.com
www.CatholicExchange.com
www.SophiaInstituteforTeachers.org

Sophia Institute Press® is a registered trademark of Sophia Institute. Sophia Institute is a tax-exempt institution as defined by the Internal Revenue Code, Section 501(c)(3). Tax ID 22-2548708.